Management for Professionals

The Springer series *Management for Professionals* comprises high-level business and management books for executives. The authors are experienced business professionals and renowned professors who combine scientific background, best practice, and entrepreneurial vision to provide powerful insights into how to achieve business excellence.

More information about this series at http://www.springer.com/series/10101

Timo Wagenblatt

Software Product Management

Finding the Right Balance for YourProduct Inc.

Springer

Timo Wagenblatt
Bornheim, Germany

ISSN 2192-8096 ISSN 2192-810X (electronic)
Management for Professionals
ISBN 978-3-030-19870-1 ISBN 978-3-030-19871-8 (eBook)
https://doi.org/10.1007/978-3-030-19871-8

This Springer imprint is published by the registered company Springer Nature Switzerland AG
The registered company address is: Gewerbestrasse 11, 6330 Cham, Switzerland

For Yvonne, Lena, and Leo

Preface

I'm a stranger in a strange land ...

I started in Software Product Management right after I graduated from university, which is unusual because most people begin their careers in "respectable" professions such as software development, sales, or consulting.

Since then, I have worked for more than 20 years in Software Product Management, and I have never been anything else other than a product manager. Yes, I have had all kinds of titles, such as System Analyst, Business Analyst, Solution Manager, Director of Solution Management, Director of Product Management, Senior Development Manager, Product Manager, Product Owner, Chief Product Owner, Head of Product, Head of Product Area, VP Product Management, and that is likely not the complete list, but I have always been a product manager.

Throughout the years, I read countless books, articles, and blogs and participated in many training sessions. I have always thought that something is missing in all these learning activities. Don't get me wrong, there are many brilliant books, blogs, and podcasts available out there. There are fantastic virtual and classroom trainings. I gained a lot from all of these and many were brilliant and inspirational. I got educated in different frameworks that mostly seemed sound and reasonable. I learned about tools and methods to improve my personal bag of tricks. I learned about the different interpretations and biases in Software Product Management.

Still, I did not feel fully truly equipped for the day-to-day challenges, as the focus of all the above was on introducing individual tools, or on one dedicated product management aspect, but nothing on the most critical, yet foundational challenges. I was lacking guidance on what is most important for my products in my context. Where should we focus our time and work efforts? How can I engage the team and the entire organization? How can I find the right balance?

I found little to no guidance to equip me properly for my day-to-day job as a product manager. Therefore, I invented the Product Yield Potential Radar framework early on in my career. Since then, I constantly think about and experiment how to master the job and strengthen the essential focus, alignment, and engagement for product teams and entire organizations.

I tapped into a Software Product Management career by a fortunate coincidence. I joined a local[1] start-up company where I directly reported to the co-founder of the company. As the CTO, he was responsible for product engineering while his brother took care of the finance, sales, and services departments of the company. At first, I didn't recognize that I was learning firsthand about Software Product Management because in those days the term Software Product Management was not well established far in the woods of Southwest Germany and it had not been a topic at university either.

In hindsight, I experienced a fantastic opportunity by beginning my career in this start-up. It allowed me to gain insights in all aspects of a software company, but more importantly into all diverse activities of successfully managing software products. When I joined CAS, there were only about 40 employees and agility and can-do attitude was the only way to survive (and get the next paycheck). Those were the days where I began organizing learning lessons about Software Product Management, first for myself, then for my team that I established in the start-up.

Due to our success, I was hired by SAP where I learned about the good, the bad, and the ugly working in a multi-billion, global enterprise. However, my Software Product Management philosophy remained the foundation of my work. The main thing is the product, everything else is secondary.

I basically started the same career path and learning cycle over again—just on a slightly bigger scale. Again, I started as an individual contributor responsible for one product and became responsible for a product management team over time. With my experiences from working in a 40 people start-up to a 90,000 people global enterprise, I could hone and improve the Product Yield Potential Radar until it became today's framework.

Why am I writing this? It is not to tell you how well my career progressed; it is about context as context is important in Software Product Management. Different products and different companies need different types of Software Product Management organizations, processes, and governance models. However, I learned that any software product company regardless of size, location, or maturity needs to master focus, alignment, and finding the right balance for everything that matters for a successful product no matter the context. Some people would call this: product mindset. I will not get into any definitions or details here about product mindset, as the entire book and my framework are at its core about instilling a product mindset to any product organization.

As a manager of product managers, I was likely more a coach than a traditional manager. I'm a product manager by heart and Software Product Management is my passion. I wanted to share what I learned about Software Product Management and with that help "my product managers" to be successful. My experiences and my view of Software Product Management manifested themselves in the Product Yield Potential Radar framework.

[1]Local being the key attribute here.

Ever since my early days at university, I have always wanted to write a book. I always had this thought, I just never started. Triggered by many questions from others about the Product Yield Potential Radar, and inspired by Toni Morrison's[2] quote: "If there's a book you really want to read but it hasn't been written yet, then you must write it," I took Toni Morrison's quote as my north star and I decided to write this book as a New Year's resolution in 2018.

Over the last few months, I have put my heart and soul into this book with the hope and motivation that everyone can benefit and improve in this strange land of Software Product Management. My hope and motivation in writing this book is that it will help you to become an excellent product manager, working with a great product team in a product-led organization. It has been a long and rollercoaster journey, but writing this book helped me to become a better product manager. I have been reflecting and thinking about everything I know on Software Product Management. I thought about everything I believe in, everything I took for granted in my day-to-day dealings, and the best way to structure and explain the Product Yield Potential framework to people.

I took Toni Morrison's quote as my north star for writing this book. My goal in writing this book about Software Product Management is to provide practicable, usable information and recommendations with all one needs to be successful in "product." I was looking for a practical framework that could be applied in all day-to-day business activities, which would help me find the right balance for my product and my context.

In this book, you'll learn how to

- plan, coordinate, and execute activities required for software products
  - consider all product dimensions along the product life cycle and
  - align all product stakeholders inside and outside the organization
- be a role model of product mindset and an ambassador of holistic product focus
- find the right balance for delivering customer value and long-term product success.

Adopting the Product Yield Potential Radar (short: PYPR) is like going to the gym. You start with PYPR because you want to improve yourself as a product manager, Software Product Management as function and the product mindset in your organization. You go to the gym for 30 minutes, come back home, look in the mirror and you see … nothing. The next day you do the same thing again. Still nothing. You do this for a week and you might think, I should stop, there is no effect and there will be no effect.

Or you continue and after a few months, maybe a year, you will recognize that you are in good shape, and others likely will have recognized it already.

[2]Toni Morrison is a Nobel Prize-winning American author.

Who Should Read This Book

The book focuses on the unique challenges of working in "product" or any related roles, whether you are a founder of a small to midsized software company or working in the complex ecosystems of large software enterprises or corporate IT departments.

This book is for product managers, product owners, product marketing managers, VPs of Product, CEOs, and start-up founders and anyone interested personally or professionally in Software Product Management. I truly believe that you, your product team, your product, and with that your customers and your organization can benefit from this book.

Whether you're a seasoned practitioner, new to Software Product Management, or just want to learn more about the best-of-all disciplines and advance your skills, this book offers a comprehensive overview for beginners as well as proven practices, a novel, holistic methodology, and in-depth tools for experienced product managers.

How This Book Is Organized

My advice is that you read the book from start to the end. You will get some useful nuggets out of every chapter that you can put to work immediately.

The book is composed of three parts. The first part provides the required context and introduces a novel Software Product Management framework. The second part details every aspect of leveraging the Product Yield Potential framework, and the third part provides case studies about how product managers and product teams have successfully adopted the Product Yield Potential Radar framework.

Part I will set the scene and provides a robust foundation.

Chapter 1 leads you through a definition of Software Product Management in the context of this book, the role of software product managers and product teams, rounded off with data-driven insights and a broad view about "the State of the Software Product Management nation" supported by recent survey results.

Chapter 2 introduces a novel and "business" tested way to structure the vital dimensions of Software Product Management. You will learn how to create focus and alignment on the things that matter for product success. You will learn about the Product Yield Potential Radar and how this framework can drive an ongoing discipline that helps the whole product team and product organization to

- understand all the required ingredients for product success in your context
- consistently assess the weak and strong parts when holistically assessing your product
- decide, based on a common understanding where focus and time investments are required
- find the right balance for product longevity and continuous improvement.

Chapter 3 describes how the Product Yield Potential Radar supports you in being the General Manager of YourProduct Inc. and how the framework can be leveraged as a communication tool for all stakeholders. Furthermore, some tips and tricks will show you how to jump-start the out-of-the-box setup and adapt the framework continuously for your own context.

Part II of this book is structured like a reference book for each Software Product Management dimension. You can use Part II as a textbook if you are interested in or have the urgent need to improve one of the following dimensions: *Product Viability*, *Product Development*, *Go-to-Market/Product Marketing*, *Software Demonstrations and Training*, *The Market/Your Customers*, or *Organizational Maturity*.

Chapters 4–9 detail each Software Product Management dimension and provide you tools and techniques to assess, understand, improve, and monitor each dimension.

Part III, Chap. 10, describes how PYPR has been used to improve the success of various products with different characteristics and setups. I will introduce how product teams applied the Product Yield Potential Radar, which insights they gained, and the benefits they could achieve. The chapter outlines how the framework has been applied successfully in practice by various product teams over the last 20 years.

Bornheim, Germany Timo Wagenblatt

Acknowledgements

Thanks to everyone whom I have had the pleasure of working with throughout the last 20 years of my product management career.

Thanks to Gregor Johann who encouraged me early on to write this book.

Thanks to Christian Kern who shared with me his broad experience about writing a book.

Thanks to Stefan Meinhardt who helped me getting formally started with the book.

Thanks to Mark Osborn for his excellent feedback, encouragement, language skills, and ongoing advisory.

Thanks to Greg McNitt for providing early feedback and his experience to the Pre-sales enablement chapter.

Thanks to everybody who provided both formal and informal feedback along the way, especially Alexander Braun, Birgit Grüne, Tobias Keller, Raphael Leiteritz, Colby Sheridan, and Adrian Zwingli.

Thanks to Hans van Delden for joining my product management journey since the early days. Thanks for your contributions about successful and sustainable partnership.

Thanks to Noah Askin for being inspirational and educational to the product management community. Thanks for your contribution about brokers and brokerage.

Thanks to all product managers who care about their product, product team, customers, and their organization.

Thanks to the ones who work with PYPR already today.

Thanks to SAP for providing me the opportunity to learn and grow.

Thanks to my teams at SAP, for your dedication, openness, and passion delivering beautiful products.

Thanks to my team at CAS who showcased product mindset before the term was even coined.

Thanks to Matthias Joneck for hiring me from university and paving my way into product management.

Thanks to Lars Farnstrom for elevating me to the next level.

Thanks to PMF for doing what you do.

Thanks to Elisabeth Aseritis for your professionalism, speed, quality, and kindness.

Thanks to Christian Rauscher and everybody at Springer for publishing my book.

Thanks to Lena and Leo for being such great kids and keeping me balanced.

Thanks to Yvonne for everything—always, forever.

Contents

About the Author

Timo Wagenblatt is VP of Product Management at SAP in Walldorf, Germany. As Head of Product Management team, he shapes and drives the incubation of cloud-native products that service underserved customer needs all the way to valuable product adoption for both customers and SAP.

Timo is dedicated to Software Product Management for more than 20 years working with clients and product teams across the globe building world-class enterprise solutions. His passion can be best described as continuously improving product management maturity while focusing on customer and employee success by evangelizing and showcasing product mindset.

Timo's experience is based on working in organizations that range from 40 employees to more than 90,000 employees. Before he joined SAP, he established Software Product Management at a start-up, gaining hands-on experience as the first product manager reporting directly to the CTO and co-founder.

In 2018, Timo started PYPR Software Product Management, his own start-up that is dedicated to helping product managers and founders adopting PYPR. He focuses on balancing and consistently improving all aspects of Software Product Management toward an aligned product mindset in the product team, department, and the overall organization.

Timo holds a diploma in Business Administration with specialization in operations research, commercial information systems, and industrial management. He is a conference board member of one of the largest product management conferences in Europe (Product Management Festival, Zurich).

https://www.linkedin.com/in/wagenblatt/
www.timowagenblatt.com
www.pypr.works

Talk is cheap, show me your PYPR
Go out and build awesome products!

List of Figures

Part I
Setting the Scene and Introducing the Product Yield Potential Radar

Software Product Management Fundamentals

1

Software Product Management is one of the most important and rewarding, and yet challenging, domains in the software industry. The benefits associated with Software Product Management excellence are significant and the notion of being a product-led organization is a hot topic and a prerequisite to attracting the best talent in the industry.

Fortunately, the need to justify the importance of Software Product Management is no longer necessary to many companies. I distinctly remember how people first regarded me when I told them that I was a product manager, and the many perplexed or curious questions that I received about my job function.

"You are defining requirements, you write user stories, you do presentations all day, you are in meetings all day, you control the development project, you are in marketing, you are in sales, you are a software developer, you are the boss of the software engineers" were many of the comments I received.

All these statements and assumptions were interesting, but my simple answer was: "No, I am a Software Product Manager."

Nowadays Software Product Management is widely recognized as the key discipline for software and digital product success. Successful products are the lifeblood of every software company, whether it is a young startup or a mature software organization. Consequently, to be a Software Product Manager is to have one of the hottest job titles in the industry and the demand for talent is growing exponentially.

This chapter introduces and defines my view of Software Product Management after 20 years in the industry, where I started as a business analyst, contributing individually, to my current position as Head of Product, where I lead a product organization at SAP today. We'll discover how Software Product Management can relate to a forest ranger's job and why Software Product Management is actually required as a practice in every software company and corporate IT organization.

We will examine all the stakeholders involved in the process and how they relate to the six dimensions of software product management: Product Viability, Product

T. Wagenblatt, *Software Product Management*, Management for Professionals,
https://doi.org/10.1007/978-3-030-19871-8_1

Development, Go-to-Market/Product Marketing, Software Demonstrations and Trainings, The Market/Your Customers, and Organizational Maturity.

In this chapter, we will also define the following terms:

- Management and its special form of Software Product Management
- Product and the specialties of software products, digital products and data products
- Software Product Managers and the T-shaped superhero capes they wear
- Product teams and the role of product managers.

The definitions and groundwork will be followed by an interpretation of the latest Product Management Festival survey (Trends & Benchmarks in Product Management 2018), which provides brilliant insights into the current state of Software Product Management, the role of Software Product Managers and the importance of their managers.

1.1 Defining Software Product Management

The title of my book is Software Product Management. How do we define the discipline of Software Product Management? Some definitions are academic, some define the discipline by enumerating the essential tasks and skills, some are narrow, and some are broad. To avoid any misunderstandings, I define Software Product Management the way I interpret the discipline and then use the term accordingly in this book.

In this chapter I will introduce my definition of Software Product Management and clarify some of the other commonly used terms that are widely, and even "wildly," used to describe Software Product Management, such as product-led, software, digital or data products, consumer and enterprise products. Then we will explore who are these product guys with "superhero skills."

But before we get there, let's start with a very basic question: Why do we need Software Product Management at all, if …

- … engineering builds technically superior products?
- … marketing maximizes awareness in the market and generates demand?
- … sales is closing the deal with customers?
- … DevOps safeguards that the solution is delivered as cost effectively as possible?
- … customer support ensures customer's incidents are timely resolved?
- … project management (PMO) delivers projects according to plan?

Interesting and kind of provocative questions, which we need to sort out. We will get some preliminary insights when we analyze the driving forces and objectives of the various teams named above. What inspires them and what is their intrinsic motivation?

Is it the product that they are focusing on? Do these teams share the same purpose? Generally, no!

Let's examine the driving forces of these teams:

- Engineering or software development teams focus on the latest technology trends, they strive for perfect software design, the cleanest coding, and if there is anything new in the developer community, they want to try it out …
- Marketing teams have clearly different objectives—they make some noise and if the market is listening and the message is spread—mission accomplished …
- Sales teams do whatever it takes to close the next deal, so the next deal is the target, the next customer is the most important one. The next customer knows best what the products direction needs to be …
- DevOps teams target full automation from development to operations, enabling a smart and short development lifecycle with increased frequency of new features. A portion of development time is required to keep them happy; there can always be more automation …
- Customer support teams prefer a stable system. New features are a risk and likely more work for them; keep the code stable, no risky experiments, please …
- Project management offices are measured by delivery according to the project's plans, minimizing deviations in time and budget. Changes to plan mean unwanted risks. Consequently, this strict approach might hinder focus on value and increasing flexibility …

While the descriptions are obviously stereotyped and generic, they emphasize that different teams and departments have different, sometimes even conflicting, objectives by design. Developing software or digital products is a challenging and complex task. There are many more teams and stakeholders involved than the few listed above. They all have high expectations toward the product, so they can achieve their own, sometimes self-serving and in sum, sub-optimal objectives for the organization.

As we discuss stakeholders for the first time, it is worth noting that product management thought leader Marty Cagan has a simple test to determine whether someone is really a stakeholder, or someone with merely an opinion, thought, or expectation toward the product. He proposes a practical test asking whether the person or team "has veto power or can otherwise prevent your work from launching." Using that practical test, you can determine real stakeholders for your product (Cagan, Inspired—How to create great tech products customer love 2018). Who can seriously hinder or even prevent the success of your product?

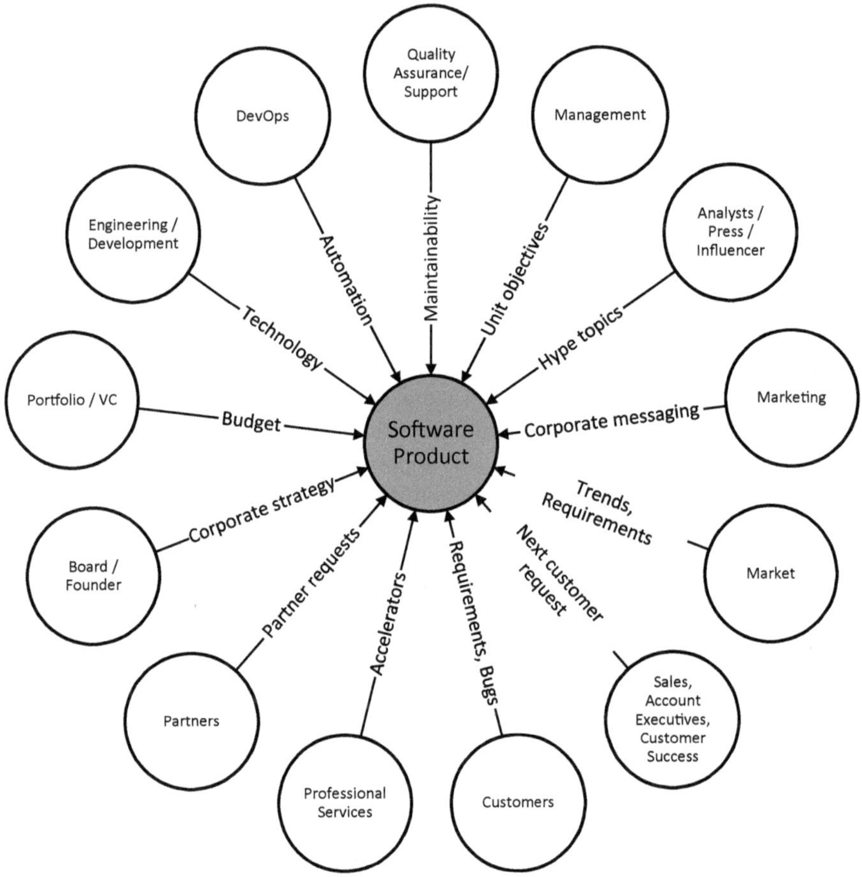

Fig. 1.1 Software product stakeholders (there are likely many more stakeholders with different titles in your organization: such as legal, procurement, bid management and the likes. Give the test and see who needs to be included and who needs to be removed from your stakeholder list. In Sect. 3.2, I will provide a tool on how to structure the interaction with stakeholders)

In Fig. 1.1 we explore who cares about the product's needs. Who is responsible for the product, ensuring it prospers and provides the expected yield from all the hard work of the contributing stakeholders? Who is the liaison between the different stakeholders, who orchestrates and brokers the information between the actors, who provides guidance and direction, and who ultimately makes the decisions in favor of product longevity?

Yes, in my opinion, that is the purpose of Software Product Management. It is not quite my final definition of Software Product Management, but we are getting there.

Let's try out the following metaphor illustrating the role of Software Product Management: Imagine every product is a tree, some are saplings in early stages of ideation or in alpha, beta, or release 1.0 status, others are already big, strong trees like flagship products, already well introduced to the market.

In this example, Software Product Management can be seen as the forest ranger's office that cares for the trees, nurturing them and protecting them from the wild. Their main responsibility is ensure that the trees grow and yield a large crop. There are many risks facing our trees: Some are home-made and others are higher forces outside of our control, such as severe weather conditions.

Like trees in the forest, products face equally great risks if no one nurtures and protects them. If there is no one dedicated to and responsible for the product—timber!

Products might not survive for a multitude of reasons even if the idea was great and a market exists. Any product failure comes with a reason. There is always a story and some are listed below as examples:

- Sales teams forcing a customer request into the product, although it does not match the product vision and strategy. The engineering team develops the best technical solution for a requirement that is not particularly of interest for the product's target market. However, it is a technically interesting challenge, Sales close the deal, Engineering is pleased with delivering against the challenge, and the product … suffers!
- Influencers and analysts create hype about the new cool thing in tech. The company's board falls in love with the healing charms, the developers spend extra hours to put it into the product, the marketing team is close to ecstasy as there is a great story to tell, and the product … suffers as it might be too early to consider the premature technology for the product. There is no customer segment to appreciate the cool thing. The time and work would have been better spent for more valuable topics instead of hyped tech!
- Last but not least … the portfolio team decides not to fund the next release, or the venture capitalist doesn't see a reason for the next infusion of money as the product updates are taking more time than expected and the user adoption is very limited after the first year of product availability. The engineering team is already preparing to hop to the next development project and the product … dies!

Unfortunately, the product pile in the software forest is growing (see Fig. 1.2). Many products are based on bright ideas for solving relevant problems, great technologies and talented people, but they could not survive the rough conditions, frequently due to shortcomings in the implementation or application of Software Product Management.

Fig. 1.2 Sad pile of lumbered products (and opportunities)

The mandate of Software Product Management and the reason for its existence is the holistic view and understanding of how all the pieces must fit together for a successful product from the first seed to the big, strong and healthy tree.

Everyone involved in product-related activities needs to understand that there is

- no next deal,
- nothing to add new features or latest technology to,
- no opportunity for showcasing great engineering skills, and
- nothing to announce and market,

if there is no longer a product because the product did not survive the agendas of individuals, teams or departments … or if the objectives and strategies are not aligned among the stakeholders.

Software Product Management sits in the middle of all of this, acting as a hub between all different stakeholders that have their own agendas, constraints and objectives. Software Product Management motivates, brokers and leads stakeholder alignment, or in other words Software Product Management evangelizes product mindset in the following dimensions:

- **Product Viability**: Comprises all necessary activities to ensure that those new product or product feature ideas make business sense, provide an appropriate return on investment and have customers that understand the value of the product enough to pay for it.
- **Product Development**: Guides the engineering team from product vision and strategy to release scope and backlog prioritization. Provides clarity and direction to the product team, to bolster the team spirit and develop a quality product.

- **Go-to-Market/Product Marketing**: Broadcast and position the product's values in the optimal way to the ecosystem in sales, professional services and the partner community, and—no brainer—to the market and the company's current and future customers.
- **Software Demonstrations and Training**: Showcase the product and train people how to use it in the best possible way, underlining the positioning and showcasing the various values for the target groups in an engaging way.
- **The Market/Your Customers**: The market can be represented by the target market segments, communities, analysts, press and media, while the customers are the people and companies who write the checks. Account managers and customer success teams provide a steady stream of feature gaps identified by their customers. Beware the bias!
- **Organizational Maturity**: Defining Software Product Management as a leadership role and improving the processes and tools continuously. Managing up the hierarchy and cross-teams to showcase the value that Software Product Management adds to the organization. Software Product Managers help infuse product mindset to the organization. Not everything can be directly influenced or fixed by Software Product Management; however, constant dripping wears away the stone.

Each dimension has its special set of stakeholders: people, teams and departments that have their stake in one or more, but likely not all dimensions. Each stakeholder focuses on one or two dimensions, articulating self-interested demands and frequently prioritizing his/her own objectives over and above the product in its entirety. While Software Product Management cares about the long-term product success, the various stakeholders might not always share the same objective.

Successfully utilized Software Product Management means increased chances of success for your product and an expanded yield potential for your product. Increasing the chances of success and the yield potential is about finding the right balance for the dimensions outlined above. This book is all about finding the right balance for your product and finding balance for yourself as a product manager in order to be successful in the best of all jobs

Figure 1.3 visualize another important aspect of Software Product Management. The ability to align all stakeholders and motivate everyone involved, thus moving as one team into the same direction. In 100% product-led organizations the Software Product Management team might be the formal authority; in others working with all the stakeholders means leading without formal authority. We will discuss this topic in more detail in later chapters as part of the soft skills mandated to succeed in Software Product Management.

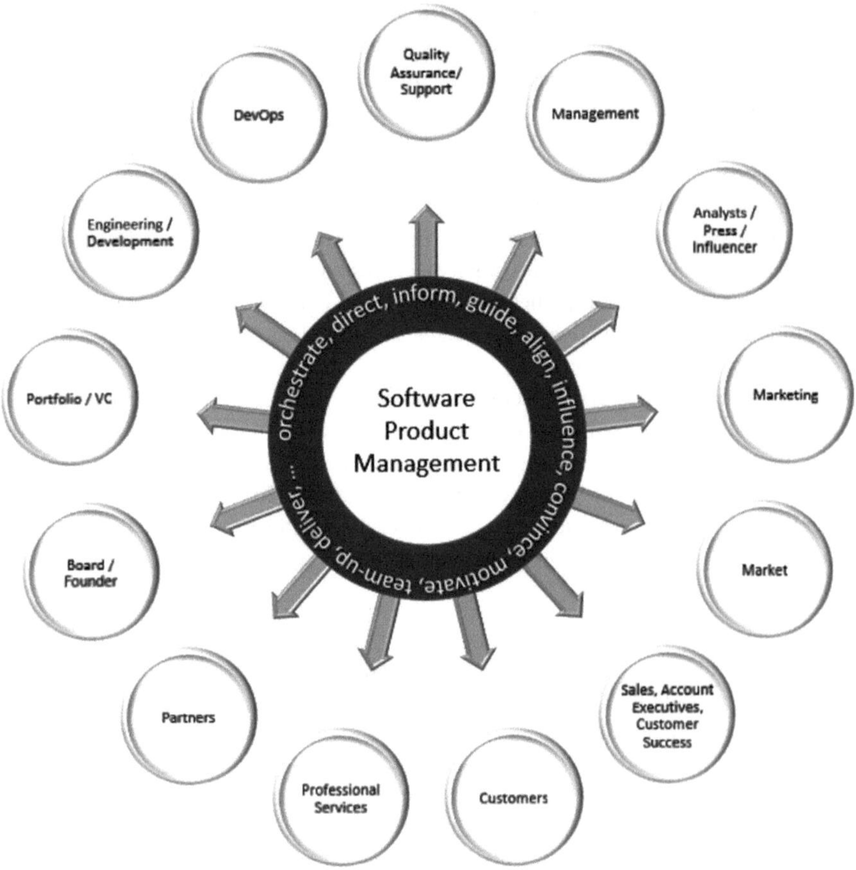

Fig. 1.3 Software product management interactions

1.1.1 An Approach to Define Software Product Management

Management and leadership—equally strong and loaded terms. There are many methodologies, checklists and sentiments out there and most have very limited value for us focusing on Software Product Management. People enjoy reading about the management and leadership styles of successful people. Is this time well spent?

As Noah Askins, Assistant Professor of Organizational Behavior at INSEAD, stated in a lecture that I attended: "The only theory of leadership that matters is your own." This doesn't mean that you should just care about yourself. It actually means the opposite. Methodologies or top 10 checklists will not do the job—in best case they are inspirational. You need to do the job. Noah emphasizes that communication and empathy tailored to your context is most important for any management.

Keep this in mind as we get into more detail about the required soft skills in Software Product Management.

We must further fine tune the definition of Software Product Management in order to clarify this book's focus and scope. By substituting the words "software product" for "product" and the phrase "software product vision and strategy" for "corporate policy" in a generic management definition from the Business Dictionary (Business Dictionary 2018) we simply arrive at a generic definition of Software Product Management:

Software Product Management = Organization and coordination of all activities important for a software product in order to achieve product success

According to the management guru Peter Drucker (1909–2005), the basic task of management includes both marketing and innovation. Practice of modern management originates from a 16th century study of low-efficiency and failures of certain enterprises, conducted by the English statesman Sir Thomas More (1478–1535). Management consists of the interlocking functions of a software product vision/strategy and organizing, planning, controlling, and directing an organization's resources in order to achieve the objectives of that vision and strategy.

That's a lot of heritage in the definitions above, however we always must keep in mind that software development is substantially different from production. Most management philosophies and lots of good advice are derived entirely from a production environment. There is all the talk about "working smarter," however, unfortunately, for many organizations the sense of great management is only about getting people to work harder and longer hours.

Management of software products is not primarily about productivity as derived from the production environment. Applying the efficiency focused style of management in Software Product Management will be directly at odds with its purpose or as stated by Tom DeMarco: "If you follow this management style then you might win battles, but you lose the war." (DeMarco and Lister, Peopleware 2013)

This book will provide a novel methodology that fosters communication and strategic thinking, to prioritize the multitude of software product management tasks. Discovering what is most important at any given stage for your product's and team's success in order to deliver business value.

Let's summarize what we have learned so far about Software Product Management:

- Software Product Management is the discipline and business process that comprises all planning, coordinating and execution activities, taking into consideration all product dimensions and aligning all product stakeholders inside and outside the organization, which leads to customer value and long-term product success.
- Software Product Management is the only department that focuses solely on the product and the product is the reason for the department's existence.

- Software Product Management is not a short-term production and efficiency play.
- Software Product Management represents the product and is the key driver for sustainable success in a product organization.

Given the volumes of work already available on the topic, we won't dive much deeper here into the discussion or definition of Software Product Management. We will focus instead on further strengthening the understanding of required practices and team aspects for all dimensions of Software Product Management throughout this book. We will do an in-depth study of every single Software Product Management dimension and learn about the challenges-overcoming tools and essential skills to successfully manage software and digital products. And most importantly, we will examine a methodology to finding the right balance in both Software Product Management and the products you manage.

1.1.2 An Approach to Define Software Products

Let's clarify how the term Software Product is generically used in this book. I have been using the term software product loosely. The term software product comprises various categories of products because software products come in many forms, sizes, and shapes. A software product may be:

- an enterprise resource planning software
- a customer relationship management application
- a database system
- your car service app
- a consumer app for download
- a game or entertainment software
- your mobile banking app
- the search capability of an e-commerce shop
- a company homepage
- an insurance claims administration capability
- a carrier service provisioning
- a service billing capability
- an ATM in a banking branch
- a data-driven benchmark
- a data-driven recommendation service
- a data-driven forecasting or optimization service
- a well-defined application programming interface (API).

The examples are endless and, unfortunately, classifications are ambiguous. Some common classifications for software products are

- enterprise software (e.g. enterprise resource planning, customer relationship management),
- consumer software (e.g. car service app, games or entertainment software, mobile banking app),
- digital products (e.g. your car service app, mobile banking app, search capability of an e-commerce shop, a company homepage),
- corporate IT products (e.g. search capability of an e-commerce shop, company homepage, a telecom service billing capability (if you work for a telecom company), in software supporting a business capability),
- services (e.g. insurance claims administration capability, data-driven forecasting or optimization service, telecom service billing capability, ATM in a banking branch), and
- data products (e.g. data-driven benchmark, data-driven forecasting or optimization service).

As you see, some of the examples do not fit into just one classification. In particular, the classification of a digital product (i.e. the delivery of digital touchpoints of a product or service) is rather new, but also very generic as any software product delivers digital touchpoints. Some terms are clearly hype terms and might disappear; however, they all try to highlight certain aspects of software products.

In this book, I will strictly use the term Software Product that comprises all the classifications above, unless there is something special to be mentioned for a given topic. Then, I will outline the differences explicitly.

Software products can be further classified and attributed emphasizing certain aspects of the product that highlight Software Product Management dimensions (Kittlaus and Clough 2009). Software products could be attributed further by

- target customers (Business-to-Consumer (B2C), Business-to-Business (B2B), corporate (internal) business users)
- development focus (standard software, services, individual software)
- commercial terms (freeware, shareware, perpetual license, subscription, etc.).

The same authors provide a generic definition of product and software product (Kittlaus and Clough 2009):

Product = Combination of (material and/or intangible) goods and services, which one party (called vendor) combines in support of their commercial interests, to transfer defined rights to a second party (called customer)
Software Product = Product whose primary component is software providing value/benefits by solving a problem for a group of users (human or technical users).

There are a few items that I would emphasize that are Software Product Management's responsibility. The values and benefits of software products are derived from the extent the product solves user problems. The focus needs to be on understanding the group of users and their underserved needs. The group of users can be generally described by target market segments. I emphasize both early on as this is a key concept and touches many if not all dimensions of Software Product Management.

If a Software Product Manager does not fully understand the real problem, then the team will not understand what the value for the user might be, and consequently the product team will have a hard time deriving a high-quality value proposition for your Software Product. Look at the examples of Software Products listed above and the actual problem the product is trying to solve. That's likely the hardest part, but we will find ways to get there throughout this book.

Furthermore, if you are interested in more comprehensive definitions and explanations regarding Software Products, you can find a full reference of definitions for many other terms like embedded software, OEM software, and product lines in the same reference (Kittlaus and Clough 2009).

For all above examples, classifications, and attributions we will use the term: Software Product.

Software Products are fantastic products to work on as they come with high flexibility and can be changed relatively easily. They are highly complex, i.e. interesting and solve engaging problems, and the marginal costs of production are almost irrelevant—once they have been developed.

Software products are delivered by software vendors ranging from one person to global software companies or corporate IT organizations. Software product customers can be internal or external businesses (B2B software), or private people, i.e. consumers (B2C software).

Sometimes organizations introduce and use the terms Solution and Solution Manager. I will not make this distinction as in my interpretation a solution that is comprised of a mix of products or services is still a product, maybe a new one or a different kind of product; however, it is still a product according to the definitions above, i.e.:

- Product + Product = new Product $\neq$ Solution
- Product + Service = new Product $\neq$ Solution
- Service + Service = new Product $\neq$ Solution

1.1.3 Software Product Taxonomy

A crystal-clear software product definition in your organization helps to avoid misunderstandings. Companies show great creativity when describing their products, services and projects. Defining what a software product is and isn't eases the confusion and level-sets the expectations. For Software Product Managers working in an organization with multiple Software Products can result in confusion for all involved. A Software Product Taxonomy can help here.

In my experience a defined and shared Software Product Taxonomy drives consistency across the organization. Everyone understands what to expect for the software developed in the organization. For example, with a Software Product Taxonomy people understand why one software piece has no roadmap, while another software mandates one, or why one software can be sold multiple times, while the other is sold only once.

A consistent and well-defined understanding across the entire organization clearly shows everyone what to sell, deliver and support. Figure 1.4 may provide you a basis for tailoring your own Software Product Taxonomy.

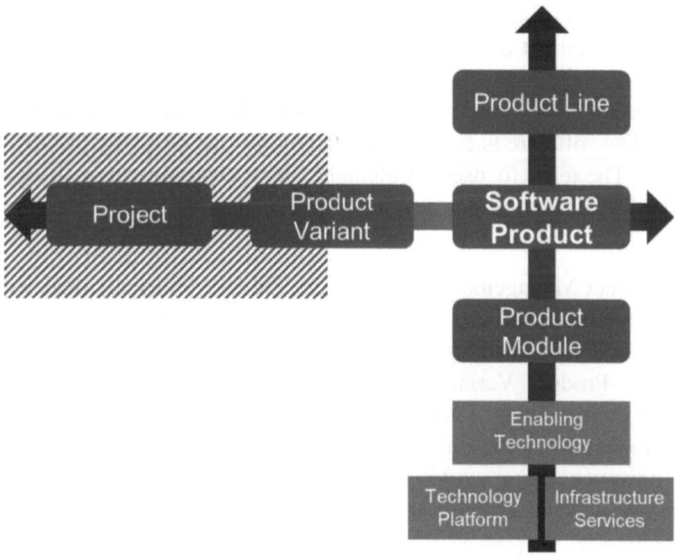

Fig. 1.4 Example of a software product taxonomy © Timo Wagenblatt 2019. All rights reserved

- **Product Line**
  Grouping of independent Software Products that belong logically together in the problem space.
- **Software Product**
  Grouping of Product Modules that the customer licenses or subscribes.
- **Product Module**
  Lowest level of a Software Product that is visible to the customer and can be licensed or subscribed individually. Generally, the Product Module is sold as part of the Software Product.
- **Enabling Technology**
  Service and functions that are required to develop and deliver a software product. Technology Enablers may be used for multiple Software Products, but are not individually sold to customers.

- **Technology Platform**
  Technology platform for one or multiple Enabling Technologies. Technology Platforms may be used for multiple Software Products, but are not individually sold to customers.
- **Infrastructure Services**
  IT infrastructure supporting Technology Platforms, Enabling Technologies, and Product Modules.
- **Product Variant**
  Specific customization or usage of alternative base technology to support the same problem as an existing Software Product for one or multiple customers. Product Variants may or may not be treated as Software Products and therefore may or may not have a dedicated Software Product Manager in charge. The more customers and ongoing developments, the more critical is the need for a Software Product Management discipline.
- **Project**
  The development of a one-off software project has a dedicated start and defined end-date. The software is created specifically for one or a very limited number of customers. The team focuses on efficiency over customer value in development, hence the fixed scope is not developed in a repeatable or re-useable way.

Software Product Management and Software Product Managers deal with Product Lines, Software Products, Product Modules and product managers with a technical bias deal as well with Enabling Technology, Technology Platform and Infrastructure Services. Product Variants and Projects are different animals that we will explore to a limited extent later in the book, as I do not consider both as part of Software Product Management. Both would benefit from Software Product Management; however, those working on both are generally not applying a product mindset as we will get to know throughout this book.

1.1.4 Software Product Management for Corporate IT Products

Software Product Management is becoming more favored in corporate IT departments that traditionally organized their work in projects and programs to deliver what "the business" wants or requires. In this case "the business" is the synonym for the internal users, the peers working for the same company.

Corporate or internal IT projects are frequently perceived as long-runners, not reliable and not flexible enough to handle changing business priorities. The age of digital transformation and its derived requirements are catalysts for even faster changes in business necessities.

Frequently, these business requirements or business deliverables include a detailed description of the solution "the business" would like "IT to implement." Unfortunately, these requirements are not originated by the users, but rather by the business management, COOs, process offices or other layers between the end user and the delivery/development team. Generally, this is where the problems usually start as many of these requests create only limited value, and together they do not form a coherent product.

IT departments have talented engineers and the teams to build lots of software products or work on adaptations of software products. For example, a corporate IT department could run project after project, in worst case with an ever-changing team set-up to support the business capability: Manage Order. The better way would be to consider the software developed, customized and delivered to the internal users as a software product. Most companies deal with orders and the order management requirements will change over time. So why use project-mode instead of product-mode for supporting the internal users dealing with orders? IT Software Products can be defined in the following way:

IT Software Product= Combination of software and run-services, which internal IT combines to

- **provide value/benefits** by **solving a problem** for a **group of users** (human or technical users) or in other words;
- enable an **internal** organization/business unit/line of business to achieve its desired outcomes.

Modern IT departments are organized around products with stable software development teams and a product-mindset. Corporate IT departments can work more efficiently by applying some product development best practices and Software Product Management is clearly one of these essentials.

Let's recall our earlier questions about why we need software product. These questions are biased toward commercial products; however, one can ask similar questions about the validity of corporate IT products. Why do we need Software Product Management at all, if …?

- … Program or Project Managers efficiently manage the project outcomes?
- … Communications maximizes awareness in the company?
- … Digital Transformation Office clarifies priorities with customers?
- … DevOps safeguards that the solution is delivered as cost effectively as possible?
- … Enterprise Architects provide the enterprise capability map?
- … Customer Support ensures customer's incidents are timely resolved?

Well, the same answers apply as before when introducing Software Product Management. What inspires these teams and what is the intrinsic motivation?

Is it the joint product focus? Do they share the same purpose and objectives? Generally—No!

Let's examine the driving forces of these teams:

- Project management office is measured by delivery according to the project's plans, minimizing deviations in time and budget. Changes to plan mean unwanted risks. As a consequence, this strict approach might foil the focus on value and increasing flexibility …
- Digital Transformation teams want to transform something. They want to infuse the latest technology and showcase how state-of-the-art the company and its business teams are. The next technology hype defines what the product's direction needs to be …
- DevOps teams target full automation from development to operations, enabling a smart and short development lifecycle with increased frequency of new features. A portion of your development time is required to keep them happy; there can always be more automation …
- Enterprise architectures can become very complex over time, capability maps can become very complex over time. Projects are nice ways to improve siloes …
- Customer support teams like a stable system; new features are a risk and likely more work for them, so keep the code stable, no risky experiments please …

While the descriptions are obviously stereotyped and generic, they emphasize that the different teams and departments have different objectives by design. Developing internal IT Products is a challenging and complex task.

So, there is not really much of a difference here: Software Product Management as a discipline and product managers as the people living the discipline are essential for Software Products and equally for IT Software Products.

I recently read an interview in which Microsoft® CEO Satya Nadella spoke about innovation, disruption, and organizational change, and I concluded that Software Product Management was probably a central part/topic of what was discussed: "Microsoft's next act" (London and Nadella 2018).

> For example, when the business is doing well, in the name of accountability, in the name of efficiency, in the name of lower transactional costs, you get organized by business unit or what have you. This reinforces the next level of productivity gains, efficiencies, and accountability. The issue is that then it becomes hard to reconflate [recombine] some of the capabilities across these divisions to build new products. This is always a challenge. In tech, it's even worse because we don't have long periods of stability. If anything, the periods of stability are short and getting shorter. So, you can use structure sometimes in order to reduce transaction costs and improve efficiency, but in the long run, we [in the technology sector] are much more capability driven. I want a silicon capability. I want a cloud-computing capability. I want an AI capability. I want great product aesthetics in devices. Then we want to be able to take [these capabilities] and apply them to different markets at different times. Without this strategic flexibility, it's very, very hard." Change is happening in business and change is happening in technology. Every successful organization needs to react to these fundamental changes. This is where Software Product Management comes into play and can unfold its power. Strategic flexibility lifts new technology capabilities into product value.

The speed of change is ever increasing and the orchestration and prioritization skills as well as all other traits of a great product manager are more and more essential for success of any product company. Incrementally better has been the paradigm of the past, and we need to prepare and cater for flexibility achieving best value for customers, users and our own organization. Design for agility and flexibility to be fundamentally different always striving for improving the value of products. Same thing but different: Product managers are acting as a hub between all different stakeholders that have their own constraints and objectives. Software Product Management motivates, leads and brokers stakeholder alignment, or in other words evangelizes product mindset in the following dimensions:

- **Product Viability**: Product Viability comprises all necessary activities and insights to ensure that the IT product makes business sense, provides an appropriate return on investment and the IT product is adopted and delivering the planned business benefits—or more.
- **Product Development**: Guiding the engineering team from product vision and strategy to release scope and backlog prioritization. Providing clarity and direction to the core product team, keeping the team spirit up and developing a quality product.
- **Go-to-Market/Product Marketing**: Broadcast and position the product's values in the optimal way to the internal user community.
- **Software Demonstrations and Trainings**: Showcasing your product and training people how to use your product in the best possible way, underlining the positioning and showcasing the various values for the target groups in an engaging way.
- **The Market/Your Customers**: The market can be represented by IT communities, analysts, press and media, while the customers are the countries, line of businesses and business units using the product. Internal references praising great IT products are nice as well.
- **Organizational Maturity**: Defining the role of Software Product Management as a leadership role and improving the processes and tools continuously. Managing up the hierarchy and cross-teams showcasing the value that Software Product Management adds to the organization. Infusing product mindset to the organization. Not all can be directly influenced or fixed by Software Product Management; however constant dripping wears away the stone.

Product managers must help overcome unaligned strategies, objectives and agendas of individuals, teams or departments. Everyone involved in product-related activities must understand the consequences when an IT product does not survive, for example:

- no opportunity to shine as a program manager with a successful roll-out of functionality
- no opportunity to be recognized as a functional leader supported by great technology
- no next roll-out or investment into the line of business or business capability
- no opportunity to showcase great IT engineering and delivery skills
- no IT product to foster and expand positive digital transformation results.

While the dimension descriptions above are slightly different, the dimensions are the same for corporate IT products. We will investigate the differences when we discuss the detailed items of each dimension in Chap. 2. I will detail variations for corporate IT products if there is a significant difference, or if the general concept changes, but not if the transfer is simply from managing Software Products to IT products. The differences will be summarized at the end of the chapters so as not to disturb the flow. I believe the content will be easier to read and digest, while readers interested in IT Product Management will find the few differences handy at the end of each section.

1.1.5 The Promise of Software Product Management

Software Product Management is one of the most important functions, which, when done well, helps make companies and software products much better, and when done badly, can really hurt a company and lumber any product.

Let's wrap up this chapter, which provides the foundation for the subsequent chapters and the outline for the book. We had a first look under the hood of the Software Product Management practice followed by a generic definition of the discipline. We got a first overview of the Software Product Management dimensions, the involved stakeholders and why Software Product Management matters. We screened through the many variations and classifications of software products.

You might not agree 100% with all these definitions and explanations, as they might not seem complete for your context. Maybe the departments or activities have different names in your organization; however, that is perfectly fine and expected. Consider this chapter as the stable foundation that can be adapted to your context—the definitions are by no means meant to be exclusive or absolute.

If your organizational objective is sustainable optimization of product success, then there is no other alternative than Software Product Management and its proven benefits (Lawley and Schure, Product Management for dummies 2017; Narayan 2018), as listed below:

- Delivering software products that better meet customer needs and solve customer problems
- Increasing revenues, business value and profitability
- Enabling sales and marketing teams to scale market and customer success
- Creating delighted customers who generate positive word-to-mouth referrals
- Capturing and owning markets long term because of a solid product strategy that drives overall product efforts
- Helping engineering teams to be successful without wasted time, and invested efforts to do something meaningful and impactful that customers value
- Minimizing siloed agendas that do not act in the best interest of the collective organization
- Ability to reorient quickly and prioritize for best outcomes and value, not only work outputs.

This list is not comprehensive, nor will Software Product Management always be able to deliver all these benefits. It requires tremendous effort to establish and continuously optimize Software Product Management. However, the promise and benefits of Software Product Management are worth these efforts.

Properly chartered and set-up Software Product Management can transform organizations into high-performing, market-focused, and user-focused enterprises—no other function in a software product company can fill this role. Software Product Management is the only department that focus es solely on the product and the product is the reason for the department's and product team's existence. Software Product Management is not a short-term production and efficiency play. Software Product Management excellence will significantly increase the chances of product success and longevity.

With that in mind we can re-phrase the previous definition of Software Product Management to:

Software Product Management is a discipline and process that

- comprises all planning, coordination and execution activities required for software products
  - considering all product dimensions along the product lifecycle and
  - aligning all product stakeholders inside and outside the organization
- governs the topics that matter for successful products
- leads to customer value and long-term product success.

Many people want hard proof that Software Product Management is so influential for building and establishing Software Products. While I do not believe in metrics to prove and measure the effect of Software Product Management as an independent function, potentially useful metrics would be

- Customer satisfaction
- Product profitability
- Product team satisfaction and churn
- Number of releases.

All these metrics should and will improve over time, if you apply good Software Product Management practices and assign a strong Software Product Manager to your Software Product. Nevertheless, I would not credit any improvement or decline to just Software Product Management or to the role of Software Product Manager. Successful software products are and always have been a team effort and can be compared to winning the Super Bowl:

> Whenever you make the Super Bowl, so many things—you have to have the good general manager and the coach and the great players, and you have to have not too many injuries—everything, game plans and everything, has to fall very much your way for that to happen.
> **Paul Allen**

Improving all the above metrics or any other you might define in your organization is equal to getting to the Super Bowl. Very often the success of the product and the product team is personified in the role of the Software Product Manager. Why is that?

In the next chapter we will dig into responsibilities and variations of the Software Product Manager role and you might already wonder which superpowers are required to master one of the most challenging and rewarding positions in any software company. The required skill set probably requires much more than what it takes to become an astronaut[1]; however, being a successful Software Product Manager feels equally brilliant and is still less risky—as of today. Further, I will detail the importance of product managers and product teams as incubators of product mindset.

1.2 The Role of Software Product Managers

Software Product Management stands for longevity of products with enduring product success. The role of Software Product Managers[2] commonly represents Software Product Management the most. A product manager is not always in charge of a complete software product. A product manager can be responsible for a whole product line or for a module or piece of functionality of the software product.

Despite many hands and many brains are required to build products, to introduce these products to the target customer segments and to keep these products in the market, the product manager symbolizes the product, and as the leader of the product team is generally considered the key driver for sustainable success.

Product managers are accountable for the sustainable success of their products. Product managers wear many hats: they are information brokers, discoverers, prioritizers, communication hubs, subject matter experts and, yes, humans. The last hat requires special attention given the demanding role.

Some standard definitions of the role that product managers play include:

- "Product Managers play a central role in Product Management. They are business managers. With the mindset of a general manager or "mini-CEO" for the product's business, they lead a cross-functional team to achieve the product's strategic intent" (Haines, The product manager's desk reference, 2nd edition 2015).
- "PMs manage products, not people, so they must achieve everything using soft influence, effective communication, leadership, and trust—not orders." (Anon and González de Villaumbrosia 2017).

[1]Soft skills requirements: "Astronaut candidates must also have skills in leadership, teamwork and communications." (Astronaut Requirements 2018).

[2]For better readability, I will use the short form product manager instead of software product manager going forward.

In this chapter, we will examine the traits of product managers and why these individuals seem to require superpowers. As there is so much material available via books, blogs, videos, podcast, etc. and so much is written and said about the role of product managers, I will keep this section rather condensed and focused by introducing:

- T-shaped superhero capes for product managers
- Various types of product managers
- Product teams and how they are formed
- How product managers lead product teams.

Instead of defining the role of product managers solely in one chapter or section, my interpretation of the product manager role will be further defined and refined throughout this book.

In most software companies and corporate IT departments, one of the pivotal roles of a product manager is brokering and coordinating the needs of all stakeholders ranging from customers, engineering and product support to sales and marketing, ensuring that the teams move in the right direction to customer value and long-term product success. As a product manager, you are acting as an information broker between distinct people networks. For example, the sales team and the software development team are distinct groups of people with very limited connections. Both are normally closed networks, likely not talking to each other, and if they are talking they are likely not understanding each other.[3]

Properly positioned as a product manager you are empowered to become the focal point for anything product related. Frequently this means, responding to a ton of product-related challenges and questions about financial results, such as how do you innovate, what's the vision, how do you focus on the user, all sorts of things. Product managers must derive insights from market inputs, not simply observe them. The better the insights, the more likely the product will address the market's needs. It takes time out of the office spent with external stakeholders representing the market to derive the appropriate level of insight. A product manager will need appropriate levels of insight to reach the real goal of creating successful products that bring value to your customers and to your business. It sometimes feels that these challenges and questions come at you all at once, which can become very hard to navigate.

As a product manager, your role is to handle these challenges in an appropriate way. If you do not respond appropriately, then this might become a downwards spiral weakening you, the product team or even the product. The main question is: How do you get ahead of these situations? What can you do to survive or even have fun and create the value and purpose you have in mind? How can these challenges be backed up by a strong team or organizational product mindset?

[3]Later in the book, Noah Askin will detail the topic of brokers and brokerage (Chapter: Organization, Processes and Governance).

That's where the Product Yield Potential Radar kicks in. The Product Yield Potential Radar is a novel framework that will help you with the above questions. I will introduce this framework in all detail in Chap. 2.

But first, I want to introduce you to the foundational concept of a vendor's tray. I got to know the concept years ago as part of communication training for managers. Traditionally, a vendor's tray is strapped in front of a person to attract customers and directly serve their demands. The tray is properly organized and is holding, carrying, and exhibiting all items that are likely in demand. The vendor has oversight and can easily access every item in the tray while being able to do other activities with his hands. Some people might call this a bag of tricks, but I like to use the analogy of a vendor's tray as I like the transparency aspect. You can directly see the empty spot that you have to refill (read: improve) on the tray. Your product manager's tray or bag of tricks requires a collection of skills, methods and tools how to accomplish your role and the various responsibilities and challenges.

My strong advice to you is to never stop maintaining your product manager tray, keep your bag of tricks current and flexible. As a product manager, you must always be open and curious about learning new tools, methods and skills. Properly equipped, you can leverage your product manager tray to master the daily challenges. Throughout the book, I will provide some interesting options to be included in your personal bag of tricks.

If you stop reading here, I want you to remember one thing. As a product manager, you need to enrich your bag of tricks and keep learning throughout your career. Product contexts are changing as the world is changing, new situations will arise—you cannot prepare for everything that might be ahead of you. Therefore, keep an open mind and work continuously on your bag of tricks to weather the storms ahead.

Let me summarize the role of a product manager in simple words.

As a product manager, you know everyone, and everyone knows you. You know the customers, the engineers, as well as the including the management team. You lead them all while they are telling you, what is the most important points to getting the job accomplished. Everyone wants to be understood by you, while they don't understand exactly what you do. Everyone requests your empathy, while you might not receive the same. You continuously work on your bag of tricks to be prepared for all situations, as each day is different. You decide what's important and what's not. You decide whether a new feature is done or needs further refinement. You are always responsible for everything. In a product mindset organization that is a dream job because the product is the most important thing, and therefore you lead them all.

Not every product manager is and does the same. People are different, organizations are different and therefore requirements are different. The role of product managers changes across different software product types, different departments, organizations and companies. The responsibilities of product managers change across different software product types, different departments, organizations and companies.

Besides all differences in the details that likely reflect each company's culture or a company's bias toward sales, marketing, or engineering, there are many similarities over and above all variations that you can observe in the industry:

- Product managers are working with many different stakeholders and need to communicate effectively with all of them. Specifically, that means receiving and considering feedback from stakeholders and broadcasting and explaining product decisions and priorities to stakeholders
- Product managers are the only ones that focus solely on the product and the product is the reason for their existence
- Product managers are generally not the HR manager of anyone in the product team
- Product managers are information brokers, discoverers, prioritizers, communication hubs, and humans
- Product managers are ultimately representing the product and are responsible for sustainable success
- Product managers need superpowers organized in a vendor's tray (remember Skills, Vendor's Tray, and Traits, the SVAT[4] of product managers).

Note that there are many definitions and opinions out there, but the only one that works is the one that works for you, your product team and your organization. When working with my product management team, we summarized the role of product managers with the following mission statement:

> Being responsible for a profitable and valuable product offering that satisfies/delights our customers while enjoying work.

This mission might not work exactly for you; however, it covers various important aspects for us: We want to be responsible for a product, the product needs to be financially viable, we want to solve customer problems and we want to enjoy our work.

After reading this book, I guarantee you that you will understand my view of what it is to be a product manager and keeping the promise of Software Product Management. I will provide you with a novel methodology that will help you to become a better product manager and that will support you improving product mindset in your product team and eventually in your organization.

Let's go to the next chapter to see how product managers with their superhero capes look like.

1.2.1 Software Product Managers—T-Shaped Superheros at Work

In this chapter I will describe the T-shape model and detail T-shaped product managers. We will learn the importance of soft skills and examine which soft skills are most important for product managers. If you read the endless listings of required traits, it sounds like product managers need superpowers to be successful in their

[4]Some people like to call this SWAT (Special Weapons and Tactics), but I like SVAT somehow better these days.

role. These superpowers traits are frequently described as the essential soft skills and hard skills for product managers.

Being a product manager is as rewarding as the role is demanding. Product managers have end-to-end accountability for product success and therefore care about each dimension and each detail as important for product success. Which traits, which skills—the hard ones and the soft ones—are required to be cut out for the role of a product manager?

As with many of you, I have been constantly striving for doing the right things at the right time for my products and product teams throughout my Software Product Management career. However there have been many occasions where tasks have been overwhelming and doubts and fear about priorities, my tasks, my role, or even my skills frequently popped up. You might have asked yourself similar questions at times: I do not code and I do not sell … what is my contribution, do I add value to the organization at all?

As I was roaming through the internet I found a website selling t-shirts. A special t-shirt caught my attention: the caption showed in big letters: "Being a product manager is like riding a bike, just the bike is on fire, you are on fire, everything is on fire and you are in hell (*Spreadshirt.com* 2018)".

That does not sound like the role anyone wants to be in, right? And it definitely does not sound anywhere close to being a superhero. I assume that it is no surprise to you that I disagree from the bottom of my heart with the fun message on this t-shirt. Rather than someone riding a bike on fire in hell, I hope this book will help you to be a successful product manager as it will provide you with insights, superpowers, and, if you like to wear them, a superhero cape, rather than the alternative.

In hindsight things tend to get clearer. I have no doubt that as product managers, we are adding tremendous value to product teams and product organizations. We are increasing the yield potential of products dramatically. Or as Marty Cagan stated: "… behind every great product you will find a good product manager … We have yet to see an exception to this rule." (Cagan, Silicon Valley Product Group—Behind Every Great Product, The role of the product manager 2018)

With agile development practices and design thinking became the de facto standard in the last decade, the mention of T-shaped skills has also arisen. I use the concept of T-shaped skills, or T-shaped persons as a metaphor to describe the abilities of product managers as illustrated in Fig. 1.5. The vertical bar of the T represents the depth of hard skills, expertise in product management and the domain knowledge of the problem (product). Hard skills are very relevant to your role and the work you are doing. These are your core Software Product Management and domain skills.

The horizontal bar represents the soft skills required or supportive to be successful in the challenging product world. Soft skills are not directly related to your job. Soft skills will help you in just about any job, and even in your personal life. Traits like communication, time management, and focus are as valuable to an astronaut, forest ranger, or product manager. In your product manager role, soft skills will help you to collaborate and communicate horizontally across disciplines.

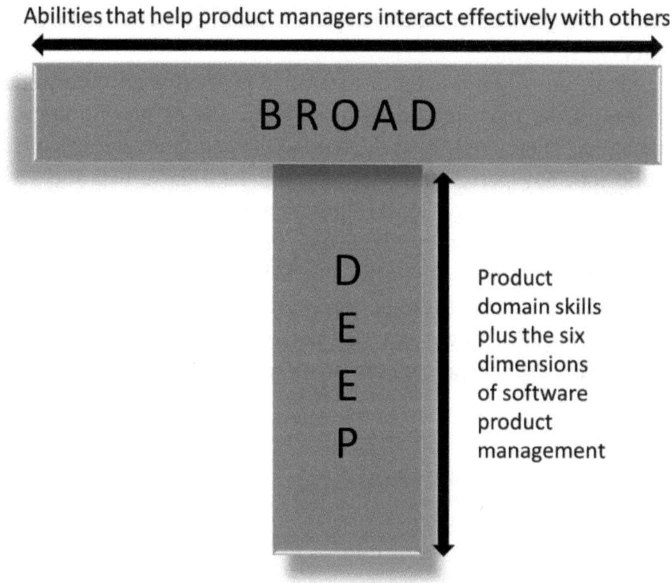

Fig. 1.5 T-shaped product manager © Timo Wagenblatt 2019. All rights reserved

What are the traits, the hard and the soft skills of successful product managers?

Product managers are experts in the domain of their product. In addition, to the domain expertise within the product scope, hard skills are required in the six product management dimensions: product viability, product development, Go-to-Market/product marketing, software demonstrations and training, market and customers, and organizational maturity. The techniques, processes, frameworks and tools required to improve and master these dimensions are the hard skills of a T-shaped product manager.

Throughout the book, you will find many proven practices that you might consider for your bag of tricks. These hard skills such as defining a product vision, writing user stories, prioritizing everything, or crafting business cases, to name a few, are embedded into the Product Yield Potential Radar, a framework that I will introduce in detail in later chapters.

However, that is only half of the equation needed to be a great product manager. Soft skills are the abilities that help product managers interact effectively with others and as you know, there are many "others" in Software Product Management.

I collected these soft skills (in alphabetical order) mentioned in relation to product managers: ability to influence, assertiveness, business acumen, boldness, collaborative, communication skills, confidence, consensus builder, coolness, critical thinking, cultural awareness, curiosity, decisiveness, effectiveness, empathetic, empathy, enthusiasm, entrepreneurial spirit, focus, forward thinking, humility, influence without authority, innovativeness, inspires others, leadership behaviors, networking, passion, persuasiveness, positivity, presentation skills, proactiveness, self-awareness, storytelling, synthesis, team worker, tenacity, time efficiency, and writing skills.

Let's be clear, no single human in the world possesses all these traits. One can easily find lists of the most important five, seven, ten or more traits of successful product managers. There are lists of the hard skills and there are lists of soft skills to survive in the job. My personal advice: Do not take these lists too serious, especially the ones that list the soft skill requirements.

In its most recent 2018 survey (*Trends & Benchmarks in Product Management* 2018) the Product Management Festival (PMF) asked: What are the three most important soft skills and what are the top 3 product manager responsibilities? The results shown in Fig. 1.6 might not be true for you, your product, or your organization, but it reflects the perception of more than 1000 product managers that responded to the survey.

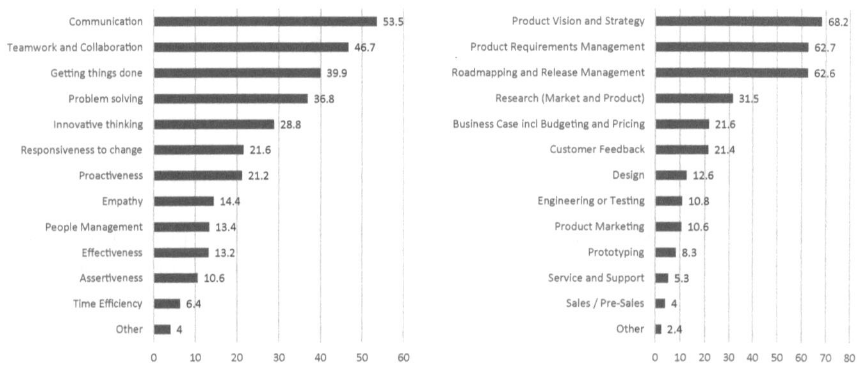

Fig. 1.6 PMF survey results—soft skills and hard skills of product managers © Timo Wagenblatt 2019. All rights reserved

The bad news is that hard skills are easier to gain and learn. The good news is that you do not need to gain all the soft skills listed. You already have some of these soft skills naturally. Everybody is born with some soft skills. Good product managers continuously improve their soft skills over time. Find out which soft skills you already have, and which ones would be interesting, or necessary for your job in your current context of product, stakeholders, and organization. Therefore, it would be beneficial if you have one soft skill (particularly self-awareness) or you benefit from a mentor, peer, coach, or manager providing you with valuable feedback.

First up in the PMF result list of required soft skills is (not surprisingly) communication. The product manager role requires lots of communication in all shapes and forms and in any direction. Product managers need to avoid being a bottleneck of communication flow, while they need to be on top of everything related to the product. As a product manager, you communicate upwards to your management and senior executives, for example to inform whether you are on track with your product achieving its vision. You communicate "downwards" with the team to stay agile and be able to course-correct developments quickly. And product managers communicate to the outside direction, to customers, partners, press, and analysts.

Communication might be in person, via phone, e-mail or via any other medium to one individual or to thousands of people. Product managers should be comfortable communicating with, not only members of your own team, but also multiple internal and external stakeholders. Remember that communication is a two-way street. Good communicators are great listeners, too.

In the early days of my career, I frequently got the feedback from my managers that I should improve my communication skills. I always heard the same feedback in my first years. One day, in another feedback meeting with another manager, I just answered to his question, about the area I wanted to improve, what seemed to be common sense before. My manager surprisingly responded to me: "What do you mean, you are a great communicator, maybe not on stage, but the engineering team knows why and what they need to build, the customers understand what and why we develop in a certain direction, sales teams know how to position the product, and the management team trusts you as a product leader, so what exactly do you mean with lack of communication skills." In hindsight it seems that I confused presentation skills on stage with communication skills, which I considered to be part of my regular work. Despite this is more than 15 years old feedback, I still remember my managers clarification very well. He nicely summarized the communication needs of a product manager as part of my feedback session. I'm not sure I thanked my manager properly at that time for this lesson.

I will not explain all the soft skills listed above and likely the list is anywhere near complete. The only other topic I would like to examine briefly is decisiveness. As a product manager, you are the one who needs to make the call if no one else does. The Product Yield Potential Radar is a framework that will help you prioritize the many product-related activities.

If you don't make the decisions, your product activities might come to a standstill or stakeholders will make the decisions on their own. We all know these situations when decisions are pending, no one talks about the white elephant in the room, and progress is halted. Phrases like: "Let's discuss this offline" or "Let's hold off on this issue until the next meeting." are common. I'm all for collecting data to make fact-based decisions, but nothing decides itself. Too much data might lead to analysis paralysis, and decision-making gets delayed until the best of all solution arrives—and it never does. As a product manager, you need to be decisive to get things to move forward. Postponing decisions only increases the risk of delays and unwanted deviations that you will have to deal with later.

As mentioned previously, being a product manager is one of the most exciting and challenging jobs in today's industry. Throughout my entire career, it felt great being a product manager. And yes, I admit, that there are times of external pressure, forced commitments, high workload, high energy, and emotional reactions.

However, as a product manager your role is to stay focused on the thing and lead the product team to success.

Keep in mind there are many diverse characters involved in building software products, so discord and friction are inevitable. I like to think that discussions, disputes, and friction indicate that all involved are passionate about their assignments. However, this might not be the case at times and you experience just (bad) human behavior. Remember to be always respectful and kind, especially at crunch time.

As a new product manager, you likely will be overwhelmed at times. Software Product Management is known for having one of the longest ramp-up times of any role in product. Keep calm and keep working on your bag of tricks. Learn the hard skills and leverage your soft skills at the beginning. It's completely normal to take a lot of time, sometimes as a long as a year to be comfortable in your role and become an effective contributor to the company. Perfect product managers do not exist. As explained before, you do not need to have every skill possible. Nevertheless, every soft skill and every hard skill you can add to your bag of tricks over time are potential superpowers that will help you, your product, and your organization. Sometimes the capes are not visible, but everyone who works with a good product manager recognizes those superpowers in action.

Remember that you need to enrich your bag of tricks and keep learning throughout your career. Contexts are changing as the world is changing, new situations will arise—you cannot prepare for everything that might be ahead of you. Therefore, keep an open mind and work continuously on your bag of tricks to weather the storms ahead.

At SAP we have a great concept called Smarties, which are half day training sessions that provide the fundamentals of various soft skills. In my role as manager of product managers, I encourage and sometimes advise my team to take at least two Smarties a year. Building up of knowledge and expertise can never be a one-time effort, and the Smarties provide a great starting point.

Remember to use the above list of soft skills, assess what you have and what you need, and start broadening your horizon and continuously working on improving your bag of tricks. And do not forget to get your skills out of the bag and use them for the benefit of your product. Put your cape[5] on and be a superhero product manager.

Note that I did not mention one of the most important traits and responsibilities of a product manager which is using "The Power of No". I will detail "The Power of No" in Chapter General Manager of YourProduct Inc.—What's on the radar, but no product manager role description would be complete without mentioning this superpower.

Last but not least, investing in the traits of a product manager is a good investment as shown in an article that lists "10 skills employers will want the most

[5]If you wonder how the cape looks, just imagine the T from Fig. 1.5: T-shaped Product Manager is a cape and the horizontal bar of the T you put over your shoulders as you require your superpowers.

in 2020" (*10 skills employers will want the most in 2020*, 2018). Note that the article is about the global workforce and not limited to product managers.

1.2.2 Types of Product Managers—Same, Same, but Different

In this chapter I will summarize the little differences and vast similarities of product manager role variations. Product managers are frequently classified by

- the customers they target (e.g. B2B, B2C, Internal)
- the main part of the Software Product Management discipline they are focusing on (e.g. product marketing manager, product manager, product owner)
- their seniority level (e.g. business analyst, proxy product manager, product manager, Head of Product)
- type of company they are working for (e.g. industry, size, company culture).

These classifications and the types of product managers derived are confusing. You can find special advice for any permutation of these attributes.[6] In my opinion, these are really not adding much value for the readers. In best case they are entertaining. Frequently they are confusing or trying to separate where no separation is required. I acknowledge that the roles and responsibilities of product managers change across different software product types, different departments, organizations and companies; however, in my opinion, the similarities overcompensate by far any variation in the details.

As a product manager, getting Software Product Management right is all about balance:

- Building awesome products requires balance of domain expertise, technical expertise and soft skills
- Balancing the needs of all stakeholders internally and externally
- Balancing your and your team's time against impact, and your work time versus your life time
- Balancing customer requests including balancing existing versus new customer demands
- Balancing new feature requirements versus technical debt
- Balancing team and organizational politics versus the main thing, while this time it is likely more about protecting than balancing
- Finding balance and reducing imbalance for the things that matter for the product.

[6] I admit I have not yet found a publication with the title: "The 10 essential skills of a B2C product marketing manager in Brazil working in a bureaucratic social media enterprise software company to become the Head of Product". But some came very close.

Generally, this list holds true for any type of product manager. Finding the right balance for your product and for your role remains the key challenge, whether you are, for example, a B2B product manager, a B2C product manager, or you are managing internal products.

For completeness, I will describe the most prominent type of product managers as I understand them. I will start with the separation by customer type. Although the roles have very different customers and demands, they do have many similarities. The primary difference in these roles is their target market, the involved stakeholders and the resulting consequences.

- **B2B Product Manager**: builds products that are bought by companies to help their employees, partners, or customers. Other companies buy the product and purchase decision makers are generally not the actual users. These products tend to be low volume as sold to companies,[7] and sometimes they're sold by sales teams instead of purchased or downloaded like a consumer app. Example: SAP® Trade Management, SAP® S/4HANA.
- **B2C Product Manager**: works on products that are usually for everyone, with the target users being a consumer. Normally the same person buys and uses the product. These products target millions, sometimes billions of users. They are normally not sold by a special sales team; hence marketing, ratings and influencers are more important. Examples are not required as you know about all these apps on your mobile phone, travel booking sides and social media platforms out there.
- **Internal Product Manager**: delivers products for users within their own company. Functional leads decide what their people (their coworkers) require. Their contribution for cost coverage is agreed based on company policies. Major internal stakeholders are the CIO and COO. Product Managers are focused on program management and execution, and less on design, because their success is mostly based on timely delivery and roll-out of functionality. However, it is easier to get requirements and feedback from real users since they're your coworkers. Example: Opportunity Scoring system for own sales teams, user authorization for internal systems.

I'm convinced that the skills and traits required to master each role are very much the same. All products need to be viable, feasible and desirable. The bag of tricks might be different based on the challenges, and there might be a bias based on frequent usage, but the lines are continuously blurring. A standard example used in the past has been A/B testing. Traditionally, A/B testing has been used to compare two different product versions with more or less functional differences, for example two versions of the same web page with user group A getting slightly different options than user group B. The approach allows to determine, which option is measurably more effective to achieve the targeted outcome.

[7]Compared to consumer products because there are more consumers than companies in the world.

For many years, I was not familiar with the method because I was working as a B2B product manager and the method originates from the B2C product side. However, given the current public cloud offerings, there is little difference left. Nowadays I can run the same experiments as the B2C product managers and A/B testing has made it into my bag of tricks.

That's one of the reasons why I like to attend product management conferences. It is important to get out of your corporate bubble, hear about new things from others and learn. Product management conferences or meet-ups are great for this purpose. Do not restrict yourself by focusing on further optimizing your existing skills. Talk, listen and connect with B2C product managers, internal product managers and B2B product managers. Be curious as the lines are blurring, and everyone will benefit from each other experiences.

I will explore the separation of responsibilities (e.g. Product Marketing Manager, Product Manager, Product Owner) in later chapters. The classification by seniority level and type of company will be covered in a later chapter about organizational maturity as well. In Chapter 360° Stakeholder View, I will explain how to leverage the Product Yield Potential Radar to clarify the roles and responsibilities of everyone in the product team.

Until then, the following list provides a solid foundation for the product manager role in this book:

- The Product Manager is ultimately accountable for the success, quality, cost management and delivery of the product and the product modules throughout the whole product lifecycle
- The Product Manager is responsible for everything related to product. The role typically includes all strategic planning, innovation, and the long-term roadmap across the product and the product modules
- The Product Manager typically acts as the most senior product executive with deep customer, market, product, and subject matter expertise
- The Product Manager gives structure to and supports the product team as a leader. The Product Manager is also focused on relentlessly improving product management practices
- The Product Manager ensures the efficiency, effectiveness and continuous improvement of processes and tools
- The Product Manager is responsible for driving product adoption across releases, will represent the product at major customer and company events to ensure that the product roadmap is clearly conveyed and results in further adoption.
- The Product Manager is building strong interaction across organizational boundaries
- The Product Manager works closely with the Head of Products driving product excellence to support the purpose and mission of the product and the entire organization.

1.2.3 Quick Side Note About Job Titles

As with the product manager role, there's much confusion about Software Product Management job titles. Personally, I had titles like System Analyst, Business Analyst, Solution Manager, Director of Solution Management, Director of Product Management, Senior Development Manager, Product Manager, Product Owner, Chief Product Owner, Head of Product, Head of Product Area, VP Product Management, and that is likely not the complete list. Just to be clear, I was always working as a product manager.

These titles are especially misleading when they include role names. If a product organization is clear on roles and responsibilities, the titles could be just the role names. However, people generally like fancy titles and therefore organizations start blurring title clarity.

For example, at SAP we have no consistency on titles and we generally don't care too much. Titles do not really matter. We have global job profiles and associated titles; however, product managers are not assigned consistently to the product manager job profile. In addition, we add complexity for new SAP'ers or external people by distinguishing between solution management and product management. Note that if you meet three SAP employees introducing themselves as Product Owner, Solution Manager, and Product Manager, they could have the same role and responsibilities or completely distinct ones.

But, even if the titles would be clear in one organization and used unambiguously, they might be hard to compare with another person with the same title from another company. This makes it hard to compare jobs. I propose to not read too much into any title.

If you are lucky the title indicates internally and externally that you work in product, that you are a "product person". If you are interested what people do, talk about responsibilities to find out what other people do. Don't assume two people with the same title do the same thing.

And within your organization, just try to be as consistent as possible. I would love to see the title Product Manager becoming a brand within your organization so peers know what you do and what to expect and not expect from you.

1.2.4 Product Teams

As much as has been written and said about product managers, as much this is true for product teams. The do's and don'ts of working as a product team, co-location and office layout instructions, the right staffing of a cross-functional team, rules of meetings for product teams, rules how to use e-mail and much more guidance has been written and recorded.

You can easily find great and not so great advice about every aspect via a simple internet search. Or you can read a good book like the product management books listed in the bibliography at the end of this one. Still, I see the need to include a chapter about product teams for the following reasons:

- Product teams are important, and I'm using the term product team frequently. Therefore, I want you to clearly understand the definition used in this book
- I introduce and use two definitions for product teams, the core product team and the extended product team
- Product teams are incubators of organizational product mindset.

I base my definition of a product team on Marty Cagan's definition: "A product team is a group of people who bring together different specialized skills and responsibilities and feel real ownership for a product" (Cagan, Inspired—How to create great tech products customer love 2018).

I like to extend Marty's definition, which he details throughout his amazing book, by only one thing. I want to emphasize the part of experiencing real ownership by extending the product team; I want to include everyone in the organization that owns and is responsible for any piece of the Software Product Management dimensions beyond the product manager, the designer, the engineers and other product development focused roles.

As a result, I distinguish between the core product team and the extended product team as illustrated in Fig. 1.7.

The core product team comprises exactly Marty's definition plus the people who work exclusively on your product. The titles or roles of these people are not important, the skills required to do the required job are important. Bringing products and new functionality successfully to the market demands several diverse perspectives and skills. Hence, product teams are generally described and best set-up as cross-functional teams.

I admit that the feelings and contributions of people outside the product development organization are frequently not exclusive as they work on more than one product. That's especially true in larger product organizations that generally have more than one product. But as people understand the holistic product approach and the importance of balance that is supported and enabled by the Product Yield Potential Radar, they frequently find their role in the extended product team and deliver nicely against both, the team's expectations and product's necessities.

In my definition, the extended product team includes everyone who contributes non-exclusively to the product success and still feels ownership for a piece of the product success ingredients.

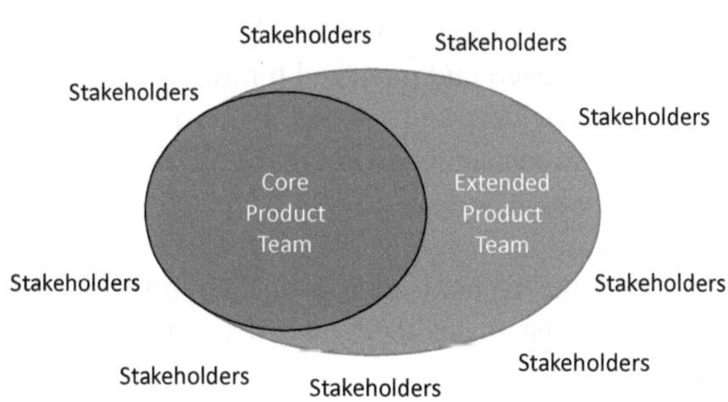

Fig. 1.7 Core product team, extended product team and stakeholders © Timo Wagenblatt 2019. All rights reserved

As a product manager, it is important to get others in the product team or the whole product organization to take ownership of product success and product issues. Note that I have frequently seen teams better performing that foster and value diversity. Throughout this book I want you to remember: The framework that I'm introducing with the Product Yield Potential Radar will strengthen the core product team. The framework will likely lead to an extended product team because more stakeholders will understand and consider a holistic product approach.

In my opinion, product managers have a key role in instilling a product mindset to the product team and to the entire organization. In my experience, as I introduced and exemplified my Software Product Management style of working more people joined the team and took real ownership over the product.

Product teams build and shape the product, and the product manager is responsible for the work results of the product teams. The product manager provides direction to what the team will work on, which is one of the main reasons why the product manager is ultimately responsible and accountable for the success of the product and the product team.

Based upon the earlier definition of stakeholders, everyone else is either a stakeholder, or not important—for product success and thus its yield potential.

1.2.5 Leading the Product Team and Instilling a Product Mindset

Successful products are the result of everyone on the team or the entire organization doing what is required. Generally, any fault with the product and with the ineffectiveness of the product team is personified in the product manager. I will not judge this, I just acknowledge it. Great product managers take the blame and share the success.

The analogy to any team sport is obvious. Let's use my favorite team sport as an example. In football (i.e. soccer for some of you), you have the team manager being criticized or even fired if the team is not doing well. The team manager does not score, tackle, sprint or pass. To win games, the team manager leads the team with a strategy, provides clear guidance on everyone's task on the pitch, and directs the team about what is important to succeed.

Everyone in the team is a football player, but they have different traits, skills, and tasks that need to be orchestrated and managed for the best results. Every team has a goalkeeper, defenders, midfielders and strikers. Every player has a clear role in the team's game strategy. Team managers do not make all the decisions. They don't tell the equipment manager which jerseys to use at match day. The players need to make 100% of decisions on their own while playing. Depending on the opponent, the game dynamics and the tactical approach, their roles need to be differently interpreted. The players must make their own decisions and need creativity and focus on the pitch to succeed.

In addition, the team manager thinks also about the best training to gain and improve the right skills for his (or the club's) vision of playing football. The team manager will hire new players and keep existing players to close any gaps in skills or traits to increase the chances of success. The best teams do not always have the best players, but they have certainly the team spirit and the ultimate will to win. Generally, the main thing is winning the next game, and everyone from the equipment manager to the players to the chairman of the club knows that everything else is secondary. But, the team manager is held responsible and accountable for the success of the team. Great team managers take the blame and share the success.

In your role as a product manager, there is no difference. As you are held responsible and accountable for product success, your mandate is to manage all product aspects and lead the product team toward product success by instilling a product mindset and keeping the main thing the main thing.

As a product manager, you provide the service of leadership to the team. Product managers lead product teams without organizational authority. These days, the concept of Servant Leadership has become very popular; however the concept is not new. In 1987, Tom DeMarco and Timothy Lister excellently summarized what people would now name the concept of servant leadership. They called a style of leadership without positional authority, as leadership as a service (DeMarco and Lister, Peopleware 2013), which requires:

- Step up to the task
- Be evidently fit for the task
- Prepare for the task by doing the required homework ahead of time
- Maximize value to everyone
- Do it all with humor and obvious goodwill.

You stepped up to be the leader of the product team, because you are a product manager. You might sometimes set explicit directions, but you understand your main role is that of a catalyst who makes it possible for the magic of real teams to happen. The magic that happens when a team understands what is important for their shared goal and effectively and trustfully works together toward achieving the product vision and successfully delivering awesome products. You are part of the core product team and you are leading the team at the same time. You instill a product mindset to the product team as you are the role model of product mindset.

I'm a passionate advocate of product mindset. I've been using the term already several times in this book, but the meaning might still not be clear. For me a product mindset means that we consider the success of the product, its impact and value for our customers and our organization as the main goal, everything else is secondary.

Your role as a product manager is assuring that everyone keeps the main thing being the main thing. This leads to the shortest form of a product mindset definition I could come up with: "Having a product mindset means keeping the main thing the main thing and use the power of no for everything else."

As a product manager you are on duty to keep product teams or even the whole product organization aligned. Hence, you remind everyone involved about keeping the product the main thing or in other words sign-up for and live a product mindset.

As a product manager, you are the natural leader of the product team and a role model of product mindset. The best product managers foster a product mindset by:

- Relentlessly focusing on outcome for your customers and company instead of pure output while increasing the product's yield potential
- Putting a stake in the ground by saying no to everyone and everything that would harm anything related to the product
- Providing product teams the vision, strategy, autonomy, and accountability that will result in the best product for your customers
- Persistent execution to make the product vision a reality by showcasing a "whatever it takes to win"—mindset
- Leading product teams with a whole product approach that supports them building and delivering the best products
- Sharing and aligning the elements for product success and the contribution of every product team member to increase the product's yield potential and chances for success
- Stimulating team members to take on work instead of pushing it to the team, even if the task at hand might not be one's core responsibility, but will help the product to grow overall.

Indicators of product mindset are many, but there is no checklist required as clearly everyone in product will notice this warm feeling once it arrives.

Great product teams become incubators of product mindset. Product teams with a strong product mindset can become epidemic in the best sense within product organizations. I will share some examples throughout the book, where the product mindset epidemic started with a single product manager, infected the product team and other product managers in the organization and finally a whole product organization signed up for product excellence.

I will share how the Product Yield Potential Radar could spark the product mindset. The Product Yield Potential Radar explains what the product requires overall, the product's current status, and the weak areas that need improvement to ensure product success and to increase the product's yield potential.

Key Takeaways

- As a product manager, you offer leadership as a service to the product team
- You are an essential part of the product team with distinct responsibilities
- Product success is a team effort and you are the team captain
- Product teams require diverse skills and other people for product success.
- Keeping the main thing the main thing is the result of a working product team and a lived product mindset
- Scaling and extending product teams are key achievements

- The Product Yield Potential Radar supports the required orchestration and clarity, pinpoints focus areas, and helps with alignment. These points are the ingredients of people engagement and ultimately drive a shared product mindset.

Later in this book, we will learn how applying the Product Yield Potential Radar guides everyone involved to continuously improve the conditions for product success. The product teams benefit from a holistic product mindset that enables all stakeholders to

- understand the required ingredients for product success
- consistently assess the weak and strong areas of the product
- decide where focus is indicated, and time investments are required on the foundation of a shared understanding.

1.2.6 Ikigai for Product Managers

Have you ever heard about Ikigai? I was not familiar with Ikigai until I read an article while waiting for my flight back home from a customer visit. Somehow the concept resonated directly with me and the simplicity and clarity felt great.

The Wikipedia entry describes Ikigai as a Japanese concept that means "a reason for being." The word translated to English roughly means "thing that you live for" or "the reason for which you wake up in the morning (*Ikigai* 2018)." In their book about Ikigai, Héctor Garcia and Francesc Morales explain that Ikigai translates roughly as "the happiness of always being busy," which drew for me the connection to Software Product Management and the role of Software Product Managers (Garcia and Morales 2017).

We already discovered the dimensions and the multiple tasks and responsibilities of Software Product Management as well as the reasons product managers wake up in the morning. Most product managers I worked with love their job, which is a great start. And I cannot remember anyone not being busy, yet happiness I could not always observe.

Finding Ikigai in your role as product manager would be wonderful and I hope I can contribute with this book at least a bit toward this aspirational goal that is said to bring nothing less than fulfilment, happiness and can even make you live longer (or at least extend the life of your software product).

Note that I'm neither a life coach nor an Ikigai expert, but I like to think about the best product managers finding their Ikigai, which means living their life in the intersection of what they love, where they are skilled, what the world needs, and what the world pays for as shown in Fig. 1.8.

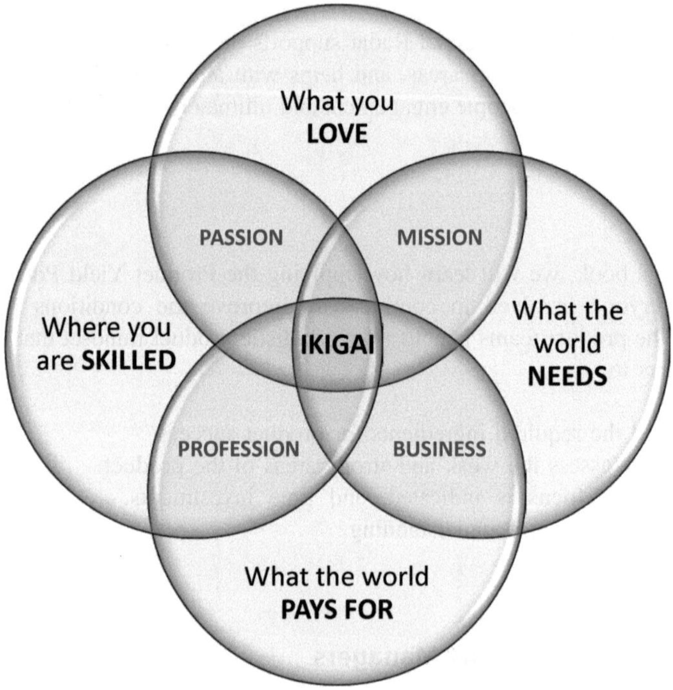

Fig. 1.8 Finding your software product management Ikigai

As a product manager who has not yet found his or her personal Ikigai, you might find yourself at one of these intersections where at least one ingredient is missing:

- Satisfied, but feeling of uselessness
  Represented by the intersection of three of the four circles, but where the real problem to be solved is missing (what the world needs)
  → product managers need to identify real problems and should be obsessed with solving these problems. The product is not great because it has tons of features, but because it solves one or multiple problems for its users.
- Delighted and feeling of fullness, but no wealth
  Represented by the intersection of three of the four circles, but where no one wants to pay for your outcomes
  → product managers need to be clear on value, positioning, and a viable business model.
- Excited and feeling of complacency, but sense of uncertainty
  Represented by the intersection of three of the four circles, but where you are **not** skilled

→ The Product Yield Potential enables product managers to understand the gaps in skills. If you know where you, the product team, and the organization might require improvements, you can fix and learn specifically.

- Comfortable, but feeling of emptiness
  Represented by the intersection of three of the four circles, but where the ingredient of what you love is missing.

The role of a product manager is likely not finding Ikigai in most jobs; however I like to think Ikigai is achievable and moreover I like to think that great product managers support the product team incrementally toward this aspirational goal.

1.3 Excursus: Defining the Journey from Total Addressable Market to Customers

The term Market is as unspecific as it is prominently used; one hears the term Market very frequently on various occasions and contexts. How often did you hear phrases like?

- "The market requires this product feature"
- "We are late to the market and almost missed the market trend"
- "A new competitor entered the market"
- "The market will tell you whether your product reached market-fit status"
- "We need to have a differentiation in the market, a unique selling proposition"
- "The total addressable market is *x* million/*y* billion"
- "Our market share declined by *x*%".

Market, market, market ...

Phrases we have all heard in the past and likely we will hear in the future. And the phrases above are just a little subset of the endless usages of the term Market. Generally, whenever someone states something with the term Market in it, there is some explicitly added or implied context.

The software product market comprises existing and potential customers (prospects) who need the software product and have the ability and willingness to pay for the software product. Hence, I recommend structuring any conversation about the market and customers using the terms Total Addressable Market, Market Segment, Target Customer and Customer. Understanding these basic terms brings clarity and will be useful throughout this book:

- **(Total Addressable) Market**
  The problems you solve, the needs you address, the pains you relieve with your product for the companies and people out there define the market.
  The Total Addressable Market is a term that is used to reference the revenue opportunity available for a software product. The Total Addressable Market helps

to prioritize portfolio and investment decisions by serving as a quick metric of the underlying potential of a given software product (Steve Blank 2012). In the diagram to the right the lighter icons indicate business or individuals that are not part of the Total Addressable Market as our software product features are of no benefit, no advantage, and not motivational to even consider buying—yet!

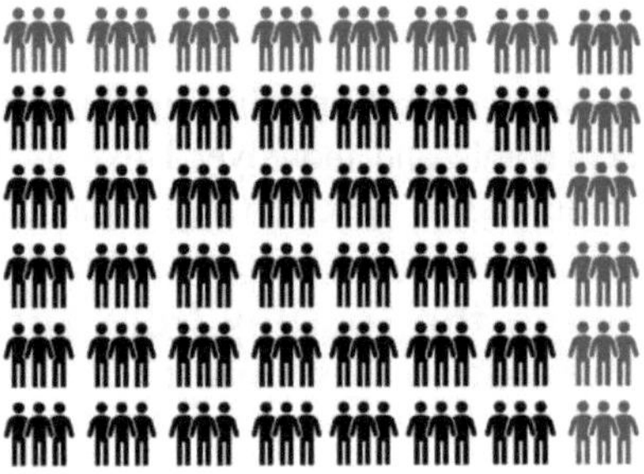

- **Market Segment**
  Different target customers in your Total Addressable Market have diverse preferences, needs, and satisfaction criteria. Although there is the notion and trend of individualism by addressing the "Segment of One," realistically all individual target customers need to be clustered in groups of target customers aka Market Segments. One basic type of segmentation is already completed by defining your software product in one of these categories: Business-to-Consumer (B2C), Business-to-Business (B2B), corporate (internal) business users. These classifications determine whether the segmentation criteria are for example by geography, size in terms of revenue, size in terms of people, size in terms of locations or any other sizing metric for B2B software product markets, age, income, values, interests, hobbies, education, or operating system for B2C software products, or line of business, location, business capability, budget for corporate IT software products. Independent of the software product classification, it has been always good advice to focus on the most promising market segment at the beginning if you can't serve all at once. Sect. 4.1 will detail the importance and strategic approach addressing market segments. In the diagram above each shade indicates a market segment for our software product as part of the Total Addressable Market.

- **Target Customers**
  After defining market segments, it gets really simple. Target customers are the ones that belong to at least one market segment that we address with our software product. Some people might use the term prospect and others would not differentiate to the term customer. I will try to stick to the term Target Customer until there is a financial transaction.
  Please note that one target customer can belong to multiple market segments—that's important to understand and to consider in many aspects of your product manager role. Sometimes that is not obvious.
  For example, I had to learn that many of my target customers who are global food and beverage manufacturer are actually not only part of the Large Customer market segment. Some of them operate in 150+ countries and even that single fact should make it clear that one legal entity called customer, is actually multiple customers considering preferences, needs, and satisfaction criteria—and I still need to remind myself once in a while. Consequently, there isn't one way to address these kind of target customers.
  Keep this in mind the next time someone tells you, she or he talked to the customer and the customer wants *x*, *y* or *z*. While this might work out for a single person, it will likely not for a 300,000-employee global company.
- **Customers**
  Customers are the ones using our software products—legally, because they bought them. We have used the term customer quite a lot already, however the term customer is used ambiguously in B2B software for the enterprise as a legal entity, any person working at the customer enterprise and the users. In B2C the term customer and user is likely the same person, but even that is not always a given. And for corporate IT products, the term customers might not be even used, but internal users, business units or line of businesses might be treated like customers.
  And in the example above, watch out if someone uses the term customer; for example if someone tells you: "I talked to the customer, and the customer wants, needs, etc. this feature."

These are basic definitions to avoid misinterpretations throughout this book as too often the phrases from the beginning of this chapter are ambiguous and full of interpretation.

1.4 The State of the Software Product Management Nation

In this chapter I will introduce some key findings and insights from a survey issued by the Product Management Festival (PMF) team. In my role as a PMF board member, I helped design the survey questionnaire and spent a significant amount of time analyzing the answers of 1011 respondents from 59 countries from around the world.

PMF is an organization whose aim is to support product management as a profession. It contributes to the development of product managers and establishes their role in their organizations by offering them all the resources and tools to empower them to create products. Its mission is to amplify the impact of product management—not only on the products themselves, but also on their organizations, to help product managers be more successful, and to make a real difference.

The complete survey results can be downloaded at www.ProductManagementFestival.com/survey. Therefore, I will not just replicate the freely available Trends and Benchmarks Report (2018). I will focus on the aspects that matter most for this book.

The survey was structured around these areas

- People
- Organization
- Process
- Product
- Product Culture and Product Mindset
- Product Management Leadership.[8]

Before I guide you through some findings, insights and learnings we gained from the survey, you can find below some stats about the frame of the survey:

- Geography: 0.4% Africa, 12.0% Americas, 72.4% Europe, 12.4% Asia, 2.8% Australia.
- Gender distribution: Female 32.1%, Male 67.7% and Other (Transgender or preferred not to state) 0.2% of the respondents.

[8]Insights in this chapter will be covered later in Chapter: Leadership, Vision, and Strategy.

- Experience: 2.7% more than 20 years, 12.0% between 11 and 20 years, 26.3% between 6 and 11 years, 33.9% between 3 and 5 years, 15.9% between 1 and 2 years, and 3.1% less than a year in product management. Software Product Management is still a new discipline and product managers are more experienced in work than in the new discipline as most people do not start their career as product managers.
- 38% have direct reports and 62% are single contributors without direct reports. The direct reports are mostly other product managers, product owners, and product marketing managers.
- 58.6% of the respondents have never attended a product management training.
- Size of organizations: 36.8% with more than 2000 employees, 14.2% have 501–2000 peers, 24.5 have 101–500 peers, 9.1% have 51–100 peers, 10.4% have 11–50 peers, and 5% have less than 11 peers.
- Customer focus: 39.3% B2B, 19.2% B2C, 38.1% B2C and B2B, 3.3% Internal.

The last point is another indicator that the lines between B2B and B2C product management are blurring. Product managers need to be prepared and understand the consequences of their role. Remember this as you continue to optimize your bag of tricks as a product manager.

1.4.1 People

Question: How do you feel in your job?

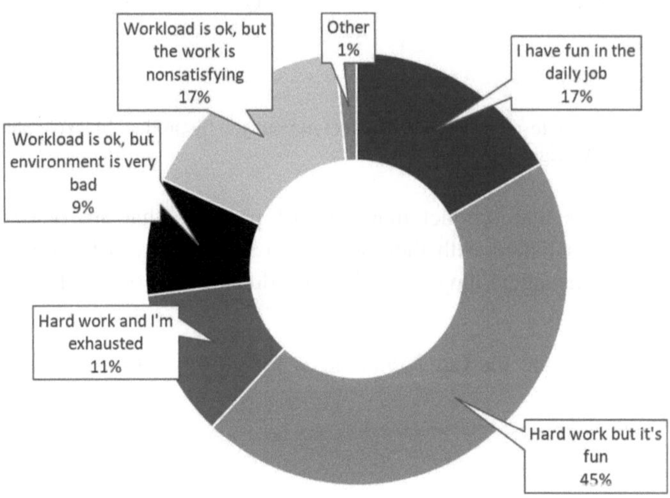

Fig. 1.9 PMF survey results—how do you feel in your job? © Timo Wagenblatt 2019. All rights reserved

Insight: Fig. 1.9 illustrates that product managers feel rather good in product management. More than 60% responded that they actually have fun in their job. However, it is not all rosy and shiny as 56% also report that product management is hard work. And 11% feel exhausted in their role and 17% rate their work as nonsatisfying.

Note that none of these numbers tells anything about the size of the organization they work for or the maturity of product management in their organizations, or the success of their products. Digging into the survey data one can learn that employees are feeling most fun in their product management role when they are

- working in really small (1–10 employees) or large (>2001 employees) organizations
- working in organizations with higher product management maturity
- working on a product in either ideation or growth phase.

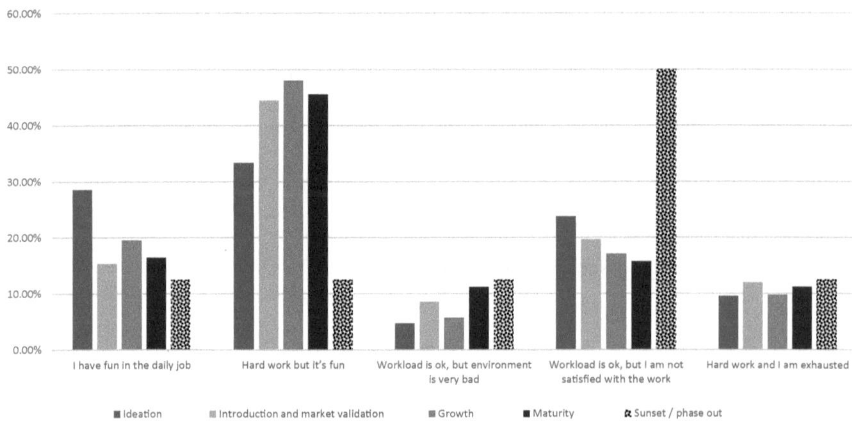

Fig. 1.10 PMF survey results—how do you feel in your job by product lifecycle phase? © Timo Wagenblatt 2019. All rights reserved

Figure 1.10 shows that product managers of products that are phased out (i.e. Timber!) are not satisfied with their work. No surprise given the emotional connection product managers have with their products based on all the blood, sweat and tears of the past.

Question: What are the top 3 challenges for you as a Product Manager to be more successful?

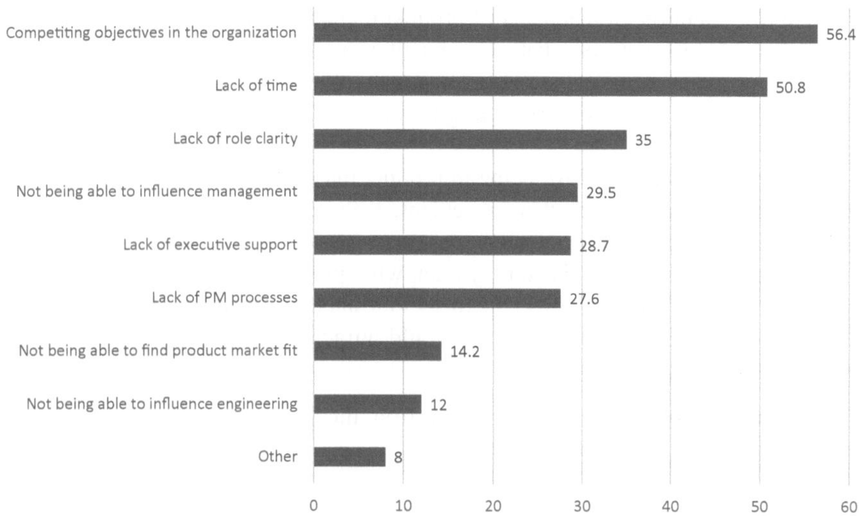

Fig. 1.11 PMF survey results—top 3 challenges © Timo Wagenblatt 2019. All rights reserved

Insight: I'll keep this one short. The numbers in Fig. 1.11 speak for themselves and I will come back to these challenges in several ways throughout the book. I admit that some of the challenges are related to each other and many challenges point toward management; however, we will sort this out later.

Question: Are you open for another job?

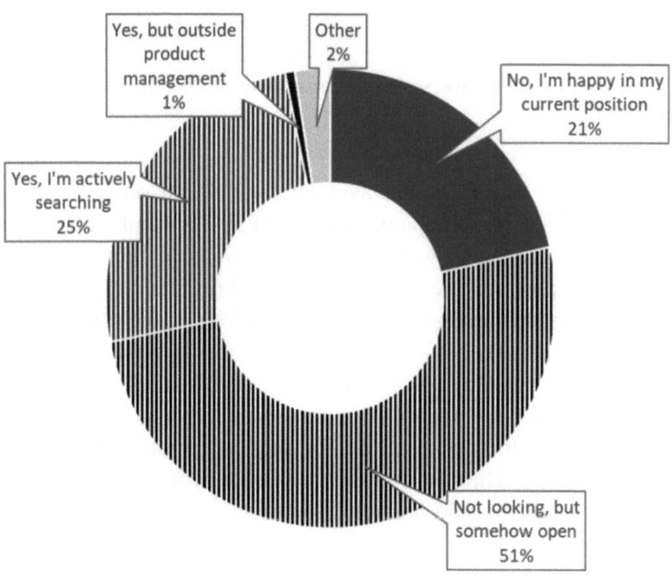

Fig. 1.12 PMF survey results—are you open for another job? © Timo Wagenblatt 2019. All rights reserved

Insight: Attention all managers of product managers, all Heads of Product, VPs of Product Management or whatever your title might be, the numbers in Fig. 1.12 should ring alarm bells in your organizations. Watch out as more than 75% of product managers are actively searching for or are at least somewhat open to joining another company.

And product managers love being in product management. Only 1% would look for a position outside product management. I heartfeltly agree that product management is the place to be.

I will explain, based on the survey data, what product managers value most and what might keep them or attract them to join another party. I will introduce the attributes of a job or organization that could attract them away from their current product and product team.

Question: If you analyze your calendar from the last 4–8 weeks, how much time did you spend on the following activities?

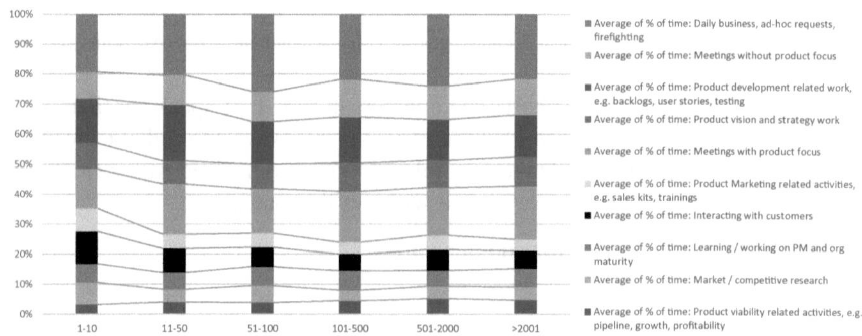

Fig. 1.13 PMF survey results—average product management calendar © Timo Wagenblatt 2019. All rights reserved

Insight: Fig. 1.13 illustrates the average time spend on the various product management activities by company size from 1–10 employees to over 2001 employees. Product managers work in all dimensions of Software Product Management. While the numbers are averages across all respondents, the results provide a great overview about the variety of tasks in a four to eight-week timeframe of product management work. No wonder that most product managers report that no two days are the same as they solve so many problems across so many disciplines.

Across all company sizes, the mix of activities is rather stable. Product managers spend roughly 30% of their time on ad hoc requests, firefighting and in meetings without product focus. That's a number we must work on. Remember that on average 30% of our time could be better spent more effectively and more product focused.

Question: What would you be looking for in the new job?

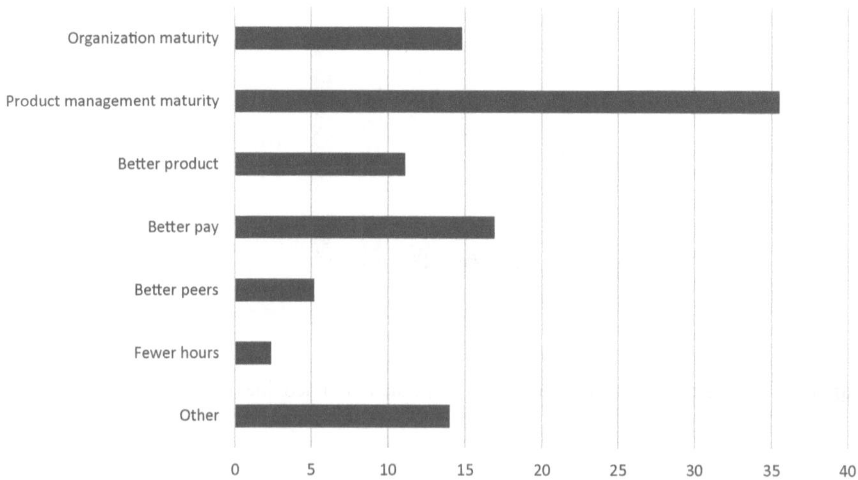

Fig. 1.14 PMF survey results—what would you be looking for in the new job? © Timo Wagenblatt 2019. All rights reserved

Insight: Product managers who are looking for a new job are craving maturity as illustrated in Fig. 1.14. They want to work in mature organizations and more importantly they want to work in mature product management organizations. Certainly, better pay is always welcome; however, fewer hours are not expected.

Product managers are looking for the right environmental qualities to be successful. They take organizational and product management maturity as a proxy for these environmental qualities. In Chap. 9 I will focus explicitly on this product management dimension. Note that I do not believe product management maturity is something only the Head of Product, Founder, VP Product Management or the likes are responsible for. Instead I see every product manager as being accountable for improving the discipline and their work environment toward product management excellence and a product mindset.

Based on the assumption that higher levels of organizational and product management maturity lead to less firefighting and less non-product focused meetings, the data shown in Fig. 1.15 explains the correlation between job satisfaction and how product managers spend their time (or should I say, need to spend their time).

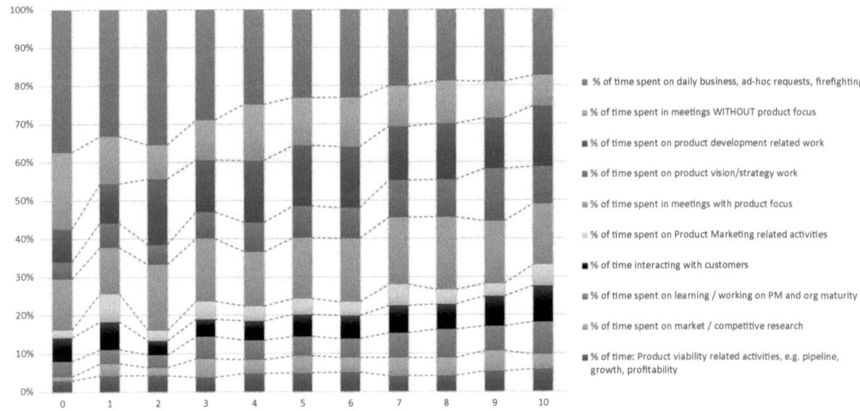

Fig. 1.15 PMF survey results—satisfaction as a function of activities © Timo Wagenblatt 2019. All rights reserved

What a clear trend in comparing job satisfaction of product managers against the time they spend with firefighting, ad hoc requests and meetings without product focus. Product managers care about the main thing—the product. The more time product managers can spend on improving the product, the more satisfied product managers are within their job.

Call to action for all product managers, you are the master of your own destiny. If you want to be more satisfied with your job, help your organization to become more mature. Call to action for all product organization leaders, if you want to keep your best product managers, treat them well and provide the best environment for your product managers, your product teams, and with that your products will be successful.

With this book, I want to help you on your journey by introducing a framework that is lightweight enough to scale with the level of adoption you and the organization can handle, and which is flexible enough to be customized for your context.

Product managers want to be product managers and they want to work in mature product management organizations. For me those are the key insights of the survey. Despite all the challenges, difficulties, complexities and hard work, product managers like the profession, they understand the impact they can have in their role, and they know that great products are the lifeblood of any product organization. In fact, some might even have found Ikigai.

In the following chapters, I will introduce some specifics concerning the role of the organization, effectiveness of processes and product work, and finally take a look at the data that provides some insights about the culture in product organizations.

1.4.2 Organization

Question: What is your organization's planned investment and in which product management area will you invest?

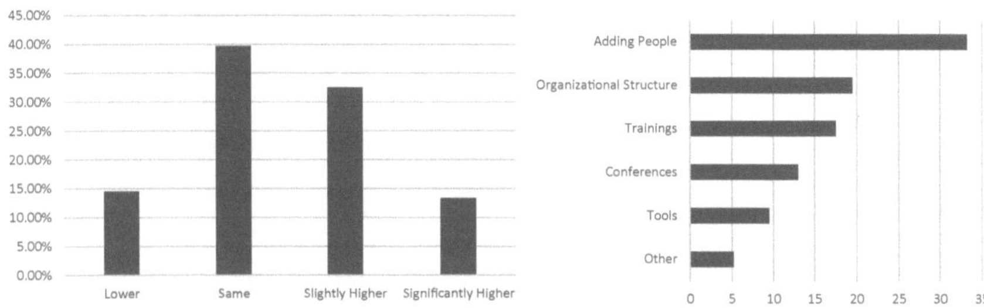

Fig. 1.16 PMF survey results—investment in product management © Timo Wagenblatt 2019. All rights reserved

Insight: More than 85% of the organizations invest the same or more in product managers and product management. Mostly organizations want to hire more product managers, which is especially interesting given the statistics about the product manager's desire and challenges shown in Fig. 1.16.

It is good to see that organizations recognize the need and plan to invest in their organizational structures and product management trainings, which will hopefully lead to improved product management maturity.

Question: How easily do you find/recruit product managers?

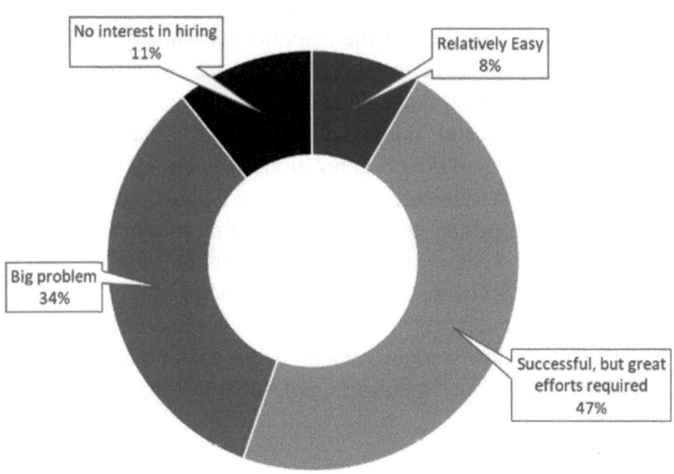

Fig. 1.17 PMF survey results—how easily do you find/recruit product managers? © Timo Wagenblatt 2019. All rights reserved

Insight: Finding product management talent is hard as shown in Fig. 1.17. Keep this in mind as you have seen how many product managers are open or actively searching for new jobs in product management. If you want to keep your product managers, or if you want to attract new talent, work on your processes, your organization and your reputation as a product organization.

Question: How well is the product manager role defined and lived by in your organization?

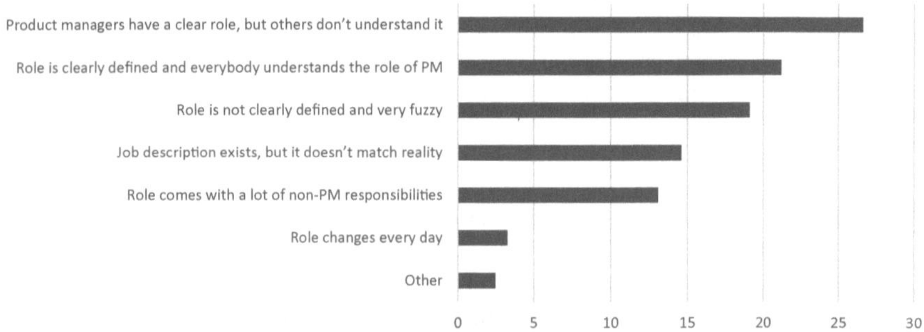

Fig. 1.18 PMF survey results—product manager role clarity © Timo Wagenblatt 2019. All rights reserved

Insight: Fig. 1.18 shows that only for less than 22% surveyed the role of product managers is clearly defined. As we will see later, that is a set-up for failure or at least poses severe problems for product managers. No wonder that lack of role clarity made it to the top three product management challenges.

The role of executives is significant in this matter. In organizations where executives are perceived to value and understand product management, lack of role clarity is in the top three for 26% of the respondents while lack of role clarity is a top three challenge for 45% in organizations where executives do not or only somewhat understand product management.

Executives that value and understand Software Product Management are attracting product managers to their organization. Role clarity is just one example of organizational maturity. As an executive or as a product leader it is vital to attract new talent and as it is important to keep your existing product management talent. Therefore, organizations need to continuously invest and improve, and the same is true for the function of Software Product Management.

I will introduce a framework that includes both factors: focus on continuous product management maturity improvement while considering the effect of organizational maturity on product managers and software product management as a corporate function.

1.4.3 Process and Product

Question: Do you have a product management process in your company? If yes, where do your product processes originate from?

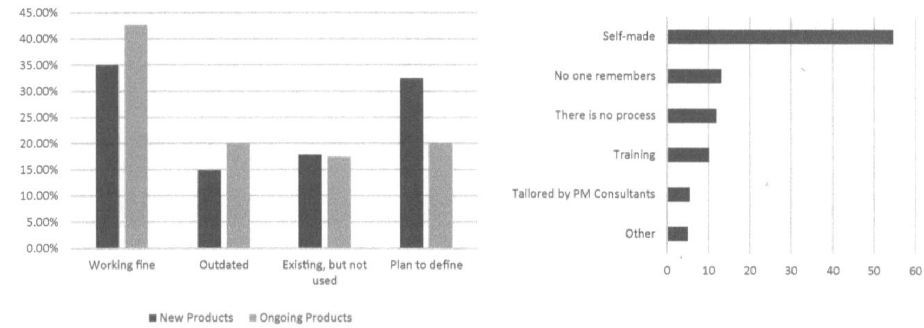

Fig. 1.19 PMF survey results—product management processes

Insight: Product management processes are an area that requires improvement as illustrated in Fig. 1.19. Less than 45% of respondents stated their processes work fine for existing products and less than 35% would rate the process for new product to be good. Generally, current processes focus more on managing existing products, while the plan to define product management processes is significantly higher for new products. Only 10% of product management processes originate from training and negligible 5% have been tailored by the support of a product management consultant.

Questions: Who is responsible for the product vision and strategy? How frequently do you review and adjust your product vision and strategy? With whom do you share updates?

Fig. 1.20 PMF survey results—vision and strategy

Insight: The good news first. Software Product Management is responsible for the product vision and the product strategy and the data underlines this common sense. Product manager, product team, and product management team combined show that clearly (>70%) in Fig. 1.20.

The fact that most product managers do a bad job in communicating updates needs special attention. Not communicating updates are a root cause for misalignments, wrong expectations, any many more unwanted side effects. I will explain the importance of a clear and shared product vision and strategy in Sect. 5.1.

Question: How do you prioritize where to focus your time/work effort as a product manager?

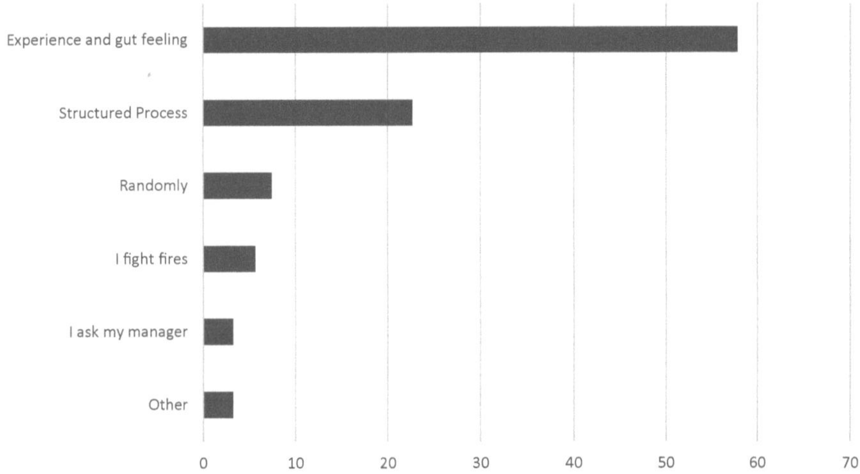

Fig. 1.21 PMF survey results—prioritization © Timo Wagenblatt 2019. All rights reserved

Insight: The numbers in Fig. 1.21 are interesting, right? We already discussed that lack of time is a top concern for any product manager out there and the clear majority relies on past experience and their gut feeling. Likely the product team members utilize the same way of time prioritization and the stakeholders join the tribe.

This means that frequently the prioritization and derived work focus relies on assumptions that are likely not shared with others. The consequences are obvious and misaligned and sub-optimal results are inevitable. The framework that I introduce with this book has its core strength exactly in this area. I will introduce the Product Yield Potential Radar in the next chapter. You will learn in detail how you can leverage Product Yield Potential Radar toward a focused and aligned product mindset.

On a side note, another data point showed that product managers that utilize a structured process to prioritize focus on time/work effort reported that they are significantly more confident than the ones using experience and gut feeling, or prioritize randomly.

In this book, I will dive much deeper into processes and product topics. You will find guidance and clarifications on improving all aspects of the ingredients for product success embedded in a novel and practical framework. Next up is a glimpse into the state of product mindset or product culture.

1.4.4 Culture

Question: How would you rate the product management maturity in your organization?

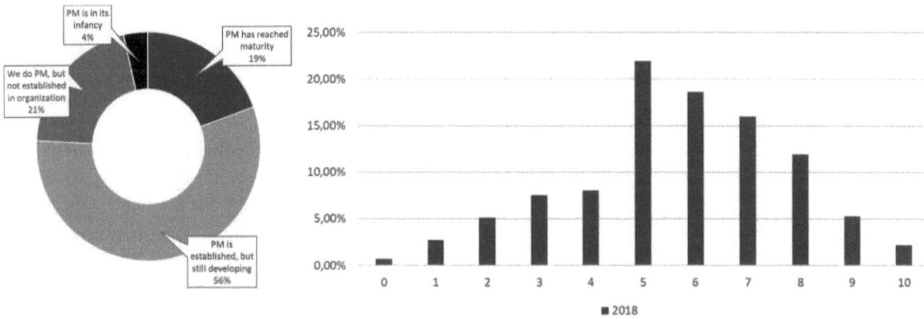

Fig. 1.22 PMF survey results—product management maturity

Insight: Product management maturity is a hot topic and I will pick up this topic specifically in Chap. 9. In particular, an approach to define product management maturity might be interesting in this context as the survey asked the question without exposing the criteria of product management maturity to the respondents. We did this on purpose to understand the perception of product managers without getting into a criteria-based assessment or academic discussions whether we defined the right criteria.

The good news is that compared to 2017, the maturity improved slightly in 2018. But only 20% of product managers consider themselves being part of a highly mature product management organization (8 or higher) as illustrated in Fig. 1.22. Combining this data with the obtained insights that product managers want to work in more mature product management organizations, explains the openness for another job in another organization of product managers.

Data shows that there is no significant difference between internal, B2B, and B2C product managers. The only thing worth mentioning here might be that the product managers that stated their products target businesses and consumers are reporting a slightly higher product management maturity on average.

As a result, investments in product management will not only help with your product's chances of success, but it will also attract product management talent as maturity improves. Don't forget to constantly talk about the great things you do in product management. B2C companies seem to understand this earlier than B2B companies. Product managers and product management leaders with B2C background are sharing successes and advancements way more often than their peers from the B2B world.

Purely based on the data, the top three key influencers that impact product management the most are product team health, product mindset of the organization, and product mindset of the product team.

These are the topics we will have a look at next.

Question: How would you rate the "product-mindset" of your product team, your manager, and your organization?

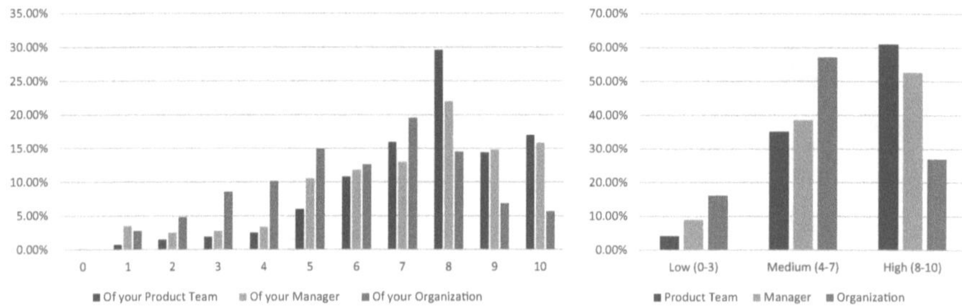

Fig. 1.23 PMF survey results—product mindset © Timo Wagenblatt 2019. All rights reserved

Insight: Note the significant difference in the ratings between product teams and organizations in Fig. 1.23. More than 60% of the product managers would rate the product mindset of the product team as high. At the same time, they rate the product mindset of the whole organization at 27%. That is a significant mismatch and a source of tension and dissatisfaction.

My read on this data is that organizations (read: executives and other functions outside of the product team) do not fully understood the impact of successful product management. It is a cultural change to keep the main thing the main thing. It is hard to give autonomy to product teams and overcome competing objectives within the organization.[9]

As an executive, that should and needs to be one of your highest concerns. Closing this gap should be your focus area for improvement. I will introduce the importance of product management leadership, organizational set-up and key principles to support a mindset change in Chap. 9.

Applying advanced analytics algorithms on the survey data exposed that the top 3 key influencers impacting job satisfaction of product managers are career path, product mindset of the organization, and team health. Next, I will introduce the product team health ratings to complete the picture of product culture.

Question: How would you rate product team health? We defined attributes to measure team health by considering team culture and delivered outcome.

[9]Remember that competing objectives within the organization was named #1 challenge for product managers.

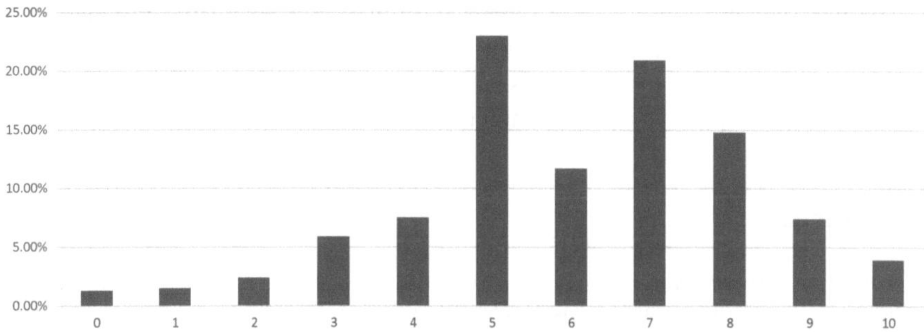

Fig. 1.24 PMF survey results—product team health

Insight: The numbers in Fig. 1.24 speak for themselves. According to the 1000+ product managers, most product teams are perceived to be on average or good health. Therefore, I would like to focus on another observation in the data.

The data analysis discovered that product managers who report lack of time as a key issue rate team health higher, or in other words, the more product managers work closely with the team the healthier the team. Almost two-thirds of the product managers that rated the team health 8 or higher, stated lack of time as one of their key challenges. That is significant as only one-third of the product managers who rated team health 7 or lower listed lack of time in the top 3 challenges.

What does this mean?

My interpretation and derived implications are:

- Spending time with the product team pays back
- Time prioritization and work focus needs to be aligned between the product manager and the product team
- Transparency of all product management dimensions beyond the product development focused items helps with alignment
- Expanding the product team beyond the core product team helps as more experts are available.

In this book, I will dive much deeper into various aspects of product culture and product mindset. In fact, the whole book is meant to support you, the product team, and your whole organization in improving Software Product Management excellence.

Product managers report back that mostly processes (i.e. compromise over outcome, unclear decision/prioritization criteria) and the organization (i.e. unclear responsibilities) are hindering them from having more impact. Let's start and sign-up for continuous improvement and drive continuous improvement of the whole discipline as a product manager.

The next chapter introduces the main and novel concept of the Product Yield Potential Radar, which is a lightweight, practical and proven framework that will help you to overcome the above listed hindrances and support your journey to provide awesome products to the market.

References

10 skills employers will want the most in 2020. (2018, December 23). Retrieved from Business Insider: https://www.businessinsider.com/10-skills-employers-will-want-the-most-in-2020-2018-1?IR=T#1-complex-problem-solving-10.

Anon, J., & González de Villaumbrosia, C. (2017). *The product book: How to become a great product manager.* Product School.

Astronaut requirements. (2018, December 23). Retrieved from NASA: https://www.nasa.gov/audience/forstudents/postsecondary/features/F_Astronaut_Requirements.html.

Business Dictionary. (2018, May 30). *Management.* Retrieved from businessdictionary.com: http://www.businessdictionary.com/definition/management.html.

Cagan, M. (2018a). *Inspired—How to create great tech products customer love.* Hoboke, New Jersey: Wiley.

Cagan, M. (2018, September 20). *Silicon Valley Product Group—Behind every great product, the role of the product manager.* Retrieved from SVPG.com: https://svpg.com/assets/Files/productmanager.pdf.

DeMarco, T., & Lister, T. (2013). *Peopleware.* Upper Saddle River: Addison-Wesley.

Garcia, H., & Morales, F. (2017). *Ikigai—The Japanese secret to a long and happy life.* New York City: Penguin Random House LLC.

Haines, S. (2015). *The product manager's desk reference* (2nd ed.). New York City: McGraw-Hill.

Ikigai. (2018, January 18). Retrieved from Wikipedia: https://en.wikipedia.org/wiki/Ikigai.

Kittlaus, H.-B., & Clough, P. N. (2009). *Software product management and pricing.* Berlin, Heidelberg: Springer.

Lawley, B., & Schure, P. (2017). *Product management for dummies.* Hoboken, New Jersey: Wiley.

London, S., & Nadella, S. (2018, September 20). *McKinsey.* Retrieved from www.mckinsey.com/industries/high-tech/our-insights: https://www.mckinsey.com/industries/high-tech/our-insights/microsofts-next-act?cid=eml-app.

Narayan, S. (2018, September 20). *martinfowler.com.* Retrieved from Product over Projects: https://martinfowler.com/articles/products-over-projects.html.

Spreadshirt.com. (2018, July 4). Retrieved from Spreadshirt.com: https://www.spreadshirt.com/product+manager+women-s+t-shirt-D13504839.

Steve Blank, B. D. (2012). *The startup owner's manual.* Pescadero, California: K&S Ranch Inc.

Trends & Benchmarks in Product Management. (2018, November 25). Retrieved from Product Management Festival: https://productmanagementfestival.com/survey/.

2 The Product Yield Potential Radar

After setting the stage in the first chapter, it is time to focus on the main theme of this book, which is a novel approach to holistically managing software products. I will attempt to support you in your product manager role by detailing how the Product Yield Potential Radar can help you in your journey toward Software Product Management excellence. My hope and motivation in writing this book is that it will help you to become an excellent product manager, working with a great product team in a product-led organization.

The previous chapter provided data-driven insights, a deep understanding, and a broad view about "the State of the Software Product Management nation" supported by the latest survey results from the Product Management Festival team. I analyzed data from more than 1000 product managers across the globe about what's HOT and what's NOT in Software Product Management.

However, as product managers, do we really need a survey to understand what keeps us awake at night?[1]

If you ask yourself: what is the number one issue or challenge facing product managers, the chances are you would say something similar to the examples below:

- "I do not have enough time (to do everything I would like or need to do for product success)."
- "My to-do list is too long for a day, a week, a month, and probably a lifetime."
- "I'm the jack of all trades and need to do everything on my own as others do not care as much about the product as I do."
- "Everything is urgent, what's the topic I should focus on?"

[1]Hopefully, this is only a metaphor for you and you sleep well! Sleep helps your brain work properly (Sleep Deprivation and Deficiency—Why Is Sleep Important?, 2018).

T. Wagenblatt, *Software Product Management*, Management for Professionals,
https://doi.org/10.1007/978-3-030-19871-8_2

- "People do not know what I do, and they do not know what is expected from them, so everyone does something (with best intentions) leading to limited success."
- "The product is great, why don't we have the success that we deserve for all the blood, sweat and tears we put into it?"

Not surprising, lack of time, or to be more precise, lack of efficient quality time seems to be a recurring theme and one of the biggest challenges. For product managers, the lack of time is supported and underlined in the PMF survey results described in the previous chapter. Very likely the challenge of having not enough time is true for product teams and all supporting teams and team members in sales, marketing, support or any other involved team working in your organization. We are living in busy times and Software Product Management is the epicenter of busyness.

Everyone feels time pressure, so everyone needs to prioritize and focus. How can we orchestrate all these events? Although perceived as urgent, are these items really important at a given time and at a given stage for our software product? Everyone seems to be driven rather than driving.

Product managers often act in an operational and tactical manner rather than being strategic. In fact, product managers need to be operational, tactical and strategic—not a surprise either—but how can that be achieved, given that there are only 24 hours in a day? How can we get quality time in our job that allows us to overcome the daily firefighting, and provides us the breathing room to focus on the vision, strategy, positioning, relationship building and relationship maintenance? How do we get more innovation, thinking and decision-making time?

As a product manager, getting Software Product Management right is all about finding and maintaining the right balance.

In the previous chapters about Software Product Management and the role of product managers, we only scratched the surface of the many different tasks and items that need consideration, or in other words, are required to increase the chances of product success and to improve the yield potential of software products.

This chapter introduces a novel and "business" tested way to structure the vital dimensions of Software Product Management. You will learn how to create focus and alignment on the things that matter for product success that product managers and product teams must master day to day.

You will learn about the Product Yield Potential Radar and how this framework can drive an ongoing discipline that helps the whole product team and product organization to

- understand all the required ingredients for product[2] success in your context
- consistently assess the weak and strong parts when holistically assessing your product

[2]PYPR can be applied on any level of the product taxonomy (Sect. 1.1.3), i.e. product line, product, and product module. For better readability, I will refer to product throughout this book.

- decide, based on a common understanding where focus and time investments are required
- find the right balance for product longevity and continuous improvement.

We will cluster all important Software Product Management activities into six dimensions. We will examine and detail each dimension by defining for each dimension, the tasks and items that are important to achieve the product's full potential. Then we will look at how all dimensions together define and limit the yield potential of a software product. We will further examine how to agree and define for each stakeholder the role and responsibilities within each Software Product Management dimension.

Additionally, I will introduce the law of the minimum and the law of tolerance that together illustrate how well product managers can use the Product Yield Potential Radar to recognize the limiting factors of product success. We will leverage the knowledge and insights from other research disciplines to improve our understanding of managing software products, from the initial idea to market leadership.

2.1 Introducing the Product Yield Potential Radar

In the past years I've set and hit many product-related goals, but my constant challenge has been trying to find balance for my products and product teams. How can I balance all planning, coordination and execution activities for highest customer value and long-term product success while aligning all product stakeholders inside and outside the organization? How can we improve the sales pipeline, product quality, marketing materials and the sales kit, product backlog, software demonstrations, look after our customers, current and future, and do all this and more at the same time?

Beginning from a Business Analyst up to the Head of Product role, these challenges and difficulties drove me at every stage on my product management journey. I constantly asked myself where I should focus and when I should focus my time on a certain topic to improve the chances of success for "my products" in the best possible way. And when I got this part sorted out for myself, questions such as what's the most effective way to improve each identified imbalance while avoiding missing out on something perhaps more important crossed my mind immediately.

Sounds familiar? And yes, you are right! There is even more to consider, such as the constant challenge to align and engage the product team and the entire organization,[3] and how to provide the best value to future and existing customers at the same time.

[3]Managers of product managers such as VP of Product Management or Head of Product roles generally are focused on how to improve Software Product Management as a discipline in their organization. However, in my opinion, everyone can and should contribute in this endeavor.

Most product managers are driven by the question of how to be more successful in their role and how to keep the product team engaged throughout the product lifecycle. How to inspire and set up the product team or the whole organization for sustainable optimization of product success is likely the most difficult issue facing everyone working in "product."

Let me summarize the main concerns of most product managers:

- How do I know what is important for my product right now and in the long run?
- How do I need to organize my day-to-day work and get the product team aligned to increase the product's yield potential?
- How can we communicate status quo and prioritization decisions best to everyone in the organization?
- How can we infuse and strengthen the product mindset (or in other words: how can we keep the main thing the main thing)?
- How can we improve the product management maturity in our organization?
- How can I balance and consistently improve all things that matter for my product's success?

I believe that there is little to no guidance in all the product management literature and trainings to equip me properly for my day-to-day job as a product manager. I perceived the situation to be worse in my role as Head of Product. The lack of mastery and guidance might be one of the main reasons why so many people in our profession still report a bad work-life balance and feel overwhelmed at times, which is reconfirmed in almost every product management survey.

When talking to product managers within my current company, or to product managers working for B2C, hardware, corporate IT or traditional companies, I perceive that not much has changed in the last 20 years concerning the main Software Product Management challenges independent of the type of software product. The survey results showing global data from more than 1000 product managers that we looked at in the previous chapter support my perception.

To avoid any misunderstandings, I admit that Software Product Management has evolved and the importance of the role of Software Product Management in developing great and successful products is common sense. We have more great tools and methods available for all tasks and responsibilities in product management. And I'm certain that there will be more innovative tools coming in the years ahead. We can adapt our bag of tricks with many useful new ways of working as we continue our career in Software Product Management.

My comment about Software Product Management inertia focuses solely on the main Software Product Management challenges that seem to persist throughout the years. The list below summarizes where most product managers still require help over and above the currently available and applied methodologies, tools and techniques:

- Understanding the required ingredients to be successful with their product in their context
- Leveraging checklists to not forget anything that matters for their product longevity
- Clarifying the role of the product manager, the responsibilities of the product team as well as the supporting teams
- Visualizing and making transparent the limiting factors for product success
- Engaging and aligning the product team toward fully exploiting the product's yield potential
- Balancing their and the product team's work efforts against impact
- Thinking and strategizing consistently with the team about overcoming the limits
- Embedding a steady communication and prioritization framework into the day-to-day business activities.

I have combined all the challenges listed above in a novel concept called the Product Yield Potential Radar; or in short—PYPR. The Product Yield Potential Radar is a thinking framework and evolved to an ongoing discipline that fosters communication and strategic thinking within product organizations.

PYPR orchestrates and helps prioritize the many product-related tasks at any given stage of the product lifecycle to maximize the product yield potential. Furthermore, PYPR clarifies the role of the product manager, defines the core product team as well as illustrates the responsibilities of the supporting teams.

Wow—that's quite a bit, right?

I will explain how PYPR works in three steps:

- First, in this chapter I will introduce
  - why focus and alignment are the keys to keeping the product team and all stakeholders engaged
  - the four steps to unfold PYPR's full potential
  - the PYPR dimension items and how these dimensions interact
  - the underlying PYPR concepts that will change your interpretation of Software Product Management
- Second, in Chap. 3, I will detail how you
  - leverage PYPR as the General Manager of the virtual company named YourProduct Inc. that represents the holistic view of your product
  - guide stakeholders toward increasing the yield potential of the product
  - introduce and utilize PYPR to your team, department, or organization
- Finally, after you understand the PYPR methodology, its components, and the best way to adopt PYPR in your organization, you will then find various examples of PYPRs and how the Product Yield Potential Radar has been adapted and adopted for B2B software products, B2C software products as well as corporate IT software products in Chap. 10.

I named the product yield potential concept a Product Yield Potential RADAR[4] because PYPR is a detection system that uses the product management dimensions to determine the yield potential and identify the constraining factors of product success. And radar charts are "commonly used methods for comprehensive evaluation, particularly useful for holistic and overall assessment through multivariate data. Its advantages lie in vivid visualization and ease of use. Through comparison and analysis, people can figure out their current situation: improving or falling behind." (Use Radar Charts for Data Analysis, 2018).

2.1.1 PYPR—Providing Focus and Driving Alignment

PYPR as a concept and methodology grew and improved with me over time. I designed PYPR as a concept and methodology that would be open, flexible and continuously improving. As stated in earlier chapters, I'm totally convinced that product managers need to be constantly driven and open minded in order to improve their bag of tricks, and PYPR provides guidance and support along this continuous evolution.

PYPR is a culmination of all that I have learned in my career in Software Product Management. PYPR evolved naturally over time as I was trying to organize and overcome the challenges and sometimes madness of the job, first for myself, and then educating my boss, then my teams, and then finally for my organization, which reflects the various stages of my Software Product Management career.

PYPR makes transparent and more tangible what you might feel in your guts, what you don't see at the surface, and it helps to uncover the tools needed to improve product success and longevity for you, the product team, and the organization.

PYPR helps to bring focus, alignment, and engagement to your product team and organization as illustrated in Fig. 2.1. All three points are key to establishing a product mindset in your organization, as successful products are never achieved by an individual product manager. It takes an entire team and sometimes organization to make impactful products happen.

To foster collaboration in the product team you need to provide guidance so that everyone knows and internalizes what the top priorities are and where the joint focus needs to be. One of the main duties of product managers is to make these priorities transparent and easily comprehensible. Once everyone understands what is most important for the product, every member of the product team and the product organization can make sure that their work efforts contribute to a steadily increasing yield potential and the improvement of the product's chances for continued success.

[4]"Radar is a detection system that uses radio waves to determine the range, angle, or velocity of objects." Source: Radar—https://en.wikipedia.org.

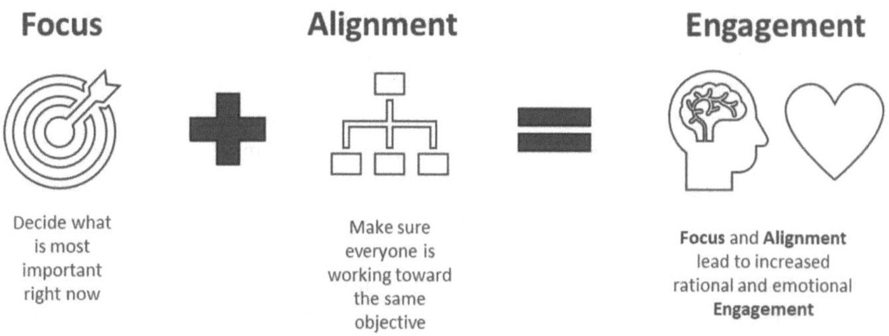

Fig. 2.1 PYPR benefits for software product management organizations © Timo Wagenblatt 2019. All rights reserved

I'm sure you also hate those exhausting and time-wasting "blah blah blah" email trails and "product" meetings. It's proven that when you discuss contextually around an artifact like the Product Yield Potential Radar, you can have more productive conversations and get to alignment more quickly. This results in less waste and more quality time for each team member and for you, the product manager, as well.

Alignment ensures all product-related activities contribute to the product vision and strategy. Alignment increases the product's success potential without wasting time on topics that are already in good shape or topics that require united activities toward the same direction, something almost every product team not using PYPR struggles with.

Alignment also allows all stakeholders to see how they fit into the bigger picture and why they are or should not be working on certain topics. This is a great way to increase engagement by giving the product team, and especially the product manager a voice, and shows every contributor and stakeholder how their work has an impact.

I have worked with many product teams that had skilled individuals, motivated and ready to rock, to solve a real problem. But they could not get a great product out or keep a brilliant product in the market because they were missing focus and alignment. The risk increases with the size of the organizations. This lack of focus and alignment frequently leads to declining engagement amongst the product team members. A vicious cycle that must be avoided by all means, otherwise … timber

Developing great software products always requires cross-disciplinary stakeholders working together. These stakeholders are likely not sharing the same language across functions. One of the most successful PYPR applications is providing a shared language across the product team and all involved stakeholders. Stakeholders from product marketing, sales, engineering, operations, finance, and so on can all work together around a PYPR and with that share a language to discuss their challenges, status quo, and work activities.

In summary, the question how PYPR helps product managers, product teams, all stakeholders, and the whole software organization to build better software products, will be the core topic throughout this book. PYPR provides focus and drives alignment that consequently leads to improved engagement. That's one of the reasons why product teams and entire organizations are adopting PYPR. I introduced some general benefits, but PYPR's potential to improve Software Product Management and the chances of product success is even more impactful.

The Product Yield Potential Radar (PYPR) helps product teams and makes the life of product managers simpler, as PYPR

- brings together the key elements that define how the product manager and the product team work together to improve the product's yield potential over time
- enables the product team and all stakeholders to overcome the language barriers between stakeholders and avoids getting lost in translation
- provides a holistic product view to make conversations more effective and more strategic
- leads to focused and aligned activities that improve the product's chances of success
- becomes the central, unifying tool to focus the conversation about any product activity on the things that matter.

2.1.2 Unfolding PYPR's Full Potential—Applying PYPR in Four Steps

The Product Yield Potential Radar is a thinking framework and comes with an ongoing discipline that fosters communication and strategic thinking within the product organization while enabling product team engagement. To reach this valuable end state by applying PYPR and unfolding its full potential, I have found the outlined approach below to be particularly useful:

1. Define, understand and structure all product-related artefacts important for your product in your context to be successful using PYPR;
2. Clarify the roles and the set-up in the product team and all involved stakeholders;
3. Conduct an initial assessment of the PYPR dimension items with the responsible team members;
4. Analyze the PYPR scores and prioritize the product-related activities toward best impact.

Each step comes with its own benefits. However, the value of applying PYPR increases as you follow the logical order. You could think about it like maturity levels of applying PYPR. Therefore, I recommend that you apply all steps sequentially. This section introduces a standard and straightforward way of applying PYPR. All aspects of this first introduction will be detailed in later sections, providing you deeper insights toward PYPR mastery:

- Detailing of all PYPR dimensions (Sect. 2.2)
- Proven practices, assessment guidance and PYPR dimension items details for each item in the respective chapters of part 2.
- Roles and responsibilities (Sect. 3.2)
- Detailed PYPR examples (Sects. 2.3 and 10)

There is a recommended order of four steps to follow to unfold PYPR's full potential as shown in Fig. 2.2. In the following sections, I will introduce and familiarize you with the PYPR framework. I will provide information with increasing details that will allow you to leverage PYPR in your daily work throughout the book.

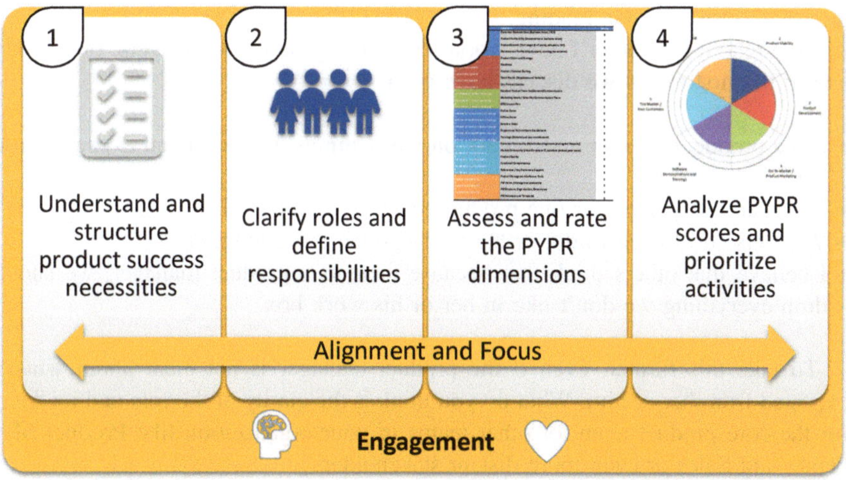

Fig. 2.2 Applying PYPR to unfold its full potential © Timo Wagenblatt 2019. All rights reserved

PYPR as a software product management methodology is completely customizable and flexible, making it easily adopted by any product team or product organization regardless of size, maturity or development approach. We will learn how to customize PYPR for your needs in your organization as part of Chap. 3.

2.1.3 Step 1: Define, Understand, Structure, and Transparentize (DUST) Product Management Dimensions

In earlier chapters we defined Software Product Management and the multiple tasks and objectives needed to deliver successful software products. In this first step, we list all essential items that are important for the product's healthiness and yield potential, or in short, the things that matter. You list the things that matter to your product based on a new or enriched view learned from the previous chapter, or on your existing corporate understanding. The objective of this foundational step is to simply list all the activities that are required and expected, implicitly or explicitly.

It might sound too simple and you might think that this step is too basic. If you think that way, do a quick field test and interview your product team or peer product managers about their tasks and responsibilities or about the tasks and responsibilities of Software Product Management in general. Ask several product team members what it means for your product to be successful. What do your peers or stakeholders think matters for YourProduct Inc?

Be prepared that you might get many different answers and perspectives, and maybe no single answer will be the same. If you get consistent answers, then you are one step ahead of most teams and organizations. If you get consistent answers and are comfortable that everything that matters is covered, then move directly to Step 2, or else continue reading.

Throughout my career I have worked with many product managers. Frequently, one of the first topics we discuss have been

- I'm a product manager and I work on many things, but is this all expected from me?
- How can one person, or one product team, accomplish all of this?
- What else do I need to do, or have I forgotten something, etc.?
- I believe that others think that because there is a product manager, we should drop everything we don't like in her or his work box.

To take this further, even if the product manager is not clear about what is expected from her or him. What do you think is the clarity of the role and its duties for the core product team, or other teams in your organization like Product Marketing and Sales or even more distant stakeholders?

These few examples are obviously a symptom of low Software Product Management maturity, as the role is not clearly defined nor the required activities for product success are organized in a process that people can follow. I acknowledge that there are trainings, great books or well-known Software Product Management frameworks[5] that define the tasks and objectives of a product manager and Software Product Management in general in various levels of detail.

Still for most of us the question remains, how can we distinguish urgent, important, and unimportant items for our product, our product team and our organization, thus optimizing for product success and longevity? Stay tuned, we will get there in Step 3 of applying PYPR.

In its simplest application PYPR defines and organizes the essential dimensions of software product management and all important items within each dimension. This very basic step will help the product team and the stakeholders to understand the things that matter for product success. For the product manager PYPRs'

[5]For example, the International Software Product Management Association (ISPMA) (2018), Pragmatic Marketing (2018), Product Focus (2018), or The 280 Group (2018) are widely recognized frameworks supporting many product managers globally.

simplest form can also serve as a checklist in times of chaos or as a reminder of what has not been looked at in a long time.

Furthermore, if you structure all the items into buckets or dimensions, then it will be handier to work with the large list of topics. What is important to be successful as a team will become more transparent and the discussions will strengthen the common understanding what it takes to deliver a great product.

As part of evangelizing product management in your organization, I recommend iterating this step multiple times to all stakeholders. For example, as you work with the engineering team detailing the dimensions, as a side-effect the team will learn about the ingredients of product success beyond clean source code, well-structured product backlogs, and a great software architecture. They will start to learn about essential product management responsibilities over and above the product owner role in the scrum team. They will learn why you might not participate in every daily stand-up, do not take every call or do not respond to every chat as they recognize the full responsibilities of your role. You will sense the same positive effects with any other role in your organization. I like to use the verb "transparentize" (merriam-webster.com, 2018) to describe this effect.

Figure 2.3: PYPR dimensions illustrate the definition of Software Product Management and the role of product managers from the previous chapter. The dimensions outlined in Fig. 2.3 are proven to work for various product teams in start-ups as well as in global software enterprises.

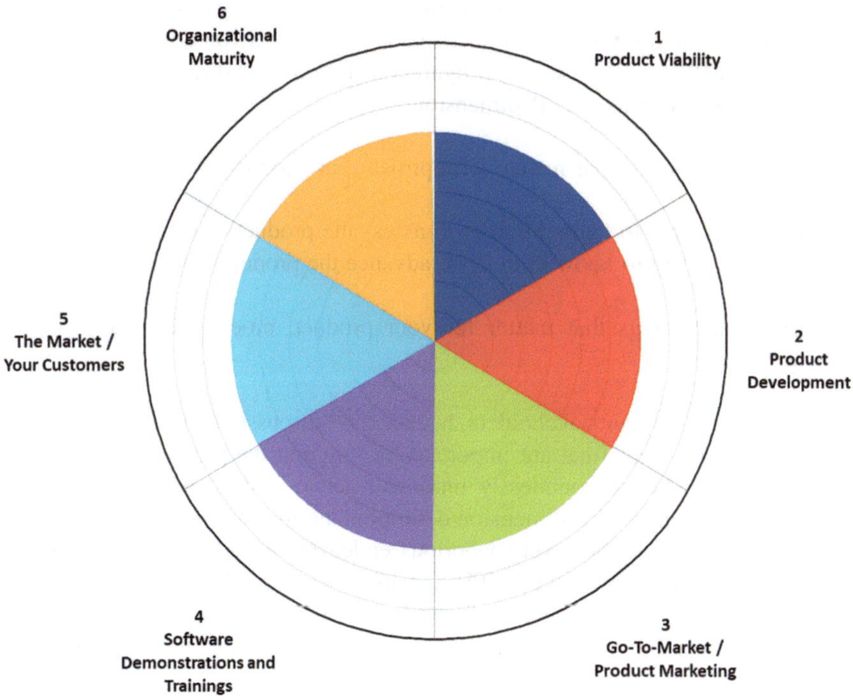

Fig. 2.3 PYPR dimensions © Timo Wagenblatt 2019. All rights reserved

Make sure that the Software Product Management dimensions listed below are understood by everyone, including the team and experts, so as to get a complete view of your product and organization.

- **Product Viability**: Product Viability focuses on ensuring business value for you and your target market segments or user personas.
- **Product Development**: Product Development concentrates on providing clarity and direction to the core product team, keeping the team spirit up and developing a quality product against the product vision and strategy.
- **Go-to-Market/Product Marketing**: Broadcast and position the product values to sales, professional services and partner community and—no brainer—to the market and your current and target customers.
- **Software Demonstrations and Trainings**: Showcase your product and train your product in the best possible way for each target group in an engaging way.
- **The Market/Your Customers**: Engage customers and understand the market while pleasing analysts and influencers to reaching a thought leadership position. That's what it is all about in this dimension.
- **Organizational Maturity**: Software Product Management is a leadership role and improving the processes and tools continuously is mandatory to gain and keep product success.

To accomplish this step, certainly we cannot remain at this 10.000-foot view level. It is important to define all items in detail that are critical within each dimension so as to improve the product's yield potential. If you do not want to stick to the default PYPR dimensions configuration, I recommend asking these leading questions when defining PYPR dimensions:

- What are the things that matter to improve your product? Define this for each dimension!
- What is important to know in order to assess the product's chances for success?
- What is important to know in order to advance the product's yield potential over time?
- What are the things that matter for your product, product team and product organization?

Brainstorm with your stakeholders, have a good discussion and cluster the items you agree on, the items that are important for you and the product team, into the right dimension. Iterate countlessly until you get to a stage where all involved stakeholders are fine with a dimension definition and its comprising items. Starting with a clean sheet can be a very laborious endeavor. As a good starting point, I recommend beginning with the PYPR dimension items as described and clustered in Sect. 2.2. These dimensions and dimension items are proven starting points that have worked well for many product managers and product teams in the past.

As a first glimpse, I provide a complete set of dimension items that worked well for most product teams I have worked with in Fig. 2.4. We will further detail all important components of each dimension in the next chapter. In Part 2 of this book, there will be one chapter detailing each PYPR dimension. In each chapter, you will find explanations and guidance with templates, tools and learnings.

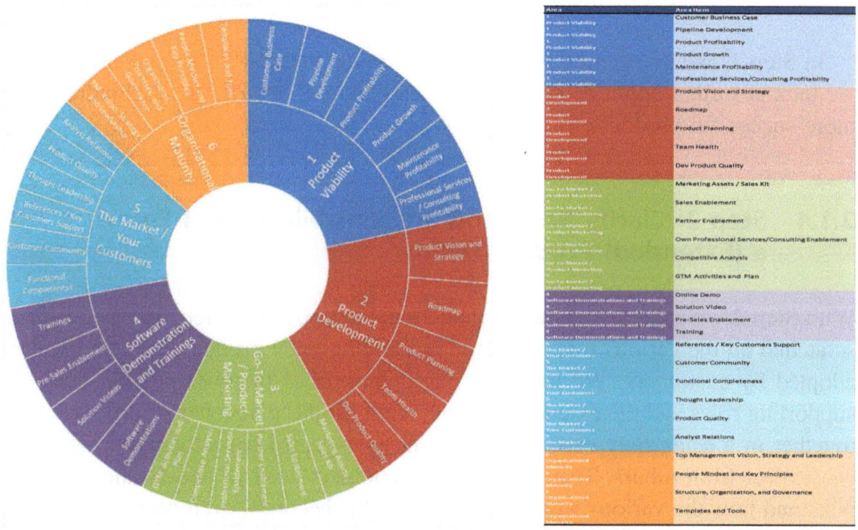

Fig. 2.4 PYPR dimension items and dimension table © Timo Wagenblatt 2019. All rights reserved

The Software Product Management artifacts and derived dimensions of product success illustrated in Fig. 2.4 are biased toward commercial products (e.g. B2B, B2C). However, in principle, these steps are equally valid for corporate IT products. For some dimensions, there are slight variations on item level that we will investigate in Sect. 2.2. In addition, you will find PYPR examples for corporate IT products in Chap. 10.

As a result of this step you have documented the context of our software products. You have defined all things that matter for your product and clustered all items into PYPR dimensions. You arrived at an aligned definition of what Software Product Management means for YourProduct Inc. and what Software Product Management stands for in your organization.

As outlined before, dimension details might deviate from the above examples and the dimensions or dimension items might be different for your organization, but PYPR is completely customizable and we will discover several variations in Chaps. 3 and 10.

Purpose and benefits of Step 1:

- Document the context of your product
- Define and understand the required ingredients for product success and structure the "ingredients" into buckets/dimensions transparently for all interested roles
- Get consensus as a team what's important for your product
- Use as a checklist of important product management activities.

In Step 1, we discovered the most basic, yet valuable PYPR applications, now we look at further applications in Step 2, and address one of the key hindrances of more successful products.

2.1.4 Step 2: Clarify Roles and Responsibilities and Form a (Extended) Product Team

With Step 2 we approach another foundational but powerful step. We have already scratched on the various roles involved in building great products and getting them adopted by customers. We looked at the definition of the core product team, the supporting roles and the extended product team. Nothing new here—if people work together in a team, they need to know what is expected from them and what they can expect from others. Teams and all stakeholders need to understand who does what and how the various work fits together. This becomes even more important as product organizations grow and more people are involved.

In Step 2 we utilize PYPR to define who is driving which items. We clarify who is accountable and responsible for each dimension and each dimension item. It is important to clarify upfront who does what and who can decide what within the product team. This is not a one-off process as you need to validate the assignments frequently and balance the work efforts and work peaks.

Watch out: It is important to have defined responsibilities; however, it is even more important to keep the team spirit and don't go back to silos.

As in football, no single player wins if the team loses the game. Don't get too bureaucratic or strict on role responsibilities as the product will suffer. All dimensions require care and work, and if someone is overwhelmed, give her or him a hand. Live the team spirit or substitute the players who value egos over outcomes.

Whether you go the route of extending the dimension table (Fig. 2.4: PYPR dimension items and dimension table) into a responsibility matrix (Wikipedia, 2018) using RACI or DACI or any other variation, the essence of this step is as follows:

- Build on a common understanding of PYPR, its dimensions and dimension items aligned within the extended product team **and**
- Clarify activity and decision responsibilities for each item

– Who is responsible and who is accountable for each activity (RACI)?

Responsible: stakeholder who performs an activity or does the work
Accountable: stakeholder who is finally accountable and has yes/no veto rights
Consulted: stakeholder that needs to provide feedback/contribute to the activity
Informed: stakeholder that needs to know of the result of the activity

– Who drives which part of PYPR and who is on duty to contribute to or approve decisions in each dimension and each dimension item (DACI)?

Driver: stakeholder who drives the decision process
Approver: stakeholder who is ultimately approving the decision
Consulted: stakeholder that needs to provide feedback/contribute to the decision
Informed: stakeholder that needs to know of the decision

By going through each dimension and dimension item you can appoint several responsibilities (D/A/C/I for decisions or R/A/C/I for activities) for each role involved. A discussion about role clarity and the things that matter for the product will strengthen everybody's understanding of the PYPR dimensions and the PYPR dimension items. In my experience, this will make the work going forward much smoother.

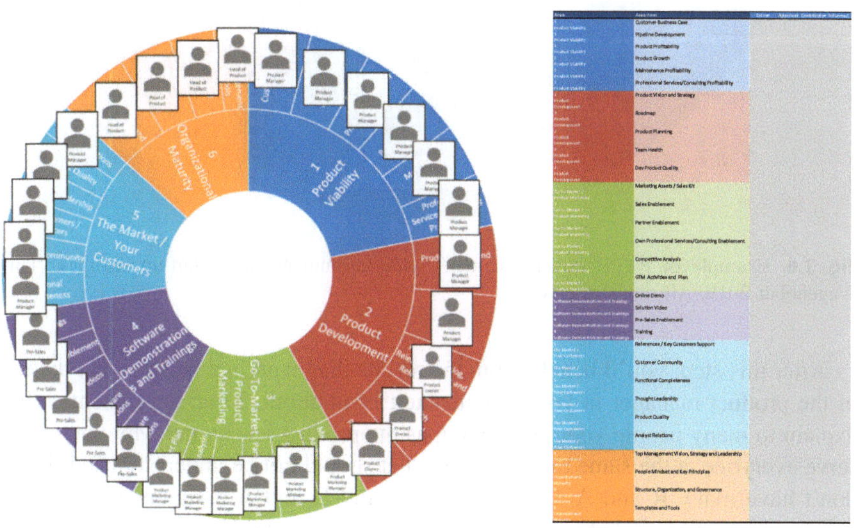

Fig. 2.5 PYPR dimension items with assignments © Timo Wagenblatt 2019. All rights reserved

Whether you are a product manager in a global software company and live in a specialized roles world as shown in Fig. 2.5, or in a start-up environment with more coarse grained assignments as illustrated in Fig. 2.6, likely you will have many R and A assignments or many D and A assignments in your role as a product manager.

Fig. 2.6 Example of PYPR dimension items with assignments in a start-up set-up © Timo Wagenblatt 2019. All rights reserved

After this step, you'll benefit from the results that everyone knows what the role of the product manager in your organization is all about. Your assignments might explain to many people your positioning as the product leader and why you cannot serve everyone at the same time—a value that should not be underestimated. If you don't have many R and A assignments or many D and A assignments, then you have much more work to do, educating your team and the organization about Software Product Management or you are factually not the product manager.

Another outcome of this step is the clear assignment of all the PYPR dimension items. Teamwork is still appreciated, but nothing should fall through the cracks anymore because of vague assumptions within the product team.

Now here comes the ugly truth of Software Product Management that stresses the team management the most and is one of the reasons for many debates about terms like "mini-CEO" as a description of the product manager role.

As a product manager, you focus likely on your important Responsible, Accountable, and Driver assignments; however, you know that every piece of the puzzle is important for product success. Therefore, you want to improve the product's yield potential by balancing all dimension items toward the optimum. That's why you care about everything and have your ears and eyes everywhere to stay informed about what's going on related to your product. You are interested in everything that is part of PYPR, because you care about the product. So far, so good.

But, some people like to play this card in a way that many product managers are "misused" implicitly or explicitly. They become a "drop anything here" product manager instead of being the product leader. People bet on the product manager doing the essential firefighting and last-minute work. They might even rely on this behavior. We need a test case, we need a user story, we need a demo, we need someone to give a presentation to customer a, b and c—great, we have a product manager. Sounds familiar?

We will discuss in later chapters how to manage these situations. I will explain how you become the general manager, the trusted, most senior product executive avoiding "drop anything here" Software Product Management in your product team and organization.

Step 1 educates the team and in the best case the whole organization about what it takes to build and market awesome products. The product manager introduces and moderates the aspects of the holistic product view. Now in Step 2, the clarification of the roles and responsibilities in your organization is another important step toward sharing ownership and instilling a product mindset in the organization. I frequently experienced that the product team attracted new members after these first steps of introducing and applying PYPR.

Steps 1 and 2 provide the foundation of how to avoid "drop anything here" Software Product Management. These steps help you to clarify and inform everyone to what extent you need to be directly involved and to what extent the responsibility or accountability is with another role. As a product manager, one of your duties is to ensure everyone focuses on the "main thing" as a team. Your job is to ensure the right things get done, it is not necessarily required to do them all yourself.

In Sect. 1.2, I asked you to remember that PYPR will strengthen the core product team based on the holistic approach to optimizing product success. I think you will acknowledge how PYPR supports you with this responsibility.

Purpose and benefits of Step 2:

- Define the role of product managers in your product context and with that shine some light into the black box of product management in your organization (i.e. people understand holistically what product management means in your organization as most stakeholders normally only see limited pieces of the puzzle).

- Define responsibilities of all involved roles in your product context and form the product team
  - Clarify who is responsible and who is accountable for the work package of each dimension and each dimension item (RACI).
  - Clarify who drives the decisions for which part of PYPR and who is on duty to contribute to or approve the required decisions for each dimension and each dimension item (DACI).
- Extend the feeling of ownership to the product team.
  - In the team = everyone who contributes to the product success, either exclusively as part of the core product team or with a shared focus as an extended product team member.
  - Not in the team = everyone who does not contribute to the product directly. Still this person could be a stakeholder (e.g. I cannot sell this product in my region; the documentation cannot be released as it does not comply with the latest brand guidelines, etc.). Stakeholders that are not part of the core or extended product team need special care as they might harm your work. I will introduce later in Sect. 3.2 how to deal with stakeholders.
  - According to the above logic, there will be a role/person responsible and accountable for each item within PYPR. If you have a gap then discuss who can fill the gap and which skills are required. This will help you to understand which skills need to be trained for or hired for the optimal team set-up.
- Explicit responsibility map for improving the product yield potential that can be used as an information radiator.
- Strengthen the common understanding about what is important for increased product yield potential as a team and with that improved chances for product success.

Steps 1 and 2 will be rather simple and fast to accomplish if you work in a mature Software Product Management organization. If you work in a greenfield environment, the default PYPR configurations introduced in Sect. 3.1 as well as the various examples in Chap. 10 are a good starting point for your PYPR adoption.

Extra benefits of Steps 1 and 2:

- The required T-shapes get defined—as people get clarity about their roles and responsibilities, they can work on gaining or refreshing the knowledge about the essential hard and soft skills needed for a successful job.
- The organizational maturity will be positively impacted as discussions and debates about role names or titles are de-emphasized. Each part of PYPR has a clear assignment and therefore product owner, product manager, product marketing manager, business analyst, solution manager, outcome owner, program manager, … all do not (shouldn't) matter anymore and likely can be rationalized over time.

In Step 2, we discovered an organization-oriented application of PYPR. In Step 3 we look at further insightful and value-adding applications of PYPR based on these two foundational steps.

2.1.5 Step 3: Assess and Visualize the Product Yield Potential

Steps 1 and 2 are the foundational steps that are important; however, the super-power value of PYPR starts with Step 3. This step is about assessing and visualizing the balance or imbalance of the things that matter for your product.[6]

In Step 3 our objective is to understand the status quo of each dimension item and document what's normally hidden in everyone's head or guts. We rate the strength of each item with a value between 0 (hell) and 10 (heaven). In this exercise you will find out the mismatches in perceptions, thoughts and feelings across the entire team—one dimension after the other—a great starting point for fact-based clarifications and discussions within the product team and all stakeholders.

Understanding the status quo of all dimension items leads to better judgement of your product's chances for success. It is essential for you as the product manager to realize the good and the weak areas of your product. Knowing where you are and knowing your current situation should be the basis for every future action; and visualizing your assessment supports this understanding and is sometimes eye-opening for everyone on the product team. Determining whether the things that matter for your product are balanced or imbalanced will guide you, the team, and the whole organization.

I found the following approach particularly effective when working with various product managers, product teams, and stakeholders:

1. Start with a full rating based on your own assessment of the PYPR dimension items. Document your assumptions for each rating, but don't stop here. I strongly recommend following the next steps. This will boost focus and alignment in the team.

   Note that only as an "old-fashioned" product manager that wants to "lead" the team the outdated way, you might stop here. As an aspiring General Manager of YourProduct Inc. you go ahead with Steps 2–5. However, I know that even aspirational product managers would like to stop here for multiple reasons. For example, some product managers are thinking that they know everything and there is no need for another view. Another reason might be that product transparency will consequently lead to more work as we continue to understand the weak parts or reveal the areas where the product manager did not pay enough attention.

[6]A product manager can be responsible for an entire product line or for a module or piece of functionality of the software product. Remember that PYPR can be applied on any level of the product taxonomy (Sect. 1.1.3), i.e. product line, product, and product module. You might consider PYPR at all levels understanding different aspects of your product capabilities.

This is an outdated interpretation of being the General Manager of YourProduct Inc. By gaining transparency, your product will benefit, your team will benefit, and you will benefit as well.
Be bold, read on, and benefit from the full PYPR value!

2. For each dimension, invite the relevant stakeholders for a rating session (i.e. with the default set-up as described in this book, there will be six meetings every two to three months). Think about the required participants with a focus on getting the critical mass of key stakeholders for each dimension, but still have a manageable team size for an effective working session. The results from the definition of the responsibility matrix above will support you in finding the required people. As a rule of thumb, invite all the RAC or DAC of each dimension to the meeting.

3. For each dimension rating session:
   a. Define one facilitator for each dimension, likely the responsible or driver as defined in the responsibility matrix.
   b. Discuss each item regarding expected deliverables and document the status quo and obstacles.
      i. If it isn't your first meeting, consider and revisit the last rating, agreed actions and notes.
      ii. Discuss what happened since last time that either improved or deteriorated the dimension item ratings.
   c. Have a joint discussion about the PYPR score of each item.
      i. Leverage the default item weights and assessment guidance for each item in Part 2 of this book.
      ii. Rate each item with a value between 0 (hell) and 10 (heaven), but beware of any bias, positively or negatively. Honest assessments are the only basis for good decisions on future activities.
      iii. In case of conflict, the product manager clarifies the expectations and necessities, leading to higher scores.
      iv. In case the stakeholders cannot agree on a rating, the product manager decides on the rating. Do not allow decimals, i.e. no 6.72 rating and no 5.5.
   d. Document the PYPR scores for each item and the underlying rating assumptions.

4. Visualize the assessment with PYPR
   a. A picture generally tells more than 1000 words; hence plotting the assessment results into a Product Yield Potential Radar diagram will provide better

clarity and direct insights. In Fig. 2.7, the circle represents the potential yield that is limited by the item assessments of the Software Demonstration and Training dimension. PYPR visualizes the imbalance of all defined Software Product Management dimensions.

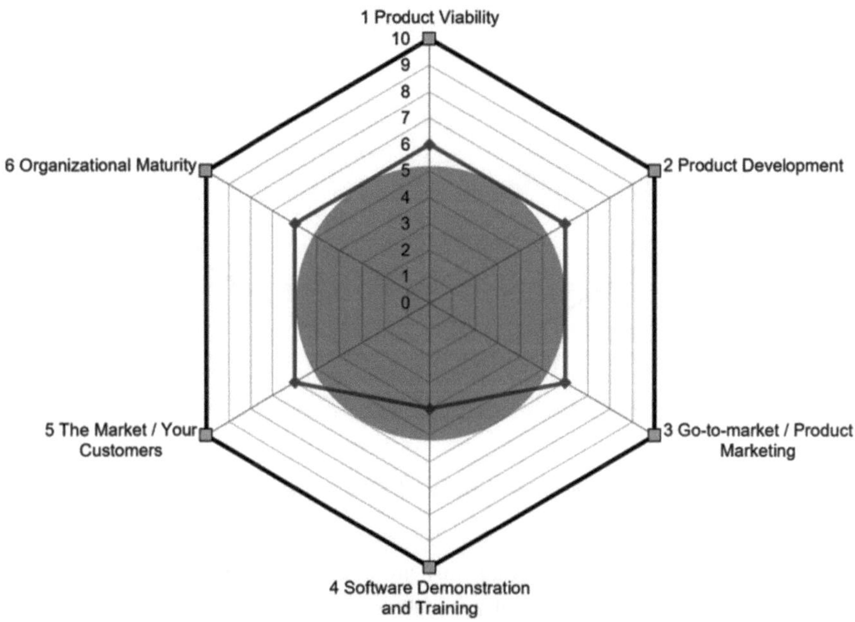

Fig. 2.7 Radar diagram to visualize the product yield potential and the limiting factor © Timo Wagenblatt 2019. All rights reserved

b. In addition, visualize both, the PYPR dimension scores and the total PYPR score, and track the results over time to understand trends and changes. In Fig. 2.8, you can see how the Software Demonstration and Training dimension declined over time. The PYPR scores were perfectly in balance in the previous assessment, and now visualize a limiting Software Demonstration and Training dimension. This basic example is just for illustration of the concept. I will introduce how to effectively work with PYPR in later chapters.

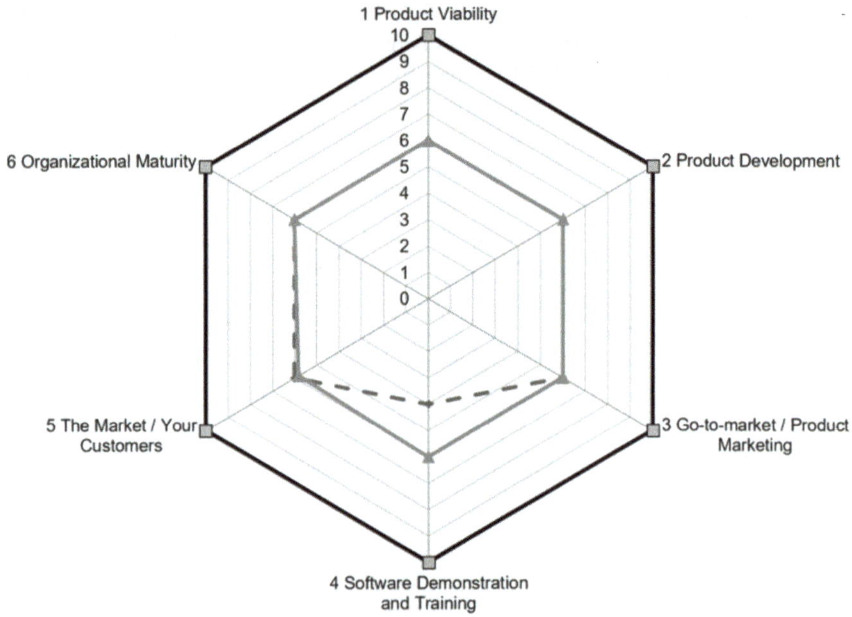

Fig. 2.8 Comparing two PYPR assessments in a PYPR diagram © Timo Wagenblatt 2019. All rights reserved

5. Store all results centrally so that they are available to the entire product team, product organization or company (whatever fits best to your corporate culture).

Figure 2.9 illustrates the increasing alignment and trust within the product team as you follow the described process. We started with the definition of the dimensions that determine product success for your product. In the next step, we clarified the details of each dimension and the respective driver of each dimension/dimension item followed by assessment sessions. In the last step, we aligned on dimension scores that lead to the Total PYPR score.

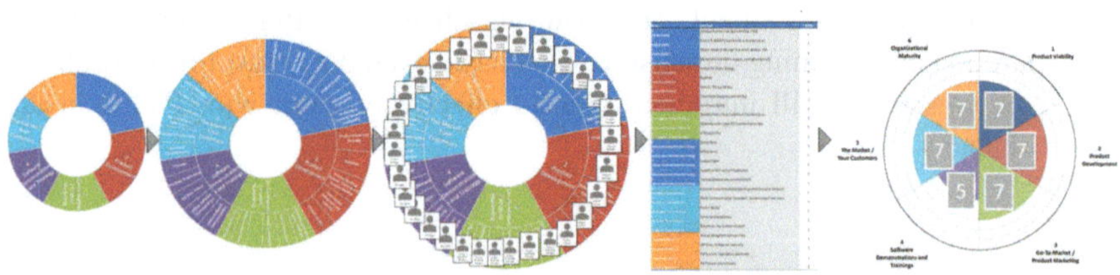

Fig. 2.9 Alignment from software product management dimensions to total PYPR score © Timo Wagenblatt 2019. All rights reserved

Note that while the example above shows an equal share of each PYPR dimension, experience shows that Software Product Management dimensions as well as the individual items of each dimension contribute with different importance to the success of products.

In Part 2 of this book, based on my experience working with various products and product teams in the last 20 years, I will recommend default weights for each dimension and dimension item considering the needs and contexts of your products and your organizations. In Chap. 3, I will explain how to best leverage Part 2 of the book for this purpose. Furthermore, in Chapter Listen—PYPRs in Action you can find some real-life examples for various products ranging from B2B and B2C products to corporate IT products that will help you to further strengthen your understanding how PYPR works.

Although Steps 1 and 2 are foundational, these steps are reviewed less frequently unless there is an urgent reason for changing the factors of product success and the assigned drivers. However, Step 3 should be part of your daily affairs. Step 3 feeds your radar; you get insights for questions like: Where are we standing with all these items that determine product success and longevity? How can we get better and improve the yield potential of our product?

As a product manager, you are mandated to keep an eye on all dimensions in parallel. Using PYPR as your software product management tool enables you to manage your product holistically. PYPR provides you overview and insights about your product's yield potential and overall healthiness. Increasing the PYPR scores over time will increase the chances of product success.

Frequent reviews and assessment sessions will bolster the alignment in the team working toward the same objectives. Increasing the PYPR score in all dimensions becomes the joint goal and hence you have a lever to keep the main thing, which is the product, the main thing. Alignment and transparency on the product status quo provide the base to incrementally improve the product's yield potential with every future activity.

Purpose and benefits of Step 3:

- Document the product status quo and the underlying rating assumptions
- Engage and align the product team toward fully exploiting the product's yield potential
- Think and strategize with the team about product's status quo in each PYPR dimension
- Align and document
  - how we got there
  - how we assess the dimension and how we rate each item
  - how to improve toward the joint objective.

With Step 3, we have gathered lots of information and insights about the status quo of the product including ideas of how to improve the status quo. Trying to improve something means generally more work and more work effort requires prioritization and decision-making about where to focus and where to pause given time is a scarce resource for everyone.

In Step 4 we take this to the next level and derive the required actions and priorities to improve the PYPR scores and with that the Software Product and its yield potential.

2.1.6 Step 4: Prioritize and Strategize Actions Based on PYPR Scores Analysis

I will keep Step 4 rather concise as there is a dedicated chapter later in the book (Sect. 3.1) on how to leverage PYPR to become a better product leader. You will learn how to run your product like your own company, being the General Manager of YourProduct Inc. leveraging PYPR as a framework. Thus, I will keep the description of this step on a slightly higher level as with the previous steps.

The proverb “What gets measured gets managed” frequently attributed to management expert Peter Drucker or to quote Tom DeMarco: “What you cannot measure you cannot control” (DeMarco, 1989) both emphasize that management requires insights about status quo. Management needs a baseline for decisions.

PYPR supports product managers here. We aligned measures and ratings in the steps before. We gained a foundation to manage our Software Products more efficiently. As we base our management to some degree on the PYPR scores, the importance of an accurate and aligned rating exercise in Step 3 is obvious (Fig. 2.10).

In my experience, Step 4 provides the highest value benefiting from all the efforts spent in the subsequent steps. Step 4 sometimes already starts naturally as people discuss the scores of each item. As part of the rating exercise in Step 3, team members will likely mention reasons and sometimes even root causes, therefore requiring counter-measures.

As discussed before, there are many tasks and objectives to be mastered by product managers and product teams. As a product manager, your job is to

Fig. 2.10 Focus is the answer, but one question remains: where? © Timo Wagenblatt 2019. All rights reserved

understand and manage the product success factors holistically. What is the standard reaction or advice when dealing with time pressure or too many tasks at the same time?

Focus … yes, it is that simple! Who has not heard this from a peer, manager, friend, spouse, trainer or consultant? And yes, if the advice stops exactly at this level, without providing any guidance about where to focus, then the advice is as useless as it is simple.

You might have noticed that I like metaphors. I also like playing on words: The above problem is exactly in focus of Step 4.

Step 4 addresses some of the biggest challenges of Software Product Management:

- Aligning all stakeholders to the next product activities
  - Explaining why we focus on certain topics while we keep others a bit on the side
  - Engaging the team to improve the product's yield potential
- Spotting Software Product Management imbalance
- Keeping the main thing the main thing over and above adverse conditions of daily business.

In our role as product managers, we need to be efficient in time management—there is always more to do than time available. Freeing up product time is pivotal by prioritizing tasks and sorting out just urgent from important topics.

As a result of Step 3, PYPR provides measures for Software Product Management, for the product team's achievement and for the product's yield potential. Figure 2.11: PYPR Assessment and Visualization shows a strong PYPR dimension score of 7 for all dimensions but the Software Demonstrations and Training dimension has been rated with an average 5.

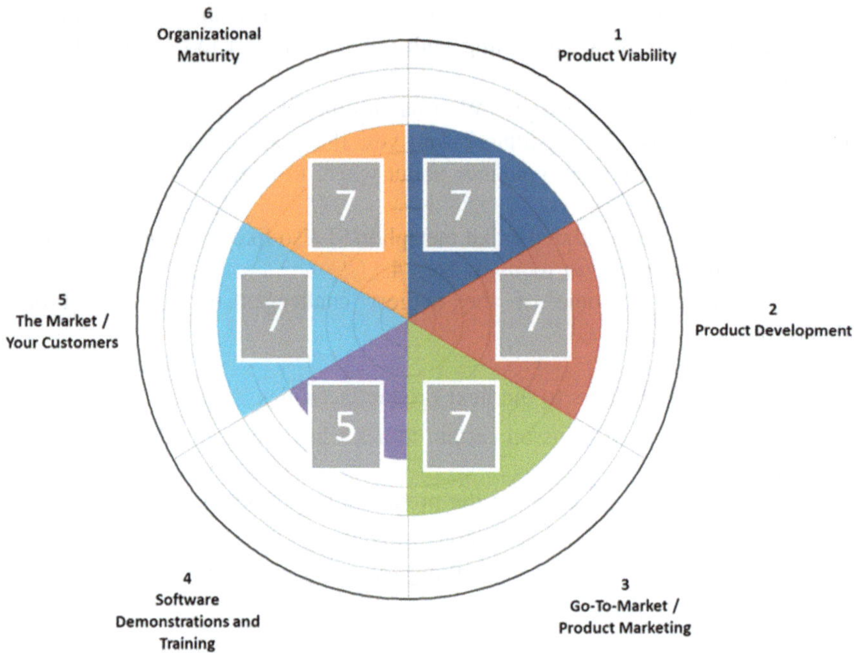

Fig. 2.11 PYPR assessment and visualization © Timo Wagenblatt 2019. All rights reserved

Aligning the stakeholders on the next product activities should be simple. You can explain why the focus on Software Demonstrations and Training items are required. PYPR visualizes nicely how the dimension limits the product success. Everyone can understand that the other dimensions are in a better shape. Likely the outcome of your meeting will be: Let's work together and improve the Software Demonstrations and Training dimension.

Yes, that is a happy day scenario and unfortunately not all days are happy days in a product manager's life. Lots of urgent ad hoc activities pop up and fires might start without warning. This won't disappear in your daily business; however, you have arrived at great insight. You have some indication of the weakest spots in your software product. You know where to focus and you can influence and manage toward this direction.

Purpose and benefits of Step 4:

- Align all stakeholders on the next and most important product activities
  - Explain why the focus is on certain topics while others have lower priority
  - Engage the team to improve the product's yield potential
- Spot unbalanced areas of product success requirements
- Keep the main thing the main thing over and above adverse conditions of daily business.

In the next chapter, I will introduce a proven practice to embed PYPR in your work environment that will benefit your product, your product team and help you to become a better product manager.

2.1.7 Proven Practice to Leverage the PYPR Assessment

Using PYPR as a one-off activity or as a Software Product Management checklist provides some value; however, the full lever pushing everyone toward Software Product Management excellence and a continuously strengthened product mindset only comes with embedding PYPR into your work environment. As a coach for my direct reports and as a product manager within my product teams, the following approach worked well over the years to get PYPR embedded thus providing value to the product teams.

After you have defined and structured the product management dimensions (Step 1), clarified the roles and responsibilities (Step 2), and did the first assessment of your product (Step 3), Step 4 is the actual step-change. To unfold the full value of leveraging PYPR:

1. Analyze the limiting factors and discuss the root cause with the stakeholders.
   - Brainstorm on strategies and tactics to resolve shortcomings.
   - Discuss and document the successful parts that worked as well. You might have a similar need to improve the dimension in the future again or other teams can learn from your success
2. Define and document an action plan for the next 12 weeks[7]
   - which limiting factors will you determine to improve?
   - what are the key activities to improve the limiting factors? Plan for the fact that 30 to sometimes up to 80% of your time and your team's time is likely already used up by your day-to-day business activities depending on your organizational maturity
   - In addition, schedule 30 min check-in meetings every two weeks
     - Instantaneous feedback is important and more effective
     - The more frequently you get feedback the more effectively you are adapting and managing toward improvement
3. Make sure the action plan is accessible for everyone in the team. Leverage PYPR as an information radiator that publicly transparentizes the product yield potential and agreed strategy and actions.
4. Latest after 12 weeks

[7] 12 weeks cadence is a default value. I recommend a cadence that reflects the ability to change dimension items effectively in your context. However, you should at least have four meetings every year. This is the absolute minimum as a recommended cadence.

- Go back to Step 1 of the overall process and do a quick check on the already defined dimensions, dimension items and assignments as described in Steps 1 and 2
- Execute Step 3: **Assess and Visualize the Product Yield Potential**
- Execute Step 4: **Prioritize and Strategize Actions based on PYPR Scores Analysis** (Fig. 2.12).

When reading the How-To guide above, you might think that these are a lot of

Fig. 2.12 Embedding PYPR in your day-to-day business © Timo Wagenblatt 2019. All rights reserved

meetings and you will not have time for this process. You might argue that the other stakeholders will not have time or are willing to spend the required time either.

In fact, this approach might require not more than two days in a quarter altogether. However, these two days come with the promise of being the most effective, most targeted and most important days for you as a product manager and as well for the core and extended product team.

In case you have doubts, please analyze your calendar. How much time did you spend in the last four weeks, the last 12 weeks, or the last year on activities to discuss the product success necessities anyway? These meetings were ad hoc and not planned, these meetings were firefighting activities, and a consequence of missing alignment, focus and sometimes engagement.

To summarize—the proven process above consists of the following meetings in each 12-week cycle:

- 6 meetings to assess the PYPR dimensions individually
  - Meetings should be time-boxed and prepared (max two hours per dimension)
  - Everyone should be invited to all PYPR dimension meetings (stakeholders mandatory, others optional)
- 1 "Strategy & Action" meeting to prioritize and strategize actions for the next 12 weeks
  - Meetings should be time-boxed and prepared (max two hours)
  - Everyone should be invited to all PYPR dimension meetings (all mandatory)

- 5 check-in meetings, 30 min each to discuss status, obstacles and progress of action items.

PYPR meetings are characterized by a holistic product-focus and are targeted explicitly to improve the product yield potential, which will be of benefit for any stakeholder. You create alignment and engagement and after a few iterations you will reach an established standard approach that will actually provide more quality time and less firefighting activities to all participants.

Note that it will take time to introduce the process to your product team and stakeholders, if you do not have the essential management support or if your organization is not mature enough yet. I will share more about the consequences of a low organizational maturity in later chapters. Introducing PYPR and unfolding its full potential will not happen overnight, even if you have management support and you are part of a mature organization. Transparency is not always welcome everywhere.

However, I still have to find the first product manager or product team that did not get value out of the outlined approach. Not all could reach the full potential due to all kinds of reasons, but certainly the benefits of Step 1, which by itself is an achievement, have been reported by all. We will discuss how to best introduce PYPR to a team and a whole organization in more detail in Sect. 3.3.

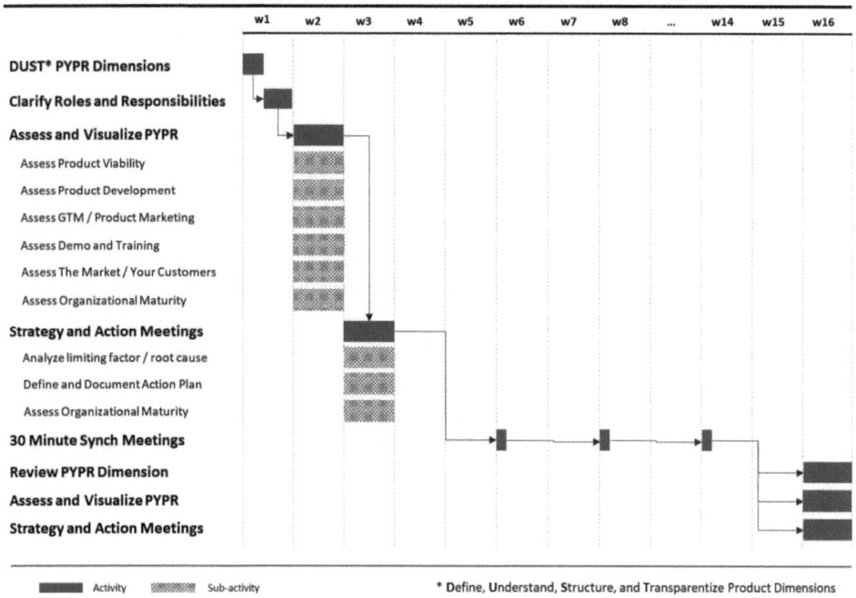

Fig. 2.13 Example of initial PYPR activities and meeting © Timo Wagenblatt 2019. All rights reserved

The meeting plan depicted in Fig. 2.13 is obviously only a schematic example as there will be weekly, if not daily, changes to one or the other dimension item that are worth considering and documenting (e.g. new deal, new learning in dev, people leave the team, training happened, bad feedback about xyz, etc.) Note that the same way behaviors and traditions define our personality and values, cadences and routines define a team.

Let me reassure you that PYPR is a lightweight framework that gains time as it provides focus and alignment. PYPR is the framework that enables you to remain focused in the fast-paced world of today's "try different things—fail fast—learn" environment. PYPR enables product teams with the clarity required to make good product decisions at speed.[8] Give it a try and you will quickly see some if not all of the improvements listed below:

- Teaches transparency about roles, product management activities and product success indicators
- Understands and structures product success necessities for your context
- Clarifies roles and responsibilities
- Assesses and rate your product's yield potential
- Aligns with all stakeholders how to overcome challenges and improve the product holistically

Let's observe in a short, imaginary story, how an established team is working with PYPR:

My name is Tom, I'm a Product Manager at ACME enterprise and I'm the General Manager of MyProduct Inc., our best-selling product at ACME. My days are super busy, and no two days are the same. I solve so many problems across so many disciplines. It's the best job I ever had.

Since we introduced PYPR at ACME, everyone understands my contribution to the company's success. The team emphasizes the importance of my role as a Product Manager. They think I'm a key player that ensures that the company is creating something customers want and I execute the product roadmap to stay ahead of the curve, focusing on long-term success.

We have clarity about all the items that are important for the success of MyProduct Inc. It was eye-opening for all of us and it became clear to everyone that product success is a team effort. We aligned on who drives what and who contributes where. As a team, we did an honest assessment of where we are with MyProduct Inc. We even invited the guys from sales and product marketing into our circle. Interesting perspectives about MyProduct Inc. And, they are actually nice—wasn't obvious from some distance.

Another aha-effect for all of us.

We are a great product team and we take care about a lot, but the Software Demonstrations and Training dimension needs work. It didn't require much time to prioritize the joint counteractions. Tim from engineering and Sue from Product Marketing joined forces to improve the situation there. We will meet every two weeks for 30 min to discuss progress or corrective actions.

[8] I will detail the importance of product vision and balancing fast-paced developing toward the vision in Chap. 5.

Sure, we meet once in a while anyway, but it is good to have these regular alignments in the calendar.

We also have our Strategy & Action meetings every 12 weeks. At first, I thought not another meeting, but now, they are naturally part of how we work, and we celebrate success that we improved some items and increased the product's yield potential frequently.

I think that our actions and our thoughts are much more focused on improving the product's chances of success. I can relate many things that I normally do back to PYPR and I can explain why I say no to one or the other. We finally keep the main thing the main thing. It feels great to be part of our product team.

There is another secret to this. I know I should know about everything I need to as a Product Manager from the top of my mind; however, let me tell you a secret: "We all look from time to time into PYPR just to reassure there is nothing left blindsided. It is the checklist we all ever wanted." And yes, I haven't checked for some time what our competitors do, and the next customer council is approaching soon as well. Do we already have a customer speaker lined-up?

Great that I can use PYPR as a checklist. Another fire is avoided, as I can plan the necessary time into my days and leave early to buy some flowers for my dear.

Then I woke up, got my first coffee of the day and decided to introduce PYPR to my company.

What's the essence of this little story? Yes, PYPR becomes part of the Software Product Management practice. It seems natural to use it as a checklist. It can be the source of justification for saying no. And I have seen the effect many times where people think much more strategically about their work and question why they do or not do certain activities. Based on this we come naturally to a recurring Step 5 as part of the PYPR proven practice. Reviewing Steps 1 to 4 frequently becomes a routine over time and is shown as Step 5 in the diagram Fig. 2.14.

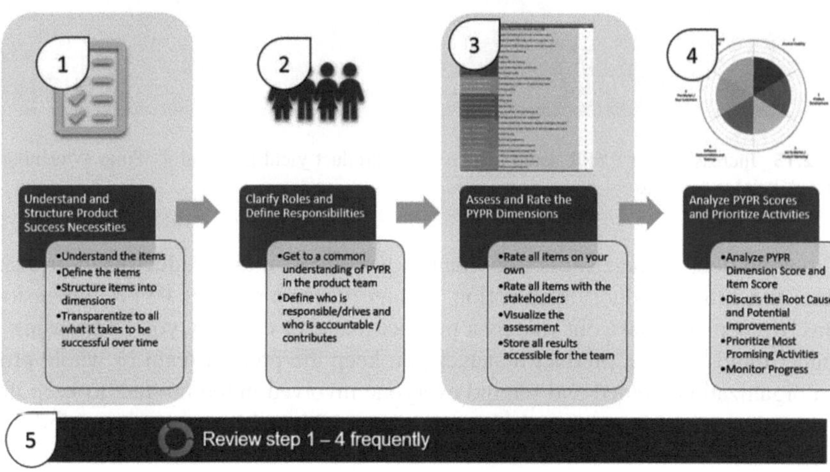

Fig. 2.14 Five steps applying PYPR to unfold its full potential © Timo Wagenblatt 2019. All rights reserved

2.1.8 Summary and Next Steps

This section is our first introduction to PYPR. I believe you now have an idea of how significant this novel methodology and holistic approach is for you, your product team and your organization. The outlined process steps have been a quick run through. You have a first understanding of how to work with PYPR and PYPRs potential in Software Product Management.

I hope you understand how the elements of focus and alignment have been consistent through all the steps with an increasing impact. Clear focus and product team alignment wins the hearts and minds and leads ultimately to a joint product mindset. Everyone realizing the importance and impact of their activities should aim to increase their PYPR scores and with that the product's yield potential over time (Fig. 2.15).

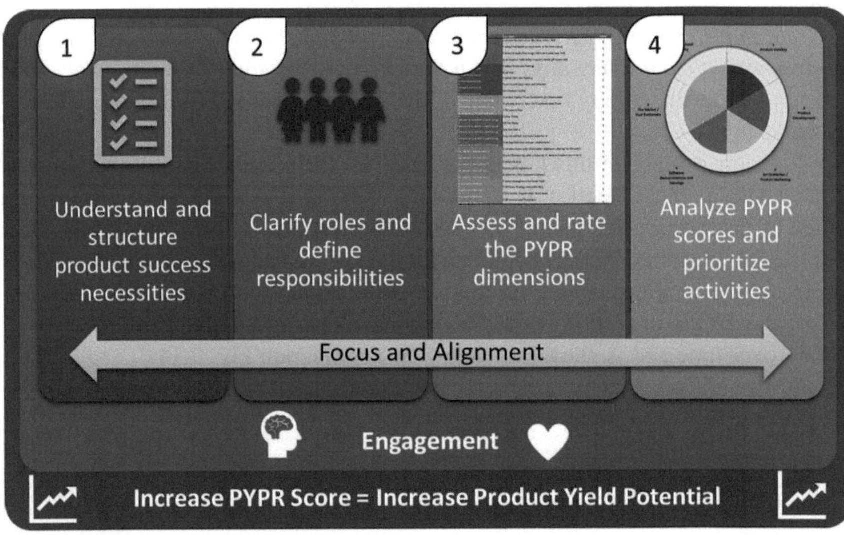

Fig. 2.15 Increasing the PYPR score increases the product yield potential © Timo Wagenblatt 2019. All rights reserved

As a product manager, it is important to get others in the product team or even better, the entire product organization, to feel ownership of all PYPR dimension items. Remember, that your role as a product manager commits you showcasing a product mindset. As a product manager you keep the product team or whole product organization aligned and remind everyone involved in the product to keep the product the main thing or in other words sign-up for and live a product mindset.

PYPR provides a robust communication and prioritization framework that can be embedded in day-to-day business activities. The process of using PYPR is straightforward and its benefits come fast and early in the process. Organizations that are more mature in Software Product Management are likely to adopt PYPR faster than others due to a robust starting point.

If you find yourself in less mature environment, PYPR will help you as an individual to become a better product manager. I worked with many product managers that used PYPR on their own and got great benefits that helped them gain many insights about themselves, their work, and the product they care about. They used these insights when working with their stakeholders, although the stakeholders did not know about PYPR at that stage. They became more self-confident in their role as they had a guiding framework. They used PYPR to understand when to say "no." And with that they became more successful as a product manager; they were no longer firefighters or overworked superheroes.

The next sections will deepen your understanding of PYPR and provide you with guidelines, examples, templates and hopefully inspiration for your day-to-day-business and product manager role, whether you are individual contributor, manager or on an executive level.

As PYPR is still a new concept for you, I recommend you continue reading the next sections. As a teaser, the next sections explain:

- A definition and detailed description of each dimension, a definition of all items in each dimension, how it feels in heaven and hell for each dimension item, and a list of the various stakeholders to work with and communicate to in each dimension.
  a. Don't skip the next sections even if you think that they are more targeted toward commercial products (e.g. B2B, B2C). In principle these dimensions and dimension items are equally valid for corporate IT products or other non-commercial products.
  b. In addition, you will find further details of PYPR examples applied in various concepts in Chap. 10.
- The Law of the Minimum and Law of Tolerance that will change your understanding of Software Product Management
  a. You will gain great insights about interdependencies of dimensions
  b. You will understand the importance of keeping all items in balance
  c. You will be surprised by the severe impact of a single dimension item becoming the limiting factor of product success.

After you gained a solid PYPR foundation by reading the next sections, there are two further options depending on your needs and interest:

- **PYPR Expert option**: On your journey to become a PYPR expert, you continue with Chap. 3 and learn
  a. how to leverage PYPR to become the General Manager of YourProduct Inc.
  b. how to better understand your stakeholder network and how PYPR can support here
  c. how to jump-start leveraging the out-of-the-box PYPR set-up and how to adapt PYPR continuously to your own context
- **PYPR Dimension Expert option**: Part 2 of this book is structured like a reference book for each PYPR dimension and the dimension items. You can also use Part 2 as a textbook if you are interested or have the urgent need to improve one of the following dimensions: Product Viability, Product Development, Go-to-Market/Product Marketing, Software Demonstrations and Training, The Market/Your Customers, or Organizational Maturity.
  Part 2 will help you to
  a. detail your understanding of each Software Product Management dimension
  b. learn tools and techniques to assess, understand, improve, and monitor each PYPR dimension item.

Furthermore, Part 3 of this book rounds out the PYPR approach by providing case studies about how other product managers and product teams have successfully adopted PYPR in Chap. 10. I recommend reading this section only after completing the sections of the **PYPR Expert option above**.

My objective is to guide and support you on your journey in leveraging PYPR in the best possible way to make you a better product manager. As you follow the recommended reading sequence you will gain a solid foundation of how to utilize and benefit from PYPR.

As part of this journey I promise you interesting sights as you will

- learn how to measure each PYPR dimension item
- investigate how to improve each item and understand potential positive and negative side effects
- learn how to adapt PYPR, especially how to customize the dimension items and dimension weights
- work with PYPR in various common business situations
- embed PYPR in your day-to-day work and your product organization and develop Software Product Management excellence.

2.2 Detailing the PYPR Dimensions

As you are applying PYPR you will experience how it boosts engagement in all important product dimensions. As previously mentioned we cannot stay at lofty levels and discuss Software Product Management dimensions in generic terms. In this chapter, I will detail what you need to know about each PYPR dimension to improve the product, the product's success and the product's yield potential.

Before we dig deeper into the underlying PYPR philosophy, I will detail the default PYPR dimensions. I will introduce the items that are part of each dimension, as this will make it easier to understand the underlying concepts. The Software Product Management dimension descriptions in the next sections are likely biased toward commercial products (e.g. B2B, B2C). However, PYPR can be customized for non-commercial products as well. I will showcase how to customize PYPR and its dimensions for this specific product context in Part 2 where each dimension is detailed in a dedicated section.

Briefly, the PYPR dimensions to be balanced are as follows (see also illustration in Fig. 2.16):

- **Product Viability**: Product Viability focuses on ensuring business value for you and your target market segments or user personas.
- **Product Development**: Product Development concentrates on providing clarity and direction to the core product team, keeping the team spirit up and developing a quality product vis-a-vis the product vision and strategy.
- **Go-to-Market/Product Marketing**: Broadcast and position the product values to sales, professional services and partner community and—no brainer—to the market and your current and target customers.
- **Software Demonstrations and Training**: Showcasing your product and training your product in the best possible way for each target group in an engaging way.
- **The Market/Your Customers**: Engaging customers and understanding the market while impressing analysts and influencers and reaching a thought leadership position. That's what it is all about in this dimension.
- **Organizational Maturity**: Software Product Management is a leadership role and improving the processes and tools continuously is mandatory to gaining and maintaining product success.

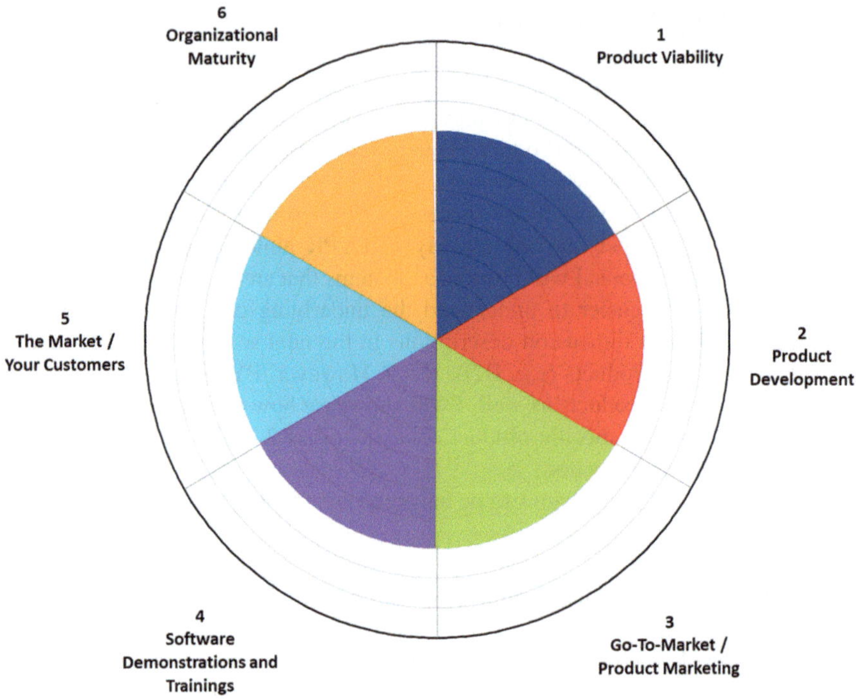

Fig. 2.16 PYPR dimensions © Timo Wagenblatt 2019. All rights reserved

In principle these dimensions are equally valid for corporate IT products or any other software product as well. There are slight variations on the dimension level and some more on the dimension item level that we will investigate in Sect. 3.3. In addition, you will find further details in the various PYPR examples, e.g. for corporate IT products in Chap. 10.

For each PYPR dimension I will provide:

- a definition and detailed description of the dimension
- a definition of all items in each dimension
- an outline how it feels in heaven and hell for each dimension item
- a list of the various stakeholders to work with and communicate with in each dimension.

2.2.1 Product Viability

The term Viability at its core definition says it all—capable of living. All products must be capable of living, which means in most organizations profitable. For most customers, a viable product needs to be cost-effective and, even more importantly, generate value.

Economic viability represents one of the three areas of the design thinking approach (Design Thinking, 2018) leading to the optimal product. Understanding and focusing on Product Viability comprises all necessary activities to ensure that these new product or product feature ideas make business sense, provide an appropriate return on investment and that many customers understand the value of the product in order to pay for it.

Very often viability aspects are checked at the end of the process, sometimes when it is too late. Therefore, the general recommendation is to test and learn early about the viability aspects of your product. The Business Model Canvas (initially proposed by Alexander Osterwalder (The Business Model Canvas, 2008) is a powerful tool, providing a strategic management as well as a lean startup template for developing new or documenting existing business models already in early stages. The Business Model Canvas helps to clarify various viability aspects and provides other insights that are beneficial in later stages of the process (Barquet, 2011).

For us product managers, viability means that we are able to justify the investments into our products and services, commercialize and successfully monetize our products and services with suitable business models in a sustainable and repeatable manner for the various phases of our product's lifecycle. Besides the pure financial focus, product viability is also determined by market share growth considerations and customer adoption.

In summary, the Product Viability dimension represents "The Financial Part of your Software Product Manager Role." Chapter 1 explains the Product Yield Potential Radar dimension in much more detail, focusing on the techniques to assess, improve, monitor, and communicate the financial part of your product manager's role.

We will discover and evaluate the tools, templates, and key performance indicators I used in my career, as well as the practices I learned and developed to assess and improve the Product Viability dimension. I detail the following topics in Chap. 4:

- **Business Model Canvas**

  Although technically not part of the Product Yield Potential Radar, we'll explore how to use this method due to its importance of reaching across many other PYPR dimensions and dimension items. Every viable product requires a working business model as a basis for a long, prosperous product life. There are many proof points that it is easier to realize a mediocre idea with a good business model than the best idea without any. The Business Model Canvas organizes all important elements of a successful business model into a framework that scales for new ideas as well as existing products. The Business Model Canvas helps to:

  - understand how products create value
  - find the right business model for new products
  - develop existing business models to the next level with the understanding how to operate the product in two, three or five years
  - compare various business models and iterate the ideas
  - get an idea of the cost/revenue balance

  The Business Model Canvas is the common language for describing, communicating and evolving product business model and viability to all stakeholders. In fact, it is a comprehensive framework for product strategy articulation.

- **Customer Business Case**
  A customer business case explains and details the customers' financial valuation of the product, including the perceived customer/stakeholder benefits derived from the product's attributes. Defining and capturing value mandates interaction with customers and industry experts, getting their input about the stakeholders and processes that are most impacted. These values could be cost reduction, revenue generation, customer satisfaction, total cost of ownership savings, defect avoidance, time savings, etc. Customer business cases are more than providing a ROI calculator; however, having one will not harm either.
- **Sales Pipeline Development**
  Monitoring the product license pipeline and renewal rates might not be the daily business of product managers; however, having a strict discipline will help you understand the chances of successfully reaching financial objectives. By applying good practice, you will understand the pipeline dynamics, deal conversion rates and with that sales forecasts will be of much better quality. Understanding the sales pipeline dynamics enables you to influence sales in the right direction with a higher chance of success. In short, we will learn how you can score when talking to important stakeholders, including Sales and your management, in this dimension.
- **Product Profitability**
  Profitable products are probably the primary objective for most organizations. For example, profitability for software products compares the revenues from incremental license deals and subscription revenues versus such costs as developmental, cloud center, sometimes sales. Understanding the hard-financial facts of your product and how to influence them positively is an important asset. We will discover what information is required to be at your fingertips and how to work with special situations for mature products and newly launched products.
- **Product Growth**
  How is your product doing in the market? Products that grow faster than competition in terms of market share are great. That's what you need to understand to measure and to achieve with your product. Product growth is important for any product, whether it is a new mobile app, website, corporate IT product or enterprise B2B solution. We will learn how to define the metrics that matter most for software products and how to rate and interpret the measures accordingly. The product vision and strategy should have a component focusing on growth as well. As great as growth can be, there is healthy and controllable growth and unhealthy or at least risky growth that needs to be managed. Growth hacking might be a strategy you favor, but take care that your product, the product team and the organization survives.
- **Maintenance/Run Profitability**
  Getting a product into the market is one side of the coin, keeping the product profitable in the market another. As a product manager, monitoring the maintenance profitability will help in various aspects; you will get insights into the software quality perception of your customers as well as the patterns of issues

during usage. Running your product in production-mode needs to be cost-effective and sustainable.

- **Professional Services/Consulting Profitability**
  Most enterprise software products require implementation services, whether they are deployed on-premise or as part of a private or public cloud offering. Yes, even with a public cloud offering, consider change management, master data integration, business process configuration etc. There is not much of a difference whatever the software deployment model looks like. Assuming professional services teams are required for your product, then you should know and monitor topics like whether your product can be implemented as fix price bids; implementations require lots of rework, professional services and customers require lots of handholding during go-live from the product team.

The financial part of your product manager role comes with many facets. Internal viability and external viability—how healthy is your product in this dimension?

Let's have a closer look. Figure 2.17: Heaven or Hell: Product Viability is a summary about what it means living in hell or enjoying heaven in the Product Viability dimension. Most likely your product assessment will be neither 0 nor 10 in all items. 0 in all items would probably mean you should start finding another idea to work on as there is no customer or user seeing any value in your product offering. You lose money every minute and so does anyone who gets close to your product. Sounds like a nightmare, so let's better look at the perfect 10 scenarios.

In the perfect 10 scenarios your customers cannot exist without your product, their desire to own it is overwhelming. Everyone dealing with your product experiences enormous values—the customers, the partners and your own company. So, if you think you are dealing with a perfect 10 product—congratulations! Or your assessment is not accurate. We will discover how to realistically rate all Product Viability dimension items later in this book. However, I have never seen a product that scored a perfect 10 throughout all items in this PYPR dimension.

	Hell		Heaven
Dimension Item		0 … 10	
Customer Business Case	No value for your customer		Customer cannot exist without your product
Pipeline Development	No pipeline		Pipeline with exponential growth, x times rev objective
Product Profitability	Negative ROI after 3 years of market introduction		ROI significantly above company / BC expectations
Product Growth	Market share with significant decline		Market share grows significantly vs competition
Maintenance Profitability	Negative ROI after 3 years of market introduction		ROI significantly above company / BC expectations
Professional Service Profitability	Negative ROI after 3 years of market introduction		ROI significantly above company / BC expectations

* ROI as measure of profitability

Fig. 2.17 Heaven or hell: product viability © Timo Wagenblatt 2019. All rights reserved

In Chap. 4, I will discuss each item, how to assess it, how to rate it and how to improve it. The Product Yield Potential Radar is not a rating tool for product managers. This is easily misunderstood and hence I will repeat this many times. The Product Yield Potential Radar is a thinking framework and ongoing discipline that fosters communication and alignment. Additionally, the Product Yield Potential

Radar helps to prioritize product management work, discovering what is most important at any given stage within your product's lifecycle.

Who are the likely stakeholders we will work with and communicate to in the Product Viability Dimension?

- Business Operations team
- Controlling team
- Sales team
- Portfolio Management/Venture Capitalist
- Customer Support team
- Consulting Partner
- Own Professional Services team
- Management/Founder for internal viability
- Customers, especially the users/buyers for external viability.

The fact that there are so many stakeholders and people involved stresses the importance of product viability for every product. Throughout my career I have discovered that everyone buys into the importance of product viability; however very often product viability considerations have been ad hoc activities or "maybe if there is time" activities.

Product managers need a framework and a process to stay on top of their product's viability measures. It is essential to have a structured process to validate and detail the viability aspects. Product managers need to communicate with the various stakeholders, and common standards will support communication among people.

Facts, especially facts, about your product's viability, are important for your business case whether you talk to your founder, as you work in a start-up company, a venture capitalist gets your own company going, or a corporate portfolio team successfully competes against other great ideas and investment requests in a multi-billion, multi-national enterprise organization.

Corporate IT products: Internal product managers care about the same dimension items, with the following aspects to consider. I will detail the differences in the respective sections:

- Sales pipeline development and professional services profitability are likely not relevant and not part of the default PYPR configuration for corporate IT products
- In my experience, the other items are equally valid for internal products also, sometimes with a different interpretation that I will explain in later sections.

2.2.2 Product Development

The Product Development dimension is probably the most apparent dimension for product managers. The 2018 Product Management Festival survey asked more than 1000 product managers globally the question: "*What are the most important product management hard skills?*" which resulted in these top three answers:

- 68% Product Vision and Strategy
- 63% Product Requirements Management
- 63% Roadmap ping and Product Planning.

All these hard skills listed above belong to the Product Development dimension. I'm excited that the product vision made it to the top three product management hard skills as I'm 100% convinced that the process of defining the product vision and strategy is most important in the Product Development dimension, and perhaps the most important part of all the product manager's responsibilities, or as the phrase goes:

> The ones who do not know where they want to arrive, should not wonder about the place they get to (Proverb)

No doubt that it is crucial for every product manager to be a—if not THE—product expert. Most product managers know every bit of her or his product, they know best what it can do, why it does what it does, the strong parts, the weak parts, and where the product needs to be in the future. In fact, many product managers spend the most of their time in the Product Development dimension as they are passionate about their product. They know what the product needs to do, because they know what the market, the customers and the users want. For the product team, you are the voice of the market and customers, and you represent these most important stakeholders in every critical decision that needs to be made.

As product managers, the ones who are responsible for the product team, we must ensure that the product team stays healthy while delivering outcomes. Clear communication and direction, transparency about the guardrails and decision implications, as well as appreciation of all diverse skills required in the team, are some of the vital ingredients. Our role is to foster the collaboration within the team, be a lively part of the team, support, represent and protect the team in the best possible and professional way.

Your role as a product manager in the Product Development dimension is essential because of all the reasons above, but also because without a product you are obsolete in your role. Software Product Management is the only department that focuses solely on the product and the product is the reason for the department's/team's existence.

In summary, the Product Development dimension represents "The Essential Part of your Software Product Manager Role." We will learn about the important tools, templates, and key performance indicators that I used in my career as well as the practices I applied and advanced to improve this important dimension. Below is a short overview of what we will focus on in Chap. 5:

- **Product Vision and Strategy**
  The Product Vision and Strategy describes the "To-be-state" of your product, the re-imagined world as the result of all your efforts; why your product is compelling for your customers and the key principles for your journey. A common understanding of the product vision and strategy will guide the product team in every aspect from requirements and backlog prioritization to product positioning and Go-to-Market activities to sales meetings and even customer support interactions. A well-defined Product Vision and Strategy includes an inspiring component to show the team that there are multiple, maybe unknown steps in the journey and operational guidelines or key principles acting as a decision-making framework (e.g. speed over quality, adoption over revenue, action over research). We will learn how to practically create and maintain a product vision and strategy as well as the tips and tricks required for keeping it the guiding light.
- **Product Development Planning**
  Actively planning and preparing the backlog of work for development (e.g. requirements, product features, user stories, epics, etc.) is the home turf for product owners and as discussed before the product owner is either a peer very close to your heart or is the name of your role as a product manager in the agile development process. Balancing market requirements and customer requirements in an efficient and transparent way needs a clear decision-making framework as if a paying customer calls out a demand or a problem; it's hard not to listen to it, even if it doesn't fit the product vision and strategy. Be prepared—be strong! Organizing, prioritizing and communicating the backlog of work continuously will be the focus of the dedicated Product Development chapter later in this book.
- **Roadmaps**
  Roadmaps are a tool to communicate the plan to deliver the promise of the product vision over product releases and time. As a product manager, you own the product roadmap or better said, you own the product roadmaps. There are lots of different audiences and occasions for presenting your product roadmap. For example, development, sales, your management and finally partners and customers are interested in where the product is heading. They frequently request product roadmap updates as they base their decisions and activities on your

product plan. Therefore, we will deep-dive and look at examples of roadmaps that meet the needs of the various audiences as well as different ways to use this important tool efficiently.

- **(Internal View of) Product Quality**
  Generally engineering teams have a good understanding about product quality. They know the parts that are robust and the features and functions that might be technically a bit shaky. As a product manager you are THE expert of your product. You know why a new capability is developed and you know how it fits into the overall product scope. You know how it should work to deliver value to your users. This means you are theoretically an ideal functional tester as you can best represent the customer. However, you will likely not get to an understanding of the product quality to the extent an engineering team does until you start reading the code. This item is about an aligned core product team perception of the product quality, not the customer's perception. And yes, there is frequently a deviation.
- **Team Health**
  A highly motivated, skilled, stable, and happy product team delivering high-value software capabilities is the holy grail and therefore the goal of your interaction with everyone in the product team and specifically in the engineering team. The basis for success is a trusted and respectful relationship with the team that is outcome focused based on shared objectives—easily written and still an area that is explosive and a major area of concern, whether you are located in one room or spread across the world. We will learn how you can improve or at least positively influence the chances of success for working together as a healthy team.

The Product Development dimension focuses on understanding and rating the interaction between the product team and the product manager as well as the required work results. It focuses on the process from defining a shared product vision and strategy, to product development planning that is transferred into and communicated via product roadmaps. Figure 2.18 illustrates the downstream dependencies delivering software against the product vision.

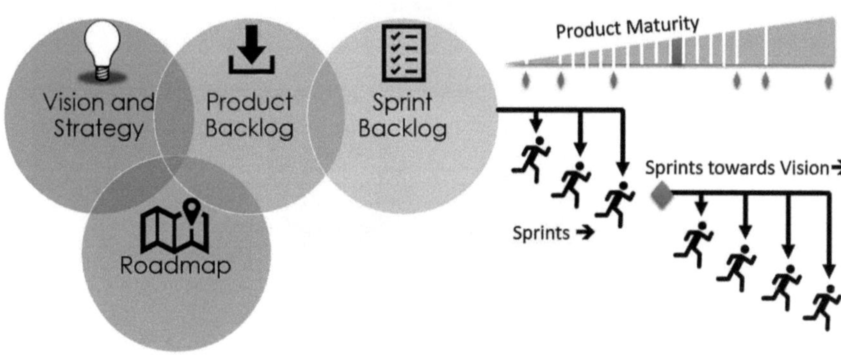

Fig. 2.18 From shared vision to increasing product maturity © Timo Wagenblatt 2019. All rights reserved

In a case where the process results in a high-quality product offering and the relationship between the product manager and the product team remains healthy and trustful, then you know that you have done a brilliant job and you should celebrate.

The essential part of your product manager role comes with many facets and with various responsibilities. Product vision and strategy, tailored roadmaps and backlogs, interaction with the product team and development stakeholders and the resulting product quality—how strong is your product in this essential and core dimension?

In Fig. 2.19 I summarize what it means to live in hell or heaven in the Product Development dimension. Most likely your product scores neither 0 nor 10 in all items. 0 in all items would probably mean you should start finding another development team to work with or radically change the way of working, and 10 would probably mean that you should hire me as I want to be on your team. But only if your rating is honest and accurate. I have never seen a product that scored a perfect 10 throughout all items.

Dimension Item	Hell	0 – 10	Heaven
Product Vision and Strategy	No product vision, no strategy, nothing		Clarity and alignment of vision/strategy for all decisions/stakeholders
Roadmap	No product roadmap		Themed roadmaps for all relevant target audiences
Product Planning	No product backlog, no release backlog, no plan		Structured, transparent, embedded, customer focused product plan
Team Health	Team doesn't know / trust you and vice versa		Trusted relationships with joint focus on outcomes
Product Quality	Product not properly tested; defects hinder releases		Fully automated testing, no defects, nothing breaks with new features

Fig. 2.19 Heaven or hell: product development

In Chap. 5 for each item listed above, we will learn how to assess it, how to rate it, and how to improve it. PYPR is not a rating tool for product managers. This is easily misunderstood and hence I will repeat this again. PYPR Radar is a thinking framework and ongoing discipline that fosters communication and strategic thinking. Additionally, PYPR helps prioritize all product management tasks to discover what is most important at any given stage of your product's lifecycle.

Who are the likely stakeholders we will work with and communicate to in the Product Development?

- Product Owners
- Developers, Architects and Development Managers
- UX Designers
- Project, Program, and Delivery Managers
- Scrum Masters
- Testers and Quality Managers
- Documentation and Training Teams
- Customers and End Users
- Partners

Depending on the chosen software development methodologies and your organizational maturity, stakeholders might have a different name for your role (like product owner in the scrum methodology). However, it is important for everyone to understand that there are more dimensions than product development in a product manager's life as I described before.

Product managers can be leveraged in various roles in the Product Development dimension and you can easily be assimilated in this dimension with 100% of your time. Therefore, it is very important to keep the right balance and focus to scale best in your role. As a product manager, you are in fact essential in product development and you will be required to work closely with all stakeholders securing product success. You need to be effective and you need a good plan to stay on top of all duties and actions in the Product Development dimension. The hard skills of defining a product vision and strategy, planning the product and being an expert in requirements management should be accompanied by being an expert in your product's problem domain. These hard skills need to be supplemented with plenty of soft skills and a great level of discipline.

Sounds as simple like a T-shape, right? Not really! Keep calm and continue reading.

I'm absolutely convinced that this book and the concepts of the Product Yield Potential Radar will help you master your daily job and interact better with your product teams, architects, and development managers as well as in your interpretation and perception of Software Product Management far beyond the Product Development dimension.

In Chap. 5 you will learn how to effectively lead the product team from the product vision and strategy to great product quality as an outcome. I will introduce the important fundamentals as well as some proven practices that worked in various situations over the last decade.

2.2.3 Go-to-Market/Product Marketing

This section comes with two headlines: Go-to-Market and Product Marketing. Sometimes the terms are used interchangeably; in some organizations they have a completely different meaning. Go-to-Market comprises all activities and assets required for positioning your product—a new feature or a new release of your product to the market, to the prospects and to your customers and users. In my interpretation, Product Marketing is a function and sometimes is its own department with the primary goal to create demand for the product through effective messaging and product positioning, which clearly explains the product's value proposition and capabilities. Product Marketing is not a generic marketing function, it needs to be very focused on the product.

According to these definitions, I will use the term Go-to-Market throughout the book, which includes the function of Product Marketing. I do this for the following reasons:

- One, you might have a situation where there is no Product Marketing department in your organization to support you in your product manager role; hence you are responsible for product marketing as well.
- And two, it is more critical focusing on activities and assets than emphasizing the organizational set-up variations and specific role definitions, which we will cover as part of Sect. 2.2.6.

Within this section we focus on understanding the PYPR items in the Go-to-Market and Product Marketing dimension rather than organizational topics. Someone needs to do the job and through transparency and communication, other teams or team members will better understand the importance of this dimension and likely support product marketing as a way to increase the success of the product.

In the Go-to-Market/Product Marketing dimension product managers need to mainly focus on:

- supporting sales and marketing teams with useful assets
- enabling the ecosystem in professional services and the partner community
- analyzing and sharing your knowledge about competitive threats if required
- enabling the market and your customers to understand the positioning and value of your product.

Focusing on your sales teams is pivotal because the sales teams are the ones who finally push and convince your customers to buy your product. While sales team focus is important, and sales assets are bundled into sales kits, one important aspect is often overlooked. The sales teams not only need to be aware of the sales kits, but also, they need to be trained how to use the sales kit.

Ideally your product ecosystem, which might comprise in-house professional services and partners, shares the same view about your product's value and positioning. Whether you consider competition as part of your ecosystem or outside is not too important. However, competitive intelligence is very important as part of the Go-to-Market dimension. At times, you need to position your product likely against your competition. You can increase your chances of success the more you know about your competition, the more you share with your ecosystem, the better you tailor your positioning in given competitive situations—independent whether you are the new challenger or the undisputed market leader.

Last, but not least—the market and your customers need to be informed about your product or a new release of your product. If you do something great, then talk, write, post, communicate by any means about it. What a waste of time, work and budget, if the outside world doesn't know the great piece of work that you deliver. There is a multitude of options for public relations and marketing activities. This area of your Go-to-Market launch activities is very often the core of the Product Marketing function comprising all communication to potential and existing customers.

You now have an impression about the scope of the Go-to-Market/Product Marketing dimension and the multitude of activities in this dimension. The Go-to-Market/Product Marketing dimension represents "The Outbound Part of your Software Product Manager Role." I will describe the tools, templates, and key performance indicators I used in my career as well as the practices I learned and developed to assess and to improve this important dimension. As a recommendation, the following dimension items are central to score high in this dimension.

- **Marketing and Sales Assets/Sales Kit**
  There is marketing and sales assets and there is the collection of these assets that are frequently called Sales Kits. Rule number one should be a no brainer, but too often this rule is broken: Don't just produce assets for assets' sake. Always consider the goal of the asset and the target group of the asset, which means the people and their roles that you are trying to reach. A well-maintained sales kit is a silver bullet containing the best marketing and sales assets. It will not only help your sales teams to close more deals—it will also help yourself freeing up time that you normally spend for repetitive education, frequent responses to the same questions, clarifying positioning of your product internally and with your customers and many more time killers of that kind. You need to take care that assets are available and up to date and classified and target group oriented. The attributes of importance are timely and qualitative. Timeliness will help to allow cross reading and involve a sales champion as it is always good to ask the target audience for early feedback and consequently the quality will come. Make sure everyone on your sales team is on the same page. It contains everything a sales rep needs to know about your sales process, buyer personas, sales metrics, and talk tracks before they go selling.
- **Sales Enablement**
  Enabling sales teams requires understanding the specifics of their job. Do they only sell your product, or do they carry a sales bag of 100 products they can choose from? Do they have a regional focus or are they acting globally? In any case sales colleagues will not have much time and will regularly not deep dive

into the bells and whistles of your product. All they are interested in might be: the value for the customer, pricing, positioning, objections, existing references, experts, partners and where to find the latest assets that cover these topics at the time they need them. A central, structured and known one-stop-shop approach might be a good option here and a great time saver as otherwise everyone might approach you directly. A special focus in sales enablement is the unending requirement to offer enablement and train sales teams. Generally, sales team members' churn is higher than other employees and the value and clear positioning of your product might be diminishing in the dynamics of Sales.

- **Partner Enablement**
  We focus on two kinds of partners, value-added resellers (VAR) and system integrators (SI). VARs are partners that are reselling a vendor's hardware or software solutions directly to customer, hence they are sometimes called the indirect sales channel and similar work and tactics like in the section above (**Sales Enablement**), tailored to and external partner, can be considered. VARs may develop and sell add-on applications to meet the needs of vertical markets and may expand your product functionality. In this case, VARs need to be enabled and orchestrated considering the Product Development dimension as well.
  SIs are companies focused on integrating IT systems and providing related consulting. This is a classic channel used by large software vendors, large hardware vendors, and original equipment manufacturers. Therefore, similar work and tactics like in the section below (**Own Professional Services/Consulting Enablement**), tailored to an external partner, can be considered.
- **Own Professional Services/Consulting Enablement**
  If you have your own professional services team that works with customers implementing and adapting your product, it is essential that your people know about your product's vision, roadmap and values. Providing the right assets and enabling these teams with latest updates enables one face to the market. In consequence your customers and prospects will perceive your company as interconnected and cohesive.
- **Competitive Analysis**
  Chances are high that your competitors will come up at least once in conversations with a prospect. It's critical to be well-equipped for these discussions by knowing exactly what advantages (and disadvantages) you have compared to each (key) competitor. Some factors to consider are pricing, usability, performance, functionality, time-to-value, and customer support. Competitive battle cards are an adequate and powerful tool for anyone in your organizations to be prepared for these discussions. The competitive analysis can help you in various other dimensions as well; hence it is of true value covering up-to-date information in a structured form at least for the top competitors, which might include internal competition in bigger organizations with a lack of portfolio management. If you provide a clear positioning tailored to each competitor, conduct a regular review and also update, there is great changes of high scores in this dimension item and more important, staying ahead of your competition in multiple aspects.

- **Go-to-Market Launch Activities and Launch Plan**
  Assets creation, reviews, enablement sessions, public relations and marketing activities, trade shows, fairs, industry events, webinars, trial offerings—there are so many options. Some have a defined cost and date not in your control, others can be budgeted and scheduled by yourself. They all have in common that they require time, effort, budget and need to be staffed. Also, there is likely dependencies on other activities and people, so in consequence all that needs to be covered in the Go-to-Market Launch Plan. If you don't have one, you might be in good company, but you are on track for stressful and chaotic times, leading to miscommunication or poor execution, and most importantly, you are risking that your superior product is outperformed by mediocre products just because you failed with an appropriate Go-to-Market approach.

If you luckily have a Product Marketing team supporting you, you should become best friends and work closely together as product managers are always accountable and frequently responsible for core content, technical facts, initial drafts and just know their products and customers best. And if you are not in this luxurious, maybe mandatory, position, then you might not split work and responsibilities between people, but maybe just between your two roles as you are the one with both hats on. Or in other words as product managers you are experts in "What to say" and as Product Marketing Managers you are experts in "How to say it." Maybe you need to be an expert in both.

The outbound part of your product manager role comes in many facets. Marketing and sales assets, internal and external audiences, subject to time and budget conditions—how healthy is your product in this dimension?

In Fig. 2.20 I summarize what it means to live in hell or heaven in the Go-to-Market/Product Marketing dimension. Again, most likely your product scores neither 0 nor 10 in all items. 0 in all items would probably mean you have no aspiration to tell anyone about your product; you enjoy the product all yourself and scoring 10 would probably mean that you have a great support from your product marketing teams and enough time to get everything well set-up and aligned. I have never seen a product that scored a perfect 10 throughout all items, however some came pretty close.

	Hell		Heaven
Dimension Item		0 … 10	
Assets / Sales Kit	No assets available		Up-to-date, quality sales kit for each target group
Sales Enablement	No sales team enabled		Sales fully equipped and trained for all situations
Partner Enablement	No partners enabled		VAR/SI enabled as own sales teams above/PS below
Professional Services Enablement	No professional services enabled		Professional services fully informed about news
Competitive Analysis	No competition identified and analyzed		Clear positioning tailored response to competitors
GTM Activities and Plan	No plan for new product or new release, no events		Staffed, aligned and funded GTM activities and plan

Fig. 2.20 Heaven or hell: go-to-market/product marketing © Timo Wagenblatt 2019. All rights reserved

Again, PYPR is not a rating tool for product managers. This is easily misunderstood and hence I will repeat the right interpretation again in this section. PYPR is a thinking framework and ongoing discipline that fosters communication and strategic thinking, and it helps to prioritize all product management tasks as to what is most important at a given stage for your product's healthiness.

In Chap. 6 we will discover how to assess each item above, how to rate it and how to improve it. We will also examine the difference in Business-to-Business where there are multiple audiences that influence the buying decisions to be targeted versus Business-to-Consumer where typically the user is the buyer.

Who are the likely stakeholders we will work with and communicate to in the Go-to-Market/Product Marketing Dimension?

- Product Marketing Managers
- Marketing Managers and Marketing Agencies
- Project and Program Managers
- Sales Managers and Account Executives (Regional, Global)
- Customer Success Teams
- Pre-sales Specialists
- Value Added Resellers (VARs)
- Consultants and Consulting Managers
- Consulting Partners/System Integrators (SIs)
- Customer buyers (IT, business, user)
- Public Marketing Event Managers

Working in this dimension is very often a challenge for product managers as the assets are customer and market facing and hence should be pixel-perfect as well as crisp. If you benefit from a Product Marketing team, an effective Go-to-Market plan will support the whole team in achieving great results. If you are alone, frequently wearing the product marketing manager hat and not benefitting from the existence (or interest) of a supportive Product Marketing team with all the items above, you need to be selective and effective in the assets you create, broadcast and keep up to date.

There is lots of moving parts and therefore you must consider any change in your product, competitive landscape, industry trends, technology trends, buyers or user persona, etc. that might entail significant investments of time and budgets to maintain this dimension. This is true whether you are in good company with a dedicated Product Marketing team or fighting alone; however, being the one-man army means you need to compromise somewhere else.

Another common issue I have encountered in this dimension is that the focus can turn quickly to features rather than values and therefore the audience is not effectively reached. The same issue is true for the dimension introduced in the next section: software demonstrations and trainings. While I could include software demonstrations and trainings in this chapter, I decided to consider it as its own dimension due to its importance and unique challenges.

Corporate IT products: Internal product managers care about the same dimension items with one major difference. Instead of the enablement of Sales, Professional Services, and partners, internal product managers focus on their market-reaching peers (e.g. the corporate communications team). In my experience, the other items can be equally valid for internal products as well, but with a different interpretation that I will explain in later sections.

2.2.4 Software Demonstrations and Training

Your software product demonstration: Lights, Camera, Action!

Software product demonstrations are normally the first impression of the product for your prospects, customers and future users. Every user and every buyer wants to see and observe the result of the team's hard work in action. We all know how important first impressions are in private life, and it is no different for software and digital products. Hence, software product demonstrations are super important for software products, and maybe even more important for business-to-business software products than for business-to-consumer software products or digital products.

There are many reasons for software demonstrations along the product's lifecycle, whether you are building a software demonstration showcasing your product to secure investments, create awareness and boost sales or create a training exercise. It is vital to understand the best ways of demoing a software product to achieve the targeted top results. When executed effectively, software product demonstrations and training can lead to excitement and buzz around your product.

On the downside, a chaotic software demonstration or a doubtful training exercise can confuse investors, buyers and users in terms of functional completeness or even product readiness, which might lead to doubts about the to-be-expected values and benefits of the product. In contrast, a perfect software demonstration and training environment, including online, offline and video options aligned with the product positioning and the internal stakeholders, as well as the market and customer requirements, sets the stage for your product to grow successfully.

You might ask: What's the role of the product manager here?

In my view product managers should not typically deliver software demonstrations to customers as part of a sales cycle. My general guidance might become clearer, when you think about one of the frequent cases of software demonstrations, for example as part of a Business-to-Business software sales cycle. Delivering the demo to your customers will have several drawbacks, including something basic such as not being an expert in delivering professional software demonstrations, or something more hidden that could weaken your position as a product manager. Some people think in boxes where the person who delivers the software demonstration and the person who is accountable for the product do not fit in the same box in their mind.

Just to be clear—I admire the skills of sales engineers and Pre-sales teams. It is an art to deliver compelling demos and tell the story of a software product. However, some people do not value the role as they should—sales engineers and Pre-sales specialist can be of tremendous value for the customer.

You are the product manager, the product executive taking end-to-end accountability; you want to be perceived as a trusted advisor and the product executive by your customers and partners.

Don't get me wrong—I do not want to give the impression that product managers should not do software demonstrations. Or in other words—I'm totally convinced that exactly the opposite is essential! Therefore, I expect every product manager to be able to demonstrate their products. Choose the situations where you want to drive the product demonstration: showcase new features, the new, cool stuff, wow the business-critical customer, or demo to executives, but all of these will be different types of software product demonstrations within different contexts.

Like software product demonstrations, there are numerous methods for trainings and using training materials. Trainings are required for all key roles in the product lifecycle—internally and externally. The role of the product manager comes with many variations, as the initial trainer in the first teach, delivering early knowledge transfer sessions for consultants, Pre-sales and sales teams, or training the end user, the customers.

Guess who is the first contact for all these requests? Yes, it's you and the product team. There is nothing wrong here as you are the expert and you know about the latest developments; you know the various stakeholders and you are doing everything to make your product successful. You are a known and hence an easy target.

In your role as a product manager, you should not do all the tasks on your own, but rather you should focus on:

- consistency
- professionalism
- scale

The storyline of software demonstrations and training needs to fit to the value proposition and positioning of your product. The delivery needs to be consistent in messaging and addressing the key customer pain points that are resolved with your product. The same is true for the training—if the training material is outdated or not delivering the key parts, that's a negative.

The Software Demonstrations and Training dimension represents "The Showcase Part of your Software Product Manager Role." There are still many issues with software demonstrations and scale in the industry. Due to its importance, I consider Software Demonstrations and Training as its own unique dimension. As a recommendation, the following dimension items need to be considered to score high in the Software Demonstrations and Training dimension.

- **Software Demonstrations**
  Software demonstrations showcase your product in various ways and forms. Online software demonstrations are product demonstrations that showcase your product by using the software live in front of the audience. Software demonstrations are part of most B2B sales cycles responding to customer pain points. As they are live, they require special attention and special skills including flexibility to react to the audience. Hence, software demonstrations require a variety of options to showcase the product in the best possible way in any given context. One common option is the preparation of offline (recorded) software product demonstrations that showcase your product in a pre-defined flow or with a pre-defined focus and message. The best part of offline software demonstrations is that you can plan them; they are reliable and deliver scale. The drawback is that they are not as powerful in many situations like sales cycles. Consider your best fallback solution in the event the live software demonstration struggles.
- **Product Marketing Videos**
  Product Marketing videos are similar to software demonstrations. The main difference is that they can be planned, they are reliable and Product Marketing videos are a great way to scale your messaging. However, Product Marketing videos cannot be tailored, and the messaging is recorded (i.e. the message is the message and cannot be adapted to the audience on the fly). Software demonstrations can be adapted as there is someone presenting to the audience and thus can adapt accordingly to their reactions. Product Marketing videos can be used for software feature demonstrations, and many other situations like overview videos, positioning videos, feature-specific videos, draw-on, customer testimonials, etc. to distribute your product related message to the masses.
- **Pre-sales Enablement**
  There are Pre-sales/sales engineering teams that deliver professional software demonstrations to prospects, customers, analysts etc., especially in Business-to-Business software organizations, and more so for Business-to-Consumer focused organizations, It is essential that your people know and deliver the message according to product vision, roadmap and positioned values. Enabling Pre-sales and sales engineering teams requires the understanding of the specifics of their job. Do they only demo your product, or do they demo a variety of

products supporting multiple lines of business and multiple industries? Do they have a regional focus or are they acting globally? In any case, Pre-sales colleagues will not have much time before the next customer. They need to know where to find the latest software demonstration assets for the region, line of business, or industry allowing them time to fine-tune the demonstration for the next audience.

- **Trainings**
  Professional, high-quality trainings and trainers are available to support all audiences, internally and externally, underpinning the professionalism of your product. For example, trainings can range from user trainings, sales trainings, business process trainings or software demo trainings. As with any document you write or contribute to—be smart and re-use. That will also help with consistency.

Figure 2.21 summarizes what it means to live in hell or heaven in this dimension. Living in hell in all items would probably mean your product cannot be demoed to anyone and if there is a technical reason for this, then you might consider replacing the whole dimension from the Product Yield Potential Radar. We will discuss how to tailor and adapt PYPR in the next section. Living in hell throughout would probably mean that you are part of an elite circle of storytellers in your organization supported by software demonstrations that are up to date showcasing every value of your product while underlining your superior positioning, both adapted for all relevant target audiences and markets. Qualitative trainings and trainers are available to support all audiences, internally and externally, underpinning the professionalism of your product. And as perfect 10 owners, you are accompanied by the self-motivated, objectives aligned and fully enabled elite circle of Pre-sales specialists and sales engineers. I have never seen a product that scored a perfect 10 throughout all items.

	Hell		Heaven
Dimension Item		0 10	
Software Demonstrations	No live or recorded software demonstration		Variation of value focused, reliable, adaptable demos
Product Marketing Videos	No videos		Variation of target audience ready videos
Pre-Sales Enablement	No pre-sales engineers enabled		Pre-sales fully equipped and trained for all situations
Training	No training		Up-to-date trainings aligned with product positioning

Fig. 2.21 Heaven or hell: software demonstrations and training

In Chap. 7 we will discover how to assess, how to rate, and how to improve each topic above. The Product Yield Potential Radar is not a rating tool for product managers. This is easily misunderstood and hence I will repeat this again and if you are bored by now, that's a good sign. As the phrase goes: If you are bored listening to yourself, that's the point when people start to understand. And there are just two more repetitions to follow in the next two chapters. PYPR is a thinking framework and ongoing discipline that fosters communication and strategic thinking across the product team. Additionally, PYPR helps to prioritize all product management tasks to determine what is most important at a given stage for your product's health, and in this section, considering software demonstrations and training.

Who are the likely stakeholders we will work with and communicate to in the Software Demonstrations Dimension?

- Product Marketing Managers and Marketing Managers
- Sales Managers (Regional, Global) and Account Executives
- Solution Experience Team
- Sales Engineers and Pre-sales Specialists
- Pre-sales Management
- Value Added Resellers (VARs)
- Consultants and Consulting Managers
- Consulting Partners/System Integrators (SIs)
- Customer Business and Technical Teams, Customer C-Level
- Training Department
- Training Consultancy

The stakeholders can be clustered in two groups, the ones that are delivering and the ones who receive the software demonstrations and training. We'll learn more about these stakeholders and their specifics throughout this book.

Note that you need to be selective about who delivers the software demonstration or training, as experience shows that ad hoc support on average hurts more than helps. Anyone who is part of the software demonstrations and training group needs to understand the basics, the product vision, the product's positioning, the target audience and the key messages to be delivered.

For example, I have seen developers and frequently product managers delivering software demonstrations as part of a sales cycle that started off well, but turned into feature and function shows, tech deep-dives or educational sessions. However, the goal of most customer meetings/software demonstrations in a sales cycle is not to distribute product knowledge or show how great you are as a developer. It is to advance the sale to the next stage. Often these goals get confused if you are too attached and hence too proud of every feature you have built.

Note that software demonstrations and trainings are the way everyone outside of the development or core product team perceives your product the first time. You might have the best and deepest functionality; however, if your software product demonstration is off target or your trainings are perceived as time-wasting, then you are screwed. You will not make it to the next round in sales, investment decisions, analyst sessions etc., which all have in common the missed opportunity of leveraging the limited face-to-face time (or phone time or online time) with your target audience.

Corporate IT products: Internal product managers care about the same dimension items with one major difference. Instead of Pre-sales enablement, internal product managers focus on the enablement of peers in Support and Roll-out teams. In my experience, the other items are equally valid for internal products as well. Sometimes with a different interpretation that I will explain in later sections.

In Chap. 7 we will examine in much more detail the various software demonstration and training types, the essentials to be considered as well as some proven practices that worked in various situations over the last decade and more.

2.2.5 The Market/Your Customers

Turning the anonymous market into prospects interested in our software products and becoming satisfied customers that value our software product—that's the purpose of product teams and we do whatever it takes to build and deliver beautiful products.

In The Market/Your Customers dimension we need to focus primarily on these items:

- Understanding your market perception in terms of functional completeness and product quality
- Engaging customers and building a customer community
- Motivating customers to support you and act as references
- Establishing thought leadership
- Engaging with influencers and analyst

In best case product managers work every day with customers and target customers. In every team meeting I ask my team about current and planned customer interactions. As we talk, chat, e-mail, call, and meet with customers, every interaction is important in many dimensions.

Very often product managers focus on the aspects of problem assessment, solution idea validation, shaping of the best business model, requirements gathering and validation, presenting to customers in sales cycles or in software product demonstrations. We explored these interactions in the respective sections Product Viability. Go-to-Market/Product Marketing, Software Demonstrations and Training.

While the interactions and priorities might be different within each product lifecycle stage, it remains imperative to understand market trends, derive market segments, target customers' and customers' needs, etc. These insights cannot be found internally. Some people call this market research, I call this understanding the purpose of Software Product Management. I do not buy into the concept of defining market research as a special, separate discipline unless we deal with a completely new product idea. However, even then I would consider market research as part of Design Thinking or Business Model Canvas activities. In my view, market research or better market segment, target customer and customer research are part of the daily interactions and work of a product manager.

The Market/Your Customers dimension focuses on understanding or expanding the total addressable market, researching existing and new market segments, engaging target customers and existing customers, and leveraging other players in the ecosystem such as influencers and analysts. Figure 2.22 visualizes the power of this PYPR dimension. Your software product's full potential will be limited if you do not score high in this dimension.

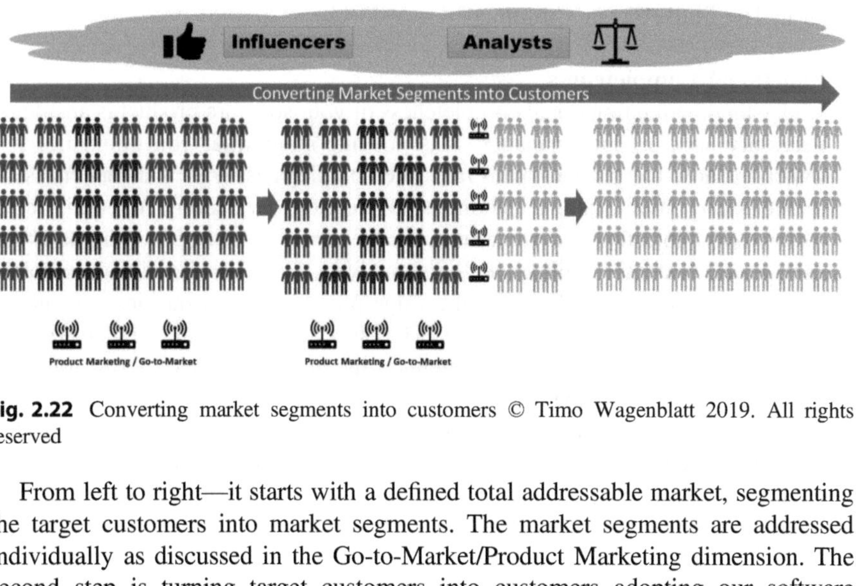

Fig. 2.22 Converting market segments into customers © Timo Wagenblatt 2019. All rights reserved

From left to right—it starts with a defined total addressable market, segmenting the target customers into market segments. The market segments are addressed individually as discussed in the Go-to-Market/Product Marketing dimension. The second step is turning target customers into customers adopting our software products, thus increasing the market share of the software product. Always keep in mind—happy customers are worth a mint. All of these three steps are accompanied by the voice of influencers and analysts.

As outlined above, the market comes with various facets like target customers, market segments, analysts, influencers, press and media, while the customers are the people and companies who write the checks. Balancing market requirements (i.e. non-customer requirements and customer requirements) directly impacts the perception of the functional completeness of our software products. It is important to know how the total addressable market, the market segments, and our target customers and customers perceive our software products in terms of functional completeness and product quality. The outside view might be fundamentally different than the internal perception, sometimes in a good and sometimes in a disastrous way.

Additionally, the interaction directly with customers, but also with analysts and influences requires product manager attention. As product managers, being considered as thought leaders in our area is truly beneficial in many ways. We should not underestimate the effect of building out our brand as a software product company or product manager. If you are the one who defines and shapes the market, you are likely more trusted and recognized, which in consequence will help you in many dimensions. Blocking time for such activities will pay back in many ways.

The Market/Your Customers dimension represents "The Purpose of your Software Product Manager Role." Having clearly defined target customers and market segments by clustering and profiling potential customers is the foundation of any market and product strategy. Converting target customers into active customers is the reason we develop products and is the basis for allowing us to continue our journey. As a recommendation, the following dimension items are vital for scoring high in The Market/Your Customers dimension:

- **Functional Completeness**
  Understanding the functional completeness of your software product is absolutely necessary as a product manager. It is not important what you think, nor it is important how the product team rates the completeness—all that matters is the market's and your existing customers' perception. Evaluating functional completeness is subjective and sometimes we feel unfairly treated looking at ratings from users, customers, influencers, and analysts. However functional completeness ratings correlate highly with the value proposition and business model you offer and what competitors provide. Therefore, understanding perceived functional completeness provides tremendous value in a multitude of ways. And keep in mind: Perception is reality!
  The perceived functional completeness can be scored against current product capabilities, competition, known customer requirements, perceived value of features and functions, and industry standards. Additional insights can be derived by usage tracking and product research whether product features are really used. In the ideation phase your task is to understand the functional completeness of the vision and problem statement.
- **(External View of) Product Quality**
  Like the item above, the perceived product quality means how the market and the customers perceive the quality of the product. There are lots of internal key performance indicators such initial response times, maximum response time and average response times or the number of reported bugs; however, all of these do not tell you the full story.
  The market and your customers perceive product quality based on other indicators or experiences. Think about positive news of successful customer go-lives or negative news about customer escalations. Think about how one small bug can

hinder a go-live even though it is only one bug in the internal KPI framework. Think about the product that is not available for use because the server is down, when the user needs your product. These and many more occasions shape the perception of your software product quality in this dimension. You will be surprised how the scoring in this dimension items deviates from the product quality score in the Product Development dimension.

- **Engaging Customers and Building a Customer Community**
  There are many ways to engage with customers either in 1:1 situations or in communities and councils addressing groups of customers all at once. These opportunities are distinct, and their objectives may vary along the product journey. In my experience, customers like to be in a community; sometimes they organize the community on their own and sometimes you can form (and steer) customer communities. Independently of the scenario, engaging customers comes with multiple, priceless benefits for both parties. Therefore, this dimensional item will have significant dependencies to other Product Yield Potential dimensions depending on the scope and form of engagement.
- **Support of Key Customers/Official References**
  Satisfied customers that value your product are the best sales assets you can and will ever have. Therefore, it doesn't matter whether the customer is a user praising your product publicly with top ratings at a website or enterprises allowing you to reference their (valuable and successful) usage of your product. There is no better marketing than word of mouth marketing. Nurture your latest customer like you did with your first one and don't be shy to ask for references. Your customers know your market segment and your target customers, their peers. If your product delivers value, they will communicate about it. Identify customers who are willing to give testimonials, be featured in case studies, give you a like, or agree to be a reference customer.
- **Thought Leadership**
  A thought leader is a person or a company that is an expert in a certain area of knowledge. Other people or companies highly value the opinion of a thought leader to topic-specific questions and concerns. Even more, thought leaders influence opinions in the area of expertise and decide who and what is important. No wonder that everyone wants to be a thought leader as thought leadership is a powerful marketing and sales tool. The only caveat is that one cannot appoint oneself as a thought leader—despite that some people and companies try hard. Interested public, customer communities, and the software product ecosystem recognizes and appoints thought leadership. One of the best ways to establish authority about your topic is to gain and frequently broadcast deep insights on the subject. You have to present a depth of knowledge that no one else has. As a thought leader, the market and your customers expect you to show innovation and mastery in the problem space of your product.
- **Analyst/Influencer Relations**
  Analysts and influencers can be considered as thought leaders as well. In the B2B space you should especially know the players in the analyst camp. Analyst ratings might be very important in your particular market segment. These ratings can stay

relevant for a year or more despite the release of new features after the last analyst report that did not appreciate your product at that time. The logic and market dynamics are very simple:

- great analyst review results = great "free" marketing = less time and budget required
- poor analyst review results = negative marketing = tons of extra work to explain every target customer who read the review that your software product is not as bad as stated in the "official and independent review"

Similarly, influencers should be known and influenced in the best possible way or at least you should not be an easy target to be blamed.

In Fig. 2.23, I summarize what it means to live in hell or heaven in The Market/Your Customers dimension. Most likely your product scores neither 0 nor 10 in all items. 0 in all items would probably mean you deal with a product that no one outside your organization cares about or even worse no one outside your four walls wants to be mentioned or seen in close proximity to your offering. You might want to rethink whether you need to find another market or another product, but clearly that means hell to any product manager. In contrast a perfect 10 throughout all items would probably mean that you are a black belt in applying Kano.[9] Customers, users, analysts, everyone perceives the product offering to be complete and valuable with highest quality standards from the thought leader. The entire business world wants to be recognized with your product and your customer community shows up with T-shirts and other merchandising items highlighting they are part of the community using your product.

Once more and likely not surprising to anyone, I have personally never seen a product that scored a perfect 10 throughout all items. In times of a real hype, there might be products that are close in public perception; however quite often it's more like a flash in a pan than reality. Nevertheless, the perfect world scenario is what we should strive for.

	Hell		Heaven
Dimension Item		0 10	
Functional Completeness	Product not considered by any market segment		No requirements nor perceived gaps from anyone
Product Quality	Customers cancel contracts due to quality issues		No customers reporting any product issues
Customer Community	No customer community or other engagement		Active customer councils and vibrant community
Key Customers Support	No customers speak for the product		Relevant, value focused, audience ready references
Thought Leadership	Not perceived in the market as a player		Market looks at you for guidance
Analyst / Influencer Relations	No analyst or influencer communication		Analysts / influencers provide top ratings

Fig. 2.23 Heaven or hell: the market/your customers

In Chap. 8 we will discover how to assess each item above, how to rate it and how to improve it. PYPR is not a rating tool for product managers. This is easily misunderstood and hence I will repeat it for the last time. PYPR is a thinking

[9]The Kano model is described in Sect. 5.5.5

framework and ongoing discipline that fosters communication and strategic thinking. Additionally, PYPR helps prioritize all product management tasks, discovering what is most important to increase your product's achievement potential.

Who are the likely stakeholders we will work with and communicate to in The Market/Your Customers Dimension?

- Customer/Prospect Business Users
- Customer/Prospect IT Organizations
- Customer/Prospect C-Level
- Customer/Prospect Purchasing Team
- Analysts
- Industry Organization Representatives
- Press Representatives
- Event Managers

The list of stakeholders could be extended by everyone we trained and enabled internally to address the market segments/target customers/customers, but they are not explicitly mentioned here. However, there is obviously a link to all these internal roles that influence The Market/Your Customers dimension for good.

In this section we reminded ourselves once more, that customers are different than the market. Software products need to focus on the targeted market segments (aka The Market), not a single customer, maybe that is one of the main differences to projects. Still customers are what makes you successful and not the anonymous market. Listen to customers, to the business users at customers and to customer executives. Evaluate strategic customers for your product. Strategic doesn't necessarily mean large customers, but customers who are willing to work with you and adopt the product and the new features early. If you further balance and find the right mix of strategic customers so that they represent the market, then you are likely in a good shape.

Corporate IT products: Internal product managers care about the same dimension items, with the following aspects to consider. I will further detail the differences in the respective sections:

- Customer community and analyst/influencer relations are likely not relevant and therefore not part of the default PYPR configuration for corporate IT products. Instead, internal product managers should focus on the extended internal stakeholder community and peer community.
- In my experience, the other items are equally valid for internal products as well, sometimes with a different interpretation that I will explain in later sections.

In Chap. 8 we will examine in much more detail how to work with customers, customer councils, analysts and influences—the essentials to be considered—as well as some proven practices that work in real life.

2.2.6 Organizational Maturity

Even the best product managers cannot provide the full value to their organization, if the organization doesn't provide some basic environmental conditions. We will discover and evaluate the most important areas that need to become more mature as an organization and a place that attracts and welcomes the best Software Product Management talent.

Beauty and success can be found even in rough environments, but you find both more often in better environmental conditions. Compared to many other disciplines Software Product Management is still in early stages according to various industry surveys and research. Consider Software Product Management in your organization as a product, likely it would be in introduction or growth phase of its lifecycle.

Consequently, the maturity level of most organizations is not at the high-end level. For example, the Product Management Festival Trends and Benchmarks report 2018 reported 80% of the product managers perceive their organizations as not being mature where Software Product Management (80% rated below 8 of a scale from 1 to 10) is concerned.

That is no surprise as Software Product Management is still a rather new discipline although it is steadily improving. The discipline comes with many facets and variations without a simple guidance for reaching organizational maturity over time.

Maturity models are very popular tools and have been around for some time in various disciplines. Maturity models promise help to organizations to level-set how well they're doing versus best practices (i.e. what does ''mature' looks like, for example, in Software Product Management). Maturity models assess the current capabilities and help figure out what capabilities need to be acquired to improve performance. Commonly maturity models are presented from the basic level of "we do it somehow" to the mastery level of "we strive for perfection", as shown in Fig. 2.24.

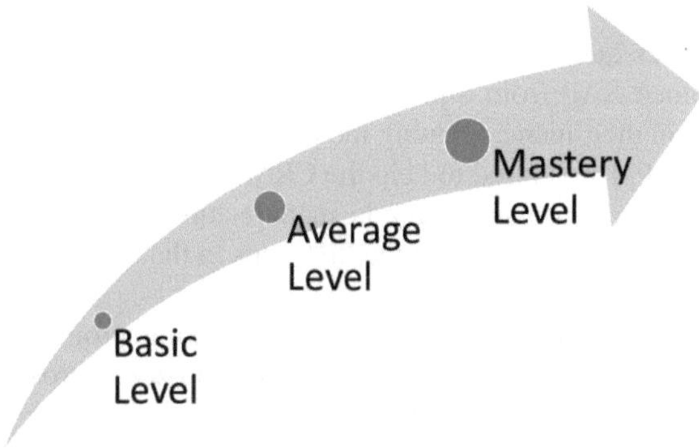

Fig. 2.24 Organizational maturity scale © Timo Wagenblatt 2019. All rights reserved

Maturity models, like any model, are simplifications to support an argument. In my view, the key point of Software Product Management maturity models is to highlight the importance and existence of maturity enablers across:

- Product Management Leadership, Vision and Strategy
- Organizational Set-up, Processes and Governance
- People Mindset supported by key principles
- Templates and Tools

Reaching higher maturity indicates Software Product Management improvements in your organization. The environmental qualities for software products improve as higher maturity levels are reached. Remember that the best product managers cannot provide full value to their organization if the organization doesn't provide some basic environmental qualities. And if product managers are not at their full potential, the products they care about are likely not at their full potential either. Organizational issues cost not only time, create anger and churn or in short make everything harder; organizational issues significantly cost money.

Increasing organizational maturity is expected to lead to:

- Higher user satisfaction
- Higher revenue/profit
- Less friction between stakeholders
- Keeping and attracting (Software Product Management) talent

The business case is clear; companies still struggle to change their organizations toward a product organization. One aspect of this resistance might be that such a change would require current line managers to give up parts of their organizational kingdoms (i.e. the functional leader part) or become product managers themselves —which they might not like as suddenly they are in the spotlight of accountability. However, as product managers, they would be in a true leadership position—a leadership that focuses clearly on outcomes and value for their customers and their own company at the same time.

Product managers struggle if there is no guidance about what software product management stands for in the organization. This needs to come from top management and be bought into and evangelized by everyone in the executive and product team. So, you are not the strange guy in the room who doesn't code or doesn't have a sales quota or a marketing KPI, but you are the product manager.

In 2006, I joined SAP from a product-minded start-up company that had been rather successful in their niche, winning most deals against much larger competitors at that time. At SAP, I was hired to help the CRM team close a gap in their offering to support fast-moving consumer goods manufacturers. SAP did a great job in onboarding me technically. I enjoyed the first steps in the new world of such a large enterprise software company.

The organization prepared for a huge co-innovation project with one of the leading brands in the fast-moving consumer goods industry. A cross-functional team had been established and I was the dedicated product manager. So far, so good.

I met the development team the first time, sitting in a room with about 20 software engineers, who had worked for many years in the CRM development team at SAP. When it was my turn in the introduction round, I introduced myself, my background, where I'm coming from and how I interpret my future role as product manager in the product team.

Silence! In fact, painful silence and lots of confused faces.

After some time, one guy asked me: "What's your role again? What are you actually doing?" I explained my interpretation of the product manager role again and the team literally freaked out … like screaming kids that lost their cuddly toy.

At that time, we were experiencing some low Software Product Management maturity—lack of leadership, lack of processes, lack of role clarity regarding Software Product Management. Luckily these days are over, and the maturity of Software Product Management improved significantly at SAP over the years.

The more organizations understand the role and the importance of software product management and their product managers the better are the chances for product longevity and success. Figure 2.25 depicts the critical items within the Organizational Maturity dimension of PYPR.

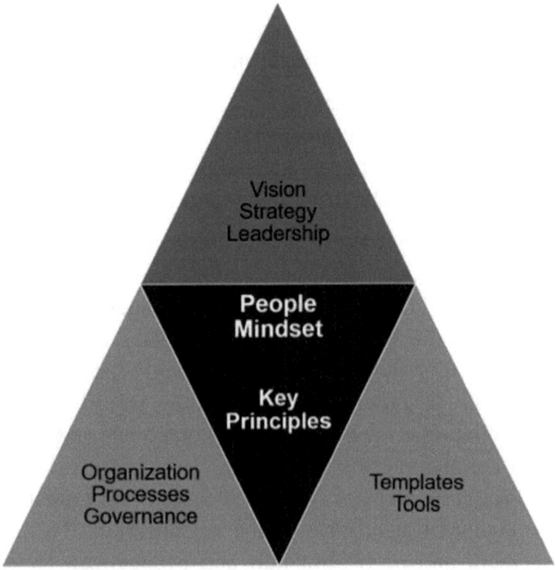

Fig. 2.25 Elements of product management organizational maturity © Timo Wagenblatt 2019. All rights reserved

At the core of organizational maturity, you find the people mindset based on key principles valid for the product organization. Some people would call this culture or product culture.

And since Peter Drucker, we know: **Culture eats strategy for breakfast!**

The Product Yield Potential Radar as a thinking framework and implemented as an ongoing discipline within Software Product Management becomes an enabler of a joint product culture also known as Product Mindset. And transferring above elements into Peter Drucker's quote leads to: **Missing Product Mindset and Key Principles eat Vision, Strategy, Leadership, and Organizational Set-up for lunch!**

The Organizational Maturity dimension represents "The Environmental Quality in your Organization." As a product manager, your working environment is not an unchangeable thing. You set the tone in many aspects. You have the lever and the overview to change things directly or at least recommend changes that are out of your direct influence. Let's discover the PYPR dimension items worth improving in the Organizational Maturity dimension:

- **Product Management Leadership, Vision and Strategy**
  Does your leadership team understand the value of Software Product Management? Is there a sponsor in the executive team or do you need to fight for attention? The management methods require a level of trust with product managers and product teams as autonomy of teams doesn't match that well with the old-fashioned style of leadership.
  Note that Product Vision and Strategy is different than the ones described in the Product Development dimension, as the vision of product management for your organization or company is in focus here. Does your organization aspire to be a product-led organization or are you on a different mission? As a product manager, you can re-use your knowledge and learning about vision and strategy for the benefit of the whole organization.
- **Product Management Organization, Processes and Governance**
  There are many ways to set up Software Product Management as a function in your organization. Independent of your approach, organizational set-up and processes need to be aligned. Organization and process is just the vehicle, not the main thing. Keep that in mind, Communication and collaboration rules, aligned metrics, in short, a proper governance of the processes across teams, is a winner. As in my story above, if there is confusion about who does what and how, then there will be too much of friction between people not adding any value. A lack of aligned processes and missing role clarity is one of the most common reasons for bad execution, lack of accountability, average outcomes and weak product mindsets. If the product manager is not properly positioned in the organization this is like kryptonite for the guys in their superhero capes.

- **Product Management Templates and Tools**
  Do you have standardized templates for business cases, launch plans, roadmaps, user stories? The list is endless and without templates and guidance, everyone in your organization will find their own way of doing it and interpreting the work results. What you want to achieve is a status of productizing Software Product Management. Productizing product management requires templates and tools. Note that this is not a one-off activity. If something works, share it with your peers and vice versa, learn from your peers what worked for them. And if a tool or template does not work, change it. In the same spirit I will add proven tools and how to work with them throughout the book.
- **People Mindset and Key Principles**
  This item might be the hardest one to crack as ultimately that is a result of everything: your product, your organization, yourself and the people you work with. Changing people mindset toward a product mindset is the aspiration. We strive for outcomes that provide value to our customers and the organization, and therefore outcome over ego is a fundamental key principle. Key principles help people with decisions and guidance about values in your organization. If people benefit from clearly communicated principles, these principles are forming the people's mindset over time.

In Fig. 2.26 you find an overview what it means to live in heaven or hell in the Organizational Maturity dimension. Most likely your product or in this case your organization scores neither 0 nor 10 in all items. 0 in all items would probably mean you feel completely displaced in your organization and there are no chances for success or impact. My advice would be to no longer waste your time and skills as a product manager in such an organization. There is plenty of opportunities out there that appreciate your talent.

Scoring a perfect 10 in organizational maturity likely means you work in a very successful company and enjoy your business and as well your private life. Congratulations! Please, give me a call!

	Hell		Heaven
Dimension Item		0 10	
Vision, Strategy and Leadership	Product Management – what's this again?		PM on the Board, PM excellence focus
Organization, Process, Governance	Total confusion on who does what and how		Roles and responsibilities agreed between all actors
Templates and Tools	Paper, pen, and no guidance or support		Continuous improvement of well-established standards
People Mindset and Key Principles	Ego over outcome, no shared principles		Outcome over ego, shared values/principles, product!!!

Fig. 2.26 Heaven or hell: organizational maturity © Timo Wagenblatt 2019. All rights reserved

In Chap. 9, we will discover how to assess, how to rate, and how to improve each item above. As promised, I re-iterate your new mantra for the last time. PYPR is not a rating tool for product managers. PYPR is a thinking framework and ongoing discipline that fosters communication and strategic thinking across the product team. Additionally, PYPR helps to prioritize the many product management tasks, discovering what is most important at a given stage for your product's success, and in this case, maybe even more for your success as a product manager.

Who are the likely stakeholders we will work with and communicate to in the Organizational Maturity Dimension?

- Product Management Peers
- Your Line Managers
- COO
- CEO
- Founder
- Department Head
- Human Resources
- External and internal Product Management Consultants
- External and internal Product Management Trainers
- Head of Product/VP Product Management

The Organizational Maturity dimension is an indicator about the state of Software Product Management and the environmental conditions for the product manager species in your organization. Leveraging PYPR with many product departments and organizations, I experienced that more mature organizations reach the full potential of PYPR faster. For less mature product teams and organizations, PYPR provided immediate value by applying the foundational Steps 1 and 2 as depicted Fig. 2.14, however leveraging the full potential as a team requires more time.

As a Software Product Manger working in an organization with a lower maturity, you will still benefit by applying PYPR to your product. You can use PYPR on your own and with your core product team. You can also conduct Steps 3 and 4 by yourself or better with your core team, but the boundary conditions in your organization are not in your favor. Therefore, you need to plan more time and effort to manage upward and educate your organization what value you and Software Product Management add. Evangelizing and educating Software Product Management becomes an important lever for product and ultimately organizational success.

In that sense PYPR is a kind of maturity model that includes organizational maturity as one dimension in concert with the other required capabilities of product success. The higher the overall PYPR score across all products the higher the Software Product Management maturity might be in your organization. We will examine this idea in Chap. 9.

In the next section, I will introduce how Organizational Maturity limits, in concert with the other dimensions (Product Viability, Product Development, Go-to-Market/ Product Marketing, Software Demonstrations and Training, and The Market/Your Customers), the yield potential of your software product. And I finally explain why I actually use the term yield potential in context of Software Product Management.

2.3 Software Product Management Governs the Product's Yield Potential

In the previous section, we covered the six PYPR dimensions and the vast number of factors influential to the chances of product success determining the product's yield potential. In this section, I will introduce how the ingredients of product longevity organized in PYPR dimension and dimension items govern every product's yield potential.

Figure 2.27 summarizes the six dimensions of Software Product Management and all the items of each dimension we have discovered so far. I will focus on how to improve all dimensions and dimension items over time in the dedicated sections for each dimension.

Fig. 2.27 Software product management dimensions and dimension items

PYPR dimensions are not independent and the items within any dimension aren't either. The dependencies and effects of the PYPR dimension items are super interesting and I will introduce them in this section. Furthermore, I want to invite you to time travel back to the year 1828, which will improve your understanding of Software Product Management today and for the future.

We will discover the Law of the Minimum and the Law of Tolerance that together illustrate how product managers can use the Product Yield Potential Radar to recognize the limiting factors of product success and understand the interdependencies of the PYPR dimensions and their items. We will leverage the knowledge from other research disciplines, gaining insights to improve our understanding of managing software products from the first idea to market leadership.

In our roles as product manager it is crucial that we understand the interactions and dependencies among product viability, product development, Go-to-Market activities, software demonstrations and training, the market and customers and our organizational maturity.

Understanding how a positive or negative change in one item affects

- another item in the same or a different dimension
- the overall product yield potential (as a measure for the chances of success)
- a huge advantage in improving as a product manager.

As we defined the role, product managers have end-to-end accountability for product success and therefore need to focus on each dimension and each dimension item that matter for the product. Do you feel like there is too much work, too much priorities and not enough time to get everything done? How do we know what is important at a given time? Why does the hard work improve one dimension item sometimes or a whole dimension not increase product success?

That's what PYPR is all about: Finding the right balance and right priorities that work best for you, your stakeholders, your organization and your product.

Most product managers I have been working with throughout my career love their products and were emotionally attached to their product in a way that they talk and act like parents. Like good parents they do everything possible and impossible so that their babies stay healthy and develop well. They invest all their time and energy caring about the product baby like helicopter parents. In fact, I have been the same for a major part of my product management career.

However, upon reflection, a more appropriate metaphor is likely found in flora. Like a sapling, at the beginning of its lifecycle every product requires special care and focused attention that evolves and changes over time as the product grows, becoming a healthy, beautiful tree—ideally a giant "profit" sequoia.

The tree metaphor becomes even more tangible when examining the law of the minimum in biology and agriculture. There the Law of the Minimum states that growth is controlled by the scarcest resource (limiting factor (Salisbury, 1992)). What does this mean in agriculture and chemistry and more importantly how can this concept be transferred to Software Product Management—that's what we will discover in the remainder of this chapter.

We will take a little excursus into a completely different and ancient—not outdated—area of knowledge, which is super important for any product manager—the Law of the Minimum. As we take the time to understand and internalize the concept, we will work much smarter, not harder. The goal is to stay and be successful in Software Product Management for the long haul. PYPR has the potential to help you to balance the quality of life and the success of your products. Working hard until exhaustion while still not exploiting the full potential of our software products needs to be avoided.

Before we will learn how the Law of the Minimum nicely corresponds with Software Product Management, let's take the already advertised excursus and understand the basics of the Law of the Minimum.

2.3.1 Introducing the Law of the Minimum

The German agronomist and chemist Carl Sprengel published the theorem of minimum in 1828. Justus Liebig, a German chemist who made major contributions in a variety of different fields, extended the theorem and popularized Carl Sprengel's "Theorem of minimum" (known as Law of the Minimum) in 1855, stating that plant growth is not determined by the total resources available, but by the scarcest available resource (water, sunlight, nutrients). A plant's development is limited by the one essential resource that is in relatively shortest supply. This resource is also called the minimum or limiting factor.

The impact of limiting factors is commonly visualized as "Liebig's barrel", a barrel in which each stave represents a different element. A nutrient stave that is shorter than the others will cause the liquid contained in the barrel to spill out at that limiting level (Liebig's Law of the Minimum, 2018).

Before we transfer these insights to Software Product Management, let's explore the origin of the Law of the Minimum. In agriculture, fertilizing fields benefit significantly by understanding the Law of the Minimum. Farmers understand and leverage the Law of the Minimum in their daily work. The yield potential depends on the plant's growth and if one crop nutrient is missing or scarce, plant growth will be poor even if the other elements are abundant as illustrated in Fig. 2.28. For example, a lack of phosphate cannot be compensated by an increased ingestion of potassium or nitrogen. The potential of the crop is represented by Liebig's barrel with staves of unequal length. The capacity of the barrel is limited by the length of the shortest stave (e.g. phosphate) and can only be increased by lengthening that stave. The capacity of the barrel is the potential yield of the crop or whole land.

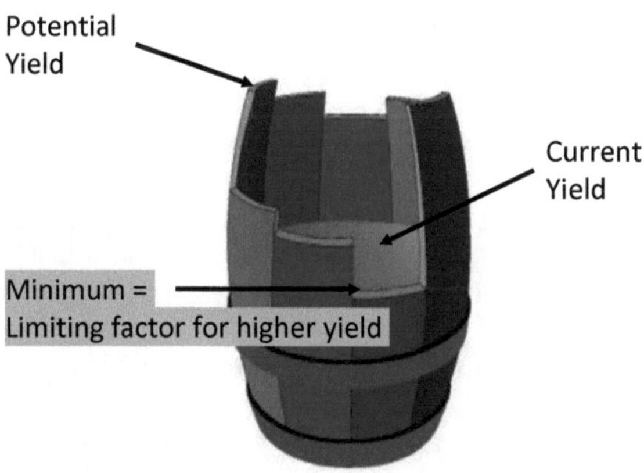

Fig. 2.28 Liebig's barrel © Timo Wagenblatt 2019. All rights reserved

When a stave is lengthened (e.g. phosphate-rich fertilizer), another one becomes the limiting factor restricting the plant's growth and the fields yield now. To maximize the yield, the crop nutrients need to be perfectly balanced for the field and plants (read product context). Farming and fertilizing are only effective if the limiting factors are continuously monitored. That's why Justus Liebig is also called the father of the fertilizer industry, but that is another story in another book that is already written.

Key Takeaways

- **Understand growth drivers and limiting factors**
- **Optimize nutrient mix for the given situation/context**
- **Balance cost and effort against yield potential**

2.3.2 Applying the Law of the Minimum to Software Product Management

Let's take a different perspective when we look at the Product Yield Potential Radar again. With the knowledge about the Law of the Minimum, we can easily transfer the concept to PYPR visualizing the nutrients required for software products to grow and provide the expected and deserved yield for all the hard work developing a software product from initial idea to user excitement and generating value for you and your customers.

Fig. 2.29 Product yield potential staves © Timo Wagenblatt 2019. All rights reserved

The Product Yield Potential Radar in Fig. 2.29 depicts all nutrients required to grow your product from a little sapling to the giant "profit" sequoia mentioned before. The art and science of Software Product Management is orchestrating the product team and all involved stakeholders and working smart to get all these product success nutrients in perfect balance.

Figure 2.30 illustrates the limiting factors to reach a higher product yield. There is one item in the Product Development dimension that requires special attention. However even if the team takes all the effort to get this item on par with the other items in the Product Development dimension, then the full yield potential will not be reached as the limiting factor will change to the items in The Market/Your Customers dimension and the one in the Organizational Maturity dimension. The minimum of any dimension governs the overall product's yield potential.

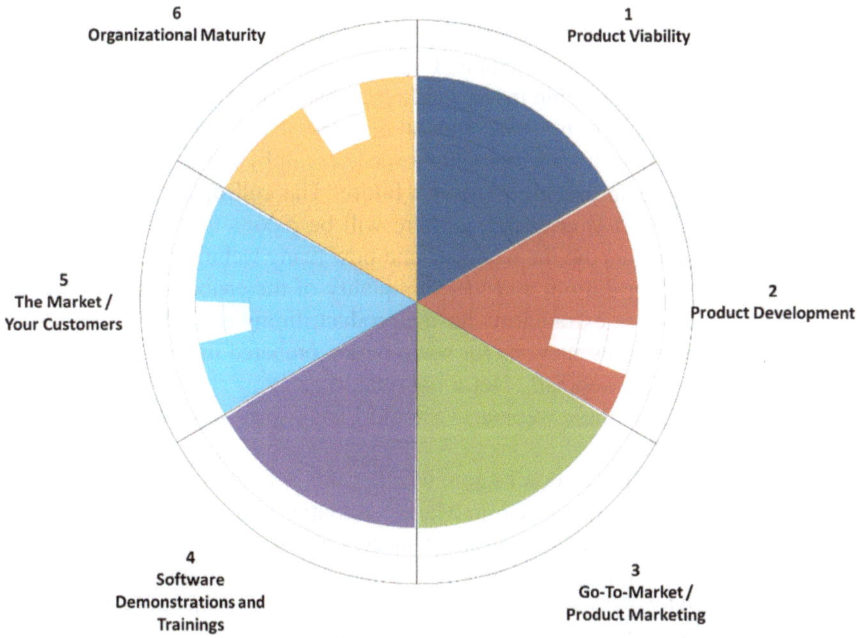

Fig. 2.30 Product Yield Potential Radar with limiting factors © Timo Wagenblatt 2019. All rights reserved

In my daily business, I'm trying to remind my team and myself that focusing on one dimension or even one single item in one dimension is important at certain times in the year or within a release cycle; however, keeping the balance with all other PYPR items is essential to a healthy product and will not harm the growth and success potential of the product plant. I found this to be true in any stage of any product's lifecycle whether I was working on a completely new product or taking over a mature product that has been in the market for over 10 years.

There are differences in the importance of the various radar dimension items—no doubt that most of the time the customer business case is more important than having a polished product video as a marketing asset. However, imagine you are in a critical sales cycle and finally get 30 min with the decision maker, and the unexpected happens—the wireless network at the customer is not usable or you cannot get access to it. Then it suddenly becomes tangible that only a balanced approach considering all aspects of PYPR leads to success and one shortcoming can easily turn out to be the limiting factor.

PYPR supports product managers' decision to say "Thanks, for considering my involvement, but no thanks!" to activities or tasks that are not important for the product at a given time. As an example, I have been approached a hundred times by colleagues who are responsible for all kind of enablement sessions. They asked me to do a short 30–60 min webinar for internal or external audiences. They claim how important it is that I do it for the product's success and by not doing the important webinar means I jeopardize my product's future. The colleagues had great arguments why my support is critical, e.g. there will be reports to management about which product managers did the webinars and how many webinars were conducted. Surprisingly reporting did not consider the quality of the enablement sessions nor the importance of these extra efforts for the product. In my early days, I took these tasks and worked on presentations for some hours, prepared myself for the various audiences and did the webinars. Not a big deal, right?

Should I have done these webinars? Should I have spent some hours on each of them?

It is hard to judge if you don't know whether this activity helps you to improve your product's limiting factor. Go-to-Market activities and product marketing are clearly very important factors for product success and webinars are a great tool for enabling a remote or bigger audience to understand the product better. In my situation, I quickly realized that I'm not working on the right thing for product success, as most webinars had no measurable effect on anything in the Product Yield Potential Radar. After all the webinars, the effect (e.g. on the sales pipeline) was not measurable or merely noise in the data. I was working for someone else's objectives, which were all for the best intention, but did not fit with my product. I tried to do everything for my product to achieve the perfect 10 in the Go-to-Market dimension by supporting these webinars.

In consequence, not everything needs to be perfect and saying no to certain requests that cannibalize more important activities should be a strong tool in your bag of tricks. We will realize the "power of no" as an important part of your product manager toolkit in more detail in later chapters.

Let's get back to PYPR—how is the Product Yield Potential Radar helping here? How does PYPR help us to understand whether something is important for the product or just useful?

2.3.3 Examples How PYPR Helps Transparentizing the Limiting Factors

Let's investigate three different products that have been assessed and rated according to the PYPR dimensions. The three products show significant differences considering their rating of Product Viability, Product Development, Go-to-Market, Software Demonstrations and Training, The Market/Your Customers and Organizational Maturity.

We will investigate two important questions with these product examples:

- Which product has the highest potential in terms of product longevity and success?
- Where should the product manager and product team focus all efforts to increase the potential?

Let's investigate how PYPR can support with these questions using an example of a well-managed software product called AverageJoe 5.0. The product scores average in all PYPR dimensions. The product scores 5 out of 10 in each dimension as shown in Fig. 2.31. Figure 2.32 shows the potential of this product plotting a circle until it reaches the radar line. The circle represents how much potential the product has, or in other words, how healthy the product is to reach its potential given the current PYPR.

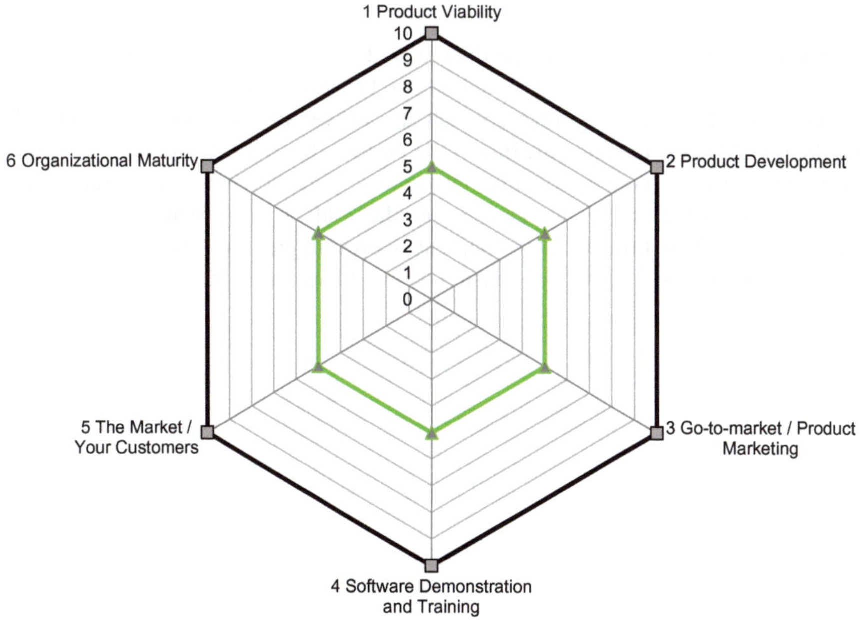

Fig. 2.31 AverageJoe 5.0 rating © Timo Wagenblatt 2019. All rights reserved

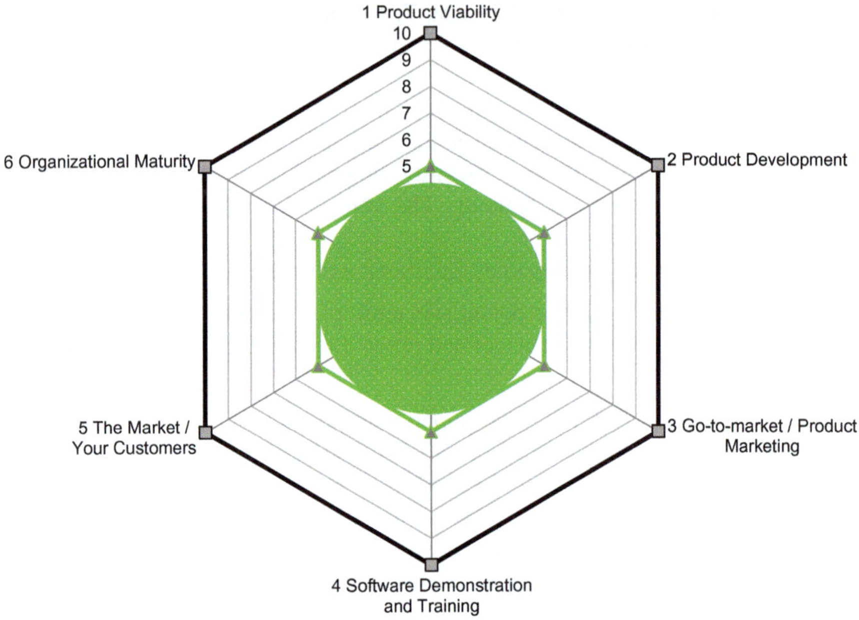

Fig. 2.32 AverageJoe 5.0 yield potential © Timo Wagenblatt 2019. All rights reserved

The product manager and the product team did a nice job scoring equally well in each dimension from Product Viability to Organizational Maturity. They did manage to balance their work across all the important dimensions. Imagine the Product Yield circle reaching the line of the perfect 10—that's the ultimate potential of product success (potential yield) that we are trying to reach as a product team.

In the second example, we analyze another old product friend, called Great-DevNoDemo. The Product Development scores higher; however the Software Demonstrations and Training dimension scores lower than the previous product.

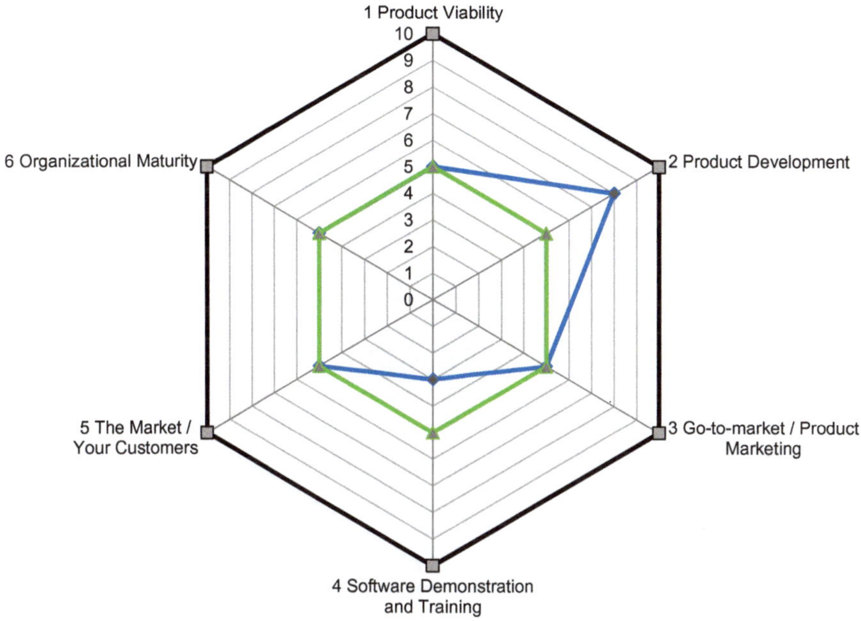

Fig. 2.33 GreatDevNoDemo rating © Timo Wagenblatt 2019. All rights reserved

What is the yield potential of product GreatDevNoDemo shown in Fig. 2.33? Is the product strong and healthy enough to exploit its potential in the market? Is it stronger than AverageJoe 5.0?

Let's plot another circle into the radar and let it grow until it reaches the line for product GreatDevNoDemo as illustrated in Fig. 2.34. The blue circle represents the yield potential or health of product GreatDevNoDemo.

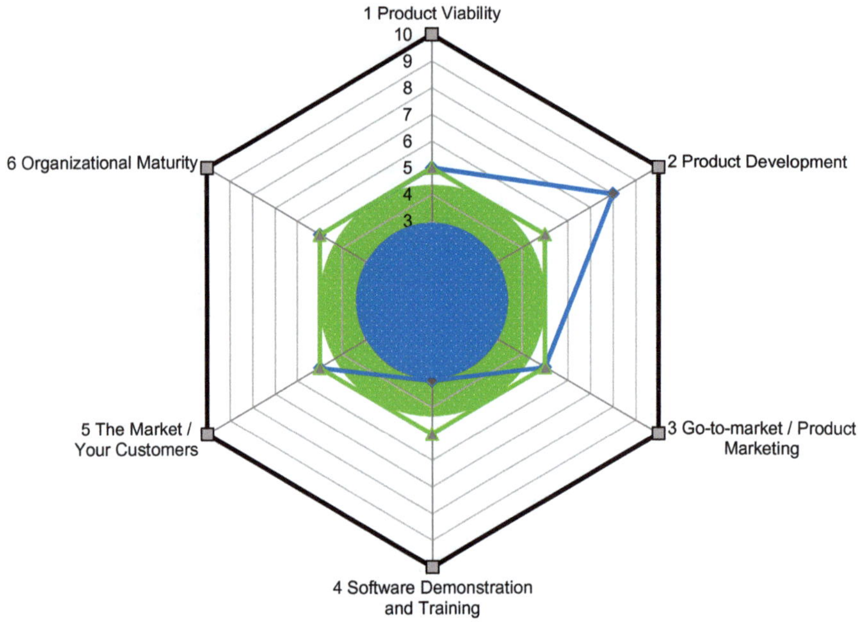

Fig. 2.34 GreatDevNoDemo Product Yield Potential Radar © Timo Wagenblatt 2019. All rights reserved

Look at the difference of the AverageJoe 5.0 circle versus the GreatDevNoDemo circle in Fig. 2.34. The product's yield potential of GreatDevNoDemo compared to AverageJoe 5.0 is lower despite the fact that GreatDevNoDemo scored much better in the Product Development dimension and only slightly lower in the Software Demonstrations and Training dimension. There you go—we found THE LIMITING FACTOR of GreatDevNoDemo in order to fully exploit its potential for longevity and success!

As product managers we might argue who cares about software demonstrations; we have a development system where we are able to show the latest and greatest. We might argue what more do we need than having customers who love the product and that our development team is just great like in Fig. 2.34. So, why should our product's yield potential be limited?

Not having a robust and reliable score in the Software Demonstrations and Training dimension limits for sure the potential of any product. The development system is there for development sake so either stop development and stabilize the customer demo, or one might like the thrill of not knowing what happens next during a demonstration. You might be the only one that can do the demos because there is no demo system or scripts others can rely on, and they are not able to transport the message that is important for you. However, we will explore this topic in more detail in Chap. 7.

The important point here is that the limiting factor hinders your product's success and limits its potential. In addition, one low scoring dimension might be like the rotten apple infecting the others. Imagine what happens to the other dimensions if new customers cannot see the product or existing customers cannot see new features that are ready to be used. Then maybe the ratings in the other dimensions will be impacted and your product becomes only a flash in the pan. Not convinced? We will explore the interdependencies of the Product Yield Potential Radar dimensions in the next section. Before we go there, let's inspect another product to stress this important lesson.

The product in the next example is called AllButDevSuperior. The product is a poster child for introducing a product to the market. The product management team took care to ensure that everything is nicely set up from a great business case internally, to a wonderful product launch, great customer connections and analyst recognition. Extraordinary software demonstrations showed the value story of the product as well as its broad and well-trained ecosystem of Pre-sales colleagues, professional services and partners.

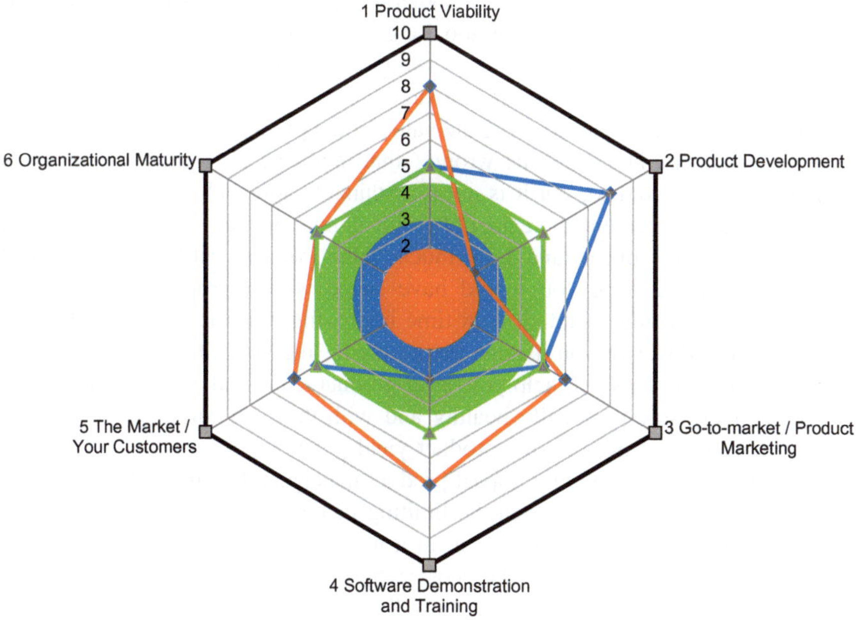

Fig. 2.35 AllButDevSuperior Product Yield Potential Radar © Timo Wagenblatt 2019. All rights reserved

Given the visualization of the PYPR assessment in Fig. 2.35, there is obviously something shaky in the Product Development dimension. As a product manager analyzing the Product Yield Potential Radar in Fig. 2.35, you have a visual proof of what you probably (and hopefully) already knew.

What does this mean for AllButDevSuperior as a product. Will it be a failure in the market? Will it have a short product life? AllButDevSuperior likely will be a "flash in the pan product." Like Icarus the product might experience quick success flying high, then burning and crashing down at earth.

Sound familiar? Timber!

The current potential of AllButDevSuperior is limited by the Product Development dimension. The product is not in a healthy condition. Yes, the Giant "Profit" Tree is still a metaphor; however the AllButDevSuperior tree will not grow to its full potential and one cannot earn the yield, if you as the product manager do not trigger the corrective actions. To trigger corrective actions, you need to know the status quo of your product. Then, you can dig into the Product Development dimension and find out why the vision, backlog, velocity, test environment or all together are not in good shape. The Product Yield Potential Radar provides this transparency for yourself, your product team, your management and all other stakeholders.

I have seen product teams that could compensate for shortcomings in one or another dimension of a product; however all compensation has not been healthy in the long run. Frequently, something or someone suffered by investing extraordinary efforts above reasonable limits for too long duration. For example, the product manager had been involved in every single software demonstration because Pre-sales teams were not properly prepared and therefore the product manager travels around the world showcasing the value of the product to strategic and not so strategic customers. Don't get me wrong—that might be the right tactic for some time or in a given context, but it is not a sustainable approach.

You will experience that there are only critical, must-win customers in the world, if your sales teams understand how much value you can add to close a deal. Imagine how much time you would have saved with a proper Pre-sales team enablement. You could spend all your time improving other areas of your Product Yield Potential Radar or you use the extra time to live your life and be with your family and friends. This will help you, your product team, and your product as you will more likely stay personally healthy and with that you can continue being a product manager and increase the product yield potential.

Unhealthy products not only impact product managers. It is likely that you have experienced these situations, when the limiting factors became real for yourself or someone in the extended product team in a negative way. One can possibly find examples for any stakeholder in the ecosystem.

Let's investigate another example: how limiting factors might be compensated short term, but the boundaries of compensation become tangible, in the next section.

Example of Unbalanced Focus on the Limiting Factor

Some years ago, I was accountable for a product that had very similar characteristics and ratings as the AllButDevSuperior product above. We had the opportunity to take over the ownership of a product that had been in the market for almost a decade and reached a decent customer base of top-notch consumer products manufacturers such as Nestlé, Red Bull and Colgate-Palmolive.

The product has been developed in a stop-and-go approach in terms of investments and had been moved around and spread across various engineering teams over the years. The implementation of the product required significant change management at the customer side as most customers used to work with Microsoft Excel® and the product's technology required a specialized skillset for the implementation teams. To cut a long story short—the product has been perceived internally as well as externally as hard to implement and hard to sell due to its complexity and depth of functionality.

Nevertheless, it was clear to me that I could convince my management team that the product had potential and could solve a major problem for our customers. When we took over the product we did an assessment of the various dimensions, including all the stakeholders, to understand where we needed to focus as a product management team. The result of the PYPR assessment is illustrated in Fig. 2.36.

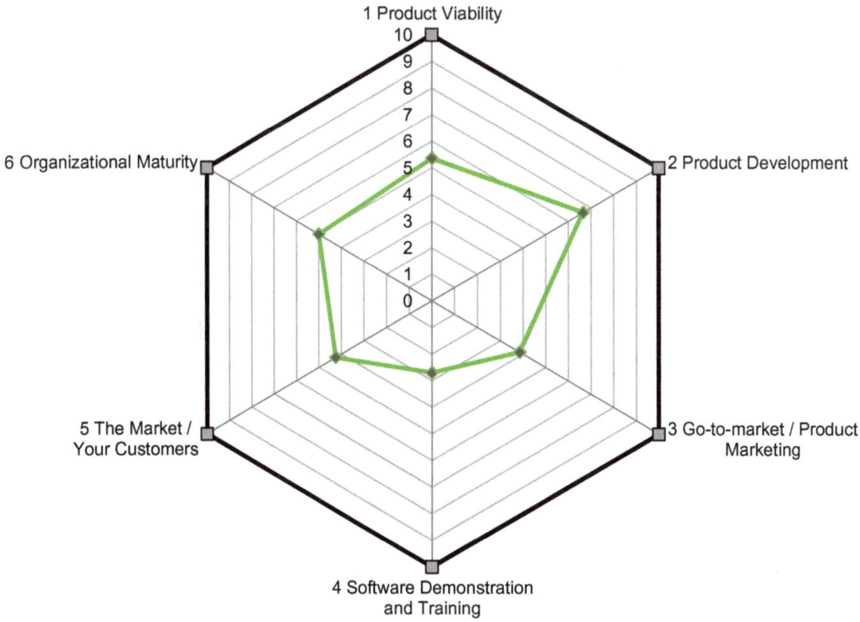

Fig. 2.36 Product assessment before takeover © Timo Wagenblatt 2019. All rights reserved

Clearly the product's further success and growth was limited by the low ratings in the Software Demonstrations and Training dimension as well as in the Go-to-Market dimension.

We will get into the details of the assessment, including the ratings and the derived actions, in later chapters. What's important for now is that we were able successfully change the damaged perception of the product internally and externally, invest time and money, and increase the sales pipeline significantly while surpassing the revenue and profit goals.

This was not only a product management achievement—not at all. Sustainable product success will never be the success of a single function. We did it as a team. Everyone from engineering to the industry Go-to-Market team to sales executives deserve the credit. Nevertheless, it was the product management team that provided the transparency of status quo, guided heavily on the vision and derived the roadmap including the backlog of features and functions delivered in releases. We changed to a radical outside-in approach taking along great customers, partners and analysts. We controlled our efforts using the Product Yield Potential Radar quarterly and adjusted focus and speed as required. Look at the ratings in Fig. 2.37 from an assessment we did after 12 months:

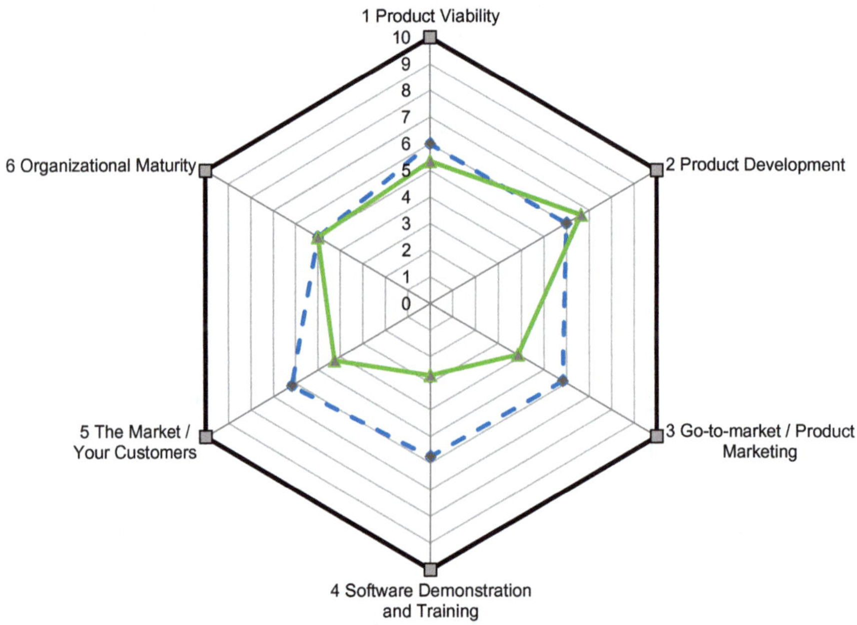

Fig. 2.37 Product assessment after 12 months © Timo Wagenblatt 2019. All rights reserved

Fantastic—what a great success improving the product and the PYPR dimensions so well and, yes, team, what a lot of work to get there. Everyone did recognize the successful turnaround of the product, as we changed the perception of the product both internally and externally, which is the hardest thing to do. Also, we created a viable product and with that secured the future of the product. However, there was something wrong … the product team thought we should have more success and we should be much happier about what we achieved. Again, we leveraged PYPR to get to the root cause. If you pay attention to the radar in Fig. 2.37 and try to find the limiting factor, you'll realize that the limiting factor is in fact in a completely different area now.

The Organizational Maturity dimension and the Product Development dimension became the limiting factors. The Product Development dimension received a lower rating than in our initial assessment. As we will see in the later sections that might happen as the ratings are sometimes relative to external factors. However, when looking deeper into the dimensions the perception got a tangible reason—the development team focus and velocity went down and the number of incidents reported internally and created by customers increased. We were driving fast with shipping multiple new releases since we took over the product. We focused on all weak aspects that we detected after applying PYPR.

Nevertheless, we took for granted that the Product Development dimension would remain strong as we got such great feedback in all other dimensions. In hindsight, the product team did sense early on that there is something cooking under the hood during the journey, but we successfully ignored it. It is easy to ignore sub-optimal items if you are successful and score high in all other dimensions. It caught us finally. So why did this happen?

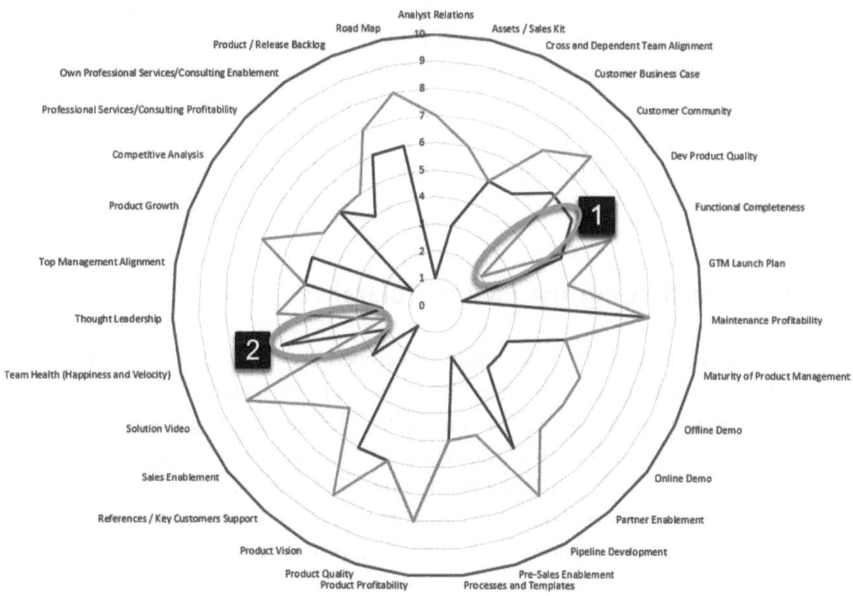

Fig. 2.38 Dimension item view after 12 months © Timo Wagenblatt 2019. All rights reserved

Looking more closely at the changes at the detailed dimension item level would have provided better insights as shown in Fig. 2.38. The rating for (1) Internal (Dev) Product Quality significantly dropped over the course of 12 months. It was not visible in the quarterly review though, but it steadily declined over the year, hence this dimension item was overlooked and blended with the successful improvements in the other dimensions. The same happened with the rating for (2) Team Health and very likely both items were dependent.

We did not understand or recognize early enough that the limiting factor was significantly shifting over time. We were too focused in getting the original weak spots solved, and the engineering team was not communicating about overload and everyone was ignoring reasons of fluctuation in the team—this might be the reason why we missed getting the even higher yield for all the hard work that we did as a team.

What does this little story tell us?

Basically, the story explains how sometimes doing more of one item (e.g. Software Demonstration, Go-to-Market, The Market/Your Customers) helps to overcome less of another item to some extent. This is a strategy that comes naturally into play especially if the other item cannot be changed or influenced directly by the product team or in the short term (e.g. Organizational Maturity) or is overlaid by success (e.g. Product Development). If you think about your daily product management work or even your private life you will find many more examples.

This insight is nothing new as you can see from the two guys who published the underlying theories over hundred years ago. Isn't that charming that some other folks expanded the Law of the Minimum in their field of interest with the Law of Tolerance that we can apply today to Software Product Management?

Let's check how the Law of the Minimum can be enhanced by the Law of Tolerance. We will do this only to a certain extent as this is still a Software Product Management book; nevertheless, I strongly believe that looking beyond our own backyard can continuously improve product management as a discipline and profession.

2.3.4 Understanding the Law of Tolerance

The Law of Tolerance is a principle developed by American zoologist Victor Ernest Shelford and further elaborated by Ronald Good. It states that an organism's success is based on a complex set of conditions and that each organism has a certain minimum, maximum, and optimum environmental factor or combination of factors that determine success. It points out a limitation of Liebig's law of the minimum – that factors act in concert rather than in isolation. A low level of one factor can sometimes be partially compensated for by appropriate levels of other factors. (Shelford's Law of Tolerance, 2018)

How does this translate to the example introduced above?

The product had still good success although we could not improve in the Product Development dimension. We compensated for the lack of improvement by increasing other factors. We were successful, but only to a certain level and not to the full yield potential that we were targeting.

Specifically looking at the Product Development dimension, the product vision and strategy was great and improved, releases went out, but testing did not cater for all the new functionality. The regression and code reviews got too little attention as the engineering team supported many new customers that were implementing the product. The Product Development dimension itself declined only slightly; however some items in the dimension significantly deteriorated.

We were buying ourselves some time with the Law of Tolerance. The lack of complete regression testing and code reviews did not directly impact the success of the product and we could compensate for some time the decline by focusing on other limiting factors.

An issue in a single dimension item that is not rated precisely or timely has the capacity to limit the overall product potential. Even worse you might work hard improving other areas, while missing that you are not targeting the root cause, which limits a more successful product. As an example, let's think about the consequences if your product is not tested well enough. Let's assume you did not concentrate on this aspect. Surely the customers who experience the mediocre quality will let you know, and you can conclude this simple dependency between the internal product quality item in the Product Development dimension and the external product quality item in The Market/Your Customers dimension.

You must spend time and effort with these customers and safeguard the relationship. You might also see that in parallel your product gets less sales support and overall you recognize a decline in license pipeline and revenue bookings. As you discover the decline in sales support, you might do some counter action and focus on better enablement, better sales kits, or even visit more prospects, etc.

However, you overlooked the root cause. The limiting factor of your product health is hidden in the Product Development dimension. I introduced the 12 weeks cadence for a full PYPR cycle as part of introducing PYPR. Because of the risk not learning fast enough, I have seen teams working in a four-week cycles.

The decline in Product Viability has nothing to do with demand generation or sales enablement in this example. Why is that? Generally, sales teams are like timid fawns when they sense a risk to their client relations, and if they have a choice to sell another product in their sales bag to make their quota, they will most likely go with the safe bet.

Another example of interdependencies of Product Yield Potential Radar dimensions we already discovered in the example above. The product success in the market puts stress on the development dimension.

Or looking at the situation from another angle—the Product Viability dimension looks great as you score high in most items. Customers get great value using your product; service teams are happy with utilization and the pipeline is prospering. There is just one little issue … you are not selling enough to compensate for your costs. Your product's profitability is not at the expected level. If you are not able to improve the situation and explain to your internal stakeholders, the reasons you analyzed and the corrective actions to your plan you do not need much imagination to know what will happen. You will receive less budgeting, meaning fewer engineers meaning less new features and less Go-to-Market budget. You see where this is going, and you get a sense of the interdependency of PYPR dimensions or Software Product Management activities in general.

The dimension and dimension item interdependencies work—as the word implies—in at least two directions. Changes in one dimension or one single dimension item can help to tolerate shortcomings in other dimensions or dimension items. However, changes can also create stress and pressure for other dimensions that will need to be analyzed and managed. The dependencies will be different product by product. However, understanding these forces and its implications on your product will make you a better product manager.

The Product Yield Potential Radar framework is an ongoing discipline that supports you in this challenging task. It enables you to understand and communicate the effect and limitations of the work of the product team. PYPR enables you to become a better product manager.[10]

2.3.5 Summary and Conclusions

Let's summarize the above lesson about the Law of the Minimum and Law of Tolerance for product managers:

If one Product Yield Potential Radar dimension is missing or deficient, product growth and success will be poor even if the other dimensions are abundant.

Dimensions act in concert rather than in isolation. A lower level of one dimension can sometimes be partially compensated for by appropriate levels of other dimensions; however the product will not reach its full potential over time.

And adapting the above for one dedicated PYPR dimension item:

There are lower limits in the Product Yield Potential Radar dimension items that your product can tolerate. The dimension items in each dimension act in concert rather than in isolation. A lower level of a single dimension item can sometimes be partially compensated for by appropriate levels of other dimension items; however product growth and success will not reach full potential over time in these situations.

As promised, that's enough about the Law of the Minimum and the Law of Tolerance. I'm not an expert in the origination of this science and we will end our excursus here. The ones who are experts in this area might forgive me for not being 100% precise; for all others I think these two concepts of the Law of the Minimum and the Law of Tolerance illustrate well the importance of the Software Product Management role, its focus, limitations, levers and most prominently the importance of balance.

Figure 2.39 illustrates the yield potential determined by the limiting factor (inner ring) and the maximum potential yield determined by the dimension with the strongest PYPR score (outer ring). The Software Product Management dimensions that matter are imbalanced leading to idle product potential. Additional time and work into product development will be without longevity effect as the product success is determined by the balance of the six PYPR dimensions. The yield potential of such a product could be improved by improving all other dimensions and keeping the product development dimension at status quo for some time (Fig. 2.40).

[10]Emphasizing the word manager as in General Manager

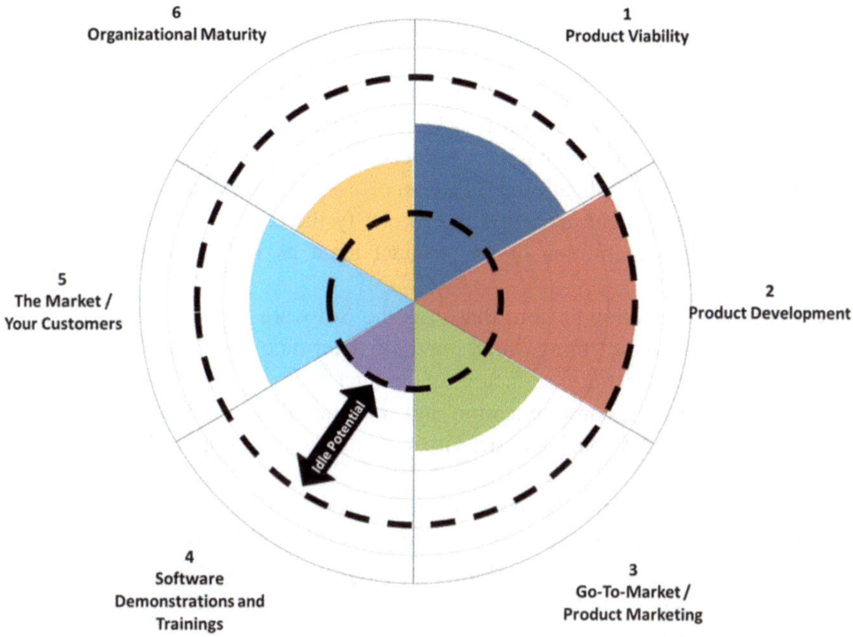

Fig. 2.39 Yield potential and potential yield © Timo Wagenblatt 2019. All rights reserved

As a product team or an individual product manager, you tend to focus on areas you believe are strong. Your expert areas, the areas where you always receive positive feedback, or the areas you are personally most interested in, more likely get attention than the work that is outside of these comfort zones. Unfortunately, this holds true even if work on the successful and healthy part of your product does not result in increasing its yield potential. We know these efforts will have none or very limited effect unless the focus shifts toward the weakest dimension lifting the limiting factors to the appropriate and required levels.

As product managers, we need to avoid expertise bias within our team and even for ourselves. We need to balance all PYPR dimensions and their elements. If we can manage to get the PYPR dimensions in balance, then we have done our job. We increase the chances of product success and longevity significantly and our product stays healthy and grows as we grow as a product team and organization.

PYPR dimension scores and PYPR dimension item scores are indicators of your product's yield potential. Raising the PYPR scores will increase the product's yield potential and with that the chances for success. Additionally, I found the PYPR score to be useful as an indicator of product mindset for the product team and the complete organization. I will detail this interpretation in Chap. 9.

Key Takeaways

- Introduce PYPR and the PYPR practice to the product team and to your organization as a foundation in which to review and improve your company's processes for managing products.
- In its most basic application, PYPR can be used as a checklist for important product management activities and to clarify the role of the product manager, the responsibilities of the product team as well as all supporting teams.
- PYPR is a detection system that uses the Software Product Management dimensions and the "things" that matter to determine and visualize the yield potential and constraining factors of product success.
- PYPR provides a communication and prioritization framework embedded in the day-to-day business activities to drive and support key product decisions.
- PYPR visualizes the balance or imbalance of your work efforts that determine the product success and the product's yield potential.
- PYPR strengthens the core product team by aligning on the product as the main thing based on the consideration of a holistic approach for optimizing product success.
- PYPR expands the product team by aligning and engaging more roles (and people) focusing on the product as the main thing based on the consideration of a holistic approach for optimizing product success.
- Product mindset prioritizes the success of the product, its impact and value for our customers and our organization, everything else is secondary.
- TALK IS CHEAP, SHOW ME YOUR PYPR.

Later in Part 1 of this book, we will learn how applying PYPR will continuously improve the conditions for product success. The product teams benefit from a holistic product mindset that enables all stakeholders to

- understand the required ingredients for product success
- consistently assess the weak and strong areas of the product
- decide where focus is indicated, and time investments required
- balance cost and work effort against yield potential
- leverage a framework that is lightweight enough to scale with the level of adoption you and the organization can handle, and which is flexible enough to be customized for your context.

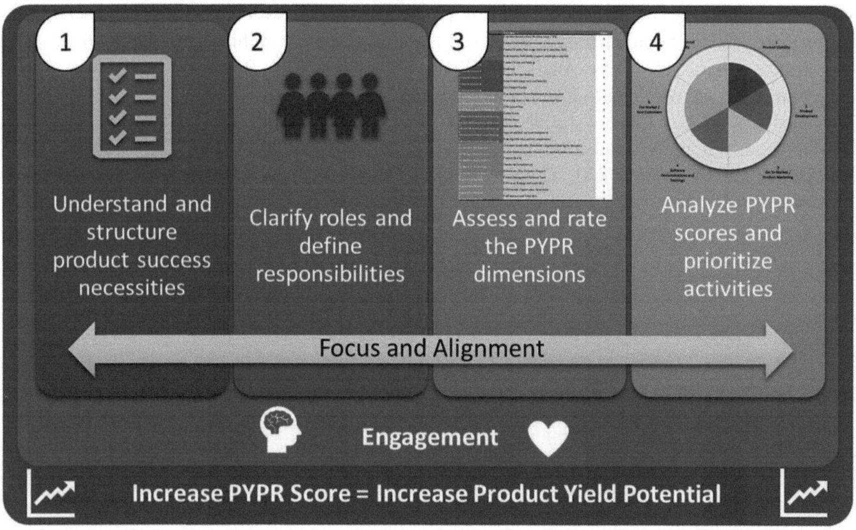

Fig. 2.40 Increasing the PYPR score increases the product yield potential © Timo Wagenblatt 2019. All rights reserved

In the next chapter, we will investigate how PYPR supports you as the General Manager of YourProduct Inc. and how PYPR can be leveraged as a communication tool for all stakeholders. As the General Manager, your success depends on managing the limiting factors and understanding the level of tolerance between the dimensions and maybe even more importantly within one dimension.

References

280 Group. (2018, December 13). Retrieved from https://280group.com.

Barquet, A. P. (2011). *"Business model elements for product-service system." Functional thinking for value creation.* Berlin, Heidelberg: Springer.

DeMarco, T. (1989). *Controlling software projects: Management, measurement & estimates.* Pearson Education; Prentice Hall PTR.

Design Thinking. (2018, June 28). Retrieved from IDEO U https://www.ideou.com/pages/design-thinking.

ISPMA. (2018, September 21). Retrieved from https://community.ispma.org/.

Liebig's Law of the Minimum. (2018, January 27). Retrieved from https://en.wikipedia.org/wiki/Liebig%27s_law_of_the_minimum.

Merriam-webster.com. (2018, August 11). Retrieved from https://www.merriam-webster.com/dictionary: https://www.merriam-webster.com/dictionary/transparentize.

Pragmatic Marketing. (2018, October 26). Retrieved from https://www.pragmaticmarketing.com/.

Product Focus. (2018, December 12). Retrieved from https://www.productfocus.com.

Salisbury, F. (1992). *Plant physiology* (4th ed.). Belmont: Wadsworth.

Shelford's Law of Tolerance. (2018, January 4). Retrieved from https://en.wikipedia.org/wiki/Shelford%27s_law_of_tolerance.

Sleep Deprivation and Deficiency—Why Is Sleep Important? National Heart, Lung, and Blood Institute. (2018, September 12). Retrieved from https://www.nhlbi.nih.gov/node/4605.

Use Radar Charts for Data Analysis. (2018, November 27). Retrieved from https://www.edrawsoft.com/radar-charts-for-data-analysis.php.

The Business Model Canvas. (2008, July 5). Retrieved February 12, 2018 from http://www.nonlinearthinking.typepad.com.

Wikipedia. (2018, March 18). Conway's law. Retrieved from https://en.wikipedia.org/wiki/Conway%27s_law.

PYPR—On Your Mark, Get Set and Go Toward Software Product Management Excellence

3

Excellence is an art won by training and habituation. We are what we repeatedly do. Excellence, then, is not an act but a habit.

—**Aristoteles**

These wise words are absolutely relevant for the Software Product Management discipline in today's world. Becoming excellent as a product manager, a product team and a product organization is what we are all striving for. Delivering excellent products that make a difference is our goal.

Excellence is defined as the quality of being outstanding or extremely good. Malcolm Gladwell explained to us the 10.000 h rule toward excellence with an emphasis on the training part (Gladwell, 2010). Practicing Software Product Management is no different. I introduced you to the foundation of PYPR. I want you to be successful and elevate Software Product Management and yourself to the next level. Therefore, reading this book is a start, but you need to practice and live PYPR.

We are close to the end of Part 1 of this book. You already have gained a solid foundation of Software Product Management and the PYPR framework:

- You know the importance and promise of Software Product Management, the role of the product manager, and how he or she represents the discipline
- You understand the traits of T-shaped product managers and why continuous optimization of your bag of tricks is a mandate
- I introduced PYPR to you and the four steps to unfold PYPR's full potential
- I presented how and why the six PYPR dimensions and their respective dimension items represent the components for product success and the product's yield potential
- You know why your garden might not be blooming as you would like to see it.

Thank you for reading and working through all of this. If you started directly with this chapter, you might want to consider going back as some essential concepts were introduced in the previous chapters.

T. Wagenblatt, *Software Product Management*, Management for Professionals,
https://doi.org/10.1007/978-3-030-19871-8_3

I have already used the PYPR definition several times and in slightly different formats, and is summarized in all the points above. But let's revisit the PYPR definition once more:

> The Product Yield Potential Radar is a Software Product Management framework that fosters communication and strategic thinking within product organizations. It is an ongoing discipline supporting orchestration and prioritization of all product-related activities to discover what is most important for the product, the product team and all stakeholders in order to maximize every product's yield potential.

I doubt anyone can easily recite this definition or wants a t-shirt with the definition on it either. Not even the many iterations of the definition in the previous chapters helped, right?

Let's break and dissect my bulky PYPR definition into reasonable and consumable pieces[1]:

- **Software Product Management framework**: The main objective using PYPR is driving product excellence with continuously improving product management maturity. You will not instill a product mindset by only defining the roles and responsibilities according to a default PYPR configuration.[2]
  PYPR provides a holistic view to Software Product Management, highlighting the importance of orchestration of all PYPR dimensions and their dimension items. PYPR provides a framework to keep the details that matter for product success in balance, taking into consideration the limiting factors, strategies and responsibilities required for the overall product yield potential.
- **Foster communication and strategic thinking**: When analyzing PYPR assessments your challenge is to go beyond the numbers and dig deeper into the story the PYPR ratings are telling you so that you can extract the motivating questions that may lead to future product-related improvements. PYPR, when applied as an ongoing discipline, facilitates a team's critical and strategical thinking about the product and its potential for longevity and success.
- **Ongoing discipline**: Using PYPR represents a commitment to continuously improve the Software Product Management practice in your organization toward excellence. To ensure you benefit from PYPR, you must commit to repeatedly using the framework. This comprises conducting the PYPR meetings,[3] leveraging PYPR as an information radiator, analyzing PYPR ratings as a team, and adapting your ongoing work priorities toward improving the dimension items that are limiting success.

---

[1]I highly recommend the book Objectives and Key Results (Niven & Lamorte, 2016), which inspired me for this breakdown of the PYPR definition, if you are interested in OKRs. PYPR and OKRs work nicely together as outlined in Sect. 9.1.1.

[2]Or training your teams in any other Software Product Management framework.

[3]You might like the term ceremonies better.

- **Support orchestration and prioritization**: PYPR clarifies the role of the product manager, shapes the core product team as well as illustrates the responsibilities of the supporting teams. I will explain this part of the PYPR definition in Sect. 3.2 in more detail. Alignment and transparency on all important aspects provides a balanced view across all stakeholders. Jointly assessing the limiting factors of product success leads to clarity and transparency about prioritization decisions.
- **Maximizing any product's yield potential**: The maximum, theoretically reachable yield in your context is defined as potential yield (the perfect PYPR score 10), while the status quo that is restricted by limiting factors defines the current yield potential (Evans & Fischer, 2018) No size fits all and hence PYPR requires and offers the flexibility to be adapted to your product's context. PYPR enables the product team to identify the limiting factors and to smooth them out. PYPR discovers and transparentizes the factors that will help the team reach the maximum yield. Note that the yield does not necessarily need to be monetary, but any kind of overall value.

In this section, I will detail how PYPR supports you in your job as a product manager, providing the leadership that the product team, your organization and especially the success of your product requires.

First, I will explain, how the Product Yield Potential Radar supports you in being the General Manager of YourProduct Inc. As the General Manager, your success depends on your ability to align all stakeholders and constantly improve the limits of what matters for your product and organization.

Second, I will describe how the Product Yield Potential Radar can be leveraged as a communication tool for all stakeholders. As a product manager you need to understand your stakeholder network and clarify the roles and responsibilities, and your level of engagement, within the product team and with all other stakeholders.

Third, I will provide you with some final tips and tricks to get PYPR started, or in other words how to finally leverage the out-of-the-box PYPR set-up and adapt PYPR continuously to your own context as it becomes a habit for you, the product team and the organization.

3.1 General Manager of YourProduct Inc.—What's on the Radar?

Part of the challenge of being an entrepreneur, if you're going for a really huge opportunity, is trying to find problems that aren't quite on the radar yet and try to solve those.

—**Sean Parker**

While Sean Parker likely was talking about problems that prevent companies from becoming larger and more successful, I like the quote and how it applies to PYPR and Software Product Management. PYPR is a detection system that uses product management dimensions and the details that matter to determine the yield potential and constraining factors of product success.

As part of the previous chapter, I defined six dimensions that matter. You might have more, or less, but I don't think it really matters how many you have. For example, I started with five dimensions and during my time at SAP I added Organizational Maturity as a sixth dimension to PYPR. What matters most is that you identify the dimensions and dimension items that help your product and your organization to detect problems on the radar early and reliably as a product team. I introduced how to define and structure the PYPR dimensions in Step 1 of the PYPR introduction process before (Sect. 2.1).

Until now, the six dimensions had the same weights in the examples and explanations. You likely wondered why all dimensions are equally important and that the dimensions items contributing to the success of your product had the same weight. You are absolutely right, not all things that matter for your product are equally important. As a product manager, you cannot and should not put equal time and work into all six dimensions and the 32 dimension items. The default PYPR configuration for the six PYPR dimensions that I recommend are as follows:

Dimension	Internal PM	B2B PM	B2C PM
Product Viability	17,5	20,0	20,0
Product Development	27,5	25,0	22,5
Go-to-Market / Product Marketing	15,0	15,0	17,5
Software Demonstrations and Training	7,5	7,5	5
The Market / Your Customers	20,0	20,0	22,5
Organizational Maturity	12,5	12,5	12,5

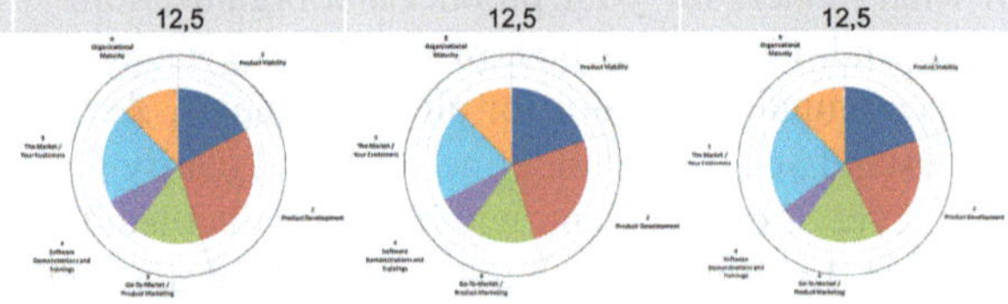

Fig. 3.1 Default PYPR dimension weights by software product manager type

In Fig. 3.1 you find default weights for B2B, B2C and internal products. As a leader you can hone the weights as you are accountable for product success. However, the default PYPR configurations listed in Fig. 3.1 are a robust starting point for most B2B, B2C and internal products.

As you can see in Fig. 3.1, there are some slight differences in the weightings; however, the ranking of the dimensions is mostly in the same order. Product Development is generally at the top, directly followed by The Market/Your Customers dimension. Another interesting observation might be that the relative importance of the Product Development dimension is the highest for internal products and the lowest for B2C products. Note that the dimension items are different, especially for the internal products, and overall the dimension item weights show more significant differences. At the beginning of each chapter that details a PYPR dimension, I will share a similar table that illustrates the default dimension item weights that I use with my product managers and product teams.

It is always possible to achieve some local objectives with dedicated efforts in one dimension or one dimension item, which will lead to imbalance for the product as a whole, therefore limiting the product's yield potential. As a product manager, one of your main duties is to check whether the achievements in one area are creating problems in another. This is where PYPR as a detection system brings the limiting factors on the radar, allowing you to resolve them. Limiting factors are often hidden below the success and improvements in one or the other dimension. PYPR shows them on your radar.

As you and the product team put time and work in one or two dimensions, the others will naturally fall behind. PYPR visualizes the balance or imbalance of your work outcome that determines YourProduct Inc's yield potential on your radar.

For example, if you focus on polishing up your sales assets, update your competitive analysis and spread the word to your sales teams and partners, you will likely improve the Go-to-Market and Product Viability dimensions short term. But you will have less time working with your engineering team, talking to customers, or improving the product management practice in your organization. So, the short-term positive effects might be negatively impacted by not doing other activities.[4]

3.1.1 CEO, Mini-CEO and Lots of Debate

When Ben Horowitz compared product managers to CEOs (Horowitz, 2018) many years ago, a heated discussion started whether this is a correct or incorrect analogy. I'm not getting into this, but instead I will focus on another related analogy.

I'm introducing YourProduct Inc. as a company with a clear mission and vision, with various functions and departments working together for the sustainable success of the company measured by market penetration, profit and customer satisfaction. The company YourProduct Inc. represents your product.

As with most companies, YourProduct Inc. is led by a General Manager. But this General Manager is different. The General Manager of YourProduct Inc.

- doesn't fire or hire people, he or she leads without hierarchical authority
- doesn't manage people ultimately reporting to her or him, but manages product teams and stakeholders
- practices the servant leadership style, which is to be very clear on vision and strategy setting the direction for the product and the product teams.

As a product manager, you are the General (Stakeholder) Manager, you are the leader of the company called YourProduct Inc. As a product manager. you share power and responsibilities, put the needs of the product success first and help people develop and perform as highly as possible. Instead of the people working to serve the product manager, the product manager exists to help the people be more

[4]Some people would call the effect: opportunity costs.

successful while keeping the main thing the main thing. As a General Manager of YourProduct Inc., PYPR is your tool to find problems that are not quiet on the radar yet.

As a product manager, you provide the service of leadership to the team, a style of leadership without positional authority (DeMarco & Lister, 2013). In my view the discussions whether product managers can be compared with CEOs or mini-CEOs are not productive. Some confusion might come from the outdated view of CEOs solely practicing an efficiency-focused style of management. However, that's not true for many CEOs I know and that is definitely not true for the General Manager of YourProduct Inc.

Being a successful product manager requires strong leadership skills as you direct and guide the product teams and all stakeholders. PYPR enables you to become a better product manager with the emphasis on "manager" as in General Manager. Being General Manager of YourProduct Inc. is as rewarding as the role is demanding. PYPR guides product managers and product teams to think and act holistically and systematically about their product's business and improvement potential.

As the General Manager, PYPR enables you to add context to all product conversations and decisions. You can provide a clear purpose to your product team and all stakeholders as to why you are working on certain topics, how the work improves the yield potential and product success, and why everyone should care about their work contribution. You can leverage PYPR as your leadership radar. You are leading everyone toward a balanced product mindset.

When working with product managers who are starting to adopt PYPR, I have seen them introducing PYPR to their team members after only the first iteration. But the ownership of PYPR remained with the product manager for some PYPR cycle iterations. With improved product mindset, the whole product team owns PYPR and the product manager facilitates the honing, assessments, and strategy and action meetings. However, as a General Manager of YourProduct Inc., you are ultimately accountable for product success and therefore you give direction and make decisions when there are doubts.[5]

Your role as a General Manager means:

- teaching the product team and the organization how to think holistically and systematically about the product's business and improvement potential
- leading the product team and the organization to act holistically and systematically about the product's business and improvement potential
- consistently improving the PYPR scores over time as a proxy for improving the product's yield potential and chances of success.

[5]He who pays the piper (PYPR), calls the tune.

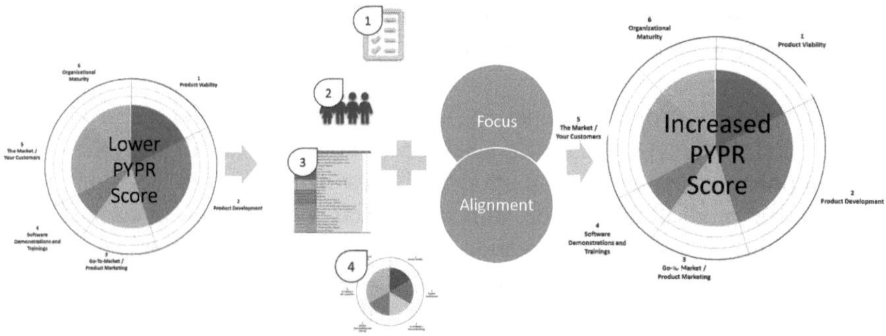

Fig. 3.2 General Manager of YourProduct Inc.—Improving the PYPR score © Timo Wagenblatt 2019. All rights reserved

At the initial stages of using PYPR, the main focus will be on clarification, transparency and alignment. With the first iteration trough the four-step process, you know where to focus and your team will understand where to focus their time and work. Focus and alignment as a result of using PYPR will lead to improved engagement. You made the first steps toward product management excellence. By using PYPR ratings, identifying limiting factors and deriving strategy and actions to increase PYPR scores, everyone looks holistically at the product increasing the total PYPR score (see Fig. 3.2).

As the General Manager, your success depends on your ability to align all stakeholders and constantly improve the limits of what matters for your product and organization. PYPR visualizes the first law of bad management: "If something isn't working, do more of it" (DeMarco, 2002). As you do more of one thing, and you cannot detect any positive impact, you might think it is due to bad execution, but likely it has been because you missed out on the limiting factor.

You are the role model for product management excellence when you think and act holistically and systematically about the product's business and improvement potential and keep the main thing the main thing.

There can be only one General Manager for each product, but there can be multiple product managers, product marketing managers, and product owners. For larger products, the General Manager sometimes has a title like Head of Product or CPO, and for smaller products, the title might be simply Product Manager.

Independent of your title, as a General Manager of YourProduct Inc., you are part of an organization, the company you work for.[6] You are likely not leading the entire organization and with that all the internal stakeholders unless you are the founder of your own startup. For all others, I quickly introduce two of the most important traits and responsibilities of a product manager, which is using "The Power of No" and being the firewall for organizational craziness.

[6]Likely the most used argument by the ones who are arguing against the CEO or analogy.

3.1.2 Firewall Against Organizational Craziness and the Bold Usage of the Power of No

The firewall against organizational craziness means that your duty is to serve the product and the product team as a gatekeeper. You “gate keep” ideas that sound great in principle and are in the corporation’s best interest, but in fact would harm the team or product directly or indirectly.[7] You are the firewall against these directions that destroy value but started with best intentions. For example, the need of weekly status reports, the guidance to use the latest technology in the next release, or the addition of many more people to deliver more scope faster. There are many of these ideas that are intended to help you but should not go through and negatively impact the value-generating efforts.

As the firewall against organizational craziness, you will benefit from another trait: the power of saying no. Saying no will be required to almost every stakeholder from time to time. Saying no can be challenging as most of us like to satisfy others. And when we say no, we likely disappoint someone. The list below provides guidelines for how you can use the power of no, politely but firmly (Cohn, 2019):

- Be clear with stakeholders: is this no? Or no, for now?
  If you are clear that you have to say no, then do it. However, if you lack time to analyze the impact, or for any other reason, you might consider saying no for now, and leave the door open to reconsider the request when time and priorities allow.
- Express appreciation and empathy for customers.
  Indicate your understanding of why the request is important to that stakeholder
- Offer only one reason for saying no
  Provide one compelling reason rather than a list of reasons. When offered a list of reasons, people tend to pick the weakest reason and argue against it.
- Convey that you each have the same goal
  Referencing a common, higher, product-level goal helps to convey why you need to say no, even if stakeholders still don’t fully agree with the answer.
- Offer an alternative
  An alternative might be a subset of the features requested, a slightly different approach, a bit less of detail. Be careful and only offer an alternative if you really mean it or can deliver the alternative.
- Explain the consequences of saying yes to the stakeholder
  Explaining the consequences of saying yes could help the stakeholder to see why you feel compelled to decline, and hopefully empathize with why you are saying no.

Note that you likely cannot just say no to all the corporate guidance without causing harm. As a rule, let one or two out five senseless ideas go through and manage its impact properly. Be clever and select the ones that you let go through

[7] And are therefore likely not in the corporation’s best interest.

the firewall as the least harmful for the product. If you are perceived as a naysayer, your management or the corporate police that controls adherence to corporate guidance will label you as not being a team player. This perception could become an issue for you personally and the product over time. As the most senior executive of YourProduct Inc. you will work with and need the support of management and other stakeholders at times.

As the General Manager of YourProduct Inc. you need to be decisive, so it is very important that you have and know your decision-making plan. PYPR transparentizes how you will make decisions (focus on prioritization) and where you will spend your and the team's time (balance and prioritization). It should be easy to accept the fact that everyone has only 24 hours in a day. It is harder to appreciate that the time spent on any given dimension needs to be balanced with any other dimension and with your quality of life, otherwise you will face the risk of feeling overwhelmed and stressed out, while not achieving your goals. As a servant leader of your product team you take care of the right balance.

3.1.3 Avoid the "DIY Product Manager"—Syndrome

Seeing yourself as a General Manager will hopefully prevent you from succumbing to a frequent and harmful syndrome: The "DIY product manager"—a syndrome that generally starts with the best intentions. For example, you are about to release the next software version and notice that the support documentation needs to be updated. You could turn to a teammate and ask them to jump in. But instead you think, "I'll just do it this once—it will be quicker this way." Before you know it, you are spending lots of time in an area where your colleagues are experts (Yang, 2019). You have become the DIY product manager. In fact, I probably did everything on the radar once on my own. I wrote test cases and user documentation, did software demos, created marketing material, and so on. Sometimes for good reasons, sometimes because I thought I could do it best.

"You might be thinking, solving problems is an important part of the job. But it is not your responsibility alone. Being a successful product manager means setting the team up for success. You cannot do this if you are constantly jumping in to fix every little thing. The instinct to fix is a good one. But if you find that you frequently have your head down working through issues that could be solved by others, you will struggle to achieve anything meaningful. It feels great to be the person who can solve everyone's problem" (Yang, 2019).

As the product manager, you are the one having the holistic view and understanding how all pieces need to fit together for a successful product from first idea (seed) to a prospering product (giant "profit" sequoia). You are the ultimate product expert and you are the most senior product executive. Being the DIY product manager is an important hat you might need to wear from time to time as the limiting factor requires it, but as the General Manager wear the hat with the right balance.

As a result of the PYPR assessment, you already have great metrics for the product. And as Peter Drucker stated: what gets measured gets managed. PYPR enables you to be a General Manager with clear measures. As a General Manager you frequently check what's on the radar. Repeatedly utilizing PYPR allows you to measure consistently YourProduct Inc. and therefore is the basis for your management.[8]

Management is a complex discipline. Software Product Management is a complex discipline. PYPR helps to sort and prioritize the complexity into smaller, manageable pieces based on a holistic understanding of the product.

In the next chapter, I will detail how General (Stakeholder) Managers can leverage PYPR to clarify roles and responsibilities among product managers, product marketing managers, and product owners and how to work with stakeholders that are external to the product team.

3.2 360° Stakeholder View

I generally distinguish between two kinds of stakeholders. There are stakeholders that are part of the product team and then there are stakeholders that are external to the product team. For the product team, we will focus on the clarification of roles and responsibilities, which is one of the key challenges for many product managers as we have seen in the PMF Product Management survey results (The State of the Software Product Management Nation).

Interest and goal alignment, and communication and transparency are vital for any stakeholder relationship, but especially for the second group of stakeholders that are more loosely coupled with the product. I will use an approach to answer these questions in the second part of this chapter:

- Do you know the stakeholders of your product?
- Do you effectively engage the stakeholders of your product?
- Are your stakeholders aligned and support key product decisions?

3.2.1 Clarify Roles, Responsibilities and Titles in Your Product Team

The results of the 2018 Trends and Benchmarks survey from the Product Management Festival (Fig. 1.11) show the lack of role clarity as being the #3 challenge for product managers. This section explains how PYPR helps you to define and align roles and responsibilities for all defined product success ingredients.

[8]What you cannot measure you cannot manage (DeMarco, 1989).

I already explained how PYPR helps with clarifying roles and responsibilities as Step 2 of the Product Yield Potential Radar introduction (Sect. 2.1). I mentioned that organizational maturity will be positively impacted because:

- discussions and debates about role names or titles are de-emphasized
- each dimension item of PYPR has a clear role assignment.

In theory, roles and job titles such as product owner, product manager, product marketing manager, business analyst, solution manager, outcome owner, program manager, or in short simply all roles and titles, should not matter anymore. There are jobs to be done and the success and longevity of the product is the main thing.

In practice and at least in my experience, most people like roles and titles!

Your organization and especially your product teams need and want clarity about who does what. They want to understand how the various parts fit together. In fact, the entire organization needs to understand how to work with product teams. This becomes even more important as companies grow and work that was done by one person in the past is now done by a team or even a whole new department.

You can use PYPR as an information radiator that publicly displays what the role and title of everyone in your product team means in terms of RACI or DACI assignments. The idea about public (meaning transparent, but still internal to the organization) information radiators is twofold:

- It promotes transparency within the product team and the organization
- It makes the information more accessible versus logging into a system, querying an application or looking up a report or dashboard.

Good information radiators spark conversation (Narajan, 2015).

Let's look at some typical examples of information radiators in the role of Product Managers, Product Owners, and Product Marketing Managers in a B2B software enterprise. Figure 3.3 illustrates an example of an organization that has three defined roles filled by three different people.

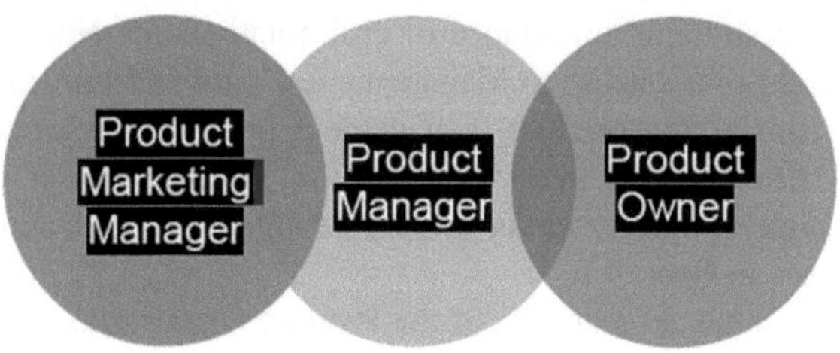

Fig. 3.3 Roles in software product management © Timo Wagenblatt 2019. All rights reserved

Figure 3.4 illustrates an example of the product manager role. On the left-hand side, you see the assignment of the product manager role to PYPR dimension items depicting her core responsibilities to increase the yield potential. These assignments are transparently defining the role for everyone in the organization. Therefore, the lack of role clarity should be less of a problem going forward.

In this example, the product manager is responsible for various items in all PYPR dimensions. Responsible being defined as the one who performs an activity or does the work. The product manager might be also accountable, but that is not depicted in the radiator. Instead the information radiator shows the items in grey color where the product manager needs to provide feedback or contribute to the dimension item.

Note that you might want or need to show the role for all assignments of D/A/C/I for decisions or R/A/C/I for activities. You could do this with shades of grey or distinct colors, but be careful with information overload and diminishing effect of the information radiators. Figure out what information your organization needs and cater to it accordingly.

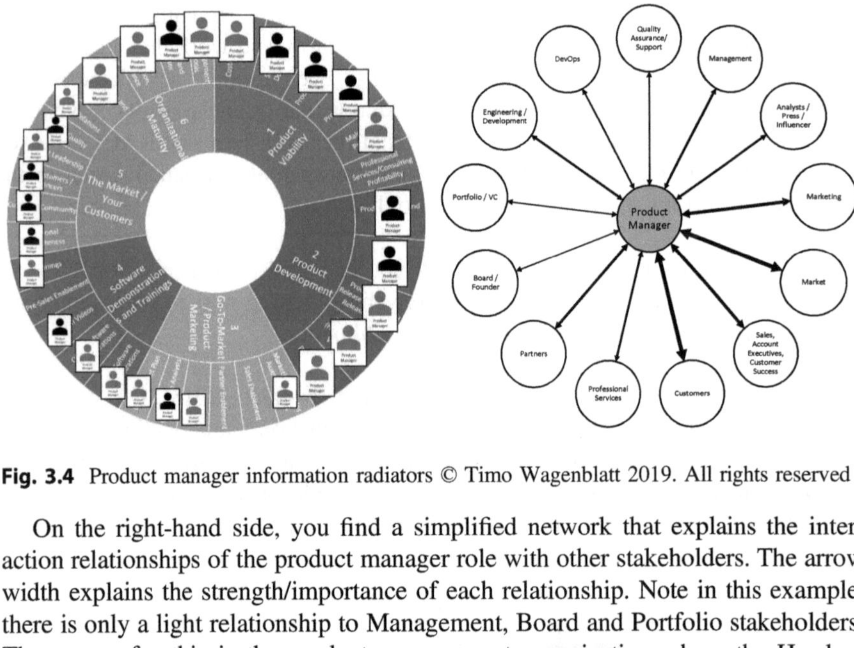

Fig. 3.4 Product manager information radiators © Timo Wagenblatt 2019. All rights reserved

On the right-hand side, you find a simplified network that explains the interaction relationships of the product manager role with other stakeholders. The arrow width explains the strength/importance of each relationship. Note in this example, there is only a light relationship to Management, Board and Portfolio stakeholders. The reason for this is the product management organization where the Head of Product mostly takes care of these relationships. We will further investigate how Product Management organizations drive role interpretations and product management processes in Sect. 9.2.

Figure 3.5 illustrates an example of the Product Owner role. While the Product Owner role is clearly defined as being a product development role (Product Owner: Agile Alliance Org., 2018) mostly as a scrum product owner, the role is frequently used inconsistently.

The assignments of the Product Owner role to PYPR dimension items depicts his or her core responsibilities and support duties. Predictably, the Product Owner is responsible for product backlog management, team health and product quality.

However, you will also find responsibilities in the Product Viability and The Market/Your customers dimensions in this example.

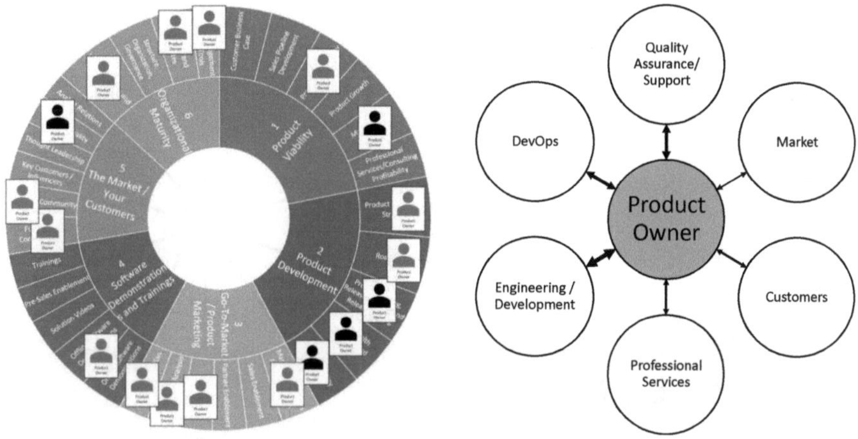

Fig. 3.5 Product owner information radiators © Timo Wagenblatt 2019. All rights reserved

On the right-hand side, you see a simplified network that explains the interaction relationships of the Product Owner role with other stakeholders. The arrow width explains the strength/importance of each relationship, and clearly the most important and frequent interactions are with the engineering, DevOps and QA teams.

Note that the Product Owner interacts with the same departments and people as the Product Manager, which is obviously a no brainer, but that is very often the root cause of misunderstandings and ultimately leads to product and product team issues.

The clarification and shaping of roles and inherent responsibilities are essential for coherent products and product success. This is true for all roles in your organization, but lack of clarity especially for the core product roles are the epicenter of product failure and revoked trust in the product people.

In this example, just imagine you are a developer in a scrum team and the product owner prioritizes the backlog for the next sprint. The next day the product manager shows up in the daily and decides on a different priority and the day after you receive an email from the product marketing manager trying to influence your work directly. What would you do?

Most people would ignore the "product guys" over time, some faster—some slower, which likely won't be good for the product. I guess it is clear that role clarity helps provide "one face to the customer," but also consistency to all other teams and departments they are working with.

Let's finish this part with the Product Marketing Manager role (see Fig. 3.6). Not surprisingly, the Product Marketing Manager role works mostly in the Go-to-market/Product Marketing, Software Demonstrations and Trainings, and The Market/Your Customers dimensions. The role might be called outbound product manager, solution manager or marketing manager in your organization, but the focus of the role remains generally toward the world outside of the company.

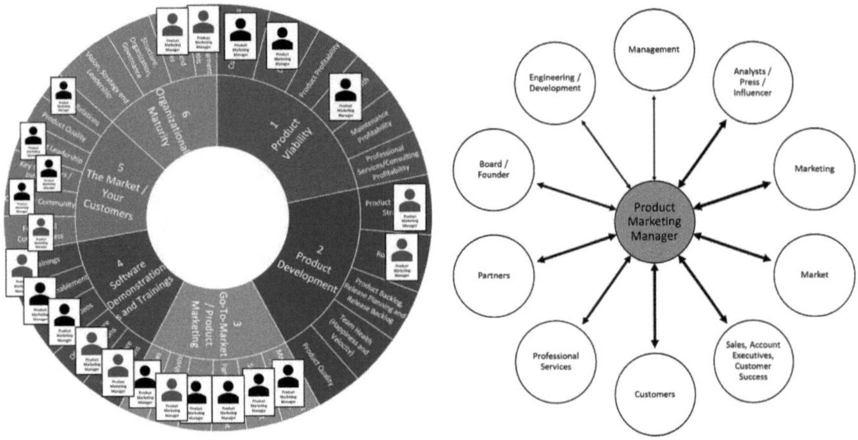

Fig. 3.6 Product marketing manager information radiators © Timo Wagenblatt 2019. All rights reserved

These are just three examples for roles in Software Product Management, and you might not even have these roles in your context. That is not the main point here. The key takeaway should be that defining all roles and responsibilities is important, but sharing this information is equally important and valuable.

The organization information radiators broadcast the roles and responsibilities to the product team, all stakeholders and the ones who have the roles themselves. Whether you print them out and have them available in the offices or you have them in the intranet, wiki or whatever most people in your organization are frequently visiting is not important. The organizational information must radiate. The public accessibility provides many benefits and, to repeat myself, will certainly help to resolve one of the top product management challenges: Lack of Role Clarity.

For all these radiators, you can still have the PYPR-related RACI or DACI matrix printed out next to the visuals. However, most people will ignore them as the information radiators are visual and therefore easier to consume.

Applying PYPR as an organizational information radiator will be of value for

- all roles in the core product team that contribute directly to the product,
- all roles living outside the core product team as part of the extended product team or
- all "lone wolf" stakeholders.

In my experience, the people and roles that are involved in the daily business become part of the flow anyway and do not need extra attention. The roles and responsibilities get sorted out in one way or another, and PYPR as an information radiator can support the job. But there are still the "lone wolf" stakeholders who are not part of the daily work of the core product team and hence need special attention to secure product success.

3.2.2 Understand Impact and Interest of "No Product Team" Stakeholders—Working with Stakeholder Maps

The first step is to define the real stakeholders you are working with. Remember to find out whether the person, role or team "has veto power or can otherwise prevent your work from launching (Cagan, 2018)".

There are important people that are not part of the core product team. Some of these people might not even be aware that they are part of the extended product team and that their contribution is required to increase the product's yield potential. They will not become team members just because you think they should. You need to work with them in order to widen and exploit your product's yield potential.

Stakeholder maps are visual tools that help you and the team to better understand

- who has interest in your product
- who has leverage/impact on your product
- what special attention/care do these people require (people—yes, stakeholders are human).

Noah Askin, Assistant Professor at INSEAD, explained to me that this part of the Software Product Management skills is defined as brokerage in organizational behavior research. Brokers are connecting the closed networks of diverse stakeholders (i.e. the Sales team with the closed network of your core product team). Noah details the concept of brokers and brokerage in Sect. 9.2.

In most software companies, and particularly in enterprise software organizations, a pivotal role for software product managers is brokering and coordinating the needs of stakeholders ranging from customers, engineering and product support to sales and marketing to ensure that the teams move in the right direction, which will lead to customer value and long-term product success.

Each PYPR dimension has its special set of stakeholders: people who have their stake in one or more, but likely not all, dimensions. While Software Product Management cares about the long-term product success, the various stakeholders might not always share the same objective.

You want to understand how you can activate the stakeholders to support your product and your goals as a product manager. There are likely too many stakeholders for you to handle with special care. Your stakeholders that are part of other corporate teams likely have different goals than you. Their goals are passed down through the functional silos of the organization. Every silo and department perceive their goals as ultimately correct and being most important. Therefore, the likelihood that all your stakeholder's goals nicely align with your interest to increase your product's yield potential is very limited. That's where a stakeholder map might be a helpful visualization tool.

The stakeholder map illustrates in a 2 × 2 matrix the actual impact that a stakeholder has on your goal versus the actual interest that a stakeholder has helping you to reach your goal. In other words, a stakeholder is likely more interested in helping you and the product, if her or his goal correlates with your goal.

Figure 3.7 depicts multiple stakeholders that are positioned by their relative interest and impact for a given product, dimension, dimension item or anything else you want to analyze the stakeholders for.

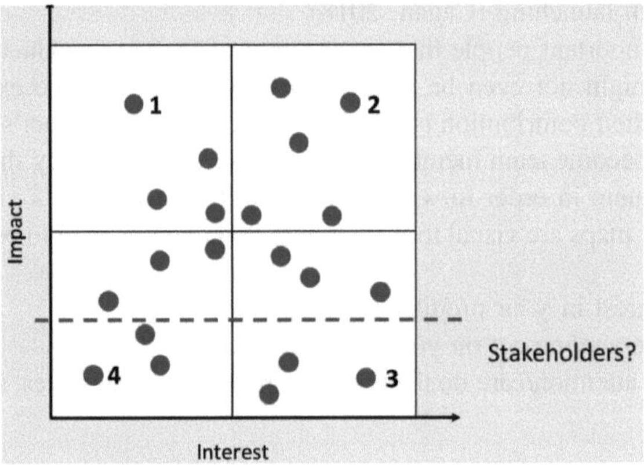

Fig. 3.7 Stakeholder map © Timo Wagenblatt 2019. All rights reserved

The dotted lines in the chart indicate the band people that likely will not pass the stakeholder test above. If they really have veto power, then they would obviously be having a much higher positive or negative impact on your product.

The usage of the stakeholder map can be best described by looking at the four highlighted stakeholders:

- **Stakeholder 1**: This stakeholder has a relatively low interest in your topic compared to the others, however the impact is relatively high. Stakeholders in this quadrant are the ones you likely need to work the hardest to get their support. You need to think about strategies to increase their interest. Network with them, understand their goals and their pains and show them how your work and your product can contribute to their success. You should have or seek an active relationship with stakeholders in this sector and manage their concerns and veto power properly.
- **Stakeholder 2**: stakeholder has a relatively high impact and fortunately a high interest to support you and the product. Just keep the relationship at that levels and find countermeasures only when required. You might not even need to contact this stakeholder and just let the good things happen. Stakeholders in this quadrant are the ones that have positive interest and impact at the same time. Foster them and do not give them any reason to fault their support of you and your product.

- **Stakeholder 3**: This stakeholder has high interest and marginal impact. Stakeholders in this quadrant are the ones that are likely supporting you while having little impact. Spend less time with these stakeholders; however keep the allies as potential support and multipliers.
- **Stakeholder 4**: This stakeholder has little interest and little impact on your product. This is the simplest sector to manage. Be nice and ignore them as much as possible.

Note that high impact could be positive impact or negative impact for your product. Most stakeholders can work in both directions. Keep an eye on stakeholders like Stakeholder 1 in the above example that have little interest, but could have negative impact on your product. This is the toughest species to manage. In this group are people that might have totally unaligned or even conflicting goals as well as the power to severely impact your product negatively. The extra time and attention you spend with them might be worth a million in later stages of the product lifecycle. Understand their special needs and concerns and deliver against these.

The stakeholder map visualizes your view of the humans that you work with and also have a stake in your business called YourProduct Inc. These people have a vested interest, demand, entitlement or requirement concerning YourProduct Inc. In addition, these people can impact the success of your work results. That's the reason they are called stakeholders. Ask yourself, as shown in Fig. 3.7, where can you draw the line and ask the question: Is this really a stakeholder?

In my experience, some product managers have many concerns, sometimes even fears, about working with many stakeholders, but generally these concerns and fears are exaggerated. Note that stakeholders

- have a vested interest in understanding what is going on
- are disconnected from product advances and news or at least get delayed information about the same as they are not part of the core product team.

Nothing more and nothing less!

These stakeholders are "lone wolves" who simply need basic communication and transparency, which holds true whether they are internal stakeholders like your management team, or external stakeholders like your most important customers.

The success of your stakeholders is likely dependent on your work results; their jobs might be dependent on your work results and they know they are not in the driving seat. They need and want to understand what is going on with YourProduct Inc. as it relates to their goals and success.

Help them to understand what is going on, reduce their fear of missing something important. Understand their objectives and special interests and take them with you on the journey to your product success or at a minimum do not let them disturb the product's positive development.

Don't be scared. Determine the level of communication and transparency that works best for you and the "lone wolf" stakeholders in your product's context.

3.3 On Your Mark, Get Set, Go!

That's it—the last chapter of Part 1, which introduces and explains PYPR. In this section, I describe the three milestones in the race to improve product success[9] and with that your personal success as a product manager by utilizing PYPR. I bring all you have read about PYPR into perspective, and I summarize the commitment needed for continuous improvement of the Software Product Management practice in your organization toward excellence (Fig. 3.8).

Fig. 3.8 On your Mark, Get Set, Go! toward increasing the Product's yield potential © Timo Wagenblatt 2019. All rights reserved

Being your new Track and Field coach, I prepared you for the race with the following training plan:

- I laid the foundation with a solid understanding of Software Product Management and the role of the product manager. I advised you that keeping your bag of tricks lively is part of the commitment to continuous improvement.
- I introduced PYPR to you and explained the four steps to unfold PYPR's full potential
- We discovered the six PYPR dimensions and their respective dimension items. We learned that they represent the ingredients for success and together depict the product's yield potential. We understood how the concepts of the Law of the Minimum and the Law of Tolerance influence the product's yield potential.
- Just before racing day, I introduced the race strategy to you, since your mandate is being the General Manager of YourProduct Inc. and we discussed how to deal with fellow-runners during the race.

Now, we arrived at the point where the race[10] starts. On your Mark, Get Set and Go!

[9]Remember that PYPR can be applied on any level of the product taxonomy (Sect. 1.1.3), i.e. product line, product, and product module.
[10]Note that we plan for a marathon as we focus on product longevity and not on "flashes in the pan".

On your Mark

"On your Mark" instructs contestants taking part in a competition to assume the correct starting position. You signed up to build and deliver awesome products. What is the correct starting position for you? Well, I actually don't know. I can only contribute that Winston Churchill once said: "Perfection is the enemy of progress."

I have worked with many talented people who were hesitant to start any new endeavor because they thought something was missing for the best possible start. However, once they started they continued to think that something was still missing. You get the point?

On your Mark doesn't mean you wait for the perfect start. You do not need your role announced with nice words and best wishes introducing the product manager, the Head of Product, the CPO, or any other shiny title. All that is required is continuous improvement of the product's yield potential, yourself as a product manager, and Software Product Management in your organization.

You have a product, you have a product team, you accept the responsibility to delight customers and deliver awesome products, you know your T-shape, and you strive to continuously improve it—you are "On Your Mark."

Get Set

Get Set means seriously preparing for the starting shot. In terms of using PYPR on your own, directly involving the product team or the whole organization, getting set comprises the following topics:

- Introducing PYPR as a novel way to understand status quo of your product and prioritize the things that matter for your product
  - Enabling the group you want to start with the basic understanding of PYPR. Consider a PYPR fundamentals training or provide a brief summary of your own learnings
  - Explaining the basic principles and concepts of PYPR, for example:
    - The six PYPR dimensions and the item details
    - The importance of the limiting factor
    - The four step process to apply PYPR and unfold its full potential
    - The role and responsibilities of the product team to increase the yield potential
- Getting the meetings on the calendar right after introducing PYPR
  - The outlined process consists of the following meetings in each 12-weeks cycle:
    - six meetings to assess the PYPR dimensions individually
    - 1 "Strategy & Action" meeting to prioritize and strategize actions for the next 12 weeks
    - five check-in meetings, 30 min each to discuss status, obstacles and progress of action items
  - Getting an assistant, scrum master or project manager to support you

- Preparing yourself for these meetings.

PYPR as a Software Product Management methodology is completely customizable and flexible, making it easily adopted by any product team or product organization regardless of size, maturity or development approach.

In my experience, some teams or product managers will start immediately to discuss single dimension items, and why one item is part of dimension A and not part of dimension B. Sometimes there is lots of energy in the room that items or whole dimensions are missing, need different names or any other type of cosmetic changes. That's not what PYPR is about.

Sometimes discussions about weights come up, but my strong recommendation would be to start with the provided defaults and change only after experiencing a few PYPR cycles. There will be plenty of opportunities to finetune PYPR for your context as you use the framework for your Software Product Management approach.

Provide this confidence to your product team and showcase that PYPR is all about focus and alignment.

The dimension items are based on my experience of doing Software Product Management for the last 20 years. The item weights within each respective dimension are based on the same foundation. At the beginning of PYPR I had to adapt the items and their weights from time to time; however, in the last few years they have stabilized. That's especially interesting as more teams with diverse contexts adopted the PYPR framework and the dimension items and weights remained rather stable. I admit that this is not a scientific proof and by no means would I claim that I have found the silver bullet for any product that definitely lead to product success.

I strongly encourage you to find the right mix for YourProduct, Inc. as dimension items and weights might require adaptations by business unit, product team, organization, or any other attribute defining your context. However, don't let this be a hindrance for utilizing PYPR. The default PYPR configurations are a decent starting point and you can hone the approach as your team or organization learns to use PYPR.

Last but not least, I like to mention two levels of buy-in:

- Stakeholder buy-in: not too important for Get Set; you can leverage PYPR and the stakeholder map to get them on board as you showcase success.
- Management buy-in: management buy-in is always desirable, but not a hard prerequisite either. You will find the support of your management beneficial, if you need extra resources like team rooms, meeting rooms, training budget, or an easier start due to management's blessing. However, I know many product managers that benefit from the PYPR framework and their management team does still not even know that PYPR exists and is being leveraged.

Go

If you were on your mark and got set for delivering beautiful products, there is just one more thing: **Go!**

- Go means being bold and signing up for Software Product Management excellence
- Go means leading the team to deliver awesome products
- Go means starting to leverage PYPR
- Go means embedding PYPR into your daily business
- Go means continuously improving and resolving the limiting factors in order to improve the product's yield potential and its chances for success

As I explained before, using PYPR represents a commitment to continuously improve the Software Product Management practice in your organization toward excellence. To ensure you benefit from PYPR, you must commit to repeatedly using the framework. This comprises conducting the PYPR meetings (read: ceremonies), leveraging PYPR as an information radiator, analyzing PYPR ratings as a team, and adapting your ongoing work priorities toward improving the dimension items that are limiting success.

Using PYPR as a one-time exercise for the team or even just for yourself might be an interesting and valuable team-building or self-reflection experience; however you are missing out on the ongoing discipline part of the PYPR definition. By not including PYPR in your product work and product-related communication regularly, you are actually not utilizing PYPR by definition.

The best way to avoid the "Set it and forget it"—syndrome is to commit as a product team to the assessment meetings, the check-in meetings and the Strategy and Action meetings as mandatory PYPR meetings (read: ceremonies) for the product team. Remember to always celebrate success. These meet-ups are excellent opportunities.

If you do not feel ready to start, that's okay. Be bold and overcome the doubts. You are a product manager. Applying PYPR will help you to become an even better product manager. You will recognize the positive PYPR impact soon, and your team will recognize it as well.

As you Go! PYPR, Part 2 of this book acts as a reference guide to help with each PYPR dimension and PYPR dimension item. Be bold and leverage the process you have learned from the introduction of the Product Yield Potential Radar (Sect. 2.1). I recommend reading Sect. 2.1 again, as with all the information you have by now, you will certainly gain a deeper understanding.

Once more—don't be scared to start using PYPR! You are a product manager.

Start, adapt, learn, improve, and grow! Personally, and in terms of your product's yield potential.

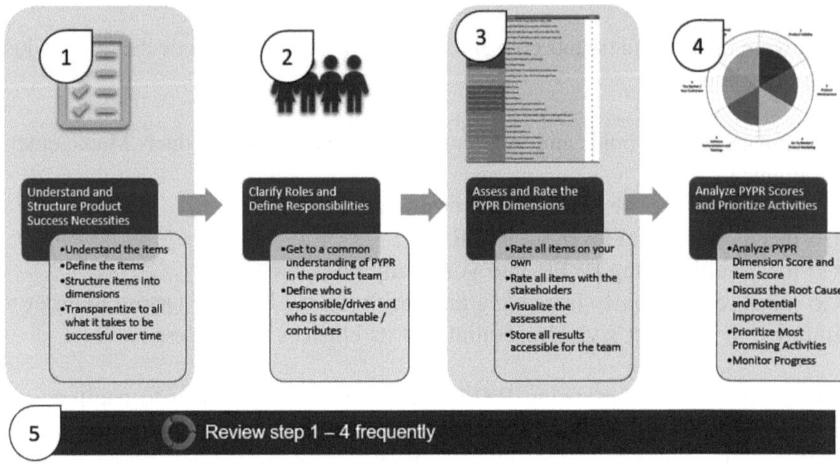

Fig. 3.9 Five steps applying PYPR to unfold its full potential © Timo Wagenblatt 2019. All rights reserved

As you go, you can use Part 2 simply as a textbook to learn more about PYPR and Software Product Management. Or you can pick and choose the content that is important to you. You might want more details about the dimension items that require improvements, you might want to understand others better, or you might need some inspiration or are looking for proven practices. For all these requests, Part 2 is your go-to reference book (Fig. 3.9).

3.4 How to Benefit Most from Part 2 and the Default PYPR Configurations

You can use Part 2 as a reference book for each PYPR dimension and its dimension items.[11] Each chapter is structured in a very similar way. Each dimension chapter starts with an overview about the PYPR dimension and a default PYPR configuration for this dimension. The default PYPR configuration is comprised of the default dimension items and their respective importance.

In Sect. 2.2, I introduced PYPR's six dimensions and 32 dimension items in total. These dimensions are the most important and need to be in balance. These dimension items are organized in three default PYPR configurations adapted for B2B product managers, B2C product managers and internal product managers.

[11] I admit that the dimension descriptions and dimension item details are comprehensive; however, for many topics there are dedicated books that only deal with that matter. If you require or seek more details or more variations than provided in Part 2 of this book, I recommend you either use the referenced bibliography or attend a dedicated training course to enrich your bag of tricks.

In Part 2 of this book, I explain for every item of the default PYPR configuration

- my interpretation of the dimension item in more detail
- a proven practice that works for me to improve the dimension item
- the default PYPR dimension item weight and criticality by product manager type
- how to assess and rate the PYPR dimension item score
- examples of direct and indirect impact of PYPR dimension item changes on other PYPR dimensions.

I describe my interpretation of each dimension item and I clarify why each dimension item is a factor that contributes to the product's yield potential. For most dimension items, I will further provide a proven practice that worked for me, my product teams and my products.

The proven practices that I introduce in Part 2 of this book do not represent a complete how to guide for Software Product Management for all products and every product team. Instead, I would like you to consider the proven practices as an initial filling of your bag of tricks if you are a new product manager or as alternative options that you can add to or exchange with your existing tools.

Remember, as product managers, our mandate is to continuously improve our bag of tricks as one size does not fit all. One tool or practice that works for me or your peer doesn't necessarily work for you and your context in the exact same way.

However, you will get one proven practice for each topic, but if you have established methods that work better for you, the team and your organization (i.e. your context), then there is no harm in keeping them unless you are not satisfied with the results. When applying PYPR, you will likely experience one useful side effect. PYPR will make it visible where you need to improve as a product manager and product team by learning or hiring additional skills.

As you Go! with PYPR, you might not need to reference some dimension items for several months as your product success is not limited by these dimension items. But, whenever there is a need you can leverage a proven practice that generally will help to improve the situation.

For each dimension item, I'm providing the default PYPR dimension item weight and the criticality of the item for each product manager type (B2B, B2C, Internal PM). The type of product manager derives the type of product or the market segment you are targeting.

The dimension item weight represents the relative importance of an item within its PYPR dimension. It depicts the width of the stave in the Liebig barrel of product yield. Criticality classifies the importance of the dimension item from low to high.

Finally, you see instructions how to assess and how to rate each dimension item. Each dimension item should be rated between 0 (hell) and 10 (heaven). The explanation of each dimension item will help to clarify the expectations. As a shortcut, I provide guiding verbiage of what it means to score low, medium or high. For example, a Low PYPR score means your assessment has most overlaps with the respective description. Therefore, the rating should be between 0 and 3 and you discuss about the final rating and fine-tuning within the Low range.

The verbiage and the ranges guide the team toward what is important. Remember do not fall into the trap of debating whether it is a 5 or a 6, only debate whether it is a Low or High rating. Follow the proven practice outlined before in

Sect. 2.1. As you Go PYPR you will find this part most valuable, most insightful and most communicative on your journey toward Software Product Management excellence.

All the information about dimension item weights, criticality and how to rate PYPR dimension items are summarized in a format like Table 3.1 for every PYPR dimension item.

Table 3.1 PYPR defaults by software product manager type © Timo Wagenblatt 2019. All rights reserved

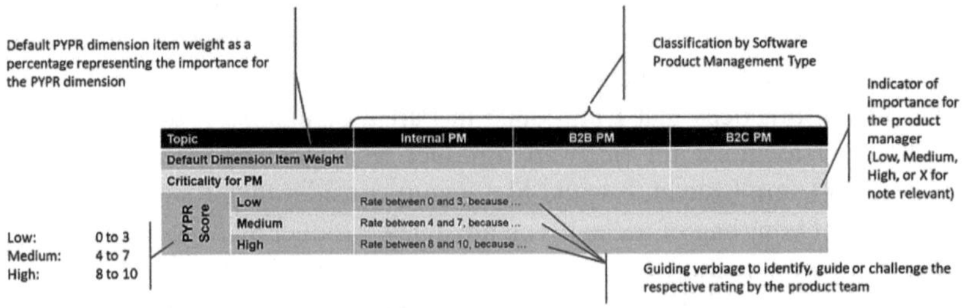

As we have seen in the chapter about the Law of Tolerance, dimension items act in concert rather than in isolation. Therefore, I added a few examples to each dimension item chapter, describing how PYPR dimensions are potentially (directly or indirectly) impacted by a change in a given dimension item.[12] These are only examples and you might experience the cross effect as well or you might not in your context. However, the examples will remind you to always take a whole product perspective. There are only very limited, fully isolated, actions that do not affect the product.

I did not explain how the Total PYPR scores and PYPR dimension scores are calculated. I mentioned and used the scores already several times. The calculation is rather straightforward.

- **Total PYPR score** = sum of all PYPR dimension scores
- **PYPR Dimension score** = sum of all PYPR dimension item scores
- **PYPR Dimension Item score** = dimension item rating times dimension item weight

I recommend checking Chap. 10 for more details about how the PYPR scores have been utilized by various product teams.

That's it—you are fully prepared to use PYPR.

[12]You'll find a table PYPR Dimensions Impact Examples that describes how a given dimension items impacts a PYPR dimension. Sometimes I described examples for all dimensions, sometimes only for a few.

You might have wished for a more concrete guide to start using PYPR. However, you have what it takes to start. You already got to know the general approach in the introduction. Now, all I can do for you is to encourage you to start, and in your journey, you might find it useful to read Parts 2 and 3 of this book if you require special help on any dimension item or want to see real-life case studies.

You signed up for Software Product Management excellence, which will lead the team to deliver awesome products. You are cut out to be the General Manager of YourProduct, Inc.

Be bold! Experience what PYPR can do for your product, your product team and for yourself.

And now: Go PYPR!

Key Takeaways

- PYPR is a detection system that uses the product management dimensions and the things that matter to determine the yield potential and constraining factors of product success
- PYPR visualizes the balance or imbalance of your work outcomes
- As a product manager, you are the General (Stakeholder) Manager, the leader of the company called YourProduct Inc.
- Use information radiators to clarify and remind the team about roles and responsibilities
- Understand the interest and impact of your stakeholders and cater to their basic needs, which are transparency and involvement
- Introduce PYPR and the PYPR practice to the product team and to your organization
- Adapt the PYPR dimensions and weights only after your first iteration as you become familiar with the approach
- Avoid "Set it and Forget it" Syndrome
- Leverage the dimension and dimension item details of Part 2 as a reference book
- Improve the product mindset within the product team, the organization, and overall in the industry
- Always remember: TALK IS CHEAP, SHOW ME YOUR PYPR
- Or better: TALK IS CHEAP, LET'S IMPROVE OUR PYPR

Part 1 started with a generic definition of Software Product Management. Using PYPR, we can update our definition of Software Product Management at the end of Part 1:

Software Product Management is a discipline and process that

- comprises all planning, coordination and execution activities required for software products
  - considering all product dimensions along the product lifecycle and
  - aligning all product stakeholders inside and outside the organization
- governs the product's yield potential
- enables product mindset and holistic product focus
- leads to customer value and long-term product success.

References

Cagan, M. (2018). *Inspired—How to create great tech products customer love*. Hoboke, New Jersey: Wiley & Sons Inc.

Cohn, M. (2019, January 2). *Six guidelines for saying no to a stakeholder*. Retrieved from https://www.mountaingoatsoftware.com: https://www.mountaingoatsoftware.com/blog/six-guidelines-for-saying-no-to-a-stakeholder.

DeMarco, T. (1989). *Controlling software projects: Management, measurement & estimates*. Pearson Education: Prentice Hall PTR.

DeMarco, T. (2002). *Slack: Getting past burnout, busywork, and the myth of total efficiency*. Crown Business.

DeMarco, T., & Lister, T. (2013). *Peopleware*. Upper Saddle River: Addison-Wesley.

Evans, R. A., & Fischer, R. A. (2018, November 27). *Crop science abstract—SYMPOSIUM-1998 ASA MEETING -BALTIMORE*. Retrieved from the Alliance of Crop, Soil, and Environmental Science Societies (ACSESS): https://dl.sciencesocieties.org/publications/cs/abstracts/39/6/1544?access=0&view=pdf.

Gladwell, M. (2010). *Überflieger: Warum manche Menschen erfolgreich sind - und andere nicht*. Frankfurt, New York: Campus Verlag.

Horowitz, B. (2018, December 31). *Good Product Manager/Bad Product Manager*. Retrieved from https://a16z.com/: https://a16z.com/2012/06/15/good-product-managerbad-product-manager/.

Narajan, S. (2015). *Agile IT organization design*. New York: Addison-Wesley.

Niven, P. R., & Lamorte, B. (2016). *Objectives and key results; driving focus, alignment, and engagement with OKRs*. Hoboke, New Jersey: Wiley.

Product Owner: Agile Alliance Org. (2018, November 18). Retrieved from www.agilealliance.org: https://www.agilealliance.org/glossary/product-owner/.

Yang, R. (2019, January 2). *The problem with being a fix-it product manager*. Retrieved from https://blog.aha.io: https://blog.aha.io/the-problem-with-being-a-fix-it-product-manager/.

Part II
PYPR Software Product Management Dimensions in Detail

Product Viability

4

The (Financial) Value-Based Part of your Software Product Manager Role

Product viability is the ability of a software product to maintain itself or recover its potentials. Product viability is determined by three dimensions. Viable products need to be profitable, implementable, and scalable. Profitable products are probably the primary objective for most organizations. Generally, software product profitability compares revenues versus product-related costs. Products need to be implementable as the ease of implementation determines the speed of adoption. Products need to be scalable as the ability to scale determines the product growth potential.

Viability considerations differ for software products that

- exist in a proven, vital market where the focus of the product team is to maximize the success and market share growth
- exist in a declining or non-strategic market where the focus of the product team is to optimize the efforts with less investment of time and budgets by streamlining the processes and making the most of existing assets
- are in ideation or development phase or are targeting an unproven market where the focus of the product team needs to be on verification (i.e. reduce the risks by making sure that the product will be viable with a working business model).
- reached the end of their lifecycle as technology gets outdated or obsolete, markets are vanishing, the customer interest is gone and the focus of the product team is to sunset the product in a professional way and help the customer and user base transition.

This chapter describes in detail the Product Viability dimension that represents "The (Financial) Value-Based Part of the Software Product Manager Role." The chapter explains the Product Viability dimension in much more detail, focusing on the techniques to assess, understand, monitor, and improve the financial and value-based part of the product manager role. I will introduce some of the tools,

T. Wagenblatt, *Software Product Management*, Management for Professionals,
https://doi.org/10.1007/978-3-030-19871-8_4

templates, and key performance indicators I used in my career, as well as the practices I learned and developed to assess and improve this important dimension.

Please note that there are complete books available for most if not all items described in this chapter. Therefore, the tools and templates provided are selected, proven practices that worked in my context. If you have already filled your bag of tricks with more advanced options or options that better fit your context that is absolutely fine. The descriptions and proven practices are meant as directional options that will help you improve the PYPR scores in the Product Viability dimension; hence it is not necessary that the descriptions match 100%. Likewise, the proven practices can be substituted with better matching ones for your specific context. The main thing remains the product, not the tools and methods to improve it.

I propose to start with the default PYPR configuration in Fig. 4.1. As you leverage PYPR for your product, consider the recommendations from Sect. 3.3

Dimension Weight 20 %		Dimension Weight 20 %		Dimension Weight 17,5 %	
B2B		B2C		Internal PM	
Dimension Item	Weighting Factor	Dimension Item	Weighting Factor	Dimension Item	Weighting Factor
Customer Business Case	20,0%	Customer Value Case	25,0%	Customer Business Case	30,0%
Pipeline Development	18,0%	Traffic Development	20,0%	Pipeline Development	not relevant
Product Profitability	20,0%	Product Profitability	20,0%	Product Profitability	25,0%
Product Growth	20,0%	Product Growth	20,0%	Product Growth	20,0%
Maintenance / Operations Profitability	12,0%	Maintenance / Operations Profitability	15,0%	Maintenance / Operations Profitability	25,0%
Professional Services/Consulting Profitability	10,0%	Professional Services/Consulting Profitability	not relevant	Professional Services/Consulting Profitability	not relevant

Fig. 4.1 Product viability: PYPR dimension defaults © Timo Wagenblatt 2019. All rights reserved

In this chapter I will detail the following PYPR dimension items[1]:

- **Customer Business/Value Case**
  A customer business case explains and details the customers' financial valuation of the product including the perceived customer/stakeholder benefits derived from the product's attributes. These values could be cost reduction, revenue generation, customer satisfaction, total cost of ownership savings, defect avoidance, time savings, etc.
- **Sales Pipeline/Traffic Development**
  Monitoring the product license pipeline and renewal rates might not be the daily business of product managers; however having a strict discipline will help you understand how to reach your financial objectives. In short, we will learn a lot how you can score when talking to important stakeholders in this dimension including Sales and your management.
- **Product Profitability**
  Profitable products are probably the primary objective for most organizations. Profitability for software products compares the revenues, for example, from

[1]The descriptions are short reviews from Sect. 2.2.1.

incremental license deals and subscription revenues versus such costs as development costs, cloud center costs, and even sales costs.

- **Product Growth**
  Product growth is important for any product, whether it is a new mobile app, website, corporate IT product or B2B product. We will learn how to define the metrics that matter most for software products and how to rate and interpret the measures accordingly.
- **Maintenance/Run Profitability**
  Getting a product into the market is one side of the coin, keeping the product profitable in the market another. As a product manager, monitoring the maintenance profitability will provide insights into the software quality perception of your customers as well as the patterns of issues during usage. Running your product in production-mode needs to be cost-effective and sustainable either.
- **Professional Services/Consulting Profitability**
  Most enterprise software products require implementation services, whether they are deployed on-premise or as part of a private or public cloud deployment. Assuming professional services teams are required for your product, then you should know and monitor topics like whether your product can be implemented as fix price bids, implementations require lots of rework, and professional services and customers require lots of handholding during go-live from the product team. In best case all implementations are rather self-contained and smooth.

Figure 4.2 illustrates all PYPR dimension items that determine the viability of YourProduct Inc. This chapter will introduce, assess, and improve the PYPR dimension that is best described with the value-based part of your product manager role.

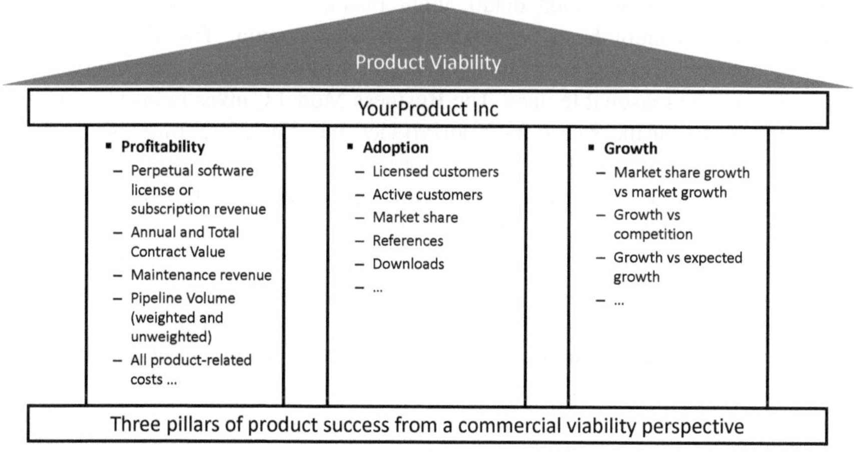

Fig. 4.2 Three pillars of product viability for YourProduct Inc. © Timo Wagenblatt 2019. All rights reserved

As the General Manager of YourProduct Inc., you need to be able to clearly articulate the business benefits of your product, describe the business model, and provide information about the business performance. I did not explicitly include a chapter about product business cases, which might be still important for conversations with your management, founder, venture capitalist, bank, or enterprise portfolio team. I acknowledge that there is legitimate demand to validate and detail the viability of organizing all important facts in a given format. However, all information that is required is part of the PYPR Product Viability dimension. Together with an up-to-date Business Model Canvas any business case work boils down to the basic task sorting all relevant facts in a given template.

4.1 The Business Model Canvas

The Business Model Canvas (Osterwalder & Pigneur, 2010) has become a global standard used by millions of people to describe and design business models from scratch to improving existing business models. At its core, Product Viability as a PYPR dimension must answer questions about

- how a product is creating value
- how the value is delivered by the product
- how the value is captured for the organization.

The Business Model Canvas helps exactly with that by plotting the nine key elements that answer the above questions on one single page.

Gone are the days of 90-page business case or business plan documents. If you are still living these days, the Business Model Canvas has the potential to ease your pain. I will not get in much detail about business cases as the processes and templates vary widely from organization to organization. The Business Model Canvas captures all components that you need for most business case templates out there, at least the reasonable ones. The Business Model Canvas helps you to create and improve the business case for YourProduct, Inc. Therefore, business cases and their cumbersome approvals are merely formal acts.

Let's focus on the value generating part of the process, which is finding the right business model for YourProduct, Inc. Business Model Canvases work well whether you are developing, improving or adapting a business model for a single product start-up company or a product out of a 1000-line items large product portfolio.

Economic viability requires a working business model for your product. Although this should be common sense by now, the development of many software products begins without the proper foundation of a business model. Great products that are desirable and feasible did not grow and ended up on the pile of sad, lumbered product trees, just because their product managers missed the importance of creating and validating a working business model.

Product managers need to work with all stakeholders to carve out a profitable business model with validated revenue streams. An early, ongoing dialog with representative customers helps—no, actually that is essential. The unique value proposition is only unique if you can identify a real differentiator in the market. I assume you already sense the importance of these topics. Let's see how the Business Model Canvas is beneficial in this process.

Applying the Business Model Canvas delivers many benefits. The selected list below helps us on our journey to deliver a valuable and profitable software product to our customers:

- Understanding how your product can create value by
  - recognizing the key problems of the target customer segments
  - better understanding the needs of the target customer segment
- identifying weaknesses and unknowns in your business model
- verifying critical assumptions of your business model
- gathering all information for a formal business case to invest in a new product (company) or new release of an existing product.

There is already many great books, blogs and videos about leveraging the Business Model Canvas. I would recommend you visit the source at https://strategyzer.com/canvas/business-model-canvas for expert advice and insights.

In this book I will focus on the relevancy for product managers and provide

- an overview about the Business Model Canvas
- the process that works for me (which is likely not much different to how it works for most) and
- how the Business Model Canvas maps to the PYPR dimensions.

The Business Model Canvas is a communication and discussion tool to test your assumptions and hypothesis of how to capture value for your organization with your product. As product managers, we need to own the process and if we do not own the process, then we should lead the process of business model generation for our products. We are accountable for our product's success. Hence, we cannot sit on the bench and watch the game.

The Business Model Canvas depicts the flows between your organization, your customer segments and your partners in nine building blocks. The nine building blocks structure the answers for the essential product questions of what, who, how and why.

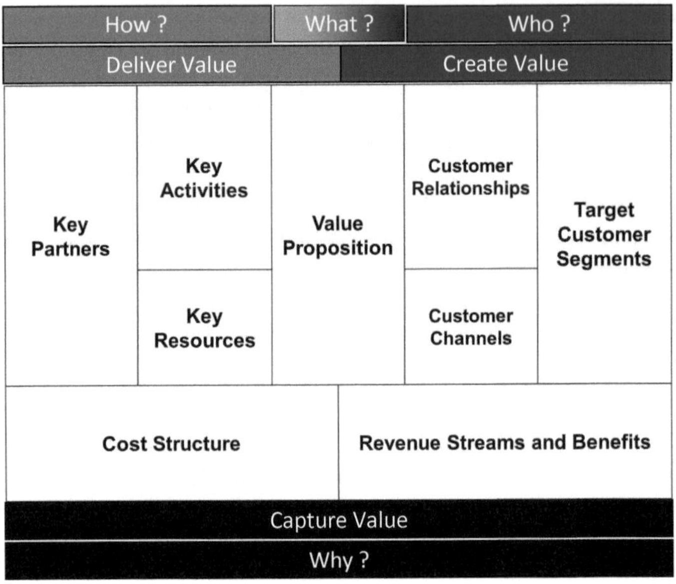

Fig. 4.3 The Business Model Canvas by Strategyzer.com under creative commons license

The Business Model Canvas as shown in Fig. 4.3 consists of the following building blocks:

- **(Target) Customer segments**
  Who do you help and for whom do you create value? Each product manager, whether from a start-up or global enterprise, is focusing on or searching for at least one customer segment of the total market, which is gaining high value from their product. This section and the next section are frequently worked out in quick iterations and hence in parallel, so that the customer segments are sharpened and fit perfectly to the value proposition. For consumer-focused products, customer segments might be user personas or socio-demographic groupings.
- **Value proposition**
  How do you help? Which one of our customer segments' problems are we helping to solve, and which customer needs are we satisfying? Software Products provide value/benefits by solving a problem for a group of users (human or technical users) defining a customer segment. The promise of value and benefits realized by using your software product is called value proposition. And that is what you describe in this canvas section. The Value Proposition Canvas (Strategyzer AG, 2019) is a great complementary tool to the business model canvas to support you in this important task (see chapter: Focus on the Value of Your Product).
- **Customer channels**
  How do you reach the customer segments throughout the phases from awareness to after sales providing post-purchase customer support? In this section you describe how you are channeling your value propositions to your customers, in the future, or currently at any given phase of the customer interaction.

- **Customer relationships**
  How do you interact with the customer segments and how do you win, maintain or upsell your customers? Note that the design of the customer relationship is a vital part of your business model and needs to be defined clearly. Are your target customer segments expecting personal assistance, self-service, communities, or even co-development?
- **Revenue streams and benefits**
  After you have discovered how you create value for your customer segments, it is time to uncover the essential questions like: What monetary benefits do you expect? There might be multiple ways earning money with the same value proposition. The Business Model Canvas helps you to generate multiple alternatives or options to identify undetected revenue opportunities. Besides the strategic nature of how to generate revenue streams, pricing plays an important role here as well. Consider multiple pricing models as part of your journey to find the best business model for your product.
- **Key activities**
  What do you do? What are the most important activities to get the business model to live and stay alive. Realizing the value proposition of your product requires software development, support activities, Go-to-Market activities, etc. Be specific and creative.
- **Key resources**
  What do you have and who are you? What key resources does your value propositions, distribution channels, customer relationships, and revenue streams require? The type of resources might be physical resources like IT infrastructure and servers, intellectual property like patents and copyrights, data like market research data, human resources like a skilled product team and special know-how.
- **Key partners**
  With whom do you work? Your business model might benefit or essentially require a business partner. Strategic partners could be complementary organizations (non-competitors), suppliers, or service providers. Key partners help mitigate risk and allow your product and business to scale, otherwise they are not key for your product.
- **Cost structure**
  Activities create costs, resources create costs and partnerships have the cost creation potential as well. Which costs do you expect? What are the most important costs inherent in our business model? Which key resources are most expensive? Which key activities are most expensive? Document your fixed costs and your variable costs and you have the last element to understand Product Viability and the viability of your business model.

Note that the Business Model Canvas pictures the nine essential blocks of a business model for new and existing products, generating new business models, adapting and improving existing business models. The method mandates to iterate and allow for rapid changes and even pivots of the business model approach as the product idea matures and assumptions are validated. Build, buy, or partner considerations are covered as part of the business model generation and finding process as well (Fig. 4.4).

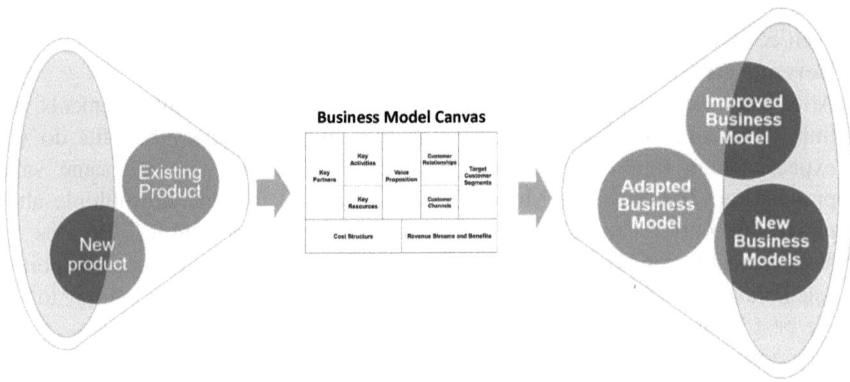

Fig. 4.4 Business Model Canvas for new and existing products © Timo Wagenblatt 2019. All rights reserved

The Business Model Canvas should not be a one-off exercise. There are many moving parts, assumptions to be validated, risks to be managed and the world never stands still. Keep the Business Model Canvas updated over your product's lifecycle and you will see benefits in ideation, growth, maturity and sunset phases of your product. Figure 4.5 Illustrates how the Business Model Canvas can be a constant companion for your Software Product journey—from understanding and validating Product/Problem Fit and Product/Market Fit to Growth Hacking strategies or product extension to finally sunsetting the software product.

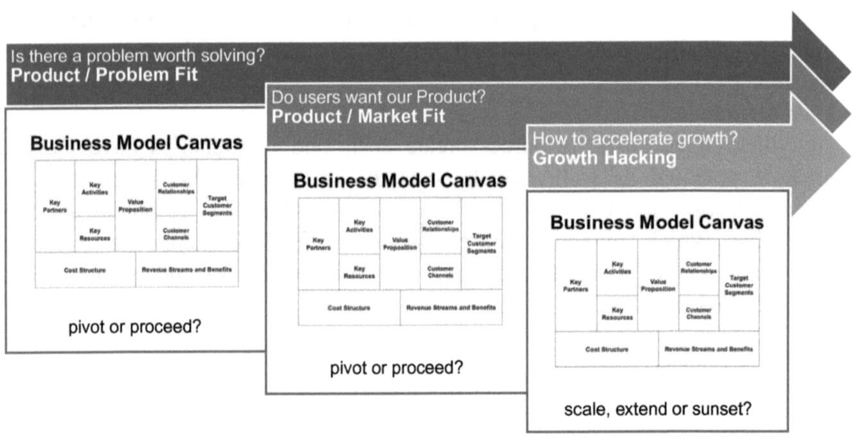

Fig. 4.5 Business Model Canvas: product-problem fit, product-market fit, Growth Hacking © Timo Wagenblatt 2019. All rights reserved

Now that we have a basic understanding about the Business Model Canvas and its benefits for Software Product Management, we will strengthen our understanding by learning a proven practice of working with the Business Model Canvas and investigating how the Business Model Canvas could impact and resonate with PYPR.

4.1.1 Proven Practice

One more repetition, a Business Model Canvas describes a current or future business model with nine simple building blocks, including customer/prospect segments, channels, and relationships; value proposition, key activities, resources, and partners; cost structure and revenue streams. The Business Model Canvas combines the economic viability of a solution with its desirability and feasibility.

Note that these building blocks carry all information of most business case templates I have seen. The canvas therefore can be used as a business case or as the highly valuable prework of any business case or investment case exercise. Figure 4.6 illustrates the proven process steps.

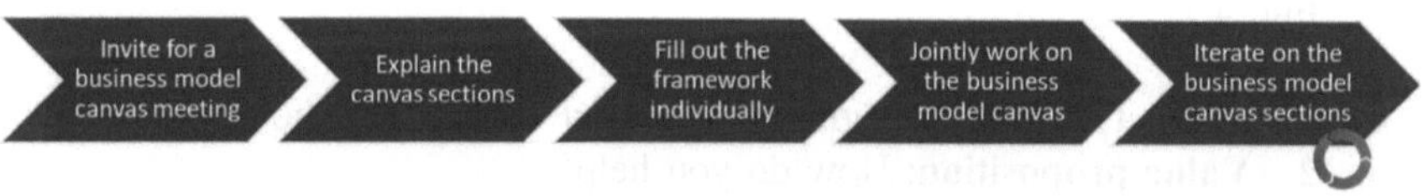

Fig. 4.6 Business Model Canvas proven process © Timo Wagenblatt 2019. All rights reserved

1. Invite the core or extended product team for a Business Model Canvas meeting. There is no difference whether you start with a new Business Model Canvas or iterate on an existing one.

   a. Time-box the meeting to maximum four hours
   b. Make sure that all participants know the context of the meeting and are available to meet in the same room
   c. Prepare the required material:

      - One printed canvas for each participant (and some extra to be safe)
      - Colored sticky notes to remind everyone to use one color for each target customer segment
      - One large printed canvas (A0 format) or draw the canvas on a whiteboard before the meeting starts

2. Get together with the team, explain the canvas sections briefly and hand out the printed canvas to all participants
3. Ask everybody to fill out the framework individually

a. Time-box the first iteration, for example 15–20 min
b. Ask everyone to use the colored notes extensively, one idea per sticky note
c. Ask for more than one idea for each block, go for quantity like in a brainstorming session

4. Start the group work and begin with the target customer segments of your product and ask the participants to contribute their ideas and discuss openly

   a. Ask everybody to share their view about the customer segment and the problem that is solved for the segment
   b. If you define different segments, keep them separated by color throughout the exercise
   c. If there are too many segments work with them practically
      - Prioritize the segments and focus on maximum three segments in this workshop
      - Invite everyone for another workshop to address the remaining ones

5. Fill out all the remaining canvas blocks accordingly

   a. The following order worked best for me and the teams I worked with (see Fig. 4.7):

      1—**(Target) customer segments** (covered in Step 4): who do you help?
      2—**Value proposition**: How do you help?
      3—**Customer channels**: How do you reach the customer segments from awareness to after sales?
      4—**Customer relationships**: How do you interact with the customer segments?
      5—**Revenue streams and benefits**: What monetary benefits do you expect?
      6—**Key activities**: What do you do?
      7—**Key resources**: What do you have and who are you?
      8—**Key partners**: With whom do you work?
      9—**Cost structure**: Which costs do you expect?

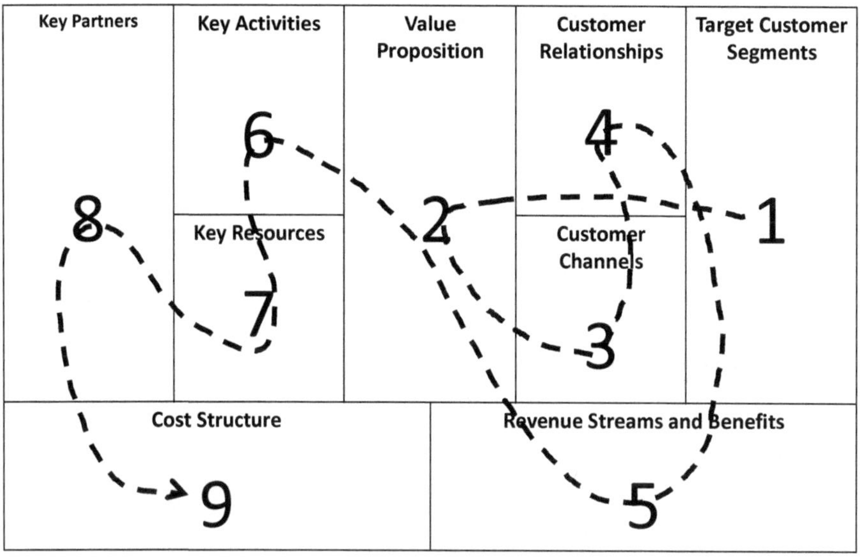

Fig. 4.7 Proven Business Model Canvas sequence © Timo Wagenblatt 2019. All rights reserved

a. Ask everybody to share their content
b. Don't always start with the same person
c. If the team gets stuck in one area, continue with the next block
d. Keep the time-box approach for each block

6. After the first iteration take a break
7. Start the next iteration

a. Add new ideas and detail or eliminate existing ones
b. Discuss the strengths, weaknesses and risks of each item in the canvas blocks
c. Mark and document assumptions and hypotheses in the canvas blocks

8. Close the workshop and capture the ***baseline*** Business Model Canvas digitally

a. Make sure you do not lose the work
b. Make the work available to everyone
c. Define actions to

- research the gaps in the canvas and learn more about the problem space
- evaluate the assumptions and hypotheses with customers and end users
- think about potential improvements

9. Iterate and start with Step 1 (or in other words—validate your canvas) until you get to a mature stage and the Business Model Canvas becomes stable indicated by

a. there are no new questions and ideas (analyze and improve)
b. assumptions are validated (reduce risks, test and verify)
c. you all are comfortable with the outcome (challenge and change).

4.1.2 PYPR Dimension Details

See Table 4.1.

PYPR dimensions mapping to business model canvas blocks

Dimension	Direct impact example	Indirect impact example
Product viability	Revenue streams, cost structure	Value proposition, customer segments
Product development	Key activities, key resources	Key partners
Go-to-market/product marketing	Value proposition, customer segments, channels, customer relationships	Key partners, cost structure
Software demonstrations and training	Customer segments, channels	Value proposition, customer segments
The market/your customers	Value proposition, customer segments, channels, customer relationships	Key partners
Organizational maturity	Key resources	Key activities

4.1.3 Summary and Conclusions

The Business Model Canvas provides value for all dimensions of PYPR. Using the Business Model Canvas provides you with great insights in your role as General Manager of YourProduct, Inc. Leverage the Business Model Canvas from inception to the sunset of your software product.

The Business Model Canvas has been adapted for special situations over the years, and one of the most prominent adaptions is the *Lean Canvas* by Ash Maurya (Maurya, 2010), which works well in the earlier stages of your software product journey.

The main difference between the Lean Canvas and the Business Model Canvas is that the How part of the canvas (i.e. Key Partners, Key Activities, Key Resources) is de-emphasized and the Product/Problem fit question is in focus. The Lean Canvas focuses on problems (instead of key partners), solutions (instead of key activities), key metrics (instead of key sources), and unfair advantages (instead of customer relationships).

The proven process as outlined above still works in a very similar way but with a slightly different order of working through the building blocks.

Key Takeaways

- Consider the status quo and potential improvements or risks of your product's business model and that product viability is a key responsibility for each product manager

- Product managers need to own, drive and refine the business model of their product
- Use brainstorming and other creative techniques to iterate to the best business model for your software product
- Use color codes consistently to map target customer segments with the eight other parts of the canvas; if there are too many, split the canvas to stay focused
- Use the Business Model Canvas for your key competitors to gain great insights about competitive strategies and your competitor's business model. You might be able to leverage this information in many areas. The competitive Business Model Canvas enriches your competitive analysis (see Sect. 6.4)
- Use the Business Model Canvas to better understand your target customer segments. For example, you might be able to leverage the gained insights in crafting a better customer business case (see Sect. 4.2)
- Use the Lean Canvas in the Product Problem Fit phase as illustrated in Fig. 4.8
- Check out the source of the Business Model Canvas to stay up to date and get the canvas template and background from https://strategyzer.com/canvas

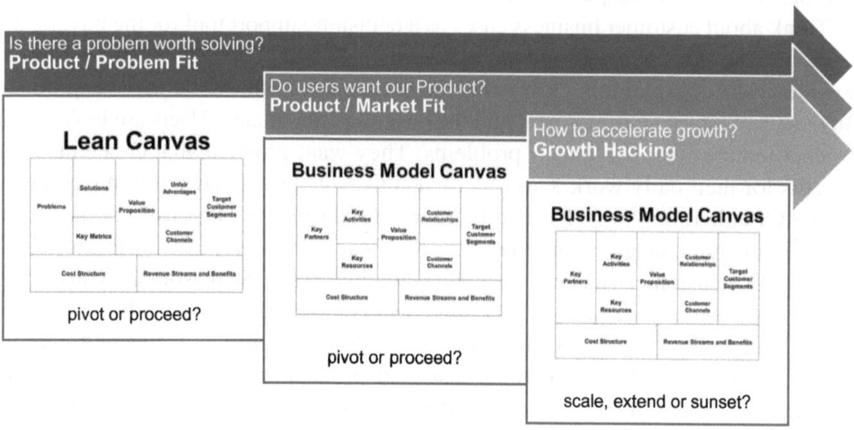

Fig. 4.8 Lean Canvas and Business Model Canvas in sequence © Timo Wagenblatt 2019. All rights reserved

4.2 Customer Business Case

Price is what you pay. Value is what you get.

—**Warren Buffet**

Who could argue with Warren Buffet when it comes to financial matters? As a product manager, you ensure that the customer does not perceive the value of your product as less than its price. Your product's viability would be rather limited in such a case. In this section I briefly touch on pricing; however, the more important part covered here and revived in later sections is the value that your product provides to your customers. If the value is not clear to your customers, the price will always be perceived as too high.

Customer business cases explain and detail the customers' financial valuation of the product and the perceived customer and stakeholder benefits from your product's features. As a product manager, you are the one who will either create the generic (i.e. not customer-specific) customer business case for your product or, my preferred option, supports a sales colleague[2] with all the required content for a fit-for-purpose customer business case template that can be adopted and tailored for each customer. If you as the General Manager of YourProduct Inc. cannot convey a compelling customer business case for your product, someone is already sharpening an axe and your product likely will not survive very long.

I have seen customer business cases in various shapes and forms over the years. While they were all different, there are common ingredients in most customer business cases. If you took the time to create a Business Model Canvas and kept it updated, building a customer business case will be just a matter of formatting the information you have already captured in your Business Model Canvas. The value proposition for each customer target segment combined with the revenue streams and benefits (which represent the costs for your customers) is all you need to know in order to create a compelling customer business case.

Think about customer business cases as a decision-support tool for the buyers, the users, and the executive decision team of your customers. The purpose of a customer business case is explaining each persona (see Sect. 5.2) the value of your product. Buyers want return on investment and the best price negotiated. Users are looking for product features that solve their problems. They want products that create tangible benefits for their daily work. Customer executives generally have nothing against a great ROI either; however, frequently they are focusing on other aspects like reputation, innovation, or risk reduction.[3,4] As the General Manager of YourProduct Inc., a compelling customer business case must clearly convey the reasons why investing money and time in your product is a good decision. Actually, it is the best decision.

As a side effect, a customer business case also helps product teams and internal stakeholders to understand the value that your product provides to your customers and target market segments. Based on the value you create for your customers, the

[2]Colleagues working on the standard customer business case asset might be in different departments, like Pre-sales, Marketing, or Value Engineering etc. However, I prefer to work directly with someone from the target user group that crafts those kinds of assets. The ones that will leverage the customer business case as part of the sales cycle are the best candidates to let you know what needs to be covered in the asset or what of information they need to build the asset on their own.

[3]For B2C products, frequently, but not always, the buyer and the user are the same person. Executive teams are not existent unless you consider spouses or parents that way.

[4]For internal products, your customer persona does not include a buyer. Still a customer business case is useful as it explains the expected financial and non-financial benefits that your product provides to a group of internal users of business units, subsidiaries, line of businesses, or your whole organization.

best and fair price for your product can be defined. I will not get into any details of product pricing in this book. In my career I have been involved in many pricing councils and my voice has been heard, sometimes more and sometimes less, but I almost never have been responsible for making the final pricing decision. This has been either the domain of the founder of the company for whom I was working, or the responsibility of a global pricing team that must consider factors not directly related to my product, such as the pricing of other products in the portfolio, industry trends, geographic specialties, or overall company strategy.

If you are interested in software pricing as a topic on its own, I recommend the book *Software Product Management and Pricing* (Kittlaus & Clough, 2009) by Hans-Bernd Kittlaus and Peter N. Clough. Their book, which provides an in-depth analysis of the business side of the software industry, introduces and details a software pricing framework.

Note that there are financial and non-financial benefits that should be part of any customer business case. Customer business cases do more than provide an ROI calculator; however, having one will be appreciated during each sales cycle. I will mostly focus on a B2B customer business case, but I will also provide a brief B2C customer business case example. As an internal product manager, you can leverage and adapt the alternative that best fits your purpose and context.

Almost certainly, at a certain stage of every B2B sales cycle, your prospect wants guidance about the expected benefits and ROI of your product. As a product manager, you are the go-to person for such insights. Therefore, building a generic ROI calculator and customer business case will help you save time and avoid firefighting activities as sales teams will likely bother you when you are busy with more important tasks. Therefore, customer business cases are essential, and you need to be prepared whether they are freely available on your website or secretly kept in your bag of tricks for special customer situations. In my opinion, customer business cases are sensitive, semi-confidential assets for various reasons. For example,

- your competitors are keen to understand how you try to convey the value of your product
- good customer business cases require customer input
- generic customer business cases might be misleading and not making the point
- customer business cases are used in sales cycles by other people (if part of your sales kit as detailed in Sect. 6.2).

As a product manager, your job is normally not to talk about pricing or even negotiate discounts with customers. However, when you are involved in sales cycles, you need to be super careful as you are the senior product executive. You might explain the value of your product and you might be forced to take part in cost and pricing discussions. If you discuss costs too early because costs are part of many value discussions and of any business case, you expose information that certainly will not be appreciated by your sales team as it weakens their negotiation potential.

Instead I recommend focusing on the pains and gains of your customers and defer pricing discussions to the sales team. A full customer business case including a cost-benefit calculator should only be considered in later phases of a sales cycle. For example, if you consider a sales cycle as having the standard phases "Recognize, Consider, Evaluate, Select, Negotiate, and Purchase," in no way should you get into the details of a cost-benefit analysis before reaching phase "Evaluate." The earlier phases need to focus on a deep understanding of the customer pains and gains and then craft the best possible business case tailored to the customer's situation. As a product manager, you need to know each customer stakeholder's goals and issues and you need to recognize which product features address them.

4.2.1 Proven Practice

When pitching to prospects or internal customers, at one stage, someone needs to convince them on the business value of your product. A cost-benefit calculator as part of a customer business case will help as you can show exactly what type of return your prospects can expect and when they can expect the return of their investments. The proven practice illustrated in Fig. 4.9 provides a standard approach ready to be tailored for your product.

Fig. 4.9 Customer business case process © Timo Wagenblatt 2019. All rights reserved

1. Understand your target market segment[5]

   a. Identify your stakeholders, e.g. buyer, user, executives
   b. Understand each stakeholder's pain points and gain points
   c. Understand the financial estimation of how much money could be saved per eased pain and how much money can be attributed to each gain

2. Conduct an objective-benefit analysis

   a. Re-use the standard pains and gains based on past experience (or your product's value proposition) as a starting point
   b. Calculate the amount of money that can be attributed to each pain and each gain
      i. Enter one line for each pain and each gain, detailing the stakeholder, the current status as a baseline, and the potential for improvement
      ii. Calculate the financial benefit for each pain and gain that's in focus for your customer

[5]Remember that we want to define a generic customer business case that reduces the workload of the product manager and can be tailored to any prospect in the target market segment.

1. Note that you could either work with generic benchmark numbers in this calculation, but estimated numbers directly from your prospect will have a much higher impact
2. Create a model with variables that can be used by your sales team or by the customer directly[6]

iii. Include intangible benefits if they are important for the customer's overall business purpose or major business goal

c. Iterate with trusted internal (e.g. sales) and external stakeholders (e.g. partners) to verify and generalize the analysis (Table 4.2)

Example of an objective-benefit analysis

Pain/gain/objective	Stakeholder	Baseline	Improvement	Expected benefit
Labor efficiency savings due to efficient planning	VP sales	8 weeks	2 weeks	750k $
Marketed customer service levels cannot be achieved	CEO	Reputation is endangered	Reputation is undamaged	intangible
Analyze sales data with less IT personnel	CIO	4 FTEs for two months	2 FTEs for three weeks	170k $

3. Derive a customer business case

a. Based on the objective-benefit analysis, you can derive a projected cost-benefit case from your prospect's point of view. A cost-benefit case comprises

i. All costs from a customer perspective including

1. one-time costs like perpetual software licenses, implementation services, training, hardware costs and any other one-time cost components related to your product
2. ongoing costs like subscription fees, maintenance costs, operations costs, data cleansing costs, or any other ongoing cost components related to your product

ii. All one-time and recurring benefits as a result of the objective-benefit analysis

[6]This kind of generic objective-benefit analysis could be used directly on your website, whether you offer a B2B, internal, or B2C product. The objective-benefit analysis is a simple self-service tool for your prospect customers.

   iii. The projected net benefit, which is simple to calculate; for example, for a year as (one-time benefit + all recurring monthly benefits * 12) – (one-time costs + all recurring monthly costs * 12) based on the great pre-work you have done

b. Independent of the format of your customer business cases, they are normally comprised of these elements: key assumptions and data input summary, projected cost-benefit analysis, projected cash flow and ROI, and expected benefits summary
   i. The financial evaluation should be represented in table and graphical format
   ii. The benefits should be clustered in categories like labor efficiency, operational efficiency, or benefits due to increased demands and profits.
   iii. The detailed financial evaluation is complemented by the intangible benefits
c. Iterate with trusted internal (e.g. sales) and external stakeholders (e.g. partners) to verify and generalize the analysis

4. Complement your Go-to-market approach with your customer business case as detailed in Sect. 6.2.

4.2.2 PYPR Dimension Items Details

See Tables 4.3 and 4.4.

PYPR defaults by software product manager type

Topic		Internal PM	B2B PM	B2C PM
Default dimension item weight		30	20	25
Criticality for PM		High	High	High
PYPR score	Low	Neither the user nor the buyer perceives your product as valuable to address their needs. You might have some arguments and a customer business case documentation, however the users and buyers tend to heavily challenge or ignore your assets		
	Medium	A customer business case is available, however there is obvious room for improvement as the customer business case is either not fully leveraged, outdated or not as impactful as you would wish. Another indication for medium PYPR score is that sales and marketing is either not knowing about the asset or not using the asset consistently within their processes		

(continued)

(continued)

Topic		Internal PM	B2B PM	B2C PM
	High	Customers cannot exist without your product. The benefits of your products are tangible and attestable for every target customer segment. The intangible benefits are accepted as a fact as well. Supporting teams in sales and marketing are consistently leveraging the customer business case insights throughout the sales and Go-to-market processes		

PYPR dimensions impact examples

Dimension	Direct impact example	Indirect impact example
Product viability	Pipeline development and product growth activities will directly benefit from a well-crafted customer business case	Less discounts impact product profitability
Product development		Product vision and strategy improve constantly the customer business case
Go-to-market/product marketing	Assets and enablement activities are supported with tangible and intangible customer benefits	
Software demonstrations and training	Storylines pick up insights from customer business case providing a consistent messaging to the customer segments	
The market/your customers		Customer community more motivated due to increasing customer base and perceived value of your product
Organizational maturity		People mindset improved as customer business case clearly explains the value generated for customers

4.2.3 Summary and Conclusions

Key Takeaways

- As product manager you need to understand executives, buyers and users to provide compelling reasons to all, so that they will consider your product over another. The customer business case is the asset that combines all this information in one document addressing the special needs of all personas.

- Customer business cases are normally comprised of
  - key assumptions and data input summary
  - projected cost-benefit analysis
  - projected cash flow and ROI
  - expected benefits summary
- Focus on the pains and gains of your customers and defer pricing discussions to the sales team
- Customer business cases are sensitive, semi-confidential assets as they explain clearly the financial and non-financial depiction of your product's value proposition. Therefore, in the wrong hands, this information can severely harm your product.

Last but not least, a special note for internal product managers. Some internal product managers argued with me, asking why you would need a customer business case at all for internal products. In my opinion, internal product managers are especially in a difficult situation. On one side of the extreme spectrum, a business case is not of interest to anyone in the organization as the delivery of the product or the requested new features for your existing product is called strategic, likely mandated by a Head of LOB,[7] or even a board member.

On the other end of the spectrum, a customer business case seems essential as any other investment in delivering or updating internal products is frequently questioned. Too often delivering internal product features are treated as isolated projects and not in product-mode. For internal products you are either advanced and cross-charge your internal customers (i.e. your product comes with a price tag), or the products are delivered without charging a license or subscription fee. In both cases, I would recommend doing your homework as described in the proven practice above and set the "to be expected" business value, the cost savings, time savings or extra revenue in relation to the costs to build the product. If you can provide a customer business case that clearly explains the benefits for your internal customers against the costs, your next investment budget is more likely to be approved.

4.3 Pipeline Development

B2B product managers especially need to understand the healthiness of their product's sales pipeline. Sales pipelines are the early warning and course correction system of your product's viability. If you have worked as a B2B product manager, you know that pipelines are frequently maintained tactically by sales teams. The numbers maintained are generally not the numbers that realistically reflect the pipeline value. Let's face it—sales people are smart, they want to stay in job and know the rules of the game.

[7]LOB = Line of Business, e.g. Sales, Marketing, Finance …

As a product manager, you need the ability to decode the sales pipeline. With some experience you will be able to derive valuable insights to steer your direct engagements in sales deals, understand structural issues and prioritize marketing activities responding to pipeline gaps.

The health of a sales pipeline can be determined by answering the following questions:

- Are there enough opportunities in the all stages to hit targets considering past conversion rates?
- Are there enough opportunities in the pipeline? For all target market segments, regions, etc.?
- Is the pipeline trailing, i.e. are opportunities rolling from one week to the next week, from one quarter to the next quarter without advancing in the sales funnel?
- As a product manager, do you know what opportunities are most important to focus on? Which one requires your attention and engagement, which ones can you ignore and consequently decline support requests?
- Do you have access to the sales pipeline information and is the data up to date?

Monitoring the product's sales pipeline and subscription renewal rates is not the daily business of product managers. Obviously, that's the domain of sales teams and whole sales operations or controlling departments. As a product manager, taking the time to understand the sales pipeline will help you to qualify the chances of success for reaching your financial objectives. With applying a proven practice, you will understand the pipeline dynamics, pipeline specifics, or deal conversion rates. Equipped with these insights, influencing sales in the right direction has much higher chances of success and judging whether your involvement is required will finally be possible.

As B2C product manager, you likely want access to a sales pipeline and similar insights, but the customer journey from Recognize to Evaluate is likely anonymous and not available in a clean and standardized sales pipeline for you. As a proxy, different data sources are used to track and evaluate the consumer buying decision process. The phases of the sales funnel are very much the same, whether a company or a consumer buys your software product. The difference really is in the speed of transition from one phase to another.

For example, think about yourself looking for an app to organize your shopping list: you likely recognize a need, you consider downloading or buying something, you evaluate different alternatives and select the product you like the most, you look for the best deal, purchase and give a thumbs up if you are satisfied.

Figure 4.10 illustrates the phases from recognizing the customer need to a purchasing customer that is happily using the product. The further down the sales process the smaller the number of businesses or consumers in a given phase. The final objective remains a happy and positive customer, no matter whether you are after likes from consumers or seek an official reference testimonial from a company representative.[8]

[8]More details about customer support and official customer references are described in Sect. 8.4.

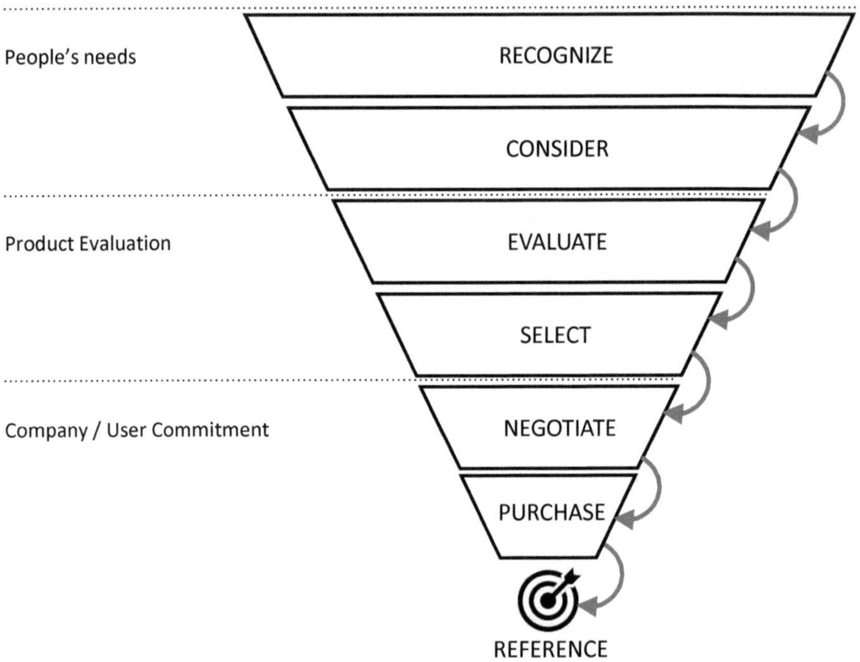

Fig. 4.10 Sales funnel phases depicting customer/buyer journey © Timo Wagenblatt 2019. All rights reserved

It is a good practice to track and calculate the conversion rates from one phase to the next phase. For example, you should know how many opportunities move from phase Consider to phase Evaluate as a percentage figure. Over time you will get valuable insights to structural issues in pipeline development early on and you will be able to forecast revenues, users and references directionally correct. That is a powerful tool for any product manager.

4.3.1 Proven Practice

You do not need to become a sales expert, but you need to understand how to read a sales pipeline and derive the right conclusions. Let the sales teams sell. As a product manager, you concentrate on whether or what you can do to support deal closure and renewals and how to increase traffic, downloads, etc. As THE product expert, you can have a tremendous effect, if your time permits. Your sales team will learn this quickly. They will try to involve you as often as possible if they think the chance of success increases with your involvement.

Therefore, I recommend checking frequently whether you must get involved. Consequently, only get involved if it is really required. Otherwise you will do someone else's job, just without any scale, and risk missing critical areas that really require your attention.

The proven practice shown in Fig. 4.11 will support you in shining light into the darkness of sales pipelines. A similar process likely exists for B2C product managers as well; however, the data source and key performance indicators are a different focus on the customer journey:

Fig. 4.11 Pipeline analysis process

1. Take note of the most important prerequisite: Where do you get reliable data that enables an early warning and course correction system? In best case you get data as a service from another team. Someone in sales cares about the underlying data even more than you do. Get the same data to avoid misalignments.

   a. B2B product managers focus on getting access to sales pipeline data.
   b. B2C product managers focus on getting customer journey data.

2. Analyze the most important pipeline measures and calculate the expected revenue for each sales funnel phase:

   a. Proven key performance indicators are listed below as a starting point for your tailored analysis:
      i. Basic indicators (as needed by customer segment, region, etc.):
         1. Number of opportunities
         2. Weighted and unweighted revenue total and for relevant timeframe, i.e. timeframe of target revenue
         3. Top x opportunities (x is determined by the time the team can spend on following up individually on opportunities)
         4. Trend (monthly, quarterly, yearly).
      ii. Advanced indicators:
         1. Linearity across the fiscal year
         2. Average deal size
         3. Opportunity last changed/consumer's last activity
         4. Delta between current and last data points

These are only a limited selection of key performance indicators. I recommend that you work on the ones you need and are comfortable with to get the insights you need for your context. Leverage what's available anyway and don't over-complicate the task.

b. Calculate the expected revenue directionally as shown in Table 4.5. Do this for each target customer segment:

Example: expected revenue calculation

Sales funnel phase	Opportunities	Purchase phase weight (%)	Average deal size	Expected revenue
Recognize consider	100	10	250 k	100 * 10% * 250k = 2.500.000
Evaluate select	20	50	250 k	20 * 50% * 250k = 2.500.000
Negotiate purchase	5	90	250 k	5 * 90% * 250k = 900.000
Expected revenue			5.900.000	

c. Some teams I worked with applied an even simpler calculation:
   i. Sum of unweighted pipeline divided by a conversion factor from the past, e.g. last year unweighted pipeline = 25 million, last year's revenue = 5 million, pipeline conversion factor = 25/5 = 5
   ii. At the beginning of the year: unweighted pipeline for the year = 30 million, expected revenue = 30/5 = 6 million
   iii. During the year: unweighted pipeline for the remainder of the year = 10 million, revenue to date = 5 million, expected revenue = 5 million + 10 million/5 = 7 million

3. Rate the PYPR dimension item based on the expected revenue compared to your revenue targets. This will become your base for defining your next actions:

   a. Note that your sales teams will likely convert opportunities from one phase to the next phase or consumers will purchase your product without your direct interaction. The question at hand is which of your actions are most valuable.
   b. List the potential activities and time-box your involvement as a product manager (i.e. maintain your balance with all other required activities out of the PYPR assessment).
      i. **Issues in People Needs—Sales Funnel phases**: Consider Product Marketing activities, targeted campaigns, product collateral and positioning improvements.

ii. **Issues in Product Evaluation—Sales Funnel phases**: Value, value, value—how can your product stand out and help your customer to "feel" the value? Storytelling or envisioning are techniques to help the customers at this stage. Basic tactics like customer business cases, trials, references and other risk-reducing actions might be a lever to support customers with their decisions.

iii. **Issues in Commitment—Sales Funnel phases**: Likely this part requires the least of your involvement. Your main concern in this area should be: How can we make it as simple as possible for the customer to purchase the product? Complex contract and ordering processes should not be exposed to the customer, whether your customers are businesses or consumers.

4. Prioritize and execute required actions based on impact and costs:
   a. Target the customer segment, the region or product with the best impact/cost ratio.
   b. Consider also opportunity costs in your prioritization, as for example the 60 min-presentation to a customer at the customer's location will include travel time and you easily "lose" a whole day. Time that you could spend more wisely and effectively, including meeting friends or quality time with your family.

4.3.2 PYPR Dimension Items Details

See Tables 4.6 and 4.7.

PYPR defaults by software product manager type

Topic		Internal PM	B2B PM	B2C PM
Default dimension item weight		0	18	20
Criticality for PM		X	High	High
PYPR Score	Low	No or very limited pipeline or traffic generated so far, less than 15% of what would be required to reach the planned numbers		
	Medium	Pipeline and traffic that is in a range of ±10% of required level to reach planned numbers		
	High	Pipeline and traffic with exponential growth and well suited to reach planned numbers		

PYPR dimensions impact examples

Dimension	Direct impact example	Indirect impact example
Product viability	Product Profitability improves	
Product development		Team Health increases sharing good news
Go-to-market/product marketing	Re-work assets and positioning, GTM plan adaptations, value selling	
Software demonstrations and training	Tailor to area of improvement, e.g. region customer segment, industry	
The market/your customers		Complete the funnel until the reference phase, ask for references as you give away goodies on the sales cycle
Organizational maturity	Process and templates	

4.3.3 Summary and Conclusions

Knowing your sales pipeline and understanding its dynamics is a powerful skill for any B2B product manager. These insights help steer your own sales efforts and engagement. You will become more credible if you understand at least the basics when talking and negotiating with sales teams. The same is true for B2C product managers, independent what kind of software product you manage, knowing the sales funnel and the decision phases, collecting the right information and using it in product marketing and development will support you tremendously in offering a better product and ultimately a more viable product.

Key Takeaways

- If a salesperson wants to involve you as part of the sales cycle with a customer, do your homework:
  - Check the pipeline entry, if there is none, ask for one. If the entry is too low, ask why.
  - Ask that travel costs be covered, if you are required to travel. Sales teams that do not pay for your expenses are likely not seeing the value of your contribution or that the deal can be closed.
  - Be tactical and use sales pipeline discussions to improve the PYPR dimension item by enforcing better data and realistic pipeline maintenance.
  - It is your decision to get engaged. You are the product manager. The ales team is asking for support. Make sure they really need you and only you

can support them. Saying no is a valid answer. It is hard to say no to support a sales cycle, but remember the opportunity costs. Evaluate whether you need to run for every deal or you can be tactical and spend your time on more important things for the product leveraging PYPR.

- Know and emphasize your role as a product manager. You are not a cheap and available Pre-sales, consulting, or customer entertainment resource.
- If a customer is of strategic importance, or if you hear good and reliable arguments from the sales team why you should support, you might still do it.
- Talk frequently to sales colleagues to understand their concerns and objectives. Understand how they operate and how they are organized.
  - Discuss your ideas and observations with account executives and sales teams.
  - Ask for current and special sales incentives, sales campaigns and focus areas.
- Review and validate the opportunity phase for the top x[9] opportunities, if you have the bandwidth pro-actively ask how you can support in deal closure activities.
- Understand the conversion factor for your product by continuously monitoring the sales pipeline.
- Monitor actual revenue and bookings versus the incremental pipeline.
- Trigger demand generation activities; align your marketing plan (e.g. refocus regionally, customer segments) based on your sales pipeline analysis.
- Re-use data, reports, dashboards and all you can get from controlling, portfolio teams and sales. Make sure they know that you are interested in their work and in their data.

4.4 Product Profitability

Products need to be profitable, perhaps not in the first two to three years, but certainly over time only very few unprofitable products and organizations will survive. Hence, no wonder that in many organizations, product profitability is the most important pillar defining product viability.

Product profitability is an important factor that affects your product sustainability and long-term success. This is true even for non-profit organizations, because commercial viability considerations are essential to ensure that your product will

[9] X being a placeholder for a reasonable number of opportunities that the team can handle; for example, we had a rule of supporting only two to three opportunities by one product manager at a given time.

continue to be available even without constant incoming funding from donors or governments.

Consequently, profitable products are probably the primary objective for most organizations. Generally, software product profitability compares the revenues from, for example, incremental license deals and new or renewed subscription revenues versus product-related costs such as development costs, cloud center costs, sometimes sales costs. As a product manager, you should have the hard-financial facts of YourProduct Inc. always handy and up to date. At the beginning of a product's lifecycle (for example, in the first two to three years), product profitability is sometimes not the north star for YourProduct Inc., and finding product-market fit with fast-paced learning and customer adoption are common proxies.

As a product manager, it's beneficial being fluent in financials. If you are not, you need at least a basic understanding of the key figures that matter in your organization to validate commercial product success. You need to understand what key figures matter to which stakeholders the most. As mentioned before, to calculate profitability measures you basically need two data sources: revenues and costs.

Sounds simple, but in many cases these data sources are not easily available. There is no alternative, you need to either get the data on your own by asking people who know or have access to these data, or you get a service from, for example, a central operations team. As you are getting access to the data, you need to verify whether the data is accurate and do a sanity check against the actual data points you know, for example, deals in which you were personally involved. Sometimes deals are missed, or costs are not properly recorded.

Product profitability data needs to be accurate as the data is key to all stakeholders concerned with investment decisions (e.g. founder, venture capitalist, management, bank or enterprise portfolio team, etc.). It is embarrassing to be in front of your executive team and they recognize data issues at glance. Even a little mistake will make all your data and maybe even you look noncredible. Part of accurate data preparation is also following the standard definition of revenue and costs applied within your organization; for example, do you report in euros, US dollars, constant currencies. Is cost of sales part of product profitability calculations, etc. If there is no standard definition, create one on your own and use it consistently going forward.

As a product manager, you are the most senior product person. You must always be prepared and have your act together. I recommend adding this task as frequent cadence into your daily business, like every Friday or every month, so product profitability assessment becomes a habit. As you analyze the data periodically and determine whether you are within range of your viability targets, you can leverage your insights in many ways (e.g. talk to executive in the language that matters to them, or steer Go-to-market activities according to regional needs or gaps).

One interesting trick of the trade is that you should understand your company context and commercial north star. If you consider for example your company's margin, your target should be delivering a product margin that is at least at par with this benchmark, over and above your agreed product objectives or business case numbers. Try to be better with your product and become a positive contributor to your organization's north star. With this approach you talk the executive's language, and you are likely de-risking future budget decisions.

Product profitability is the result of your business model. The Business Model Canvas (Sect. 4.1) covers all important dimensions, including revenue streams, cost structure, and value proposition for each target market segment. Remember to keep your business model updated or consider another canvas iteration if you see your product profitability off track.

In the next section, I will introduce a proven practice that allows product managers to monitor all aspects of product viability from an internal perspective. The Product Scorecard combines the three pillars of product viability: Product Growth, Product Adoption and Product Profitability, supported by PYPR dimension item Pipeline Development.

4.4.1 Proven Practice: Product Scorecard

Note that you do not need to become a finance expert, but you need to understand the basic financial measures of YourProduct Inc. and derive the right conclusions. The product scorecard is a proven way to get your act together. If properly set up the product scorecard will become a valuable resource for all your responsibilities within the Product Viability dimension.

1. Take care of the most important prerequisite: Where do you get reliable data that is required for keeping your product scorecard accurate and up to date? In best case you get data as a service from another team. Someone in controlling or operations teams normally cares about the underlying data even more than you do. Get the same data to avoid misalignments.
2. The product scorecard consists of the following components:
    a. Actual software sales revenue: actual/booked incremental perpetual license, subscription revenues.
    b. Planned software sales revenue: expected revenue based on pipeline analysis, for example, as described as proven practice in Sect. 4.3.
    c. Incremental product costs: Incremental costs that can be allocated to the product. Incremental means they are born by working on further improving the product. Depending on your product and your organization, these costs might include development, sales, marketing, etc.

    For a full product scorecard view, I recommend additional key figures for product growth and product maintenance/run analysis, which are covered in Sects. 4.5 and 4.6.

3. Determine which key performance indicators (KPIs) are appropriate for your product within your context. Table 4.8 lists common KPIs that you might want to consider. The descriptions or calculations might be different within your context. Clarify the standards and adhere to the existing ones or create a new standard and modify the example to reflect your KPIs.

Example: product profitability calculation

Key performance indicator	Description	Formula	Example
Actual license revenue	Total recognized software license revenue	–	200k USD
Actual subscription revenue	Recognized cloud subscription revenue	–	100k USD
Total actual revenue	All recognized product-related revenue	Actual License Revenue + Actual Subscription Revenue	300k USD
Expected revenue from pipeline	For current year, the outcome of the sales pipeline analysis. For past years, 0	See proven practice in Sect. 4.3	800k USD
Latest estimate total revenue	Forecast of total product revenue considering already recognized revenues and expected pipeline conversion	Total actual revenue + Expected revenue from pipeline (per year)	1.100k USD
Direct product costs	Recognized cost of product development	–	40
Indirect product costs	Sales Costs	–	30
Total costs	All recognized costs	Direct product costs + Indirect product costs	70
Latest estimate incremental profitability	Forecast of product profitability	(Total actual revenue − Total costs)/Total actual revenue	20%

Key Figures	2016	2017	2018	2019	Lifetime
Actual License Revenue	100	500	1.000	300	1.900
Actual Subscription Revenue	-	-	-	-	-
Total Actual Revenue	**100**	**500**	**1.000**	**300**	**1.900**
Expected Revenue from Pipeline	-	-	-	800	
Latest Estimate Total Revenue	**100**	**500**	**1.000**	**1.100**	**2.700**
Product Costs	300	300	300	40	940
Sales Costs	200	100	120	30	450
Total Costs	**500**	**400**	**420**	**70**	**1.390**
Latest Estimate Incremental Profitability	**-400%**	**20%**	**58%**	**77%**	**27%**

Fig. 4.12 Product scorecard example—product profitability

Figure 4.12 illustrates an example of a product scorecard focusing on (incremental) product profitability.

4. Check in with your product team and stakeholders as to the appropriate frequency for updating the product scorecard and reviewing the data (e.g., weekly, monthly, quarterly, annually).
   a. I recommend reviewing the product scorecard as part of the standard PYPR meeting cadence and derive the PYPR dimension item ratings accordingly with the team.
   b. As a product manager, you might monitor latest development more frequently and derive appropriate actions.

Obviously, the outlined proven process is only an example, but the sketched product scorecard might be a good starting point for your adaptation or you leverage the product scorecard going forward.

Section 4.5 outlines another component that should not be missed in any product scorecard. In addition, you might consider adding product services profitability to the product scorecard as outlined in Sect. 4.7, if your context benefits from implementing partner needs.

4.4.2 PYPR Dimension Items Details

See Tables 4.9 and 4.10.

PYPR defaults by software product manager type

Topic		Internal PM	B2B PM	B2C PM
Default dimension item weight		25	20	20
Criticality for PM		High	High	High
PYPR score	Low	Your product contributes negatively to the main profitability/viability indicators that are relevant for your organization. No or very limited contribution after two or even three years of market introduction. Examples are negative product margin or return on investment. In case financial measures are not important for your business model/organization, customer adoption would be a possible proxy, e.g. adoption significantly behind agreed business plan objectives		
	Medium	The company is not losing money, but your product's contribution is either marginal or close to the average margin/ROI of your organization. In case financial measures are not important for your business model/organization, your product has customers, but at par with expected numbers		

(continued)

(continued)

Topic		Internal PM	B2B PM	B2C PM
	High	Your product contributes positively to the main profitability/viability indicators that are relevant for your organization. Significant/recognized contribution of your product quickly after market introduction. Examples are positive product margin or return on investment significantly above company average. In case financial measures are not important for your business model/organization, customer adoption would be a possible proxy, e.g. adoption significantly higher than agreed business plan objectives		

PYPR dimensions impact examples

Dimension	Direct impact example	Indirect impact example
Product viability		Increasing profitability will have a positive impact on maintenance/run profitability over time (given your product works)
Product development	Profitable products ease future investments	
Go-to-market/product marketing	Faster selling of your product requires speeding-up partner and services enablement	
Software demonstrations and training		Pre-sales enablement could include showcasing product viability showcasing product strength
The market/your customers		Analysts are monitoring customer successes closely, adoption is key metric for improved analyst ratings
Organizational maturity		Accurate data to measure profitability leads to higher maturity levels and product manager satisfaction

4.4.3 Summary and Conclusions

Key Takeaways

- Product managers monitor and analyze product profitability and its components to determine how well the product is performing in the market and what's the contribution to the organization's key performance indicators.

- Product profitability determines your product sustainability and long-term success. Sometimes there is a grace period where learnings and adoption are in focus, but every grace period ends.
- Understand the north star performance indicator relevant for your product in your organization (e.g. license revenue of 5m per year, 100 live customers in two years, 1M annual contract value subscription bookings per year).
- Maintain your product scorecard and have it ready for your management and other stakeholders.
  - Know your actuals, discounts, average deal size
  - Know your latest estimate numbers and consider your pipeline insights as introduced in Sect. 4.3
- Get the operations team to get you the data, if not, you need to find a way to get the data.
- Update the product team and the stakeholders frequently.

4.5 Product Growth

Among the product viability key pillars product growth is next in line. Product growth is important for any product, whether it is a new mobile app, website, corporate IT product or enterprise B2B solution. Your product vision and strategy will be aspiring if it includes a component focusing on growth. For example, it feels great being part of a product that is growing faster than competition in terms of market share. However, product growth is a double-edged sword. The upside of product growth is so attractive that the downside of product growth is often overlooked.

As product managers, our main target is best described as sustainable product growth. Sustainable product growth depends on two key factors: product-market fit and positive net growth (Sequoia, 2018). Only products with a positive net growth of the north star metrics and high product-market fit are set up for sustainable product growth. Figure 4.13 illustrates the dependencies between these two key factors:

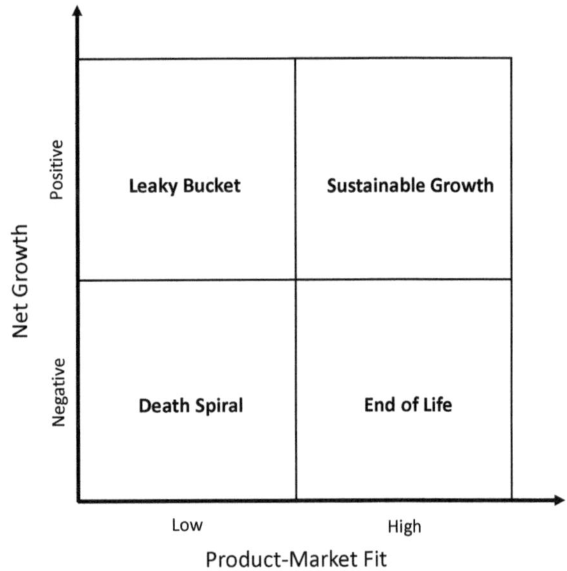

Fig. 4.13 Net growth and product-market fit relationships

The quadrants are self-explanatory. For further details, please check the referenced source that explains the four quadrants in detail.

There are some stumbling blocks regarding product growth that need to be balanced. Product growth needs to be planned and managed to be sustainable. YourProduct Inc. needs to be well-prepared for product growth, from a functional, technical, and organizational perspective. In that case, product growth needs to be treated as a risk for product longevity and continued success.

For example, if your product is growing too quickly and

- new users are churning in large numbers due to missing product-market fit, those users may never try your product again, and you will permanently lose the chance to make them active users (Sequoia, 2018).
- your product infrastructure is not laid out for millions of users or your product is not prepared for high-data volumes from hundreds of large enterprise customers. The positive effect of product growth will negatively impact your product's reputation to the extreme that it might be disinvested.
- your organization is not set up to service the great results of product growth, therefore, the product team will suffer big time and all future innovation will be delayed due to firefighting activities that keep the business going.

As a General Manager of YourProduct Inc., it is your responsibility to balance product growth as you understand and manage the trade-offs. You need to know and test the limits that your product, your product team and your organization can handle without harming the product's future.

As a product manager, you use many tactics for healthy product growth; for example, understand and communicate the expected quantity structure in terms of users, data volume, etc. to the engineering team as part of business model, product vision, and product strategy milestones. You need to balance and proactively prepare all aspects of the product to handle the planned product growth.

For example

- rightsizing Sales and Pre-sales support
- balancing professional services and partner ecosystem
- adapting your Go-to-Market planning and enablement programs.

Phases of product growth are phases of crisis for your product. The better you plan and prepare to handle these crises, the greater your chances to benefit from the tremendous upside of sustainable product growth.

Some product managers and product organizations are obsessed by product growth. No wonder growth hacking[10] became an industry buzz. Growth hacking might be appealing at first sight, but be careful that your product, the product team and the organization survives. Excessive focus on product growth improving the wrong north star key figures has hurt even large sequoias. Growth hacking frequently puts unnecessary stress on the product team and organization; therefore many product managers advise against growth hacking as a marketing or sales tactic for sustainable product growth (e.g. Johns, 2018; Gilad, 2018). Adding your growth strategy as a component to the product vision and strategy is generally perceived as being superior to growth hacking. Once more it is all about finding the right balance for YourProduct Inc.

McKinsey proposes the following three crucial questions be answered methodically in order to become successful at driving growth in your organizations. In addition, being deliberate, persistent, and disciplined in the way you go for product growth is important (Cvetanovski, Hazan, Perrey, & Spillecke, 2018):

1. Where is my growth going to come from?
2. How do I grow now and tomorrow?
3. How do I set up my growth engine?

Before answering these questions, there is one fundamental topic to be clarified and defined. Product growth comes from many directions, but what is the growth direction that matters most for your product and your organization. Product growth could be measured by market share, year-over-year revenue, sales pipeline, customer adoption (e.g. live customers, downloads, monthly active users, total active users, etc.), conversion, retention, or in short, product growth can be measured in any key figure that best reflects your growth aspiration and product vision.

As a product manager you need to align and drive the decision toward your north star measure, the only measure that matters for product growth. The north star measure might change for your product as part of your product strategy, but many companies retain their north star measure for a very long time.

[10]**Growth hacking** is a process of rapid experimentation across marketing funnel, product development, sales segments, and other areas of the business to identify the most efficient ways to grow a business (Growth hacking, 2019).

Eric Ries describes innovation accounting as "a quantitative method aiming to show if the company is working in the right direction" (Ries, 2011). Innovation accounting is a great tool for your bag of tricks in order to understand whether you develop new features growing toward your north star or you waste time and money building features that have no effect on the metrics that matter for your product and organization.

At the 2017 Product Management Festival event, Chris Long (at that time Product Growth Lead at Spotify) spoke on the topic, "How to Lose Your Hair and Grow a Product." Chris' message changed my view about product growth. Product growth should be focused on increasing the total value that your product delivers to your users and customers. And therefore, product growth needs to be the focus of everyone in the organization and not just the goal of a dedicated function in Marketing, Sales or Product Management. Chris explained a simple, but powerful formula: **total customer value = value per user × total number of users getting value**.

As you grow your product, the north star for sustainable growth should be growing the total value for your users and customers (if there is a difference for your product). That's ultimately customer centricity. Therefore, I would recommend picking your product growth metrics along this guidance. Revenue and profit are great (and essential), but both only come sustainably if your product delivers value to your customers. Think about the value your product delivers for each target market segment and each persona therein. I'm sure you already see the direct linkage to other PYPR dimension items like Product Vision and Strategy, Product Development Planning, and Functional Completeness or Understanding Your Level of Product-Market Fit.

It's the balancing act of getting more people to use products and building more value for users that probably best describes the essence of sustainable product growth. As part of the February 2018 PMF Connect Session, Chris further explained the challenges of implementing growth strategies. He consistently focused on defining the right north star and how to best structure the team to help achieve those aligned metrics that represent the "quality of the user experience," which is to grow every product that provides value (Long, 2018).

Generally, your product strategy needs to fit your product's lifecycle phase. For product growth this becomes even more important. Product growth considerations differ for software products that

- are in ideation or development phase, or are targeting an unproven market where the focus of the product team needs to be on reducing product risks by making sure that the product will be viable with a working business model. While product growth might be tempting in these early phases, uncontrolled product growth might add too much risk.
- are existing in a proven, vital market where the focus of the product team is to maximize the success and outperform competition.
- are existing in a declining or non-strategic market where the focus of the product team is to optimize the efforts with less investment of time and budgets.

Obviously, these products are likely not having product growth as a major component in their product strategy.

Note that focusing on product growth before your product has reached market fit is most likely a setup for failure. Before reaching product-market fit, the odds of being successful with YourProduct Inc. are dramatically against you in almost every dimension.

Consider that your product might have different parts, modules, customer segments; each could be a growth target that is healthy to grow at a certain point. There might be parts of your product that are ready for growth, while the whole product and organization is not yet ready.

As part of your product manager role, I recommend thinking about product growth as relative growth. Do not use vanity metrics but think about real growth indicators and analyze them in perspective with the market, competition and the likes; otherwise your north star might guide you in the wrong direction. Product growth should be reflected as part of your product scorecard. The example in Fig. 4.14 focuses on growth metrics for customer retention, deal sizes, market share and customer adoption.

Number of incremental customers and renewals	100	120	140	150	
Average Deal Size	1	4	7	7	5
Size of target customer segment	1.000	1.500	2.250	3.375	
Market Share	10%	15%	16%	15%	
Number of new live customers	40	50	60	70	220
Total Customers	100	220	360	510	510
Adoption Rate	40%	41%	42%	43%	43%

Fig. 4.14 Product scorecard—growth measure examples

Growth strategies can differ (as well as revenue or pipeline implications) by customer size (large enterprises to single consumer) and market size. Relative growth measures like year-over-year comparison or percentage shares are good indicators over absolute indicators like revenue.

Whether you define the one metric or a balanced set of product growth key performance indicators that matter for your product is not too important, as long as the metrics fit to your product and organization. As a product manager, you need to stay on top of practicability of the selected measures, balancing the impact of growth and keeping the focus on product longevity.

If your product and organization is ready for product growth, you need to pick the best growth tactics for your context to increase the slope of product growth. Product growth tactics could be new releases, addressing new market segments, or even introducing new products. The ideal pattern for sustainable product growth might look like Fig. 4.15, where each phase of growth is manageable and supported by the right timing for reaching the next level. Chris Long used a nice analogy for this sustainable product growth approach: use a ladder not a catapult to get from one level to the next. If you think you need a catapult, then the step might be too risky for your product in its current state.

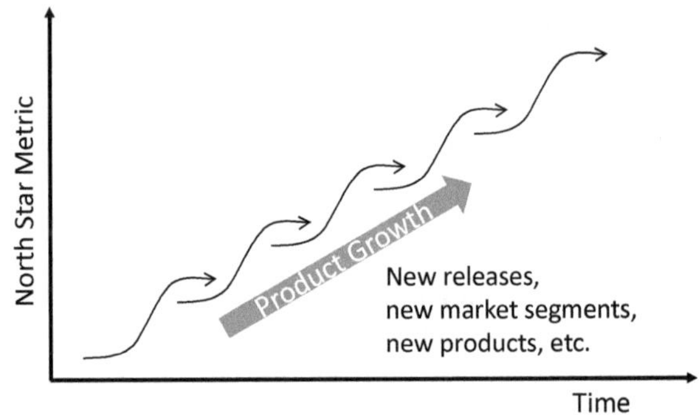

Fig. 4.15 Growth strategies © Timo Wagenblatt 2019. All rights reserved

4.5.1 PYPR Dimension Items Details

See Tables 4.11 and 4.12.

PYPR defaults by software product manager type

Topic		Internal PM	B2B PM	B2C PM
Default dimension item weight		20	20	20
Criticality for PM		High	High	High
PYPR score	Low	The net growth of your product is negative and you have not reached product-market fit. Another indicator of low product growth rating might be to not know whether your product is growing, in which direction or at which speed		
	Medium	The net growth of your product is either slightly below or above 0. Your product maintains the same level of customers and users over a period of time. "Leaky bucket" products are ranked in the medium range as well. For these products, in particular, you have to take corrective measures before they get burned by their success. Another indicator might be that your product has reached end of life and the focus might shift on maintaining status quo or on sunsetting the product to a transitioning to a new product		
	High	Your product has reached market fit and the product is growing towards your north star. The organization as well as the product is prepared for incremental growth manifested in a brilliant product vision and strategy. Everyone is focused on keeping the right balance of growth and associated risks. The team considers multiple growth scenarios and aligns on the best approach for the current product lifecycle phase and further product context		

PYPR dimensions impact examples

Dimension	Direct impact example	Indirect impact example
Product viability	Sales pipeline increases due to product growth tactics	
Product development		Team health deteriorates due to ill-paced product growth
Go-to-market/product marketing	Enablement needs to fit to growth strategy	
Software demonstrations and training		Brilliant product marketing videos can create buzz that needs to be handled
The market/your customers		Unhealthy product growth could lead to decreased product quality perception
Organizational maturity	Non-optimal organization, process, and governance issues are even more painful	

4.5.2 Summary and Conclusions

Key Takeaways

- Product growth is essential for any product; therefore, finding balance and the right timing for product growth keeps the risks associated with product growth under control.
- It is the role of the product manager to balance the efforts of the product team to continuously create more value for users and customers, while capturing the most value from the product. This balancing act requires a mindset of a farmer and a hunter, being obsessed by resolving user problems and growing against the north star.
- As a product team you need to align on the metrics that matter most for your product, and your organization.
- Growth hacking can become a great strategy to out-innovate or outperform your competition but pick your battles at the right time one the right foundation. List different product growth scenarios and pick the ones that work best for YourProduct Inc. growth. Only awesome products can sustainably grow.
- Product growth and growth hacking has its base in B2C Software Product Management. Itamar Gilad provides an excellent overview of a template for growth (Gilad, 2018). Product growth is an area where B2B and internal product managers can learn a lot. So, if you are not a B2C product

manager, leverage the learnings from your peers and adapt for your context. Your bag of tricks requires product growth tools, so you can pull them out when your product and your organization are ready.

4.6 Maintenance/Run Profitability

Product managers likely do not work directly on fulfilling maintenance contracts or maintaining the technical infrastructure of running software products. Nevertheless, monitoring and optimizing service and support activities are part of the holistic PYPR-based Software Product Management understanding. As a product manager, paying attention to the following topics is beneficial for the product (Kittlaus & Fricker, 2017):

- Consider, manage, and monitor supplemental product services for supporting and running your product
- Service and support resource management matching product strategy and success
- Analyze incoming service requests frequently.

The first bullet point might create some additional revenue opportunities, as all topics are a learning opportunity about your product. Lessons might include insights about where customers require and ask for support, whether YourProduct Inc. is properly staffed to handle the current and planned workload without sacrificing quality, and the likes. The incoming service requests especially require a structured monitoring and analysis process. As a product manager, you can learn about problems with product quality, performance, usability or functional completeness, when digging into the pool of reported issues.

As part of the Product Viability dimension, you need to understand whether the product is viable in terms of running and maintaining the product. Therefore, enhancing the product scorecard introduced before by maintenance/run-related key figures is a proven practice. Remember that a product scorecard is a proven way to respond professionally to any product viability questions or concerns. If properly set up the product scorecard will become a valuable resource for all your responsibilities within the Product Viability dimension.

Running your product in production-mode needs to be cost-effective and sustainable for yourself and your customers. We already covered the viability part for customers operating your product on their own within the customer business case (see Sect. 4.2). In this section, we discover the maintenance/run profitability for our organization. The following process likely looks familiar, but this time we focus on a different set of key performance indicators related to maintenance/run profitability:

1. Take care of the most important prerequisite: Where do you get reliable data that is required for keeping your product scorecard accurate and up to date? In best case you get data as a service from another team. Someone in controlling or operations teams normally care about the underlying data even more than you do. Get the same data to avoid misalignments. Note that you need to get or agree on a split of maintenance revenues from license (subscription) revenues. Furthermore, you need to define and agree about all costs in profitability considerations. Some might be simple, like infrastructure costs, but some are hard such as development fixes to a service request with adding or improving a feature. This is not about becoming an accountant, but it is necessary to consistently monitor and optimize the maintenance and run profitability for YourProduct Inc.
2. The product scorecard consists of the following components:
   a. Actual software maintenance revenue: actual/booked service and support revenues
   b. Planned software maintenance revenue: expected revenue based on support contracts
   c. Maintenance/run-related product costs: Costs that can be allocated to maintaining or running the product.
3. Determine which key performance indicators (KPIs) are appropriate for your business within your context. Table 4.13 lists common KPIs that you might want to consider. The descriptions or calculations might be different within your context. Clarify the standards and adhere to the existing ones or create a new standard and modify the example to reflect your KPIs.

Example maintenance profitability calculation

Key performance indicators	Description	Formula	Example
Actual maintenance revenue	Total recognized software maintenance revenue (including the split from the subscription revenue)	–	110k USD
Expected maintenance revenue	Total expected software maintenance revenue (including the split from the subscription revenue) in the current year	–	1.100k USD
Latest estimate total maintenance revenue	Forecast of total product revenue considering already recognized revenues and expected pipeline conversion	Total actual maintenance revenue + Expected maintenance revenue (per year)	1.210k USD
Actual maintenance/run costs	Recognized cost for maintaining and running the product	–	75
Latest estimate maintenance/run profitability	Forecast of maintenance/run profitability	(Latest estimate total maintenance revenue − Actual maintenance/Run costs)/Latest estimate total maintenance revenue	94%

Figure 4.16 illustrates an example of a product scorecard focusing on maintenance/run product profitability.

Product Scorecard: YourProduct Inc

Actual Maintance Revenue	10	50	100	110	270
Expected Maintance Revenue				1.100	1.100
Total Maintenance Revenue	**10**	**50**	**100**	**1.210**	**1.370**
Actual Maintenance / Run (e.g. Cloud Operations)	**75**	**80**	**85**	**75**	**315**
Latest Estimate Maintenance / Run Profitablity	**-650%**	**-60%**	**15%**	**94%**	**77%**

Fig. 4.16 Product scorecard example—maintenance/run profitability

4. Come to an agreement with your product team and stakeholders about the appropriate frequency for updating the product scorecard and reviewing the data (e.g., weekly, monthly, quarterly, annually).
   a. I recommend reviewing the product scorecard as part of the standard PYPR meeting cadence and determine the PYPR dimension item ratings accordingly with the team.
   b. As a product manager, you might monitor latest trends more frequently and determine appropriate actions.

Obviously, the proven process is only an example, but the sketched product scorecard might be a good starting point for your adaptation, or you can leverage the product scorecard as is going forward.

4.6.1 PYPR Dimension Items Details

See Tables 4.14 and 4.15.

PYPR defaults by software product manager type

Topic		Internal PM	B2B PM	B2C PM
Default dimension item weight		25	12	15
Criticality for PM		High	Low	Low
PYPR Score	Low	Costs of running your product and maintaining current status quo is significantly higher than the internal benefits (for IT products) or revenues (direct or derived). Your product contributes negatively to the main profitability/viability indicators that are relevant within your organization. No or very limited contribution after two or even three years of market introduction. Examples are negative product margin or return on investment		
	Medium	The company is not losing money maintaining and running your product, but your product's contribution is either marginal or close to the average margin/ROI of your organization		
	High	Your product contributes positively to the main profitability/viability indicators that are relevant for your organization. Significant/recognized contribution of your product quickly after market introduction. Examples are positive product margin or return on investment significantly above company average		

PYPR dimensions impact examples

Dimension	Direct Impact Example	Indirect Impact Example
Product viability	Maintenance and run profitability can be of significant impact to make or break any business case	
Product development	Outstanding product quality and great software design provide consistently better maintenance and run profitability	
Go-to-market/product marketing		Product positioning and product marketing focus on outstanding TCO
Software demonstrations and training	Feedback about training material and operations guides quality	
The market/your customers		Product quality perception correlates with technical support experience
Organizational maturity		Accurate data to measure profitability leads to higher maturity levels and product manager satisfaction

4.6.2 Summary and Conclusions

Running your product in production-mode needs to be cost-effective and sustainable. The maintenance/run profitably dimension item represents one of the key pillars of overall product profitability. While maintenance/run profitably is an important topic, stakeholders ultimately care only about total product profitability taking into consideration all aspects of the product.

As a product manager it is useful to understand your organization's context. As you know your company's margin, profitability, or any other key performance indicator requirements, there is one single thing that secures the longevity of YourProduct Inc.—to be at least at par or better with your product KPIs.

For a full product scorecard view, I recommend additional key figures that take into consideration product growth and product maintenance/run analysis that are covered in Sects. 4.5 and 4.6. Figure 4.17 illustrates an example of a product scorecard that combines all three pillars of product viability.

Product Scorecard: YourProduct Inc

Key Figures	2016	2017	2018	2019	Lifetime
Actual License Revenue	100	500	1.000	300	1.900
Actual Subscription Revenue	-	-	-	-	-
Total Actual Revenue	**100**	**500**	**1.000**	**300**	**1.900**
Expected Revenue from Pipeline	-	-	-	800	
Latest Estimate Total Revenue	**100**	**500**	**1.000**	**1.100**	**2.700**
Product Costs	300	300	300	40	940
Sales Costs	200	100	120	30	450
Total Costs	**500**	**400**	**420**	**70**	**1.390**
Latest Estimate Incremental Profitability	**-400%**	**20%**	**58%**	**77%**	**27%**
Actual Maintance Revenue	10	50	100	110	270
Expected Maintance Revenue				1.100	1.100
Total Maintenance Revenue	**10**	**50**	**100**	**1.210**	**1.370**
Actual Maintenance / Run (e.g. Cloud Operations)	**75**	**80**	**85**	**75**	**315**
Latest Estimate Maintenance / Run Profitablity	**-650%**	**-60%**	**15%**	**94%**	**77%**
Total Product Profitability	**-423%**	**13%**	**54%**	**94%**	**58%**
Number of incremental customers and renewals	100	120	140	150	
Average Deal Size	1	4	7	7	5
Size of target customer segment	1.000	1.500	2.250	3.375	
Market Share	**10%**	**15%**	**16%**	**15%**	
Number of new live customers	40	50	60	70	220
Total Customers	100	220	360	510	510
Adoption Rate	**40%**	**41%**	**42%**	**43%**	**43%**

Fig. 4.17 Full product scorecard example—profitability, adoption, and growth © Timo Wagenblatt 2019. All rights reserved

As you carefully review the product scorecard example, you might see that the number of live customers is not in line with the same growth rate as the number of total customers. Despite many reasons, there might be a hidden issue with professional services/consulting profitability that we briefly touch on in the next section.

4.7 Professional Services/Consulting Profitability

The last pillar of product viability is the ability to implement your product. Assuming professional services teams are required to implement and run your product then you should know and monitor topics like whether your product can be implemented as fix price projects; implementations require lots of rework, and professional services and customers require lots of handholding during go-live from the product team or conversely product implementations can be self-contained and smooth. The easier the implementation the better. The less involvement is required, the less time you need to invest and the faster your product receives positive references.

As a product manager, you need to understand the ecosystem and partner landscape. You need to clarify whether you focus on your own professional services team, go completely with a partner approach, or try a blended strategy.

Professional services profitability, as with all profitability considerations, requires attention on the two core components: revenue and costs. Professional services revenues are the costs that impact the customer business cases as discussed in Sect. 4.2. Professional services costs are a function of the number and time of people required to implement your product and their seniority levels.

I asked a longtime colleague from my product management career, Hans K. van Delden, Partner at PwC, to contribute his view on working with implementation partners, and the role of product managers in this interaction.

4.7.1 On Working with Implementation Partners by Hans K. van Delden, Partner, PricewaterhouseCoopers

One topic that deserves special attention is the often-challenging relationship between the product vendor's own professional services resources and the implementation partners'.

The business of implementing enterprise software can be lucrative, especially for complicated software products that have to be highly configured and/or tightly integrated into an enterprise's other corporate systems. The success of these implementation programs is critically important to the software vendor as a failure in the implementation will often reflect very negatively on the software vendor even if the software vendor is not at fault. For these reasons, a software vendor may maintain a professional services team that focuses on the implementation of its own software product. If the vendor's professional services team is large enough relative to the market size, it will be a direct competitor to the vendor's implementation partners.

This relationship—a combination of competition and cooperation—is challenging to manage for both the software vendor and the implementation partner. Product managers may not have the official role as the "Alliance Manager" within their organization; nevertheless, they have one of the most important roles to play in this complex relationship.

As a veteran implementation partner—having been on the good and bad side of this relationship with many software vendors—I'd like to share a few thoughts on how you can help with this relationship.

For starters, you need to decide what role you want your own professional services to play relative to your implementation partners. Do you want to focus entirely on building and selling software, leaving implementations entirely to your partner community? Do you want or need to own all the implementations of your software? Do you want to provide just enough professional services support to a few implementation partners to ensure implementations of your software are successful? Any of these choices (or others you might image) may be a fine choice for your business. Think through this decision carefully as it can make an enormous difference to the success of your product.

When engaging potential implementation partners, be clear with them on how you see the role of your own professional services relative to theirs. Being vague or even passive-aggressive will only waste time and cause frustration. Most professional services firms want to have healthy relationships with the software vendors they support and would prefer to have an open dialogue upfront with the software vendor about the roles each party can best play in the common interest you have in serving your joint clients.

I should provide a word of caution here. Don't push your own professional services unless you are certain they are highly qualified (i.e. they can consistently implement your product successfully). While the profits from implementation services can be tempting, pushing your own implementation services can backfire if you establish a reputation for poor implementations that then erodes your core software license revenues.

As with any relationship, the relationship between a product manager and his implementation partner will have its difficult moments. Nothing is more helpful in these situations than being able to trust each other. That means maintaining an honest, open dialogue with each other even when it's hard to do so.

Implementation partners have a responsibility to be good actors with their clients. You should not expect anything less. If you want to keep a good relationship with your implementation partner, don't expect them to serve you at the expense of their clients. This can become a sticky issue during the Pre-sales cycle, when an implementation partner is advising their client about your software product. The implementation partner has an obligation to be honest with its client about the relative strengths and weaknesses of your product. That's not a betrayal of trust. That's a good partner.

Both parties also need to be realistic about their position in the market and what that means for their relationship. Rarely does it make sense for either party to have an exclusive relationship with the other.

The software vendor will likely have multiple implementation partners. That is usually good for their business and good for their clients. Implementation partners have a responsibility to be competitive on their own merits. They should not be dependent on an exclusive relationship with the vendor to sell their services.

Similarly, the software vendor should not expect an implementation partner to advocate their product over others when that is not in their client's best interest. That is hard for a software vendor to understand (especially for sales people), but how you each handle such a situation is a good measure of the strength of your relationship.

4.7.2 PYPR Dimension Items Details

See Tables 4.16 and 4.17.

PYPR defaults by software product manager type

Topic		Internal PM	B2B PM	B2C PM
Default dimension item weight		0	10	0
Criticality for PM		X	Low	X
PYPR Score	Low	Costs of implementing your product are significantly higher than costs for implementing competitive products or the expected benefits derived from your product. Your product contributes negatively to the profitability measures of your professional service teams and implementation partners. Other indicators are the lack of implementation partners, despite your product requires implementation services and project escalations due to project delays or implementation quality issues		
	Medium	Professional services teams do not lose money implementing your product You manage to handle current demand. You have to approach partners, and partners are not approaching you. Product adoption and growth is not hindered, but also not positively impacted		
	High	Professional services are balanced for all target market segments, are a strategic pillar of product viability and driver of product growth and adoption. Professional services are enabled on latest capabilities and assets. Costs of implementing your product are significantly lower than costs for implementing competitive products or the expected benefits derived from your product. Partners are constantly approaching you to extend the collaboration. New partners are filling up the waiting list		

PYPR dimensions impact examples

Dimension	Direct impact example	Indirect impact example
Product viability	Professional services profitability can be of significant impact to make or break any business case	
Product development		Implementation partner strategy is part of the product vision and strategy considerations
Go-to-market/product marketing	Enablement, enablement, enablement …	
Software demonstrations and training		Train and enable all implementation partners on the latest product capabilities
The market/your customers		Analyst relations improved due to balanced implementation partner strategy
Organizational maturity		Process to deal with combination of competition and cooperation

4.7.3 Summary and Conclusions

Key Takeaways

- Implementation partners have a responsibility to be good actors with their clients. Mandate the same professionalism from your professional services partner (whether your own or external does not matter) than you mandate from your product team.
- Your professional services approach needs to balance regional focus, capabilities, reputation, and many more aspects. Think through this decision carefully as it can make an enormous difference to the success of your product. Your approach needs to match your business model and product positioning.
- A good professional services strategy can foster product adoption and growth. An unclear approach might harm both, although mediocre implementation is not your fault.
- The outlook on profitable implementation services attracts partners and your own professional service teams. Have a clear strategy for all professional services that might be required to implement, run, and maintain your product.

Professional Services Profitability can be interpreted as a proxy for how interesting your product might be for partners and your own professional services.

References

Cvetanovski, B., Hazan, E., Perrey, J., & Spillecke, D. (2018, December). *Growing faster than the market: Three questions the C-suite should ask.* Retrieved from McKinsey.com: https://www.mckinsey.com/business-functions/marketing-and-sales/our-insights/growing-faster-than-the-market.?cid=other-eml-alt-mip-mck&hlkid=4bfce93557c74a54adba861952671be9&hctky=10359493&hdpid=46c53923-e8c0-46f3-ae12-4939b91cb0b4.

Gilad, I. (2018, February 27). *The mechanics of growth.* Retrieved from Hackernoon.com: https://hackernoon.com/video-the-mechanics-of-growth-37ddca3e63f5.

Growth hacking. (2019, February 10). Retrieved from Wikipedia: https://en.wikipedia.org/wiki/Growth_hacking.

Johns, A. (2018, December 5). *Indispensable growth frameworks from my years at Facebook, Twitter and Wealthfront.* Retrieved from YouTube: https://www.youtube.com/watch?v=OxNrMeRme0E&feature=youtu.be.

Kittlaus, H.-B., & Clough, P. N. (2009). *Software product management and pricing.* Berlin, Heidelberg: Springer.

Kittlaus, H.-B., & Fricker, S. A. (2017). *Software product management.* Berlin: Springer-Verlag GmbH, Germany.

Long, C. (2018, February 15). *PMF connect sessions #3: Chris Long – Shopify – challenges of implementing a product growth strategy.* Retrieved from YouTube: https://www.youtube.com/watch?v=dSioeiPmyVw.

Maurya, A. (2010). *Running lean: Iterate from plan A to a plan that works.* Sebastopol, CA: O'Reilly.

Osterwalder, A., & Pigneur, Y. (2010). *Business model generation: A handbook for visionaries, game changers, and challengers.* Haboken: Wiley.

Ries, E. (2011). *The lean startup.* New York: Crown Publishing Group.

Sequoia. (2018, June 26). *Sustainable product growth.* Retrieved from Medium.com: https://medium.com/swlh/sustainable-product-growth-541fa786df01.

Strategyzer, A.G. (2019, March 1). *The value proposition canvas.* Retrieved from Strategyzer.-com: https://www.strategyzer.com/canvas/value-proposition-canvas.

Product Development

5

The Essential Part of Your Software Product Manager Role

This chapter describes in detail the Product Development dimension that represents "The Essential Part of the Software Product Manager Role." Without a product, Software Product Management is not required. The product is the reason for the department's and the product team's existence. In that sense, this PYPR dimension is truly essential.

In Sect. 2.2.2 I mentioned that I will detail the Product Development dimension, but I must put this statement in perspective. In the Product Development dimension, it is obvious just how broad the field of Software Product Management really is.

You might think that the Product Development dimension should be the main part of this book. In fact, many product managers spend most time of their day working in this dimension as they are passionate about their product. In fact, this chapter is the largest of all PYPR dimension chapters in Part 2 by number of pages, but it would be beyond the scope of this book getting into all the bells and whistles of software product development and accompanying development methodologies.

In addition, you can find valuable resources that detail every single important aspect of current knowledge, particularly in this PYPR dimension. There are entire books available for almost every topic of product development, software engineering and disciplines within their proximity. You just need to find out what works for you, your product team, your organization, and your product.

In my opinion, the other five PYPR dimensions are equally important, but are underrepresented in the current literature and communities. In this book, I will not discuss agile development, design thinking, requirements engineering, agile software engineering, backlog grooming, or estimation games for story points or value points, to name only a few topics that you might have expected.

In this chapter, I will focus on key concepts and proven practices that will help you as a product manager to be more successful. The focus will be on the role of the product manager, and how to leverage PYPR as a framework to instill a holistic product perspective—the main focus of this book. The role of the product manager is to lead the team to an aligned product vision and strategy, plan the product activities to achieve the vision and support the execution toward the product vision.

T. Wagenblatt, *Software Product Management*, Management for Professionals,
https://doi.org/10.1007/978-3-030-19871-8_5

Developing software or digital products is a challenging and complex task. Engineering teams have the aspiration to build the best product in the market—technically. Your role as a product manager is essential in orchestrating the noisy product development process. Yes, every software product development process is noisy. Things will go wrong—always. As product managers, we must maintain flexibility to react and adjust to the noise, a good attitude in convincing the product team to follow the strategy, and we are especially diligent in keeping the shining and guiding light of the vision in everyone's mind.

I propose to start with the default PYPR configuration shown in Fig. 5.1. As you leverage PYPR for your product, consider the recommendations from 3.3.

Dimension Weight 25 %		Dimension Weight 22,5 %		Dimension Weight 27,5 %	
B2B		B2C		Internal PM	
Dimension Item	Weighting Factor	Dimension Item	Weighting Factor	Dimension Item	Weighting Factor
Product Vision and Strategy	25,0%	Product Vision and Strategy	25,0%	Product Vision and Strategy	20%
Roadmap	15,0%	Roadmap	10,0%	Roadmap	22,5%
Product Planning	20,0%	Product Planning	20,0%	Product Planning	20,0%
Team Health	25,0%	Team Health	25,0%	Team Health	22,5%
Dev Product Quality	15,0%	Dev Product Quality	20,0%	Dev Product Quality	15,0%

Fig. 5.1 Product development: PYPR dimension item defaults

In this section I will detail the following PYPR dimension items[1]:

- **Product Vision and Strategy**
  The Product Vision and Strategy describes the "to-be-state" of your product, the re-imagined world as the result of all your efforts; why your product is compelling for your customers and the key principles for your journey. A well-defined Product Vision and Strategy includes an inspiring component to show the team that there are multiple, maybe unknown steps in the journey and operational guidelines or key principles acting as a decision-making framework (e.g. speed over quality, adoption over revenue, action over research).
- **Product Development Planning**
  Actively planning and preparing the backlog of work for development (e.g. requirements, product features, user stories, epics, etc.) is the home turf for most product managers. Balancing market requirements and customer requirements in an efficient and transparent way needs a clear decision-making framework. Everything shouts "Prioritize!" as business demands are always above and beyond capacity.

[1]The descriptions are short reviews from Sect. 2.2.2.

- **Roadmaps**
  As a product manager, you own the product roadmap, or better said, you own the product roadmaps. There are many different audiences and occasions for presenting your product roadmap. Frequent product roadmap updates are required as the basis for communication and customer plans. Therefore, we will deep-dive and look at examples of roadmaps that meet the needs of the various audiences as well as efficient ways to use this demanded tool.
- **(Internal View of) Product Quality**
  Generally engineering teams have a good understanding about product quality. They know the parts that are robust and the features and functions that technically might be a bit shaky. As a product manager you are THE expert of your product. However, you will likely not get to an understanding of the product quality to the extent an engineering team does until you start reading the code. This PYPR dimension item is about an aligned core product team perception of the product quality, not the customer's perception.
- **Team Health**
  A highly motivated, skilled, stable, and happy product team delivering high-value software capabilities is the holy grail and therefore the goal of your interaction with everyone in the product team and specifically in the engineering team. The basis for success is a trusted and respectful relationship with the team, which is outcome focused based on shared objectives. We will learn how you can improve or at least positively influence the chances of success when working together as a team.

The items that are part of the Product Development PYPR dimension are the most critical hard skills of product managers, according to most product management surveys. So, if you are already an expert in one or the other topic (which you likely are as a product manager), you might at least get a new perspective on each listed item in this secion. In addition, you can master the referenced great books for further details if the provided level of detail is not sufficient for you. For the PYPR dimension items you are not an expert yet, but this section will provide you a great overview and at least one addition for your bag of tricks for each item.

What product teams need, and what they want from product managers more than anything else, is to know that they are building products that users and customers really need to solve their problems. Product teams like to understand how their work is going to lead to value for the organization, because users and customers are using and paying for their product, which gives them direct feedback that their work and time was not wasted.

PYPR helps clarifying to everyone the elements that matter to achieve a viable product over and above the Product Development dimension. By doing so, PYPR clarifies Software Product Management's contribution to product success and longevity.

As part of the Product Development PYPR dimension, we translate problems into software requirements. We need to understand problems that are hidden in customer requests or in proposed, potential solution. We discover the underserved needs of customers and users and consequently derive target market segments and value propositions. That's all great, but there are always too many problems that we will discover, too many needs that are not served, and too many customer requests trying to improve the current product in their direction.

As a product manager, it is your core responsibility to balance all demand with the available development capacity. You need to lead the product team in the right direction and be decisive about priorities and the next most important things to do. I'm not referring to PYPR here, I'm referring to a process that consistently and transparently prioritizes along the journey from problems to a viable software product. Figure 5.2 illustrates the process beginning with user problems and underserved needs that need to be prioritized as everything cannot be discovered and clarified at the same time.

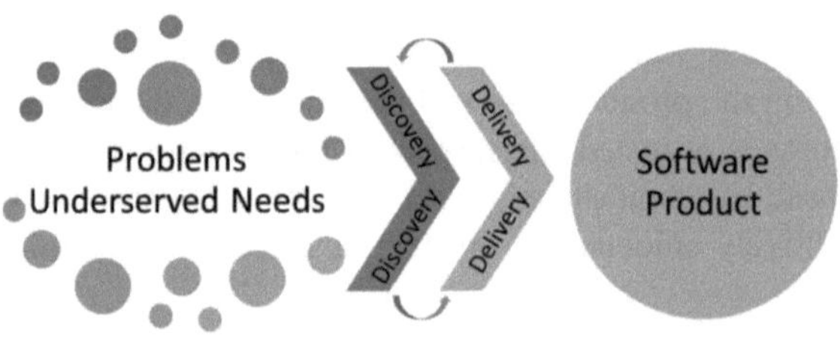

Fig. 5.2 Product development essentials © Timo Wagenblatt 2019. All rights reserved

The items that went through discovery need to be prioritized for delivery leading to a new or improved software product. Obviously, this is a very lightweight illustration of a very complex process that requires strong prioritization skills and leadership. As part of this book, I do not detail the ideation phase or the discovery phase, but these are obviously foundational steps for start-ups or organizations building new products.[2] PYPR kicks into manage a product closely before first release and already launched products in-flight.[3]

Figure 5.3 summarizes the scope of this section visually, the dimension with the highest weight of all PYPR dimensions across all product types.

[2]If you are ideating on a new product, and are not clear about the target market and what problems you want to solve, I recommend reading chapter The Business Model Canvas. In addition there are excellent books that cover these topics like (Cagan, 2018; Olsen, 2015; Ries, 2011) to name a few of the best.

[3]Product focus (https://www.productfocus.com/) calls this "in-flight" product management (Product Focus, vol. 15).

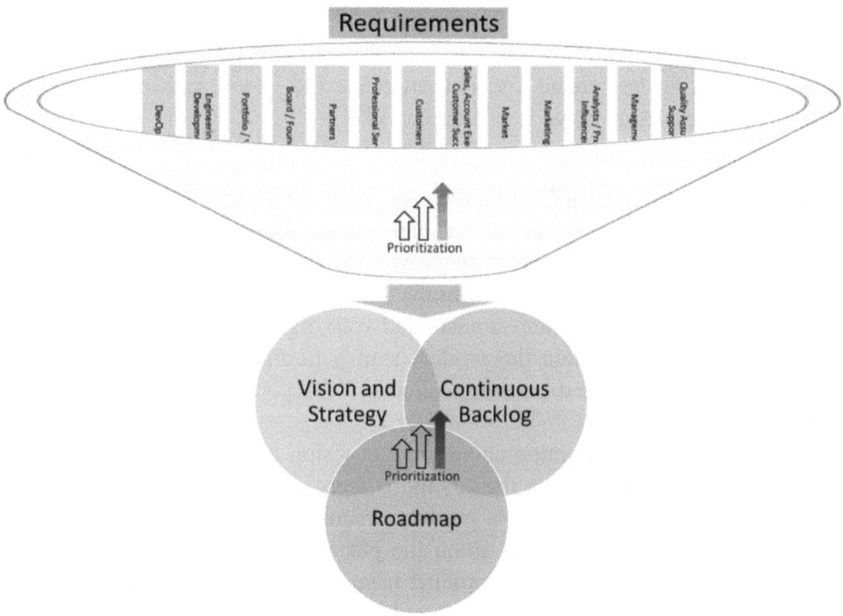

Fig. 5.3 The role of the product manager in the product development dimension © Timo Wagenblatt 2019. All rights reserved

This dimension requires a product manager that leads product development, provides transparency, and has clear communication paired with empathy. If I'm adding team performance and team culture to the mix, and not leaving out product quality, then we complete the Product Development dimension and the focus of this chapter.

Last but not least, I would like to mention one critical stakeholder that needs special attention in the Product Development dimension. In many organizations, product managers have to deal with one or even multiple development managers. The development manager is focused on maximizing engineering utilization and development quality. That's great, however, there is more. Sometimes development managers tend to be dominant based on their experience, formal authority over engineers, or because they have been employed longer in the company than you. Based on their context, they might have their own priorities and are used to running their own little pet projects on the side. Business impact and customer value are not priorities for these kind of dominant development managers.[4]

My advice would be to leverage your empathic superpowers that you frequently use with customers, but this time with your colleagues. Demonstrate your value with a holistic product understanding, fast and smart decision making, and showcase joint successes based on your understanding of your colleague's motivation and objectives.

In the next section, I will introduce the purpose and direction of YourProduct Inc, communicated via your product's vision and strategy.

[4]I acknowledge this is stereotyped and there are many exceptions to this outline.

5.1 Product Vision and Strategy

Good business leaders create a vision, articulate the vision, passionately own the vision, and relentlessly drive it to completion.

—**Jack Welch**

As the General Manager of YourProduct Inc., you are leading the product team and all product stakeholders. Product vision and product strategy provide a crystal-clear sense to your teams of why everyone is working on the product, why the product matters, who you are building your product for, the phases along the journey, and how value is derived for your customers and your organization. The product vision and product strategy explain the product team's north star. The north star is the foundation and the agreed common direction everyone in the product team is pulling toward.

I have a very strong opinion about product vision and strategy. In my opinion, product vision and strategy are the key ingredients of any successful product. Note that product teams or even whole product organizations that do not know where they are going will be surprised about the place they finally get to.[5] Vision and strategy are the foundation of the product team's effectiveness. A brilliant product vision and strategy has the potential to guide the team in every aspect. The engineering team might be super-efficient developing new features and functions, but if the end goal is wrong or not clear they progress in the wrong direction. Hence, the default PYPR configuration reflects the value and importance of product vision and product strategy.

Frequently, product vision and product strategy are mentioned as they would be one artifact. However, they are not the same thing. Product vision and product strategy belong together like Yin and Yang.

The product vision outlines the re-imagined world as the result of all your efforts. The product vision needs to be inspiring and motivational for the entire product team. Otherwise, the product vision cannot match the high expectation that forces you to wake up every day as the guiding light for you, the product team and the organization.

A compelling vision articulates how the world will be a better place if the product team succeeds with their product. Great vision statements require time and many iterations. A vision needs to explain how the work of the product team creates value for the target market segments. A vision should be customer-centric, simple to understand, constant over time, and easy to agree. Last, a product vision requires innovation capacity in a sense that the product vision cannot be achieved in only a few quarters.

A product vision has no value if it is not shared with the product team and all stakeholders. Use the product vision statement frequently in meetings, presentations and the likes. Remember the saying: "Once you get bored listening to yourself, people start to understand your message."

[5]And frequently that is not a pleasant surprise.

Many people think a product vision should be one of the first steps when building a new product. I would not argue with this. A product vision should be solidified during early phases, the very latest before the development of a new product (or a new release) starts.

If you have already built a product without documenting and sharing its vision, a little story will illustrate that it is never too late to start. A few years ago, I was supporting the handover of an established product from one development organization to my development organization. I asked for the product vision firmly believing that every product needs a vision. The product manager described the vision to me and after some minutes the development architect joined the conversation. He was wondering what we are doing and asked us to use the time for something more meaningful as the product had already been introduced to the market for some years. He piqued my interest enough for me to dig further into the topic.

We stopped the meeting and agreed to have another session the next day with a broader audience, including more people from the product team, professional services, and line-of-business and industry go-to-market teams. People were confused when I introduced the session with the objective being to write down the product vision. The crowd thought that we would be finished in ten minutes as they had already worked together for a few years on this product for a few years. The product manager started to explain his view of the product vision and after a couple of minutes the meeting turned into a complete chaos. While everyone understood the current capabilities of the product, the desired future state was obviously not aligned. In fact, some views were even contradicting each other. To keep the story short, we were not finished after ten minutes, but after four hours we left the room with a good first version of a product vision. We did a couple more iterations and, despite the fact that everyone initially expected the exercise to be a waste of time, the team still uses the product vision to this day.

Discussing, aligning and clearly documenting the product vision is a critical task of each product manager—it explains the product's DNA. I recommend including a product vision review in the product planning process and reaching several milestones throughout the year for review. Typical checkpoints are releases, GTM events, or extended product team meetings as part of the PYPR meeting cadence.

Driving a product vision toward completion requires a strategy. A compelling product strategy details the phases toward reaching the product vision. Product strategies describe the most important stages along your journey. While the product vision should be stable after a few iterations, the product strategy needs to be flexible enough to correct course and react accordingly to the unknowns in your journey. While discovering product-market fit, product strategies need to be iterated on and refined. Frequently minimum viable products (MVPs) depict early stages of product strategy. All product phases together depict the product strategy explaining how you plan to bring the product vision to life. For example, the product strategy stages could include new markets or lines of business you are interested in exploring, strategic technology themes, key customer requirements or a mix of business and technical topics.

As a product manager, you lead the team and facilitate joint discussion within strategy reviews to define and refine the right phases leading to frequent strategy updates. This is not a one-man show, it requires many hands and brains to deliver on the vision.

Together, product vision and product strategy ultimately have the purpose of providing clarity about the north star of YourProduct Inc. to the product team and the whole organization.

I have tried various product vision and strategy methods in my product management career. Elevator Pitch and Business Motivation Model worked best for me and the teams I'm working with. Both methods are described with a proven practice in the following sections. Independent of format and method, product vision and strategy need to be crisp and easy to understand, while not losing the power of inspiration. Elevator Pitch and Business Motivation Model have these traits. Remember that no one typically reads and fully comprehends a 20-page or longer document. In addition, as a product manager, it is your job to compile the vision and strategy and keep it up to date. As always there are more methods out there; if you learn better methods—share them with the community and put them in your bag of tricks or vice versa.

5.1.1 Proven Practice: Elevator Pitch

The Elevator Pitch method (Moore, 2014) is concise and easy to learn and it provides great value to the team who jointly creates the resulting product vision. If you have already done the Business Model Canvas, you will be able to re-use many of the insights to define the product vision statement and shorten this exercise as illustrated in Fig. 5.4. In addition, the Elevator Pitch Method and your product's value proposition share many things in common (see Sect. 6.1).

The set-up scenery is very tangible. Imagine you meet a senior manager in the elevator. You have 30 s to 3 min—the time it takes to get to the executive level—to convince the senior manager of the value and vision of your product. Do you have your crisp and compelling vision statement ready?

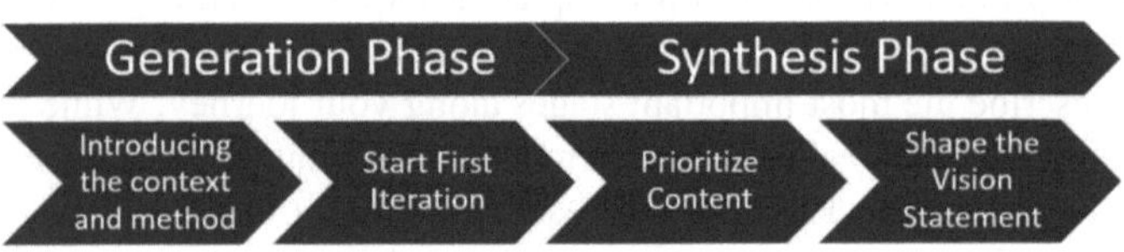

Fig. 5.4 Elevator pitch process © Timo Wagenblatt 2019. All rights reserved

1. Meet with the product team and invite stakeholders as well. Everyone who should know or considers the product vision should be represented in the workshop. As a starting point, share and review the existing product vision, if this is not your first workshop.

2. Welcome the participants and explain the brainstorming format and the iterative approach to answering the following questions:
   a. Who should buy or use the product?
   b. What value does the product provide to the customers?
   c. Which customer needs does the product address?
   d. Which product attributes are critical, differential and unique?
   e. What is the alternative option for the customer?
3. Introduce the Elevator Pitch template and write it on a whiteboard/flipchart:
   a. For (**target customers**)
   b. Who are dissatisfied with (**the current market alternative**)
   c. Our product is a (**new product category**)
   d. That provides (**key problem-solving capability**)
   e. Unlike (**the product alternative**)
   f. Our product (**describe the key product features**).
4. Start with the first iteration:
   a. Decide whether you need to organize the team into small working groups, as smaller groups tend to be more effective at arriving at a final vision statement (max 8 people/group)
   b. Everyone in a group writes answers on individual sticky notes for any of the template variables (5–10 min)
   c. Jointly insert the sticky notes into the Elevator Pitch phrase in each group
   d. Discuss the brainstorming results, and remove duplicates (max 20 min).
5. Consider a short break after the initial iteration. After a short break (15 min may be sufficient) the groups reconvene.
6. Prioritize and shape the elevator pitch itself. Consider the various ideas that are available from the brainstorming exercise. Try out different wordings and present their draft versions of the pitch.
7. The exercise is successfully completed when the group agrees on what the elevator pitch should and should not contain. Frequently the groups arrive at separate statements for different target customer segments. Don't be a perfectionist and aim for final wording. Use the team for quality time and assign one or two persons to follow-up for the final wording after the major decisions have been made in the exercise.
8. Share the product vision with the product team and all stakeholders and use it frequently in meetings, presentations and the likes. Remember the saying: "Once you get bored listening to yourself, people start to understand your message."
9. Don't forget to validate and update the product vision statement throughout the product lifecycle.

Example of a vision statement that resulted from an Elevator Pitch workshop:

For manufacturers selling goods through the consumer distribution channels (e.g. grocery chains, e-commerce platforms) that are dissatisfied with costs, speed and overall benefits of 3rd party data integration,
YourProduct Inc. is a strategic, open, enterprise-class platform for integrating 3rd party data that provides a foundation for Sales, Marketing and Supply Chain processes.
Unlike isolated, single business areas, or limited data source focused products, our product

- Provides master data harmonization for each product and location in the world
- Delivers 3rd party data logistics (acquisition, loading, tracking)
- Provides data quality management to assure data completeness, correctness and consistency
- Enables integrated analysis, insights and planning processes
- Allows partners building applications utilizing 3rd party data.

That's a vision statement example that can act as the guiding light for the product team and that is easily conceivable at the same time. The team can leverage the product vision statement for any topic from prioritization and product positioning to product marketing activities and more.

5.1.2 Proven Practice: Business Motivation Model

A more detailed approach to describe your product's vision and strategy is the Business Motivation Model. The Business Motivation Model (BMM) is an OMG Specification (OMG, 2019) for support of business decisions about how to react to a changing world. The Business Motivation Model specification provides a scheme or structure for developing, communicating, and managing business plans in an organized manner for organizations. As product managers, you can leverage the BMM to detail the vision and strategy of YourProduct Inc.

The BMM is much broader than outlined in this proven practice. If you are interested in more details, I recommend visiting the OMG homepage and reading the latest BMM specification. I will explain only two of the many BMM elements:

- **Ends**: What (as opposed to how) the product wants to accomplish. Ends broadly describe the product's purpose as vision, goals, and objectives.
- **Means**: How the product team intends to accomplish its ends. Means describe general action plans as mission, strategy, and tactics.

The ends and means elements of the BMM are paired on three levels as illustrated in Fig. 5.5. The ends describe the purpose of your product with increasing detail from vision to goals to objectives. The means describe the action plan to achieve the product purpose with increasing detail from mission to strategy to tactics.

Fig. 5.5 Elements and levels of the business motivation model © Timo Wagenblatt 2019. All rights reserved

In Software Product Management, most people talk only about vision and strategy. As shown in Fig. 5.5 the BMM details product vision and strategy by adding the element of mission on the level of the vision and the element of goal at the level of strategy. Action plans can be changed without changing the purpose of your product, however vice versa is likely not advisable.

The process of getting to a BMM for YourProduct Inc. follows the same pattern as described in the proven practice for the Elevator Pitch. You meet with the product team and invite all required stakeholders. You introduce the context of the workshop and the fundamentals of BMM. You generate the first ideas for each BMM element and use the work results to prioritize the best content to shape the BMM for YourProduct Inc. Several iterations might be required and a frequent review of the BMM results should be part of your product meeting cadence.

Instead of focusing solely on the vision statement, the team details the vision statement by considering all elements shown in Fig. 5.6.

Ends	Definition	Means	Definition
Vision	Describes a state you would like to achieve with YourProduct Inc in the future. The vision needs to be inspirational and aspirational to become a cornerstone for your stakeholders motivation.	Mission	The mission communicates what YourProduct Inc. does to achieve the vision. A mission outlines the ongoing operational activity on the level of the product vision. The mission describes what the product team is or will be doing on an ongoing basis.
Goal	A goal amplifies a vision as it indicates what must be achieved on a continuing basis to effectively move towards the product vision. A goal is a statement about a state or condition of YourProduct Inc. A goal can be reached through appropriate strategies.	Strategy	A strategy represents the essential course of action to achieve ends (goals in particular). A strategy usually channels efforts towards those goals. The strategy statement communicates and details how you plan to achieve the goals to deliver on the product vision.
Objective	An objective is a statement of an attainable, bound, and measurable target that you and the product team want to achieve towards delivering on the product's goals.	Tactic	A tactic is a course of action that details the strategies. A tactic implements strategies . Tactics generally channel efforts towards objectives.

Fig. 5.6 Elements and levels of the business motivation model © Timo Wagenblatt 2019. All rights reserved

From my experience, I recommend focusing on each level, one after the other. Start with vision and mission, and then derive goals and strategies as a second step. Level three, the level of objectives and tactics, is frequently not required to describe the product vision and strategy. However, I listed level three for the following reasons:

- Objective and tactic are elements of the standard OMG specification
- Objectives can be easily confused with objectives as defined in the OKR framework, which I will briefly introduce in Sect. 9.1.
  - If you are familiar with OKR, note that an objective in BMM is rather a key result in the OKR framework.
  - Consequently, a goal in BMM represents the objective in OKR. If you are not familiar with OKR, check out the introduction in Sect. 9.1.

Consider the BMM for your bag of tricks, if your product team, your stakeholders, or your organization require a detailed and structured way of defining the product vision and strategy. Consider the Elevator Pitch if you require less details and a more lightweight approach is sufficient. I had good experiences with both practices.

5.1.3 PYPR Dimension Items Details

See Tables 5.1 and 5.2.

Table 5.1 PYPR defaults by software product manager type

<table>
<tr><th colspan="2">Topic</th><th>Internal PM</th><th>B2B PM</th><th>B2C PM</th></tr>
<tr><td colspan="2">Default dimension item weight</td><td>20</td><td>25</td><td>25</td></tr>
<tr><td colspan="2">Criticality for PM</td><td>High</td><td>High</td><td>High</td></tr>
<tr><td rowspan="3">PYPR score</td><td>Low</td><td colspan="3">No up-to-date, clearly documented product vision nor a product strategy that is shared with all stakeholders. Stakeholders might know the product vision and strategy, but might not share a common understanding or agree to its direction. They were not asked or showed no interest to contribute. Consequently the product vision is not considered in most product decisions like Go-to-market assets, value propositions, demo, sales positioning, backlog prioritization, etc.</td></tr>
<tr><td>Medium</td><td colspan="3">Product vision and strategy is available, but not all stakeholders share a common understanding or agree to its direction. Some product decisions consider the product vision and strategy as an important factor</td></tr>
<tr><td>High</td><td colspan="3">Up-to-date, clearly documented product vision and strategy that is shared with all stakeholders. All stakeholders know the product vision and strategy and share a common understanding. They were asked and showed interest to contribute. Consequently the product vision is considered in all product decisions like Go-to-market assets, value propositions, demo, sales positioning, backlog prioritization, etc. All product decisions and product development work targets to either get closer to the product vision or reduce the risk of activities in the same direction</td></tr>
</table>

Table 5.2 PYPR dimensions impact examples

Dimension	Direct impact example	Indirect impact example
Product viability		Stronger value proposition due to clear vision and strategy
Product development	Product vision and strategy is part of this dimension and directly impacts the rating due to its high weighting	Product planning is driven by product vision and strategy
Go-to-market/product marketing		Go-to-market assets benefit from the clear guidance of the product vision and strategy
Software demonstrations and training		Software demonstrations underlining product vision
The market/your customers	Thought leadership could be based on strong product vision and strategy	Strong vision and strategy attracts the market and keeps your current customers engaged
Organizational maturity	Product management vision and strategy reflects product vision and strategy	

5.1.4 Summary and Conclusions

The product management manifesto nicely summarizes your responsibilities as the General Manager of YourProduct Inc.: "I have a strong vision for my products and have developed winning strategies that align with my company's goals to ensure that our investments of time, money and energy are well-spent." (Product Management Manifesto, 2019).

Key Takeaways

- Discussing, aligning and clearly documenting the product vision is a critical task of each product manager—it explains the product's DNA.
- Product vision and strategy usually need to be validated and updated several times during a product's lifecycle.
- A product vision needs to be future-looking, inspiring, comprehensive and ambitious. A product strategy outlines how to realize the product vision.
- Everyone in the product team should buy into product vision and strategy. Vision and strategy guide all efforts but leave enough room for creativity and autonomy. Vision and strategy align everyone's focus.
- Less is more and therefore contains only information critical for the success of the product.
- Relentless execution ultimately determines whether the vision becomes a reality.
- Adjust vision (e.g. if you need to pivot) and strategy (if required to go faster toward the vision) and keep both up to date.

5.2 Product Development Planning and Review

Planning, preparing, and reviewing the work for product development is the home turf of the product owner role. As discussed previously the product owner is either a peer very close to your heart or the name of your role as part of the agile development process within your product team. Discussing all details of product development planning or getting an in-depth explanation of the various frameworks, tools and methods is beyond the scope of this book.

In fact, many books are required to cover the topic completely. The good news is that there are already excellent books available for almost every topic in product development. Books that are dedicated to single aspects of product development planning. Instead of boring repetition, I will reference the books I can recommend for further details. Nonetheless, I will explain some key concepts and proven practices that I find essential for this PYPR dimension item. Otherwise this book would not be complete.

Product development planning is the process of crafting and preparing a plan with associated actions to

- move as a team toward product vision along the product strategy
- satisfy the information needs of the product team and all stakeholders
- track progress of product development.

Product development planning starts with gathering requirements from all stakeholders. Requirements are coming from everywhere. Stakeholders either approach you directly, or requirements come to you via user reviews, your support portal, interviews, or in-app feedback to name a few alternative channels. Typical classifications of requirements are functional, non-functional, business, or user requirements. Requirements gathering is an ongoing process that needs to be properly managed. As a product manager, you should be in control or at least have an overview of all channels for requirements gathering. You might want to limit the official channels and set up one central repository for all relevant product requirements. Otherwise requirements gathering might be overwhelming and you run the risk of missing important requirements.

Collecting requirements is the first basic step, but an endless list of requirements leads to nowhere. As product managers, we need to focus on getting quality into our requirements. Analyzing requirements means understanding the market problem (i.e. the problems of the customers in your target market segments), behind the raised requirement. Requirements need to be classified and qualified, for example, some requirements might not be valid for your product, outside the product vision, or the market problem is not clear. Product development planning benefits from qualified requirements in many ways. In the next section I will introduce proven practices, particularly the topic of qualifying user requirements.

Once you have a qualified list of requirements, you can start to prioritize product development. Requirements prioritization considers various aspects that benefit from the skills of all in the core product team. I will introduce various prioritization techniques in the next sections, and they all have in common that a product manager should not prioritize alone in isolation. Take into consideration the knowledge of your product team and benefit from higher engagement levels.

As with all plans, the product development plan needs to be communicated and tracked. A plan that is not communicated is equal to not having a plan. The same is likely true for tracking plan progress. The process of product development planning and reviewing includes product plan communication for all relevant audiences (e.g. management, customers, media) and agreed principles for progress tracking (e.g. sprints, discovery phases, releases).

In summary, product development planning provides the following outcomes for the product team and stakeholders:

- Understanding the target market problem space and gathering the respective requirements
- Prioritizing requirements management and product backlog
- Constructing a product roadmap
- Validating product vision and strategy.

Managing requirements and planning product development are not one-off tasks. In fact, as a product manager you must deal with an ongoing stream of incoming requirements, including changes and additional insights along the way, that must be managed throughout the development cycle. The same is true for product plan communication and product progress tracking as illustrated in Fig. 5.7.

The second step of requirements analysis focuses on discovering the underlying problem and validating the best solutions for this problem. As a product manager, you need to prioritize which requirements are important and should be further explored. Only the problems that are worth being resolved are the next step's focus. Marty Cagan describes this process as "Dual-Track Agile" (Cagan, Dual-Track Agile, 2019a, b), one track focusing on discovery and the other one on delivery and both requiring proper prioritization.[6]

Fig. 5.7 Product development planning process © Timo Wagenblatt 2019. All rights reserved

[6]If you are idea ting on a new product, and are not clear about the target market and which problems you want to solve, I recommend reading Sect. 4.1. In addition there are great books covering these topics like (Cagan, 2018; Olsen, 2015; Knapp et al. 2016; Ries, 2011) to name a few of the best.

In the next sections, I focus on the topics I consider most important in the product development dimension plus some tips and proven practices that might be beneficial. I will introduce the following concepts and proven practices:

- Writing and organizing user-centered requirements
- Working with backlogs which is valid for discovery and delivery backlogs
- Conducting product development planning workshops
- A proven process for structuring requirements managing complexity into consumable pieces in Sect. 5.3
- Various prioritization techniques with focus on
  - The Prioritization Board in Sect. 5.4
  - The Kano Model—Adding Empathy to Requirements in Sect. 5.5
- Dealing with product roadmaps in Sect. 5.6.

For product managers, Product Development Planning and Review, or in short, Product Planning consists not "just" of planning and tracking activities. Obviously, there is a lot of execution required, as you work with user stories, use cases, user story maps, and personas, showcase your domain knowledge, create roadmaps, and make decisions, including big ones concerning vision and strategy and smaller ones as part of your daily business of backlog prioritization.

5.2.1 Proven Practices[7]: Requirements, Personas, User Stories, Use Cases, and User Story Map

The headline of this section might be slightly misleading. The important part of this section is not the proven practices, tools and methods listed in the headline. The main topic is to understand and communicate the requirements that will solve a customer problem before the coding starts. In my experience the format to capture and communicate these requirements is secondary, but some practices have proven to deliver better results than others.

Requirements, personas, actors, user classes, user stories, use cases, and user story maps are common concepts, but sometimes people get either confused or very dogmatic, and sometimes both, about these concepts. As a product manager and for the product team, the main focus is to build the right functionality based on a clear understanding of problems and underserved user needs.

As a product manager, you must satisfy the information needs of the product team or enable the team to gather the required information on their own. The key questions to be answered include[8]:

[7]For more details I recommend some great books, but there are so many great resources that these are just a food starting point. Find the ones that resonate best with your needs.

[8]The Value Proposition Canvas is a great tool structuring this part (see Sect. 4.1).

- What pain are we solving with our product, what gain does the user and customer get?
- How are the users and customers addressing the pain today?
- What can we possibly do to ease the pain in the future by providing a better option to users and customers?

There are various strategies to understand the pain points, problems and underserved needs. Generally, the closer you are to the source, the real user of the product, the better.[9] For example, if you want to learn more about how to play football, you can read a document written by a person that probably interviewed some football players, or you can talk to a guy that knows someone who plays football, or you read a book about football, or you talk to a guy who plays football, or you take a ball and play with your friends. Which strategy do you prefer to gain the most insights?

As a product manager, you need to understand the problem domain. Therefore, you need to get in touch with existing as well as future users and customers, interview them, listen to them, and capture everything relevant that can help the product team to better understand the problem to be solved. If possible, you might even shadow users for some time. In my experience, the part of requirements gathering and capturing domain knowledge is good organization and structure. Otherwise the team might not see the wood for the trees anymore, drown in tons of ideas, information snippets, solution approaches, and a variety of document formats, and that's not including all the information available to build an outstanding product.

Product managers must derive insights from market inputs, not simply observe them. Therefore, product managers and the product team have to think, reflect on the inputs and learnings, and validate their hypothesis. That part is not mentioned often, but you must think about the best solution now and then. Many people tell you to see customers all day, but that is only a starting point. It is important to set some time aside for thinking and reflecting on user problems. Some people like to think as a team, discuss and brainstorm in a group setup; I prefer some hours to reflect on my own. Find and agree to the best working model that fits you and the product team.

As described in a simplified way before, product managers gather requirements to solve stakeholder problems, express them as user stories and add them to a central repository. Let's structure and examine this statement in the remainder of this section.

As a product manager you should start by falling in love with the problems you are solving for your target market segments (Sankaran, 2019). In short, all you need to do is focus on the problem, transform the problem into small pieces and prioritize

[9]Note that not all users and customers are equally a great source for understanding and clarifying requirements. Barry Boehm defines the necessity of finding and recruiting CRACK users that are collaborative, representative, authorized, committed, and knowledgeable (Boehm & Turner, 2004) for this task.

them. I describe the part of transforming a problem into smaller pieces and prioritizing them in Sect. 5.3.

Let's focus on the problem first as most people already struggle with capturing the basic user problems. Frequently, problems are mixed with potential solutions, before the underlying problem is even discovered and clearly understood. I recommend the following structural approach to describe a problem (SkillsYouNeed, 2018).

Document the goal and barrier components of the problem. The goal is best described in the format "I want to…" and the barrier can be described straightforward as "but…". For example, I want to communicate the user requirements to the product team, but I don't know how to best organize and communicate them most efficiently. That's the starting point: someone (a user) has a problem.

As product managers, we analyze the problem, understand the user needs, and derive user requirements from the problem. For example: I want to organize and communicate user requirements to the product team. That's a clearly stated requirement, but we need to clarify what "I" means, who has the requirement that my product should cover to resolve the problem?

There are multiple proven practices to describe users. I will introduce the most common ones (user classes, actors, personas) that describe the people who are actually using the product:

- **User Classes**: Classification of a distinct group of users for a product. User classes can be prioritized by importance for the product. User classes can be refined by any attribute (e.g. age, skill level, frequency of usage, job function).
- **Actors**: Actors are more abstract than user classes. Note the difference between user classes and actors. Sometimes this differentiation becomes important, though the actor (e.g. approver) is the same for various user classes; different user classes (manager, administrator) may have different requirements for the product.
- **Personas**: Personas are fictional characters developed to represent different users of your product. A persona is an aggregated user profile of a specific actor based on user research. The persona description contains characteristics that are relevant in terms of the usage of the product such as goals, pain points, behaviors, and sometimes a background history and a name to bring them to life. Working with personas makes the requirements clarification and discovery process more tangible. Personas help to envision how to satisfy the actor's needs with the product.

The idea behind user classes, actors, and personas is creating emphasis on the user to enable the product team to make better design decisions. Building on the short example from above: A product manager wants to organize and communicate user requirements to the product team.

As a product manager, it is your responsibility to understand the dedicated users of your product. The tools described above should be part of your bag of tricks as they will help you to communicate the characteristics, diversity, and importance of your target users.

Remember, the best way to understand your dedicated users better is talking and listening to your users. Get as many exposure hours as possible for yourself and for the product team with real users that are interacting with the product in any form (Spool, 2019). The interaction might be in early phases with wireframes or mock-ups, during sprint testing, or later with usability assessments of the finished development.

One more thing on personas; is there really any interest in whether the persona is 37 years old, has two kids, a cat, and a black car? Yes, it makes the persona more real, more tangible, but spend your creativity more on the hooks for each persona (e.g. Eyal, 2014; Startup Grind, 2018):

1. What internal trigger is the product addressing?
2. What external trigger gets the user to the product?
3. What is the simplest behavior in anticipation of reward?
4. Is the reward fulfilling, yet leaves the user wanting more?
5. What "bit of work" is done to increase the likelihood of returning?

Product teams need to understand the users of their products and build hooks to retain their users. These are essential requirements for B2C products, but B2B and internal products will also benefit from this reasoning.

That's it on users, let's shift gears and look at requirements.

There are multiple proven practices to describe requirements. I will introduce the most common ones (user story, user story mapping, use cases, and use case model) that describe what users require the product to do:

- **User Story** (e.g. Patton, 2014; Cohn, 2004; Leffingwell, 2010): A user story is a brief description of desired functionality from the perspective of a persona. As introduced before, users share ideas, solutions, needs, requirements, and problems via various channels and formats. Product managers gather these requirements to solve these problems, express them as user stories and add them to a central repository called backlog.[10] Large user stories that need to be broken down into consumable user stories are called epics. User stories should be detailed enough for the product team to start working on the requirement that follows from the user story. User stories are a simple tool to understand, describe, plan, and execute the product development. Note that user stories are not requirements, some people confuse this. A user story serves as an artefact for further conversations with the product team and the customers. User story details are continuously enriched and updated over time and need to be ready just before or further clarified during development.

[10]Due to the amount of user stories, the backlog works best with a hierarchical structure that is discussed in the next section.

- **The three C's of User Stories**: Remind yourself about the three C's as you work with user stories. User stories are written on a **c**ard (i.e. user stories are brief) that captures the intent of the story. The user story depicts the basis for a **c**onversation to further work out the details (i.e. user stories need additional documentation) of the intent with the requirements donor. The last C stands for the **c**onfirmation that the objectives of the user story have been reached. That's a proven practice to work with user stories in a nutshell.
- **Acceptance Criteria**: Acceptance criteria define the boundaries of a user story, and are required to confirm that a story is completed and working as intended. Like the whole user story, acceptance criteria must be expressed clearly and in simple language.
- **Format/Template**: The most common template for writing user stories is: As a *<persona>*, I want to *<need/activity>* so that *<reason/business value>*.
  The simple story format helps the product team to learn how to distill the important parts of a product requirement by identifying who, what, why, etc. The business value especially indicates importance to the persona and helps the product team to understand how they are providing value to their users.
  Writing detailed user stories also helps with understanding the business process and the feature. The Gherkin format (e.g. Williams, 2018 or Hiptest, 2018) is one of the best formats to write quality user stories. As a product manager, you need to write in an understandable language and format for your target audience (product team, customers).
- **INVEST in user stories**: It is common sense that well-written user stories follow the INVEST model (Wake, 2018):

  I—Independent from each other
  N—Negotiable
  V—Valuable for the persona
  E—Estimable by the development team
  S—Small/sized right
  T—Testable.

• **User Story Mapping** (e.g. Patton, 2014; Cohn, 2004): User Story Map ping helps you to develop and visualize your collection of user stories from a user perspective. The list of user stories can become huge and hard to handle. The product team needs to understand the big picture, how all user stories relate to each other. The main benefits of user story mapping are
  - a common understanding of the intended usage of the product from the user's point of view
  - organization of user stories into the big picture.

Storytelling is the most important part of a mutual understanding of the intended product usage, and it enables the team to thoroughly think through the flow of the story from a user perspective.

- **User Story Map Components**: A user story map combines multiple aspects in one visualization. User story maps are structured in two parts.
  - The part above the bold line in Fig. 5.8 is called the backbone of the product, listing all essential activities or epics that the product supports. On the left side all identified personas are listed (each color-coded) and the activities or epics illustrate a day in a life of each persona from left to the right timing-wise. The user story map can be further structured by introducing a usage sequence that clusters epics and activities that logically belong together.
  - The part below the bold line in Fig. 5.8 details the activities and user stories. The user stories are ordered by priority. The following sections detail the proven practices used to prioritize user stories that can then be shown in a user story map.
  - Figure 5.8 illustrates all components of a user story map and shows another useful application of user story maps. User story maps can be used as a prioritization tool, or at least as a visualization of the prioritized user stories. Due to the graphical view of the user stories, the product team can spot imbalances in functional coverage or holes in the usage sequence more simply. The dotted line indicating user stories being in or out of scope is called the walking skeleton.
  - The walking skeleton describes the product we build that supports the least number of necessary tasks across the full span of user experience (i.e. prioritized list of user stories in scope for product release).

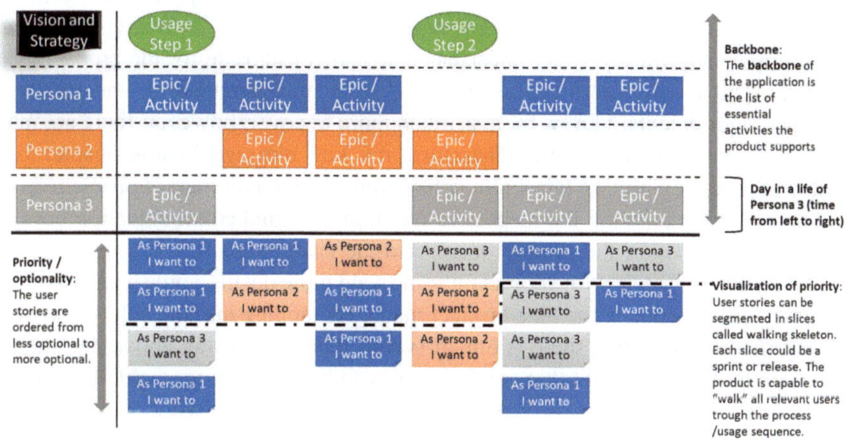

Fig. 5.8 User story map © Timo Wagenblatt 2019. All rights reserved

- **Use Case**: Use cases have been used as a proven practice to define requirements for some time and people still confuse the value and purpose of use cases. I will briefly outline what use cases are and guide you to the definitive books on that subject (Cockburn, 2000; Adolph, Bramble, Cockburn, & Pols, 2002). A use case is a definition of product use, from an actor's perspective, for accomplishing a specific goal within a product. A use case describes the human-product interactions that are necessary to process exactly one workflow step. A single use case describes a set of steps, a sequence of user interactions, to successfully accomplish the user's goal. A use case also shows alternative paths to success, failures, and associated data used in the interactions. Good use cases are typically written in natural language writing, reflecting user requirements and specifying the goals of one or more actors, but not how these goals are to be implemented. Note some basic rules for working with use cases (e.g. first broad than deep). It is not necessary to detail each use case to the full extent until the use case is stable and prioritized. Most use cases need several iterations until they are stable. Therefore, you must constantly ask yourself if you have found the "right" use cases at the "right" granularity. I acknowledge that writing good use cases takes time, however the time is well spent, in my opinion, as the requirements will be well described and then the work can be leveraged for test planning and deriving test cases.
- **Use Case Model/Diagram**: A use case model or use case diagram defines and relates all user interaction for an entire product. Use case diagrams show the actor who processes the use case, all relevant use cases that describe the functionality of the product or product module, and the connections between use cases. A use case model provides overview of how use cases are included in other use cases, how use cases extend other use cases, and which use cases belong to each actor.

User stories, user story maps, use cases and use case diagrams are all means to explain requirements. Once more, the format is not too important, the requirements need to be complete (i.e. verifiable, modifiable, traceable e.g. Leffingwell & Widrig, 2000), and most importantly (in my view) understandable and consumable for the product team.

That's all I will contribute to the broad field of understanding and managing product requirements. I know there is much more to cover; however, there are many books available on this topic. Therefore, my key message in this chapter is as follows: product planning takes into consideration the target market problem space, gathering and organizing the respective requirements, and communication between the product manager, the product team, and the customers.

Find your own style with your team: some want more details, some want less, some want technical depth, some hate product managers tapping into the solution area.

For product manager, there is lots of (valid) guidance to stay above the line and focus on building the right things and not how to build the things right. That is very important for team morale. As a product manager, you should work on the problem, ask the right questions and think about what the product should do, while the product team works on the solution, the answers and how the product accomplishes the task. In addition, as a product manager, your job is to provide the why to the product team. The why is important for the team to understand that everything they do is for a higher purpose. Consequently, the team should either work in discovery (e.g. building wireframes or prototypes to shape the product and reduce the risk in delivering new features), or work on backlog items that are contributing to solve a user/customer problem.

In the next section, I will show how requirements are organized in product backlogs.

5.2.2 Proven Practice: Working with Backlogs

I already mentioned the central repository where all gathered requirements are added to. The central repository is frequently called product backlog or continuous backlog.[11] Continuous backlogs emphasize the continuous update and work that happens in the product backlog.[12] The backlog is continuously updated, refined, groomed, new items added, outdated ones are consequently deleted.

Due to the amount of user stories, backlogs work best when organized in a hierarchical structure:

- **Theme**: A collection of user stories that logically belong together.
- **Epic**: A large user story that needs to be broken down into consumable user stories.
- **User Story**: A description of desired functionality from the perspective of a user (persona).
- **Backlog Item**: Break-down of a user story into engineering tasks.

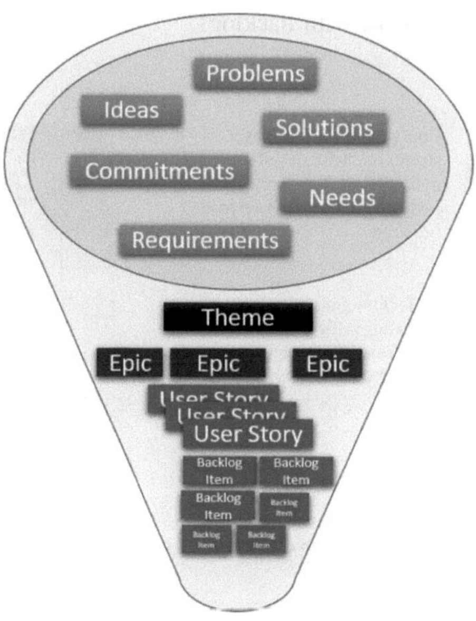

[11]Especially in agile development frameworks backlog might be called continuous backlogs.
[12]Continuous delivery might be one reason of more frequent backlog updates.

The appropriate level of detail depends on the priority. Items that are close to implementation are fine grained, need to fit into a sprint and can be realized by one team. Topics with lower priority are coarse-grained and will be broken down when required. Working with the backlog is one of the core tasks of the product owner role. There are various options for estimations of value, risk, and criticality. I will introduce proven practices in Sects. 5.3 and 5.4.

Product backlogs or continuous backlogs should be DEEP (Pichler, 2010):

- **D**etailed appropriately (e.g. with use cases)
- **E**mergent (i.e. dynamic, iteratively adjusted, living)
- **E**stimated
- **P**rioritized.

A product backlog represents all requirements gathered for a product. Sometimes product backlogs are split into two or three backlogs due to better handling options than working with large backlogs as illustrated in Fig. 5.9. The release backlog are the ones that are considered for the next release cycle, the next quarter or whatever is an appropriate cycle for items that are groomed and refined with the core product team. The sprint backlog represents the items that are prioritized and fine-grained enough for the next couple of sprints.

Find the best path for yourself and the product team. I have seen both working in sub-optimal ways and they worked fine. The structure needs to fit to your organization and working style; it is the content in the backlog that matters. Figure 5.9 summarizes how to best work with backlogs.

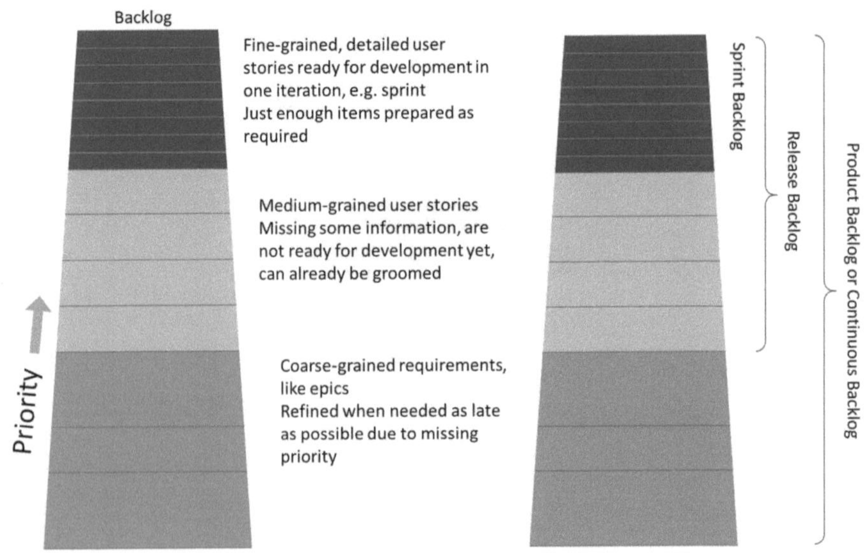

Fig. 5.9 Working with backlogs © Timo Wagenblatt 2019. All rights reserved

In my experience, the software tool you use for backlog management is of secondary importance. The tool that you prefer should support the attributes that you require for managing your backlog. The prioritization board approach explained in Sect. 5.4 describes all attributes that work effectively with backlogs. Most tools I'm aware of allow for hierarchical structuring, but in my experience the prioritization or ranking features were basic and transparency in large backlogs were always an issue. I'm sure the software tools have improved and are already better by the time you read this book.

Finally, I will briefly introduce two great concepts to you that are important for the following reasons:

- Developing products or new product features starts with ideas for solving customer problems
- The description of the Product Development dimension would not be complete, if these concepts are not mentioned

There are all these ideas to solve customer problems and requirements, but how can we solidify the assumptions and understand what ideas are worth pursuing and what ones should be dismissed early. Dual-track backlogs and GIST Idea Flow are two interesting concepts that can help with this common challenge for any product team:

- **Dual-track (agile)** (Cagan, Dual-Track Agile, 2019a, b): Dual-track agile recommends solidifying ideas first in a discovery phase. In the discovery phase the objective of the product team is to quickly generate validated requirements, user stories, or items in the product backlog. The ones that endure the discovery phase are phased into the delivery phase. For all items that made it into the delivery phase, the product team focuses on generating releasable software fast. The concept focuses on risk reduction and delivering only with a solid understanding of the requirement and solution approach.
- **GIST Idea Flow** (Gilad, 2019): The GIST Idea Flow concept is part of the GIST planning framework. GIST is named after its main building blocks: Goals, Ideas, Step-projects, and Tasks. Itamar Gilad recommends collecting all ideas in a so-called idea bank rather than product backlogs. Ideas are constantly added to the idea bank and prioritized. Prioritized ideas shall be solidified with experiments to learn more about the impact of the idea, increase the confidence and gain insights into the required implementation efforts. The product team focuses on step-by-step learning and validating how to best deliver value for the users until a new feature is launched. As with the dual-track concept before, GIST idea flow focuses on risk reduction investing time in the most impactful ideas that the team confidently builds in the fastest way.

5.2.3 Proven Practice: Product Development Planning Workshop

Product development planning workshops' goal is to align with the core product team on what's most important for product development. The workshop is not to be confused with a sprint planning workshop,[13] but rather working with the team to achieve a prioritized, aligned view on what we are doing next (i.e. what do we target in the next sprints, quarters, or whatever planning window works best for the team or is mandated in your organization).

The outcomes of a successful product development planning workshop are as follows:

- Prioritized backlog (continuous, product, release, or sprint)
- Aligned and shared focus on the things that matter in product development
- Engaged and motivated team.

Like every workshop, product development planning work benefits from an excellent preparation, smooth workshop execution, and professional post-processing of the workshop results. Let's have a look at these three steps in more detail.

1. **Workshop Preparation**:
   a. Each product development planning workshop is an excellent opportunity for a repetition (or maybe re-validation) of the product vision and strategy. Product vision and strategy should be a prerequisite before getting into product development planning (see Sect. 5.1).
   b. You benefit from the pre-work of having a consolidated, clean list of requirements where your insights about value, cost, and risk are included. If you do not, then Sects. 5.4, 5.5 and 5.3.1, and the proven practices introduced in this section, will be useful for the workshop preparation.
   c. Reserve a proper size room for all participants and provide the required workshop materials and technical infrastructure.
   d. As you can see there is significant pre-work required; however, product development planning workshops are certainly very important, and the level of preparation reflects this importance.

[13]However, sprint planning could be an application or side product of a product planning workshop. The same proven practice applies to sprint planning workshops.

2. **Workshop Execution**:
   a. Present the product vision and strategy or ask a product team member to do so.
   b. Explain the objectives of the workshop and introduce the tools you are going to leverage to reach the objectives.
   c. Apply the tools taking into consideration the pre-work and the team's preferences. If a tool doesn't work, stop and try another one that brings the team closer to the objectives.
   d. Split, group, re-group as the topic or situation requires. Be flexible about the desired outcomes. Have some fun!

3. **Workshop Post-processing**:
   a. Transfer all workshop results, pictures, refined estimations, identified risks, clarified questions, and anything else into a re-usable format. Store the results electronically and centrally for better re-use.
   b. Summarize overall workshop results and share it with the workshop participants and all required stakeholders. The RACI or DACI matrix will help you to not forget and annoy anyone.
   c. Leverage the results in your daily work until the next product development planning workshop.

Workshop duration and cadence are driven by the purpose of the workshop (e.g. if you focus on product strategy you might run this kind of workshop twice a year for two days; however, if your focus is on execution you might do the workshop for one hour every week.

Product development planning focuses on finding the balance between building the right things (your role), building things right (engineering team's role) and building it faster (i.e. reduce the feedback loop time (product team's role).

5.2.4 PYPR Dimension Items Details

See Tables 5.3 and 5.4.

Table 5.3 PYPR defaults by software product manager type

Topic		Internal PM	B2B PM	B2C PM
Default dimension item weight		20	20	20
Criticality for PM		High	High	High
PYPR score	Low	Product development is either planned in an unstructured, nontransparent, isolated, or purely internally focused approach or not planned at all. Symptoms are for example, that there is no central, organized requirements repository, no single product backlog, no aligned standards, e.g. for writing user stories or capturing requirements, no aligned prioritization approach, no consideration of constraints, no involvement of the whole product team, etc.		
	Medium	Product development is planned, but there are obvious areas for improvement. Medium scores should have at least the following attributes. All incoming requirements are stored in a central database, which is accessible to the product team and all relevant stakeholders. A clear process and quality guidance/support exists for all planning artefacts, e.g. requirements, user stories, backlog items, roadmap, etc. Prioritization happens in a consistent and transparent way. The planning results are communicated at least to the core product team		
	High	Product development planning is a major differentiator. All stakeholders benefit from structured, transparent, integrated, and customer-value focused product planning results that consider the known boundaries and constraints in an optimal way		

Table 5.4 PYPR dimensions impact examples

Dimension	Direct impact example	Indirect impact example
Product viability		The dimension benefits as a whole due to a balance product plan considering internal and external stakeholders and market insights
Product development	Product team health benefits from an aligned and transparent approach. Roadmaps become more reliable due to good product development planning	
Go-to-market/product marketing		Go-to-market planning can be based on a robust product development plan
Software demonstrations and training		Digital asset creation, software demonstrations build, and training material creation can be planned
The market/your customers	Engaging trusted customer community in planning will have positive impact	
Organizational maturity		Key principles can be derived from successful product development planning and shared with other teams

5.2.5 Summary and Conclusions

Key Takeaways

- The ultimate objective of product development planning is to increase the chances of developing a working product; that is a product that covers the important features for the problem space (completeness), that is stable even after major upgrades (stability), that is flexible and offers some degrees of freedom for the implementation (flexibility), and efficient for the user (performance).
- Collect everything from individual customers, the market, technology, competition, channels, press, analysts, trends and anything else that might be interesting for your product. Understand the value for your customers and the fit to your product vision.
- Solidify the assumptions and understand which topics are worthy to pursue and which ones should be dismissed early.
- The appropriate level of detail depends on the priority of a requirement. The closer the requirement is to the actual implementation the more clarity is required.
- Structure, detail and communicate requirements in the form of epics, user stories or any form of clear documentation. Understand, prioritize, and communicate the requirements that will solve a customer problem before the coding starts.
- Plan for technical debt reduction if the product team does not consider this as a priority.
- Product development planning needs transparency as all stakeholders outside the core product team, product development might appear to be a black box otherwise. Therefore, I recommend not just explaining the results of the product planning but the product planning process itself to your customers and all stakeholders (Fig. 5.10).
- Find the balance between building the right things (your role), building things right (engineering team's role) and building it faster; that is, reduce the feedback loop time (product team's role).

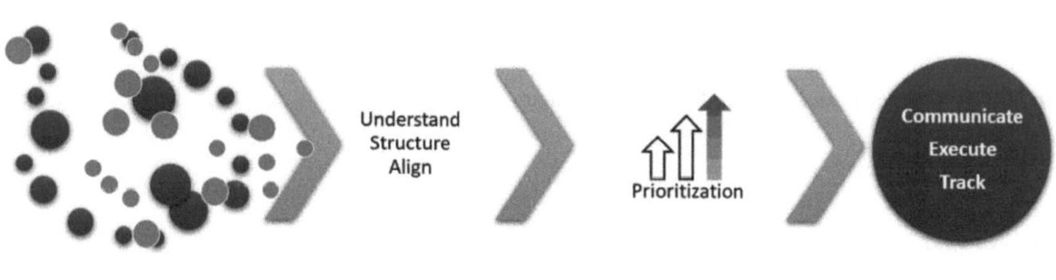

Fig. 5.10 From ideas, problems, and requirements to product plan transparency © Timo Wagenblatt 2019. All rights reserved

5.3 Leading and Prioritizing in Product Development

The role of leadership is to transform the complex situation into small pieces and prioritize them.

—**Carlos Ghosn**

Wikipedia provides a standard and useful definition of the term Prioritization: "Prioritization is the activity that arranges items or activities in order of importance relative to each other (Prioritization, 2018)."

Sounds simple in theory, however as we all know, prioritization is one of the most difficult tasks to master in our day-to-day Software Product Management work. One can easily find many books, methods, directions, blogs, and other materials attempting to explain the process, but still prioritization seems to remain a key issue as most product management related surveys indicate.[14]

As a product manager, prioritizing "things" is a major part of your role.[15] In the Product Development dimension, "things" can be a lot of different topics and can come with multiple names from business or technical requirements, epics, user stories, backlog items, tasks or roadmap themes. I will summarize all "things" and use the term requirements instead as the principles and methods I introduce apply to all these "things" listed above and more.

When prioritizing requirement "things," there's a whole bunch of information to consider, and it's more than just the cost and value of a given requirement. As we all painfully know, capacity and demand are never in balance. I have never experienced a situation in my product management life, where the capacity in product development was even close to solving all known problems and underserved needs (Fig. 5.11).

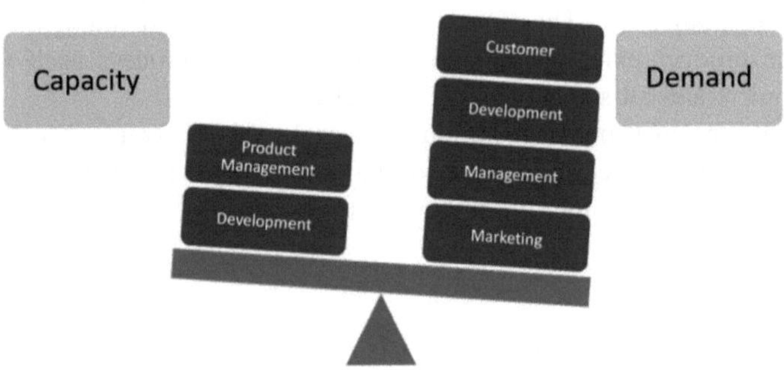

Fig. 5.11 Capacity and demand—an imbalanced couple © Timo Wagenblatt 2019. All rights reserved

[14]For example, check the PMF survey results: https://productmanagementfestival.com/survey/.
[15]In most organizations, backlog prioritization is the responsibility of the Product Owner as agile development methodologies is applied.

In addition, there are boundary conditions that might come from product team dynamics (read: organizational politics), existing product team skills, or the capabilities of the whole organization that need to be considered. Some requirements even have non-negotiable deadlines. In addition, many unknowns are lurking beneath the surface ready to pop-up when you think everything is under control. All these topics define your context. Your context has a big impact on how you prioritize.

Your context illustrates the complex situation you are required to master in your role. While managing software products, everyone encounters many complex situations in their daily work. Each situation must be analyzed, categorized and clustered into smaller pieces, so these pieces can be prioritized into consumable work packages. This process requires your best leadership and prioritization skills.

So, what is so complex about prioritization? Prioritization is complex as it requires smart consideration and handling of too many directions from various stakeholders, contradicting objectives, budgetary constraints, and tight deadlines in parallel. Prioritizing requirements means deciding which set of requirements need to be implemented first and which ones can be delayed till a later phase.

This is a perfect example of another significant element of prioritization. Prioritization means making decisions. That's what I introduced as one of the superpowers of a T-shaped product manager, the trait of being decisive. Making decisions means taking responsibility. Things can go wrong, people might debate your decisions, people might ignore your decisions and you must deal with it. That's one of the reasons why many people are scared to make decisions. Note that you will never please everyone. "If you try to please everybody, you will almost please nobody" (Cagan, 2018).

In this section we will cover

- how you can transform a complex situation into smaller and prioritized pieces
- key prioritization principles and techniques
- tools that support me in leading and influencing the product development decision process.

The topics and practices that I discuss in this section have helped me to be less anxious when making the necessary decisions required in Software Product Management. They also provide the stable foundation needed in Software Product Management. From this robust base you can expand and lead all aspects of PYPR.

5.3.1 Nine Steps to Transform a Complex Situation into Consumable and Prioritized Pieces

Summarize why prioritization is hard: Product Development and Product Development Planning is a complex problem due to many directions, stakeholders, contradicting objectives, constraints and boundaries—all at the same time. It also requires confidence to lead and guide the process and make decisions if decisions need to be made.

You might find the following proven process useful to transform the complexity into smaller, prioritized pieces:

1. **Collect all requirements (read: "things")**
   Collect everything you hear from individual customers, the market, technology trends, competition, channels, press, analysts, engineering and anything else that should be considered for your product. That's an ongoing task that never ends. Have your ears and eyes everywhere and consider any requirement you become aware of. Just add everything to the list. If you hear something often and frequently—take note. The objective is to fully digitize all requirements information centrally for better backlog management.
2. **Cluster to same or at least similar granularity**
   Of course, requirements come to your attention in different shapes, forms and especially levels of detail. Requirements can be stated on very generic terms, such as we need a new online-banking app, to very detailed granularity, such as I would like to store the hair color of my customer in a free-text attribute. Document the granularity level of the requirement and cluster by a defined taxonomy that works for your product team and organization. For example, use the schema illustrated in Fig. 5.12 for any requirement you received and collected. Assign them to one of the levels from left (lower granularity) to right (higher granularity) and enrich the requirement with context.

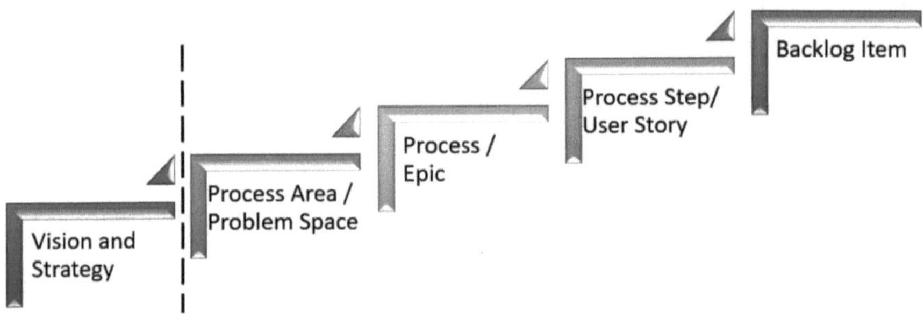

Fig. 5.12 Granularity levels of prioritization

   This context will become the basis of the prioritization process. Note that sometimes there are huge requirements that should be directly split (or refined as in Scrum) to a workable granularity. Splitting requirements could be, for example, along personas, clarified parts versus parts that need clarification, or simply the basic transactions like CRUD[16] versus the rest (Leffingwell, 2010).
3. **Breadth before depth**
   You will not make good progress or create coherent backlogs when you waste time writing detailed requirements or user stories. Document and collect only the directly accessible information. If there is nothing available, then at least document when you received and where you received the requirement. The objective is to balance detailing (and splitting/refining) requirements for better

[16]CRUD = create/retrieve/update/delete.

prioritization and get an overview about the available requirements first. Note that probably 80–90% of the requirements will not be considered in the next development cycle, e.g. sprint (see Sect. 5.2.2).

4. **Spiral your prioritization approach**
   Leverage the clusters from Step 2 and prioritize only items in each iteration that are on the same level. I would propose to start at the first or second level (i.e. problem space or epic in the example from Step 2) depending of the number of items. Prioritize requirements in an iterative, breadth-first approach, with each iteration requiring increased precision and accuracy of the requirements set.
   With this approach, disregard fairly early on whole requirement sets in areas that are not currently important. Still there might be high-value items in these requirement sets. One approach could be that you screen the requirements list for these high-value, low effort requirements and add them to the prioritized list in the last iteration. But be careful with this approach. Don't let the exception become the rule.
   For all requirement sets on the same granularity level, Steps 5–7 represent one iteration of the prioritization process. Start with lower granularity requirement sets, detail the prioritized ones and prioritizes the next granularity level in the next iteration.
5. **Define decision attributes and weights (with your stakeholders)**
   Define the underlying principles for decision making and prioritization. The decision influencing factors could focus on value, cost, technology, competition, speed, or anything else that the team or organization considers as important. Align with the stakeholders which factors should be considered in the prioritization process. Define the weight of each factor compared to the other factors. Note that the PYPR assessment and the strategy and action meetings are a great source for this step. The outcomes of the assessment uncover the weak areas of YourProduct Inc. that you might consider for future prioritization.
6. **Rate the items (with your stakeholders) and seek support**
   Use a prioritization board (like the prioritization board introduced in Sect. 5.4) to rate each requirement in your prioritization list for each granularity level. Spiral to the next level of detail for the top items and seek information about technical complexity, development effort and associated risk levels. Get to know the requirements better and include early user feedback. The Kano model[17] could be a valuable tool at this stage as it works with limited requirement details.
7. **Rank the requirements and analyze the results**
   Random and unstructured information transformed into smaller and consumable pieces is a complex starting situation. You can leverage aligned information to rank and analyze the requirements clutter. The requirements can be ranked in a unique order and the ordered list can be analyzed, considering specifics like required skills, etc.
   Note that the ranking position is not a strict order as, for example, some items might require scarce development skills, and complex or dependent requirements mandate a certain experience level, while juniors can take high rank and low complex or medium complex requirements. Another example would be not

[17]You can find a detailed introduction of the Kano model in Sect. 5.5.

to take only high-risk items in scope, but balance with items that might have a lower rank, and a lower risk.

8. **Double check PYPR assessment, roadmap theme and vision**
   After you have spiraled through course-grained to fine-grained requirements in Steps 5–7, you have arrived at a ranked list of requirements. Before you start with development, I recommend one last sanity check for each item on your list:

   a. Will the prioritized requirement get you closer to the product vision or does the work reduce the risk level?
   b. Do the prioritized requirements fit to one or two, maximum three common themes?[18]
   c. Will the prioritized requirement improve the PYPR scores for one or more items, for example product quality, functional completeness, but also software demonstrations, thought leadership, etc.?

9. **Decide final prioritized list**
   For the ones who passed the sanity check, start implementing and start adding all the details required to build the best product ever. The time of breadth before depth is over, you have arrived at an aligned and prioritized requirement list and, therefore, you should do your best to arrive at the best possible result by working hard on all details for your selected scope. For all others, keep them in your backlog until their time is ripe.

Figure 5.13 summarizes the nine steps from requirements acquisition resulting in requirements clutter to better understanding and structuring the clutter. In other words, align with what is important for the product and the stakeholders to finally prioritize product development, which means arriving at a product plan for the next development cycle.

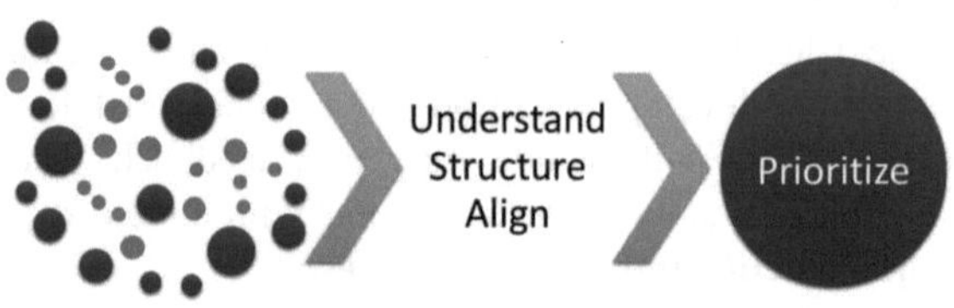

Fig. 5.13 Understand, structure, align to be able to prioritize © Timo Wagenblatt 2019. All rights reserved

The nine-step process is a rather generic approach and mandates the use of some tools and proven practices. Some of them I have already mentioned such as the Prioritization Board, Ranking, the Kano Model, and Themed Roadmaps. I will introduce all mentioned tools and proven practices later in this book.

[18]Themed roadmaps are a great asset. You can find more details in the Sect. 5.6.

I continue emphasizing the importance of prioritization especially in the Product Development dimension. This is our home turf, we need to master this part. Everyone in the product team expects us to lead and guide this essential part of Software Product Management. Whatever the setup and organization, prioritization mandates special focus as most product managers will spend a great deal of their work time and efforts in the Product Development dimension.

In the next section, I will explain some more key principles I found useful for leading and prioritizing product planning. These key principles will support you as a General Manager of YourProduct Inc.

5.3.2 Prioritization Key Principles and Guidelines

There are many ways of prioritizing "things." The best choice for you and YourProduct Inc. depends on the specifics of your stakeholders and the type of your product. But all forms of prioritization have certain characteristics and underlying logic in common. Here are useful key principles and guidelines agnostic of most prioritization approaches.

- If we could accomplish all the work, a prioritization process would not be necessary. Consequently, the product team and all other stakeholders need to understand that prioritization will require a compromise. The perfect prioritization result is a theoretical construct that cannot be achieved, but still the objective is to get as close as possible.
- No matter whether the prioritization is quantitative or qualitative, analytical results are not enough to convince all stakeholders. Aligned prioritization decisions require empathy and other soft skills to develop convincing arguments. You need to activate the willingness of most stakeholders to compromise. Working in a product-led organization with high organizational maturity will help you as a product manager. You are likely empowered to make decisions if decisions are required. Everyone else should know the escalation path in the event compromises are not in sight, and hence you need to reach to an authority with power stronger than the involved stakeholders (Kittlaus & Fricker, 2017).
- The decision process how to best leverage scarce resources (time, people, budget) in product development is as complex as this process is critical for your product's success, but also how you are perceived as a product manager is important. In simple words:
  - You are responsible for the prioritization results and hence you need to lead the process and make the decision process transparent.
  - You need to reach an expert level in this area otherwise your stakeholders lose trust in your decisions and in your leadership.

- Prioritization should be a team effort. Excluding very simple prioritization problems, all other prioritizations require the involvement of someone else from the core or extended product team in the process. It's not advisable that the product manager alone will set the overall priorities. Product managers should focus on leading and moderating the process and only make the decision if the team gets stuck.
- Every prioritization process and supporting tool should focus on determining the best portfolio and sequence of "things" to advance the product. Advancing the product means to deliver the most value at each point in time, given the existing boundaries and constraints.
- Prioritization processes and tools need to provide answers for the basic value questions like (how much and to whom?) and the basic delivery questions (how much, which risks, which skills?) to achieve consensus about what and when enabled by transparency and clarity.
- Time is money. All stakeholders should be aware that any delay in prioritization decisions immediately translates into potential scope reduction, waste of budget, and deferred business value. In addition, external pressures might lead to reduced quality when the team is trying to catch up the initial delay by shortening required testing and quality assurance activities.
  Just to state the obvious: The above guideline doesn't mean to fast-track prioritization, just to encourage everyone to find the right balance and to acknowledge that complete details are never available, and the perfect prioritization result is a myth.
- Whatever you prioritize, keep the "things" to be prioritized on the same or comparable level of granularity as otherwise you are comparing apples and oranges, which lead to less valuable prioritization results.
- A prioritization process makes it easier to justify the decisions. Visualizations of the prioritization results make the decisions more accessible for the stakeholders.
  - Conceivable decision criteria support leading the product team and convincing stakeholders.
  - If decision criteria or decisions are not transparent, there are risks are that your product will be developed in the wrong direction, decisions will be made for you, the results will be less predictable, and your time will be wasted.
- Distinguish what is urgent versus important by applying this simple rule:
  - Urgent means that there is a deadline coming up with consequences if something is not completed. The deadline needs to be valid for your product and have impact on your product if not respected. Everything else is not urgent.

  - Important means that something is getting you closer to your vision or reduces the risk of doing so. The importance might also be the result of the proper prioritization process as outlined below using a prioritization board.
  - Always remember that urgent does not automatically mean important!
  - Focus first on urgent and important "things," then urgent "things," then important "things" and only if you still have capacity for everything else.

- Product lifecycle affects the decision criteria and prioritization process (Kittlaus & Fricker, 2017).
  - Ideation and inception: Focus on onboarding first customers, testing the product vision.
  - Market validation and growth: Extend the minimum viable product scope, manage complexity due to product functionality depth.
  - Optimization: Focus on delighters, extending customer segments, maintainability and implementation accelerators.
  - Phase-out and sunsetting: Retain customers with minimal investments, prepare conversion to enable smooth transition to successor product.

And one last comment: Remember that many people hesitate to make decisions because they fear making wrong decisions. Most prefer to make no decision or tend to wait for more data, or any other excuse to delay decisions.

This is where you come in. As a product manager, your role requires you to lead and guide the team by understanding, structuring and aligning all requirements (and opinions), guiding the team with transparency through the process and getting the product plan to a conclusion. Providing a clear ranking and priority of requirements to the product team is your accountability. With the outlined approach you add the required transparency to the decision process.

Next time someone calls out a prioritization decision as wrong, ask confidently: why?

Why wasn't the concern raised during the prioritization process, but only after the fact. Is there new data, new direction, new whatever? Sometimes wrong means that people cannot understand the decision or have a different opinion that has not been considered or simply has been less prioritized in the decision process. Remain confident and reflect whether there is a problem in the process, in prioritization transparency, or whether someone just wants to aggrandize oneself.

5.3.3 Selected Prioritization Techniques

There are many aspects to prioritization and decision-making processes and there are many techniques available for your choice. I will introduce only a few techniques that I use routinely and have passed the real-life test throughout my product management career:

- Two-dimensional matrix analysis
- The Prioritization Board
- The Kano Model
- User Story Map ping as already introduced in Sect. 5.2.1 also represents a prioritization technique, in this case for user stories.

Most approaches to prioritizing "things" consider a value and a cost or risk dimension. Value criteria can be anything from revenue, margin or profit measures to softer values like validating hypothesis, winning a customer or aligning to organizational priorities. Examples of cost and risk criteria are the estimated cost of development, confidence in required skills, or level of complexity. As described previously, the decision influencing factors commonly focus on value, cost, and risk derived from technology, competition, speed, or anything else that the team or organization considers as guiding principles.

A common and simple approach is to plot the interesting dimensions into a matrix. One axis represents the value criteria and the other axis represents the cost or risk criteria. I'm sure you have used or at least seen similar matrices like the examples in Fig. 5.14.

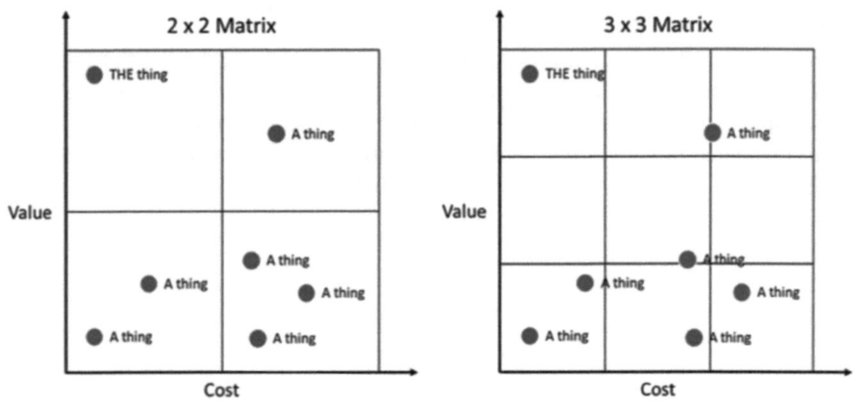

Fig. 5.14 Example of a 2 × 2 and 3 × 3 matrix © Timo Wagenblatt 2019. All rights reserved

That's it, very simple, which is one of the reasons why these models are so prominent.

Well, but there are some limitations/requirements:

- Garbage in, garbage out. You require representative and qualitative data for value and cost dimension
- Two dimensions only[19] in one view
- More dimensions require parallel assessment of these multiple matrices. There is theoretically one matrix for each combination of available prioritization criteria
- Clear definition and meaning of each matrix sector, i.e. the upper right sector versus the sector below.

You might have seen other kind of matrices, such as the unbalanced matrices, which are not balanced like a 3 × 2 or 2 × 4 matrix or the matrix has simply more segments like 4 × 4 or 10 × 10. These are variations to the concept, but it remains the same concept with the same limitations. The same is true if you swap the dimensions or rename the dimensions to something like impact versus feasibility.

Note that I do see value using a matrix to illustrate or underline correlations or dependencies, yet I'm not convinced that matrices are proper prioritization techniques on their own. You will find some examples in other chapters, where I consider the two-dimensional matrices useful.

Stakeholders often have differing views on objectives, priorities and decision factors. Hence lack of transparency and clarity in decision making (aka prioritization) leads to dissatisfied and sometimes even frustrated stakeholders. That too should be avoided for many reasons. A prioritization board is a useful tool if you want to consider more than two or three dimensions.

Furthermore, I will introduce the Kano Model, which is a theory to gain insights about the feelings of users concerning product requirements. Additionally, the Kano Model provides guidance on investment levels for individual requirements.

The prioritization methods I explain in this book need to satisfy two basic requirements:

- Enable a defendable and strong product decision
- Personally worked for me and my teams and stakeholders.

Numerous methods on how to prioritize requirements have been developed over the years. While some work great on a small number of requirements, others are better suited for many decision-makers and decision influencing factors. There is much material available on the internet and a broader selection of prioritization techniques can be found in many places. Some colleagues came up with an

[19]Experienced people might add a third dimension by applying, for example, a bubble chart to the matrix; professionals add icons to represent a fourth dimension. I would not recommend both approaches, if your goal is prioritization of things, but go for it if you like good looking charts with little workable output.

interesting approach to structure prioritization techniques such as the Periodic Table of Elements (Zacarias, 2018a). A more traditional overview of common techniques that can be used when prioritizing requirements is shown in Fig. 5.15.

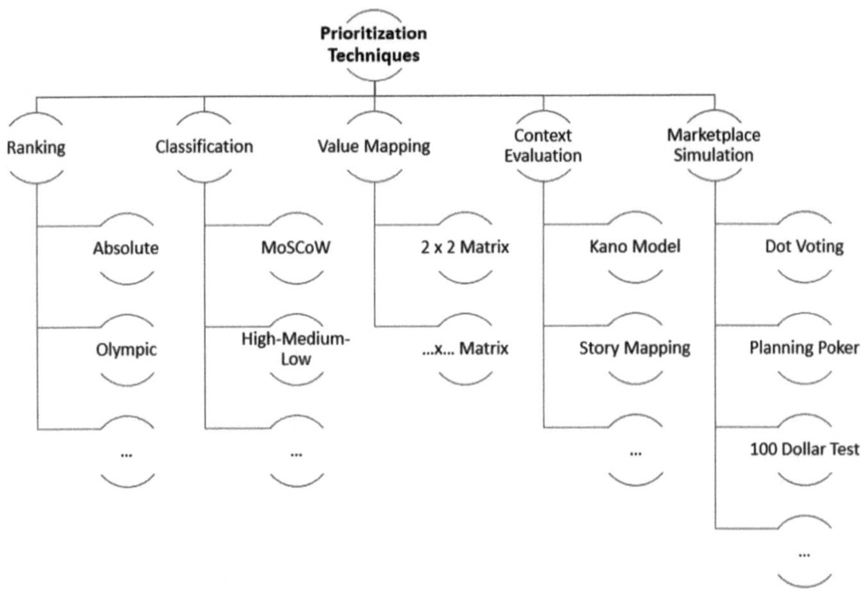

Fig. 5.15 Structuring common prioritization techniques

No prioritization method is perfect. Nevertheless, using prioritization techniques is much better than letting fire or loudness define your priorities. Another reminder: Most important in your role as a product manager is keeping your bag of tricks open and being bold enough to try out something new. Perhaps you will find a better, more suitable approach for yourself, your team and your product along your journey.

The prioritization board approach described in the next section introduces a practical and valuable approach to dealing with backlog and roadmap prioritization. Open your bags!

5.4 The Prioritization Board

Considering the multitude of stakeholders and the other players with opinions, it will be hard to find any situation where two or three dimensions will cover all decision influencing factors. The prioritization board approach described in this section combines various techniques in one process:

- Weighted average prioritization
- Classification
- Qualitative assessment
- Ranking

- The process of managing scope derived from my #1 recommended book about requirements engineering (Leffingwell & Widrig, 2000).

Take the template and adapt it for yourself, your teams, or your organization's needs. The main benefit that I have seen when using the prioritization board for myself or observing my teams using this tool: transparency and traceability of prioritization decisions. The prioritization board approach will strengthen your understanding of the generic description to transform a complex situation into smaller, prioritized pieces, as described in Sect. 5.3.1.

Transparency in decision making is probably one of the most important aspects of prioritization. Therefore, guide the stakeholders through this exercise and there will much less friction.

The Prioritization Board

The process of applying the prioritization board consists of the following steps that I will detail in the following sections:

1. List of items/requirements to be prioritized
2. Decision attributes, decision influencing factors
3. Priority rating
4. Development Assessment
5. Ranking and decision process (Fig. 5.16).

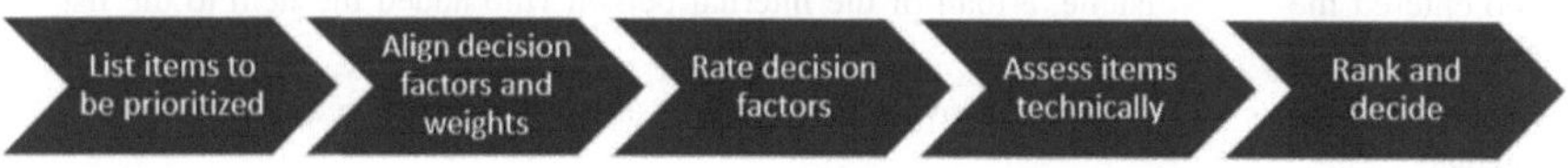

Fig. 5.16 Prioritization board process © Timo Wagenblatt 2019. All rights reserved

5.4.1 Step 1: Prioritization Scope—List of Requirements

The list of requirements represents the collection of all the requests (functional, technical, non-functional) that you collected for your product. Some people call this list product backlog. The requirements need to be explained (read: documented) to a level that each requirement can be understood by everyone involved in the prioritization process.

The attributes that are important for this area are dependent on the level of granularity and the requirement type respectively (e.g. epic, user story, business requirement, technical requirement, backlog item, task etc.). No one list of attributes fits all. However, in my experience most prioritization tasks can follow a standard format and a standard structure.

In addition to the requirement attributes in Table 5.5 I found it useful to introduce the administrative attributes in Table 5.6. They will be beneficial for later reference and almost complete the transition into backlog items.

Table 5.5 Requirements attributes

Attribute	Explanation
Unique identifier	Unique identifier
Functional classification	Useful to categorize requirements that require special team skills
Process or business capability	Depending on your approach to work with a standard process or with a business capability model, reference here the process area/process/process step or business capability that will be improved by implementing the requirement
Persona	Reference to persona requiring the requirement, high-level requirements might require multiple personas
Related requirement item	Reference to similar or dependent requirement items, if known
Details	Description of the requirement/product use case/feature/user story or whatever you prioritize. Make sure there is enough description available, but not a novel for each item
Customer/requestor	Who requested the requirement
Customer value	Rough information about the expected value for the requestor. Documented as • an absolute number for value KPIs like cost saving, ROI, revenue, etc. • rating between 1 (low) to 5 (very valuable) with additional information in which area the perceived value will happen

Table 5.6 Administrative requirements attributes

Attribute	Explanation
Who entered the item	Name, e-mail of the internal person who added the item to the list
Assigned product manager	Who can provide more details about the item if required
Release cycle/theme	Tag or keyword for the item, might be useful for clustering at a later stage in the process
Item status	Status of the item in the prioritization board: • New • Rated • Considered in development

5.4.2 Step 2: Align on Decision Influencing Factors

Step 2 is all about alignment for what is important for the product and organization. What are the underlying principles for decision making and prioritization. As described previously, the decision influencing factors (DIF) could focus on value, cost, technology, competition, speed, or anything else that the team or organization considers as guiding principles and important for decision-making.

Align with the stakeholders which factors should be considered in your prioritization process. Define the weight of each factor according to these principles:

- Define minimum 3 and maximum 6 decision influencing factors
- The sum of all weights needs to be 100%
- The minimum value of a single dimension factor should be 10% and the maximum value should be 70%. If you set the weight below 10%, why would you consider the factor as important for this exercise. If you set the weight above 70%, why do you need a matrix—the key driver for decision-making is obviously the one that is overweight (Table 5.7).

Table 5.7 Requirements attributes—continued

Attribute per DIF	Explanation
Influencing factor description 1–6	Description of the factor that influences the prioritization
% Weight 1–6	Percentage weight of the influencing factor

For example, the team could define user satisfaction (50%), incremental revenue (30%) and product differentiator (20%) as the right mix and importance of decision influencing factors.

Do not overcomplicate the prioritization process with too many assessment criteria. This might lead to many requirements that have very similar priority scores. If you can't resist having more than three or four dimensions, then consider removing those with the lowest weightings and spend time with the stakeholders about what is "really" important for the product and the organization.

5.4.3 Step 3: Rate Decision Influencing Factors and Understand Priority Rating and Rank

Rate all items from Step 1. Discuss and agree with the team for a rating value between zero to 10 for each decision influencing factor. The rating value describes the degree to which a requirement satisfies an influencing factor. You can use the mandatory flag if a certain requirement is an absolute must. Note that you should be cautious using the mandatory card, and you might consider limiting the use of the mandatory flag to a small number. We used to call the mandatory flag the "boss guidance." As a result of the exercise you can calculate the attributes as outlined in Table 5.8 that represent the relative priority of the requirements.

Table 5.8 Requirements attributes—priority and ranking

Attribute	Explanation
Priority rating	Sum of all weighted dimension ratings calculated as $\sum DIF\ rating\ value * DIF\ weigth$ for all items The sum ranges between 0 and 10, while it is set to 10 once a requirement is marked as mandatory
Priority classification	A verbal classification of the priority rating for each item. The classification uses the terms: Critical, Important, and Useful. This means that every

(continued)

Table 5.8 (continued)

Attribute	Explanation
	requirement that is considered is classified at least as useful which avoids offending requestors and supporters **Classification**: $0 \leq$ Priority Rating < 6 ➔ Useful $6 \leq$ Priority Rating < 8.5 ➔ Important $8.5 \leq$ Priority Rating $\leq$ 10 ➔ Critical
Rank	The absolute rank of the requirement compared to the complete list that is prioritized

With this step we have already gained valuable insights about priorities and arrived at a ranked order of the items in question. That's already a great achievement. The initial prioritization should be done without too much influence from the engineering team. Though we do the prioritization because we cannot realize all the work. We still haven't figured out how much we can achieve in one takt, sprint, release, or whatever is the name and duration of your development cycle.

5.4.4 Step 4: Development Assessment

As part of Step 4, we work together with the core product team or sometimes with only the development architect to document the rough level of effort required for each requirement implementation. To get to an estimation make sure to balance the team's required work effort versus the directionally right "rough order of magnitude" assessment that is preferred in this step (see Table 5.9).

Table 5.9 Requirements attributes—complexity, effort, and risk

Attribute	Explanation
Technical complexity	Information about the complexity of implementing the requirement on a low-medium-high scale: • New technology (High) • Known/done before (Medium) • Commodity/minor (Low)
Effort estimation	T-Shirt Size estimation that fits to your product e.g. Small (1–50 person days), Medium (50–200 person days), Large (200–500 person days), X-Large (more than 500 person days) Alternative approach for stable teams: • Small (effort equal or less of one sprint for one team of ten) • Medium (effort equal to two sprints for one team of ten) • Large (effort equal or larger than three sprints for one team of ten) Note that this is clearly not at sprint backlog level as all items should be small (so they fit in one sprint). Otherwise further splitting and refinement is mandatory

(continued)

Table 5.9 (continued)

Attribute	Explanation
Development risk rating	Information about the risk of implementing the requirement on a low-medium-high scale. Estimation of the probability that the requirement will impact schedule or budget negatively. For example, requirements that likely require new technology the team has never used before are of higher risk than others, or requirements that have hard dependencies to customer or other teams deliverables are of higher risk, than if the team can work completely autonomous

Note that most items will not get developed in the next cycle and it is likely you will not have complete information available at this early phase of the development process. A counter action would be to focus continuously on estimating product backlogs, but this would be a tremendous waste of time.

Understand that this exercise is hard for the team, especially during the first few iterations of working together. It requires trust and the ability to abstract the requirement estimation process from the actual development process as there are limited details available for most items in the list.

Role play conversation[20]:

Software Product Manager: What's roughly is the effort needed to build this requirement?

Product Team: We don't know. We do not have enough details or a design idea.

Software Product Manager: I understand, but is it a kind of an easier thing that we have done before?

Product Team: No.

Software Product Manager: Is it the most difficult requirement in the list?

Product Team: No.

Software Product Manager: Would it be okay to give it a medium on a scale of low-medium-high?

Product Team: Medium sounds about right

Software Product Manager: Thank you. How about the next requirement?

The role playing is not scientific, but it does work. You can even expand the role playing to cover more insights concerning technical complexity and risk rating. The important aspect of the exercise is that we want to make directionally right decisions despite incomplete information. You can spend much more time here if you can afford it. However, most items will not be built anyway, and the details and refinements can and need to happen later in another phase anyway.

[20]Inspired from Leffingwell and Widrig (2000), p. 198.

Spending more time at an early phase might likely be a waste of time and should be used for more value-adding activities. Manage and explain the expectations properly, especially to your product team. If the team figures out in a later process that something is way more complex or requires dramatically less effort, that's fine and will be considered.

A pragmatic approach in Step 4 is to ask the team to estimate the list until we are 50% over capacity. In Step 5, we will see why it is useful for not stopping the exercise at sharp capacity level.

5.4.5 Step 5: Prioritize and Decide

Given the pre-work of Steps 1–4, the most critical step to decide about the items to be worked on can be based on robust information as shown in Fig. 5.17. You can prioritize the requirement list based on technical complexity, risk rating, effort estimation, or priority according to aligned decision criteria and absolute rank.

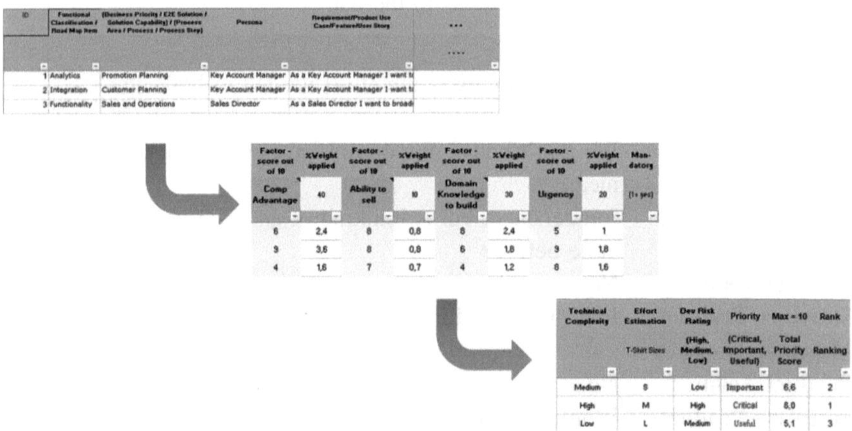

Fig. 5.17 Prioritization board results

I acknowledge that the final prioritization step might be still tricky. However, you have all information you need to move on. Be confident, lead the team and leverage the following principles.

- Do not forget that the estimations are rudimentary and have the flexibility to reprioritize as you learn more details about the requirements.
- Balance your scope based on a bell curve distribution for technical complexity, risk and effort estimation. Consider less complex, less risky or less effort requirements on lower ranks, but within the same priority classification in scope and postpone higher ranked items if the distribution is not healthy.

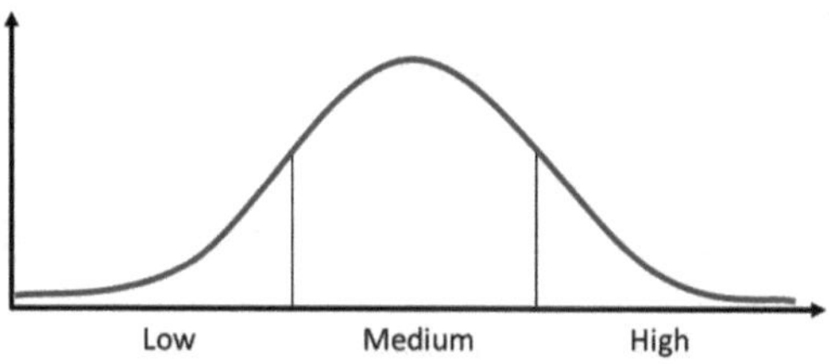

- Items classified as useful are not considered in this development cycle.
- Always be prepared to justify your scoping and de-scoping decisions through conflicting pressures and corporate oblivion.
- Communicate the prioritized list to all stakeholders and emphasize that the prioritization result is a compromise according to the agreed decision criteria. The alternative is further delays in decision making.
- Always remind yourself and others that delays in scope decisions generally translate into scope reduction, budget waste, quality reduction, or business value reduction.

I recommend supporting the decision results communication by visualizing the prioritization result, leveraging something easy like the 2 × 2 matrix or any other visual aids that work for you and your stakeholders to consume and rationalize the prioritization results. And keep in mind, we are working in product-mode not project-mode, there is no fixed scope contract. There will be a next round of prioritization, new events and insights that might require course corrections on our journey.

5.4.6 Summary and Conclusions

In your role as product manager, the objective is not to set priorities and keep the team focused on delivering them. The objective is to continuously focus on adding value toward the product vision and strategy. If there are new findings and insights along the way, then the prioritization board will be a great resource to incorporate these.

Key Takeaways

The prioritization board provides:

- Objective consideration of multiple criteria for requirement prioritization
- Integrated view considering conflicting decision influencing factors
- Easy to consume, transparent and ranked priority decision toward all stakeholders
- Transparency into prioritization logic across product team and potentially external stakeholders
- Reusable information for continuous backlog refinement.

In the next section, I will introduce the Kano Model, which is a theory to gain insights about the feelings of users concerning product requirements. The Kano Model results can be leveraged as a valuable input for the prioritization board.

5.5 The Kano Model—Adding Empathy to Requirements

For most software products, product backlogs seem endless. The requirements[21] list contains more critical items than reasonably fit into the next release or sprint or whatever development increment you are focusing on. As a product manager, you need to find the best balance for your product. Sales, Marketing, Engineering, Management, and yes, customers, in short, everyone will share their opinion with you, while you constantly ask yourself, which epics/user stories/backlog items/requirements/features should be included into the next release/sprint to maximize outcome?

Every team, every organization has a capacity limit as the achievable outcome is always constrained by time, development capacity or budget. Hence, every product manager needs to prioritize. Prioritization is king, which is not news to you. We already discovered the prioritization board method and how important prioritization techniques are in your decision-making responsibility.

As explained before, at least one criterion of the prioritization criteria is very likely customer satisfaction or user adoption, but how do you know what features will make your customers or prospects happy and satisfied?

- How do we prioritize for customer/market satisfaction?
- How do we measure satisfaction?
- How do we not just satisfy customers, but rather WOW them?

These questions are probably one of the hardest to answer in your daily job, but there is a method that I found exceptionally useful in the decision-making process and adding customer and user empathy in a structured and logical way over and above gut feeling: the Kano Model.

In this section we will discover the Kano Model theory; how customer satisfaction can be researched before requirements are developed. To deepen the theory, the section concludes with a case study showing how we applied the Kano Model in a critical situation.

5.5.1 Kano Model Theory

The Kano Model is a theory for product development and customer satisfaction developed in the 1980s by Professor Noriaki Kano, which classifies customer preferences into five categories (Must-be Quality, One-dimensional Quality, Attractive Quality, Indifferent Quality and Reverse Quality) (Kano Model, 2018).

[21]For simplification reasons I will only use the term requirement in this chapter. It might be epics, user stories, use case, backlog items, requirements, features in your terminology or granularity.

The Kano Model has gained some popularity in the last few years. I first heard about it in a product owner (yes, not Product Manager) training that was conducted at SAP in 2014. The Kano Model had been introduced as a method to prioritize backlog items and define the minimum viable product, focusing on customer satisfaction versus feature presence. The matrix depicted in Fig. 5.18 will help us to understand the correlation between the availability of a product feature and the satisfaction of the user using the feature.

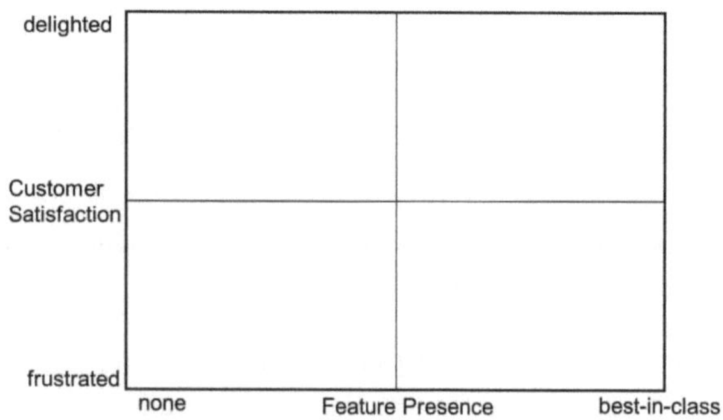

Fig. 5.18 The Kano matrix © Timo Wagenblatt 2019. All rights reserved

The feature presence axis explains the availability of the feature for the user on a scale from not available to best-in-class feature as shown in Fig. 5.19. The underlying assumption is that the effort to build the feature is a function of the feature availability, or in other words, the effort to build a best-in class feature is higher than a basic feature than not building it.

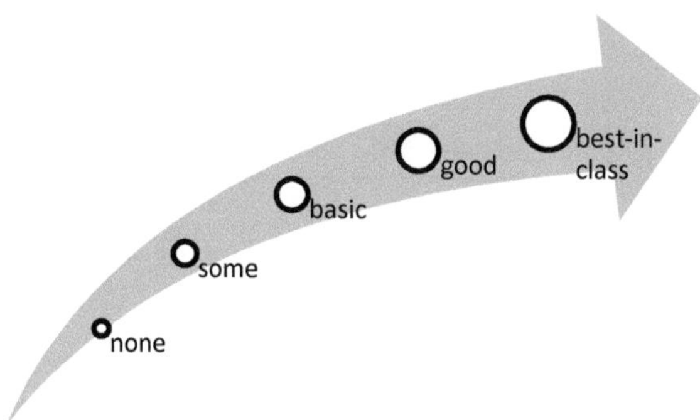

Fig. 5.19 Feature presence classification © Timo Wagenblatt 2019. All rights reserved

The customer satisfaction axis explains the feelings of the user on a scale ranging from frustrated to neutral to delighted as shown in Fig. 5.20. Understanding how the user feels about a given feature before the feature is built, that's the focus of the Kano Model. Leveraging this deeper understanding of the user's perception and feelings will help us as Product Managers make the right decisions about which features to focus on as well as balancing the level of effort building the prioritized features.

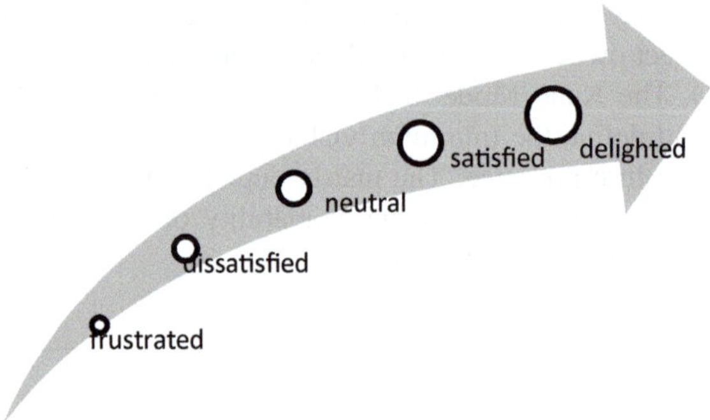

Fig. 5.20 Customer satisfaction classification © Timo Wagenblatt 2019. All rights reserved

According to Mr. Kano's theory all product features can be classified into the following categories:

- **Exciting and delighting Features (Exciters and Delighters)** (Kano, 1984)
  These product features have the specifics that even partial availability raises customer satisfaction dramatically. These are unexpected features that result in a strong positive sentiment. Imagine how you felt using the first smartphone and uncovered features that made you think: "Wow, that's really cool!" Even some level of functionality leads quickly to a significantly increased satisfaction. Features classified as Exciters and Delighters should be part of any prioritization, but only to a certain level of investment.

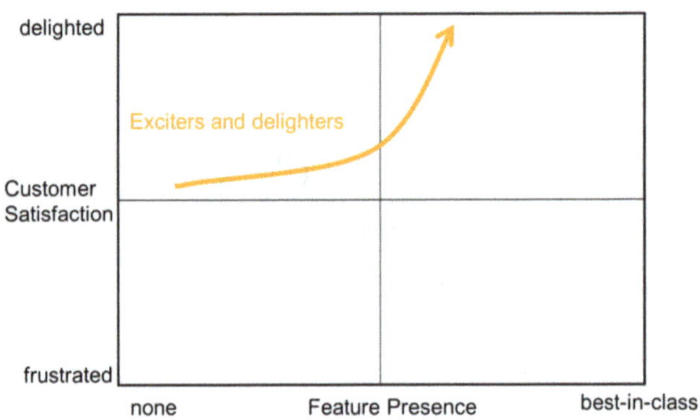

- **Performance Features (Satisfiers)** (Kano, 1984)
  These product features have the specifics that they behave the way you would expect. The more functionality available the more satisfied the users are. Imagine how you feel having more memory to store pictures on your smartphone or cloud storage or faster internet connection. The features are called One-dimensional in the original Kano Model. The availability of the feature results in satisfaction when fulfilled and dissatisfaction when not fulfilled (Kano Model, 2018). An

adapted example of this would be cloud storage that is said to have 15% more storage space for the same price will result in customer satisfaction. But if the product only offers five percent more space then it will lead to dissatisfaction.

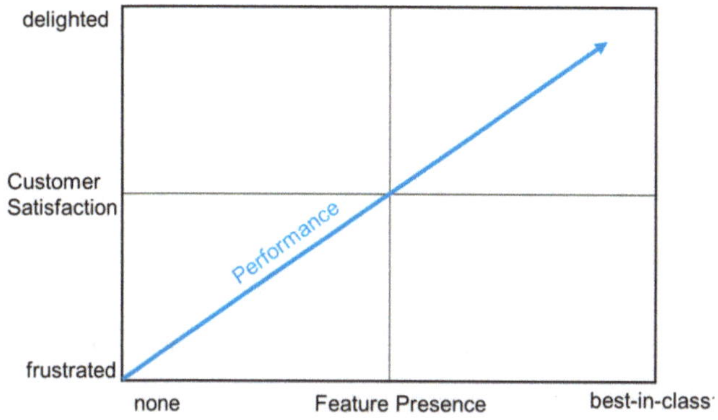

- **Must-have Features (Dissatisfiers)** (Kano, 1984)
  These product features have the specifics that they are simply expected by the customer and if they are available the customer is at least not disappointed. The satisfaction level will increase steadily, but it will not increase to a level reaching the positive side of the dimension. Imagine how you feel if you can use your smartphone to make a call, and now imagine if you cannot. Clearly making calls is a must-have feature for smartphones. Imagine how you feel if a product only comes with these kinds of features. Will you want to use and buy it?

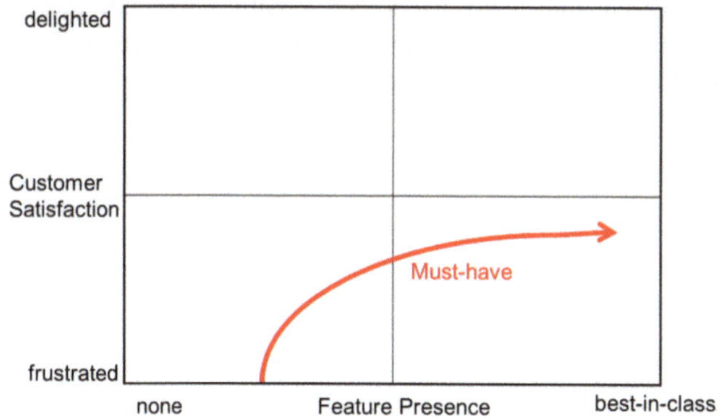

For me the beauty of the Kano Model has always been that it visually explains how customer satisfaction and the efforts to build a new product feature are related. We all have a gut feeling about this matter, but with the Kano Model it can be nicely formalized and explained. Although it seems common sense that in software development the focus should always be on the customer and the user, still too often the user's feelings are not considered during prioritization of software features. As we will discover in the case study below, the support of such a powerful method can efficiently change the normal ways of prioritizations. Mr. Kano's classification of product features is summarized in Fig. 5.21.

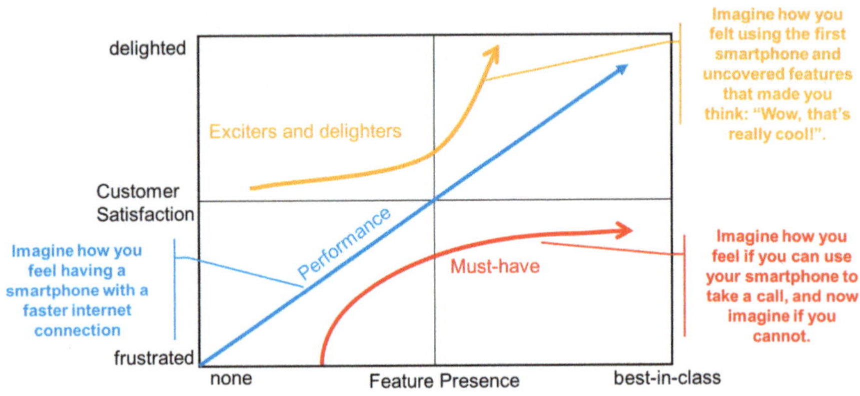

Fig. 5.21 The Kano classification with examples © Timo Wagenblatt 2019. All rights reserved

After looking at these important classifications, the Kano Model is not yet complete. There is one more feature classification missing that Mr. Kano called Indifferent qualities.

- **Indifferent Features**
  These product features are the ones that need special focus as they have a high saving potential. Identifying these features will save time and effort as users won't really care whether the feature is not available or best-in-class. The users feel indifferent or neutral for these features. That means it doesn't matter how much effort we put into them, users won't really appreciate the efforts. This is another way of saying we should really avoid working on these features, because they're essentially waste of time and budget.

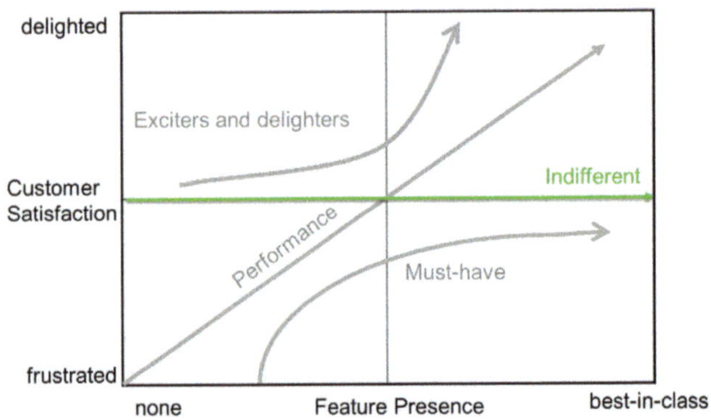

5.5.2 Kano Model Questionnaire

The training provided me with a new tool that I immediately put in my tool box as it was logical to me and did sound very interesting with lots of potential. The only issue was that I had not been trained how to get to the most important information—how to uncover customer's perceptions toward our product's attributes? When do I classify a feature as delighting, must-have, performance, or indifferent? How do I get to this essential information?

Luckily, the Kano Model was not new to the world, just new to me and maybe its application in backlog prioritization. I researched the internet and there are various great sources referencing the concept of the Kano Model questionnaire (e.g. Zacarias, 2018b; Kano's method for understanding customer-defined quality, 1993). I improved my bag of tricks and adapted the method for my purpose and for better applicability in my contexts over time.

The Kano Model consists of a pair of questions for each feature we want to evaluate:

- One asks our users how they feel if they have the feature (functional question)
- The second asks how they feel if they do not have the feature (dysfunctional question).

The answers to these questions are structured, meaning the user can select from the following answers:

Short description	Long description
I like it	This would be very helpful to me
I expect it	This is a basic requirement for me
I am neutral	This would not affect me
I can tolerate it	This would be a minor inconvenience
I dislike it	This would be a major problem for me

To classify the product features into one of the four Kano categories, we will use an evaluation table as proposed by Fred Pouliot (Pouliot, 1993). The evaluation matrix in Fig. 5.22 helps identify the correct classification (Delighter (D), Performance (P), Must-have (M), Indifferent (I), Reverse (R), Questionable (Q)). In addition to the four known classifications, it introduces two new classifications: Reverse and Questionable.

		Dysfunctional				
		Like it	Expect it	Neutral	Tolerate it	Dislike it
Functional	Like it	Q	D	D	D	P
	Expect it	R	Q	I	I	M
	Neutral	R	I	I	I	M
	Tolerate it	R	I	I	I	M
	Dislike it	R	R	R	R	Q

Fig. 5.22 The Kano classification matrix

A feature that is classified as Reverse indicates that the user wants the opposite of the feature more than the feature itself. Very interesting to understand as with this insight the dysfunctional feature could become the functional feature and user would get what she wants.

A feature that is classified as Questionable indicates that the user did not fully understand the questions or the feature we are describing in the question. If a user likes a proposed feature and in parallel likes that the feature is not there, it is a good indicator to talk to the user and check the rating.

Robert Blauth and team did research on how users react to the ratings and the long description. They proposed adding another question to the pair of functional and dysfunctional questions based on their experience using the Kano Model questionnaire (Robert Blauth, 1993). The additional question asks users how important a given feature is to them, which is likely the standard way how you have asked for priorities or rated product features in the past. The scale ranges from zero, meaning not of any interest to 10 meaning extremely important.

That's all the theory you need to know before starting to apply the Kano Model for your product feature classification and prioritization. I will illustrate the design and usage of the questionnaire and the Kano classification with a case study in the next section. This will help you to understand the insights you gain about the product features and the user's preferences as well as some watch outs when applying the method.

5.5.3 Proven Practice: Applying the Kano Model in the Wild

Since the first time I heard about the Kano Model in a product management training it felt like something I was searching for ages. The training was only a high-level introduction of the general theory, so I researched more about the method and started experimenting. Since then, I tested and applied the method in many contexts and with many user groups over the years. I experienced that not just I as a product manager found it useful as I gained new insights about my users, but also the customers appreciated the early consideration in the prioritization process.

Applying the Kano Model has been always useful in terms of supporting the prioritization process as well as gaining better insights about users. As product managers it is the purpose of our job to create products that satisfy and maybe even delight our customers. That's why I like to dedicate this section how to apply and leverage the Kano Model.

I will provide you with some context regarding the situation the product team faced and how we successfully used the Kano Model with three of our key customers, who, in fact, were very vocal customers in our long-lasting customer council. We had a two release per year strategy established, which was guided by our customer council. We frequently delivered one release in spring and the second one in the fall each year.

In this example, we faced some severe issues late in the release process that did not allow us to release to the customers and we had to postpone the release for a few weeks. However, we conducted early feedback-seeking demos in our customer council meetings a few months earlier. All signs were positive to release on time.

Therefore, it was a huge surprise to our customers to hear about the release delay and customer satisfaction dropped remarkably. It was particularly bad since we already discussed and detailed the next big things on our roadmap and our customers were prepared for these co-innovations.

With some extra work we got back on track with our release; however, we decided to mostly emphasize technical backlog items in the next release and hence the time and budget dedicated for the value generating big-ticket items was reduced. Given this situation, we understood that it was even more important to work closely with our customers and make sure that their users would be satisfied with the delivered functionalities.

On top of the list of required functionalities the customer council asked for functionality addressing a new user persona, the managers of our current user base. Satisfying your users is important, but satisfying the managers of your users, targeting them to become active users who will not just use your software but might also be the decision makers buying your product or renewing the subscription—well, you get my point.

We invited the customers to a first kick-off session and defined jointly the following process:

1. **Collecting and Understanding the Sales Director Requirements**

We started with researching the needs of the sales directors in consumer products manufacturers and there was not much news to be shared. We followed the standard process of requirements gathering, having multiple workshops with the end users and customer representatives, sometime 1:1, sometimes with the whole group. We collected many requirements, epics, and user stories and clearly, we got content for some more years of development. I will not detail much more of the process, that's well understood and in case you need a reference I would recommend you *Managing Software Requirements* by Leffingwell and Widrig (Leffingwell & Widrig, 2000).

The result of this process step is a list of user stories[22] that need to be aligned with the participating customers and users. We did know, and the customers did

[22]Or epics, depending on definition and granularity. I will use the term user story for simplification reasons, while I admit that some items are rather epics in the introduced example.

recognize as well that we could not develop all these functionalities in the next release. Prioritization of the backlog was required.

2. **Creation and Introduction of a Kano Model Questionnaire**

We created a Kano Model Questionnaire for 20 user stories with the objective of getting more data from our target users (user personas). For each user story we created three questions,

- the functional question (asking how they feel if they would have the feature)
- the dysfunctional question (asking how they feel if they would not have the feature)
- and the easiest part, the priority rating of the user story.

The quality and clearness of your questions is important for many reasons. Otherwise you might get too many user stories that are categorized as questionable. You obviously want to avoid this extra work and extra iteration as much as possible. Therefore, it is important that you test your questionnaire within your team: you can ask developers, testers, pre-sales or consulting colleagues. If they do not understand the questions, revisit and rephrase them.

The questions should be phrased as clear and concise as possible. Each question needs to focus on a single user story and if the user story is complex and requires multiple steps or sub-processes, you need to split the question into multiple questions or multiple Kano questionnaire iterations with increasing granularity over time.

Your questions should be phrased in terms of benefits to the user, and not in terms of how the problem is solved or what the product will do. For example, "If you can trigger and approve or reject workflows such as like incremental funds requests, early shipment requests, forecast approval from a central place in context of your sales plan's responsibility, how do you feel?" is better than "if we enable SAP Workflow Engine, how do you feel?"

The key points are that you need

- to be mindful of how the questions are interpreted and
- to make sure respondents understand the content and purpose of the questionnaire.

Consequently, we did not just send a short email to the users asking for the answered survey back. We introduced the questions, the pair of functional and dysfunctional questions plus the importance rating for each user story and the possible answers to all participating users.

When more details were available, like mock-ups, videos or anything else better explaining the functionality, we used it. Afterwards we asked the users to fill out the questionnaire and let us know if there were any problems with the questions or missing details. The result of this process step is a set of answered Kano Model Questionnaires like the one in Fig. 5.23 from a set of representative users from all participating companies.

Req #	Question	I like it - This would be very helpful to me	I expect it This is a basic requirement for me	I am neutral This would not affect me	I can tolerate it This would be a minor inconvenience	I dislike it This would be a major problem for me
1	If you understand the progress of a new product introduction (presented to customer, agreed with customer, part of customer plan, ...), how do you feel?	x				
	If you do not have insights about the progress of a new product introduction (presented to customer, agreed with customer, part of customer plan, ...), how do you feel?				x	
	How important is it for you to understand the progress of a new product introduction (presented to customer, agreed with customer, part of customer plan?			5		
2	If you can identify the plans that influence your key performance indicators (e.g. margin, market share...) from your KPIs down to the contributing plan or plans, how do you feel?	x				
	If you cannot track from your KPI down to the contributing plans that cause the positive/negative impact, how do you feel?				x	
	How important is it for you to identify the plans that influence your key performance indicators (e.g. margin, market share...) from your KPI down to the contributing plan or plans?			7		
3	If monitoring the planning progress of your sales teams in one view is possible, how do you feel?	x				
	If you understand the planning progress of your sales teams via 1:1 communication (talk, email, chat, phone), how do you feel?				x	
	How important is it for you to monitor the planning progress of your sales teams in one view			6		
4	If you have the flexibility to access, add and create reports/dashboards as part of your management console, how do you feel?		x			
	If you access your reports and dashbaords via a screen outside of the management console, how do you feel?					x
	How important is it for you to access, add and create reports/dashboards directly in the management console?			8		

Fig. 5.23 Answered Kano model questionnaire © Timo Wagenblatt 2019. All rights reserved

3. Analyzing the Questionnaire Results

Analyzing the answers is actually the fun part as we learn a lot about our users and their requirements. Not only how important a requirement is for them, but getting to the core—how they feel about it. A practical approach to analyzing the received questionnaires could be:

a. Categorize each answer using the Kano Classification Matrix shown in Fig. 5.22

The result of this step is a classification of each user story for every answered questionnaire. You might need to get back to the user directly in case of questionable answers. With that you already gain great insights about the user and can understand the likely satisfaction level. Figure 5.24 shows an example of a fully classified questionnaire.

Req #	Req Desc	Category
1	New Product Introduction Insights	Delighter
2	Multi Plan Analysis with Drill-Down to single plan	Delighter
3	Monitoring planning progress of your sales team	Delighter
4	Add and create reports/dashboards	Must-have
5	Planning process configuration	Delighter
6	CBP Plan scenarios broadcasting	Must-have
7	Sales Playbook and guard rails	Delighter
8	Workflow Requests and Approvals	Delighter
9	Annual plan scenarios analysis for all plans	Must-have
10	Listing Insights and Actions	Indifferent
11	Freeze Plans	Delighter
12	Plan vs Target Insights in Own Responsibility	Must-have
13	Time-bound planning	Performance
14	Insights With Direct Plan Navigation in Own Responsiility	Delighter
15	Planning Collisions within Planning Responsibility	Must-have
16	Planning Collisions across Planning Responsibillity	Delighter
17	Push Promotions	Must-have
18	Exceptions and Actions	Delighter
19	Collaborative Sales Team Meetings	Delighter
20	Mobile Enablement	Delighter

Fig. 5.24 Example: classified user stories © Timo Wagenblatt 2019. All rights reserved

b. Score the answers from the functional and dysfunctional questions and calculate the Kano priority

As you want to further work with the answers, it will be very useful to score the answers for all questions. There are various weights proposed for the scores. We applied the scores shown in Fig. 5.25 for each answer as we did rate negative feelings slightly higher than positive.

	This would be very helpful to me - I like it	This is a basic requirement for me - I expect it	This would not affect me - I am neutral	This would be a minor inconvenience - I can tolerate it	This would be a major problem for me - I dislike it
Functional	4	2	0	(1)	(3)
Dysfunctional	(3)	(1)	0	2	5

Fig. 5.25 Scoring Kano model questionnaire answers © Timo Wagenblatt 2019. All rights reserved

We did not want to create major problems for our customers and therefore applied an unbalanced score table emphasizing that the non-existence of functionality that a user would perceive as a major problem leads to a higher priority. The scores can be adapted as you design the questionnaire and should reflect your target group of users and their context, but you should not change the score on the fly or have different scores for different users in the same research project.

The result of this step is a functional and dysfunctional score for each user story for every answered questionnaire. In Fig. 5.26 you see an example of a fully scored questionnaire.

Req #	Req Desc	Question	Score	Kano Priority	Category
		Functional	4		
1	New Product Introduction Insights	Dysfunctional	2	11	Delighter
		Priority	5		
		Functional	4		
2	Multi Plan Analysis with Drill-Down to single plan	Dysfunctional	2	13	Delighter
		Priority	7		
		Functional	4		
3	Monitoring planning progress of your sales team	Dysfunctional	2	12	Delighter
		Priority	6		
		Functional	2		
4	Add and create reports/dashboards	Dysfunctional	5	15	Must-have
		Priority	8		
		Functional	4		
5	Planning process configuration	Dysfunctional	2	11	Delighter
		Priority	5		
		Functional	2		
6	CBP Plan scenarios broadcasting	Dysfunctional	5	15	Must-have
		Priority	8		
		Functional	4		
7	Sales Playbook and guard rails	Dysfunctional	2	12	Delighter
		Priority	6		
		Functional	4		
8	Workflow Requests and Approvals	Dysfunctional	0	9	Delighter
		Priority	5		
		Functional	2		
9	Annual plan scenarios analysis for all plans	Dysfunctional	5	16	Must-have
		Priority	9		
		Functional	2		
10	Listing Insights and Actions	Dysfunctional	2	10	Indifferent
		Priority	6		
		Functional	4		
11	Freeze Plans	Dysfunctional	2	12	Delighter
		Priority	6		
		Functional	2		
12	Plan vs Target Insights in Own Responsibility	Dysfunctional	5	15	Must-have
		Priority	8		
		Functional	4		
13	Time-bound planning	Dysfunctional	5	16	Performance
		Priority	7		
		Functional	4		
14	Insights With Direct Plan Navigation in Own Responsiili	Dysfunctional	-1	12	Delighter
		Priority	9		
		Functional	2		
15	Planning Collisions within Planning Responsibility	Dysfunctional	5	15	Must-have
		Priority	8		
		Functional	4		
16	Planning Collisions across Planning Responsibillity	Dysfunctional	2	13	Delighter
		Priority	7		
		Functional	2		
17	Push Promotions	Dysfunctional	5	14	Must-have
		Priority	7		
		Functional	4		
18	Exceptions and Actions	Dysfunctional	2	12	Delighter
		Priority	6		
		Functional	4		
19	Collaborative Sales Team Meetings	Dysfunctional	2	12	Delighter
		Priority	6		
		Functional	4		
20	Mobile Enablement	Dysfunctional	2	13	Delighter
		Priority	7		

Fig. 5.26 Example: scoring Kano model questionnaire answers © Timo Wagenblatt 2019. All rights reserved

In addition to the scoring of the functional and dysfunctional questions, there is also the priority rating straight from the user and the Kano priority, which simply is the sum of functional score + dysfunctional score + priority rating. The Kano priority is a great measure as it combines the scores of the satisfaction measurements and the absolute priority given by the user. Therefore, the Kano priority combines the absolute perceived priority by a user and the satisfaction level of having a feature as well as the dissatisfaction level if a missed feature.

Now we only needed to do this for ***all*** questionnaires that we received as described in the next step.

c. Consolidate all results from each user questionnaire and calculate the average priority, average functional score, average dysfunctional score and the average Kano priority

In a first step, you summarize the classification results from each user questionnaire in a matrix as shown in Fig. 5.27. You just need to count the total responses in each category for each user story. For example, requirement 6 in the first row, is a must-have for 6 people, a performance feature for 8 people, attractive (delighter) for 2 people and 2 people would not care about the feature. As most people rate requirement to be a performance feature, the requirement is classified as Performance.

Note that you should not expose this classification to your users and customers (yes, and not to your competitors). The classification is important in the next step where you decide which, in my example user stories, you are going to develop and to which level of maturity you develop the user stories.

Before we get there, it will be useful to add a few more measures supporting the decision-making process by providing additional insights. The first measures that are useful are the averages of the functional and dysfunctional scores. These measures are simple to calculate. You take the Sum of Functional Scores / # of

Req #	Requirement	Must-have	Performance	Attractive	Indifferent	Questionable	Reverse	Classification
6	CBP Plan scenarios broadcasting	6	8	2	2	0	0	Performance
2	Multi Plan Analysis with Drill-Down to single plan	10	4	2	0	2	0	Must-have
12	Plan vs Target Insights in Own Responsibility	6	4	6	0	2	0	M, A
15	Planning Collisions within Planning Responsibility	10	2	2	2	0	0	Must-have
9	Annual plan scenarios analysis for all plans	8	2	6	2	0	0	Must-have
16	Planning Collisions across Planning Responsibillity	10	2	2	2	0	0	Must-have
17	Push Promotions	4	6	8	0	0	0	Attractive
19	Collaborative Sales Team Meetings	0	0	8	6	2	0	Attractive
18	Exceptions and Actions	2	2	8	2	0	0	Attractive
1	New Product Introduction Insights	8	0	6	2	0	2	Must-have
14	Insights With Direct Plan Navigation in Own Responsiility	2	2	4	6	4	0	Indifferent
11	Freeze Plans	0	2	14	2	0	0	Attractive
3	Monitoring planning progress of your sales team	2	4	8	2	2	0	Attractive
10	Listing Insights and Actions	0	0	14	4	0	0	Attractive
4	Add and create reports/dashboards	2	0	14	2	0	0	Attractive
7	Sales Playbook and guard rails	2	0	12	4	0	0	Attractive
20	Mobile Enablement	0	2	14	2	0	0	Attractive
13	Time-bound planning	2	2	10	4	0	0	Attractive
8	Workflow Requests and Approvals	2	2	10	4	0	0	Attractive
5	Planning process configuration	4	2	4	6	2	0	Indifferent

Fig. 5.27 Kano classification consolidating all questionnaires © Timo Wagenblatt 2019. All rights reserved

participants or Sum of Dysfunctional Scores / # of participants. The insights you gain with these measures is a potential for satisfaction respectively dissatisfaction.

The second set of measures are the average priority simply calculated as sum of priority / # of participants and the average Kano priority calculated as the sum of (Functional Scores + Dysfunctional Scores + Priority Ratings) / # of participants for each individual user story.

The result of this process step is a clear understanding of

- the average functional score,
- the average dysfunctional score,
- the average user-stated priority and as well
- the average Kano priority,
- the Kano classification for each user story.

In Fig. 5.28, you can find all measures required to get to the objective of the whole exercise, the actual decision-making process to define which user stories should we build, and to which extent should the selected user stories be implemented. Yes, more statistics could be applied like standard deviation and the likes, but I find the calculations above sufficient and there was limited benefit in the cases we applied those additional measures.

Try it out on your own and include additional measures as you find them appropriate.[23]

4. **Prioritizing the Features and Feature Implementation Levels**

We gained an understanding of the satisfaction or dissatisfaction for each user story by our representative user group. This understanding can now be used to save development time and budget. In this step we prioritize the user stories and their implementation levels. This has been the objective of using the Kano Method.

Req #	Requirement	Avg Prio	Functional	Dysfunctional	Kano Prio	Kano Classification
1	New Product Introduction Insights	7,2	2,8	1,6	12,3	Must-have
2	Multi Plan Analysis with Drill-Down to single plan	8,7	2,4	3,8	15,3	Must-have
3	Monitoring planning progress of your sales team	6,4	3,2	2,6	12,1	Delighter
4	Add and create reports/dashboards	6,0	4	1,2	11,4	Delighter
5	Planning process configuration	5,5	2	1,2	8,7	Indifferent
6	CBP Plan scenarios broadcasting	8,1	3,2	4,4	15,6	Performance
7	Sales Playbook and guard rails	6,6	3,2	1,2	11,3	Delighter
8	Workflow Requests and Approvals	5,9	2,8	2,6	10,9	Delighter
9	Annual plan scenarios analysis for all plans	8,2	3,2	2,8	14,4	Must-have
10	Listing Insights and Actions	6,1	4	2	11,7	Delighter
11	Freeze Plans	6,7	4	1	12,2	Delighter
12	Plan vs Target Insights in Own Responsibility	8,7	3,6	2,6	14,8	Must-have, Delighter
13	Time-bound planning	6,2	2,4	1,2	11,0	Delighter
14	Insights With Direct Plan Navigation in Own Responsiility	8,2	2,4	1,4	12,2	Indifferent
15	Planning Collisions within Planning Responsibility	7,8	2,4	3,4	14,5	Must-have
16	Planning Collisions across Planning Responsibillity	7,6	2,4	3,4	14,3	Must-have
17	Push Promotions	7,2	4	3,8	14,1	Delighter
18	Exceptions and Actions	6,1	2,8	2,8	12,4	Delighter
19	Collaborative Sales Team Meetings	7,9	2,8	1	13,0	Delighter
20	Mobile Enablement	5,9	4	2	11,3	Delighter

Fig. 5.28 Kano questionnaire measures

[23]Examples of more sophisticated statistical measures can be found here: Zacarias (2018b).

Some useful prioritization techniques have been already introduced in Sect. 5.2 and the outcome of the Kano questionnaire fits perfectly well as a dimension in the prioritization board reflecting customer satisfaction as a decision influencing factor. If you want to consider this, the best way would be using the Kano priority and applying it in a normalized way directly to the prioritization board as one dimension.

Focusing on the user stories in leveraging our analysis, I describe below how we used the measures we derived in Step 3 to rank the user stories and define the level of effort we put into each item.

If we just look at the top 10 items, the case study showed nicely that the user-stated priority is a standard way to ask customers and users about the importance of a product feature, however it is very easily a false friend. Take a look at the average user-stated priority for the top five items compared to the Kano priority and the Kano classification Fig. 5.29.

Req #	Requirement	Avg Prio	Kano Prio	Kano Classification
2	Multi Plan Analysis with Drill-Down to single plan	8,7	15,3	Must-have
12	Plan vs Target Insights in Own Responsibility	8,7	14,8	Must-have, Delighter
9	Annual plan scenarios analysis for all plans	8,2	14,4	Must-have
14	Insights With Direct Plan Navigation in Own Responsiility	8,2	12,2	Indifferent
6	CBP Plan scenarios broadcasting	8,1	15,6	Performance
19	Collaborative Sales Team Meetings	7,9	13,0	Delighter
15	Planning Collisions within Planning Responsibility	7,8	14,5	Must-have
16	Planning Collisions across Planning Responsibillity	7,6	14,3	Must-have
17	Push Promotions	7,2	14,1	Delighter
1	New Product Introduction Insights	7,2	12,3	Must-have

Fig. 5.29 Average user-stated priority versus Kano measures

Just following the average user-stated priority we would start from top to bottom until the development capacity is fully utilized, thinking we work on the most important topics delivering the highest impact and value for our customers. However, including the Kano priority and the Kano classification the picture changes dramatically.

User story #14 is classified as Indifferent, so the users basically do not care whether the user story is available in our product, or in other words, the satisfaction of our users would not increase even if we deliver the best implementation for this user story. Consider this—the costs might be Hundreds of person days in development and the users would not value all that hard work. Therefore, we decided not to consider user story #14 at all and with that freeing up time and budget for other user stories.

Another interesting insight has been that user stories #15, #16 and #1 are classified as Must-haves; however, they are not ranked at the top and would be missed out or postponed to later deliveries.

These are just two examples where the focus on the average user-stated priority would not deliver the best outcome. Consider the different picture when ordering the user stories by the Kano priority in the top 10 list depicted in Fig. 5.30.

Req #	Requirement	Avg Prio	Functional	Dysfunctional	Kano Prio	Kano Classification
6	CBP Plan scenarios broadcasting	8,1	1,2	6	15,6	Performance
2	Multi Plan Analysis with Drill-Down to single plan	8,7	2,4	3,8	15,3	Must-have
12	Plan vs Target Insights in Own Responsibility	8,7	3,2	2,8	14,8	Must-have, Delighter
15	Planning Collisions within Planning Responsibility	7,8	1	6,6	14,5	Must-have
9	Annual plan scenarios analysis for all plans	8,2	6,4	2,8	14,4	Must-have
16	Planning Collisions across Planning Responsibillity	7,6	8,6	2,4	14,3	Must-have
17	Push Promotions	7,2	5,4	2,4	14,1	Delighter
19	Collaborative Sales Team Meetings	7,9	3,4	6,2	13,0	Delighter
18	Exceptions and Actions	6,1	2,4	3,4	12,4	Delighter
1	New Product Introduction Insights	7,2	4	1,2	12,3	Must-have

Fig. 5.30 Average user-stated priority versus all Kano measures © Timo Wagenblatt 2019. All rights reserved

There is a common rule of thumb that you should start with all the Must-have user stories, then you would do the Performance ones and finally the Delighters. I think this rule works well if your budget and time is sufficient. Hence in most cases, I would recommend another approach for the ranking of the backlog or in this case the user stories.

Using the full insights that we calculated and discovered in Step 3, we used the decisions as illustrated in Fig. 5.31 for the best investment level of each item.

Req #	Requirement	Functional	Dysfunctional	Kano Prio	Kano Classification	Order of dev	Investment level
6	CBP Plan scenarios broadcasting	1,2	6	15,6	Performance	6	Remaining budget and time
2	Multi Plan Analysis with Drill-Down to single plan	2,4	3,8	15,3	Must-have	1	MVS
12	Plan vs Target Insights in Own Responsibility	3,2	2,8	14,8	Must-have, Delighter	2	>MVS
15	Planning Collisions within Planning Responsibility	1	6,6	14,5	Must-have	3	MVS
9	Annual plan scenarios analysis for all plans	6,4	2,8	14,4	Must-have	4	MVS
16	Planning Collisions across Planning Responsibillity	8,6	2,4	14,3	Must-have	5	MVS
17	Push Promotions	5,4	2,4	14,1	Delighter	7	<MVS, but defined budget
19	Collaborative Sales Team Meetings	3,4	6,2	13,0	Delighter	8	<MVS, but defined budget
18	Exceptions and Actions	2,4	3,4	12,4	Delighter		
1	New Product Introduction Insights	4	1,2	12,3	Must-have		

Fig. 5.31 Average user-stated priority versus all Kano measures with investment level © Timo Wagenblatt 2019. All rights reserved

We considered all the Must-have user stories and ranked them according to the Kano priority, however, we did not put user story #1 into the release backlog. The rationale behind this has been the given Kano priority and the relatively low dissatisfaction level of 1, 2 in case the user story is not available. With that we could include user stories that are Delighters such as user stories #17 and #19. For all the Must-have user stories we defined a minimum viable scope knowing that a richer functionality will not increase user satisfaction. We also considered that user story #12 had a diverse rating being a Must-have and Delighter user story. Therefore, we allocated additional time to this user story, going beyond the minimum feature implementation level. I would strongly recommend always considering at least one Delighter in your prioritization, as this is what wows the users using your product.

We allocated a budget as well to the Delighter user stories #17 and #19. This allowed us to spend significant time and budget to deliver the highest Kano priority item, which is uscr story #6.

You might wonder why we did not start with the performance item. We applied the rule that we get the must-have's first, then add some delighters and use all remaining budget for the performance item, assuming the customer satisfaction is higher with a few delighters and a bit of the performance item than a fully-fledged performance item and no delighters. Of course, you could have a different interpretation, but this worked well for our context.

With this release backlog, we went back to the customers and users presenting our prioritization. And they were satisfied … just kidding!

All we did was increase the chances that our customers and users are satisfied. By getting deeper insights about the user's feelings, we increased our chances significantly. In our case study, the results have been very positive, although we did not manage to develop all items in the release and even missed on delivering some user stories classified as Must-have.

Along these lines you can never expect everyone to be satisfied. There will likely be some people that might be disappointed as in the case of user story #14, which was classified as Indifferent. Most users rated the user story that way; however, a few users said it is a Must-have user story. As product managers we need to care about the market, not the individual, but we equally need to remain flexible and open as we decide what gets built and what remains in the product backlog. Be prepared to disappoint some customers and users and make it transparent why and how you decided.

You can safeguard the impact of your decisions by having a great quality questionnaire and taking time to define and recruit a representative user group. In addition, consider the average functional score and the average dysfunctional score. These are indicators of how satisfied your users will be if you implement a certain feature or how disappointed they will be if you decide against it. In Fig. 5.30 you can see that the users would be much more dissatisfied not getting user story #15 than user story #16, and users would appreciate user story #9 much more than #15. You can work with these additional measures and build the best package for your product's success and your customer's and user's satisfaction.

5.5.4 Leveraging the Insights for Your Market Situation

The Kano Model is a superior method as it is easy, logical and puts the user in the center of the research. In addition, it allows you to see where to find the greatest leverage for your investment. There are many conclusions you can draw from applying the Kano Model in the wild. Find in Table 5.10 three strategic takeaways that can be applied as a general rule for your prioritization strategy.

Table 5.10 Kano model application by market situation

Market situation	Differential value rule
You compete on features and functions in an existing marketplace	Invest in performance and must-have features, but never overinvest in a feature that is already commoditized. Think about disruption and unique selling points by focusing on delighters
You are already competitive, but you want features that constitute a decisive competitive edge	Drive innovation by having the courage to invest heavily in delighters
If resources do not allow you to compete with the current rules of the game, play a different game	Invest in delighters even if you don't have complete feature parity or cover must-have scope

5.5.5 Human Behaviour—Attractive Today Is Commodity Tomorrow

Now that we have a complete picture of all Kano theory and how it can be applied in your daily work, it's important to recognize a fundamental fact: Kano classifications of features are not static—they change over time as illustrated in Fig. 5.32. What our users feel about some product feature now is not what they'll feel in the future.

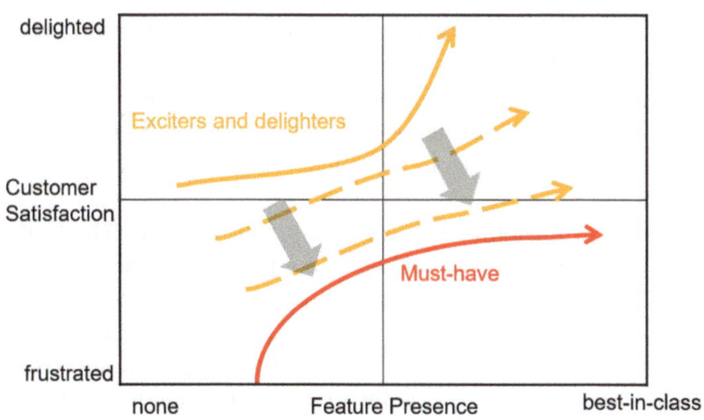

Fig. 5.32 Kano classifications change over time © Timo Wagenblatt 2019. All rights reserved

"It is a never-ending search for the next Delighter feature" (Lawley & Schure, 2017) and "Differentiators of software products tend to have a short life time, as competitors are quick to catch up. … delighter features … are quickly taken for granted, turning into performance or even must-have features." (Kittlaus & Fricker, 2017)

Delighting features turn into Performance and Must-have features over time, or in other words, over time delightful innovation becomes another basic need. Consider the smartphone example again: touchscreens by now are just a basic expectation with any mobile phone.

5.5.6 Summary and Conclusions

User centricity, user focus and other buzzwords have been around for years, but there are still many decisions and prioritization approaches that do not consider enough the user's "feelings." The Kano Model provides a brilliant option to gain insights in this direction. These insights can then be used for many decisions, from prioritization to when to stop improving a feature. Consider the results as a starting point, not the final answers. You might consider multiple Kano questionnaires with increasing levels of details. Note that you cannot just tick the box of user focus just because you did a Kano questionnaire. This is only a small piece of the puzzle to understanding the requirements and its impact on your users.

The Kano Model results can be leveraged as a valuable input for the prioritization board process as explained previously. For example, the Kano classification and priorities can be easily incorporated into one of the decision influencing factors focusing on customer satisfaction or user adoption. Furthermore, the resulting insights can help shape the scope of individual items.

You might consider leveraging the value mapping prioritization techniques to visualize the cost versus value information of each requirement together with the Kano classification. This provides another angle to look at the requirements and make better decisions.

B2C product managers might consider applying the Kano Model in an even more sophisticated way using the A/B testing feedback as an input to the Kano questionnaire. Consider questions about satisfaction in each group, some represent the functional part and some the dysfunctional part of the Kano questionnaire.

These examples above should encourage you to improve your back of tricks in prioritization techniques. Combining techniques is an option as well as experimenting and seeing what works in the context of your product, your organization and your users.

Finally, I need to mention some cautionary notes as well. The Kano questionnaire should be done with users, real users not proxies. When working with users you need to focus on finding a representative group of users. The questionnaire needs special attention as well. In best case you moderate each question and do not just send the questionnaire. Every word is important as people understand different things reading the same words. Test the questionnaire internally or with a trusted subset of users. If you have visuals, mock-ups and the likes, even better. And as a last note, do not mention to the users you interview that you are applying the Kano Method. People are smart, and the results might become biased and essentially less useful for prioritization.

The Kano Model as well as the other prioritization techniques are not directly part of PYPR. However, the Kano Model provides valuable insights that might result in improvements of multiple PYPR dimensions and items from functional completeness to team health to value for customer reflected in the customer business case item.

5.6 Roadmaps

Your customers can tell you the things that are broken and how they want to be made happy. Listen to them. Make them happy. But don't rely on them to create the future roadmap for your product or service. That's your job. **Mark Cuban**

I agree with Mark Cuban: Creating the future roadmap of your product is your job. But do not confuse product roadmap with product strategy. I consider roadmaps purely as a communication tool for the product direction for (internal or external) information purposes at the time of presentation.

The issue with roadmaps is that most people agree that they are directional by nature. However, whenever you present a roadmap to, for example, customers, partners, or your management team, no one seems to remember the bold, underlined, and flashing disclaimers, at the beginning, on top, across and below the roadmap document, stating: Everything here is subject to change without notice!

There are various roadmap formats out there. If you are looking for a comprehensive list of roadmap types I would recommend that you to simply search the internet or read any standard Software Product Management book like the *Product Management for Dummies* book (Lawley & Schure, 2017) and the likes.

Roadmaps are living documents. Everyone who is in charge of a roadmap asset knows that any roadmap is a fast-moving vehicle. Roadmaps need to change as new requirements with higher priority come in or new discoveries arise. Roadmap documents cannot be treated and should never be understood like a project plan that is set in stone, particularly if your organization values outcomes more than predictable output. Make it crystal clear to everyone exposed to the roadmap that the roadmap document is a living document.

The rise of agile development techniques, but also the improved understanding that decisions made on vague information and little data may not be the right answer once customers are engaged and further details are discovered during the development process mandates to see roadmaps in a different light.

Consequently, this means that roadmap stakeholders need to understand that roadmaps are snapshots of the current (read: today's) direction. The roadmap document represents the news of today. And tomorrow yesterday's news is old. That's a hard statement that not everyone would buy into or accepts. I would love to have roadmap documents (and presentations) in the "Mission Impossible" movie style—they self-destruct after reading.

Despite all the reasoning why roadmaps are not what people would like them to be, your customers, partners, and your executive team are unlikely to stop asking for roadmaps. Some of the reasons might be that:

- Customers have to plan for technology and business process changes.
- Customers need to understand when they can expect your software product will solve their problems and the problems of their business users.

- Sometimes customers have to build a business case of why they should upgrade to a new software version or adopt new product features[24]; therefore, customers require information about costs, timing and scope and you likely want to support their needs.
- Management wants to understand similarly what they get for their investment and the rationale behind each release. Your objective is to secure buy-in for your product vision and strategy, and to maintain continued funding and in best case enthusiasm. The roadmap document should only be a part of your management communication. However, you can re-use it nicely on top of PYPR and your product vision and strategy work results.
- Partners need to know when they need to learn the new capabilities, when they can leverage the new capabilities in their implementation project or whether they better go for a custom solution.

Each party stated above and many more not mentioned want to get insights and make conclusions based on your product roadmap. Management, internal departments, external partners, and customers will all want to make decisions on investment priorities and plans. Your roadmaps will require different flavors for each audience to best meet their (and your) needs.

That's exactly the area of conflict between the legitimate information needs and the essential agility to optimize for customer value over predictable output. In short, that is the ultimate reason of all the noise about roadmaps. David Cancel, CEO of Drift, and former Head of Product for HubSpot, summed up these frustrations well when he explained why he no longer puts together a traditional roadmap: "Either I'm going to disappoint you by giving you exactly what we thought six months ahead of time was the best solution when it's not, or by changing course and having lied to you (McCarthy, 2018)."

As great product managers we cannot disappoint our customers, partner, and executives nor we would ever lie to them. Period. But there is a demand for product roadmaps.

In the next section, I will introduce a proven way to stick to the high standards and survive in the product roadmapping area of conflict—somehow.

5.6.1 Proven Template: Current, Planned, Vision—Roadmap

Evidently roadmapping is an essential tool in your bag of tricks as a product manager. And like any tool it can be used well or in the wrong way. Have you ever

[24]For B2C products the business case might be more of a metaphor; however, consumers have the similar information demands. What's new in the game, when do I get the feature I ever wanted, when can I use these two apps together and thousands of other questions. Consumers might stay with your product, if they understand the roadmap and see the improvements coming and its vision. Without roadmap information, they might switch to your competition and miss the big thing you worked on and they ever wanted, but they are not using your product anymore and will not recognize your efforts.

tried to tighten a screw with a hammer? The roadmap format described in this section has various benefits and re-uses the great work and efforts you put into your Product Vision and Strategy and Product Development Planning and Review. Note that the product roadmap is not your product vision, it is not your product strategy and it is not a copy of your backlog. A roadmap is a roadmap.

The product roadmap enables the stakeholders to find out about your product's current capabilities and how they add value to solve their problems. Stakeholders can discover planned innovations already being worked on and get a perspective on the future direction of your product.

The product roadmap template consists of the following:

- **Introduction of the currently available product**
  Add your available product one-pager here. Re-use from the sales kit or vice versa re-use the asset in the sales kit. Basically, the introduction comprises a concise product description, list of the product key elements, how these elements solve the business pain points and anything else that fits nicely on one page and is important for your product positioning and product vision.
- **Today's capabilities, planned innovations, and product vision**
  In the main part of the roadmap document you detail on one page in an appealing way your complete roadmap (at least the part you want to expose outside of the core product team) (Fig. 5.33).

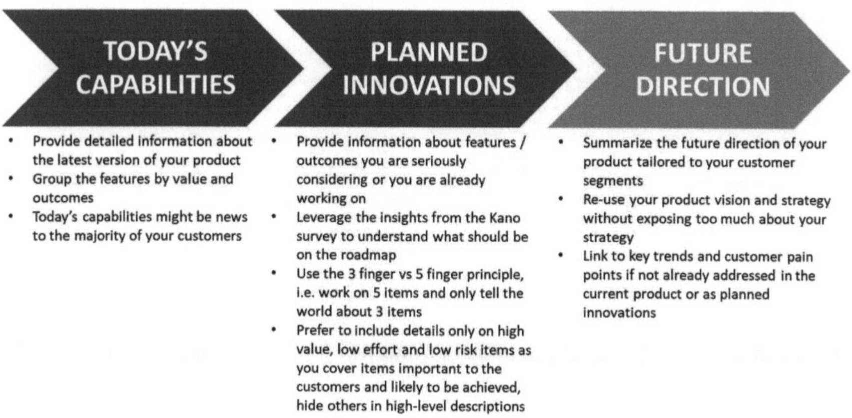

Fig. 5.33 Product roadmap structure © Timo Wagenblatt 2019. All rights reserved

You could add some details for each roadmap item in subsequent slides, but avoid any details such as screen captures or the likes. These could be perceived as promises that you want to avoid.

- **Summary and Further Information**
  Summarize the key messages of your product roadmap presentation. Provide links to further material (e.g. marketing brochures, Product Marketing videos, etc.) and how the product team can be approached.

Roadmaps are a tool to represent your product in the best possible way. As so many people are interested in roadmaps, and less in vision, use the roadmap document to infuse the vision. The template introduced in this section has proven its value in the past years. It provides a complete and clear structure, serving the stakeholders' needs in an appealing way while not being a project plan masked as a product roadmap. The product roadmap provides details where details make sense and provide directions where details could be misleading.

SAP® applies a similar format to all their roadmaps. Figure 5.34 provides an example of a SAP roadmap showing a variation adapted to the fixed release dates of new features and the rich content not fitting on a single slide. SAP shares product roadmaps with everyone on their website. Sounds scary to product managers, right?

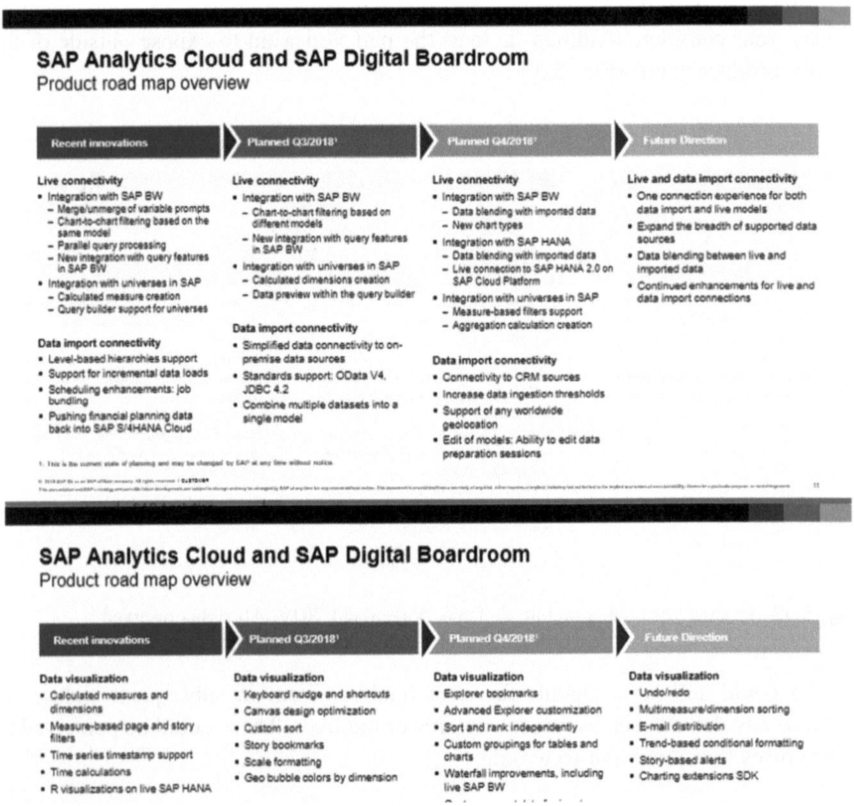

Fig. 5.34 Product roadmap example: SAP Analytics Cloud (SAP Product Roadmaps, 2018)

This kind of product roadmap is not a technical document nor a project plan nor a contract nor a commitment. This product roadmap is a tool that underlines the current and future strength of YourProduct Inc.

5.6.2 PYPR Dimension Items Details

See Tables 5.11 and 5.12.

Table 5.11 PYPR defaults by software product manager type

Topic		Internal PM	B2B PM	B2C PM
Default dimension item weight		22.5	15	10
Criticality for PM		High	Medium	Low
PYPR score	Low	No current roadmap available or roadmap that is basically a reflection of the short-term backlog and only internally available. A low scoring should also be considered for poor quality roadmap content and format due to the damage it could cause		
	Medium	Roadmaps re-available, but lack some of the qualities outlined in this section		
	High	Roadmaps are available for all relevant customer segments and tailored for all interested parties featuring the product positioning and product vision. The roadmap covers the proven template topics and is centrally available and used		

Table 5.12 PYPR dimensions impact examples

Dimension	Direct impact example	Indirect impact example
Product viability		Pipeline generation, upgrading customers improve maintenance profitability
Product development	Product development dimension improves	Dev. management perceives progress and understands high-level planning
Go-to-market/product marketing	Can be used as a sales tool and for enablement sessions	Roadmap underlines product positioning and shiny future of product
Software demonstrations and training	Pre-sales enablement improves	
The market/your customers	Functional completeness positively impacted	
Organizational maturity	Improves templates and tools dimension item	

5.6.3 Summary and Conclusions

When presenting roadmaps, you should always have a call to action; that is, a request for feedback of how the roadmap resonates with them or ask them work with you on certain roadmap items. Planned and future items of your roadmap are items that are under consideration and if there is sufficient customer interest and support the likelihood of delivery increases. It's a great way for you to have a conversation with customers about what they would like in the future and for you to get useful feedback.

Key Takeaways

- Product Roadmapping means internal and external expectation management.
- Leverage product roadmaps. Roadmaps can become great communication vehicles when used and understood in the right way.
- Connect your product roadmap to your product vision and strategy.
- Product roadmaps should address the needs and the problems of your target market segment and therefore focus on outcomes rather than features.
- Engage with customers and partners
  - Include customer and partner feedback.
  - Ask them to work with you on the planned innovations (i.e. more insights to secure their planning, but also increase product value with early feedback cycles).
  - Emphasize that the further along you are in the development process the higher the chance a feature gets released, but there is no guaranteed delivery.
- Product roadmaps are out of date almost as soon as they are published if you do not follow some basic principles. Factor probability and uncertainty into your roadmap to manage stakeholder expectations.
- Competition reads your public roadmaps as well, don't expose your strategy via product roadmaps, keep the balance and include some "smoke grenades" in the future direction section.
- De-scoping is not a sin, but frequent changes to the entire roadmap is guaranteed to hurt your internal and external credibility.

- Utilize the following roadmap checklist when you're developing and reviewing your roadmap content:

  – **Housekeeping rules**

    Do not include content/wording that commits to planned/future features associated with specific delivery dates or version numbers. This might cause legal issues and revenue recognition problems.
    Any slide with planned or future content needs to contain a statement like: "This is the current state of planning and may be changed at any time" or "Roadmap is only accurate" <today>. Details will change. Contact <your contact details> for latest version."
    If you cannot resist and add screenshots, make sure you use "**Labs preview**" sticker for any screenshots on planned or future slides.
    Include a legal disclaimer slide.

  – **Content**

    Check content is concise and relevant for your audience.
    Focus on key messages and highlight changes.
    Ensure key messages are clear.
    Be vague on dates as much as possible, so instead of stating "Planned August 25th", state "Planned Q3" or "2nd Half 2019".
    Include the current product release number.
    Planned innovations = Already in development (aggregated, not single backlog item level, maybe epic).
    Future direction (Little detail, big ticket items, key trends, 3 and 5 finger rule, themes).

5.7 Product Quality from an Internal View

I have a very clear opinion about the product manager role in product quality. Product managers need to spend time with their software product, and testing is time well invested. Your role is to verify and accept the product developments, and as a side effect, you will get to know the product better. Generally engineering teams have a good understanding about the technical product quality. They know the parts that are robust and the features and functions that might be technically a bit shaky. You need to understand the areas that seem to be fixed easier, and the ones that are on the harder side as well. As product managers, you need to know the ins and outs of your product. You need to know every little bit of YourProduct Inc. You represent your internal and external customers, the market and all other stakeholders. These are a few of the many reasons why it is so important for product managers to actively test the product.

Historically product quality was located in one department, the Quality (Management, Assurance, etc.) department. Luckily those days are over and product teams have widely understood and accepted that quality is everyone's responsibility.

This section is not about becoming a better tester or starting a QM career. I want to provide you with some foundational knowledge to better understand the various aspects of product quality. Therefore, I will explain the following tools of the trade:

- Grouping quality aspects in three clusters
- The Agile Testing Quadrant taxonomy of the various testing requirements of software products
- General quality principles and derived engineering practices.

These tools of the trade will help you become a better product manager. You will be equipped to understand how product managers can contribute and lead the team to better product quality.

One way of structuring software product quality is according to the value chain of product development (Chappell, 2019). As an example, the value chain starts with the customer problem to be solved, that leads to a software product solving the customer's problem—ideally. Product quality can be clustered into process, structural (code), and functional quality accordingly as illustrated in Fig. 5.35.

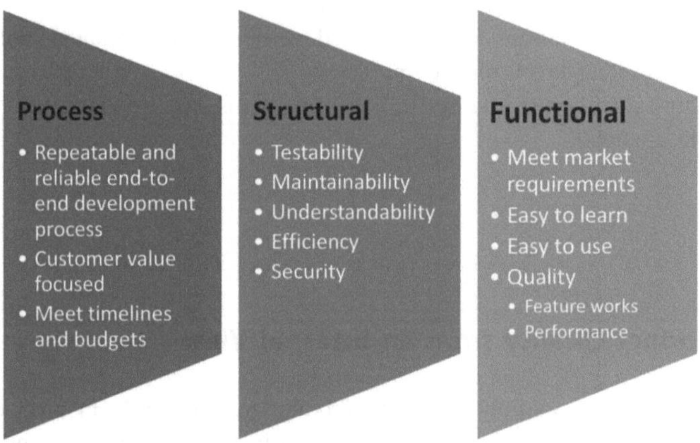

Fig. 5.35 Product quality aspects © Timo Wagenblatt 2019. All rights reserved

The Agile Testing Quadrants by Brian Marick provide a taxonomy to help teams identify, plan and execute the testing needed (Agile Testing, 2019). If you want more details of the concept, I recommend Lisa Crispin's and Janet Gregory's book that popularized Brian's model (Crispin & Gregory, 2009).

The Agile Testing Quadrant model summarizes all aspects of product quality as illustrated in Fig. 5.36. I will briefly introduce the model and use it to explain the product manager's potential playing field. In this section I focus on the core product team's responsibilities, not the customer's perception of product quality. In Sect. 8.2, I will utilize the same model to explain how and what customers perceive from the actual product quality and why there might be deviations.

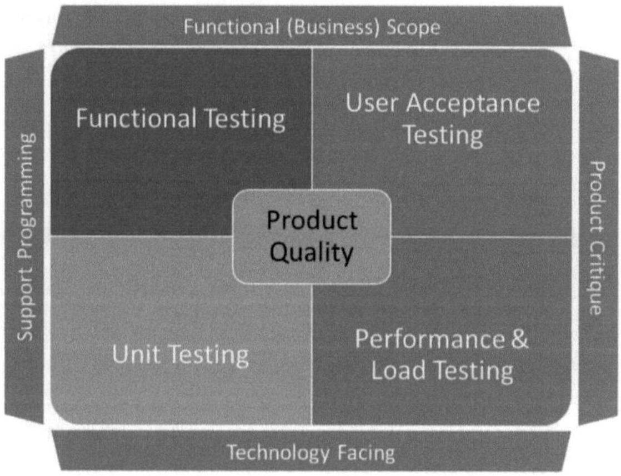

Fig. 5.36 Agile testing quadrants model © Timo Wagenblatt 2019. All rights reserved

I prefer the Agile Testing Quadrant model because all important aspects are easily explained. Functional testing and user acceptance testing uncover whether we are building the right product. User acceptance testing and performance and load testing uncover the externally exposed part of your product. Unit testing and the performance and load testing uncover whether you are building the product right.

As a product manager your playground is likely in the area of functional testing (to confirm product behavior), user acceptance testing (focus on user scenario, not single feature), and performance and load testing (provide quantity structures representing your target customer segments reality). As a product manager you are like a tourist in Product Quality Land, who cannot visit everything, hence wants to make sure to see the most important things.

Using the three aspects of product quality and the Agile Testing Quadrant model you now have the foundation to understand your product's status in this PYPR dimension item. As a product team, you can likely improve the PYPR rating if you consider some of the quality principles and apply some engineering practices that are certainly interrelated as illustrated in Fig. 5.37.

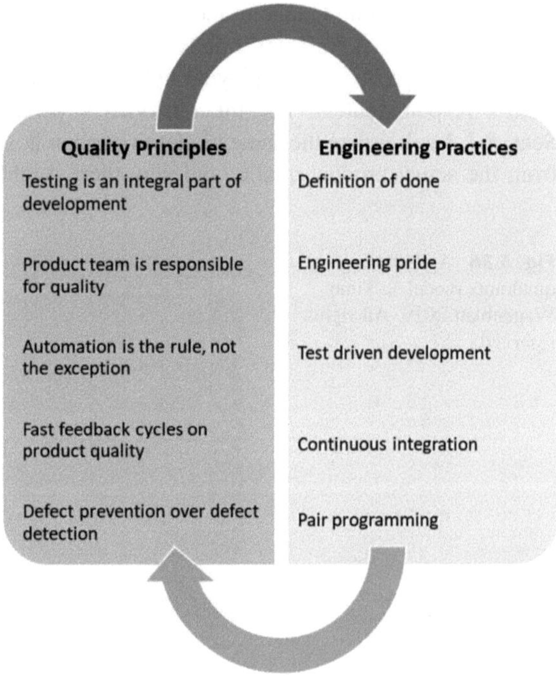

Fig. 5.37 Example of quality principles and engineering practices © Timo Wagenblatt 2019. All rights reserved

5.7.1 PYPR Dimension Items Details

See Tables 5.13 and 5.14.

Table 5.13 PYPR defaults by software product manager type

Topic		Internal PM	B2B PM	B2C PM
Default dimension item weight		15	15	20
Criticality for PM		Medium	Medium	High
PYPR score	Low	Most product functionality isn't properly tested, no one feels responsible for testing and good product quality, testing is considered as a burden and not as an integral part of delivering customer value, all tests are manually and randomly done, the number of incidents are at record levels, bugs are found in existing and new features, changing existing code leads to unpredictable side-effects, simple requirements are risky to implement, no backlog items accepted in sprint reviews and I'm sure you can find many more symptoms of low product quality within your core product team		
	Medium	The team feels somewhere in the middle. Some aspects might be rather on the low end while others work extremely well. Perceptions are deviating, e.g. product owner perceives product having great functionality, while development team suffers from technical debt		
	High	Fully automated testing for regression and new functionality, quality is everyone's responsibility, test activities ensure high quality from various perspectives like performance, integration, development standards, user interaction and customer value, very limited defects found even in edge scenarios, existing functionality doesn't break with new features, theoretically product/product features can be released any time		

Table 5.14 PYPR dimensions impact examples

Dimension	Direct impact example	Indirect impact example
Product viability	Maintenance/run profitability correlates highly with product quality	
Product development	Team health benefits from superior product quality due to pride of work and avoidance of conflict	
Go-to-market/product marketing		Great product quality allows early for enablement of Go-to-market stakeholders. Testing activities can be part of enablement plan

(continued)

Table 5.14 (continued)

Dimension	Direct impact example	Indirect impact example
Software demonstrations and training		More reliable software demonstrations and shorter time for demo build
The market/your customers	Better product quality generally leads to better perceived product quality externally	
Organizational maturity		Improved people mindset with product quality being a key principle

5.7.2 Summary and Conclusions

As much as testing is essential, testing can also become very time consuming for a product manager and the core product team. You need to help the team to find the right balance here. As a product manager, you also need to find the right balance for yourself. I would recommend clearly stating to the team that you only test new functionality that has reached a certain maturity, thus allowing you to do quality testing and avoiding basic bugs or even short dumps in even straightforward and simple scenarios.

Key Takeaways

- Product quality is everyone's responsibility in the product team. Involve everyone within the core product team.
- Assess the PYPR dimension item with your architects, your quality team (if you still have one) and invite randomly selected engineers to get a broader view. Remember to get your own view of a proper rating of all aspects of product quality.
- The primary goal is minimizing defects through a repeatable, effective end-to-end process.
- Products with higher quality are generally more valuable than lower quality.
- Testing should cover new features and regression tests.

5.8 Product Team Health

As product managers, many of us feel responsible for the product team as we feel for the product. Generally, we care that the team works and behaves like a true team while delivering outcomes. A highly motivated, skilled and happy product team delivering high-value software capabilities—that's the goal of our interaction with everyone in the product team and specifically with everyone in the engineering team.

I decided to add team health to the Product Development dimension due to the focus of most product managers and all product owners on this essential dimension of Software Product Management. The Product Development dimension is the essential part of our role as without a product team delivering an awesome product, there wouldn't be much to sell, to market, or to manage. Whether you have the core or extended team in mind doesn't matter, team health is important for any team. Note that the proven practice and the conclusions are easily transferable to any team.

Let's examine what team health actually means and whether, as product managers, we are really responsible for team health?

In my definition, team health has two major components: team culture and team performance. Both must be in balance when I think about a healthy team. Think about both (theoretical) extremes:

- **Team "Libertine"**: This team fosters creativity and collaboration. Trust and respect are the foundation of their collaboration. The team is happy to be together and enjoys each day at work. But, the team does not deliver any value to their customers. They are in "Happy land" and reject any request for change as this might be risky.
- **Team "High Pressure"**: This team is built to deliver: fast, high-quality and as much as possible. They are confident in their abilities to deliver. They can predict their speed of delivery like a well-maintained machine. But, team is only a term for them. They work together rather than team up. Each member trusts their own work much more than that of their colleagues. If something goes wrong, the blame is certain. They consider asking for help as a weakness.

Which team would you want to join? You might feel biased toward one or the other, but you likely agree that it wouldn't feel fantastic to be on any of the teams. Definitely both teams are not set-up to find Ikigai.

As General Managers, team health is another item on our list of things to balance. In my opinion, team health needs to be nonstop on our radar, as without the team, we will go nowhere. Great teams require many ingredients and (unfortunately) not all are in our control. Therefore, the team has the duty to become a great team, but we must and can certainly add our piece. And as product managers we have the traits and the lever to support the incubation of great teams.

Clear communication and direction, transparency about the guardrails and implications of decision, as well as appreciation of all diverse skills required in the team are some of the vital ingredients. As product managers, our role is to foster the collaboration within the team, be a lively part of the team, supporting, representing and protecting the team in the best possible, professional way. If we showcase the same empathy to the product team and the whole organization that we show to our customers, we are on a good track.

There is a plethora of tools available how-to best measure and visualize team health in order to understand how teams are doing and what areas need improvement. The general idea being once more: "What you cannot measure you cannot manage" (DeMarco, 1989).

The proven practice described in this section is one simple offer to help fill your bag of tricks, but keep in mind the team must be comfortable with the way team health is assessed. Before you start the assessment of your team health, the questions below should be answered, taking into consideration your product team's organizational context:

- What are the attributes that impact team health and matter for us (positively and negatively)?
- How do we measure and visualize these dimensions?

There are common elements that determine whether a team works or fails. These aspects might be different for your team and your organization. The list below provides a selection from which you can compile your own team health indicators:

- As we discussed, successfully bringing products and new functionality to the market demands several diverse perspectives and skills. Hence, product teams are generally best set up as cross-functional teams.
- The foundational aspects of well set up, cross-functional teams are as follows:
  - The team is set up with the right skills and size for the product/product feature.
  - The team is stable and has a dedicated work environment.
  - The team agrees on joint rules how to work together (e.g. effective meetings, self-organization, adherence to agreed standards, etc.)
  - Clear team cadences for planning, feedback, and reporting are established and set the pulse of the team.
- The teams share purpose and vision, have a joint understanding about the measures of success, and have clear roles and responsibilities.
- Teams are focusing their time and energy on things that add value, create impact, and are aligned with the product vision and corporate objectives. They track their progress and continuously improve for the better.
- The team members talk to each other—frequently and openly. Clear, consistent communication is a key principle of the team's agreed working model.
- Everyone can sense the feeling of psychological safety within the team due to a culture where everyone has trust and mutual respect for their peers. Team members are comfortable being themselves and are encouraged to make mistakes with a shared sense of accountability. Success is celebrated together, and mistakes are fixed as a team while being considered as a lesson.

The ultimate measure of a team is not simply what it has already achieved, but the joint understanding that balance of team culture and team performance is the goal that requires continuous improvement. In my experience, it doesn't matter how you measure and visualize the dimensions that impact team health. It just matters that you measure and visualize the status quo of team health, and then make the effort to improve as a team over time.

One last remark on working with product teams, likely with any human. The ultimate currency you deal with in a team is trust. Think about trust being the currency that is exchanged between the emotional bank accounts of each team member. You build up a positive trust balance by keeping your promises, walk your talk, with character, with integrity, and all kinds of positive actions that showcase your product mindset (and not your ego). Every positive sentiment associated with you will lead to deposits in the emotional bank account, in the trust account. You build trust as a great product manager. Trust comes one coin at a time. It takes time to gain trust.

But you need to be aware that trust is a very transient. When you do the wrong things, when you are too distant from the team, when you become unreliable, you undermine the trust levels you have already earned, and you will figure out that payouts from the emotional bank account will happen much faster than deposits.

5.8.1 Proven Practice: Team Health Assessment

The objective of assessing team health is to understand your strengths and weaknesses as a team and derive suitable actions for improvement. The purpose of the team health assessment is to evaluate how well your team is working together. The team health assessment allows your team to gather insights about jointly agreed upon attributes that impact team health. The team health assessment is a session by the team and for the team.

The proven practice described here provides an option that you can offer to the team if there is no established process. In my experience the team health assessment should not be facilitated by the product manager, but the product manager should be part of the assessment. As a product manager, you are part of the team. You might leverage a scrum master, ask for some volunteer team members, or get someone external to the team as workshop facilitator.

1. Prepare the team health assessment meeting and let it become a standard routine

    a. Define your health indicators as a team (re-use the list above or come up with your own tailored aspects.
    b. Define a regular cadence (monthly seems to work well), get the meeting series on everyone's calendar and communicate the objectives clearly. This is a meeting for the team and not for the product manager. Remember that the product manager should not initiate the meeting series.
        - Define the rules (e.g. honesty is key, adherence to standard feedback rules), clarify the best timing, and reserve a proper room. There are no right or wrong answers, and everyone's opinion is equal.

- Make sure that every team member is available on the day of the team health assessment to give everyone the opportunity to speak up, give feedback, and contribute to the session.

c. Appoint the required role of a facilitator whose task is to keep the discussion focused and productive. The facilitator can also be the note taker.

2. Conduct the team health assessment meeting

a. As a facilitator you
- welcome the core product team into the prepared room and remind everyone about the rules and objectives.
- read the definition out loud for each measure that the team wants to examine of healthy, high-performing teams.
- ask everyone to start with a quiet reflection (max 10 min). Don't expect people to come prepared. Therefore, the exercise gives every team member the time to focus.
- start the assessment session using a spider diagram for dot voting (whiteboard, flip chart or digital doesn't matter, but digital is better for tracking changes etc.).

b. As a team member
- place one dot on any of the team health indicators. Document your perception and do not get biased by other dots (negatively or positively). Note that anonymous voting might be recommended, but I believe that trust building comes with transparency. The spider diagram in Fig. 5.38 is a simplified example with each dot representing a team members opinion.

Fig. 5.38 Team health spider diagram © Timo Wagenblatt 2019. All rights reserved

- record the results of each attribute team rating on a Team Health Monitor grid.
- analyze jointly the results and look at the trend compared to the last assessment. The trend helps to balance current downs or highs.
- have an open discussion about the ratings, take a team view and discuss potential improvements.

3. Agree on actions and define the next steps
   a. Document an improvement plan for the one or two of the aspects rated the worst. Define how you as a team would like to strengthen these aspects. You might want to link these steps to your team OKRs. If you are not familiar with OKRs, I will provide a brief introduction in Sect. 9.1.
   b. Cluster the agreed actions into three categories: owned by the team, owned by the product manager, and owned by management.
   c. Consider the team health assessment results and improvement plan in your next PYPR strategy and action meeting. Some teams incorporate the team health assessment meetings into an existing team ritual, like retrospectives, or PYPR meetings, as there are likely the same participants.
4. Wrapping-up the team health assessment
   a. The result of the team health assessment can be used as an input for the PYPR dimension rating. Team health checks are likely to be done more frequently for the core product and scrum teams. Be sure to conduct at least one team health assessment during each PYPR cycle.
   b. As a product manager, you will focus mostly on your own particular action items, and as the General Manager of YourProduct Inc, you will discuss management's action items with the management team.

5.8.2 PYPR Dimension Items Details

See Tables 5.15 and 5.16.

Table 5.15 PYPR defaults by software product manager type

Topic		Internal PM	B2B PM	B2C PM
Default dimension item weight		22.5	25	25
Criticality for PM		High	High	High
PYPR score	Low	Everyone in the team feels that the team health needs to be improved. The team misses its purpose and does not know or understand the vision and strategy. The scope of their work is completely overwhelming. Team members don't feel they are part of a team, but rather individuals that neither know nor care about what the other people in the "team" are doing. Team members think that they are wasting their time working on the product. The team thinks that their way of working is not adequate and they are not meeting their own expectations. Sprint commitments are not made or way less than agreed. The team seems unable to complete anything. The work keeps getting stuck or interrupted. No one wants to work for the team, and existing team members would like to move out		
	Medium	The team feels somewhere in the middle. Some aspects might be rather on the low end while others are extremely well. Likely the team doesn't feel everywhere average, but if they do, medium ratings are the right range as well. Some aspects might be rather on the low end while others are extremely well. Likely the team doesn't feel everywhere neutral or being average, but if they do, medium ratings are the right range as well		
	High	The team members love to be in the team and they are proud of the value they provide to the product, their company and their customers. The know exactly what they need to do and they identify themselves with the vision and strategy of the product. The team has found great balance between team culture and team performance. The way of working fits perfectly to the team set-up. The team outcomes are predictable and fast. The team is proud of the quality of the work they deliver. The team is happy and sees no major need for improvement. The scope of their work is perfectly matching the team size and skills. The team is widely recognized and attracting the best talent		

Table 5.16 PYPR dimensions impact examples

Dimension	Direct impact example	Indirect impact example
Product viability		The team goes the extra mile for new and existing customers
Product development	Improved team health improves product planning and product quality	
Go-to-market/product marketing		Team members "team-up" for enablement and asset creation
Software demonstrations and training		Training is a team event
The market/your customers		Perception of product quality and functional completeness are benefits for all customers exposed to a healthy team
Organizational maturity	Team spirit, key principles and processes are impacted by healthy teams, other teams recognize and adopt the mindset and processes of successful teams	

5.8.3 Summary and Conclusions

Great product team health comes with the right balance of team culture and team performance. As a product manager, you are part of the team while you are leading the team. And in your role as the team leader, the General Manager, your word is heard, and your actions are recognized. You can be a catalyst for increasing trust and psychological safety within the product team.

Key Takeaways

- Be empathic with your product team in the same way you show empathy to your customers. Remember that no one gets up in the morning, comes to work and says, "I'm going to really screw up bad today."
  - Criticize in private, praise in public. Both should be timely and specific.
  - Actions speak louder than words. Spending time and being authentic with the product team will pay back in many ways.
  - Keep commitments and be a role model for a product mindset to create deposits into your trust account.
- Share the product vision and strategy frequently and underline the team's purpose.

- Celebrate success and share all the good news. Share only the bad news that requires a different way of working or a significant course correction. Take the blame and learn from mistakes.
- Leverage a systematic approach with clear visualization to assess and monitor team health
- Use your intuition and don't worry about establishing standardized criteria for team health assessment criteria—that only distracts from the discussion.
- Communication within product organizations enables orchestration and prioritization of the many product-related activities, discovering what is most important for the product and the product team.
- Foster a feedback culture that values continuous improvements in the way teams work together.

References

Adolph, S., Bramble, P., Cockburn, A., & Pols, A. (2002). *Patterns for effective use cases*. Upper Saddle: Addison-Wesley.

Agile Testing. (2019, January 7). Retrieved from Wikipedia: https://en.wikipedia.org/wiki/Agile_testing.

Boehm, B., & Turner, R. (2004). *Balancing agility and discipline*. New York: Addison-Wesley.

Cagan, M. (2018). *Inspired—How to create great tech products customer love*. Hoboke, New Jersey: Wiley.

Cagan, M. (2019a, January 4). *Dual-track agile*. Retrieved from Silicon Valley Product Group: https://svpg.com/dual-track-agile/.

Cagan, M. (2019b, February 17). *Dual-track agile*. Retrieved from SVPG.com: https://svpg.com/dual-track-agile/.

Chappell, D. (2019, January 5). *The three aspects of software quality*. Retrieved from YouTube: https://www.youtube.com/watch?v=1k7dWhd5_So.

Cockburn, A. (2000). *Writing effective use cases*. Upper Saddle River: Addison-Wesley.

Cohn, M. (2004). *User stories applied: For agile software development*. Boston: Addison-Wesley Professional.

Crispin, L., & Gregory, J. (2009). *Agile testing: A practical guide for testers and agile teams*. Addison-Wesley.

DeMarco, T. (1989). *Controlling software projects: Management, measurement & estimates*. Pearson Education: Prentice Hall PTR.

Eyal, N. (2014). *Hooked: How to build habit-forming products*. Portfolio Penguin.

Gilad, I. (2019, January 5). *Why you should stop using product roadmaps and try GIST planning*. Retrieved from Hacker Noon: https://hackernoon.com/why-i-stopped-using-product-roadmaps-and-switched-to-gist-planning-3b7f54e271d1.

Hiptest. (2018, June 25). *Writing scenarios with Gherkin syntax*. Retrieved from hiptest.com: https://hiptest.com/docs/writing-scenarios-with-gherkin-syntax/.

Kano, N. S. (1984). Attractive quality and must-be quality. *Journal of The Japanese Society for Quality Control, 14*(2), 147–156.

Kano's method for understanding customer-defined quality. (1993). Retrieved from http://www.academia.edu, http://www.academia.edu/29830721/Kano_s_method_for_understanding_customer-defined_quality.

Kano Model. (2018, February 25). Retrieved from Wikipedia: https://en.wikipedia.org/wiki/Kano_model.

Kittlaus, H.-B., & Fricker, S. A. (2017). *Software product management*. Berlin: Springer-Verlag GmbH, Germany.

Knapp, J., Zeratsky, J., & Kowitz, B. (2016). *Sprint: How to solve big problems and test new ideas in just five days*. New York City: Simon & Schuster.

Lawley, B., & Schure, P. (2017). *Product management for dummies*. Hoboken, New Jersey: Wiley.

Leffingwell, D., & Widrig, D. (2000). *Managing software requirements*. Longman: Addison Wesley.

Leffingwell, D. (2010). *Agile software requirements: Lean requirements practices for teams, programs, and the enterprise*. Upper Saddle River: Addison-Wesley.

McCarthy, B. (2018, April 3). *Why David cancel hates roadmaps (but uses them with customers)*. Retrieved from www.productculture.org, https://www.productculture.org/articles/2018/4/3/why-david-cancel-hates-roadmaps-but-uses-them-with-customers.

Moore, G. A. (2014). *Crossing the Chasm, 3rd edition: Marketing and selling disruptive products to mainstream customers*. New York City: HaperCollins Publishers.

Olsen, D. (2015). *The lean product playbook: How to innovate with minimum viable products and rapid customer feedback*. Hobokem, New Jersey: Wiley.

OMG. (2019, January 13). *About the business motivation model specification version 1.3*. Retrieved from Object Management Group: https://www.omg.org/spec/BMM/1.3/.

Patton, J. (2014). *User story mapping: Discover the whole story, build the right product*. O'Reilly and Associates.

Pichler, R. (2010). *Agile product management with scrum: Creating products that customers love*. New York: Addison-Wesley Professional.

Pouliot, F. (1993). Theoretical issues of Kano's methods. *Center for Quality of Management Journal*, Kano's Methods for Understanding Customer-defined Quality.

Prioritization. (2018, January 27). Retrieved from Wikipedia: https://en.wikipedia.org/wiki/prioritization.

Product Management Manifesto. (2019, February 27). Retrieved from 280 Group: https://280group.com/product-management-methodology/product-management-manifesto/.

Ries, E. (2011). *The lean startup*. New York: Crown Publishing Group.

Robert Blauth, R. R. (1993). Experience in the use of Kano's methods in the specification of BBN RS/1 Release 5.0. *Center for Quality of Management Journal*, Kano's Methods for Understanding Customer-defined Quality.

Sankaran, S. (2019, January 5). *To be a stellar product manager—You have to fall in love with the Problem*. Retrieved from ProductCoalition.com: https://productcoalition.com/to-be-a-stellar-product-manager-you-have-to-fall-in-love-with-the-problem-aad2bf704904.

SkillsYouNeed. (2018, December 27). *Identifying and structuring problems*. Retrieved from skillsyouneed.com: https://www.skillsyouneed.com/ips/problem-solving2.html.

Spool, J. M. (2019, January 5). *Fast path to a great UX—Increased exposure hours*. Retrieved from Medium.com: https://medium.com/@jmspool/fast-path-to-a-great-ux-increased-exposure-hours-afde796f2e43.

Startup Grind. (2018, November 1). *How to build habit-forming products*. Retrieved from YouTube.com: https://www.youtube.com/watch?v=-jXM4NymlcA.

Wake, B. (2018, March 29). *INVEST in good stories, and SMART tasks*. Retrieved from Exploring Extreme Programming: https://xp123.com/articles/invest-in-good-stories-and-smart-tasks/.

Williams, M. (2018, June 28). *Writing better user stories with Gherkin and Cucumber*. Retrieved from Medium.com: https://medium.com/@mvwi/story-writing-with-gherkin-and-cucumber-1878124c284c.

Zacarias, D. (2018a, November 30). *Product prioritization techniques*. Retrieved from Folding Burritos: https://foldingburritos.com/product-prioritization-techniques.

Zacarias, D. (2018b, March). *The complete guide to the Kano model*. Retrieved from https://foldingburritos.com/kano-model/.

6 Go-to-Market/Product Marketing

The Outbound Part of your Software Product Manager Role

We explored the Product Development dimension and how to technically develop a great software product in the previous chapter. We got the product on the shelf, so now it is the time to discover how we get the product off the shelf. No product will be successful, if the whole ecosystem does not know about it. Go-to-Market activities and product marketing focus on the market, your existing customers and all other stakeholders to help them better understand your product's value and benefits. Marketing software products requires a broad range of skills and knowledge as a diverse audience with special needs and demands must be reached.

This chapter describes in detail the Go-to-Market/Product Marketing PYPR dimension that represents "The Outbound Part of the Software Product Manager Role." The outbound part of the product manager role focuses on awareness creation, translating the value of your product into leads, incremental sales opportunities, and product success in the current installed base and net new customers and users. Depending on your product, success might be measured by adoption, product profitability, or any other north star that we discussed in Chap. 4.

Sometimes the responsibility for Go-to-Market/Product Marketing is not part of the product management organization, but is the responsibility of Marketing and rarely Sales departments. Independent of the organizational setup, as a product manager you are indispensable in this dimension as you are heavily involved and driving this PYPR dimension or you are significantly contributing to its outcomes. As a product manager, your attention on this PYPR dimension is vital, because the Go-to-Market/Product Marketing dimension has the potential to determine product success and could easily become a limiting factor to the product's yield potential.

To safeguard product success, your attention and focus is required on the following topics:

- Sales and marketing teams are provided with useful assets to do their job
- Professional services and partner ecosystem are fully equipped for success
- Competitive landscape is monitored; insights are derived, leveraged and shared
- The market and your customers are informed about your latest capabilities and understand the positioning and value of your product.

T. Wagenblatt, *Software Product Management*, Management for Professionals,
https://doi.org/10.1007/978-3-030-19871-8_6

I propose to start with the default PYPR configuration shown in Fig. 6.1. As you leverage PYPR for your product, consider the recommendations from Sect. 3.3

Dimension Weight 15 %		Dimension Weight 17,5 %		Dimension Weight 15 %	
B2B		B2C		Internal PM	
Dimension Item	Weighting Factor	Dimension Item	Weighting Factor	Dimension Item	Weighting Factor
Marketing Assets / Sales Kit	20,0%	Marketing Assets / Sales Kit	25,0%	Marketing Assets / Sales Kit	30,0%
Sales Enablement	20,0%	Sales/Marketing Enablement	10,0%	Corporate Communication Enablement	20,0%
Partner Enablement	15,0%	Partner Enablement	10,0%		
Own Professional Services / Consulting Enablement	10,0%				
Competitive Analysis	15,0%	Competitive Analysis	20,0%	Competitive Analysis	15,0%
GTM Activities and Plan	20,0%	GTM Activities and Plan	35,0%	GTM Activities and Plan	35,0%

Fig. 6.1 Go-to-Market/Product marketing: PYPR dimension item defaults © Timo Wagenblatt 2019. All rights reserved

In this section I will detail the following PYPR dimension items[1]:

- **Go-to-Market Activities and Plan**
  As YourProduct Inc. is going to market, there are many activities, many stakeholders, and many dependencies to manage all; consequently, there needs to be a plan. Assets creation and reviews, enablement sessions, public relations and marketing activities, trade shows, fairs, industry events, webinars, trial offerings—there are so many options. They all have in common that they require time, effort, budget and staff. The Go-to-Market "Project" Plan is the central document for your Go-to-Market activities.

- **Marketing and Sales Assets/Sales Kit**
  Marketing and sales assets need to be available, current, properly classified, and target group oriented. Always consider the goal and audience of each asset. The most important attributes for all assets are timeliness and quality. A well-maintained sales kit will free you up, giving you time normally wasted on repetitive education, frequent responses to the same questions, clarifying positioning of your product internally and with your customers.

[1]The descriptions are short repetitions from Sect. 2.2. Perhaps you missed one or more aspects of product marketing or marketing overall, but in my interpretation, this PYPR dimension is not about covering the complete 4P in marketing. I focus on the product manager role and the core tasks, responsibilities, considerations. For example, I acknowledge that pricing is an important topic, and I agree that it is worth reviewing pricing with each new launch. Nevertheless, I do not include pricing as a topic in this chapter because pricing is part of the business model overall (see Sect. 4.1) and according to the recent McKinsey PM Index, only 1% of the PM spend time on this.

- **Sales Enablement**
  Enabling sales teams requires understanding the specifics of their job. Sales colleagues will not have much time and will regularly not deep dive into functional scope of your product. All they are interested in might be: the value for the customer, pricing, positioning, objections, existing references, experts, partners and where to find the latest assets that cover these topics at the time they need them. Generally, sales team members' churn is higher than other employees and the value and clear positioning of your product might fade in the dynamics of Sales.

- **Partner Enablement**
  We focus on two types of partners: value-added resellers (VAR) and system integrators (SI). VAR's are reselling your product to customers; hence they are called the indirect sales channel. VAR's have similar requirements like your own sales force.
  SI's are companies focused on integrating products and provide related consulting. This is a classic channel used by large software vendors, large hardware vendors, and original equipment manufacturers. Therefore, SI's have similar requirements like your own professional services team.

- **Own Professional Services/Consulting Enablement**
  If you have your own professional services team that works with customers implementing and adapting your product, it is essential that your people know about your product's vision, roadmap and values. Providing the right assets and enabling these teams with latest updates enables one consistent market approach. In consequence your customers and prospects will perceive your company as cohesive and professional.

- **Competitive Analysis**
  Chances are high that your competitors will come up at least once in conversations with a prospect. It's critical to be well-equipped for these discussions by knowing exactly which advantages (and disadvantages) you have compared to each (key) competitor. Competitive analysis can help you in various other dimensions as well; hence it is of true value covering up-to-date information in a structured form at least for the top competitors.

The best Go-to-Market and Product Marketing results are achieved when considering the following basics:

- Understand the value of your product and message the value consistently for each target market segment. That's the foundation of everything you do in this PYPR dimension.
- Tailor all efforts considering the market segment specifics, the competitive landscape and adhere consistently to your product vision and strategy.
- And finally, you need a plan that summarizes all aspects and clearly captures the deliverables, timelines, resources required, responsibilities, backed up by aligned time and budget commitments.

The product launch plan is the central piece of work that puts a conclusive frame around all important aspects of the Go-to-Market/Product Marketing dimension. If you consider these basics, then your chances to deliver the right messages, to the right people, at the right time significantly increases.

The objective of all work in this PYPR dimension is to ensure successful introduction and adoption of your product. Ultimately, your product's success is grounded on the benefit a customer derives from the product delivered. Help your colleagues, partners, customers and the market to understand your product's value proposition.

6.1 Value Focused Go-to-Market, or: Be Clear on Your Value, Before You Broadcast Your Message

Our value proposition to consumers is so much more about completeness than freshness. Having the complete season is so much more valuable, in our business model, than having last night's episode.

—**Ted Sarandos**

Ted Sarandos' quote nicely explains a part of the Netflix™ value proposition as an integral part of their business model. As explained in Sect. 4.1, the value proposition for each target market segment is the central component of each business model. YourProduct Inc. is providing value and benefits by solving a problem for a group of users who together define a target market segment.

In Chap. 5, I introduced the Kano Model (Sect. 5.5) as a method to understand the attractiveness of product features to users. Within the core product team, all our efforts are focused on continuously increasing the customer value. As product managers, creating customer value and associated benefits are front and center of our thinking and decisions.[2]

[2]At times we prioritize tasks to de-risk development activities and gain more knowledge, but only to assure that we can build the topics providing the highest customer value.

All blood, sweat and tears we invested into business model generation and product development are misapplied, if our Go-to-Market approach and product marketing activities are not equally customer focused. Remember that customers ultimately buy value and not products or features.

Product teams frequently mix product features with customer benefits or customer value. For example, one-click buying, or automatic invoice matching are great product features, but these feature descriptions do not explain customer benefits. In fact, prospects and customers care very little about your product features as they do not explain how their life or business will improve if they buy and use your product. Still many software product companies focus on promoting product features and attributes over measurable benefits and the unique value provided by their products compared to the next best market alternative[3] (Merkado, 2018). Therefore, the mandate of your Go-to-Market approach, sales and marketing assets is to focus on customer value and tangible benefits.

Generally, the value your product brings to your customers is summarized in a value proposition. I will introduce proven practices to capture and communicate value propositions next. But before we go there, we need to get to the basics first, the understanding and definition of value and perceived value.

Itamar Gilad provides a great overview about how people perceive value and why a thorough understanding of value and perceived value are important for everyone in product (Gilad, 2018). He provides the following definition: "Value is the property we assign to a thing—a product, a service, a person, an experience, that indicates how important, worthwhile or beneficial we think it is for us." Gilad further summarizes that value is subjective, contextual, and relative to costs and existing alternatives. I will further detail these points in Sect. 8.1 as the perception of value and your customers perception of functional completeness are highly correlated. However, value does not only come with functionality, there are other components to perceived value like social value (what's in for us) and personal value (what's in for me personally) (Gilad, 2018). If you like a shorter definition, you probably like the following definition of customer value: "The difference between what a customer gets from a product, and what he or she has to give in order to get it." (Customer Value, 2018). As a product manager, there is lots of "value" in understanding these concepts to derive your product's values accordingly.

A value proposition summarizes the promise of value and benefits realized by using your software product. Remember that a value proposition is not a feature list, but instead the promise to your targeted customers on the value your product will deliver for them. There are many value proposition templates available. Geoffrey Moore's value proposition is a proven practice you might consider for your bag of tricks:

For <target market segment> who <pain or gain statement> our <feature/product module/product capability> so that <tangible description of benefit> (Moore, 1995).

[3]Which can be a competitive product or doing nothing.

Defining a good value proposition looks simple at first. However, condensing all your knowledge into a few, specific value propositions that easily explain your product's values to your target market segments and the relevant personas will require some iterations and really deep thinking.

As a product manager, you meant to use your superpower of customer empathy and decide what the true differentiators are. Don't be afraid to experiment a little and change what feature you highlight (by the means of derived value) to find out what resonates best with your target market segments. Your value proposition should clearly define:

- what value your product offers to prospects who are looking into buying your product
- how your product is different from competitors in the marketplace
- what features are the most appealing to buyers.

If your value proposition can't describe these components clearly and concisely, you need to re-work your value proposition until it is useful.

The Value Proposition Canvas (Strategyzer AG, 2019) is a great complementary tool to the business model canvas (Sect. 4.1) for your use in this essential activity. The Value Proposition Canvas supports you in structuring your knowledge about better understanding of each market segment and the way you provide value to each market segment. The Value Proposition Canvas zooms into the Value Proposition and Customer Segment blocks of the Business Model Canvas. On the right-hand side, the Value Proposition Canvas shows the customer profile area where you detail the customer's jobs to be done and the associated pains and gains with each job. On the left-hand side, there is a value map that structures the potential product features and how they create gains or relieve pains (Strategyzer, 2018). The Value Proposition Canvas is a proven practice for understanding the product features you might discover in product development. However, for the purpose of Go-to-Market and product marketing, the Value Proposition Canvas tells how you are creating value for your target market segments with your product features. All you need to do is listen.

It is the product team's responsibility to come up with a compelling value proposition for the product and its features. The value proposition work benefits from a sound problem analysis, market segmentation and value analysis. Then value propositions can support all product positioning and messaging activities. I hope you see the central theme from business model to product vision to Go-to-Market approach and unique selling proposition.

As the General Manager of YourProduct Inc., it is your job to establish focus on customer value in every PYPR dimension to drive consistency and become marks of professionalism. Remember, if the value isn't clear, the price will always be too high (Bar, 2018).

6.2 Going Public and Staying Public with YourProduct Inc.

In this section, I will describe the glue that holds everything together concerning going public and staying public with YourProduct Inc. What does this mean? We spent lots of work on defining and validating a viable business model for our product, we collected the market requirements, prioritized and developed toward highest customer value for each target market segment, and now … we have a product that no one knows about.

YourProduct Inc. needs to be introduced to the market, or to be more precise, to each target market segment defined in your business model as illustrated in Fig. 6.2. Some customers that you already engaged with during business model validation or requirements clarification likely know about your product, but the entire market and your internal stakeholders do not. To introduce your product and to keep your product in the market, the market, your customers, partners, and many colleagues require timely information.

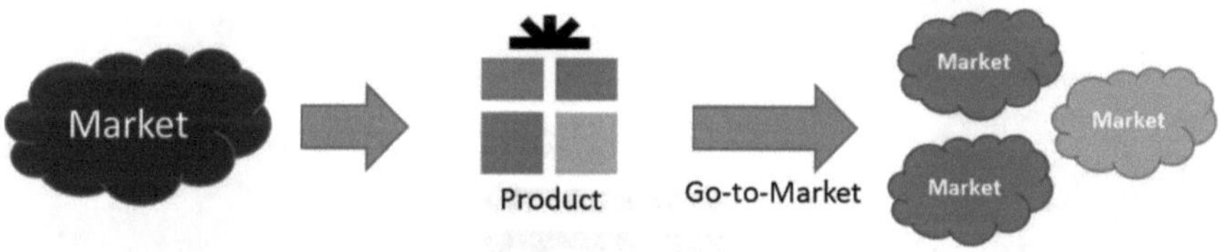

Fig. 6.2 Go-to-Market illustration © Timo Wagenblatt 2019. All rights reserved

As YourProduct Inc. is going to market, there are many activities, many stakeholders, and many dependencies; consequently, there needs to be a plan. And there needs to be a team ensuring that the plan is executed. Depending on your context, dedicated launch teams can be a good practice allowing you to scale and engage experts for the various activities. As you establish your launch team, you take care that all responsibilities, roles and milestones are clarified, supported by a budget and that the progress is monitored by aligned and communicated KPIs.

Go-to-Market planning and executing is such a broad topic that I must limit my contribution to the bare minimum of essential considerations for product managers within this section. There are numerous ways of Go-to-Market planning and execution. For example, depending on the lifecycle phase of your product, your marketing strategy and your Go-to-Market approach requires differentiation (Lawley & Schure, 2017). Please check the great resources listed in the bibliography that are dedicated to the topics of product marketing and Go-to-Market planning and execution for further details and practices.[4]

[4]One of the books that are frequently mentioned in this domain is Geoffrey Moore's book *Crossing the Chasm* (Moore, 1995).

Perhaps there will be a launch lead from Marketing or Product Marketing, but as a product manager, you are ultimately responsible for a Go-to-Market plan that is properly staffed, budgeted, and which includes all important components that will support your launch and product team in executing a successful market introduction.

Creating and executing a plan that meets your product objectives and considers your restrictions (time, budget, skills) is the goal of PYPR dimension item: Go-to-Market Activities and Plan. One basic component to success is having all the required parts of a Go-to-Market plan as illustrated in Fig. 6.3.

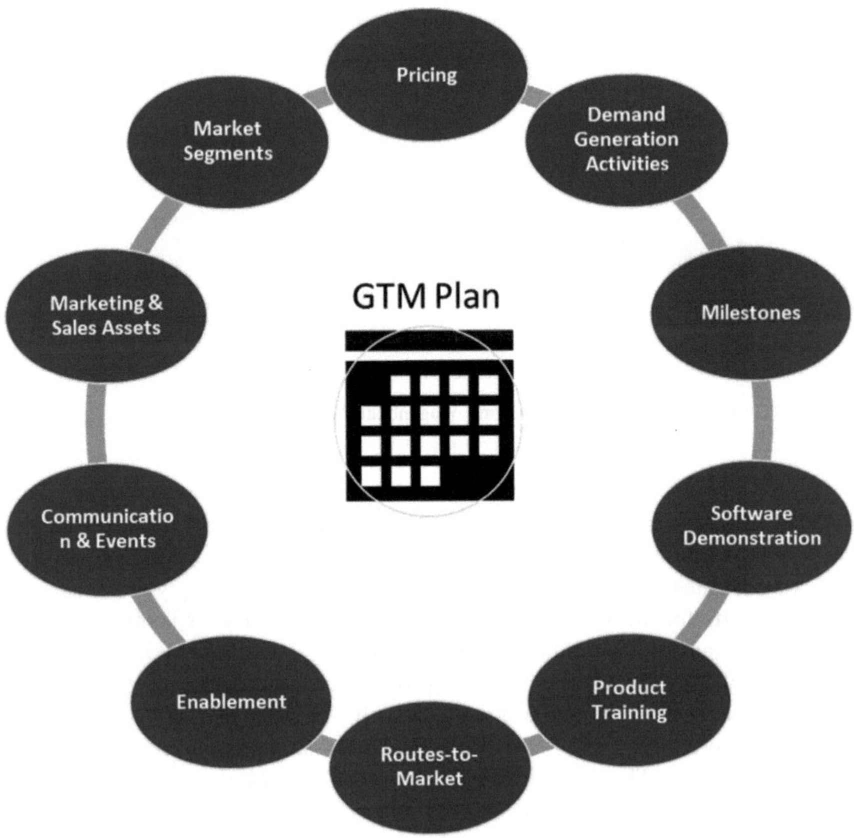

Fig. 6.3 Go-to-Market plan elements © Timo Wagenblatt 2019. All rights reserved

The outcome of a great Go-to-Market plan is delivering the right message to the right target audiences at the right time. Further, as a product manager, you want to monitor the progress against these outcomes. Therefore, each Go-to-Market plan requires measurable objectives and accountable stakeholders for each part of the plan. The Go-to-Market objectives should be in line with the overall objectives (e.g. introduction, awareness, adoption, etc.) and scope (e.g. global launch, targeted launch by region or market segment etc.) of the launch. Additionally, the product positioning and strategy and the Go-to-Market objectives are coherent. Establishing and monitoring Go-to-Market objectives and KPIs enables you to potentially course-correct during the Go-to-Market project execution.

As the General Manager of YourProduct Inc., you need to provide clarity on the main drivers of your Go-to-Market strategy as they drive the activities within your Go-to-Market plan, for example:

- Create awareness and generate leads
- Maximize revenue
- Gain market share
- Drive adoption
- Get your first five official customer references

Note that Go-to-Market plans are not only essential for the launch of your first product version, but proper Go-to-Market planning and execution is fundamental for each launch of new functionality, from going to market with a single new feature or a new product module to launching a completely new product release.

There are various launch types, but the topic of launches in a continuous delivery (agile) development requires special attention. As a product manager, you need to balance the information need and information overload for your colleagues and partners, but especially for your customers so they do not become overwhelmed or even unhappy with continuous smaller feature updates (Lawley & Schure, 2017).

Go-to-Market planning and execution requires a project approach in order to be successful. The Go-to-Market Plan is a kind of a project plan, as there is fixed scope and fixed timeline associated with launching a product feature, module, or completely new product version. Generally, Product Marketing or Go-to-Market planning and execution follows a process as shown in Fig. 6.4.

Fig. 6.4 Go-to-Market project planning © Timo Wagenblatt 2019. All rights reserved

As a product team or a dedicated launch team, you start with the assessment of your and your product's current status. The latest PYPR assessment might be of use here. Based on your understanding of status quo, you derive a Go-to-Market strategy. As a next step, you define the optimal set-up of your Go-to-Market project given your restrictions (time, budget, skills) and prepare the project. Preparation of the project includes the definition and alignment on timelines and required work results, which are then implemented and executed in the next steps. Last but not least, you monitor the progress of your Go-to-Market project, course-correct if required or scale to success.

As a product manager, you are dealing with assets creation, reviews, enablement sessions, public relations and marketing activities, social media campaigns, trade shows, fairs, industry events, analyst briefings, webinars, and many more activities. Some of these activities have a deadline not under your control, others can be scheduled as part of the planning activities.

The Go-to-Market "Project" Plan is the central document for your Go-to-Market activities. If you don't have one, you are on track for stressful and chaotic times, leading to miscommunication or poor execution and most importantly, you are risking that your awesome product will be outperformed by mediocre products just because you failed with an appropriate Go-to-Market approach.

Launching your product is one part, but staying public is another one. Frequently product teams benefit from a dedicated launch team and a dedicated Go-to-Market project manager. But when is the Go-to-Market project over? At the release date? Likely not? As discussed, there will be several launches for YourProduct Inc. Therefore, dedicated launch teams that disappear at a certain point have a major disadvantage. I recommend staffing most of the launch team with members of the product team and product stakeholders. Otherwise, "All the focus, know-how and momentum stops at this critical point which often results in major problems. Issues that would be easy to solve with the launch team are much harder to resolve once all the infrastructure and experience has disappeared." (Lunn and Dickenson, Vol 1).

That's it in a nutshell about Go-to-Market/Product Marketing planning and execution.[5] However, there are many more items of the Go-to-Market/Product Marketing dimension that are introduced in this book. The subsequent sections about marketing and sales assets, competitive analysis, enablement, and the entire Chap. 7 include all components of a sound Go-to-Market plan. Remember to always focus on the value your product delivers for your customers and your plan will pave the way for your product's success.

6.2.1 PYPR Dimension Items Details

See Tables 6.1 and 6.2.

---

[5]If you wonder where the details about Product Marketing are hidden, then I would like to direct you to Sect. 2.2.3. Product Marketing is the department frequently associated with Go-to-Market planning and execution.

Table 6.1 PYPR defaults by software product manager type © Timo Wagenblatt 2019. All rights reserved

Topic		Internal PM	B2B PM	B2C PM
Default dimension item weight		35	20	35
Criticality for PM		High	High	High
PYPR score	Low	There is no Go-to-Market plan nor clarity on responsibilities to launch new features, modules, or whole products to the market. There is no support from product marketing or marketing teams. Go-to-Market planning is not in focus of the product team. Some activities might be done, but without alignment to product positioning and strategy		
	Medium	Go-to-Market planning and activities are in focus of the product team. The success is limited due to, for example, no proper staffing, too limited budget, bad quality of activities, missing plan components, delays in execution, misaligned objectives, etc.		
	High	Go-to-Market plan comprises activities that are delivering the right message to the right target audiences at the right time for all new product developments. The Go-to-Market plan consists of measurable objectives and accountable stakeholders for each part of the plan. The Go-to-Market objectives are in line with the overall objectives and scope of the launch. Additionally, the product positioning and strategy and the Go-to-Market objectives are coherent. Last but not least, the Go-to- Market plan is properly staffed and budgeted		

Table 6.2 PYPR dimensions impact examples

Dimension	Direct impact example	Indirect impact example
Product viability	Sales pipeline stays flat or is declining due to missing awareness of your products capabilities and value proposition	
Product development		Product team needs to support roll-out activities
Go-to-Market/Product marketing	All other PYPR dimension items contribute to the Go-to-Market plan	
Software demonstrations and training	Software demonstrations need to be available according to plan, the Go-to-Market plan will not be complete without the outcomes of this dimension	

(continued)

Table 6.2 (continued)

Dimension	Direct impact example	Indirect impact example
The market/Your customers	Functional completeness perception directly correlated with quality of product launch	
Organizational maturity		Key principles emphasize the whole product approach comprising Go-to-Market activities

6.2.2 Summary and Conclusions

Key Takeaways

- Due to the amount of activities, involved people, and dependencies, Go-to-Market plans need to be treated like project plans.
- Plan backwards from your release/launch date and avoid last minute rush. Plan for review of assets and include stakeholder representatives for review and sign-off of assets. Plan proper lead time and consider dependencies of activities.
- Go-to-Market plans comprise all activities and assets that are outbound focused (i.e. everything that people outside the core product need to know about your product and how your product is marketed and sold).
- Go-to-Market planning and execution requires staffing, budgeting and consistency with product and organizational branding.
- There are different categories of product launches (i.e. launch of new product focusing on creation of new customer base and market introduction, launch of new release or significant product enhancements focusing on enabling existing community and driving adoption, or launch of continuous improvement focusing re-positioning and customer satisfaction).
- There are many launches over the lifecycle of a product.
- Establish a standard process for Go-to-Market projects and create checklists considering all important dependencies and assets.
- Leverage a visual project plan with timelines, activities, and responsibilities clearly delineated.
- Consider and inform all other, dependent processes (e.g. sales planning, demand management, global marketing, etc. about your contribution and your expectations).
- Include monitoring of the Go-to-Market plan in your PYPR assessment meetings.

6.3 Marketing Assets and Sales Assets/Sales Kit

Marketing assets and sales assets are frequently mentioned in the same breath; however, there are some fundamental differences. Generally marketing assets focus on a broader audience focusing on the early stages of the customer and buyer journey (e.g. Recognize, Consider) while sales assets are required at later stages (e.g. Evaluate, Select, Negotiate).[6]

The messaging of marketing assets and sales assets needs to consider not just different target market segments, but also different persona of customers. For B2B products, multiple personas need to be considered within a single customer (e.g. buyer, CIO or IT architects, functional leads and all addressed end-user personas). For B2C products, there are generally only the end-user personas to be targeted. However sometimes selling your product might require addressing a buyer that is not your user (e.g. parents supervising their kid's game purchases).

It is important that the messaging to each of your target market segment and customer personas fits for purpose. My strong advice to anyone who is tasked in working on marketing or sales assets: Don't work on any asset until you know and understand the target audience persona. As you craft the assets, try to working in a way that your work can be re-used in other assets even if this requires a little more time. Your time investment will pay back in many aspects as re-use improves consistency. As a product manager, you understand your target personas likely the best. Your empathy superpower enables you to provide lots of value in this PYPR dimension item.

Only creativity, time, and budgets limit the types of assets that can be used for marketing and sales activities. The right list of assets for your product-related marketing campaigns and activities, and the relevant components for your product's sales kit, depend on above three factors, as well as your product and your overall context. Finally, as a product manager, you do not forget the internal (i.e. sales and marketing teams, etc.) and the external (i.e. existing and target customer, partners, analysts, etc.) stakeholder needs. Table 6.3 lists some common examples that might provide you some inspiration.

The list is already overwhelming, with so many more options not even mentioned. Creating all these assets costs money, and sometimes even more importantly, time. The goal is not creating all these assets, the goal is to provide just enough, qualitative, and handy assets for your target audience.

I mentioned before that re-use is important. Let's clarify this to avoid misunderstandings. Re-use drives consistency, so if a piece of information is useful in multiple assets, create it in a reusable way, but do not re-use information snippets just to fill documents with unnecessary information. That will create inconsistencies and be impossible to manage. As a product team, you need to find the right balance between too many versus too little assets and too much repetition versus too many assets to get all required information.

---

[6]See Fig. 4.10.

Table 6.3 Marketing and sales asset examples

Assets (in alphabetical order)	Primary usage	Description
Blogs	Marketing	Blog posts for specific and reinforcing messaging via the social media channels your target audiences consume
Case study	Both	Description of how specific customers leverage and benefit from using your product. Case studies might be part of the customer reference assets as described in Sect. 8.4
Competitive battle card	Sales kit	See Sect. 6.4
Customer business case	Sales kit	See Sect. 4.2
Customer references	Both	See Sect. 8.4
External webinars	Marketing	Online presentations targeting external stakeholders (e.g. customers, prospects, partners)
FAQ document	Sales kit	Document that collects and answers the frequently asked questions in a way you like them to be answered
L0 to L2 product presentations	Sales kit	Product presentations to detail all good about YourProduct Inc. from executive level product presentations (L0) to functional/user-level details (L2). Make sure you understand which levels your product requires, and which granularity works best for each target audience and specific context
Press releases	Marketing	Share news about latest customer success or product updates
Product brochure	Both	Glossy asset detailing the information from the product fact sheet for download or broad distribution
Product fact sheet	Sales Kit	One-pager summarizing critical, need-to-know information (like product description, addressed needs, key product elements, technical requirements, contact channels, etc.) for **external** stakeholders. An enriched version can be considered for sharing with partners
Product landing page	Marketing	Web page representing your product and portal to all assets (e.g. documentation, training courses, videos, demonstrations, collateral, etc.) important and useful for external stakeholders
Product marketing video	Both	See Sect. 7.3
Roadmaps	Both	See Sect. 5.6
Sales discussion guide	Sales kit	Designed to help sales teams and partners conduct targeted sales calls and position YourProduct Inc. effectively. The guide contains a range of questions and starting points for both face-to face and telephone sales conversations including relevant buyer personas. The sales discussion guide might include VITO letters, telemarketing guides, etc.

(continued)

Table 6.3 (continued)

Assets (in alphabetical order)	Primary usage	Description
Sales fact sheet	Sales kit	One-pager summarizing critical, need-to-know information (like product positioning, customer profile, buying center, pricing metric, up-sell and attach products, product team contacts, main competitors, link to additional information, etc.) for your **internal** sales team and other internal stakeholders. A sanitized version can be considered for sharing with partners
Software demonstration	Both	See Sect. 7.1
Technical presentation	Sales kit	Document focusing on the technical-focused target audiences like enterprise architects, or system analysts explaining the architecture, software requirements, sizing and hardware requirements, etc.
Thought leadership and whitepapers	Both	See Sect. 8.5
Who is who document	Sales kit	List of product team members with information how and when to involve them, the documents is strictly for internal use only and should be never shared with customers and partners. Having this document will route many requests that would have come to the product manager first directly to the right person in the product team

As a product manager, you can leverage the PYPR assessment to understand how your product is doing in this dimension item. It is okay not to work on these assets every day, but there are certain events that mandate working on marketing and sales assets (e.g. product launch, new release, repositioning, pivot, change in pricing, value proposition, target market segments, or as simple as corporate document templates). Cleaning up existing marketing and sales assets is important as well. Outdated assets need to be rigorously deleted to avoid outdated messaging or other misunderstandings. Therefore, it remains a best practice to maintain a catalog of assets that links to the one location where each asset is stored with a version history.

6.3.1 PYPR Dimension Items Details

See Tables 6.4 and 6.5.

Table 6.4 PYPR defaults by software product manager type

Topic		Internal PM	B2B PM	B2C PM
Default dimension item weight		30	20	25
Criticality for PM		High	High	High
PYPR score	Low	No up-to-date marketing and sales assets available. Assets might outdated because of missing cohesiveness to vision, strategy, messaging, positioning, target market audiences, released functionality, addressed personas, industry trends, etc.		
	Medium	Limited marketing and sales assets are available with mediocre quality or only partial coverage of value proposition, personas, available functionality, target market segments etc.		
	High	World-class marketing and sales assets underlining and boosting your product positioning, available for all personas, enabling customers and the target market segments to adopt your product and get informed about all existing product functionality in the most valuable way		

Table 6.5 PYPR dimensions impact examples

Dimension	Direct impact example	Indirect impact example
Product viability	Sales pipeline increases due to successful marketing campaign	
Product development		Team health increases due to positive press releases
Go-to-Market/Product marketing	Go-to-Market planning needs to consider required list of assets and required lead times for asset creation	
Software demonstrations and training		Pre-sales enablement can re-use marketing and sales assets
The market/Your customers	Perception of functional completeness increases with market segment - tailored marketing and sales assets	
Organizational maturity		Marketing communications, product marketing and product management processes need to be aligned

6.3.2 Summary and Conclusions

As a product manager, working on sales and marketing assets and keeping them up to date can become very time-consuming. Seek help and talent in writing, graphics, and creativity. The parts you must focus are quality of the content and timeliness, there is no other option.

Key Takeaways

- The objective of marketing and sales assets is to get the attention of your target customer segments and your current customers about your latest product developments and value proposition.
- Professional marketing and sales assets are informational, attention-grabbing, and specific, providing the audience options to more details. Only create targeted, specific content that will engage with specific audiences in specific contexts. Specific is the key word here.
- Marketing and sales assets need to be available, consistent, up to date, properly classified, and target group oriented.
- A well-maintained sales kit will give you time that you otherwise would use on repetitive education, frequent responses to the same questions, clarifying positioning of your product internally and with your customers.
- Key principles of effective marketing and sales assets are consistency, accuracy, professionalism, and scale. As you follow these principles during asset creation and asset delivery, you build trust with your internal and external audiences.
- As a product manager, you are ultimately responsible for the quality of the marketing and sales assets. If they are of low quality your product will suffer and the success will be limited. Therefore, you should block some time (e.g. quarterly, every six months) as a standing call to check that all available assets are adhering to the key principles previously set.
- Brilliant marketing assets easily become a scaling machine that will ease the enablement efforts of your sales, partner, and professional services community.

6.4 Competitive Analysis

It is nice to have valid competition; it pushes you to do better.

—**Gianni Versace**

In competitive analysis we are essentially studying our competition, trying to understand who the competition really is and how to deal with them. Based on an honest evaluation and with support of some tips on how to best go about analyzing our competition overall, we will examine a Proven Practice. So, whether you have ten or more competitors or only a few, it's critically important to have a process for analyzing your competition.

You might question why I'm listing competitive analysis as part of the Go-to-Market/Product Marketing dimension and you rightly do so. A great competitive analysis delivers insights for many interesting areas. For example, competitive analysis is frequently mentioned as a great input of market research (PYPR dimension: The Market/Your Customers), pricing (PYPR dimension: Product Viability) and competitive analysis belongs to many business case templates I have seen in the past (PYPR dimension: Product Viability).

In my view, sorting competitive analysis into the Go-to-Market/Product Marketing dimension is appropriate for the following reasons:

- Chances are high that your competitors will come up at least once in conversations with any prospects.
- It's critical to be well-equipped for these discussions by knowing exactly which advantages (and disadvantages) you have compared with each (key) competitor.
- Competitive battle cards are an adequate and powerful tool for anyone in your organization to have for these discussions.

When was the last time you performed a competitive analysis for your product? Too often, a competitive analysis is only conducted during the early days of a company or the launch of a new product. Some people try to ignore competition, some blame lack of time and some are simply underestimating the value of competitive analysis. Many reasons, none is valid.

Nevertheless, many product managers are not taking full advantage of a proper competitor audit. If you see benefits in one or more of the following insights, I propose you add another action item to your list of ongoing product management activities:

- Knowing how each of your competitors are positioning their products and the messaging applied
- Knowing the way your competition segments the market and the way they approach each segment
- Knowing the strengths and weaknesses of your competitors' products and features, which value they are adding and what unique differentiators they might offer.

Once in a Software Product Management training I heard a metaphor that the competitive landscape is like the weather; it changes. Depending on where you are located, weather can change rapidly and frequently. In a similar manner, depending on your type of software product or the number of competitors, your competitive analysis may have to change frequently to reflect updated information. There is no excuse not knowing at least your top three competitors unless you are positioned in a market with less than three players.

As a product manager, you must ensure your Go-to-Market approach remains compelling to your target audiences. Whether you do a SWOT analysis, or some other method is not too important to me, but it is essential that you accept there is competition, that you know your competition and leverage the intelligence in the best possible way.

There are many ways to conduct competitive analysis. I recommend not over-complicating the process and the results. In your role, you will have lots of information and insights as part of your daily business. Only at times of new entries you have never heard of or you start losing deals to a competitor or you face users going over to the competition then a dedicated process is required. Here is a good process that will get you to a better understanding of the competitive landscape or of one specific competitor (Fig. 6.5).

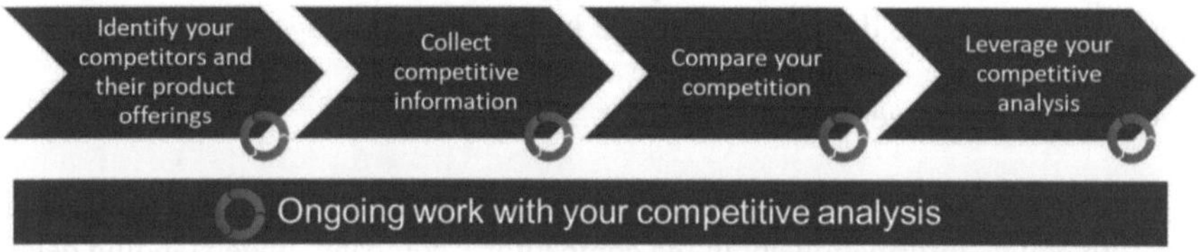

Fig. 6.5 Competitive analysis process © Timo Wagenblatt 2019. All rights reserved

6.4.1 Proven Practice

1. Identify your direct and indirect competitors and their product offerings

   a. Find and define the competition:

      - I'm certain you know your #1 and #2 and maybe even #3 competitor by name, hence defining these as competitors is simple.
      - If a prospect, customer or anyone else points out to you, who they think is a competitor, take the time to perform an honest evaluation and understand that competition is always defined from the buyer's perspective, not yours. This is also true for a product that might be in your own organization's portfolio, but you never thought of it as a potential competitive product until the customer mentioned it to you.[7]

[7]We faced the situation that some customers could not differentiate one product offering targeting sales and marketing users from another SAP® product offering targeting supply chain users. Both had components of a planning application and both leveraged machine-learning for more accurate forecasting. Our peer Software Product Managers and our team tended to ignore this perception; however it turned out that we both had to shape our product positioning for the market and for our internal sales colleagues. As a result, we saved a lot of time and we could all focus on real competitors.

b. Start with understanding your buyer's and your user's point of view. They might consider companies and products as your competition, although you had not thought or even considered it. A common reaction in these situations could be that they do something totally different and the customers are comparing apples to oranges. However, as the saying goes: perception is reality. Your competition really isn't about what you think about your product, it's what you customer thinks about your product's values.
c. The first stage determines who your competitors really are. This is essential and not as trivial as it sounds at the beginning. You should not limit your thinking by focusing your attention to the one or two major competitors and ignore those who are growing slowly but surely. These new competitors might be more dangerous than the known suspects.

2. Collect competitive information

a. Collect company information and product information. While it's important to collect information about the competitor's company, understanding details of the competitive product such as pricing, usability, performance, functionality, time-to-value, and customer support are far more valuable.
b. Do research through publicly available information sources but always be mindful of your company's code of business conduct and always respect confidentiality and privacy laws. There is no issue in gathering competitive intelligence such as reading analyst reports, listening to speeches at conferences, understanding how your competition positions itself, where they emphasize topics and which customers speak for them. In addition, the following sources might inspire if you do not have enough information available:

• Competitor websites
• Thought leader communications like blogs
• Partners
• Press releases, articles, social media posts
• Sales or any other internal team's feedback
• Win/Loss Analysis
• Any interaction with users, customers and prospects

c. Listen to prospects and customers; listen to your sales team and who they face as competition. If you develop a relationship with your prospects, they may tell you who your competitors are while you're in the presentation stages. For those customers that made the decision to go with you, use the time you interact with them to find out who they were previously using for the problem you will solve for them now. Ask questions and listen to what they say and what they do not say.

   d. Leverage tools like LinkedIn Sales Navigator® and Google Alerts® or similar tools that can help you stay up to date regarding your competition's changes including job postings, personnel changes, product updates.

3. Compare your competition
   a. Note that you need to be honest when making comparisons. I know it is hard as you might need to acknowledge that your competition might have one or the other strengths as well. If you are not ready for this step, don't waste your time with competitive analysis and do something of more value.
      - Good, you are mentally prepared.
      - Start to list what you think are your five to 10 top product features, what drives most value for your customers, which problems can you solve for them.
      - Create a little table like Table 6.6 with the product features down the left side of the page and across the top of the page list your top competitors.

Table 6.6 Product feature by competitor comparison

	Competitor 1	Competitor 2	Competitor 3	You
Product features 1				
Product features 2				
Product features 3				
Product features 4				
Product features 5				

   b. Now think about each of these items on the left, use the information and knowledge you have already gained and if your competitor has a similar feature make a checkmark, use Harvey balls or score between one and 10.
   c. Review your ratings and check
      - Is your rating honest or driven by your pride about your product?
      - Did you keep in mind is that the competitive comparison is conducted through the buyer's or user's eyes, not your own view. We need to admit that our views are biased.

4. Leverage your competitive analysis
   a. Equip your salespeople to compete during the decision stage of the buyer's journey
   b. Create a handy battle card for each competitive product using the template below
   c. Publish the battle card internally and keep it internal only, strictly internal!

   d. Make sure your work is accessible to and known by everyone who can benefit internally.
5. Ongoing considerations working with your competitive analysis
   a. Focus on only the top five competitors and add more as you need them in the sales process.
   b. Do not talk negatively about your competition to anyone, this will harm you and is not professional. When talking to others, only speak about your product's values.
   c. Keep your analysis up to date using automation tools; competitors aren't standing still nor are you, but time is a scarce resource.
   d. Don't forget to update your stakeholders in the event the competition disappears. Might be a great opportunity to excel.
   e. Keep in mind that your competitor is profiling you as well in the same way. Be paranoid about that and remind everyone in the extended product team that internal documents such as detailed roadmaps, customer lists or pricing information are strictly confidential and could be used against the product or the entire organization!

Note that you should be cautious in sharing any competitive analysis information, especially negative information, as you don't want to come across as unprofessional by bashing the competition. Your goal is to use the competitive analysis intelligently and become a trusted advisor for your prospects and current customers. You do this by using information thoughtfully and with sensitivity. The result of the right analysis leads to the format described in Sect. 6.4.2, mentioning why YourProduct Inc. is superior, which is much more credible than saying the competitive products are bad.

6.4.2 Competitive Battle Card Template

There are several different formats to capture competitive analysis. For practical reasons, I propose a very lightweight approach as not many people in our target group will take the time to digest more than provided in this template and one can save time keeping the lightweight version updated.

I prefer quality over quantity. Use whatever template fits best for you and for your organization. Define a new template or try to adapt the one outlined in Fig. 6.6 for your needs. Note that you occasionally need to provide information about your competition, so be prepared, but do not overdue it and keep the target in mind.

The competitive battle card template consists of:

- **Header**:
  Add the competitor company or product logo, the date the battle card has been last reviewed and a little teaser, in case it ends up at the other side. The header should come with a shiny confidential stamp and make it clear you mean it.

- **Competitive Product Information**
  - Short description: Use the description of the product as the buyer would find it. In case you cannot grab anything from the officially available material, provide a description in your own, unbiased words.
  - Market segment pitch: Cover three to four bullets of why the prospects in this segment should use the competitive product. Again, use what you have available or come up with your view of their USP by the market segment in which they compete with you.
- **Competitive comparison**
  This is the most important section. List three to five bullet points why your product is the best in the market segment, don't copy from one battle card to the next one. Think about how you can best compete against THIS competitive product.
- **Objection handling**
  Cover the most common questions or objections you heard in the field and provide the recommended answer for each of these questions. I do not cover too many questions as it gets hard to read so many for the busy target group, so focus on just the top ones. If you have a FAQ document, link to it from this section.

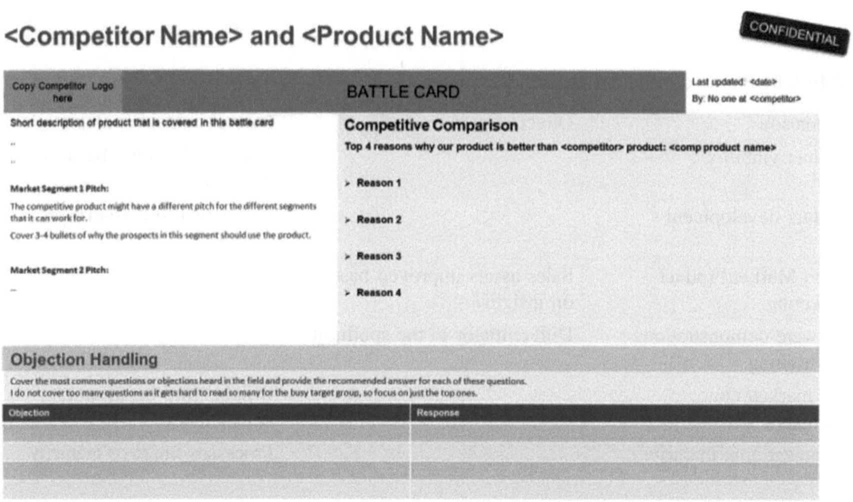

Fig. 6.6 Competitive battle card template

6.4.3 PYPR Dimension Items Details

See Tables 6.7 and 6.8.

Table 6.7 PYPR defaults by software product manager type © Timo Wagenblatt 2019. All rights reserved

Topic		Internal PM	B2B PM	B2C PM
Default dimension item weight		10	15	20
Criticality for PM		Low	Medium	Medium
PYPR score	Low	No competition identified and systematically analyzed, no process in place to keep the competitive analysis current		
	Medium	Leverage standard and easy access information, analyze only for very few competitors, limited process or ad-hoc activity		
	High	Provide a clear positioning tailored to each competitor, conduct a regular review and post updates supported by automated tools and a robust process		

Table 6.8 PYPR dimensions impact examples

Dimension	Direct impact example	Indirect impact example
Product viability		Pipeline declining because of competitor
Product development		Understand differentiation features
Go-to-Market/Product marketing	Sales assets improved based on insights	
Software demonstrations and training	Differentiator in the spotlight	
The market/Your customers		Insights into functional completeness
Organizational maturity		Processes improve maturity

6.4.4 Summary and Conclusions

Note that there are many ways to analyze your competition. The reality is that staying current on your competition can be a time-consuming task. At times, it can be too time consuming and hence is put aside. Look for allies in other teams or departments that benefit as well from competitive intelligence. Always remember, it's ultimately more important for you in your role to remind everyone of the unique value of your product and your company to the market.

Key Takeaways

- Stay current about your competition
  - Leverage tools like LinkedIn®, Google Alerts®, and other tools that include insights in your day-to-day business.
  - With that you can further strengthen your knowledge of your competition and stay current with changes in their products or organizations.
- PYPR indicates whether you need to improve in this dimension
  - Don't spend too much time worrying about competition and analyzing every single detail of your competition.
  - There is no need to have a dedicated activity or extra effort, if the assessment indicates you are doing fine.
- Never share any of your competitive battle cards outside of your organization (not to customers and not to partners and not to competitors)
- Play fair with your (human) sources and respect your competitors, keep in line with code of business conduct and certainly with the laws
- If you know your competition and if you know yourself, you need not fear the results of hundred battles (Tzu, 2015).

6.5 Enablement, Enablement, Enablement

This section is all about enabling all parties in your ecosystem, your stakeholders, and every helping hand that support the Go-to-Market approach of YourProduct Inc. The teams and stakeholders to be enabled exemplify your routes to market. The routes to market (and your customers) likely comprise many or all the following examples: license sales, inside sales, tele sales, service sales, partners, product marketing, marketing, professional services, etc. For B2B products, Pre-sales enablement needs to be front and center of this list; therefore, I dedicated Sect. 7.2 solely to the topic of Pre-sales enablement.

Still the list is likely not complete, but you get the sense that there are many people who need to be enabled. Which leads us to this question: What does enablement actually mean?

Enablement requires the following elements:

- Assets
- Communication
- Training

In this section, we cover Sales and (Product) Marketing team enablement, Partner enablement, and Professional Services enablement. The objectives and requirements of these teams are different, but enablement for all these stakeholders has a lot in common. All stakeholders require support to do their part of the job and by supporting them, they become capable of supporting you and ultimately the product.

Stakeholders require assets to successfully support your Go-to-Market strategy and plan. In Sect. 6.2, I introduced the sales and marketing assets, which are one key pillar of enablement. Remember the importance of crafting these assets for re-use as this will not only save you time, but also deliver consistency. There is no need to build a completely different asset for channel partners than for your own sales force. There are not many arguments to provide different assets to your own professional services teams than for your implementation partners.

The same is true for trainings. Training is the actual, the active part of enablement. How much variation is required for training external stakeholders and internal stakeholders? Define your strategy and balance the additional efforts with its impact.

As a product manager, you understand that all stakeholders are potential multipliers and determine scale. Professionalism and high-quality assets are essential. You will likely not have the time to review or even create all assets on your own. You will not have the bandwidth to conduct all trainings on your own. But, it is your responsibility to find the right balance for YourProduct Inc. As a product manager, you provide the guidance and guardrails for all enablement assets and activities. Brilliant enablement not only provides information about your product, it goes beyond that. Great enablement communicates your product's value and positioning, aligns your stakeholders with your overall strategy, and empowers them to appropriately represent YourProduct Inc.

Communication is not just the right messaging about your product and your organization. Communication as part of enablement is also about communicating effectively with your stakeholders. One part of effective communication is simplicity. I recommend having one central place where each stakeholder can find the relevant assets and trainings. That's the one-stop-shop for all news, where all updates to assets and trainings and changes to the one-stop shop are frequently communicated. As you start to have multiple locations for the same information, it becomes almost impossible keeping everything up to date and in synch. If you find any stakeholder using outdated assets or messaging, you likely have not found the best communication approach yet.

One last aspect of communication. Too often enablement and communication are one-way streets. However, as you enable your sales teams, marketing teams, professional services, and your partners, they like are willing to provide you with invaluable feedback. Enablement is an opportunity to discover how to improve your product, your Go-to-Market approach, and your enablement program to get better results.

Enablement comes with the ongoing requirement to find the best ways to communicate the value and positioning of your product. Enablement means keeping all stakeholders up to date as your software evolves. Enablement is never a one-off activity. Just think about the churn in your sales force year over year.

Enablement also depends on the context of your product and the number of stakeholders that need to be enabled. You require different strategies depending on your Go-to-Market approach. For example, the enablement approach, the assets, the training and the communication are different whether

- you target a limited number of large customers, small businesses, or single consumers.
- you sell in a high-touch mode or no-touch mode.
- you work completely with teams in your own organization or 100% with channel partners.

Your business model and the context of your product and your organization impact your Go-to-Market plan and activities, which has ripple effects on your enablement approach.

6.5.1 Sales and Marketing Enablement

Enabling your sales and marketing teams is pivotal as these teams are the ones who are finally pushing and convincing your customers to buy your product. We already covered the necessities of enablement (assets, communication, and training). Enabling sales and marketing teams is about understanding (or asking) what these teams require to do their job.

Sales team enablement typically comes with a sales kit and product-specific training. The sales teams not only need to be aware about the existence of the sales kits, they need to be trained how to use them. Product sales training comprises all the knowledge about the product your sales teams needs to best sell your product. Therefore, you need to understand what's really interesting for sales people. Note, it is not a deep dive on every feature of the product. The focus for sales team enablement is to ensure your sales team knows the details that will drive customers' decisions. Keep this in mind, as sales teams generally will not take the time to participate in "your" enablement activity, if they do not see value for reaching their quota. A good approach for enabling sales teams is to explain the following to them:

- why your product supports or triggers a compelling event they can use with their customers
- link between the customer problem and the unique selling proposition of your product

If you, in addition, provide them a world-class sales kit when they need it, then you are set up for success and high ratings for this PYPR dimension item. A world-class sales kit is hard to define, as it heavily depends on what your context (product, organization, sales motion, route to market, people in your sales teams, industry, etc.) requires. Generally, a sales kit is a collection of assets useful to the sales team in closing business. Think about the sales and marketing assets from Sect. 6.2 that match the demand of your context.

For example, we defined a master bill of materials for all products in my area that need to be maintained and kept to the highest standards. The core enablement material comprises

- **Assets**: Product Fact Sheet, Sales Fact Sheet, L0 to L2 Product Presentations, Customer Business Case, Competitive Battle Card, Who is Who Document
- Software product demonstration catalog (see Sect. 7.1)
- Product Training (see Sect. 7.4)

The bill of materials comprises the minimum set of assets. The product team can decide to provide more, but never less for their products. All assets are mandated to be available in the one-stop-shop for each product. We also aligned on the key principles of quality over mass, usefulness (i.e. target audience and target user of the asset in mind), completeness (i.e. all required information), and uniqueness (i.e. no repetitive assets).

Marketing team enablement can be core marketing team enablement, product marketing team enablement, or both. I define core marketing as not being product-specific, while product marketing certainly has product focus. Therefore, enabling core marketing concentrates more about working with these teams on events and feeding them with updates that are important for the whole organization. Enabling marketing teams is rather a project approach, like working jointly on an asset, preparing a tradeshow or internal company event, but not an ongoing, planned activity.

A common approach is that product marketing supports or is responsible for the Go-to-Market dimension. Product marketing enablement is best done by including the product marketing team with the core product team. Being part of the core product team, they know what's going on and what needs to be done anyway. To be very clear, I do not see value in a separate product marketing team outside of the product team. I have seen this approach in various interpretations, but I have never seen it being effective or working properly.

6.5.2 On Partner Enablement by Hans K. van Delden, Partner, PricewaterhouseCoopers

Once you have decided to work with an implementation partner, it's in your best interest to enable them to represent your solution effectively (pre-sale) and to implement your solution effectively (post-sale).

Enabling an implementation partner requires an investment of time from both the implementation partner and the software vendor. You have to decide jointly how much time you are willing to invest with any given partner, but without some investment of time, you won't have much of a partnership. In my experience, there are four areas where both parties will benefit from investing their time together.

- **Clarity on Pricing**—Partners are often involved in solving client problems and building the business case and budgets for the associated implementation programs. While your implementation partners don't need to know your exact pricing methodology, they need to be able to make a reasonable estimate of the software licenses costs.
- **Clarity on Product Roadmap**—Nothing freezes a product pipeline faster than uncertainty on product direction. As a Product Manager, you certainly want to avoid this situation, while still maintaining some flexibility in your product roadmap. At a minimum, you need to share enough information to enable effective implementation planning—which, of course, is an important service that your implementation partner provides to your joint clients.
- **Product Training**—Implementation partners will need training from time to time—for example, when you are first onboarding them as a partner and when you release a major upgrade or new product. If possible, try to provide some form of asynchronous training for your implementation partners. This is far easier to complete than classroom training for professional services staff, which are often committed to inflexible client programs.
- **Access to the Product Team**—As the foremost experts on the software product, the Product team can be an invaluable resource to an implementation partner—especially when a client has an unusual problem or possibly even a new product

need. Product Managers should seek to establish a healthy professional relationship between the key members of their product team and the key resources from the implementation partner.

Your investment in enabling your implementation partners should pay dividends in both the pre-sales and post-sales cycles. During the pre-sales cycle, large enterprises will often seek input from their SI partners on software capabilities, costs, implementation timelines, watch-outs, etc. To the extent your implementation partners are well informed, these discussions can greatly facilitate the sale of your software. During the post-sales cycle, you want your implementation partner to make the best use of your product and deliver the best results for your joint clients.

6.5.3 Own Professional Services/Consulting Enablement

Again, the key question to be answered for professional services enablement is: What is really interesting for professional services teams? And I agree with the insights of Hans K. van Delden about partner enablement. Therefore, I will not repeat the importance of product training, clarity on product roadmap, pricing, and access to the product team.

Depending on your Go-to-Market strategy, the degree you rely on your own professional services team and the guardrails provided by corporate policies, you can consider preferring your own team with, for example sharing slightly more information, or sharing earlier. However, I would recommend not making any differentiation as you work with partners and own services teams.

If you benefit from working with your own professional services teams, you might be able to drag the teams into product testing early on. Another option could be to leverage your internal team for demo build activities. These are effective ways of early knowledge transfer. And if these are valid options in your context, why not offer the same to your partner community?

6.5.4 PYPR Dimension Items Details

See Tables 6.9 and 6.10.

Table 6.9 PYPR defaults by software product manager type

Sales enablement				
Topic		Internal PM	B2B PM	B2C PM
Default dimension item weight		20	20	10
Criticality for PM		High[a]	High	Low
Professional services enablement				
Topic		Internal PM	B2B PM	B2C PM
Default dimension item weight		0	10	0
Criticality for PM		X	Low	X
Partner enablement				
Topic		Internal PM	B2B PM	B2C PM
Default dimension item weight		0	15	10
Criticality for PM		X	Medium	Low
Rating sales, partner, and professional services enablement				
PYPR score	Low	No or very limited sales/ professional services/ partner employees enabled for latest positioning, product features, etc. Sales and professional services require almost always product team support. The target market segments cannot be served properly due to missing scale		
	Medium	Some sales/ professional services/ partner employees are properly enabled and up-to-date with latest positioning, product features, etc. Sales/professional services/partner employees are a bottleneck within many opportunities and customer projects that needs to be frequently mitigated by product managers		
	High	Sales/ professional services/ partner employees are trained, up-to-date and available with decent lead time in all target regions and for all target market segments. There is a close collaboration and feedback loop between sales/ professional services/ partner employees and the product team, sales/professional services/partner representatives are active members of the extended product team		

[a]Corporate Communication Enablement

Table 6.10 PYPR dimensions impact examples

Dimension	Direct impact example	Indirect impact example
Product viability	Due to brilliant enablement of partners and professional services, product growth benefits due to smooth product implementations	
Product development		Team health improves due to missing firefighting activities
–		Marketing and sales assets improve due to two-way communication with sales, partners and professional services
Software demonstrations and training		Software demonstrations improve due to two-way communication with sales, partners and professional services
The market/Your customers	Brilliant enablement of partners and professional services leads to more references	
Organizational maturity		Organization and governance improved due to direct interaction and feedback from sales, professional services, and partners

6.5.5 Summary and Conclusions

Key Takeaways

- As a product manager, your focus remains on consistent enablement, building trust with all "to-be-enabled" stakeholders, trigger and balance the required actions to reach these goals
- Enablement requires the following elements:
  - Assets
  - Communication
  - Training
- Good enablement practices ensure consistent messaging and provide scale.
- Develop an enablement plan (milestones, enablement schedule, asset creation/updates) that fits your product planning and include the enablement plan to the overall Go-to-Market plan.
- If you rely on partners to sell or implement your product for you, then you need to enable them properly.
- Record all trainings sessions and make them available in the one-stop-shop.

- Communicate with all "to-be-enabled" stakeholders in a dialog, not in a one-way approach. Collect feedback and understand the needs of all stakeholders and be clear about your expectations as well.

References

Bar, M. (2018, December 27). *If the value isn't clear the price will always be too high*. Retrieved from https://productmanagementfestival.com/conference/value-isnt-clear-price-will-always-high-2/.

Customer Value. (2018, June 23). Retrieved from http://www.businessdictionary.com/definition/customer-value.html.

Gilad, I. (2018, October 12). *How people perceive value*. Retrieved from https://medium.com/@itamargilad/perceived-value-and-why-you-should-care-e03be4f3e3c3.

Lawley, B., & Schure, P. (2017). *Product management for dummies*. Hoboken, New Jersey: Wiley.

Merkado. (2018, May 25). *Tech companies: Sell customer value rather than products*. Retrieved from https://merkadoservices.wordpress.com/2013/07/22/tech-companies-sell-customer-value-rather-than-products/.

Moore, G. A. (1995). *Crossing the chasm: Marketing and selling high-tech products to mainstream customers*. Harper Collins USA.

Strategyzer. (2018, December 4). *StratChat: Value proposition canvas best practices*. Retrieved from https://www.youtube.com/watch?v=r0mtUQnny94.

Strategyzer AG. (2019, March 1). *The value proposition canvas*. Retrieved from https://www.strategyzer.com/canvas/value-proposition-canvas.

Tzu, S. (2015). *The art of war*. Chiron Academic Press: Authoritative ed.

Software Demonstrations and Training 7

The Showcase Part of your Software Product Manager Role

Software product demonstrations and product training are frequently your product's first impression to anyone outside the product team. There are endless options to showcase your product, for example via software product demonstrations, product videos, company videos, or product trainings to name a few. "Buyers and vendors both see hands-on experience as one of the best ways to evaluate a product. More than 75% of buyers used product demos in their purchase process, and 87% of vendor respondents shared demos with prospects. Product demos and free trials were two of the top three most helpful and trustworthy information sources for buyers. Vendors also identified demos as the most effective content type for helping to convert prospects" (Headley, 2017 (Summer)).

What's the role of the product manager here? Usually you are not the one demonstrating your product, nor will you conduct the product training. You are the General Manager of YourProduct Inc., you are the product manager and that's why you care that there are valuable software demos and relevant product trainings that underline the product position in relevant product trainings. Therefore, the role of the product manager can come in many variations in this PYPR dimension, from being the initial trainer in the first teach, delivering early knowledge transfer sessions for consultants, Pre-sales and sales teams, or training the end user customers about the latest product features. In your role as product manager, what you really need to focus on is consistency, professionalism, and scale through software product demonstrations and product training.

This chapter explains the Software Demonstrations and Training PYPR dimension that represents "The Showcase Part of the Software Product Manager Role." Due to its importance and according to my experience, that there are still many issues with software demonstrations, I consider Software Demonstrations and Training as being its own dimension and not part of the Go-to-Market dimension.

We will examine in more detail the various software demonstrations and training types to improve the items of this PYPR dimension, and the essentials to be considered as well as some proven practices that worked for me in various situations over the last decade. The tools and templates provided are selected, proven

T. Wagenblatt, *Software Product Management*, Management for Professionals,
https://doi.org/10.1007/978-3-030-19871-8_7

practices that worked in my context. If you already have filled your bag of tricks with more advanced options or options that better fit your context that is absolutely fine. The descriptions and proven practices are meant as directional options to help you to improve the PYPR scores in the Software Demonstrations and Training dimension; hence it is not necessary that the descriptions match your context 100%. Likewise, the proven practices can be substituted with better matching ones for your specific context. The main point is to improve the product, not the tools and methods to improve it.

I propose to start with the default PYPR configuration in Fig. 7.1. As you leverage PYPR for your product, consider the recommendations from Sect 3.3.

Dimension Weight 7,5 %		Dimension Weight 5 %		Dimension Weight 7,5 %	
B2B		B2C		Internal PM	
Dimension Item	Weighting Factor	Dimension Item	Weighting Factor	Dimension Item	Weighting Factor
Software Demonstrations	25,0%	Software Demonstrations or Self-explaining Software	45,0%	Software Demonstrations	25,0%
Product Marketing Video	20,0%	Product Marketing Video	40,0%	Product Marketing Video	15,0%
Pre-Sales Enablement	30,0%			Support and Roll-out team Enablement	30,0%
Trainings	25,0%	Trainings	15,0%	Trainings	30,0%

Fig. 7.1 Software demonstrations and training: PYPR dimension defaults © Timo Wagenblatt 2019. All rights reserved

Although the dimension weights seem relatively low, I frequently considered this dimension to be the stepchild of product management and with that the limiting factor of product success. In section I will detail the following PYPR dimension items[1]:

- **Software Demonstrations**
  Software demonstrations showcase your product in various ways and forms. Software demonstrations are part of most Business-to-Business sales cycles responding to customer pain points. The occasions for software demonstrations require a variety of options to pick from and showcase the product in the best possible way in any given context.
- **Product Marketing Videos**
  Product Marketing videos have some similarity with software demonstrations. The main differences are that one can better plan them, they are reliable and Product Marketing videos scale. Product Marketing videos can be used for software feature demonstrations, but also for many other situations like overview videos, positioning videos, feature-specific videos, draw-on, customer testimonials, etc. to distribute your product-related message to the masses.
- **Pre-sales Enablement**
  In Business-to-Business software organizations and also for Business-to-Consumer focused organizations, there are Pre-sales/sales engineering teams that deliver professionally software demonstrations to prospects, customers,

[1]The descriptions are short reviews from Chap. 2.

analysts etc. Enabling Pre-sales and sales engineering teams requires the understanding of the specifics of their job.
- **Training**
  The objective is as simple as having professional, high-quality trainings and trainers available to support all audiences, internally and externally, underpinning the professionalism of your product organization. Understand your role as a product manager for scaling, while staying on track with your product positioning.

The storyline of software demonstrations and your product training needs to fit to the value proposition and positioning of your product. The delivery of software demonstrations and product training needs to be consistent in messaging and how the product values are addressing the customer pain points and solving the customer's problems. If the training material is outdated, or not up to date in content and delivery channels, that's potentially a strong negative against product success as well.

7.1 Software Demonstrations

Software demonstrations showcase your YourProduct Inc. Therefore, software demonstrations should be treated with the same professionalism as product development. For example:

- You have the latest technology and best performing infrastructure within development, but your software demonstration environment consists of outdated equipment … think and reconsider.
- You have an established and great procedure to prepare for the next release, next sprint, or next backlog item, but demonstrations and trainings are always ad hoc activities … reconsider this.

Product managers need to scale and balance their involvement. Creating consistent and professional software demonstrations take time. Presenting software to customers and prospects frequently comes with traveling from one end of the country or even the world to the other. If you want to master these challenges—scaling is a must. The following strategies should be part of your product management survival kit:

- Scale with replication: Use recordings of the best, whether it is you, the Pre-sales specialist, developer, tester, etc. when explaining new software features, value cases, or a software product demonstration. Leverage the best tools and share the videos or recorded demos with your target audiences.
- Scale with more hands (and brains): Provide the right guidance, support and enablement for Pre-sales and Sales Engineering Teams. These teams could be responsible or at least strong supporters of software demonstrations creation and

maintenance. Supported with latest updates they will have positive side effects like consistent messaging to the market and your existing customers. Consequentially, your audiences will perceive your company and your product positioning as interconnected and cohesive.

Software demonstrations showcase your product by explaining the values of your software to an audience. Software demonstrations might be run from a SaaS landscape, from your laptop, from a server behind your company's firewall, or wherever your product environment physically resides. The software demonstration environment requires special focus, using the best possible equipment and infrastructure. Note that a software demonstration is likely your audience's first impression of your product. And you know how tricky first impressions can be.

Software demonstrations are part of most B2B sales cycles responding to customer questions and pain points, whether personally in a room setup or via video streaming in front of huge audiences. Since they are live, they require special attention and special skills, including the flexibility to react to the audience. Hence, the various occasions for software demonstrations require a variety of options as the task at hand is to showcase the product in the best possible way in any given context.

Let's investigate a scenario that is equally important and prominent—a customer meeting with a planned software demonstration as part of a sales cycle.

It's show time! The time for you to make your product shine. Maybe you start by positioning your organization, going over specific financial and soft facts, strategies, and future goals. Then, you move on to discussing specific problems that companies—like this customer—may be having, and finally you show them how your software features can solve them all. Right!

Do you think this is exciting for your customer? Will this standard approach advance the sale? Maybe, but likely not as your competitor might be more creative, better prepared and more exciting.

Software demonstrations should be conducted in a way that are exciting for the audience and are tailored to this audience's needs. Using real data (preferably the customer's data)—along with the customer's storyline, you can walk your audience through the software demonstration like it's a finely crafted play.

Murphy's Law applies to software demonstrations as well, so think about your best fallback solution in case the live software demonstration has problems. Who hasn't experienced this?

Yes, software demonstrations go wrong, which is typical of Murphy's Law, but why? There are many reasons, but the one of not preparing professionally is inexcusable. Software demonstrations need to be standard business for any product organization. Software demonstrations are what customers, analysts, investors, managers, and everyone who is external to the product team recognize as the outcome of your work. It should be a no brainer using the best system, leveraging the best talent and preparing bullet-proof software demonstrations … and things can and still will go wrong.

I acknowledge that even the best preparation might not be 100% bullet-proof, but always remember—crashes during a software demonstration are generally unacceptable. Put yourself in your audience's shoes; if the software doesn't work well in your fully-controlled demo environment, will your audience think your product is going to work in their real-life environment? In best case these problems will only lengthen the sales cycle or undermine your credibility, but likely you will be out of the running despite that fact that your product might be great and would be an ideal fit for your prospects.

Offline or recorded demos are one fallback option, while not being the silver bullet. As a product team, you need to think about your fallback options and plan accordingly for the software demonstration for YourProduct Inc.

One common fallback option is the preparation of offline (recorded) software product demonstrations that introduce and explain your product in a pre-defined flow or with a pre-defined focus and message. The nice part of recorded software demonstrations is that you can plan them; they are reliable and deliver great scale. The drawback is that they are not as powerful in most situations and the messaging is only one directional. There is no presenter around, who can course-correct misunderstandings or respond to questions. Therefore, recording the best talent when explaining new software features, explaining value cases, or delivering software product demonstrations is as critical as leveraging the best channels to share these assets with the well-defined target audiences.

On another topic, as product manager, you are technically the most qualified person to give the demo as you are the product team member who knows the most about the product's users, features, capabilities, roadmap, unique selling points, interfaces, etc. However, that is not correct for 99% of product managers.

In a software demonstration context, knowing your product really well means that you can speak on an expert level about all its details, which is exactly what you don't want to do to an external (read: novice) audience. The pride showcasing all the hard work is almost impossible to hide for core product team members. Generally, the audience is not interested in features and functions, but rather in solutions for their problems. Therefore, software demonstrations should tell a story about how your target audience's personal, professional life or business will be improved or made better in some way by using your product.

I think it is important that you understand the importance of this PYPR dimension item, and what it takes to provide great software demonstrations. But your job as a product manager includes finding the members in your extended product team that are most skilled at telling that story.

Great storyteller skills comprise:

- Triggering your audience's emotions
- Inspiring the audience's imaginations
- Making your product seem at least as good as it actually is

If you find such skills in your core or extended product team, then the better chances to deliver great software demonstrations. If that's you, congratulations on being one of the 1% of product managers out there. Still remember the tradeoff that you, as the product manager, are the most senior executive of YourProduct Inc. Over time you will learn whether and when you should use this superpower in this PYPR dimension, and when you should step back and let the professionals do their job.

7.1.1 Proven Practice: SUCCES(sful) Software Demonstrations

The objective of conducting software demonstrations is to achieve success, which requires SUCCES. No, this is neither a tautology nor a typo. It's simply a mnemonic that helped me remember important pieces of successful software product demonstrations.

Years ago, I learned the mnemonic SUCCES from one of SAP's best software demonstration presenters. She also introduced the term "Blackberry® line" to the "How to present impactful product demonstrations" training class. The term Blackberry® line reveals a lot and sounds like ancient times, although the training was only a few years ago. Nowadays she might call the concept Apple iPhone® line or Samsung Galaxy® line; however, I have not listened to her recently. We can be politically correct here and just call the concept smartphone line, not as sexy but you get the idea.

The smartphone line concept is easily observed in many presentations, software demonstrations, and trainings, and likely your attention followed the same pattern in the past. The audience attention follows a pattern such as shown in Fig. 7.2.

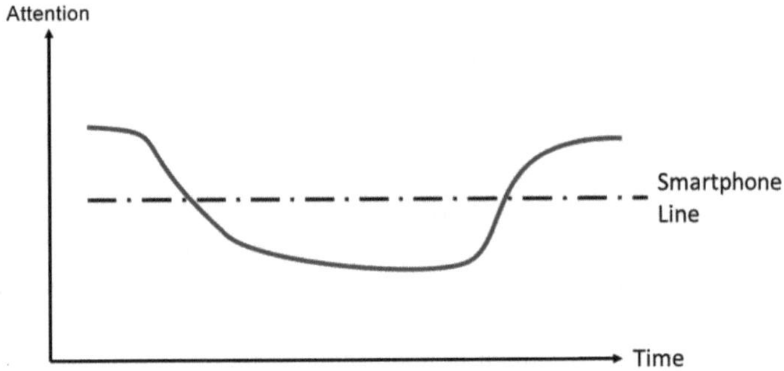

Fig. 7.2 Smartphone line © Timo Wagenblatt 2019. All rights reserved

At the beginning we are excited about the presentation, the speaker and the topic. The excitement declines as the speaker or the topic or both do not fascinate us, and the audience's attention continues declining if there is no stimulus until we reach a certain level where we pick up our smartphone and check emails, our schedule, or activities in social media, etc. Likely our attention is gone until our subconsciousness hears some key words like closing comments, conclusion, summary, key takeaways and the phrases you normally hear at the end of presentations. Suddenly our attention is back as the presentation comes to an end.

That's not what we want for our software demonstrations, correct?

Software demonstrations are a special kind of presentation. Let's check how we can be successful or help others to be successful in this discipline. To avoid the smartphone line, the SUCCES criteria are:

- Story
  No surprise, but any demo needs a story. Without a clear storyline that underlines the product's positioning and the value of its functional scope, the attention will decline even faster below the smartphone line. Products solve problems, which is the reason your audience attends a software demonstration. Consequently, the demo's storyline needs to show immediately to the audience how the most relevant problems are solved.
- Unexpected
  Plan for something unexpected in your storyline. Think about variation points that do not follow the same pattern your audience is expecting. Many software demonstrations follow the same pattern, so people will appreciate if you deviate from the norm and surprise them positively.
- Concrete
  The story must be tangible and concrete. Your story needs characters, some might call these personas. The audience needs examples they can relate back to their daily business.
- Credible
  Along these lines, the story needs to sound real. Unrealistic business scenarios or data that is not based in reality weakens the best software demonstrations and will not keep the attention level high.
- Emotional
  Probably the hardest part and not always possible is getting to the emotional level in software demonstrations, which is what we should strive for as emotions are complicated. Exploiting the pain points your product addresses might help, or getting the presenter to be passionate about the topic is another way of looking at the E of SUCCES.
- Simple
  Finally, the software demonstration needs to be simple, so that the audience can follow the story. We are the experts of our product, we know how to use the product, we know the terminology, floorplan, navigation etc. The audience does not. We need to keep this in mind as the audience cannot follow the software demonstration and then you will see some open laptops or smartphone use over time. As product managers, this might be the most difficult part of SUCCES.

7.1.2 PYPR Dimension Items Details

See Tables 7.1 and 7.2.

Table 7.1 PYPR defaults by software product manager type © Timo Wagenblatt 2019. All rights reserved

Topic		Internal PM	B2B PM	B2C PM
Default dimension item weight		25	25	45
Criticality for PM		High	High	High
PYCR score	Low	No up-to-date software demonstrations available. Software demonstrations might outdated because of missing cohesiveness to vision, strategy, messaging, positioning, target market, released functionality, addressed personas, industry trends, etc.		
	Medium	Limited software demonstrations available with mediocre quality (e.g. performance, data quality, story line) or only partial coverage of addressable market, value proposition, personas, unique selling points, functionality etc. Some fallback options are available for demo system downtimes		
	High	World-class software demonstrations underlining and boosting your product positioning, available for all personas, enabling customers and the target market segments to understand your product's value supported by clear and relevant story lines, realistic data, reliable infrastructure, and great performance		

Table 7.2 PYPR dimensions impact examples

Dimension	Direct impact example	Indirect impact example
Product viability	Sales pipeline and product growth benefit from brilliant software demonstrations	
Product development		Product quality improves due to automated demo script testing
Go-to-Market/product marketing	Go-to-Market plan needs to consider lead times for software demonstration creation and updates	
Software demonstrations and training	Pre-sales enablement and scaling	
The market/your customers	Customers and prospects perceive functional completeness generally higher if they can see relevant software demonstrations	
Organizational maturity		Key principles could include that a feature is only 'done', if it can be shown to customers

7.1.3 Summary and Conclusions

As a product manager, you play an important role in the PYPR dimension item of software demonstrations, but likely you are not the star. You need to ensure that the main parts are well cast, and the set is optimally prepared.[2] Your role in this play might be not in the spotlight, but your main concern should be that software demonstrations are available that underline the product vision and product positioning, reliably showcasing the great value YourProduct Inc. offers. Product managers frequently write demo scripts, but once more, there is likely someone else who can do better with this. Reviewing demo scripts from Pre-sales or other talented colleagues might be sufficient.

Key Takeaways

- Prepare with SUCCES for successful software demonstrations
- Maintain a software demonstrations catalogue and make sure everyone providing software demonstrations for your product knows about the catalogue. The software demonstrations listed in the catalogue should describe at least the information below:
  - Internal user type/Target Persona/Key Message/Link to demo script and demo system/customer value/supported processes.
- Understand your audience
  - Software demonstrations to train the audience or to establish the value? Overview software demonstration for an executive is different than in a vendor selection with a formal RFP
  - In a sales cycle, the goal of a customer software demonstration is not to impress with deep product knowledge. It is to advance the sale.
- Avoid showcasing new features in general sessions, always be precise about release and availability versus not released software functionality and do not mix both as there might be legal and financial consequences that you should strictly avoid.
- Demos should stay on task and not be diverted by questions from the audience. I know there will be questions, and it takes years of experience for a solution engineer not to click the button when someone asks about a certain feature. Go back to these questions after the main story line as far

[2]I admit that sometimes it might be the best option for product managers to demo the product, especially if, for example, strategic, critical customers are asking to get a sneak peak.of the latest developments or the audience are senior executives that want to see the results of their investments, but in both cases these are different types of software demonstrations.

too many software demonstrations run out of time without delivering the key messages.

- Never demo a meaningless feature to your audience. Every feature you demonstrate must be tied directly to the customer problem. Focus on what the product does to ease the customer problem and not on how the product works.
- Have a backup! Murphy's Law will apply in many ways like wireless inaccessibility, projector resolution problems, network latency, firewalls, etc.
- Special note on software demonstrations as part of a sales cycle (Kraner, 2018):
  - Uncover the customer problems, ask for a discovery session to tailor your software demonstration
  - Understand the priority and severity of the problem and who will fix the problem
  - Use customer data if possible
  - Demonstrate your competence in understanding your customer's pain and demand for improvements. Have pain questions prepared to get the conversation going.

7.2 Pre-sales Enablement

Pre-sales enablement requires special focus because it is a great opportunity for product managers to scale. Enablement comes with the ongoing requirement to train to better communicate the value and positioning of your product while keeping the teams up to date, as your software evolves and gets frequent updates that likely will affect the values and positioning of your product. If your teams don't know about the new cool demo highlighting the latest, most valuable feature and which problem it solves, they cannot leverage it in their customer interactions, and hence all the work they put into the assets and into software development will have limited impact.

I asked my colleague "Greg McNitt, Executive Solution Engineer at SAP, for his view of Software Product Management from his experienced Pre-sales perspective. He gave the following feedback that provides an excellent perspective to all product managers:

"Pre-sales has one goal: "to win." Pre-sales is a unique role in that it requires individuals who are comfortable in front of a keyboard and mouse to tell a business story. To win the customer's business, Pre-sales must demonstrate the product's ability to meet the business requirements and do so in an intuitive and easy to understand way, all while being peppered with all kind of ad hoc questions.

Software Product Management's job does not end at the development of features and functionality. The end goal is to convince customers that the product is the right solution for their business problems. This means that product managers need to deliver:

- Features and functionality to meet the business requirements
- Supporting sales material to position the solution from introductory meetings through deep dive sessions
- A strong demonstration.

Furthermore, product managers sometimes need to play a supporting role in customer presentations, especially if the customer wants to go deeper into the product and its future then a product expert is needed.

When getting more specific about Pre-sales enablement, the demonstration topic is the life blood of the Pre-sales organization. Compare it to an automobile manufacturer: when the new car model is released, where does the first model get shipped? To the dealership. It's the dealership's sales people that need to know the features of the new car, the selling points, and be able to demonstrate or "test drive" the new car. For me, it's the same in software. The new product/release needs to be delivered to the Pre-sales organization. This includes:

- A working demonstration
- Good demonstration content that tells a realistic business story (e.g. the "day in the life of …" demo)
- Supporting collateral/sales material/videos/slides/solution briefs/customer references
  - Frequent sessions designed to educate the Pre-sales organization, both about the feature and functions of the product, as well as the business value.

There is a lot of pressure within the Pre-sales organization as software companies broaden their capabilities and acquire new offerings. This pressure often forces Pre-sales resources to become generalists rather than specialists—to be able to tell the "end-to-end" story beyond one specific product. This dynamic weighs heavily on the product managers as they need to deliver content, functionality, and demonstrations that are easy for the broader Pre-sales audience to digest, as well as deep demonstrations for the specialists."

And when I asked Greg: "What makes a great user-focused demo?" His answer was short and to the point: "Beyond the table stakes of a good demonstration—the demo must show the customer business value and provide the users with a compelling, easy-to-use solution that will improve their job."

There is nothing to add from my side, the customer has spoken.

7.2.1 PYPR Dimension Items Details

See Tables 7.3 and 7.4.

Table 7.3 PYPR defaults by software product manager type (Pre-sales Enablement is substituted with Support and Roll-out Team Enablement for internal IT products. Similar to Pre-sales teams, they need to be enabled to understand the latest developments and proper positioning. The support and roll-out teams might be responsible for creating the training material and software demonstrations or embellishing the assets the product team delivers.)

Topic		Internal PM	B2B PM	B2C PM
Default dimension item weight		30	30	0
Criticality for PM		High	High	X
PYPR score	Low	No or very limited pre-sales engineers enabled for latest positioning, product features, etc. Software demonstrations require almost always product team support. The target market segments cannot be served properly due to missing scale		
	Medium	Some pre-sales engineers are properly enabled and up-to-date with latest positioning, product features, etc. Pre-sales engineers are a bottleneck within many opportunities that needs to be frequently mitigated by product managers		
	High	Pre-sales engineers are trained, up-to-date and available with decent lead time in all target regions and for all target market segments. There is a close collaboration and feedback loop between pre-sales engineers and the product team. Pre-sales representatives are active members of the extended product team		

Table 7.4 PYPR dimensions impact examples

Dimension	Direct impact example	Indirect impact example
Product viability	Sales pipeline increases and becomes more mature as opportunities advance faster	
Product development		Product team exposed to direct feedback and pre-sales team supporting testing activities
Go-to-Market/product marketing		Frequent feedback for sales assets
Software demonstrations and training	Better software demonstrations and scale	

(continued)

Table 7.4 (continued)

Dimension	Direct impact example	Indirect impact example
The market/your customers	Functional completeness perception improved by great pre-sales performance	
Organizational maturity		People mindset improved due to collaboration and pre-sales perspective

7.2.2 Summary and Conclusions

I will keep it short as Greg already summarized the Pre-sales matters well. As product managers, your Pre-sales colleagues are your opportunity to scale. Engaging Pre-sales colleagues and keeping them up to date and interested takes certainly time; however, it can pay back big time. If you need any more reason, I give you two:

- The Pre-sales team is used to present software products in a compelling way, consumable for the audience, and sticky in its message. It is their profession, not yours.
- You cannot and should not be part of all sales opportunities. Remember the amount of demonstrations that might be required to reach the financial goals for your product. You are the most senior product executive, not the one that generally demonstrates the commodity (read: already released) features and functions.

7.3 Product Marketing Videos

I use the term product marketing videos as a placeholder for any product-related digital content. Product marketing videos are marketing assets and part of most sales kits (for more details see Sect. 6.2). I will use the term for simplification reasons despite the fact that some assets might not be a video.

Product marketing videos are vital content for most SaaS products, because they are required for scaling customer onboarding. Product marketing videos can become quality material for your customer's success team that can provide a five-minute overview of your entire product's value. Product marketing videos can be a core component of your product marketing strategy that will support your Go-to-Market approach. These are just a few of the many applications of product marketing videos.

As a product manager, the first thing to decide when you consider leveraging product marketing videos is who will create them. There are essentially two choices:

- Hire a professional video production company
- Produce the video on your own within the product team.

Hiring a company to create your demo video can be a great option if you require high-quality assets and have the budgets available. Video production companies usually take care of almost all the work, from creative concepting to scripting and production. You might be interviewed and have a reviewing role, but you'll have less work compared to creating everything on your own, while generally getting better results.

If you decide to produce videos on your own within the product team, then obviously you save money, but someone needs to spend time on this topic. However, then you are in full control of your home-made videos and, for example, quick updates to reflect slightly changes in positioning or wording are much simpler. Digital assets help with great scale and they deliver your message, not a variation biased by a presenter. But note that digital assets have two interesting attributes to consider: they are sticky, and generally you are not in control of who can access them once they are on the internet. Concerning the stickiness of digital assets, I recommend having a strategy very early on to update or delete outdated product marketing videos that weaken your latest messaging and product positioning.

You might discover that many kinds of product-relates assets are required for various purposes. As a product manager, you can help to find the right balance in terms of assets and the best use of the Go-to-Market budgets. Independent of the sourcing, every product marketing video requires a clear purpose, benefits from storytelling, and needs to be consistent with your overall product marketing and product strategy.

A balanced plan considers assets that support all stages of your customer/buyer journey, such as shown in Fig. 7.3, and the digital assets required for stakeholder enablement. Plan your mix of advertisement, promotions, presentations, demonstrations, or feature explainer assets. I have seen product teams being successful with producing their own product feature videos for (technical) enablement sessions and spending more time and budget for quality assets in order to get closer to their customers.

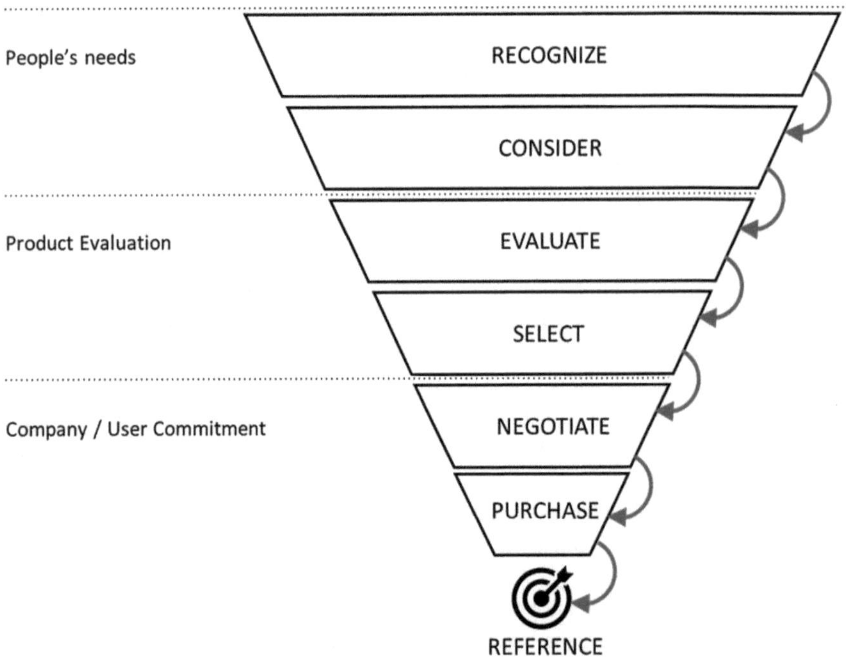

Fig. 7.3 Consider customer/buyer journey for product marketing (Videos) © Timo Wagenblatt 2019. All rights reserved

7.3.1 PYPR Dimension Items Details

See Tables 7.5 and 7.6.

Table 7.5 PYPR defaults by software product manager type

Topic		Internal PM	B2B PM	B2C PM
Default dimension item weight		15	20	40
Criticality for PM		Medium	High	High
PYPR score	Low	No up-to-date videos available. Videos might be outdated because of missing cohesiveness to vision, strategy, messaging, positioning, target market, released functionality, addressed personas, industry trends, etc.		
	Medium	Limited videos available with mediocre quality or only partial coverage of addressable market, value proposition, personas, unique selling points, etc.		
	High	World-class digital assets underlining and boosting your product marketing strategy, supporting all personas, enabling users and the market to understand your product's value		

Table 7.6 PYPR dimensions impact examples

Dimension	Direct impact example	Indirect impact example
Product viability	Sales pipeline and product growth benefit from brilliant digital assets	
Product development		Team sees their product from an external view being proud of what they deliver (if they like the digital assets)
Go-to-Market/product marketing	Go-to-Market plan needs to consider lead times for digital asset production	
Software demonstrations and training	Pre-sales benefits from variation of digital assets	
The market/your customers		Thought leadership amplification in both directions, positive or negative
Organizational maturity		

7.3.2 Summary and Conclusions

Key Takeaways

- Product marketing videos can be leveraged through social media, website, blog, or mailouts. Video marketing can introduce or update your product to your target customer segments in a fresh and scalable way.
- Balance product team's involvement by considering budget, scale, and flexibility.
- Every asset needs a story. Consider the customer/buyer journey and adapt the storyline accordingly for any product marketing asset.
- Gather feedback about content (early) and adoption (ongoing) as a base to continuously improve your product marketing assets.
- Have a plan to delete outdated assets (at least from your official channels).

7.4 Training

The main objectives improving the Product Training dimension item are maximizing product adoption and customer success. While these are rather generic objectives for any product manager, I will introduce the pivotal role that product trainings can play for software products.

While software demonstrations and product marketing videos especially target new customers, product training should focus on enabling new customers to leverage your product in the best possible way. Software products continuously evolve with each new feature being released. Hence, product training cannot be static either. Basically, everyone outside of the core product team and most importantly for your customers need to be consistently and professionally trained about product updates. There is no sense of giving users new product features without proper explanation and then awaiting the desired results.

Like software demonstrations, product trainings require multiple options in terms of content and delivery. Trainings are required for enabling all key roles in the product lifecycle—internally and externally. Guess who is the first contact for all these requests? Yes, it's likely you as the product manager, and there is nothing wrong here. You are the expert and you know about the latest developments, you know the reason for the product updates and you know the benefits they bring to the various stakeholders. The role of the product manager can be manifold, from being the initial trainer in the first teachings of a new product, delivering early knowledge transfer sessions for consultants, Pre-sales and sales teams to training the end user —the customers. Within this dimension item, I want you to focus more on the external part of product trainings as we covered the internal audiences as part of the various enablement chapters. Product training can become a very time-consuming duty in your role as product manager. As a product manager, your main responsibility is to provide material to the training departments.[3] As a product manager and within the core product team, you need to focus on re-usable material as this will help you to be most effective and save lots of time. Re-use can already start as part of writing high-quality user stories or test cases.

As a product manager, your responsibility and focus needs to be consistency, professionalism, and scale concerning product trainings. I will provide a training evaluation model and some topics to be considered as to not let product training become the limiting factor of product success.

Based on the understanding of the target audience, your product trainings (Kirkpatrick & Kirkpatrick, 2016)

- need to be favorable, engaging and relevant to their jobs (reaction)
- help your target audience to acquire the intended knowledge, skills, attitude, confidence and commitment based on their participation in the training (learning)
- impact the behavior of the participants as they apply what they learned during the training (behavior)
- deliver the targeted outcomes (results).

Once your product trainings deliver these four levels of the Kirkpatrick model, your product is likely scoring well as part of the PYPR assessment. If you additionally consider the following topics (e.g. Rollins, 2019; Ramani, 2019), your product trainings become rather a strategic weapon than a must-do at the end of the product development process:

- **Strategy**: Align your product training strategically with the specific strategy of your product and your organization. Your product strategy might aim at the foundational knowledge transfer about your product features and how they bring value to your customers, thus reducing customer support costs or even generating revenues from training. In addition, it is important that you plan for product trainings and keep them up to date with each upgrade cycle of your product. "If your product release cycles and product training content are not in sync, you risk losing your existing customers. It is important that you assess and examine your product training to see if it's relevant and revamp it as and when required" (Ramani, 2019).

[3] I strongly recommend leveraging an existing training department, or if you don't have one established in your organization, ask for one to be created. Even in the startup where I began my career, we had two people doing full-time trainings and this has been worth a million. Trainers also become experts on current functionality and hence can support you nicely with many adjacent tasks like answering questions about current functionality, enabling Sales, Pre-sales, partners and so on. In addition, having new hires going through the product training also provides the right foundation before you start working with the new colleagues within your product team.

- **Training material development**: Training material must be useful across the range of learning styles. Developing content requires creativity and time. As a product manager, you need to balance your own involvement although you are the content expert. Training material needs to start from the basics, be logical, and comprehensive. Training material should be consistent, providing great customer experience that matches your established high standards.
  Consider training material development not just outside the product but think about product training comprising "an easy-to-use interface that has a prominent "Help" or "How-to-use" walkthrough that guides and enables users to use the product with ease. People don't have the patience or time to read a huge "Help Document" to figure out how the product works. Users need just-in-time and on-demand eLearning nuggets that help them address their queries at each stage of their user-journey" (Ramani, 2019). Describe the new product benefits both for the business and each user so that the training is motivational.
- **Training delivery**: Training delivery addresses how the training is conveyed, circulated, and accessed by your target audiences. Apply a blended learning approach considering different learning styles and ways people prefer to learn. Make your training delivery diverse and find the blend that matches best your users and customer needs from the many alternatives (e.g. in-product training, online training, video tutorials, classroom training with instructor, self-paced e-learning or facilitated by virtual instructor, books, blogs, or mandated self-training). Depending on your product, you might consider a certification program.
- **Training feedback and measurement**: Measuring training success and collecting training participant feedback rounds off a professional training experience. To evaluate employees' learning, reaction, behavior and results you can leverage the Kirkpatrick model as previously introduced. Considering feedback and measuring training results will help to determine gaps and make future training more effective independent of the training delivery model.

Generally, product trainings are focused on conveying product knowledge. However, product training as any customer interaction has some sales effects as well. As your product must always shine brightly, then your product training needs to be great as well.

7.4.1 PYPR Dimension Items Details

See Tables 7.7 and 7.8.

- **Engage Customers and Build a Customer Community**
  There are many ways to engage with customers either in 1:1 situations or in communities and councils addressing groups of customers all at once. Customers like to be in a community, sometimes they organize the community on their own and sometimes you can form (and steer) customer communities. Independently of the scenario, engaging customers comes with multiple, priceless benefits for both parties.
- **Support of Key Customers/Official References**
  Satisfied customers that value your product are the best sales assets you can and will ever have. There is no better marketing than word of mouth marketing. Nurture your newest customer as you did with your first one and don't hesitate to ask for references. Your customers know your market segment and your target customers, their peers. If your product delivers value, they will talk about it to others. Identify customers who are willing to give testimonials, be featured in case studies, give you a like, or agree to be a reference.
- **Thought Leadership**
  Thought leaders influence opinions in their area of expertise, broadcasting who and what is important. Everyone wants to be a thought leader as thought leadership is a powerful marketing and sales tool. One of the best ways to establish authority on your topic is to gain and frequently broadcast deep insights on the subject. As a thought leader, the market and your customers expect innovation and mastery from you in the problem space of your product.
- **Analyst/Influencer Relations**
  Analysts and influencers can be considered as thought leaders as well. In the B2B space, in particular, you should know the players in the analyst camp. Analyst ratings might be important in your particular market segment. Similarly, influencers should be recognized and influenced in the best possible way, or at least you should not be an easy target for bad sentiments.

As the General Manager of YourProduct Inc., you balance market and customer requirements. You balance the special attention required for current product capabilities (e.g. Go-to-Market, software demonstrations, training, enablement), for future product capabilities (e.g. product vision, strategy and planning), and the manifestation of your work (e.g. user feedback, surveys, references) regarding customers, prospects, and other external matters.

8.1 Functional Completeness or Understanding Your Level of Product-Market Fit

As the General Manager of YourProduct Inc., it is your core responsibility to lead the product team in building awesome products that are functionally complete for both your target market segments and your existing customers. Clearly, functional completeness and product-market fit is a core product manager responsibility;

however, it is the customers and prospects that ultimately judge functional completeness and product-market fit.

As a product manager and expert within your product's problem domain, you certainly have an opinion about the functional completeness of your product as well. However, your gut feeling based on your deep understanding of the market and customers is not important here. The market and customer perceptions ultimately define reality. But, depending on your context, there might be good proxies such as industry reference models or something similar that could serve as a basis to define functional completeness. Sometimes even analysts define the mandatory scope of functional completeness as part of their research and publications.

Technically, I believe that a product is functionally complete when and if the complete requirements set by the target market segment is implemented. Building on that, "A set of requirements is complete *if and only if it describes all significant requirements of concern to the user, including requirements associated with functionality, performance, design constraints, attributes, and external interfaces* (IEEE 830-1993, §4.3.3, 1994)" (Leffingwell & Widrig, 2000). Note that the complete set of requirements explicitly includes functional and non-functional requirements.

Functional completeness is relatively hard to define and to measure as the term is fuzzy. In addition, the basis of the complete requirements set is volatile as the world is frequently changing. I interpret functional completeness therefore as the relative perception of customers and prospects versus the fully-fledged needs of each group with the current available product capabilities.

Understanding and assessing functional completeness needs to be related to

- established and known target market segment requirements
- customer and prospect needs (served and underserved needs)
- competitive capabilities

Consequently, you cannot assume that delivering incremental product scope automatically leads to higher levels of functional completeness. Given the features you build for the new product version add customer value because they are wisely prioritized and validated, even then perception of functional completeness might decline. For example, competitive products might leapfrog your product, new market requirements could arise, new underserved needs might be discovered and articulated, new industry trends could pop up, or functional delighters of your product deteriorate to commodity features (see Sect. 5.5.5). As part of your PYPR assessment of functional completeness, you should verify your assessment against the items listed above.

I recommend a proxy measure to assess the customer and prospect perception of functional completeness since their perception will change frequently and continuously. The Net Promoter Score®, described in the next section, could be used as a proxy measure. Independent whether you leverage such a measure, I assume that is very clear how other PYPR dimension items are connected to your product's functional completeness (e.g. Product Development Planning, Competitive Analysis, or Software Demonstrations to list only a few). Basically, every interaction with your target market segment and your customers potentially impacts the perception of your product's functional completeness and provides input for reaching or improving product-market fit.

As I have used the term product-market fit already several times, it is important to set this concept into perspective with the definition of functional completeness. Figure 8.2 illustrates how these concepts relate to each other based on a great blog summarizing a PRODUCTIZED talk from Dan Olsen (Drozhzha, 2019)[2]. A product might be product-market fit without being functionally complete. A minimum viable product (MVP) is a means to test with a minimum amount of work and a limited feature to set the product's value proposition in order to launch, learn and iterate and ultimately reach product-market fit. Generally, an MVP is a smaller slice of the functional completeness pie. In other words, you can certainly get a product to market with a very limited feature set and you might have recognizable success with your MVP piece of the pie, but functional completeness is about the full pie depicting your complete target market segment.

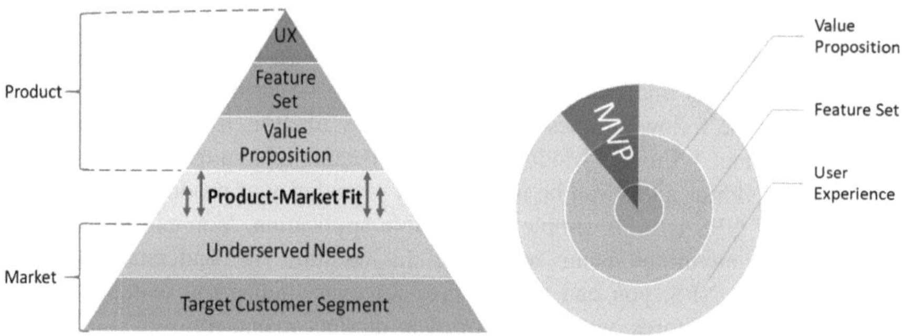

Fig. 8.2 Setting product-market fit, MVP and functional completeness in perspective © Timo Wagenblatt 2019. All rights reserved

Reaching product-market fit is a core responsibility of Software Product Management. According to Dan Olsen (2019), a product reaches product-market fit when it

- meets customer needs
- is better than other alternatives
- is easy to use
- is a good value/price ratio

As a product manager, you focus on these items for increasing levels of product-market fit until your product is perceived as functionally complete. It is all about balance. The value and benefits your customers and prospects expect from your product need to be at par with the provided capabilities. Once again, you can see the importance of a great and relentlessly iterated value proposition for your product (Sect. 6.1). As your product is properly positioned, the perception of functional completeness benefits accordingly.

[2]The concepts are based on Olsen (2015) and Walter (2011).

A great way to improve the Functional Completeness PYPR dimension item is the combination of a thorough Competitive Analysis and an excellent understanding of user needs. As you understand the delighters, performance and must-have features based on a Kano analysis (Sect. 5.5), you have all information needed to outperform your competition and provide a functionally more complete offering to your target market segments.

8.1.1 Proven Practice: Net Promoter Score®[3]

Net Promoter Score® (NPS) is a lean option to measure overall customer satisfaction about functional completeness. I'm describing the tool as a proven practice, but NPS is clearly not the full solution to achieving full product full product-market fit transparency as introduced in the previous section. Nevertheless, NPS is a simple, yet powerful tool that determines whether users and customers find value in your product.

NPS is a metric that determines customers' likelihood to recommend anything from a product, service, to an organization as a score of customer experience (Qualtrix, 2019a, b, c). We want to understand market and customer experience in this PYPR dimension. To better understand how the market or your customers are experiencing your product, the following question is asked: How likely is it that you would recommend [Product Y/Product Module X/Product Feature Z] to a friend or colleague?

Note that NPS as a tool can be used for any granularity of product functionality. The power of NPS is in its simple and flexible application. You can measure and track almost anything using an NPS. In addition to understanding your product-specific NPS, you can track scores for everything from overall NPS for your organization, stores, web pages, or even product managers.

NPS measures the market and customer perception[4] based on the responses to a simple question. Respondents provide a rating between 0 (not at all likely) and 10 (extremely likely) and, depending on their response, customers fall into one of three categories (Qualtrix, 2019a, b, c; Asya, 2019) as shown in Fig. 8.3

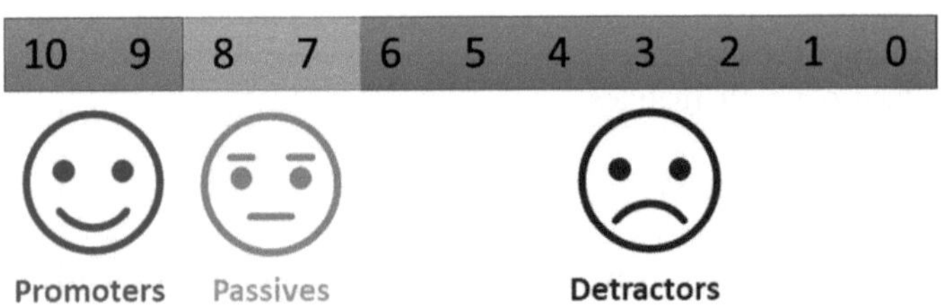

Fig. 8.3 NPS® respondent categories © Timo Wagenblatt 2019. All rights reserved

[3]The Net Promoter® Score (NPS®) is a metric developed by Fred Reichheld, founder of Bain & Company's Loyalty Practice

[4]Note that market means non-users while customers means users of your product. Segmenting your NPS by market and customers enables you to derive different insights about your product's market versus customer perception.

- **Promoters (score 9–10)**: Promoters are stereotyped as loyal enthusiasts who will continue buying and using your product. Promoters have the potential to fuel growth by referring others. They are the key product evangelists that you could consider for early testing activities and for product or product feature launches. Promoters can become influencers as they are passionate about YourProduct Inc. Create ways to keep them excited, so they will share their sentiments about your product with their communities. Promoters frequently act as reference customers for prospects and investors. They are likely willing to speak at industry conferences and act as ambassadors for your product.
- **Passives (score 7–8)**: Passives are stereotyped as satisfied but unenthusiastic users and could be customers who are vulnerable to competitive offerings. Passives are users and customers that need special attention. Find ways to keep them actively engaged in your customer communities. As a product manager, you should understand how to transform Passives into Promoters. Generally, Passives are happy with your product today, but they could change to Detractors as your product evolves. As a product team, consider whether it would be worth the effort to track the overall trend in the conversion rate from Passive-to-Detractor and Passive-to-Promoter. These might be great trend indicators about the health of your product strategy and value proposition.
- **Detractors (score 0–6)**: Detractors are stereotyped as unhappy users and customers who can damage YourProduct Inc. and hinder product growth through negative word of mouth. Detractors are the users and customers that most likely will switch to a competitive product. Detractors would not recommend your product. As a product manager, you will frequently find the most valuable feedback from Detractors concerning functional completeness and product-market fit of your product. Understanding the underserved needs of Detractors is a gold mine.

Calculating NPS is a straightforward subtraction of the percentage of Detractors from the percentage of Promoters. For example, if 25% of respondents are Detractors, 45% are Passives and 30% are Promoters, your NPS would be $30\% - 25\% = 5\%$. NPS explains whether you have more users and customers liking your product than disliking it. Note that a good NPS depends on your context; however a NPS of 5% would have some room for improvement as software and apps are averaging at 31% according to the NPS Benchmark in 2018 (NICE; Satmetrix, 2019).

Calculating a product-specific NPS provides great metrics tracking market and customer perception. Consider whether you get all insights with an NPS for the whole product or you benefit from measuring and tracking NPS on a smaller granularity. Calculating and tracking NPS is best for benchmarking your product's perception regarding functional completeness. Understanding how to improve functional completeness, and why people are Promoters, Passives, or Detractors require more data (Qualtrics.com, 2019). Consider additional questions and data sources (e.g. feature usage, performance, etc.) that can help you and the product team better understand what is really driving your product's NPS.

Sometimes NPS ratings are perceived as harsh as the calculation of the NPS amplifies the user and customer satisfaction versus average calculations. However, as the General Manager of YourProduct Inc. you can stand this.

8.1.2 PYPR Dimension Items Details

See Tables 8.1 and 8.2.

PYPR defaults by software product manager type © Timo Wagenblatt 2019. All rights reserved

Topic		Internal PM	B2B PM	B2C PM
Default dimension item weight		20	15	20
Criticality for PM		High	Medium	High
PYPR score	Low	Your product has not reached product-market fit or your product provides a very limited piece of the expected functional completeness in the problem domain that your product addresses. An indicator of a low functional completeness is "Walking skeleton" scope or even less user stories of your complete user story map. Another indicator of low functional completeness is an Net Promoter Score significantly below the average Net Promoter Score in your product context		
	Medium	Your product has reached market-fit for a recognizable scope of the know target market requirements. Your product covers the main usage scenarios of your user story map. Another indicator of medium functional completeness is an Net Promoter Score close to the average Net Promoter Score in your product context		
	High	Your product is functionally complete measured and proven by complete coverage of established definitions of reference models, good quality user story map, lack of underserved needs of your target market segments, or relative to any competitor out there. Another indicator of high functional completeness is an Net Promoter Score significantly above the average Net Promoter Score in your product context		

PYPR dimensions impact examples

Dimension	Direct impact example	Indirect impact example
Product viability		Sales pipeline impacted by perception of functional completeness
Product development		Backlog prioritization reflects sentiments from Passives and Detractors focusing on NPS improvements
Go-to-Market/Product marketing	Competitive analysis provides insights about functional completeness of competitors and validates understanding of functional completeness	
Software demonstrations and training	Perception of function completeness depends heavily on software demonstrations in early customer interactions	
The Market/Your Customers	Identified Promoters can be recruited to become official references	
Organizational maturity	Established template and tool support for NPS measurement and analysis	

8.1.3 Summary and Conclusions

Key Takeaways

- Functional completeness and product-market fit are core product manager responsibilities.
- Focus on the best value proposition supported by the right feature set and a beautiful user experience for increasing levels of product-market fit until your product is perceived as functionally complete.
- Market and customer perceptions define reality, not your opinion and gut feeling. Beware of confirmation bias.
- Perception of functional completeness is a relative assessment to the context of your product.
- Don't mix functional completeness, product-market fit and minimum viable product (MVP).
- Proxy measures and reference models can help with level-setting and assessing customer and prospect perception of functional completeness.
- Remember to collect NPS feedback from a representative group of your target market segment and do not collect from only happy customers.

- Consider the type of NPS survey and leverage both (Qualtrix, 2019a, b, c):
  - Survey customers after an important event or interaction (transactional NPS)
  - Survey customers on a regular basis, such as the end of every quarter or year.
- "The research behind the Net Promoter methodology shows that companies with scores higher than their competitive set grow faster and more successful." (NICE; Satmetrix, 2019).

8.2 Product Quality from an External View

Product quality issues override even the best functional coverage of your target market's problem space. To understand your product quality from an external view, you have to change your perspective. You need to step into your customer's and partner's shoes. Think about how someone external to your organization or even just external to the product team (e.g. your professional services team) would rate the quality of your product.

As introduced in Sect. 5.7, the Agile Testing Quadrant model summarizes all aspects of product quality. In this chapter I focus on the external perception of product quality. What can externals perceive from the various aspects of actual product quality?

As you can see in Fig. 8.4, people external to the product team generally perceive your product by the parts they use. External people recognize whether and how fast the product solves their problems. Note that the external perception is already biased if they were looking at your product before they actually used it; for example, they attended software demonstrations or peers were showing them your product.

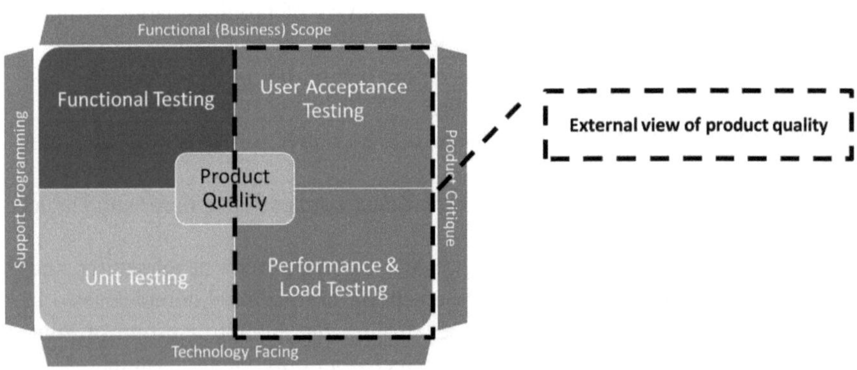

Fig. 8.4 External view of product quality © Timo Wagenblatt 2019. All rights reserved

As you rate the product quality from an external view, you need to remind everyone including yourself to stay honest. If something is not great, acknowledge it. For this PYPR dimension item, it doesn't matter what you know or believe about your product's quality, only the external perception counts. To understand the external perception you can interview externals, conduct a net promoter survey, or use some hard facts from your support database (maximum response time, initial response time, escalations, number of support messages, etc.) or you can leverage externally available ratings and reviews.

Note that the root causes for a bad or good perception are not all product related. Root causes could be that your product is just of bad quality. However, as you know, there are endless different reasons for perceived bad quality: customers/partners misuse your product, a bad or mediocre implementation, outdated technical infrastructure, or your sales team oversold the value of your product to name a few. However, customers and partners do not need a detailed analysis of poor quality to make up their mind. The product doesn't work as expected—period. Sad, but true, the root cause is hidden behind the visible parts of your product and hence the task is generally up to you.

As a product manager, your job is leading the team to delivery of an awesome product with high quality. As a proactive measure, involving and educating your customers, partners or other externals could be a useful tactic. In my experience, externals that trust your organization and more importantly trust you and the product team are likely having a better perception of your product quality. Building trust with externals is a nice addition to your to-do list. I have no silver bullet, but I have seen trust-building activities like inviting customers and partners to early testing sessions of new functionality, frequently interacting and communicating, and being honest and open about what your product can do and what it cannot do (yet), as working well. In general, I think it is a good advice to keep your commitments and tell the truth, independent of product quality.

8.2.1 PYPR Dimension Items Details

See Tables 8.3 and 8.4.

PYPR defaults by software product manager type

Topic		Internal PM	B2B PM	B2C PM
Default dimension item weight		20	20	20
Criticality for PM		High	High	High
PYPR score	Low	Customers cancel contracts or uninstall your product due to quality issues, the quality concerns are recognized in the market, customers or partners communicate product quality issues loud and clear to everyone internally and externally		
	Medium	Most customers and partners do not perceive quality issues, there might be a few concerns communicated to you and externally, but overall product quality seems to be no major concern for your existing customers, partners or target market segments		
	High	No or very limited customers and partners perceive quality issues with your product, no or very limited users rate or speak about your product quality in a negative way		

PYPR dimensions impact examples

Dimension	Direct impact example	Indirect impact example
Product viability	Product growth will be very limited if customers perceive your product as a low quality product	
Product development	Product teams exposed to customer feedback blaming bad product quality (justified or not) is unhealthy	
Go-to-Market/Product marketing		Market messaging are less impactful if they compete with damaged market perception
Software demonstrations and training		Effects of great product demonstrations and new shiny features are undermined by doubts about product quality
The Market/Your Customers		Analysts talk to customers without you, bad feedback about product quality will harm your analyst ratings severely
Organizational maturity		Doubts in product management excellence if product quality concerns from customers reach your senior management

8.2.2 Summary and Conclusions

Key Takeaways

- A happy customer tells a friend, an unhappy customer tells the world.
- The root cause for bad product quality perception matters only to you, as you want to fix it. The market, analysts, your customers, in short, everyone externally generally does not care about the underlying reasoning of not-optimal product quality.
- Set perceptions are hard to change.
- Externals that trust you and the product team likely have a better perception of your product quality.
- Consider trust-building activities in your frequent interactions with externals (e.g. invite customers to early customer testing weeks).
- Use the proven practice: Net Promoter Score® to understand your customers' product quality experience.

8.3 Engaging Customers and Building a Customer Community

A happy customer tells a friend, an unhappy customer tells the world. **Proverb**

As product managers, one of your key responsibilities is to understand customer needs and translate them into product requirements. As a product manager, you cannot compromise on having direct customer interaction. We have already discovered many interaction points with customers, for example as part of the chapters about product backlogs (dimension: Product Development), software demonstrations (dimension: Software Demonstrations and Trainings) and functional completeness (dimension: The Market/Your Customers).

There are many ways to engage with customers either in 1:1 situations or in communities addressing groups of customers all at once. The opportunities are diverse, and the objectives of the customer engagements may vary along the product lifecycle from validation of ideas over discussing requirements to even properly sunsetting a software product.

Independently of the scenario, engaging customers comes with multiple, priceless benefits for both parties. Therefore, increasing the PYPR score in this dimensional item will have dependencies to other areas of PYPR depending on the scope and form of engagement. We will examine these effects later in this chapter.

In this chapter, we concentrate on building a customer community through advisory councils. Let's have a look at the generic benefits of engaging customers via advisory councils:

Customers	YourProduct Inc
• Get early insights into your product roadmap • Increase access and engagement with product team • Peer-to peer knowledge sharing and network with peers around the focus areas • Influence the product development during the full development cycle • Get to know and build personal relationships with the product team • Securely exchange information in a clear legal framework	• Deepen customer relationships • Verify product strategy and positioning • Clarify requirements and constraints • Validate importance of product requirements • Increase revenue and product adoption • Build trust and community • Get to know and build personal relationships with the customers (i.e. real people) • Securely exchange information in a clear legal framework

8.3.1 Customer Advisory Councils

Customer advisory councils are an invitation-only, first-class group of strategic customers willing to collaborate in an open environment with you. Strategic customers don't mean large or loud customers, or the ones who paid the most. It means that these customers are supportive in delivering your product vision and strategy.

The customer advisory council can be defined by the statements below:

- Drive mutually beneficial objectives and improve the value of your software product.
- Foster frequent communications and events between council members and the product team to
- Exchange to inform, influence, and prioritize strategy, Go-to-market, roadmaps, and development of existing and new products in agreement to market and customer requirements
- Composed of senior executive and forward-thinking thought leaders who engage in bi-directional discussions on strategic topics
- Mutual commitment of resources.

There are different types of customer advisory councils that all have their own characteristics. At the top of Fig. 8.5, which illustrates the three main types, is the executive advisory council that focuses on top-to-top relationships,[5] the middle layer depicts the main part where business and IT users (or consumers in the B2C scenario) are involved, and last are the workstreams where the actual topics are detailed that have been prioritized in the functional councils.

[5]Likely will not happen for consumer applications, unless you can manage to establish a key influencer council.

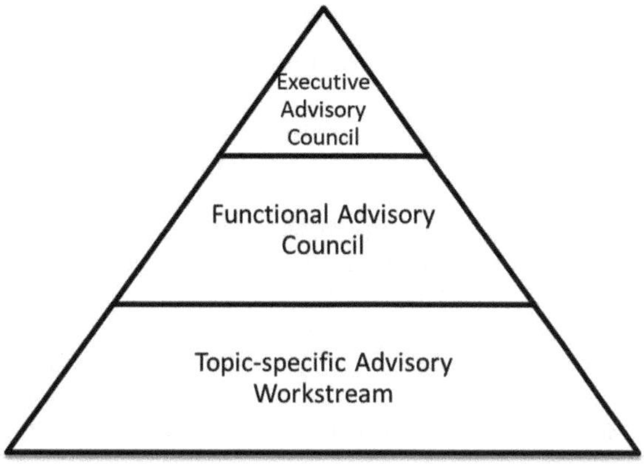

Fig. 8.5 Customer advisory council types © Timo Wagenblatt 2019. All rights reserved

Note that customer advisory councils are not project steering committees. These councils exist to provide advice to the product team about product vision, strategy, roadmap, requirements, etc. Hence, the selection of the council members is critical and should be done strategically. Take your time, think and agree early on about the mission of the councils with the council members.

And remind yourself and the product team—this is a customer council with customers using your product; no prospects should be in these meetings. Please take this advice seriously as the council will lose its effectiveness and trust level once you open Pandora's Box and let prospects or sales team into the exclusive circle.

All different types of councils have their right to exist as they fulfill a special, valuable purpose. Table 8.5 highlights the specifics of each type.

8.3.2 Proven Practice

Well-run customer councils can become a strategic lever against competition. There are some good guidelines to consider that will help you and your customers to benefit from these councils. Remember that these benefits are not free as time and budget commitments are required; however in my experience all three types of customer advisory councils are worth every minute.

As guidance, professionally run customer advisory councils fulfill these critical success factors

Customer council types

	Executive Advisory Council	Functional Advisory Council	Topic Advisory Work Stream
Host/Sponsor	Founder/Board/Head of Product	Head of Product/Product Manager/Product Marketing Manager	Product Manager
Target audience	Strategic customers, segment agnostic, key influencer	Business and IT, Consumers	Work stream topic interested customer representatives
Customer members	C-Level, decision makers	Corporate influence/impact/authority, mixture of IT + business	Influencer, stakeholder, IT- and business, all topic-related
Membership	Invitation only	Invitation only, >10 active members	Invitation only, short-term membership
Customer feedback	Interaction, feedback, guidance on strategy; customer priorities	Interaction, feedback, guidance on geographic/industry/LOB strategy; strategic dialogue and feedback on future innovation	Interaction, feedback, guidance on innovations; customer priorities
YourProduct Inc. feedback	YourProduct Inc. strategy; proven practices exchange	Understand customer segments by geographic/industry/LOB strategy, strategic plays, proven practices exchange	Ideate and validate innovations per topic
Meeting frequency	1–2 times annually, rotated by geography for customer proximity	In-person 1–2 times annually, rotated by geography for customer proximity, supplemented by 4–6 virtual meetings	As defined by the work stream, mix of in-person as a group, in-person 1:1 and virtual meetings
Meeting duration	1–3 days	2–3 days (one day usually dedicated to focus topics/deep dives for selected participants)	1–2 days
Meeting agenda	Standing agenda including trends, strategy, roadmaps	Mixture of customer-led and YourProduct-led, proven practices sharing, mixture of standing agenda (roadmap updates, new features demo, strategy update) and customer-driven agenda	Topic driven

- Demand a minimum of 10 companies interested in the executive or functional advisory council, but no more than 30 companies to keep the community closed
- Demand a minimum 3 companies interested in the topic related advisory work-stream, but no more than 5 companies to be able to reach consensus
- Designate a customer co-lead to share responsibilities

- Clarify capacity and commitment of council host/sponsor
- Clarify expected participant engagement and your own capacity to support the councils
- Agree on a recurring frequency and invite for the meetings in a timely manner, sometimes even a year ahead
- Don't make it a sales event—customers want influence, not a sales pitch
- Follow-up timely on action items and open to questions after the councils

Once you have decided to establish a customer advisory council, planning and executing customer advisory councils are projects on their own with the three steps illustrated in Fig. 8.6 to be iterated after each council:

Fig. 8.6 Setting-up customer advisory council phases © Timo Wagenblatt 2019. All rights reserved

1. Plan customer advisory council
   a. Find best meeting dates after considering other events and holidays
   b. Communicate planned meeting dates to participants
      - Use the standard communication channels
      - Follow-up and repeat as you want customers to be there in person
   c. Plan advisory council communications
   d. Determine and secure budgets
   e. Create a project plan
2. Execute customer advisory council
   a. Plan agenda and speakers
      - Balance the topics and the formats (interactive sessions, overview, deep dive, demonstrations, etc.)
      - Involve the customers and ask for their interests
      - Get something new on the agenda every time
   b. Identify customer attendees and invite attendees
   c. Communicate and confirm legal requirements (e.g. required non-disclosure agreements)
   d. Prepare council feedback surveys
   e. Conduct pre-event briefings
   f. Document meeting minutes

3. Follow-up post council activities
   a. Finalize action item list
   b. Collect and share all presentations, meeting minutes and action items
   c. Communicate feedback and lessons learned internally
   d. Optionally schedule and document a post-event update call or phase this step into your frequent communications with your customer council
   e. Measure success of the advisory council
      - Success measures are best already defined in Step 1
      - Do not sneak a sales KPI in here
      - You look for advice and customer relationship and hence your metrics should reflect the same.

8.3.3 PYPR Dimension Items Details

Engaging customers in a community comes with various facets. Whether you go with a formal advisory council approach or with alternative approaches like ramp-up programs, beta customers, customer testing (A/B testing), or user groups, there is a significant difference in terms of criticality depending on the type of product manager you represent (Tables 8.6 and 8.7).

PYPR defaults by software product manager type

Topic		Internal PM	B2B PM	B2C PM
Default dimension item weight		25	15	10
Criticality for PM		High	Medium	Low
PYPR score	Low	No customer community or other engagements like influencers, beta programs and early adoption		
	Medium	Customer council available, limited representation of customers, gritty engagement process		
	High	Active customer councils with representative customer group and vibrant, positive community supporting your product		

PYPR dimensions impact examples

Dimension	Direct impact example	Indirect impact example
Product viability		Maintenance profitability improves due to customers upgrading to latest release
Product development		Team Health improves as team exposed to customers directly
Go-to-Market/Product marketing		Improved messaging
Software demonstrations and training		Training demand verification
The Market/Your Customers	References and community strengthened	
Organizational maturity	Improves Templates and Tools dimension item	Community council processes established

8.3.4 Summary and Conclusions

Engaging customers and building a community around your product takes time and effort. Focusing on your customers beyond your regular engagements is a critical success factor and getting customers together in a community can be a great multiplier. It is all about people as you meet the abstract customers that might be called business team, company x, y, and z or consumer 1, 2, and 3. Real people behind abstract terms are more tangible as you meet Rob from the marketing team in Philadelphia, Martin from customer x and Leo, Lena, or Yvonne using our app.

Key Takeaways

- The proximity to your customers defines the criticality of formal engagements and processes.
- There are multiple options to engage with customers that require adoption by type of customer (internal, company, consumer)
  - User Communities/User Groups
  - Executive Advisory Council
  - Functional Advisory Council
  - Topic Advisory Work Stream
  - A/B Testing Segments
- Well-managed Customer Advisory Councils or other customer engagements deliver great ROI (Jensen, 2017)

- More business from customer advisory boards than from non-members
- Higher loyalty
- Strategic direction from trusted customer contacts
- Acceleration in referrals and testimonials process

• Engaging customers comes with a simple success formula
  - Provide value to your target customers like early insights, know-how sharing to
  - Get customers spending their precious time with you to support your product

• Customer communities create loyalty and a sense of shared identity

8.4 Customer Support and Official References

Once more—a happy customer tells a friend; an unhappy customer tells the world.
—**Proverb**

Customer support is priceless in many ways. I already introduced the need for official and recorded customer references in Sect. 6.2. In this chapter, I will focus on the process of getting official customer references. Furthermore, I will explain how to improve the PYPR dimension item with various ways and forms of "unofficial" customer support that is equally impactful and valuable.

Official references are all the assets that have been approved by your company and the customer, who provides the reference. Official references are always handy, once they are available. You might have your own communication or reference support team that wants to be involved in the process in order to lower your workload, or more likely, quality control the messaging according to company guidelines and requirements. If you have a product marketing manager, working on official references/recommendations might fall into her or his responsibilities. Remember to clarify the roles and responsibilities as part of PYPR Step 2.

As a product manager, you know your customers best. You know the ones who are happy with your product, reliable, and willing to work with you. These customers are natural candidates to be official reference customers. Sometimes customers that would be qualified according to these criteria cannot become official references, because many companies have policies that prevent them from participating in such activities. I spent a vast majority of my career in the consumer-packaged goods industry, supporting that industry with sales and marketing products. This industry is known for their brands and the brand and company logos are these consumer-packaged goods company's assets. There are some companies that would never allow their company or brand logos to be close to a software vendors' logo. That is just one of many reasons that customers cannot or do not want to be an official reference for your product.

This is the part where you should not give up. There are many other ways that you could benefit from happy customers and excellent customer relations. For example, your customer contact might be able to speak at events and conferences with you or for you. Conferences might be an excellent opportunity for an informal chat between peers that you could actively facilitate. Also, customer contacts might accept 1:1 meetings, phone calls, or on-site visits with your prospects as these kinds of activities do not fall under the company policy regulations. Asking these questions will show you what is possible and what is out of reach, when talking with your customer contact about being available as a reference customer.

As a product manager, you are likely getting urgent customer reference requests from sales representatives looking for their next deal. Customer reference calls or meetings can be powerful tools during sales cycles. Your customers trust the message about the value of your product much more, if they hear it directly from peers that have already worked with you and used your product.

Besides the sales teams, official references are also in high demand with other departments. For example, your marketing team would like to broadcast any reference customer to the outside world as it becomes available. Analyst relations teams would like to include customer references into their work. And Pre-sales teams have a valid demand for customer references as well, may it be as part of an RFP process they support or to strengthen the storyline of their software demonstrations.

So far, I have focused mostly on the B2B product manager role. For B2C products, official references, customer ratings and likes are equally, if not more important. However, as a B2C product manager you have much less direct interaction and influence because the number of customers is just not manageable in 1:1 interactions. Therefore, official references, likes and good ratings require different tactics and processes. I will not go into much detail; however, direct marketing campaigns, online marketing, contests, and constant, low key ask and encouragement within your product might be useful tactics.

As a product manager, you need to know how well your references cover your market segments. It is great to have references, but if they are not balanced across your target market segments, they have less value. For example, if you already have great references in North America, but you also target Europe or Asia, then the incremental value of another reference customer in North America is clearly lower than your first customer in Asia. Consider this balance as you invest time and work into your customer interactions. You can dramatically improve the likelihood of getting references as a product manager. You are the most senior product executive. You can offer safeguarding measures for your prospect reference customer, such as active participation in a steering committee, direct channel to your development team, special support activities, special discounts, and many more activities are in your control.

Whether you are a B2B, B2C or internal product manager, customer references are an important asset that mandates a clear process and strategy of how to get references, maintain references and utilize references. I recommend organizing this strategy with the extended product team and prepare for success. The next section provides a basic, but proven process—from first customer interaction to using the approved references—that has worked for B2B and internal product managers.

8.4.1 Proven Practice: Customer Reference Process

Available and approved customer references are must-have asset for any sales kit and a priceless tool for your marketing team and many other departments. Depending on your organization, you might have a dedicated reference support team. If not, the process outlined in Fig. 8.7 might be very useful for you. And even if you already have a process in place, the proven practice might provide some new insights and potential improvement ideas.

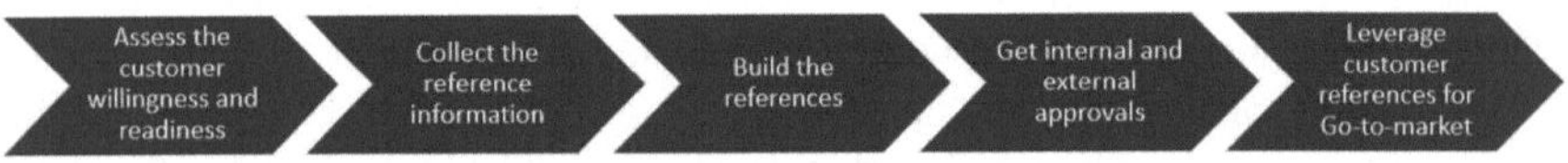

Fig. 8.7 Customer reference process © Timo Wagenblatt 2019. All rights reserved

1. Assess the customer willingness and readiness

   a. Check with the customer, if becoming a reference is an option. The best opportunities for asking are when there is a trigger event, like customer is asking for higher discount, customer went successfully live, customer asks for reference request himself, ... basically whenever it is a give and take situation.
   b. Understand whether the customer can be an official reference or whether the customer wants to act as an unofficial reference due to, for example, company policies.
   c. Discuss the possible formats: written reference, video, speaking engagement and/or customer-to-customer calls, etc.
   d. Make the process as convenient for your customers as possible. The less time investment they need, the better. Do not forget to explain the value of being a reference customer to your reference prospect, like the opportunity to demonstrate and showcase

      - industry leadership and success externally
      - accomplishments and success to their own management and other internal audiences
      - Closer relationship with you, the product team and your organization

2. Collect all required reference information for all considered customer reference types. The list below might be a good foundation from which you can adapt to the special needs in your organization.

a. Basic company information like the full legal company name, location, number of employees, revenue, official homepage URL, company mission and vision.
b. Basic customer contact information like full name and official title, openness for official quote, ask for potential "raw" quote and offer to provide a proposal for the quote.
c. Product related information like which product, product module, product version does the customer use, regional coverage and roll-outs, and the reason for selecting your products.
d. Background information about overcoming challenges, achieved benefits and future plans:

   - Challenges
     1. What were the customer's key challenges?
     2. Are there any relevant data points about the scale of the challenge?
     3. How did the challenge/problem impact the end customer/business user?
   - Benefits
     1. How did the product make an impact on the company's business?
     2. What business benefits could be achieved? Examples like x% higher customer satisfaction, x$ increased revenue, x$ lower costs, x% faster time to value, or x% faster data loads
   - What are the customer's future plans?

3. Build the references based on the information you collected. The data collected in Step 2 is a solid base to utilize storytelling as a technique. For written references consider the help of a professional writer as you save time and the quality is likely better. The same is true for other formats, get expert help internally or externally as references are priceless.
4. Share the draft reference asset for internal review with relevant stakeholders and consolidate the feedback. Likely this step requires a couple of iterations until you arrive at the final version
5. Ask for customer feedback and approval in one step to save time. Share the final and internally approved version with your customer contacts. Do not forget to directly include the ask for approval, maybe via an approval form so you can start utilizing the reference asset as soon as you get the final go from the customer. According to the new General Data Protection Regulation (GDPR), multiple approvals might be required, if customer contacts are personally mentioned. It is my understanding that every customer representative mentioned, for example, in a reference quote or shown in a video, needs to provide written consent.
6. Document the new reference assets and, finally, it is time to leverage customer references for Go-to-market activities, sales cycles and more.

8.4.2 PYPR Dimension Items Details

See Tables 8.8 and 8.9.

PYPR defaults by software product manager type © Timo Wagenblatt 2019. All rights reserved

<table>
<tr><th colspan="2">Topic</th><th>Internal PM</th><th>B2B PM</th><th>B2C PM</th></tr>
<tr><td colspan="2">Default dimension item weight</td><td>15</td><td>25</td><td>15</td></tr>
<tr><td colspan="2">Criticality for PM</td><td>Medium</td><td>High</td><td>Medium</td></tr>
<tr><td rowspan="3">PYPR score</td><td>Low</td><td colspan="3">No or very limited customers want to speak for your product, no or very limited users rate or speak about your product in a positive way</td></tr>
<tr><td>Medium</td><td colspan="3">You have some references, but cannot cover your target markets with high-quality references completely. There might be supporting processes, but not everyone understands how to get, maintain, and utilize references</td></tr>
<tr><td>High</td><td colspan="3">You have a pool of official and unofficial references that are relevant, value focused, and target audience—already covering your target market segments. Everyone knows and understands the process how to get references, maintain references and utilize references</td></tr>
</table>

PYPR dimensions impact examples

Dimension	Direct impact example	Indirect impact example
Product viability		Pipeline grows and progresses as you can utilize references
Product development		Product team gets official proof that their work is appreciated
Go-to-Market/Product marketing	Sales kit value increases, marketing messages can be bolstered with customer stories	
Software demonstrations and training		Pre-sales can underpin their storylines
The Market/Your Customers	Analysts value customer willingness to advocate for your product	
Organizational maturity		Management recognizes the impact of product management

8.4.3 Summary and Conclusions

Beyond question, customers that support your product also support you and your product team. Customers that value your work get value from your work. That's why they advocate for your product. Take any kind of customer references as a stimulus to continue being the best product manager you can be and deliver awesome products.

Key Takeaways

- Have a clear process how to get, maintain and utilize references
  - Proactively work out a structured reference process with your sales and marketing leaders, rather than dealing with them on an ad hoc basis. Define common criteria like questions to be answered in advance, and when to decline reference requests
  - Analyze what a prospect customer wants out of a reference and understand the customer's concerns. Match your existing references accordingly and saying no to a reference request is an option
- Quality of reference assets is essential. Focus on the customer and the value your product provided, instead of corporate speak. Your content should:
  - Provide value/outcome-based content
  - Emphasize benefits according to the product usage

  Focus on tangible improvements and their impact on the customer's business and IT, rather than on pure technical achievements
  Include measurable metrics
- Understand the value of new references for yourself
  - Organize your references according to your target market segments to keep the overview
  - Does the customer provide a reference that closes a gap in a region, industry, size of customer, age of reference, etc.?
  - Invest your time and work on references based on your needs
- Leverage trigger events to ask for references, such as when a customer is asking for a higher discount, customer went successfully live, customer asks for reference request himself, etc.

- Realize that references burden customers
  - Only request a reference from your contacts when absolutely necessary.
  - Likely you have only a few high-quality references, and you want to save them for when you have the highest probability of impact.
  - Use the power of no, in case you have doubts
  - Educate your marketing and sales teams on this.

8.5 Thought Leadership

"Thought leaders are the informed opinion leaders and the go-to people in their field of expertise. They are trusted sources who move and inspire people with innovative ideas." **Denise Brosseau** (2018).

Thought Leadership has been a buzz word in the last few years as everyone wants to be a thought leader, given the promising benefits that thought leadership can bring to industry. Many people claim thought leadership for topic x and industry y, or expertise z. However, thought leadership is not simply a title that you put on your social media account or on your business card; the title of thought leader is bestowed by the audience, by the market.

Let's clarify how I would define thought leadership:

- Thought leaders shape the way that the industry thinks. They lead the thinking in their area of expertise
- Thought leaders are known for their expertise. When people think of the "experts" in a particular industry or area of expertise, your name should be immediately at the top of the list
- Thought leaders are change agents because they are trying to bring change to an issue or problem about which they care deeply
- Industry leadership or recognized expertise are softer and less loaded terms for thought leadership

In your role as product manager you already fulfill the prerequisites to becoming a thought leader. Note that this doesn't mean you are a thought leader yet, just because you have the ingredients. Like a great cook, you should leverage the available ingredients to serve a fantastic meal of thought leadership. Becoming a thought leader doesn't happen overnight. Thought leadership is a journey that begins as small as gaining the trust of your product team, then it expands with a proven track record across your organization and your industry. You share your expertise so that others can learn from your expert knowledge.

The ingredients to become a thought leader are EPIC:

- Expertise and know-how: showcase that you are THE product expert
- Proficiency in your problem space (i.e. the problem your product addresses)
- Interest and engage your target audience (users, buyers and their personas) addressing their special needs
- Clarify your product vision and the problem space your product serves

To be considered a thought leader in your area of expertise is truly beneficial in multiple ways. We should not underestimate the effect of building out our brand as a software product company or as a product manager. If you are the one who defines, influences and shapes the market, you are likely more trusted and recognized than your peers. Blocking time for thought leadership activities will pay back in many ways.

The benefits of Thought Leadership and the justification for taking time out of your busy schedule are as follows:

- **Attention**
  - Your organization, your product, and last but not least, you are in the spotlight and get free marketing as

    you are referenced frequently
    you will be asked to give interviews to the press or industry journals
    you are asked to speak at conferences or write thought leadership articles

  - People want to work for you and people want to work with you to improve your product
- **Competitive Advantage**
  - "Neutral" opportunities to position your strengths tactically and implicitly
  - Constant visibility strengthens the customer relationship and builds trust
  - People trust people, and if you are trusted this will have ripple effects on your product

The benefits of more attention and gained trust are multipliers. They will save you marketing dollars and they will save you time convincing others—internally and externally. Thought Leadership is the art of positioning yourself and with that your product and your organization as a leader in its area through best-in-class content like blogs, videos, articles, or any other form of content regularly. Prospects, partners and all other members of your problem space will see you as having insight and authority. So, when a problem needs to be solved, you and the product you represent will be at the top of their list.

Note the product manager doesn't need necessarily to be the recognized thought leader, but it might help due to the ripple effects.

I had the bonus of meeting and working with a few thought leaders in a problem space that was my home for many years. I want to highlight one person from the early days of my career that I recognized as a thought leader. Rob Hand was already widely regarded as a thought leader in the consumer products industry at this time. I loved his "Monday Morning Memo" e-mails and I read all of them. Later in my career I had the pleasure of working with him on a team at SAP®. He was clearly the thought leader in our extended product team. I felt truly honored when he later called me a thought leader. For me he is the model of what a thought leader should be, and I have enjoyed his mentorship over the years.

Thought leaders can motivate people to follow them as they seek education, direction and inspiration. Followers expect innovation and mastery in the problem space from thought leaders. Let's see what we can do to further improve upon the journey to becoming a thought leader (Fig 8.8).

8.5.1 Proven Practice

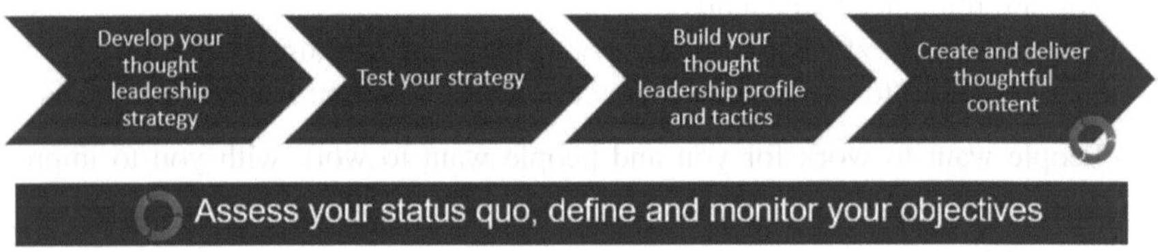

Fig. 8.8 Thought leadership process © Timo Wagenblatt 2019. All rights reserved

1. Assess your status quo using PYPR
   a. The good thing first, you do not need to artificially search for a topic to base your thought leadership. You know the problem space that matters for your product and your organization.
   b. Early in your career you might not have a great reputation, and in the ideation and introduction phases of your product, there is not much success you can leverage to start your journey.
   c. Along with your core and extended product team assess whether the market perceives you as thought leaders and who should be representing this status.
   d. If you are not in a thought leading position, then continue with the next step.

2. Develop your Thought Leadership strategy
   a. Discuss and define who should be the thought leader in your team

   b. Verify whether the predestined thought leader has the required ingredients and is EPIC
   c. Leverage your product vision to define what your future should be
3. Test your ideas with the product team, peers and trusted contacts
   a. Identify the questions your customers are asking and the topics that attract them.
   b. List these ideas and prioritize them with experts inside your company or trusted contacts outside (e.g. partners, customers)
4. Build your thought leadership profile and define your tactics
   a. Define your target audiences
   b. Define the channels (e.g. social platforms, magazines, industry journals, etc.) and content types (blogs, videos, tweets, etc.) that fit your target audiences
   c. Define your style of messaging and broadcasting
5. Create and deliver thoughtful content
   a. The most important advice I can provide here: quality over quantity
   b. The following tips and tricks might also be of use on your journey (Templeman, 2015):
      - Be confident about your expertise and show it in your shared content
      - Ask questions and leverage the Benjamin Franklin Effect: if you ask someone a question, they will like you more
      - Use the effect of social proof and surround yourself with experts in your organization or industry (great especially at the beginning of your career). The proximity of experts as shown by guest contributions showing expertise "bleeds" into your own.
      - Don't be afraid to start a controversial discussion against common sense, but only if you can support your views with data, examples and social proof as we covered above.
      - Always be honest and credible with your contents
6. Define and monitor your objectives as part of PYPR
   a. Define success measures for your thought leadership
   b. As part of your day-to-day work with PYPR document the activities to improve thought leadership and measure success
   c. Monitor your competitors' strengths in thought leadership and monitor their activities carefully. Note that the approach as outlined in Sect. 6.4 is also useful for this part.

8.5.2 PYPR Dimension Items Details

See Tables 8.10 and 8.11.

PYPR defaults by software product manager type © Timo Wagenblatt 2019. All rights reserved

Topic		Internal PM	B2B PM	B2C PM
Default dimension item weight		10	15	20
Criticality for PM		Low	Medium	High
PYPR score	Low	Neither your company, nor your product or anyone in the product team is recognized or known in your problem area/industry		
	Medium	You start reaching some of your target audiences via limited channels. Others start sharing and commenting on your content. The number of people you reach is still low, but growing steadily		
	High	The market is keen to hear and read your position and is seeking your guidance on trends and developments. You are referenced frequently and your followership is steadily increasing towards the max. Your success as a thought leader is measured by tools and a robust process		

PYPR dimensions impact examples

Dimension	Direct impact example	Indirect impact example
Product viability		Trusted customer business case numbers
Product development		Product team is proud of you
Go-to-Market/Product marketing	Positioning is trending	Reference customers easier to get
Software demonstrations and training		No one expects you to demo yourself
The Market/Your Customers		Functional completeness perception increases without new functionality
Organizational maturity	People want to work for you/in your team	

8.5.3 Summary and Conclusions

You need to work hard to achieve thought leadership. You, your product, and your organization will receive great benefits. But be cautious—never call yourself a thought leader! This is the job of your audience and followers and only they can grant you the title.

Key Takeaways

- The journey to become a well-respected thought leader does not happen overnight. We must simultaneously improve our credibility, reputation and reach.
- Build a thought leadership strategy and roadmap
  - Establish authority on your topic by frequently broadcasting deep insights and demonstrating a depth of knowledge on the subject
  - Orchestrate your thought leadership work (e.g. blogging, social media, speaking, networking, PR)
  - Leverage your network of thought leaders and experts
- Create and deliver high-quality content (webinars, blogs, eBooks, etc.) to influence customers (buyers and users), industry experts, research analysts, key editors in the press and other third parties.

8.6 Analyst/Market Influencer Relations

Analysts and influencers are frequently considered as thought leaders and industry authorities. Analysts and influencers hunt for knowledge, expertise and insights about a specific topic or industry. With this knowledge, they engage with executives, other industry experts and likely your target market customers who offer their work products. Analysts and influencers are paid for advice on strategy, trends, market threats and opportunities, or product and vendor reviews.

In the B2B software market, analysts and their publications require your attention as a product manager. These analyst work products might be the de-facto standard influencing the perception and expectations in your particular market segment. Sometimes these analyst ratings remain relevant for a year or more despite the fact that you released a ton of new features or even did a pivot with your product since the last product review. That's even more dramatic if the latest analyst publication did not appreciate your work and product superiority. The logic and market dynamics are very simple as illustrated in Fig. 8.9.

Fig. 8.9 Market dynamics of analyst reviews © Timo Wagenblatt 2019. All rights reserved

Many years ago, I faced a situation that underlined the significant impact of one overlooked analyst review in a brutal and hence memorable way. The analyst relations team "owned" the relationships to the most important analysts in my software product domain. The analyst relations team acted as a shared service team supporting all industries with which SAP works. The analyst relations team, with best intentions, took the latest, available product roadmap they found, involved someone from the industry product marketing team and conducted an analyst briefing session with the most important analyst in my area of work.

Neither I nor anyone from the core product team was part of the briefing session. In fact, we did not even know these meetings were scheduled. To keep the story short, the session went south as the analyst did not see a vision or underlying product strategy. In addition, there were no recent product demonstrations shown and there was no one to provide references of the latest customer success stories. And we did not know about any of this drama at this stage.

When I learned about the bad meeting outcome it was already too late. That same day, the analyst published his vendor panorama of all the software products serving our target market. An account executive called me approximately three hours later requesting urgent support as her software deal was in jeopardy. Her customer had read the analyst review and not surprisingly the bad press raised severe concerns. Our product was rated somewhere in the middle, while our biggest competitors obviously did a much better job presenting themselves in the best light possible.

One analyst meeting that turned out to be the basis of an important publication jeopardized not only this single deal, but the brilliant work of the product team in the following weeks and months. We were preparing a launch of a software module that did not only close a gap in our offering, but also for the whole industry. And all these efforts were not appreciated as the analyst did not know about it. We perceived the analyst report as unfair and some members even took offense. You could easily see and feel the correlation of the PYPR dimension item Analyst/Influencer relations and the PYPR dimension Team Health.

The account executive call was just the beginning of extra work to explain to every target customer who read the review that our software product was not as bad as stated in the "official and independent research." We had to do lots of firefighting, justifications, explanations and more unplanned activities for some months. We took the approach of educating the customers and prospects about the process of the review, took the opportunity to position our recent functionality that had not been considered in the publication, and reached out to the analyst for a review update when we launched such a significant functionality.

In retrospect, I need to take the blame as the responsible product manager. How could we not know about the analyst briefing, which focused so hard on product development? How could we as an organization consider an analyst review as not important enough and did not treat the analyst like our most important customer? I learned a lot in this little crisis and the whole team learned too.

In short, analysts and other market influencers should be considered as an important part of The Market/Your Customers dimension. As the product manager, you need to be part of the analyst interaction in your problem space, but certainly so when it comes to product reviews or other interactions that require product executive's insights. There is a high likelihood that analysts and influencers will affect key decision makers such as your existing and potential customers, investors or even your management team (Fig 8.10).

8.6.1 Proven Practice

Fig. 8.10 Analyst/market influencer relations process © Timo Wagenblatt 2019. All rights reserved

1. Understand the business of analysts/market influencers and identify the main stakeholders, or in other words: how do analysts and market influencers get paid?

   a. They provide work products like reports, rankings (e.g. magic quadrants, market analysis such as market size and market share, webinars and speak at conferences).
   b. They might help your target companies/buyers with their expertise in selecting the software products. Buyers may consult analyst companies to help them sort through a variety of confusing and overlapping software products.
   c. Analyst and market influencer's business mostly offer

      - research work products as part of their education of the market about news, trends, competitive analysis, market sizing, market shares and the likes.
      - consulting to direct your decisions or your target market customers' decisions.

2. Select the analysts/market influencers you have and want to work with
   a. Select the ones with the most Influence regarding reach and reputation along the dimensions that matter most to you; for example, buyers, competitors, press, or investors.
   b. Product managers should know the key analysts in their area and how to leverage them. Which analysts matter to your target market segments and which ones do you want to work with? If you do not know the analysts/market influencers, ask customers, ask peers, ask even competitors and as always search the internet.
   c. Define and agree with all internal stakeholders which analysts should be worked with, how you work with them, how you deal with the ones not on the list, and last but not least, who works with the analysts/market influencers.

3. Work with the analysts/market influencers
   a. Treat each analyst like your most important customer. Plan your analyst meetings like important customer meetings; there might be a significant multiplier effect. Define what is your goal and desired outcome of the engagement and consider what your counterpart is looking for. There is always some give and take working with analysts.
   b. Take the A-team approach for your key analyst engagements. Confirm your best relationship manager, your best industry spokesperson, your best Pre-sales engineer and your best self in the team. Deliver against the agreed agenda and ask your counterpart for feedback and whether you can help to serve the analyst's information needs.
   c. For the briefing itself, be clear on the message and image you want to convey. You likely will only have 30–90 min to cover a lot of content (e.g. company overview, vision, strategy, roadmap, key customer success, software demonstrations, competitors, small talk, your questions and information demands, etc.). Plan your key points carefully and weave them into a coherent storyline reinforced by recent customer stories. As you see, not any different to many customer interactions.
   d. Plan for ongoing engagement with analysts and market influencers. Most people like consistency in terms of contacts at your company and your presentation compared to your actions. Share interesting information and press releases, but ask for consent first and second keep the balance between interesting information bites (for the analyst) and spam.
   e. Agree openly on the rules of engagement, whether non-disclosure agreements are in place, required or not accepted. Adapt your information sharing accordingly.

4. Leverage insights and feedback
   a. You can learn a lot when you listen to the analysts and market influencers. Sometimes you might need to read between the lines, as they might be under NDA.
   b. Listen to the words they use, the topics they emphasize, the stuff they do not mention or the areas they do not react to as part of your presentation.
   c. Review your product vision, strategy, roadmap and positioning based on your new learnings. Do you need to correct course or are you on track? Did you hear about a white spot or key trend you overlooked? Did you learn about competitive strengths or weaknesses?
   d. Sometimes the analyst voice can even help to overcome internal politics, especially if you are either new to your role, your company, or you work in an organization that trusts external (paid) feedback more than their own experts.

8.6.2 PYPR Dimension Items Details

See Tables 8.12 and 8.13.

PYPR defaults by software product manager type © Timo Wagenblatt 2019. All rights reserved

Topic		Internal PM	B2B PM	B2C PM
Default dimension item weight		0	10	15
Criticality for PM		X	Low	Medium
PYPR score	Low	Analysts and influencers know about your software product and officially dislike it		
	Medium	Analysts and influencers do not consider your product in their research, communication, and work products or rate you neutral		
	High	Analysts and influencers praise your product and underline your thought and market leadership		

PYPR dimensions impact examples

Dimension	Direct impact example	Indirect impact example
Product viability	Pipeline increase based on positive feedback	Product growth
Product development	Product Vision, Strategy, or Roadmap updates	Team Health due to external recognition of their work
Go-to-Market/Product marketing	Positive vendor/product ratings need to be part of any sales kit	
Software demonstrations and training	Product marketing video update reflecting the latest trends named by analysts	New insights about what is hot and what is not can improve your software demo positioning
The Market/Your Customers		Market perception concerning functional completeness or thought leadership
Organizational maturity		Product culture

8.6.3 Summary and Conclusions

Analysts and market influencers play an important role in many industries, but their influence on buyers and users varies widely. Understand their influence on your buyers and users and react accordingly. Analysts and market influencers are not your customer as they do not pay for your software product; they will likely never use it, however they might be the one voice that is heard by all your customers.

Key Takeaways

- Analysts and market influencers are megaphones broadcasting to your target market.
- Working with analysts takes time and sometimes money, but the benefits for you and your software product might include positive sentiments in research reports, recommendations to potential customers and increased exposure to the broader industry ecosystem of your target market.
- If you think the analyst briefing sessions are not relevant for you as they are mostly high-level blah blah meeting, be clear on the missed opportunity to learn about trends, customers, competitors, buzz words, and a direct response to the positioning of your product with an industry expert.
- The benefits of great analyst reviews will save you marketing dollars and they will save you time to convince others—internally and externally.
- Listen carefully if your competitors are mentioned indirectly or directly and remember that analysts and market influencers will likely share in the same way about you as well. Keep that in mind when sharing and presenting.

Balance the risk and opportunity carefully and plan your contributing accordingly.

- Build trust by continuation in the engagement and delivery against your talk.[6]
  - Be honest and do not exaggerate too much as you certainly will get found out by someone with an analyst profile who talks to many people in your industry ecosystem.
  - Be consistent by having a clear and consistent message and pick it up in the next engagement.
  - Share customer stories to underline your vision and success. Before sharing sensitive information with an analyst, agree upfront how sensitive information is treated and whether NDAs are required and respected.
  - Check in with analysts at least every six months to stay on their radars.
- **Bonus tip**: Analysts like to be recognized as thought leaders. Ask them what they miss or would like to see more in the product. Pick one item that fits your product, something that customers would like as well and add it as a delighter prioritized as part of backlog. Show this feature in the next analyst engagement and let the magic happen—you listened, valued the opinion and delivered.

References

Asya. (2019, February 20). *The power of NPS in your product strategy*. Retrieved from productboard.com https://www.productboard.com/blog/the-power-of-nps-in-your-product-strategy/.

Bonilla, C. (2017). We've got users, so why talk to the market? *Pragmatic Marketing (Fall edition)*, 27–28. Retrieved from Pragmatic Marketing, https://cdn.agilitycms.com/pragmatic-marketing-v2/pdf/PRAGMATICMARKETERFALL2017.pdf.

Brosseau, D. (2018, September 18). *What is a thought leader*. Retrieved from thoughtleadershiplab.com http://www.thoughtleadershiplab.com/Resources/WhatIsaThoughtLeader.

Drozhzha, K. (2019, February 8). *A playbook for achieving product-market fit by Dan Olsen*. Retrieved from Medium.com https://medium.com/@Productized/a-playbook-for-achieving-product-market-fit-by-dan-olsen-3e97f7cb1006.

Jensen, R. (2017). Retrieved from pragmatic-marketing, https://cdn.agilitycms.com/pragmatic-marketing-v2/pdf/PRAGMATICMARKETERSUMMER2017.pdf.

Leffingwell, D., & Widrig, D. (2000). *Managing software requirements*. Longman: Addison Wesley.

[6]I'm happy to report that we improved our analyst rating steadily from the lower end of the rating to be the market leader after three years. We achieved this because we understood the negative impact of not being professional in analyst engagements. We delivered against the vision and strategy we outlined in the meetings; we could share positive customer stories, and showcase commitment to the industry and target market.

NICE; Satmetrix. (2019, February 18). *U.S. Consumer 2018 Net Promoter Benchmarks*. Retrieved from nice.com http://info.nice.com/rs/338-EJP-431/images/NICE-Satmetrix-infographic-2018-b2c-nps-benchmarks-050418.pdf.

Olsen, D. (2015). *The lean product playbook: How to innovate with minimum viable products and rapid customer feedback*. Hoboken, New Jersey: Wiley.

Olsen, D. (2019, February 10). *Google Ventures workshop: Lean product management*. Retrieved from YouTube.com https://www.youtube.com/watch?v=mIBccpqUcgY&ab_channel=GV.

Qualtrix. (2019a, February 16). *How to measure & calculate Net Promoter Score (NPS)*. Retrieved from Qualtrix.com https://www.qualtrics.com/experience-management/customer/measure-nps/.

Qualtrix. (2019b, February 16). *What is Net Promoter Score (NPS)?* Retrieved from Qualtrix.com https://www.qualtrics.com/experience-management/customer/net-promoter-score/.

Qualtrix. (2019c, February 25). *Software feedback*. Retrieved from Qualtrix.com https://www.qualtrics.com/blog/software-feedback/.

Qualtrics.com. (2019, February 17). *How to measure & calculate Net Promoter Score (NPS)*. Retrieved from qualtrics.com https://www.qualtrics.com/experience-management/customer/measure-nps/.

Templeman, M. (2015, December 9). https://www.forbes.com/sites/miketempleman. Retrieved from forbes.com https://www.forbes.com/sites/miketempleman/2015/12/09/thought-leadership-and-its-5-essential-strategies/#9c4c6311894f.

Walter, A. (2011). *Designing for emotion*. A Book Apart.

Organizational Maturity

9

The Environmental Conditions of Your Software Product Manager Role

This chapter details PYPR's Organizational Maturity dimension that represents "The Environmental Conditions of your Software Product Manager Role." I will outline how even the best product managers cannot provide full value to their organization, if the organization doesn't provide some basic environmental qualities. Product managers and product teams that can't provide their best deliver products that are not at their full potential.

Consequently, PYPR considers organizational maturity as one significant dimension that determines product success. I will focus on the kind of environmental conditions in software organizations that are good or bad for product managers, product teams, and product success. We will discover and evaluate what are the most important areas necessary to become a more mature product organization as well as how to attract and retain the best Software Product Management talent.

No two organizations are alike and organizational systems are complex. Therefore, maturity models are used to explain organizational systems. Product Organization Maturity models are, like any model, simplifications that highlight the importance and existence of maturity enablers across:

- Product Management Leadership, Vision and Strategy
- Organizational Set-up, Processes and Governance
- People Mindset supported by Key Principles
- Templates and Tools.

Issues in any of these maturity components can limit your product's yield potential. Let's revisit the PMF survey results from Sect. 1.3. As you can see in Fig. 9.1, chapter examines the top challenges, as identified by product managers around the globe, which prevents them and their products from being more successful.

T. Wagenblatt, *Software Product Management*, Management for Professionals,
https://doi.org/10.1007/978-3-030-19871-8_9

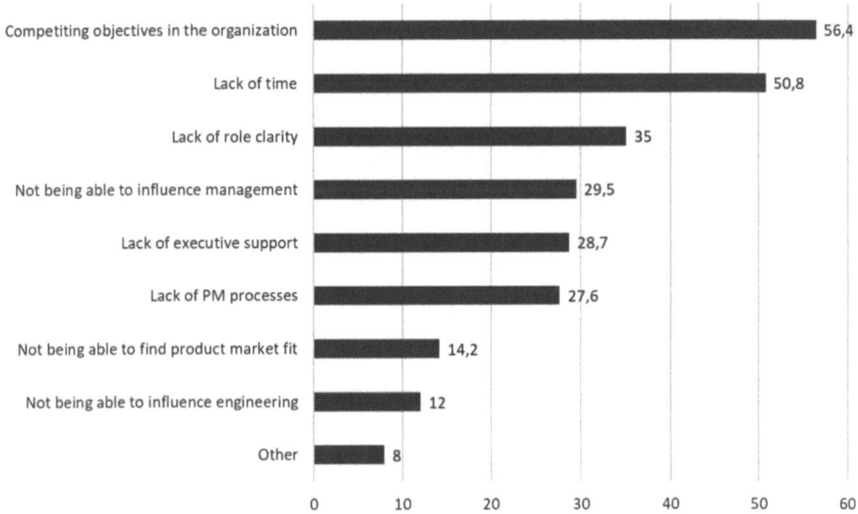

Fig. 9.1 PMF survey results—top 3 challenges © Timo Wagenblatt 2019. All rights reserved

These challenges should be a wake-up call to all executives and Software Product Management leaders out there. They need to understand that resolving these challenges will not only help product managers in their job, but will help any product organization to be more successful. Ignoring these challenges will create anger and churn within product. In addition, top management needs to appreciate that not fixing these organizational issues will significantly cost money and jeopardize the longevity of all products and consequently the entire organization sooner or later.

To be very clear—this call to action is not just for top management executives, founders, CPOs, or Heads of Product. As a product manager, you "are well placed to know what's wrong, where you can make quick wins, and where changes will take longer to bear fruit." "So rather than thinking "I'm only a product manager," think "I am the product manager so I'm going to lead within the business and improve the job that product management does" (Product Focus, Volume 13).

In my business life, I heard of way too many people complaining about their organization. Sometimes I had been one of them, until I realized—we are all part of the system. With our actions, with our behavior and with our attitude, we shape the organization and we can influence and very often change our work environment for the better. That is true, especially in your exposed role as a product manager.

You are a product manager, so you care about your product and everything around it. Therefore, you are mandated to improve your organization by showcasing product success and continuously cultivating and evangelizing the job that Software Product Management does in your organization. If you are a role model of product mindset, others will follow, and you will have an impact on your organization over and above your product's success.

Software Product Management excellence requires a strong foundation in every organization. Organizations need to focus on excellence in organizational set-up with clearly defined accountabilities, metrics that are aligned with product strategy and product success, and true empowerment of product managers and the whole Software Product Management function. A strong organizational foundation provides processes aligned to the product portfolio and the best tools and infrastructure to live up to the high aspirations of a customer-centric product-led organization. Last but not least, any organizational set-up is borne by the people. Clearly formulated expectations and exemplified values in balance with an effective recruiting process and talent mix are the backbone of great product organizations.

I propose to start with the default PYPR configuration in Fig. 9.2 As you leverage PYPR for your product, consider the recommendations from Sect. 3.3.

Dimension Weight 12,5 %	
B2B	
Dimension Item	Weighting Factor
Leadership, Vision, and Strategy	25,0%
Organization, Processes, and Governance	25,0%
People Mindset and Key Principles	30,0%
Tools and Templates	20,0%

Dimension Weight 12,5 %	
B2C	
Dimension Item	Weighting Factor
Leadership, Vision, and Strategy	25,0%
Organization, Processes, and Governance	25,0%
People Mindset and Key Principles	35,0%
Tools and Templates	15,0%

Dimension Weight 12,5 %	
Internal PM	
Dimension Item	Weighting Factor
Leadership, Vision, and Strategy	20,0%
Organization, Processes, and Governance	25,0%
People Mindset and Key Principles	30,0%
Tools and Templates	25,0%

Fig. 9.2 Organizational maturity: PYPR dimension item defaults © Timo Wagenblatt 2019. All rights reserved

In this chapter I will detail the following PYPR dimension items[1]:

- **Product Management Leadership, Vision and Strategy**
  Does your leadership team understand the value of Software Product Management? Is there a sponsor in the executive team or do you need to fight for attention? Does your organization aspire to be a product-led organization or are you on a different mission?
  These questions are the focus of the next chapter.
- **Product Management Organization, Processes and Governance**
  There are many ways to set up Software Product Management as a function in your organization. Organizational set-up and processes need to be aligned. Communication and collaboration rules, aligned metrics; in short, a proper governance of the processes across teams is a winner.
- **Product Management Templates and Tools**
  Without templates and guidance, everyone in your organization will find their own way. What you want to achieve is a status of productizing Software Product Management. Productizing product management requires templates and tools aligned to all product management and related processes.
- **People Mindset and Key Principles**
  Changing people mindset is the hardest one to crack as ultimately that is a result of everything: your product, your organization, yourself and the people you work

[1]The descriptions are short reviews from Sect. 2.2.6.

with. Changing the people mindset toward a product mindset is the aspiration. Key principles help people with decisions and guidance about values in your organization. If people benefit from clearly communicated principles, these principles form the people's mindset over time.

I have already touched briefly on product organization maturity models being simplifications of real organizations. Therefore, that is likely one of the reasons why maturity models are very popular tools and have been around for some time in various disciplines.

Product Management and organizational maturity models assess the current capabilities and help figure out what capabilities need to be acquired to improve product management or organizational performance. Most product management and organizational maturity models are structured sequentially.[2] Commonly maturity models are presented from the basic level of "we do it somehow" to the mastery level of "we strive for perfection."

I think it is not important whether there are three or five or whatever many levels in a maturity model. I personally interpret the final stage in any maturity model not as something at the end of the journey but as the aspirational vision to be achieved. Some items might be achievable earlier, some items later depending on the context of the organization. If you can achieve only some items listed at a higher maturity level early, then that's a great achievement that will have a direct impact. As Martin Fowler stated: "The vital point here is that the true outcome of a maturity model assessment isn't what level you are but the list of things you need to work on to improve." (Fowler, 2019).

In that sense PYPR is a kind of product management maturity model that includes organizational maturity as one essential dimension in concert with the other required capabilities of product success. The higher the total PYPR score across all products in an organization the higher the Software Product Management maturity might be in your organization. PYPR guides product managers and product teams to think and act holistically about their product. As a leader in a product organization, analyzing PYPR scores and visualization can help to better understand systemic problems, required learning needs, and patterns of success or limitation across teams. These insights can be the base to mature product management and the entire organization. Note that I do not propose PYPR as an organization maturity model, that is not the main point of using PYPR but rather an unplanned, but developable by-product.

In this chapter, I will not explain or detail any of the excellent work already written on product management maturity models (Haines, 2012; Product Focus, 2018a, b; Lawley, 2018). I do not want to replicate all this great work, but provide some food for thought on Leadership, Vision, and Strategy; Organizational Set-up,

[2]The sequential interpretation of maturity models is one of the reasons why at times maturity models have a more theoretical character than practical applicability. The waterfall approach might be a root cause for this reputation.

Processes and Governance; Tools and Templates; and People Mindset and Key Principles in the next chapters.

Before we start looking at Software Product Management leadership, and the vision and strategy toward Software Product Management excellence, I want to highlight one approach to judging product organization maturity that resonates well with me. Rich Mironov proposed the distance of the product team to the actual user as a proxy of organizational maturity (Tan, 2019). The closer the product team can be or is allowed to be with the customer and users, the more mature the product organization. A similar concept was introduced by Hubert Palan during his talk at WebExpo 2017 (Palan, 2019). Remember the importance of customer and user intimacy in whatever design of organization, process, and governance you are proposing.

Organizational Maturity is likely the hardest to write about of all PYPR dimensions as organizational maturity is the most specific to your context. Therefore, I provide a framework and key considerations, but the adaption and implementation need to be specific to your context. Note that I do not focus on change management, process design, and only briefly on organization set-up, but rather I want to focus on the role of people working in product management (from CPOs to associate product managers) and their mandates and responsibilities of being role-models of product mindset, transforming organizations in successful product-led organizations while not letting organizational shortcomings limit their product's success.

Finally, this is a call to action to all executives who want to retain their product people or attract new talent. Product people need to contribute from the bottom, but executives have the mandate to provide and improve the environmental conditions from the top. This chapter explains the PYPR dimension items used to improve organizational maturity.

9.1 Leadership, Vision, and Strategy

The single biggest way to impact an organization is to focus on leadership development. There is almost no limit to the potential of an organization that recruits good people, raises them up as leaders and continually develops them.

—**John Maxwell** (Qualtrics, 2018)

Applying John Maxwell's guidance to product organizations sets the frame for better understanding what is important in this PYPR dimension item. The single biggest way to impact a product organization[3] is to focus on developing its leaders. Who are the leaders within your organization?

Traditionally, organizations treat people managers as leaders.[4] Marty Cagan explains the fundamental differences of product leader and people manager responsibilities in his blog (Cagan, 2019):

[3]An organization that focuses on products, not projects.

[4]"Leadership and management are often lumped together, and it's true that many leaders are also managers, but the responsibilities are very different." (Cagan, 2019)

- Purpose of strong leadership is to inspire and motivate the entire organization with vision, strategy, objectives and key results.
- Purpose of people management is hiring and developing the actual members of the product teams by effective staffing, continuous coaching, and clear objectives.

Before we continue, let's clarify the role of the executive team in your organization. Does your executive team understand the value of Software Product Management? Is there a sponsor in the executive team or do you need to fight for attention? There are still product organizations where Software Product Management is either not valued or even understood as a key enabler of any product organization's success.

Executive teams are instrumental for effective Software Product Management. According to McKinsey, executive teams can enable a strong product management leadership development model that includes (Gnanasambandam, Harrysson, Srivastava, & Srivathsan, 2018):

- a concrete, actionable description of what the organization wants and expects from its product managers and the Software Product Management function (read: vision)
- reflection of the organization's strategy and priorities
- product management Career paths and how the behaviors and mindsets differ for each level (e.g. principal product manager vs. director of product)
- organizational enablers for ongoing growth and apprenticeship (e.g. rotational programs, regular cadence of product reviews (with focus on coaching and knowledge sharing rather than inspection), walking in the shoes of other functions (taking support calls or doing customer demonstrations, for example), conducting skip-level one-on-one sessions, providing formal mentorship programs, giving regular growth-based feedback, etc.).

Your role as the Chief Product Officer, Head of Product, and as an individually contributing product manager benefits from a strong executive team that understands and sponsors Software Product Management, Therefore, your mandate is to continuously educate your executive team why and how Software Product Management helps the entire organization to reach its objectives. However, evangelizing the importance of Software Product Management is not trivial nor it is ever done until everyone in the company embraced a product-mindset.

There are many tactics to secure management buy-in. Roman Pichler summarized a few in his blog (Pichler, 2019):

- Explain how Software Product Management benefits the company
- Address how the executive team benefits from Software Product Management

  - higher bonuses due to better product performance
  - reduced workload due to product managers acting as General Managers
- Explain that the executive team retains control (e.g. via product portfolio decisions) despite providing autonomy to the product managers and product teams.

As you have the buy-in and support of your executive team, things will go smoother and you do not have to fight daily uphill battles to better your product and the entire company. The executive team that properly supports the Software Product Management function is one part of leadership. The leadership of the Chief Product Officer (CPO)[5] or Head of Product is another important component of this PYPR dimension item. Both need to play in concert, hence organizations where Software Product Management leaders are part of the executive team are generally perceived as more mature and more successful.

Product Leaders who understand the value of Software Product Management for their organizations need to focus on:

- Articulating their Software Product Management vision and the strategy to achieve it
- Organizational set-up, processes, and governance allowing product managers, and product teams to reach their highest impact (see Sect. 9.2)
  - Clear definition of products and product portfolio priorities
  - Aligned objectives, planning processes, and prioritization guidelines
  - Well-defined roles and career paths
  - Effective recruiting process and tailored people development investments
- Tools, templates, and an infrastructure for efficiency (see Sect. 9.3)
- Organizational values and key principles that are consistent with the actions, attitude, and vision of the executive team (see Sect. 9.4).

Continuously improving across these dimensions drives excellence and showcases that the executive team understands and values Software Product Management. There is a significant impact, if product managers do not believe that their executives understand and value their role and their positive contribution to the organization. The perception of your organizational maturity and your product management maturity is the basis to retain and attract the best talent as I will detail later in this chapter.

[5]Sometimes organizations have no official lead for the product management function as either the founder or a senior executive assumes the role. Further organizational set-up considerations are part of the next chapter.

Software Product Management leaders play an important role in helping product managers reach their full potential. Product Management leaders are responsible for inspiring and motivating the Product Management organization. They need to share their vision and strategy of Software Product Management and its implementation within the organization. It is important to define whether your organization aspires to be a product-led organization or whether you are on a different mission.

CPOs, Heads of Product, and Product Managers need business context (vision, objectives, expected results) from the executive team to work out a cohesive vision and strategy, for the entire organization down to the product level. As you define the vision and strategy for the Software Product Management in your organization, you certainly benefit from your bag of tricks that you filled in Sect. 5.1.

Software Product Management leaders need to provide a clear purpose of Software Product Management to all product teams and all stakeholders; they communicate their expectations, monitor progress and impact, and course-correct as required. They need to lead and continuously improve their organization toward Software Product Management excellence.

As a Software Product Management leader, your main objective is increased Software Product Management maturity that ultimately feeds to an improved organization maturity. I have already touched on the importance of Software Product Management maturity and the product mindset of the entire organization in Sect. 1.3.

Remember the significant difference in the ratings of product mindset between product teams and organizations. More than 60% of the product managers rated the product mindset of the product team as high while the whole organization mindset rating arrived at only 27%. Product managers are looking for product and executive leaders to provide them and the product teams the environmental qualities that foster product success and longevity. Product managers are looking for leadership to:

- apply management methods that fit to the Software Product Management vision and strategy
- provide autonomy for product decisions to reach transparent objectives and innovate from the vision
- sponsor the Software Product Management function providing the time that is required to have an impact
- foster bi-directional, continuous learning.

Whether you are an organizational leader or a Software Product Management leader, "listening to your team and addressing their concerns, always being open to criticism, practicing transparency, being solely accountable for mistakes, and most importantly, deflecting credit away from yourself and giving it to others" (Mercer, 2018) will be appreciated by everyone working in your organization.

Leadership that contributes positively to organizational maturity is about transitioning toward a product-led organization. The Software Product Management vision is the north star of your transition and the strategy depicts the milestones to get there. Nothing changes the first day, the first week, or maybe even the first month, but over time consistency will make the organization and the product management function more mature.

As an executive or product leader closing the gap of product mindset between the product teams and the entire organization needs to be the focus area for improvement. Remember, that product mindset of the organization has been within the top three key influencers impacting product managers' job satisfaction.

As a product leader, PYPR enables you to add context to all product conversations and decisions. You can provide a clear purpose to your executive team and all stakeholders as to why you are working on certain topics, how the work leads to product success, and why everyone should care about their work contribution. You can leverage PYPR as your leadership radar. You are leading everyone toward a balanced product mindset.

As an executive or product leader defining the objectives for the entire organization or the Software Product Management function, the framework of Objectives and Key Results (OKR) might be a good approach as part of your bag of tricks for implementing your vision and strategy, and a transparent way of leadership. The framework enables you to ensure that each product team has a clear and relevant set of objectives. The objectives and key results should be tied to implementing the strategy and product (organization) success.

As you provide the Software Product Management function, the product teams, and the product managers a "small number of significant problems to solve (the objectives), they can consider the problems and propose clear measures of success (the key results). The managers may need to iterate with their teams and others to try and get as much coverage as possible of the broader organization's OKR's." (Cagan, 2019) This approach strengthens the sense of empowerment and the level of trust that is required for great achievements.

9.1.1 Objectives and Key Results

Objectives and Key Results, or in short OKR, combine the best aspects of goal setting into one framework. OKR is a goal-setting and management framework and many tech companies, likely most prominently Google™, adopted the framework over the last decade. The origin of OKR is often-times credited to Andy Grove during his time at Intel™.

Goal management is of course not new; in fact, it has been around for decades. Peter Drucker introduced a methodology called Management by Objectives (MBO) already in the early 1950s. Many great things have been attributed to OKRs, but some people might say it is nothing else, but a label applied to a wide range of best practices in goal management.

I will not get much further into the details of OKRs, however I will briefly introduce the OKR framework for two reasons:

- The framework is implemented at many software product organizations and due to its benefits, the OKR adoption is still increasing
- OKR as a goal management framework and PYPR as a product management framework are complimentary and can be applied perfectly together

If you are interested in a more comprehensive presentation of the Objectives and Key Results framework I do recommend the following two books: *Radical Focus,* by Christina Wodtke, takes you through a fictional case study in form of a fable, and then in the second part, Christina details how to use OKRs to help teams realize their big goals (Wodtke, 2016). The second book, *Objectives and Key Results—Driving Focus, Alignment, and Engagement* with OKRs by Paul R. Niven and Ben Lamorte, is a full-fledged reference guide on OKRs, and shows you everything about implementing OKRs effectively (Niven & Lamorte, 2016). I'm sure there is other great resources out there, but these two books are the ones I can personally recommend.

As stated before, OKR is a goal-setting framework used to focus a team, not only a product team, on inspiring, hard, but not impossible, objectives. The progress of objective achievement is evaluated by key results. OKRs are publicly available to the entire company and should not be directly related to performance evaluation of teams or individual team members. OKRs are set, reviewed, and revised quarterly (and annually). And last but not least, they need to be supported by leadership, tools, and processes. Hence, I included OKRs in this chapter. An Objective tells you where to go; Key Results tell you how to get there.

Objectives	Key results
• Qualitatively describe what the team wants to accomplish • Breaks down and operationalizes a team's purpose by maximum 5 objectives for a defined time period • May or may not be measurable but must be strategic • Objective score is the straight, equal weighted average of the key results grades • Example: Implement PYPR as a product management framework in Q1	• Quantitatively describe how the related objective will be accomplished • Make Objectives measurable by associating 2–4 key results to an objective for the defined time period • Should be a little uncomfortable so that the team is always striving • Self-rated by the team for the defined period. Since OKRs are meant to be set boldly, 70% target achievement is considered as successful, so there is room for improvement; 40% or below means a learning opportunity, not a failure • Example: Train 100% of product team members of 3 product teams in Q1

One reason why OKR and PYPR are so complimentary is that you can quantify the success via key results and qualify the objectives to be reached using the six dimensions and 32 dimension items as defined in the standard PYPR set-up.

As part of the PYPR process, I introduced the Strategy & Action meetings where the product team analyzes the limiting factors and prioritizes the most important improvement area and the required actions. Step 4 of applying PYPR is likely the most obvious link to OKR as a goal-setting framework.

When you read the paragraph below, what do you think is described? OKR or PYPR?

As the leader of the product management organization or as the General Manager of YourProduct Inc., you want to focus efforts on strategically important topics. As a leader, you like to integrate teams in strategic goal-setting while you align the activities across the organization. The assessment, analysis, derived strategy and actions enhance transparency about the current status that you constantly monitor and evaluate.

I think everyone who knows the OKR framework could easily relate the paragraph to OKR, especially if you focus on the goal-setting aspect. However, after reading this book and understanding the PYPR framework for Software Product Management, I hope that you can see how PYPR is nicely compatible with the OKR framework for goal-setting.

Unfolding the full potential of PYPR definitely works without OKRs; however, I see a natural fit and ease of adoption for product management and product teams in the event you leverage OKR as a framework in your organization.

On a side note, my objective is to increase the PYPR scores as a component of the annual employee goals in my teams. In addition, as I introduced in Sect. 1.2, I ask all product managers to constantly improve their bag of tricks and to add or refresh some blocks of their T-shape in both directions: the vertical hard skills and the horizontal soft skills of a great product manager.

Last but not least, note that OKR and PYPR are both relatively simple frameworks and most people grasp the key aspects quickly. Nevertheless, as you are leading your teams and leveraging one or both frameworks I would recommend:

- a foundational training for the team
- support by an onsite consultant who will guide the first steps
- spot consulting after some lessons to hone the framework for your context

These would be generally beneficial for you as a leader and the product team, as they would help to safeguard the success while speeding up the unfolding of the frameworks' full potential.

9.1.2 PYPR Dimension Items Details

Leadership, vision, and strategy is about to impact everything; therefore, I do not list some examples as I have for all other PYPR dimension items. However, some examples were already mentioned in the text before (Table 9.1).

Table 9.1 PYPR defaults by software product manager type © Timo Wagenblatt 2019. All rights reserved

Topic		Internal PM	B2B PM	B2C PM
Default dimension item weight		High	High	Medium
Criticality for PM		25	20	15
PYPR score	Low	You are alone and the organization doesn't value your contribution. No, this is way too negative. You can derive the right attributes to justify a low rating by not checking any of the attributes listed for medium and high ratings		
	Medium	Very much the same attributes as for the High PYPR score ratings, but the understanding and sponsoring ends at the Chief Product Officer/Head of Product level is not (completely) supported by the executive team. Software Product Management has no seat on the executive team		
	High	Executive teams understand and sponsor the value of Software Product Management. Product Management is represented in the board. Software Product Management function and the entire organization is inspired and motivated by an aligned and clearly communicated vision, strategy, and implemented by objectives and key results. Transformation plan to achieve strategic vision including required change management and training. Chief Product Officer/Head of Product lead and continuously improve their organization toward Software Product Management excellence. Product managers have the autonomy for product decisions to reach transparent objectives and innovate from the vision. Product managers and product teams benefit from good leadership practices. Product Manager is a key role and understood by everyone in the organization. Product Management is perceived as a brand. The "Power of No" is with Software Product Management. There are no forced customer commitments that need to be built into the product		

9.1.3 Summary and Conclusions

Key Takeaways

- As an executive or product leader you are defining the vision and strategy of the Software Product Management function in your organization.
- CPOs, Heads of Product, and Product Managers need business context (vision, objectives, expected results), support of their management, ongoing coaching, and true empowerment that comes from the executive team.
- As an executive or product leader defining the objectives for the entire organization or the Software Product Management function, the framework of Objectives and Key Results (OKR) might be a good approach.
- An indicator of strong organizational and Software Product Management maturity is when clear expectations about the role of Software Product Management and everyone working in "product" are established, accepted, and lived. Working in Software Product Management in such an organization is like a strong branding— a brand that is built upon reputation and trust.
- As an executive or product leader your job is to keep this brand equity.
- In product organizations, product managers need be treated as leaders. Therefore, product organizations must appreciate Software Product Management as an essential factor of product, and with that organizational success.
- The litmus test for empowerment and with that indicators of organizational maturity and strong leadership include:
  - Executive teams accept "the Power of No" from product management. As explained in Sect. 3.1.2, if the executive team constantly overrules the Software Product Management representatives, there is no autonomy and independent empowerment whether leadership calls out agile or lean principles.
  - Executive teams consider the Software Product Management opinion, or even better, Software Product Management is represented in the executive leadership team
  - The number of forced product commitments from the executive team.

- PYPR enables Software Product Management leaders to understand when the "Power of No" is required. PYPR also points out weaknesses not just for one product, but across the entire organization. PYPR identifies structural flaws that can be improved with training or hiring the appropriate talent.
- PYPR is a kind of maturity measurement on its own. The higher the average PYPR scores across products, the higher the maturity. In addition, PYPR includes organizational maturity as a dimension itself that can become the limiting factor of product success.
- "The manager's function is not to make people work, but to make it possible for people to work." (DeMarco & Lister, 2013)
- Leadership is about continuous learning and improving toward organizational maturity. Keep in mind that "Learning is limited by an organization's ability to keep its people." (DeMarco & Lister, 2013) In your Software Product Management function provide the environmental qualities to retain people.

Examples of responsibilities for Software Product Management leadership (whether founder, CPO, Head of Product, etc.)

- Defines and lives the Software Product Management vision and strategy
- Evangelizes with stakeholders to move everyone in the same direction (execution of product management) and makes sure people understand and live the strategy
- Build a strong product culture
  - Drives focus, alignment, and engagement within product teams and entire organization to establish a product mindset
  - Understand importance of continuous and rapid discovery (testing and learning)
  - Respects the product teams and acts as a firewall so the team can work on the topics that add value toward the vision
  - Focuses on continuous innovation and improvement
  - Understands that great products are the results of true collaboration
  - Add others that are important in your context
- Responsible for building the skills of product managers in line with vision
- Recruiting, training and ongoing coaching are the main priorities.

9.2 Organization, Processes and Governance

If you're not watchful, the process can become the thing. This can happen very easily in large organizations. The process becomes the proxy for the result you want. You stop looking at outcomes and just make sure you're doing the process right.

—**Jeff Bezos** (Bezos, 2018)

Jeff Bezos' warning words about processes becoming the proxy of desired work results can easily be expanded to the organizational set-up. Organizations are frequently organized or re-organized for a plethora of reasons, but not to maximize customer value and outcomes.

Different companies need different types of Software Product Management organizations, processes, and governance models. "A company's approach to Software Product Management will affect the responsibilities of the function, its reporting position within the business, and the way it interacts with other functions." (Bierl, Grüntges, Harrysson, & Williams, 2018).

In this chapter, I will not provide you with an organizational perfection vision as such a vision depends solely on your context and your aspiration. Therefore, I will focus on providing you some guidance about important aspects that should be considered to provide a solid foundation for effective Software Product Management.

I attended Large-Scale Scrum training where Bas Vodde[6] introduced the notion of the organizational perfection vision to me. As a leader in your organization, whether you are part of the executive team or a Software Product Management leader, take the time for this intellectual game. Ask yourself: "When I come back to work on Monday, how will my company look like that changed over the weekend to be the perfect organization?" Note that you will likely never achieve the perfect vision; however, it is a great north star to follow.

There are various options to structure your organization. I will mention some common set-ups in the summary and conclusion chapter. In my opinion, the more interesting point is the likelihood of bias toward one or the other function depending on your organizational structure. Product managers are more biased, for example, to marketing, sales, engineering, or finance, if they report to one of these functions rather than directly to the executive board or have a seat on the executive board. On your journey to becoming a product-led organization, Software Product Management as a separate function reporting to the Executive Board can directly help drive a product-focused company strategy. (Product Focus, Volume 13)

[6]Bas is one of the two creators of the LeSS (Large-Scale Scrum) framework for scaling agile development.

There are many ways to set up Software Product Management as a function in your organization. As you structure the organization or re-organize the company, remember Conway's Law that describes the relationship of organizational design and communication structures and product design and architecture (Wikipedia, 2018a, b). Your product will likely mirror your organizational set-up.

Software Product Management is a lever to balance this effect and the biases mentioned before as Software Product Management represents a holistic product approach across your organization. Note that PYPR provides an indicator of your organizational maturity and bias toward a certain function within your organization.

The definition and interpretation of your product taxonomy (see Sect. 1.1.3) needs special attention in this PYPR dimension as well. Think about your product definition and how your definition is reflected in your organizational set-up. Where do you organize product teams? At product line, product, or product module level? Do you require central functions for special topics like pricing or Go-to-Market, or are these functions part of the Software Product Management organization itself?[7]

As you leverage PYPR within your organization across product modules, products, or product lines, you learn in which PYPR dimension or dimension item your teams face the most issues, where you record the lowest ratings. As a Software Product Management leader, you can use these insights and dig deeper into topics like involved roles, processes, and organizational set-up. You might find structural issues, ineffective processes, or governance problems.

Which leads us to the topic of clarity about roles and responsibilities. Role clarity is essential for effective processes and smooth governance. If there is confusion in your organization about who does what and how, then there will be too much friction among people. A lack of aligned processes and missing role clarity is one of the most common reasons for bad execution, lack of accountability, average outcomes and weak product mindsets. Remember that for product managers who are not properly positioned in the organization, this is like kryptonite for the guys in their superhero capes.

As introduced before, PYPR helps you to clarify roles and responsibilities (see Sect. 2.1.4) or acts as information radiators (see Sect. 3.2). You can also use PYPR to identify gaps in your corporate skill set. By leveraging PYPR you can identify the PYPR dimension items where you lack some knowledge and skills.

As we defined Software Product Management at the beginning of the book, Software Product Management is not a short-term production or efficiency play. Working toward your organizational perfection vision will require time and leads to changes across the entire organization. As an executive team who signed up for Software Product Management excellence, you need to acknowledge that managing change is vital for success. You need to address the entire organization with proper communication, training, and coaching that is summarized in a change management plan. "Nothing changes, if you change nothing." (Vodde, 2018)

[7]If you are interested in the set-up of IT organizations, I recommend (Narajan, 2015).

Steven Haines outlines the importance of allocating enough time for change to take place (Haines 2012). As you are managing Software Product Management, you should consider this guidance and many more in his excellent book. But remember: "The fundamental response to change is not logical, but emotional." (DeMarco & Lister, 2013)

Improved organizational maturity will be recognized internally and externally as you transition to a product-led organization. Not everything can be directly changed, and Software Product Management cannot influence or fix everything either; however, constant dripping wears away the stone. As a Software Product Management leader, you need to focus on your Software Product Management vision and the strategy to achieve this vision to secure product success. You need to focus on organizational set-up, the processes, for example, in development and sales, and also the HR process concerning incentives and budgets that fit or improve your organizational perfection vision.

As a Software Product Management leader, you signed up for continuous process improvements to support higher ratings in each PYPR dimension items. The identification of the limiting factors across product teams can help you to find structural problems. As you identify these patterns, you can offer the appropriate trainings and resolve problems in governance (e.g. unaligned or even contradicting objectives across departments and functions) or mediocre processes.

As a Software Product Management leader, you manage up the hierarchy and cross-teams showcasing the value that Software Product Management adds to the organization and with that infuse product mindset to the organization.

An effective product management function is responsible for enforcing a product mindset and for managing the cross-functional interactions required to keep the product on track. Software Product Management plays a vital role as a neutral judge in decision making as the central point representing the product. Software Product Management brokers the needs and information between all involved stakeholders (see Fig. 9.1).

I have mentioned the topic of brokerage several times previously. Noah Askin shares more details on brokerage and the role of product managers as brokers between all functions in the next section.

9.2.1 On Brokers and Brokerage by Noah Askin, Assistant Professor of Organizational Behavior and Director of Product Management Executive Program, INSEAD

For years, social scientists and network scholars have been exploring the concept of brokers and the activity they engage in: brokerage (e.g. Burt, 1976, 2004; Marsden, 1982). Brokers are the people in networks who occupy positions that connect otherwise disconnected groups. But the position goes beyond a simple structural one: to engage in brokerage is to serve as a conduit for information, ideas, and communication across these disparate groups, and to facilitate interaction if or when it becomes necessary. Anyone who has spent any time as a product manager will surely identify strongly with the broker concept and its behaviors: product managers are almost always in such a position, regardless of the organization. Given how central brokering teams is to product management, it is worth understanding the concept a bit better. When done well, the act of brokerage can be a net positive for the broker, the organization, and even its users.

It is instructive to start with foundational sociologist Simmel's (1950) notion of "The Triad" as the basis for the concept of brokerage, because it illuminates the two primary functions of product managers. Simmel described two types of connectors: *tertius gaudens* (the third who enjoys) and *tertius iungens* (the third who joins).

Someone in the *gaudens* position is seen as benefitting from the broker position, extracting informational and other resource-based benefits because the position has the advantages of wide vision across the network and of being able to play two disconnected parties off one another. Think of the product manager who sits between sales and development and who tends to keep them separate from each other. If the two departments have few other means of connecting with one another, the product manager can utilize information strategically to get what she needs from either group.

Product managers stand to personally benefit significantly from their position between many of the different departments within their organization, and even external stakeholders and customers as well. Because of these benefits, we know that brokers tend to get promoted faster and have higher annual compensation than similar people who are not in broker positions (Burt, 2005, 2010).

Tertius iungens, on the other hand, is about bringing people together. Rather than benefitting as a single point of contact between separate groups, brokers in this position create cohesion among those groups, acting as an arbiter or connector. Think of the product manager who successfully brings together potential users and software developers as a means of designing a frictionless user experience.

While brokers can extract benefits exclusively for themselves in a *gaudens* role, in an *iungens* role they are often benefitting the greater good: their organization and their users alike. Brokers in these positions are more likely to be able to mobilize others and implement creative or novel ideas (Ibarra, Kilduff, & Tsai, 2005; Obstfeld, 2005).

One of the challenging but compelling aspects of being a product manager is that the role calls for both types of brokerage. Many product managers will tell you that depending on the organization, the groups being brokered, and the demands of the situation, they may need to translate information across groups uninterested in communicating with one another or bring together unusual organizational bedfellows for yet another push toward releasing the next version of a product.

Armed with a basic idea of what is meant by brokerage, I want to highlight two key aspects that are of particular relevance to product managers, as well as two potential dangers. While an in-depth review of brokerage would take an entire book unto itself (e.g., Burt, 2005), these issues are fundamental to any product manager looking to be successful.

Perhaps the most important benefit of being a broker is the social capital that comes with the position. Though deemed "mini-CEOs" by some, product managers differ from CEOs in one particularly critical way: product managers typically do not have the formal authority to demand others get things done on their behalf. Enter social capital. In terms of a definition, I refer to social capital as the "…resources embedded in a social structure which are accessed and/or mobilized in purposive action" (Lin, 2002). Essentially, social capital is about the ability to get things done based on your position within—and knowledge of—your social network, as well as what capabilities and resources the people in your network have.

Because of their connectivity to many groups within an organization, product managers are able to utilize their position to know who is capable of what, who is connected to whom, and what the different priorities are for the many teams with whom they interact. The informational benefits of such broad connectivity in an organization means that—by engaging in *gaudens* or *iungens* behavior depending on the situation—product managers can tap the right people or apply the appropriate amount of social pressure to accomplish tasks that many others would need formal authority to make happen.

To that end, **Takeaway #1**: Expand, understand, and tap into your network within (and outside of) your organization to ensure you can accomplish the tasks necessary to be an effective product manager.

A second key benefit that comes with being in a brokerage position is the increased capacity for innovative and creative insight that comes with the role. Interaction with and understanding of very different groups within organizations means a product manager must engage with a broad range of information and ideas. Doing so both requires a greater openness to new/different ideas than people in more closed network positions, and it creates the opportunity to synthesize or recombine those ideas into something new and beneficial (Burt, 2004; Lee, Mingo, & Chen, 2007). The benefits for creative idea generation more often come to those in a *gaudens* position, but the ability to put those ideas into effect is more a function of a *iungens*, integrating position (Hargadon & Sutton, 1997; Lingo & O'Mahony, 2010; Obstfeld, 2005).

Thus, product managers have the chance—but also the challenge—to switch back and forth between the ways in which they engage the disparate people inside and outside their organization as a means of generating new ideas and putting them into practice. Empathy very much comes into play here, as understanding how different network connections will respond to a product manager's behavior is essential. However, when done well, the product management position affords its occupant a great opportunity to generate, sell, and execute innovative ideas for the organization, due in large part to its location at organizational crossroads.

Takeaway #2: Though often overwhelming and always demanding empathy, engaging with colleagues from very different areas (and geographies) within your organization leads to exposure to new/different ideas and pain points that product managers can turn into innovative ideas and solutions for the organization and its customers.

But it's not all sunshine and roses for product managers. There are two key concerns associated with being a broker that are particularly relevant for product managers. The first is around trust.

As someone occupying a position between many different organizational areas but not really inside of any, product managers are likely to face some resistance and distrust. "You're no longer one of us," someone from development might say, or "you're only interested in keeping your developers happy," might be a response from someone in marketing. Product managers often lack a clear home by nature of the fact that they must interact with so many different groups in the organization. Doing so means that the trust that comes from being "one of us" is often missing, putting a greater burden of proof on product managers to demonstrate their trustworthiness. Tapping into your friends—i.e., using your social capital—can help, but many interactions will feel less comfortable than if you were a core member of the departments with whom you are trying to collaborate.

Takeaway #3: Budget extra time to establish both your own reputation (i.e., show you do good work) and trustworthiness (i.e., show you have heard your collaborators' concerns and understand their pain points) into your cross-functional partnerships. The extra time and effort put in up front will save you time and pain down the road.

Finally, there is a real concern about overload and burnout. This will come as no surprise to any product managers currently reading. Product managers, like many brokers, must not only maintain a large network, but they must regularly be adding to that network every time they facilitate a connection between previously disconnected others in their network. Otherwise, they lose their advantageous position as their network slowly closes around them.

Moreover, as the single point of contact for facilitating interactions across groups, product managers are constantly fielding incoming requests for help, information, and access. This is all while trying to get products designed and shipped! Research I'm currently conducting appears to suggest that despite being stronger performers and receiving higher bonuses, brokers who engage in *gaudens* behavior are less likely to be satisfied with their work and more likely to voluntarily leave their company than those in either *iungens* or other non-broker positions. The struggle is real!

Takeaway #4: Be aware of the potential downsides of brokerage, particularly as your own time is concerned. Product management can be an extremely exciting and fulfilling role as one of the hubs of activity in organizations large and small. But being that hub can easily come with the constant feeling that far too much is being asked of you.

Takeaway #5: To the extent possible, find ways to delegate tasks and relationships to trusted colleagues. That is, outsource tasks when possible so that not everyone and everything must go through you alone (Table 9.2).

Table 9.2 PYPR defaults by software product manager type

Topic		Internal PM	B2B PM	B2C PM
Default dimension item weight		High	High	Medium
Criticality for PM		25	20	15
PYPR score	Low	Organizational power, processes, or governance roles are more important than outcomes, business results, and customer value. Product managers and product decisions are biased toward one organizational function. Brokerage is perceived as a very bad thing		
	Medium	Product managers can do their job. Furthermore, there are some of the positive aspects of the high PYPR scores description and little from the low description		
	High	Product managers can unfold to their full potential, driving product and company success supported by established and continuously improved organizational structures, processes, and governance that fits to the product and company context. Prioritization considers what matters for product success over and above organization, processes, and governance rules. Brokerage and cross-team collaboration is not just encouraged, but mandated. All processes are aligned and accountabilities are clarified and communicated		

9.2.2 PYPR Dimension Items Details

Organization, processes, and governance impact everything; therefore, I will not list some examples as I did for all other PYPR dimension items. However, there are some examples already mentioned in the text before.

9.2.3 Summary and Conclusions

Key Takeaways

- Different companies need different types of Software Product Management organizations, processes, and governance models.
- Organize or re-organize to maximize customer value and outcomes.
- A product-led organization prioritizes what matters for product success over and above anything else when shaping or reorganizing its structure, processes, and governance approach.
- Product managers are less biased toward one function, when they report directly to the executive board or have a seat on the executive board.
- Design organization, processes, and governance for brokers to work and brokerage to happen.
- Expand, understand, and tap into your network within (and outside of) your organization to ensure you can accomplish the tasks necessary to be an effective product manager,

- Budget extra time to establish both your own reputation and trustworthiness in your cross-functional partnerships.
- Be aware of the potential downsides of brokerage, particularly as your own time is concerned.
- Continuously work and improve toward your organizational perfection vision.
- As a Software Product Management leader, you can use PYPR to find gaps in corporate skillset, structural issues, ineffective processes, or governance problems within your organization.
- PYPR is an indicator of your organizational maturity and bias toward a certain function within your organization.
- Figure 9.3 illustrates a few organization examples that need to be vetted with your company context and needs. Whatever organization design you come-up with, keep in mind that for product organizations, structure, processes, and governance need to be balanced. Things will go wrong in product development, as the process is complex and noisy. Balance the set-up and rules with the need for agility, innovation, and product mindset.

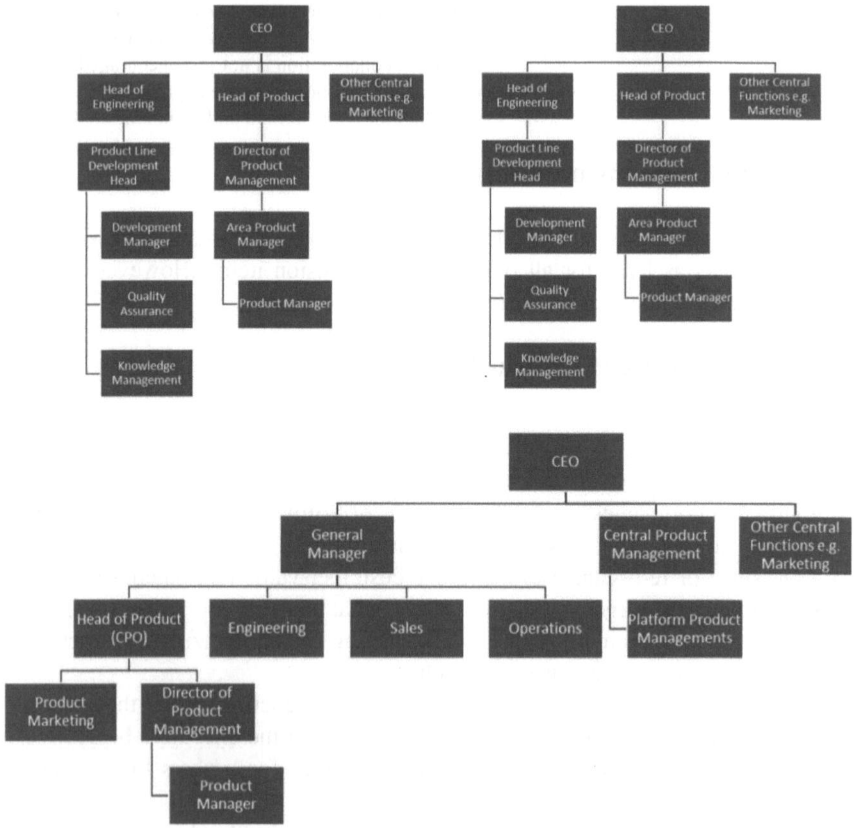

Fig. 9.3 Examples of product organizations © Timo Wagenblatt 2019. All rights reserved

- Allow your product managers to do their job. Establish and continuously improve organizational structures, processes, and governance that fits to your context and let product managers be the General Managers of YourProduct Inc.

Examples of organizations based on different company needs.

See Fig. 9.4 for an example of functional and people management dimension career paths, where the titles shown in pattern block are management career paths, while the others are functional career paths:

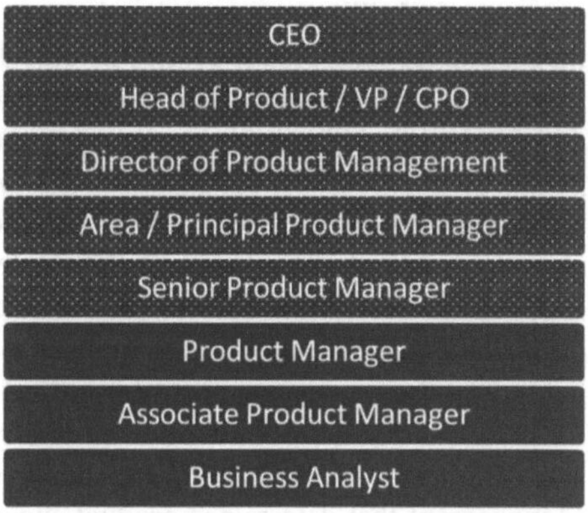

Fig. 9.4 Example of functional and management career paths © Timo Wagenblatt 2019. All rights reserved

9.3 Tools and Templates

A fool with a tool is still a fool.

—Proverb

In the previous chapters, I explained the importance of leading the Software Product Management function with a strong vision supported by a strategy to reach this vision We discovered the organizational models, the product management processes, and governance derived from the organizational set-up. In this chapter, I want to sharpen your sense about the tools[8] and templates that support or are even mandated by all the above. The best tools and templates will have limited impact, if there is imbalance in the components that determine organizational maturity.

[8]A tool can be a method like the Business Model Canvas, or a software product to leverage the method. I do not make a distinction within this chapter.

First, tools and templates need to help and support their intended users. If you consider this fundamental rule, then it is obvious that tools and templates for product managers must be discussed with product managers. Tools and templates that are based on anything else than solving the problem of the user are generally not leveraged by the targeted users, even if the usage is strongly mandated by management or central process teams. As product managers are brokers and have so many interactions with other users and stakeholders, every tool and template must take into consideration the requirements of the adjacent users and stakeholders as well. That's not news to you, right. Basically, what I am proposing is to consider all tools and templates as a product that helps everyone involved in Software Product Management.

Second, tools and templates and your organization, your processes, and your Software Product Management leadership style need to be in balance. Consider the extreme of a brilliant organizational set-up, great aspiration to be a product-led role model and a sound plan to reach this objective, but the product teams do not benefit from tools and templates they can leverage in any PYPR dimension. That sounds awkward, right? Think about the other extreme, that your talented people in the product teams worked out some great tools and templates, but the organizational set-up and processes do not appreciate the efforts or might even be hindering it. How long would you expect these people to stay in your organization given the PMF survey results from Sect. 1.3? Remember that product managers rated mature organizations as the number two reason why they are looking for a new job, just behind product management maturity?

Third, throughout this book I introduced PYPR and its PYPR dimension items as well as tools, methods, and templates to improve each aspect of Software Product Management that determines product success. As a Head of Product, or individual product manager, leveraging PYPR and mapping the tools and templates within your organization will help you with each dimension item. You might want to use the coverage as a proxy or at least a component of your organizational maturity. You will also gain a great overview about the dimensions where you are well equipped and use latest tools and templates consistently versus dimensions or dimension items where you find your organization still in medieval times.

With that PYPR represents a way to assess the status quo of the tools and templates aspect of product management maturity. PYPR further guides you toward improving product management maturity, and organizational maturity considering the holistic product approach across your organization. Leverage PYPR as you define the appropriate standards for your organization.

Lack of appropriate tools and templates can limit the success of product teams. Product managers and teams need to spend significant time and effort finding the right tools and defining the right templates. A professional approach across your whole organization will allow your product teams to spend their time on value adding work. And if you have multiple teams or multiple products within your organization, providing standardized tools and templates as a baseline with accompanied training and services easily becomes a competitive advantage. Otherwise, everyone in your organization will find their own way of doing what needs to be done and their own way of interpreting the work results. Or people just take shortcuts. Both will lead to sub-optimal results.

Productizing Software Product Management might be a great analogy here. Product management processes and the tools and templates that make your processes effective should be treated like a product not a project. An ad hoc approach will not scale, and your organizational maturity remains at low-levels. A standardized approach will ease the communication and the ability of teams working together. As a leader in your organization, you need to monitor that the benefits of standardization do not harm the autonomy and flexibility that product teams require to build awesome products. Continuous improvement of well-established standards should be a guiding principle for product organizations. Lively Communities of Practices can help with shaping, improving, and establishing valuable standards. Note that "In lean thinking, standardized work does not mean conforming to centralized standards … Rather, the idea is for a team to master a baseline against which improvement experiments can be compared. This baseline—the standard—is created by the team themselves (not by a centralized group) and is ever-evolving." (The LeSS Company B.V., 2018).

In my experience Software Product Management benefits from the usage of software products. I leverage software products for various PYPR dimension items that help me and the team to be more effective. There are many lists of the best software products for product management (Gerald, 2019; The Nag, 2018; Aha.io, 2019; Software Tools for Product Managers, 2019), or (Predictive Analytics Today, 2019). However, all products–which I am aware of–are not the best in supporting holistic Software Product Management as defined by PYPR. I look forward to leveraging Software Product Management products that better address the needs of product managers by covering all aspects of a holistic product view and provide the flexibility, which is reflected in one's own bag of tricks.

9.3.1 PYPR Dimension Items Details

See Tables 9.3 and 9.4.

Table 9.3 PYPR defaults by software product manager type © Timo Wagenblatt 2019. All rights reserved

Topic		Internal PM	B2B PM	B2C PM
Default dimension item weight		High	High	Medium
Criticality for PM		25	20	15
PYPR score	Low	Tools and templates are not existent or not used due to the lack of value or fit to organization and existing process. Everyone in the product organization uses own tools and templates, mostly not even digitally. There is no sharing of tools amongst the product teams. Tool usage and selection is ad hoc and not consistent. Tools are mis-used to follow a process a tool might not support. Tool usage is optional, even for areas where tool usage would be highly beneficial, e.g. information, transparency, consistency, etc. Product managers from different product teams only use the same tools and templates coincidentally		
	Medium	Tools and templates are used, however not across all product management processes and PYPR dimension items. Single product teams might agree on standards, but there is no standardization across product teams. For selected processes and PYPR dimension items, tools and templates are consistently rolled-out and trained considering the flexibility required by product teams, but providing the benefits required e.g. information, transparency, consistency, etc.		
	High	Every product management process and every PYPR dimension item benefits from the best tools and templates available in the market. All product managers have a set of options and exchange their experiences amongst the community of practices. Product managers can understand each other as they work with the same tools and templates. Product managers continuously improve the available tools and templates. Improvements and updates are shared with everyone. The tools and templates fit to the organizational set-up, processes, and governance model for product management and all related functions and departments. The tools and templates lead to better results and product success		

Table 9.4 PYPR dimensions impact examples

Dimension	Direct impact example	Indirect impact example
Product viability	Product scorecard exists for all products, and is the base for course-correction and product investments	
Product development	Backlogs are consistently managed and have the same attributes across product teams	
Go-to-Market/Product marketing	Sales teams enablement is smooth due to aligned sales kit structure and content	
Software demonstrations and training	Pre-sales teams enablement is smooth due to aligned demo script templates	
The market/Your customers		NPS® measured for all products and reporting available for product teams
Organizational maturity		Processes aligned with tools and templates

9.3.2 Summary and Conclusions

Key Takeaways

- Tools and templates need to help and support their intended users
- Lack of appropriate tools and templates can limit the success of product teams
- Tools and templates need to fit to all other elements of organizational maturity and to the people working with the provided tools and templates
- Productizing product management requires processes, tools and templates
- Even if tools and templates do exist, it does not necessarily mean they will improve anything unless they are used and fulfill their purpose
- Community of Practices are an enabler for tool and template improvements and adoption
- Product teams need to be able to adapt for their context, but having a general set of tools and templates will be a great foundation
- Product management processes, tools, and templates make your processes more effective and should be treated like a product not a project.

9.4 Mindset and Key Principles

A mindset is a set of assumptions, methods, or notations held by one or more people or groups of people.

—**Wikipedia**

Changing people's assumptions, methods or notions is one of the hardest issues to solve. The mindset of people within product organizations ultimately reflects their product, their organization, themselves and the people they work with. For any product organization fostering the people mindset toward a product mindset is the aspiration. At the core of organizational maturity, people's mindset is based on key principles valid for the entire organization. Remember: Missing Product Mindset and Key Principles eat Organizational Maturity for lunch!

Key principles can guide people with making decisions about values in your organization. If people benefit from clearly communicated principles, then these principles form the people's mindset over time. This is not about putting some posters on the wall stating values like empowerment, honesty, communication. That's just paper on the wall. Mindset change is not manifested in printouts, and defining key principles is not a game of "bullshit bingo" (Ledo, 2019). The actual values and derived key principles, as opposed to the nice-sounding values and key principles, are shown by who gets rewarded, promoted, or removed from the team. The real key principles are the values and rules that are practiced daily by peers and managers in the organization. Talk is cheap, show me your actions.

As you define the key principles for your product team or entire organization, ask the team about the rules and principles they value, don't tell them from the top. Ask them how they want to work together, where they need guidance. In addition, as an executive or product leader, communicate clearly how you will decide between two alternatives. For example, target market segment success over individual customer requirement. Key principles are meant to scale decisions. Product teams can leverage key principles to make autonomous decisions that adhere to the communicated key principles. Therefore, it is important that the communication of key principles is clear and comprehensible.

Note that real key principles are the behaviors and rules that are upheld by executives and product leaders in the organization. Walking the talk of this key principle is particularly hard if the customer is important for the company, and yet demands features from YourProduct Inc. that are outside the product vision and strategy. What do you think is the impact on people mindset (read: product mindset) when an executive team or product leader who is praising the values of team empowerment and product mindset is forcing commitments on the product team that are obviously (at least for the team) not getting the product closer toward the product vision or reducing the risk of doing so?

As you adopt and implement PYPR as a thinking framework and an ongoing discipline within your organization, PYPR becomes a cultural pillar and enabler of product mindset. The organization understands that the success of its products, their impact and value for the customers and the entire organization is the main goal; everything else is secondary. Indicators of product mindset include the following:

- Defining and aligning the elements of product success and the contribution of every product team member to increase the product's yield potential
- Fostering product teams with a holistic product approach
- Providing product teams the vision, strategy, autonomy, and accountability that will result in the best product for their customers and the entire organization
- Relentlessly focus ing on outcome for their customers and company instead of output.
- Stimulating team members to take on work instead of pushing it to the team, even if the task at hand might not be one's core responsibility, but will help the product yield potential to grow overall.

There are a few more topics I want to touch on concerning mindset and key principles and overall for organizational maturity. First, I would like to share some considerations about victimized behavior[9] that has been researched by Kevan Hall. Kevan Hall describes the traits of successful matrix managers and matrix victims (Hall 2013) working in a matrix organization. Matrix managers and product managers have much common including the challenges of achieving great results without authority and being accountable without full control (Kittlaus & Fricker, 2017). As explained before, you are a product manager, and you can overcome any soupçon of victimized behavior and lead the product team and the entire organization to a holistic product mindset.

Second, continuous improvement requires continuous learning. Learning requires feedback and the faster you receive feedback the better. For example, if you want to learn to sing, you start singing the first note and you hear yourself 30 min later. How fast will you learn if you hit the tone or missed it? Think about the consequence of delayed feedback to your learning curve.[10] This insight is true whether you are learning for a test, language, experiment in development (read: Dual-track agile and GIST from Sect. 5.2), or working with PYPR. As you use PYPR more frequently and conduct Strategy and Action meetings maybe not every 12 weeks, but for example, every four weeks and consider PYPR as the artifact of your weekly team meeting (extended team), you will learn faster and be able to improve the product yield potential and potentially the product mindset faster.

Finally, Communities of Practice can help with establishing values and key principles, as well as learning and strengthening product mindset. A Community of Practice is a group of people who know how to do something (their practice) and who interact regularly to learn how to do it better. Consider forming a Community of Practices for the various roles you might have in your product team. As for managers of product managers,[11] they all have a different focus and can share what they do and jointly learn how to do better. Communities of Practice follow some simple rules and gather around a defined community theme (e.g. Product

[9]People see themselves as victims of the organization, not being willing to change or influence the organization.

[10]Feedback loops need to be optimized in Software Product Management. That's how we learn.

[11]You might also consider a community of practice for each PYPR dimension.

Development PYPR dimension, or Product Planning, or by role, e.g. Product Manager). The community organizes itself and participation is voluntary. Generally, the community benefits from a core group that coordinates the regular events and active community members. There are many advantages of using a Communities of Practice, such as knowledge sharing, access to expertise, learning from peers, and team building. Communities of Practice can become incubators of product mindset and key principles that work for the community and the entire organization.

9.4.1 PYPR Dimension Items Details

See Table 9.5.

Table 9.5 PYPR defaults by software product manager type © Timo Wagenblatt 2019. All rights reserved

Topic		Internal PM	B2B PM	B2C PM
Default dimension item weight		High	High	Medium
Criticality for PM		25	20	15
PYPR score	Low	Personal objectives are always valued higher than the team or even the product. There is no common language or principles that is shared between people or within the product team. There might be one or two positive aspects in siloed areas, but they are by coincidence not by design and people-specific		
	Medium	The team has an understanding of product mindset. There are at least some aspects of the description for high PYPR scores that can be ticked		
	High	The organization understands that success of its products, their impact and value for the customers and the entire organization is the main goal, everything else is secondary. Continuous improvement and learning is a key principle in the entire organization. Feedback loop cycles are optimized. Communities of Practices are established and working. People enjoy working for the organization. The organization has a strong reputation as a role model of product mindset. Product management talent is attracted by the mindset. Clearly communicated and established key principles help with scaling consistent decisions throughout the organization		

9.4.2 Summary and Conclusions

I will keep this brief as the entire PYPR framework emphasizes a holistic approach for Software Product Management. In every dimension and in almost every item, you will find guidance and explanations toward product mindset. Be open and let a product mindset become your company DNA. Your employees, your product teams, your product managers, your product, and all leaders will benefit from a more successful organization.

Key Takeaways

- To sing well, you need good ears; as a product manager, Software Product Management leader, and product organization executive, PYPR can be your ears.
- Good tools, templates and principles are key to building a high performing team and impact the people mindset toward a product mindset.
- Create a common language and scale aligned decisions with key principles.
- Measure team or organization performance by metrics that cover customer success and adoption, not output. Set clear expectations for great Software Product Management and the required mindset.

PYPR helps to bring focus, alignment, and engagement to your product team and organization. All three points are key to establishing a product mindset in your organization. Remember that it takes an entire team and sometimes organization to make impactful products happen.

References

Aha.io. (2019, January 18). *What tools do product managers use?* Retrieved from https://www.aha.io/roadmapping/guide/product-management/which-tools-do-product-managers-use.

Bezos, J. P. (2018, December 25). *2016 letter to shareholders*. Retrieved from https://blog.aboutamazon.com/company-news/2016-letter-to-shareholders.

Bierl, B., Grüntges, V., Harrysson, M., & Williams, J. (2018, May 18). *Turn product managers into super conductors*. Retrieved from https://www.mckinsey.com/business-functions/operations/our-insights/turn-product-managers-into-super-conductors.

Burt, R. S. (1976). Positions in networks. *Social Forces, 55*(1), 93–122.

Burt, R. S. (2004). Structural holes and good ideas. *American Journal of Sociology, 110*(2), 349–399.

Burt, R. S. (2005). *Brokerage and closure: An introduction to social capital*. Oxford: Oxford University Press.

Burt, R. S. (2010). *Neighbor networks: Competitive advantage local and personal*. Oxford: Oxford University Press.

Cagan, M. (2019, March 9). *Empowered product teams*. Retrieved from https://svpg.com/empowered-product-teams/.

DeMarco, T., & Lister, T. (2013). *Peopleware*. Upper Saddle River: Addison-Wesley.

Fowler, M. (2019, March 4). *Maturity model*. Retrieved from https://martinfowler.com/bliki/MaturityModel.html.

Gerald. (2019, March 3). *Tool landscape for product managers*. Retrieved from https://pd7.group/2018/tool-landscape-for-pms.

Gnanasambandam, C., Harrysson, M., Srivastava, S., & Srivathsan, V. (2018, December 14). *The product management talent dilemma*. Retrieved from https://www.mckinsey.com/industries/high-tech/our-insights/the-product-management-talent-dilemma.

Haines, S. (2012). *Managing product management*. New York City: McGraw-Hill.

Hall, K. (2013). *Making the matrix work—How matrix managers engage people and cut through complexity*. London: Nicholas Brealey Publishing.

Hargadon, A., & Sutton, R. I. (1997). Technology brokering and innovation in a product development firm. *Administrative Science Quarterly, 42*(4), 716.

Ibarra, H., Kilduff, M., & Tsai, W. (2005). Zooming in and out: Connecting individuals and collectivities at the frontiers of organizational network research. *Organization Science, 16*(4), 359–371.

Kittlaus, H.-B., & Fricker, S. A. (2017). *Software product management*. Berlin: Springer-Verlag GmbH, Germany.

Ledo, F. (2019, January 18). *Bullshit bingo!* Retrieved from https://www.bullshitbingo.net/cards/bullshit/.

Lawley, B. (2018, August 26). *The product management maturity scale*. Retrieved from https://280group.com/product-management-blog/product-management-maturity-scale/.

Lee, F., Mingo, S., & Chen, D. (2007). Collaborative brokerage, generative creativity, and creative success. *Administrative Science Quarterly, 52*(3), 443.

Lin, N. (2002). *Social capital: A theory of social structure and action*. Cambridge: Cambridge University Press.

Lingo, E. L., & O'Mahony, S. (2010). Nexus Work: brokerage on creative projects. *Administrative Science Quarterly, 55*(1), 47–81.

Marsden, P. V. (1982). Brokerage behavior in restricted exchange networks. *Social Structure and Network Analysis, 7*(4), 341–410.

Mercer, C. (2018, October 9). *Transitioning to product management*. Retrieved from https://www.linkedin.com/learning/transitioning-to-product-management/qualities-of-great-product-managers.

Narajan, S. (2015). *Agile IT organization design*. New York: Addison-Wesley.

Niven, P. R., & Lamorte, B. (2016). *Objectives and key results; driving focus, alignment, and engagement with OKRs*. Hoboke, New Jersey: Wiley.

Obstfeld, D. (2005). Social networks, the tertius iungens orientation, and involvement in innovation. *Administrative Science Quarterly, 50*(1), 100–130.

Palan, H. (2019, March 3). *The five stages of product excellence*. Retrieved from https://www.webexpo.net/prague2017/talk/the-five-stages-of-product-excellence/.

Pichler, R. (2019, December 16). *Five tips for introducing product management to your company*. Retrieved from https://www.romanpichler.com/blog/five-tips-for-introducing-product-management-to-your-company/.

Predictive Analytics Today. (2019, January 18). *Top 20 product management software*. Retrieved from https://www.predictiveanalyticstoday.com/top-product-management-software/.

Product Focus. (2018, December 12). Retrieved from https://www.productfocus.com.

Product Focus. (2018, August 27). *Product management maturity model*. Retrieved from https://www.productfocus.com/product-management-maturity-model-blog/.

Qualtrics. (2018, November 17). *10 powerful quotes on leadership to inspire your organization*. Retrieved from https://www.qualtrics.com/blog/10-powerful-leadership-quotes/.

Simmel, G. (1950). *The triad*. Chicago: Chicago Free Press.

Software Tools for Product Managers. (2019, March 1). Retrieved from https://brainmates.com.au/general/software-tools-for-product-managers/.

Tan, A. (2019, March 2). *How to structure product management, according to Rich Mironov.* Retrieved from https://brainmates.com.au/product-management/how-to-structure-product-management/.

The LeSS Company B.V. (2018, December 18). *Continuous improvement towards perfection.* Retrieved from https://less.works/less/principles/continuous-improvement-towards-perfection.html#Kaizen.

The Nag. (2018, November 17). *17 best product management tools.* Retrieved from https://medium.com/nag-corporations/17-best-product-management-tools-f6ec6d41f1b5.

Vodde, B. (2018, November 1). Amsterdam.

Wikipedia. (2018, March 18). *Conway's law.* Retrieved from https://en.wikipedia.org/wiki/Conway%27s_law.

Wikipedia. (2018, August 1). *wikipedia.org.* Retrieved from https://en.wikipedia.org/wiki/Responsibility_assignment_matrix.

Wodtke, C. (2016). *Radical focus—Achieving your most important goals with objectives and key results.* Cucina Media LLC.

Part III
Case Studies Applying PYPR

Listen—PYPRs in Action 10

Leveraging PYPR Toward Software Product Management Excellence

Part 3 of this book shows how PYPR has been used to improve the success of various products with different characteristics and setups. We will investigate how product teams applied PYPR, which insights they got and the benefits they could achieve. The chapter outlines how PYPR has been applied successfully in practice by various product teams.

I will concentrate only on a few, diverse examples that explain the various usage options of PYPR. First, I will introduce a B2B product, well established in the market, utilizing machine learning in the product, focused on one dedicated industry. Second, I will introduce a product that focuses on a much broader target market, is highly successful in terms of product viability, but is impacted by a product manager losing focus of the product manager role responsibilities. In case study three, I will introduce a product manager who leveraged PYPR as a checklist for self-awareness and understanding all aspects to be considered in product management in the early stages of his career. Last but not least, I will introduce a case study of an internal IT product team trying PYPR for the first time in order to increase product management maturity in the IT Business Services team at SAP.

The case studies are just a glimpse of the PYPR applications; however, I think they will be useful for following reasons:

- They showcase real-world applications of applying PYPR
- They help you to understand the positive impact PYPR can generate
- They also indicate challenges that can arise as transparency kicks in when utilizing PYPR.

In my opinion, case studies are important and should be shared in the community. Therefore, I plan to post more case studies on the PYPR website (www.PYPR.works) over time. As you apply PYPR for your product, product team, and organization and would like to share with the community, you can use this platform to get in contact with me and showcase your PYPR achievements on the website.

T. Wagenblatt, *Software Product Management*, Management for Professionals,
https://doi.org/10.1007/978-3-030-19871-8_10

10.1 Summary of Default PYPR Configurations

In Part 2, I introduced the default weights for each PYPR dimension and PYPR dimension item. For a better overview, you can find the default PYPR configuration in this chapter.

Everything I describe in this book has been successfully applied and solidly tested for many Business-to-Business products over the last 20 years. PYPR has been applied and tested for internal products for about one year. For B2C products, PYPR has been discussed and calibrated with many Business-to-Consumer product managers from great companies such as Google or Facebook, so I would claim PYPR has been theoretically tested for B2C products, but the actual application and weight stabilization might need further calibration.

PYPR as a Software Product Management methodology is completely customizable and flexible, making it easily adopted by any product team or product organization regardless of size, maturity or development approach.

As you start using PYPR, the sections below are your reference point.

- Section 2.1: Introducing the Product Yield Potential Radar
- Section 3.3: On your Mark, Get Set, Go!

You might also consider a product management consultant to help you in the first steps of your PYPR journey. In my experience, having help with introducing PYPR to a product team, honing the PYPR configuration, or acting as a sounding board after each PYPR iteration comes with many benefits, including a faster adoption curve and with that positive impact to product success.

Remember the PYPR definition explained and detailed throughout the book:

The Product Yield Potential Radar is a Software Product Management framework that fosters communication and strategic thinking within product organizations. PYPR is an ongoing discipline supporting orchestration and prioritization of all product-related activities. PYPR helps to discover what is most important for the product, the product team and all stakeholders to maximize any product's yield potential.

Using PYPR represents a commitment to continuously improve the Software Product Management practice in your organization toward achieving excellence. To ensure you benefit from PYPR, you must commit to repeatedly using the framework. This comprises conducting the PYPR meetings (read: ceremonies), leveraging PYPR as an information radiator, analyzing PYPR ratings as a team, and adapting your ongoing work priorities toward improving the dimension items that are limiting success.

Start, adapt, learn, improve, and grow! Personally, and in terms of your product's yield potential.

10.1.1 Default PYPR Assessment and Visualization for B2B Products

See Figs. 10.1 and 10.2.

Area	Area Item	Driver	Approver	Contributor	Informed	Product A / Product Module 1	Product B / Product Module 2	Product C / Product Module 3	Comments
1 Product Viability	Customer Business Case					0	0	0	
1 Product Viability	Pipeline Development					0	0	0	
1 Product Viability	Product Profitability					0	0	0	
1 Product Viability	Product Growth					0	0	0	
1 Product Viability	Maintenance / Run Profitability					0	0	0	
1 Product Viability	Professional Services/Consulting Profitability					0	0	0	
2 Product Development	Product Vision and Strategy					0	0	0	
2 Product Development	Product Development Planning					0	0	0	
2 Product Development	Roadmaps					0	0	0	
2 Product Development	Product Quality (Internal View)					0	0	0	
2 Product Development	Product Team Health					0	0	0	
3 Go-To-Market / Product Marketing	Marketing Assets / Sales Kit					0	0	0	
3 Go-To-Market / Product Marketing	Competitive Analysis					0	0	0	
3 Go-To-Market / Product Marketing	Sales Enablement					0	0	0	
3 Go-To-Market / Product Marketing	Partner Enablement					0	0	0	
3 Go-To-Market / Product Marketing	Own Professional Services / Consulting Enablement					0	0	0	
3 Go-To-Market / Product Marketing	GTM Activities and Plan					0	0	0	
4 Software Demonstration and Trainings	Software Demonstrations					0	0	0	
4 Software Demonstration and Trainings	Pre-Sales Enablement					0	0	0	
4 Software Demonstration and Trainings	Product Marketing Videos					0	0	0	
4 Software Demonstration and Trainings	Trainings					0	0	0	
5 The Market / Your Customers	Functional Completeness					0	0	0	
5 The Market / Your Customers	Product Quality (External View)					0	0	0	
5 The Market / Your Customers	Customer Community					0	0	0	
5 The Market / Your Customers	Customer Support and Official References					0	0	0	
5 The Market / Your Customers	Thought Leadership					0	0	0	
5 The Market / Your Customers	Analyst / Market Influencer Relations					0	0	0	
6 Organizational Maturity	Leadership, Vision, and Strategy					0	0	0	
6 Organizational Maturity	Organization, Processes, and Governance					0	0	0	
6 Organizational Maturity	People Mindset and Key Principles					0	0	0	
6 Organizational Maturity	Tools and Templates					0	0	0	

Fig. 10.1 Default PYPR assessment template

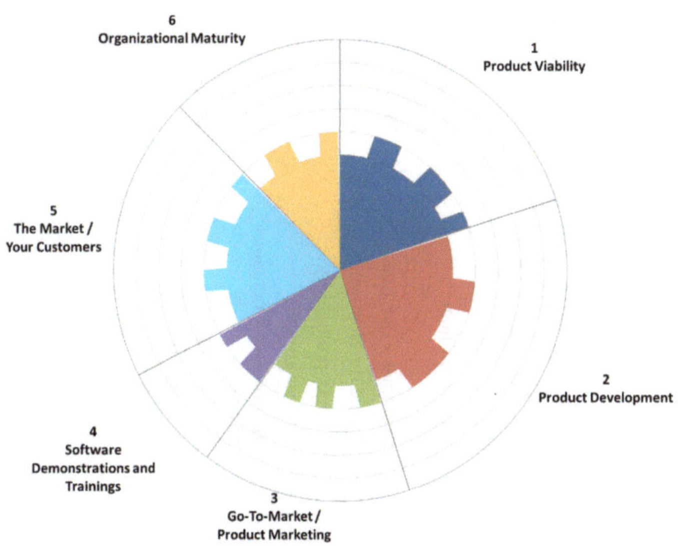

Fig. 10.2 Default PYPR assessment visualization

10.1.2 Default PYPR Configuration: Product Viability

See Table 10.1.

10.1.3 Default PYPR Configuration: Product Development

See Table 10.2.

Table 10.1 Product viability: PYPR dimension defaults © Timo Wagenblatt 2019. All rights reserved

Dimension weight 20%		Dimension weight 20%		Dimension weight 17.5%	
B2B		B2C		Internal PM	
Dimension item	Weighting factor (%)	Dimension item	Weighting factor (%)	Dimension item	Weighting factor (%)
Customer business case	20.0	Customer value case	25.0	Customer business case	30.0
Pipeline development	18.0	Traffic development	20.0	Pipeline development	Not relevant
Product profitability	20.0	Product profitability	20.0	Product profitability	25.0
Product growth	20.0	Product growth	20.0	Product growth	20.0
Maintenance/Operations profitability	12.0	Maintenance/Operations profitability	15.0	Maintenance/Operations profitability	25.0
Professional services/Consulting profitability	10.0	Professional services/Consulting profitability	Not relevant	Professional services/Consulting profitability	Not relevant

Table 10.2 Product development: PYPR dimension item defaults © Timo Wagenblatt 2019. All rights reserved

Dimension weight 25%		Dimension weight 22.5%		Dimension weight 27.5%	
B2B		B2C		Internal PM	
Dimension item	Weighting factor (%)	Dimension item	Weighting factor (%)	Dimension item	Weighting factor (%)
Product vision and strategy	25.0	Product vision and strategy	25.0	Product vision and strategy	20
Roadmap	15.0	Roadmap	10.0	Roadmap	22.5
Product planning	20.0	Product planning	20.0	Product planning	20.0
Team health	25.0	Team health	25.0	Team health	22.5
Dev product quality	15.0	Dev product quality	20.0	Dev product quality	15.0

10.1.4 Default PYPR Configuration: Go-to-Market/Product Marketing

See Table 10.3.

10.1.5 Default PYPR Configuration: Software Demonstrations and Training

See Table 10.4.

10.1.6 Default PYPR Configuration: The Market/Your Customers

See Table 10.5.

10.1.7 Default PYPR Configuration: Organizational Maturity

See Table 10.6.

Table 10.3 Go-to-Market/Product marketing: PYPR dimension item defaults © Timo Wagenblatt 2019. All rights reserved

Dimension weight 15%		Dimension weight 17.5%		Dimension weight 15%	
B2B		B2C		Internal PM	
Dimension item	Weighting factor (%)	Dimension item	Weighting factor (%)	Dimension item	Weighting factor (%)
Marketing assets/Sales kit	20.0	Marketing assets/Sales kit	25.0	Marketing assets/Sales kit	30.0
Sales enablement	20.0	Sales/Marketing enablement	10.0	Corporate communication enablement	20.0
Partner enablement	15.0	Partner enablement	10.0		
Own professional services/Consulting enablement	10.0				
Competitive analysis	15.0	Competitive analysis	20.0	Competitive analysis	15.0
GTM activities and plan	20.0	GTM activities and plan	35.0	GTM activities and plan	35.0

Table 10.4 Software demonstrations and training: PYPR dimension defaults

Dimension weight 7.5%		Dimension weight 5%		Dimension weight 7.5%	
B2B		B2C		Internal PM	
Dimension item	Weighting factor (%)	Dimension item	Weighting factor (%)	Dimension item	Weighting factor (%)
Software demonstrations	25.0	Software demonstrations or self-explaining software	45.0	Software demonstrations	25.0
Product marketing video	20.0	Product marketing video	40.0	Product marketing video	15.0
Pre-sales enablement	30.0			Support and roll-out team enablement	30.0
Trainings	25.0	Trainings	15.0	Trainings	30.0

Table 10.5 The market/Your customers: PYPR dimension item defaults

Dimension weight 20%		Dimension weight 22.5%		Dimension weight 20%	
B2B		B2C		Internal PM	
Dimension item	Weighting factor (%)	Dimension item	Weighting factor (%)	Dimension item	Weighting factor (%)
References/Key customers support	25.0	References/Key customers support/Influencers	15.0	References/Key customers support	15.0
Customer community	15.0	Customer (consumer) community	15.0	Extended stakeholder alignment	25.0
Functional completeness	15.0	Functional completeness	20.0	Functional completeness	20.0
Thought leadership	15.0	Thought leadership	15.0	Thought leadership	10.0
Product quality	20.0	Product quality	20.0	Product quality	20.0
Analyst relations	10.0	Analyst/Press relations	15.0	Peer community	10.0

Table 10.6 Organizational maturity: PYPR dimension item defaults © Timo Wagenblatt 2019.

Dimension weight 12.5%		Dimension weight 12.5%		Dimension weight 12.5%	
B2B		B2C		Internal PM	
Dimension item	Weighting factor (%)	Dimension item	Weighting factor (%)	Dimension item	Weighting factor (%)
Leadership, vision, and strategy	25.0	Leadership, vision, and strategy	25.0	Leadership, vision, and strategy	20.0
Organization, processes, and governance	25.0	Organization, processes, and governance	25.0	Organization, processes, and governance	25.0
People mindset and key principles	30.0	People mindset and key principles	35.0	People mindset and key principles	30.0
Tools and templates	20.0	Tools and templates	15.0	Tools and templates	25.0

10.2 Case Study: B2B Product–Machine Learning

In this case study I focus on Step 3 and Step 4 of applying PYPR. The product team already utilized PYPR for many years. The product manager invited the extended product team to attend the assessment sessions, and strategy and action meetings early on.

This case study spans almost a year and showcases how the product team, and the product, benefitted from applying PYPR over time (Table 10.7).

Table 10.7 Product characteristics—case study 1

	Product characteristics
Product type	B2B, On-premise
Product lifecycle	Growth
SPM and PO	Software Product Manager biased toward development, SPM also product owner
Transparency	Product marketing, lead architect, accountable dev manager part of PYPR
Dev approach	Scrum, engineering team new to agile dev approach
Team maturity	Experienced team across the board, with exception of engineering team below architect level as high fluctuation and unexperienced developers
Market segment	Large to upper midmarket target customers in mature markets
Specialty	Machine-learning product with run-service requirement as customers lack expertise of keeping the models and data feeds up to date

10.2.1 PYPR Assessment and Visualization

The PYPR Assessment provided the following results for this product. The Product Viability dimension scored highest, while the Go-to-Market/Product Marketing dimension scored low.

The PYPR dimension view provides a good first indication, where the limiting factor of the product's yield potential resides. Clearly the Go-to-Market/Product Marketing dimension needed improvement as shown in both the table and even better in the chart to the right in Fig. 10.3.

Dimension	Score
Product Viability	6,54
Product Development	5,65
Go-to-Market / Product Marketing	2,80
Software Demonstrations and Training	4,90
The Market / Your Customers	4,85
Organizational Maturity	4,50
Total PYPR Score	**29,24**

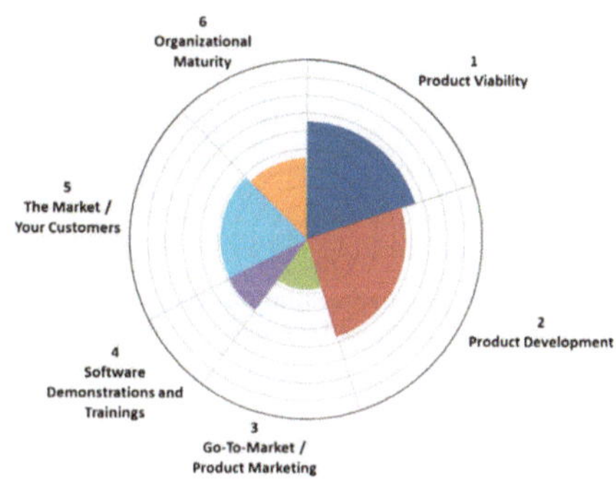

Fig. 10.3 B2B product–machine learning: assessment results © Timo Wagenblatt 2019. All rights reserved

Note that this doesn't mean that the team should focus solely on the Go-to-Market/Product Marketing dimension. Keeping all dimensions in balance requires that the team remains working in many areas to maintain their level. There is plenty of ad hoc work in the team's day-to-day business anyway, so topics fall through the cracks, or in other words, important topics fly under the radar. PYPR provides transparency. PYPR enables that the focus activities for the next improvement cycle are documented, aligned and tracked with the bi-weekly check-ins.

By analyzing PYPR one level deeper, we could identify the lowest rated items across all PYPR dimensions: Own Professional Services/Consulting Enablement, Competitive Analysis, Partner Enablement, References/Key Customers Support, and Marketing Assets/Sales Kit. Note that four out of the five items belong to the Go-to-Market/Product Marketing dimension, while References/Key Customers Support belongs to The Market/Your Customers dimension that scored okay overall.

Although the Go-to-Market/Product Marketing dimension is lacking behind badly, one dimension item has been rated really well. The GTM Plan and Activities item has been doing well as the Product Marketing team had a well-maintained event calendar relevant for the product, and the product has been positioned at all these events.

The full PYPR Dimension Items view visualizes an unbalanced status across all dimensions as shown in Fig. 10.4.

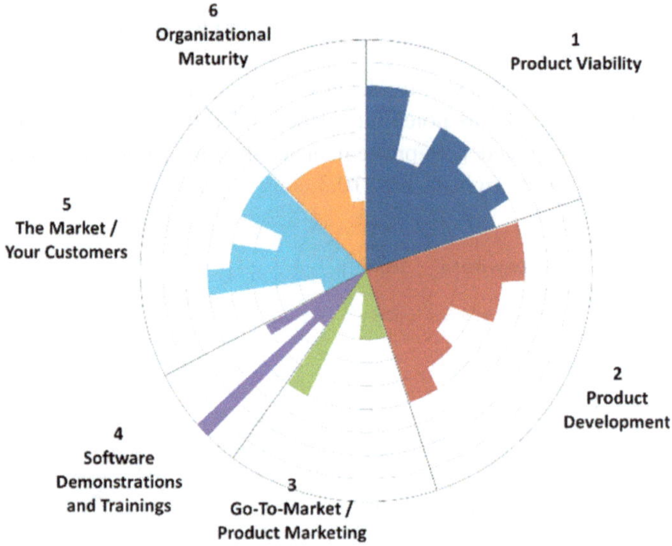

Fig. 10.4 B2B product–machine learning: dimension items radar cycle 3 © Timo Wagenblatt 2019. All rights reserved

This pattern is kind of typical, especially in early stages of applying PYPR in an organization. The product teams are at a stage of unalignment with pockets of excellence in one or the other dimension. There is no shared understanding of what it requires to improve the product's yield potential across all dimensions. As we discussed throughout this book, unbalanced focus sometimes leads to quick success although it hurts the longevity of the product and product team.

Benefits of the assessment:

- Alignment with product marketing about status quo of the product success factors
- Clarify roles as Product Marketing was not aware what is expected from their team in terms of deliverables and timelines
- Support from the Training team to help with enablement material and enablement sessions
- Identification of most limiting factors in Go-to-Market/Product Marketing and The Market/Your Customers dimensions.

10.2.2 PYPR Strategy and Action Plan

Based on the analysis of all PYPR dimensions and dimension items, the team jointly defined the Strategy and Action Plan as outlined in Table 10.8.

The PYPR assessment also discovered that the items Customer Business Case, Product Marketing Video, and Product Vision and Strategy were rated the highest. Based on this aligned understanding the team could re-use the strong base of a well-documented Customer Business Case and a clear Product Vision and Strategy.

Table 10.8 Strategy and action plan

Strategy and action plan	
Competitive analysis	From the discussions about this item, the team derived a quick win as there has been lots of information and knowledge available across the team. One person assumed the task to collect all information and condense it in a usable format that should be added to the sales kit **Key result**: provide competitive battle cards for the top three competitors (defined by lost deals in the last six months)
Own professional services/Consulting enablement	The training department committed to offer trainings tailored to own professional services as well as partners. The team could re-use the strong training assets and infrastructure already available **Key result**: define training plan and adapt content, publish training opportunity and invite for trainings
Partner enablement	
References/Key customers support	Contact the lively customer community/council and convert the positive sentiment into official references **Key result**: find two additional customer references in the next 12 weeks and get both officially approved, focusing on EMEA and North America (one each)

The team decided to leverage information from both items in the enablement activities as well as in the marketing and sales assets. This should result in a coherent message internally and externally that might spread the impact to other items as well.

10.2.3 PYPR Cycle Results

The PYPR Assessment after the 12 weeks period provided the following results. The Product Viability dimension still scored the highest, while the Go-to-Market/Product Marketing dimension remained at the bottom (see Fig. 10.5). However, the counter-actions resulted in improvements as the Go-to-Market/Product Marketing dimension score significantly increased to 4.00 from 2.80. Overall, the Total PYPR score improved to 33.70 from 29.24.

Dimension	Score
Product Viability	6,60
Product Development	6,05
Go-to-Market / Product Marketing	4,15
Software Demonstrations and Training	5,65
The Market / Your Customers	5,75
Organizational Maturity	5,50
Total PYPR Score	**33,70**

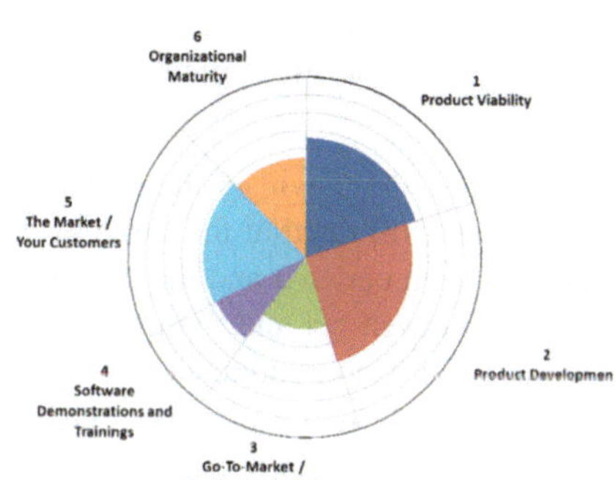

Fig. 10.5 B2B product–machine learning: dimension radar cycle 4 © Timo Wagenblatt 2019. All rights reserved

Analyzing the individual items across all dimensions shows the following results. The lowest rated items across all PYPR dimensions are: Own Professional Services/Consulting Enablement, Competitive Analysis, Pipeline Development, Sales Enablement, and Software Demonstrations. Note that three of the five items still belong to the Go-to-Market/Product Marketing dimension, while Pipeline Development belongs to the top scoring Product Viability dimension.

That is an interesting investigation that needs special attention. The product's viability is scoring high; however, the pipeline development went down to 3 from 5. There can be multiple reasons for such an effect, like changing sales team priorities (read: incentives), closed deals without new pipeline generation, new competitor entry, etc. In this case, the decline triggered lots of debates as there was no obvious reason. The result of the work process is not important here, but it is noteworthy that the team experienced the big benefits of applying PYPR, transparency, focus and alignment.

Figure 10.6 visualizes the dimension item view on the left and the PYPR change view on the right. The change view of PYPR illustrates which items improved, declined or remained at the same level versus the last assessment. The grey area shows the last assessment result (cycle 3) and the colored area the current results (cycle 4). Areas with grey areas higher than colored ones declined and areas with colored higher than grey ones improved.

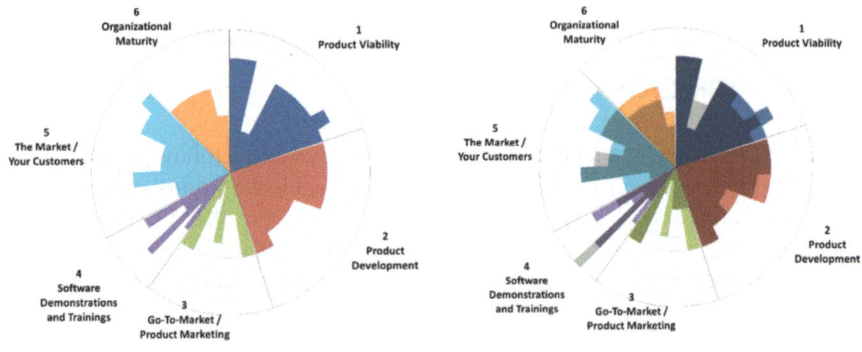

Fig. 10.6 B2B product–machine learning: dimension items radar cycle 4 and cycle 4 versus cycle 3

Note that the Own Professional Services/Consulting and Sales enablement activities are still rated at the same level as in the cycle 3 assessment. The training plans had been updated and the training material had been worked on. The material was not reviewed yet and the invitations for the enablement sessions went out, but they have not been conducted yet. The team worked on the most important items, but the impact was not effective. That's okay as some changes require more time than others, and hence it is okay that the items remain in focus.

Remember that change might happen for items you work on and for items you do not work on. That's why it is essential to always assess where you are for the full radar dimension items. Some dimension items might improve without being in current focus as the work of the subsequent cycles yield fruit. While some items might decline as there are external factors or the time just works against you and your work is outdated and lower rated today.

The world keeps turning and the only constant is change. PYPR helps to weather the storm as the guiding light, the north star, or in other words being the radar to keep your product and your product team on track.

That's what Software Product Management is all about: Continuously working on finding and keeping right the balance for your product. You are the General Manager of YourProduct Inc. In Fig. 10.7, you can see how the product manager and the product team improved the yield potential of the product over time. The dimension PYPR scores and the Total PYPR scores are trending in the right direction, indicating the continuously increasing product yield potential.

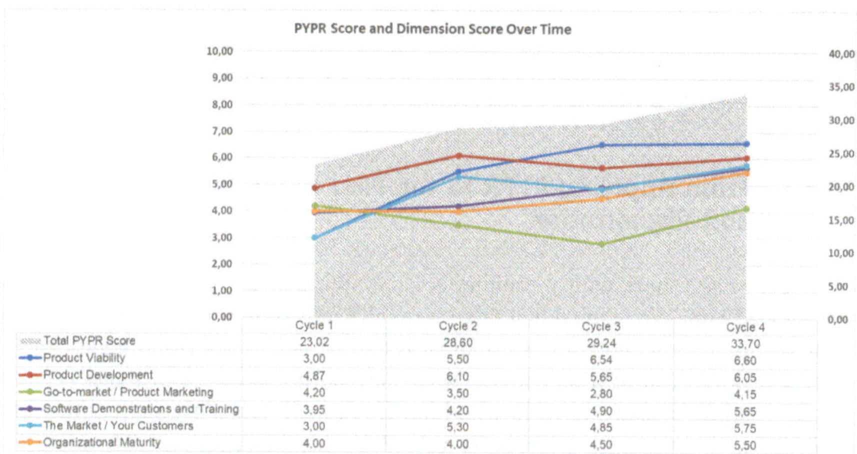

	Cycle 1	Cycle 2	Cycle 3	Cycle 4
Total PYPR Score	23,02	28,60	29,24	33,70
Product Viability	3,00	5,50	6,54	6,60
Product Development	4,87	6,10	5,65	6,05
Go-to-market / Product Marketing	4,20	3,50	2,80	4,15
Software Demonstrations and Training	3,95	4,20	4,90	5,65
The Market / Your Customers	3,00	5,30	4,85	5,75
Organizational Maturity	4,00	4,00	4,50	5,50

Fig. 10.7 B2B product–machine learning: total PYPR score and PYPR dimension scores over time © Timo Wagenblatt 2019. All rights reserved

10.3 Case Study: Cross-Industry B2B Product–Software Product Management Starter

The case study describes Steps 1–4 of applying PYPR. The product manager used PYPR for the first time. The product manager decided to work even without the core product team in the assessment and strategy and action meetings.

I selected this case study as it illustrates how PYPR supports not only Software Product Management professionals, but also delivers benefits for young talents in this discipline. The product team did not know that the product manager leveraged PYPR to balance the product team's and the his own activities (Table 10.9).

Table 10.9 Product characteristics—case study 2

Product characteristics	
Product type	B2B, private cloud, on-premise
Product lifecycle	Growth
SPM and PO	Software Product Manager new to the role with consulting background. Assigned to the role as domain expert, however no guidance on role and responsibilities. Takes also the product owner role in scrum team, not co-located with team
Transparency	PYPR not used with the product team, only for self-reflection and learning
Dev approach	Scrum, engineering team new to agile dev approach
Team maturity	Young Software Product Manager with seasoned development team. Both first time in product, used to deliver project work
Market segment	Global, large to upper midmarket customers using SAP ERP software
Specialty	Product elevated from multiple customer-specific project. Former Project Manager part of the scrum team as lead architect and scrum master

10.3.1 From Applying PYPR to the First PYPR Assessment and Visualization

This case study starts with a training session. We met the product manager and interviewed him. We learned that there were all kinds of minor problems mostly in team set-up and collaboration. He indicated that he is the jack of all trades for the team, but doesn't have a real say in what they do nor could he activate peers in product marketing teams to work with him. He decided to mainly support the sales teams as new customers were most valued by his management. Therefore, he enthusiastically accepted any sales-support request. In the interview he mentioned that it doesn't feel right, but he is busy and sees some positive results from his efforts. In short, he felt insecure as no one provided guidance to him about the expectations coming with the new role.

In the first step we used the standard PYPR set-up for B2B companies. It seemed to be the first time someone described the role and the important items to him. PYPR helped the new product manager to structure all his activities and gain transparency about items that were not on his radar.

Furthermore, the initial PYPR sessions provided guidance about the importance of the six dimensions for his product and the importance of the items in each dimension. He was absorbing all this information and keen to get to the next steps.

We spent an hour or so clarifying the roles and especially his role as a product manager. He understood that he is not alone. Many people worked on the product or in its proximity. We asked to get the stakeholders to the initial assessment session; however, he rejected this request. He wanted to understand the product yield potential status on his own first.

The initial PYPR Assessment provided the results as illustrated in Fig. 10.8. The Product Viability dimension scored highest, while the all other dimensions suffered.

Dimension	Score
Product Viability	6,54
Product Development	4,25
Go-to-Market / Product Marketing	2,40
Software Demonstrations and Training	3,05
The Market / Your Customers	3,65
Organizational Maturity	5,00
Total PYPR Score	**24,89**

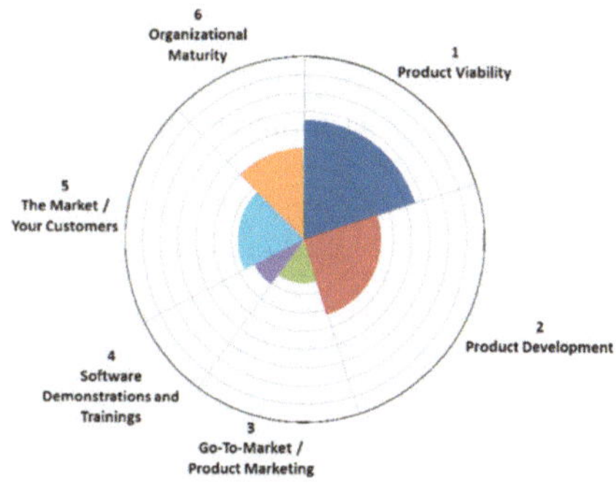

Fig. 10.8 B2B product–software product management starter: assessment results © Timo Wagenblatt 2019. All rights reserved

This pattern is fairly typical for new product managers. New product managers are generally and naturally biased to their background, work history, or context. That is understandable as without guidance anyone would focus on the items and topics close to your comfort zone. The product manager prioritizes her and the product team's efforts accordingly. Like in the case study before, the bias here is toward Product Viability, but the situation was completely different. The product manager had a forced bias. The context, i.e. the direct manager, emphasized product profitability as the most important metric for rating the product manager. Note: rating the product manager, not the product or the product team.

Multiple misconceptions and misunderstandings led to the status and low PYPR score as illustrated in Fig. 10.8.

- The product team did not understand the role of the product manager either, hence they continued in their project set-up building feature after feature without ranking for business value. After receiving some feedback from the product manager about the latest sales engagement or from a customer directly, they judged whether they like the new request and if they like it, they built it.
- The product manager did not focus on any Product Marketing dimension items as there was a dedicated Product Marketing team. However, they rarely met and aligned on activities or positioning.
- All software demonstrations where done in the quality system on the flight as only the product manager or a consultant at customer-side did software demonstrations. Certainly, there was no script or any other guidance available.
- The customers did not recognize the product as a product on its own, because the product was mainly sold as part of bigger deals, merely another line item amongst all other purchased products.

• The direct manager did not question any of these as the key metric, namely product profitability, looked great. Even the sales team appreciated the support of the product manager and sent thank you notes copying the direct manager frequently.

So, what's the point here? All okay, right? Why to worry about any of these as the product is selling well? In Fig. 10.9, the PYPR dimension view provided some insights or at least topics to discuss:

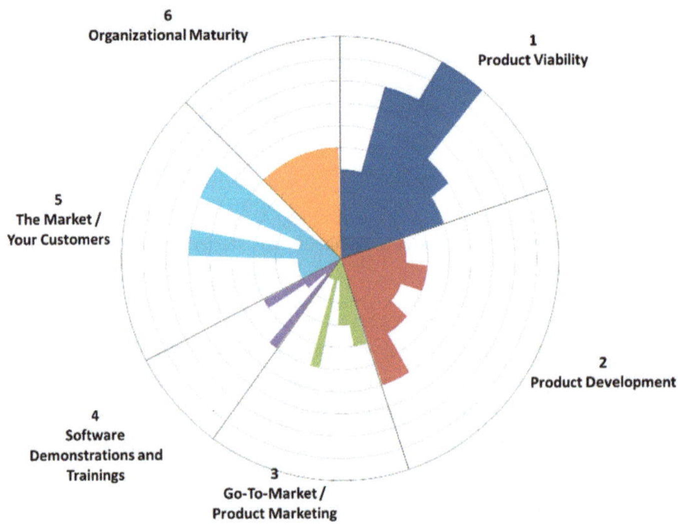

Fig. 10.9 B2B product–software product management starter: dimension items radar cycle 0 © Timo Wagenblatt 2019. All rights reserved

By analyzing PYPR at the dimension item level, we could identify that most items had a rating below 5 and the Rockstar item with a perfect 10 was, with no surprise, the product profitability. The story behind a great profitability always has two dimensions: revenue and investment. The product had ok revenue and little investment leading to a great profitability % number. However even in the Product Viability dimension, there was signs of issues as the customer business case and maintenance profitability items scored very low. This product was obviously out of balance. There would be much more to tell about the product, however, that is not the point of this case study. The main reason I picked this case study out of the many PYPR applications is the reaction and personal development of the product manager.

It was the first time that he looked at his product holistically. He understood that being a General Manager of YourProduct Inc. is much more than pleasing his direct manager short term. He could see the product was dying, slowly but surely.

10.3.2 PYPR Strategy and Action Plan

Based on PYPR, he started to prioritize his activities in order to get balance for his product and to secure its longevity. He had to admit that despite all the nice sales numbers, the product was not really recognized in the market. Customers bought the software, but did not upgrade or sometimes didn't even use the product. Internally the product was only sold, if there was personal involvement as enablement did not happen.

The product manager treated PYPR like his personal to-do list and worked on each item, one after each other. Note that he did not do it all on his own; for example, he started working on product vision and the strategy part, but he was wise enough to include the product team, a few account managers and someone from the product marketing team in the exercise. In fact, this was the first time that this extended team met in one room.

Another important outcome was that the team worked together on an investment case, pro-actively thinking about the future and proper positioning of the product. They connected with other departments addressing the same customer segments and aligned on Go-to-Market activities.

10.3.3 PYPR Cycle Results

After 24 weeks the PYPR Assessment provided the following, amazing results illustrated in Fig. 10.10. Many dimension items could be improved, and despite the product manager not sharing that he was using PYPR until he showcased the positive results, he leveraged PYPR as a tool for himself to manage the product, his time and the stakeholders in a much more effective way.

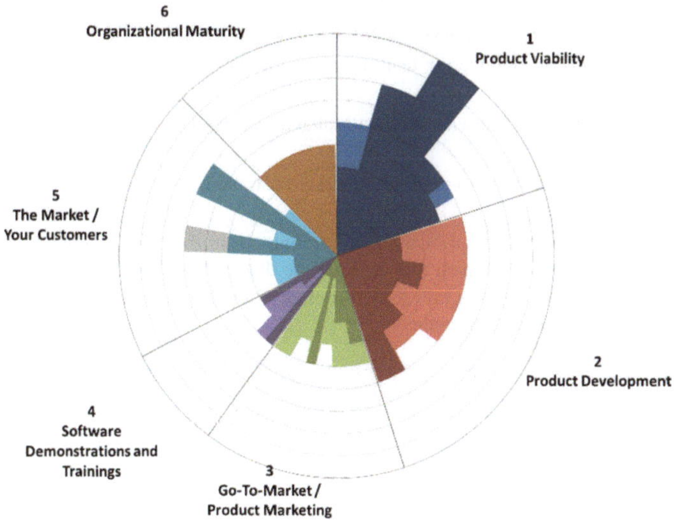

Fig. 10.10 B2B product–software product management starter: dimension items radar cycle 0 versus cycle 2 © Timo Wagenblatt 2019. All rights reserved

When I met the product manager for this assessment (together with the product team!) and a few times afterwards by chance, I could see and feel his excitement and passion. I think I met a newly confident product manager who was now on a mission well-equipped to build an awesome product.

10.4 Case Study: B2B Product–Cross-Industry Software Product

In this case study I focus on steps 3 and 4 of applying PYPR (Sect. 2.1). The product team used PYPR for the first time. The product manager decided to work only with the core product team in the assessment and strategy and action meetings.

The product in this case study was recommended as a PYPR pilot due to the outstanding perception within the company. The product was a great financial success and the product manager therefore was well respected by the management team.

I picked this case study as it illustrates how important balance is for the continued success of a software product and the product manager (Table 10.10).

Table 10.10 Product characteristics—case study 3

Product characteristics	
Product type	B2B, private cloud, on-premise
Product lifecycle	Maturity
SPM and PO	Software Product Manager biased toward sales, Product Owner proxy within the core product team detached from customers
Transparency	Lead architect, accountable dev manager part of PYPR
Dev approach	Scrum, engineering team used to agile dev approach
Team maturity	Seasoned Software Product Manager, young development team not co-located
Market segment	Global, large to upper midmarket customers using SAP ERP software
Specialty	One offering out of multiple offerings from the same company in the same functional domain that can only be distinguished by specialists. Customers and sales teams find it hard to understand the benefits of this product compared to the others

10.4.1 PYPR Assessment and Visualization

The PYPR Assessment provided the results in Fig. 10.11 for this product. The Product Viability dimension scored highest, while the Product Development and Organizational Maturity dimension scored low.

Dimension	**Score**
Product Viability	7,82
Product Development	4,80
Go-to-Market / Product Marketing	6,85
Software Demonstrations and Training	7,20
The Market / Your Customers	6,45
Organizational Maturity	5,00
Total PYPR Score	**38,12**

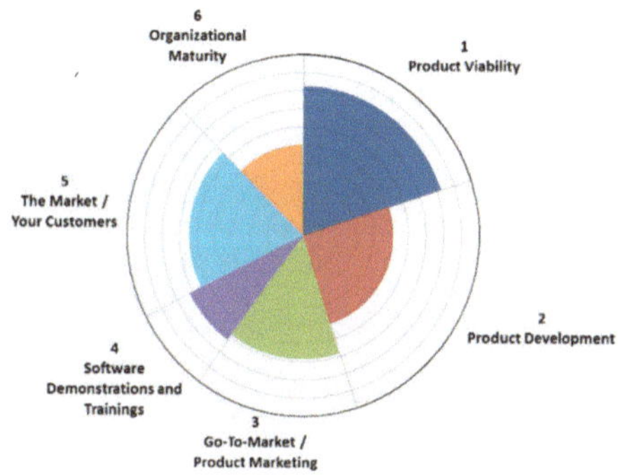

Fig. 10.11 B2B product–cross-industry: assessment results

The PYPR dimension view provides a good first indication, where the limiting factor of the product's yield potential resides. Clearly the Product Development and Organization Maturity dimensions need improvement as shown in both the table and even better in the chart on the right in Fig. 10.11.

By analyzing PYPR at the dimension item level, we can identify the lowest rated items across all PYPR dimensions: Team Health, Product Planning, Maintenance Profitability, and Internal Product Quality. Note that three of the four items belong to the Product Development dimension, while Maintenance Profitability belongs to the Product Viability dimension that scored the highest overall.

The full PYPR Dimension Items view visualizes an unbalanced status across all dimensions as shown in Fig. 10.12.

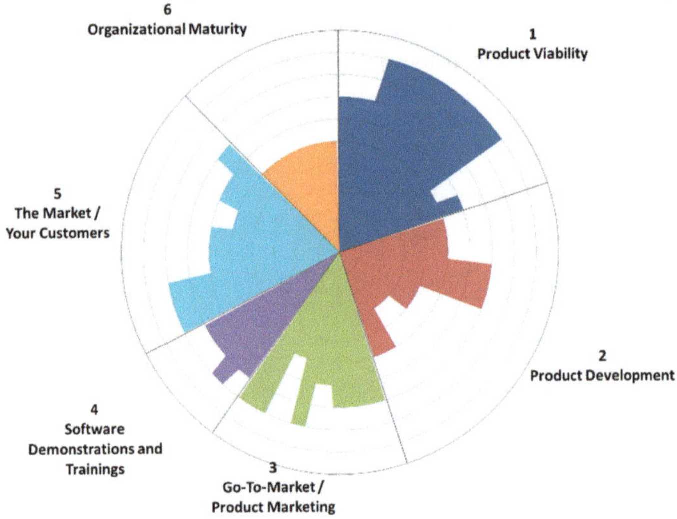

Fig. 10.12 B2B product–cross-industry software product: dimension items radar cycle 0 © Timo Wagenblatt 2019. All rights reserved

This pattern is fairly typical for product managers with a strong sales bias. The product manager focuses mostly on product profitability and anything that supports selling the product as a fast as possible. The product manager prioritizes his and the product team's efforts accordingly. The main message throughout this book has been that imbalanced focus sometimes leads to quick success while it negatively affects the longevity of the product and product team. And this case study is a sad, but a perfect example.

Benefits of the assessment:

- Identification of most limiting factors in Product Development dimension
- Spotting unbalanced areas of product success requirements
- Transparency that organizational maturity not accepted as important by the product manager nor the product team for their product
- Product manager eager to get even more out of the existing product.

10.4.2 PYPR Strategy and Action Plan

Based on the analysis of all PYPR dimensions and dimension items, the team jointly defined the Strategy and Action Plan as outlined in Table 10.11.

Table 10.11 Strategy and action plan

Strategy and action plan	
Product team health	Software Product Manager spending time with product team member to enable a proxy PO in the team. Software Product Owner commits to be available in sprint grooming sessions and sprint reviews **Key result**: Software Product Manager participates in all sprint grooming sessions and provides feedback to "done" backlog items within three working days The product team was enthusiastic about this action plan as clearly, they did not feel attached to what the product managers were doing. They appreciated the great internal and external perception, but they had a different view about their product, i.e. not delivering to its full potential
Product planning	The PYPR assessment meeting became a heated discussion about ad hoc requests during the spring by the product manager. The product manager provided direct customer feedback from his sales meetings asking for direct consideration. The team did not have the empowerment to challenge the asks trying to accommodate the requests **Key result**: team agreed to have quick synch meetings after sprint backlog prioritization. Product manager agreed to provide new priorities only via the product backlog and no longer via emails or phone calls to individual team members
Maintenance profitability	This item was forced by the product manager to be worked on despite there were other items rated at similarly low levels. The product manager only agreed to the other two items above when the maintenance profitability was also a focus topic for the next 12 weeks. Clearly this showcased the financial focus bias first hand **Key result**: the product manager asked the team to only work on priority very high and priority high customer messages. Internal messages and less important messages should be ignored. The team should reduce headcount to save budget

Note that I only facilitated the workshop and at this point tried to step out of the moderator role. Unfortunately, I could not convince the product manager to focus more on the longevity of the product versus these obviously short-term focused actions. The product team wasn't strong enough to reject the focus on maintenance profitability either. The product team was happy with the other two items that directly impacted them and did not want to jeopardize this achievement.

The product team focused solely on their product. The overall organizational maturity was discussed as not really impacting them. They could not imagine why they should spend time on this topic and hence agreed to set all dimension items to 5.

10.4.3 PYPR Cycle Results

The PYPR Assessment after 12 weeks provided the results shown in Fig. 10.13. The Product Viability dimension scored still the highest, while the Product Development dimension remained at the bottom (see Fig. 10.14).

Dimension	Score
Product Viability	7,74
Product Development	4,45
Go-to-Market / Product Marketing	6,85
Software Demonstrations and Training	7,20
The Market / Your Customers	6,25
Organizational Maturity	5,00
Total PYPR Score	**37,49**

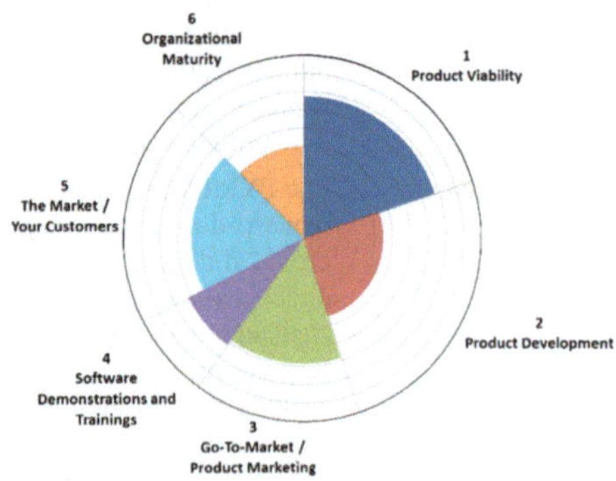

Fig. 10.13 B2B product–cross-industry: dimension radar cycle 1 © Timo Wagenblatt 2019. All rights reserved

Fig. 10.14 B2B product–cross-industry software product: dimension items radar cycle 0 versus cycle 1 © Timo Wagenblatt 2019. All rights reserved

The counter-actions did not drive improvements. The Product Development dimension score decreased to 4.45 from 4.80 and even the Product Viability dimension decreased slightly. Overall the Total PYPR score decreased to 37.49 from 38.12.

What happened during the last 12 weeks that caused this turn for the worse? A view to the dimension item level provides transparency.

Many dimension items declined while the maintenance profitability item in the Product Viability item increased. Can you see which way the wind is blowing?

Basically, nothing changed in the behavior of the product manager. The focus remained on exploiting the product (and maybe the product team). PYPR helped to make the shortcomings and the imbalanced situation visible; however the product manager had no real intention to balance the efforts.

The product manager missed most of the scheduled 30 min synch meetings during the PYPR cycle. In this situation PYPR only provides transparency. If the product manager does not take the role seriously, the product team suffers and ultimately the product suffers.

This case study ends with something interesting. The product team refused to work with the product manager going forward. They sensed that the Software Product Manager was driving his own agenda and didn't share their product-mindset and dedication. Consequently, the product faced a serious crisis.

We had meetings with the product manager's and the engineering team's line managers. Lots of emotions were in the room. We jointly analyzed PYPR as a team and derived a strategy and action plan for the next 12 weeks.

To everyone's surprise the product manager resigned after four weeks. To no one's surprise he joined a sales team and currently enjoys the work as a sales executive.

Note that this is an important lesson for the people managers among us. Sometimes you can identify patterns comparing different PYPRs in your organization. These patterns might be structural or organizational issues to be tackled for the benefit of many product teams. However, product managers might have their own agenda and management by objective is potentially dangerous.

10.5 Case Study: Corporate IT Product

The case study describes Step 1 to 4 of applying PYPR in corporate IT departments. The corporate IT product manager (called IT Product Owner) used PYPR for the first time. The product manager decided to include the core product team from the beginning when adopting PYPR.

I selected this case study as it illustrates how PYPR supports not only commercial software products, but also internal IT products. In this case study, the IT Services team was strongly biased toward delivery of prioritized backlog from Sales team representatives (called Business Product Owner). Sales team representatives shielded the Sales users from the product team (Table 10.12).

Table 10.12 Product characteristics—case study 4

Product characteristics	
Product type	Internal product, mobile application
Product lifecycle	Maturity
SPM and PO	Experienced Software Product Manager. Fills in also as product owner in scrum team, not co-located with team
Transparency	Delivery Manager, lead architect, accountable dev manager part of PYPR
Dev approach	Scrum, engineering team new to agile dev approach, efficiency and delivery focus
Team maturity	Technically experienced team, used to get clear guidance on requirements to be implemented, project mindset
Market segment	Sales users in large software company

10.5.1 PYPR Assessment and Visualization

The product team followed the standard PYPR process as outlined in Sect. 2.1:

- **Step 1: DUST[1] the Product Management Dimensions**
  The team started with the default PYPR configuration for internal products. Besides some naming and dimension weight discussions, the team reached consensus about what matters most for products in their context. The PYPR dimension item list could be used as a checklist of important product management activities for corporate IT products.
- **Step 2: Clarify Roles and Responsibilities and form a (Extended) Product Team**
  The team concluded that Step 1 will help to define the role of product managers in IT Services and with that could become the basis to position product management in the organization. The PYPR dimension item list helps clarifying who is responsible and who is accountable for the work package of each dimension and each dimension item (RACI) and who is driving the decisions for each dimension and each dimension item (DACI). The team recognized that there are some people missing in the meeting, e.g. Business Product Owner, central communications team, etc. Not all items could be assigned to roles (and people). The team agreed at this stage that it is necessary to strengthen the common understanding about what is important to increase the product yield potential beyond the team members in the current meeting set-up.

[1]Define, Understand, Structure, and Transparentize.

- **Step 3: Assess and Visualize the Product Yield Potential**
  The team did not feel comfortable rating with a scale from zero (hell) to 10 (heaven). The team decided to use an alternate scale: zero (bad), 5 (neutral), or 10 (awesome). During the PYPR assessment, there were some moments where the team considered switching to the zero to 10 rating, as zero felt too low and 5 too high. The team decided to continue with the 3-level rating but consider the zero to 10 rating next time. Figure 10.15 illustrates the results of the PYPR assessment.

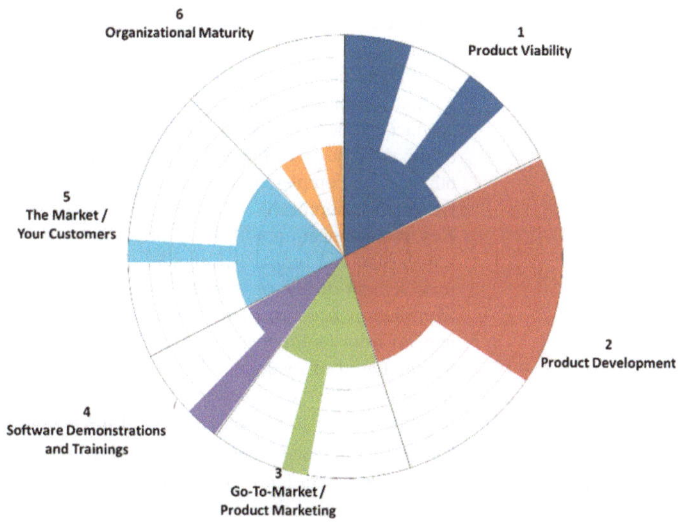

Fig. 10.15 Corporate IT product: dimension items radar cycle 0 © Timo Wagenblatt 2019. All rights reserved

- **Step 4: Prioritize and Strategize Actions based on PYPR Scores Analysis**
  The team discussed the PYPR results in detail and started digging into the various root causes of the weaker dimension items. However, some items could not be clarified due to missing information amongst the meeting participants. As the first action item, the team agreed to invite all stakeholders to the next meeting to be more effective. The team decided to focus on the improvement potential in the following dimension items: Organization, Processes, and Governance, Go-to-Market Activities and Plan, and Customer Community (Stakeholder Alignment). The product manager accepted the task to socialize all stakeholders with the PYPR framework and explain to everyone the next and most important product activities derived from the initial assessment.

10.5.2 PYPR Strategy and Action Plan

Based on the analysis of all PYPR dimensions and dimension items, the team jointly defined the Strategy and Action Plan as outlined in Table 10.13.

Table 10.13 Strategy and action plan

Strategy and action plan	
Organization, processes, and governance	Delivery manager and product manager aligned on the importance to plan and prepare for a larger mindset change. Most teams in the organization had been focused and trained on efficient delivery of business-prioritized requirements without condition, rather project-minded than product-minded. The team starting with PYPR has been one of the most advanced teams toward product mindset while others were completely thinking and working in a fix scope, fix timeline approach **Key result**: meeting with Head of IT Services to agree on action plan and further stakeholder involvement, especially involvement of line of business management team has been identified as key focus area as required change needed to happen from requirements gathering and prioritization to interpretation of roadmaps (i.e. not being a project plan) and roll-out of delivered functionality. Just becoming more product-minded in IT Services would not do the job
Customer community (stakeholder alignment)	The product manager accepted the task to socialize all stakeholders with the PYPR framework. As door-opener, an explanation about the next and most important product activities derived from the initial assessment had been identified. Getting stakeholder airtime had been very time consuming due to the availability of line of business management. Sales management teams are obviously managed by business results and consider product as a business service. Consequently, talking to IT delivery teams has been rather a one-directional communication and only became a priority for 'the business' when informing about desperately required product features. The product manager required various attempts and tactics to get the right level of attention due to the low organizational maturity

10.5.3 PYPR Cycle Results

PYPR Assessment after 12 weeks provided the results summarized in Fig. 10.16. The PYPR scores provided only limited insights due to the changes in the rating system. Still the team perceived early on positive effects of applying the PYPR framework. Among the key achievements has been the further alignment and clarification of roles, the strengthened involvement of users, which on its own lead to increased user perception as a result of being recognized and considered.

In my opinion, the most important effect has been the understanding of the management teams in corporate IT and the business-side about the challenges of the current set-up as well as the things that matter for successful corporate IT products. PYPR contributed as the artefact for discussing and showcasing the potential of a stronger product mindset.

The transformation toward a product-minded IT organization is in full swing as I write this case study.

Dimension	Initial PYPR Score	New PYPR Score
Product Viability	7,50	6,55
Product Development	8,25	7,03
Go-to-Market / Product Marketing	5,75	5,15
Software Demonstrations and Training	7,00	7,05
The Market / Your Customers	5,50	6,55
Organizational Maturity	2,75	4,75
Total PYPR Score	**36,63**	**37,08**

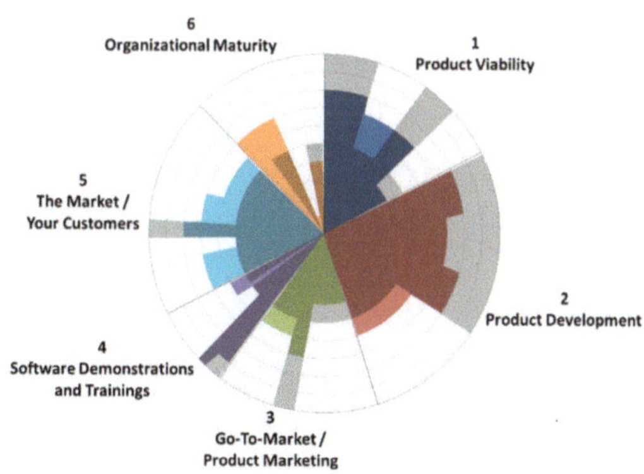

Fig. 10.16 Corporate IT product: dimension items radar cycle 0 compared to cycle 1 © Timo Wagenblatt 2019. All rights reserved

Index

T. Wagenblatt, *Software Product Management*, Management for Professionals,
https://doi.org/10.1007/978-3-030-19871-8

MIX
Papier aus verantwortungsvollen Quellen
Paper from responsible sources
FSC® C105338
FSC
www.fsc.org

If you have any concerns about our products,
you can contact us on
ProductSafety@springernature.com

In case Publisher is established outside the EU,
the EU authorized representative is:
Springer Nature Customer Service Center GmbH
Europaplatz 3, 69115 Heidelberg, Germany

Printed by Libri Plureos GmbH
in Hamburg, Germany